P9-AQL-072

THE THOUGHT AND CHARACTER
OF
WILLIAM JAMES

Briefer Version

hARpER 🔥 τORChBOOKS

*A reference-list of Harper Torchbooks, classified
by subjects, is printed at the end of this volume.*

WILLIAM JAMES, 1907

Alice Boughton

THE THOUGHT AND CHARACTER
OF
WILLIAM JAMES

Briefer Version

RALPH BARTON PERRY

HARPER TORCHBOOKS
The Academy Library
Harper & Row, Publishers
New York and Evanston

ὦ ψυχὴ καθαρά
θανοῦσα γὰρ οὐ θάνες

THE THOUGHT AND CHARACTER OF WILLIAM JAMES: *Briefer Version*
Copyright, 1935 by Henry James
Copyright, 1948 by the President and Fellows of Harvard College
This book was originally published in 1948 by Harvard University Press
and is the briefer version of the two-volume edition originally pub-
lished in 1935. The Briefer Version is here reprinted by arrangement.
First HARPER TORCHBOOK edition published 1964 by
Harper & Row, Publishers, Incorporated
49 East 33rd Street
New York, N. Y. 10016

CONTENTS

CONTENTS

PREFACE

The Thought and Character of William James was published in 1935 in two ample volumes, and was designed to serve the double purpose of a systematic account of James's development and a repository of selections from James's unpublished literary remains. The present abridged edition does not supersede the larger work, but makes its central core available to the general reader. It has been prepared with a view not only to convenience and brevity, but to simplicity of presentation. Some material and bibliographies have been omitted and James's thought has been set forth in terms that require no previous familiarity with technical problems of philosophy and psychology. At the same time this volume, like the longer version, allows James to speak for himself through his letters and writings. Here appear for the first time three recently discovered letters.

The Preface to the original edition contains my grateful acknowledgment of the help received in preparation: to the James family, and especially to Henry James for access to the rich store of James papers; to James's correspondents or their executors who have authorized the use of unpublished letters; to Harvard University for the use of the Widener Library and other facilities; and to many colleagues and friends for information and advice.

In the preparation of the present volume I have been fortunate enough to have as my collaborator Elizabeth Perkins Aldrich, whose assistance was indispensable in the preparation of the longer version. She is uniquely familiar with the material and shares my veneration for James's memory. I have relied so greatly on her understanding and editorial expertness that a mere expression of gratitude is inadequate. She is in fact, if not in name, the co-author of this book.

Ralph Barton Perry

Cambridge, Massachusetts
July 3, 1947

1

FOREWORD

The life of William James was widely spread, both in its roots and in its branches. It took its nourishment from many sources, grew in many directions, and bore a great variety of fruits. It was richly fertilized and abundantly fertile. Having a peculiar genius for friendship, James entered into relations of intimacy with a large circle of contemporaries, not only with men of his own age but with his juniors and seniors. He was gifted in the art of self-expression, and had at the same time a power to elicit self-expression from others, so that his friendships were highly articulate and his correspondence voluminous. Habits of travel and a knowledge of languages widened the scope of his sociability, and made him an important channel by which America was carried to Europe and Europe to America. In short, his life and mind were so interwoven with their context, so thoroughly socialized and humanized, that a record of them must necessarily be in some measure a history of his times.

While it is true that James and his philosophy originated in the nineteenth century and overlapped the twentieth, such an historical attribution would be misleading. James was true to his origins and his ancestry, as a man must needs be. But it was not like James to feel allegiance to the past, least of all to his own past. His philosophizing in the twentieth century was not an inference from premises laid down in the century before. He traveled with little baggage and with no inflexible itinerary, being singularly free, and wholly devoted to what he took to be the truth at the present moment of his thinking. He was modern, in the sense that is applicable to all ages. Hence it is that James is a philosopher of the twentieth century as well as of the nineteenth, and that much of his thinking, as well as of the man himself, seems formed in the fashion of today. And were he alive now, he would, as always, be looking to the future.

I

THE ELDER HENRY JAMES

The family circle within which William James grew to maturity was unusual in the degree to which it quickened and moulded its members. It was central and not peripheral to their individual lives. The father, Henry James the elder, had no recognized profession that harnessed him to its routine or summoned him to an office. His occupations of study, meditation, and writing—all of his vocational activities save occasional public lectures—were carried on in the plain sight of his household; and though its other members were unreceptive or even indifferent to "father's ideas," and knew little of what was in his books, the "felt side-wind of their strong composition" made a part of the circumambient atmosphere, and "was in the last resort the gage of something perpetually fine going on." Such, at least, is the grateful testimony of one of the most illustrious members of this family group, who also refers to them as "genially interested in almost nothing but each other." [1] Their mutual interest was due in part to the fact that the education of the children—their relation to school and church and state—was as irregular as their father's vocation. The family claimed them in default of any stable institutional attachments elsewhere. They were further united by the bond of their exceptional tenderness. The elder James complained of his love for his children as both painful and sinful. Emerson records in one of his notebooks: "Henry James said to me, he wished sometimes the lightning would strike his wife and children out of existence, and he should suffer no more from loving them." [2] That his principles as well as his feelings were involved appears from the following, written to the younger Henry:—

Cambridge, Dec. 21 [1869?]

My darling Harry,—

. . . Your long sickness, and Alice's, and now Willy's, have been an immense discipline for me, in gradually teaching me to universalize my sympathies. It was dreadful to see those you love so tenderly exposed to so much wearing suffering, and I fought against the conviction that it was inevitable. But when I gained a truer perception of the case, and saw that it was a zeal chiefly on behalf of my own children that animated my rebellion, and that I should perhaps scarcely suffer at all, if other people's children alone were in question, and mine

---

[1] Henry James, *Notes of a Son and Brother*, 1914, 163; *A Small Boy and Others*, 1913, 59. Selections from these books are reprinted by special permission of the publishers, Charles Scribner's Sons.

[2] "Gulistan," 1848.

were left to enjoy their wonted health and peace, I grew ashamed of myself, and consented to ask for the amelioration of their lot only as a part of the common lot. This is what we want, and this alone, for God's eternal sabbath in our nature, the reconciliation of the individual and the universal interest in humanity. . . . Ever, my darling boy, your loving DADDY

But if the members of this family were interested in one another it was largely because they were interesting. They shared this quality with the larger tribe to which they belonged, the uncles, aunts, and cousins who were perpetually crossing paths with them and to whose vicissitudes of fortune they could never remain indifferent. William James of Albany, New York, progenitor of the tribe, father of the "elder Henry James," and grandfather of the subject of this book, died in 1832, a decade before the birth of his illustrious grandson. But his third wife, Catharine Barber, lived until 1859, and when our William and his brother Henry were small children they were frequent visitors at her house. This scene, living in vague but poignant memories, and amplified by the vivid narratives of their father, closed the vista of their retrospect. To this scene William looked back through the events of that intermediate life which bound him to it:—

> Father's boyhood up in Albany, Grandmother's house, the father and brothers and sister, with their passions and turbulent histories, his burning, amputation and sickness, his college days and ramblings, his theological throes, his engagement and marriage and fatherhood, his finding more and more of the truths he finally settled down in, his travels in Europe, the days of the old house in New York and all the men I used to see there, at last his quieter motion down the later years of life in Newport, Boston and Cambridge, with his friends and correspondents about him, and his books more and more easily brought forth—how long, how long all these things were in the living, but how short their memory now is! [3]

"William of Albany" was an ample and dynamic person. During the forty-odd years which elapsed between his emigration from Ireland (probably in 1789) and his death in 1832, he survived three or more business partners; participated in the opening of the Erie Canal and the westward development along the Mohawk Valley; extended his interests beyond merchandizing to commerce, real estate, banking, and public utilities, and from Canada to New York City; accumulated one of the great fortunes of his day (estimated at $3,000,000); married three wives, and begat fourteen children; became one of the first citizens of his city and state, and a chief pillar of the Presbyterian Church. It is not surprising that this first William should have felt sure of himself, and sought to impose his will on others; or that he should have been loyally attached to

[3] To A.H.J., written in 1882 immediately after his father's death; *The Letters of William James,* edited by his son Henry James, 1920, I, 221, published by the Atlantic Monthly Press.

his way of salvation, and to the God who presided over his destiny. He attempted to keep both his worldly and his spiritual estate intact by making the possession of the one dependent on the acceptance of the other.

The elder William James did his best to transmit a blend of piety and acquisitiveness to his surviving offspring; but partly because there were too many of them, partly because the strictness of his rule was compromised by his own indulgence, partly because his children inherited their father's temperament without inheriting his opinions, and partly for technical reasons known only to lawyers and courts of equity, his plans, in sum, miscarried. Calvinism and churchgoing rapidly declined. Money-getting and money-keeping ceased to be a family vocation. "The rupture with my grandfather's tradition," wrote the younger Henry, "was complete; we were never in a single case, I think, for two generations, guilty of a stroke of 'business.'"[4] Money became rather a means to the leisurely amenities, the life of fashion, the cultivation of taste and its gratification, or the study and pursuit of letters.

Thus the Jamesian heredity was already brewing. Take a temperament ardent (or Irish), a piety Calvinistic, a physique nervous and energetic rather than robust; modify these with the effects of affluence and leisure; and the result is an ineradicable puritanism contradicted by tenderheartedness, and an emotional instability mellowed by urbanity. In the case of Henry, father of the third and most famous William, these ancestral and domestic influences were accidentally modified by acute suffering and permanent impairment of bodily capacity. In 1824 or thereabouts, he was tutored by Joseph Henry who was also assistant to Dr. T. Romeyn Beck, the principal of the Albany Institute, where Henry James, a boy of thirteen, was then attending school. Dr. Beck encouraged his boys to play at science under the direction of his young assistant. Perhaps this assistant reflected on the question contained in the book to which he owed his conversion to science: "Why does flame or smoke always mount upward?"[5] In any case he taught the boys in his charge to fly hot-air balloons supplied with lighted balls of tow. One of these balls having accidentally entered the window of a neighbor's barn, his pupil, Henry James, was seriously burned in a gallant attempt to stamp it out. The result was two years in bed and a double amputation of his leg above the knee.

This happened to a boy who later described himself as follows: "I lived in every fibre of my body. The dawn always found me on my feet; and I can still vividly recall the divine rapture which filled my blood as I pursued under the magical light of morning the sports of the river, the wood, or the field."

When the young Henry entered Union College in 1829 his health and spirits had fully revived. The loss of his leg prevented him from engaging in

[4] *S.B.O.*, 190.
[5] *Memorial of Joseph Henry*, Washington, 1880, 180; *cf.* also 206-10.

"the sports of the river, the wood, or the field," [6] but he could and did enter with zest into the pleasures and fashionable life of his day. Indeed he was so extravagant that the irate father, noting his son's "progress in arts of low vileness" and "unblushing falsehood," predicted that he would soon find himself lodged in prison.[7] He continued in college, however, and graduated in 1830, with a passable but not distinguished record; after which he made an abortive attempt to please his father by studying law, and became for a time (1830-1832) one of the editors of an Albany publication entitled the *Craftsman*.

These are but external events in the life of a youth who was profoundly introspective. He was too temperamentally religious either to accept his hereditary beliefs with indifference or to renounce them altogether. His worldly interests and animal spirits were at war with his humanity, and both were at war with his traditional piety. But in his case such a conflict could result only in an enrichment and intensification of faith.

Good Presbyterians tended toward Princeton. The Reverend William, an elder half-brother, had gone there in 1813. Joseph Henry, already a famous physicist, had gone there in 1832, called from the Albany Institute to a professorship in the College of New Jersey. Henry James followed in 1835, when he entered the Princeton Theological Seminary. As a theological student at Princeton James could have little in common with his fellows: to them religion was an institution, to him it was an original and personal revelation.

In 1838 he withdrew from the Princeton Seminary and took up his residence in New York City. He was now permanently alienated from the Church, "disaffected both by temper and culture to ritual or ceremonial views" of religion.[8] The ministry being closed to him, and the other recognized professions being wholly incompatible with his genius, he entered upon that career which seemed to his children so embarrassingly equivocal, and which he described by responding to their questions: "Say I'm a philosopher, say I'm a seeker for truth, say I'm a lover of my kind, say I'm an author of books if you like; or, best of all, just say I'm a Student." [9]

He was all these things, but there was a vocation underlying them, namely, to make articulate and triumphant his own peculiar religious insight. That insight was at once a development of Calvinism and a repudiation of it. Though he insisted upon the unreserved lovingness and lovableness of God, and upon the solidarity of mankind, his personal religious experience was profoundly

[6] *The Literary Remains of Henry James*, edited by his son, William James, 1885, 183. The above citation was quoted from an autobiographical manuscript left by H.J.[1], published by W.J. in the *Atlantic Monthly*, LIV (1884), and afterwards more fully in *L.R.H.J.*

[7] From a correspondence between William James (of Albany) and his friend Archibald McIntyre, November 12 and December 2, 1829; and a letter of H.J.[1] to Isaac Jackson, tutor at Union College, January 30, 1830.

[8] *L.R.H.J.*, 123.

[9] *N.S.B.*, 69.

Calvinistic. It was Calvinistic in this very idea of human solidarity. For was it not a first premise of Calvinism that the sin of Adam is communicated to his whole progeny, so that the race is like an organism which, being stricken in one of its members, must suffer in all? James was Calvinistic, too, in his unreserved acceptance of the view that man is estranged from God. Religion begins with despair. This is not an accident, but a necessary condition: there can be no upward path that does not start from the depths. He was Calvinistic in his acceptance of the doctrine of justification by faith, salvation being an unmerited bounty, proceeding from indulgent love to its unworthy object.

So far James not only accepted Calvinism, but rejoiced in it, as the highest and holiest truth. But the depth of his Calvinism only makes the more astonishing his radical departure from it—a departure so radical that it might be termed an inversion. According to Calvinism, men fall collectively, and are saved individually. They are fallen by nature, by force of their biological inheritance, while they are raised up as individuals—elected, set apart, and marked by their superior zeal and rectitude. But that which is the mark of salvation for the Calvinist, that sense of the special favor of God, which expresses itself in a preëminent capacity for righteousness, is for James the very moment of the fall. The biological man is innocent. It is when he presumes to claim individual superiority, whether on the score of his prerogatives or on that of his exceeding piety, that he is most completely alienated from God. What he must repent is his pride, and the beginning of his real salvation appears when he identifies his own hopes altogether with those of the race. In short, for James men fall individually, and are saved collectively!

James's literary career did not begin until 1850, and meanwhile he had seen the light.[10] This light came to him from two sources, Swedenborg and Fourier. They did not convert him—but confirmed and sustained him, giving him a language, a systematic framework, and support for the faith that was in him.

To Swedenborg's writings James attributed a religious revelation which he experienced in 1846:

> I read from the first with palpitating interest. My heart divined, even before my intelligence was prepared to do justice to the books, the unequalled amount of truth to be found in them. . . . Imagine a subject of some petty despotism condemned to die, and with (what is more and worse) a sentiment of death pervading all his consciousness, lifted by a sudden miracle into felt harmony

[10] The major writings of Henry James are as follows: *Moralism and Christianity; or Man's Experience and Destiny*, 1850; *Lectures and Miscellanies*, 1852; *The Church of Christ Not an Ecclesiasticism*, 1854; *The Nature of Evil, considered in a Letter to the Rev. Edward Beecher, D.D., Author of "The Conflict of Ages,"* 1855; *Christianity the Logic of Creation*, 1857; *Substance and Shadow; or Morality and Religion in Their Relation to Life*, 1863; *The Secret of Swedenborg, being an elucidation of his doctrine of the Divine Natural Humanity*, 1869; *Society the Redeemed Form of Man, and the Earnest of God's Omnipotence in Human Nature, affirmed in Letters to a Friend*, 1879.

with universal man, and filled to the brim with the sentiment of indestructible life instead; and you will have a true picture of my emancipated condition.[11]

But James's friend, J. J. Garth Wilkinson, whose writings had first attracted his attention to Swedenborg, complained later that there was nothing in common between James and Swedenborg but the "term" *Divine Natural Humanity*.[12] It was as impossible for James to be a good Swedenborgian as to be a good Presbyterian. Religion was for him a matter of experience and insight, and not of dogma or historical revelation. James was a metaphysician, a mystic, and a hereditary Calvinist, who looked to Swedenborg to deliver him altogether from the letter—even from the letter of Swedenborgianism.

James's other great source of light was Fourier, who died in 1837, and whose fame spread with such rapidity that in 1846 the number of his American followers was estimated at 200,000. It is, of course, impossible to explain this movement as an isolated phenomenon, or as proving the peculiar merit of Fourier's teachings. It is a manifestation of that same eager and confident spirit of reform which appears in the Free Soil movement, abolitionism, the peace societies, the Owenite movement, and transcendentalism. Those who belonged to one of these movements usually belonged to the rest, or at any rate were sympathetic to them, and to all other "isms." "In the history of the world," said Emerson, "the doctrine of reform had never such scope as at the present hour. . . . We are to revise the whole of our social structure, the state, the school, religion, marriage, trade, science, and explore their foundations in our own nature." [13]

There is no evidence that Fourier was influenced by Swedenborg, and it is not certain that he was even acquainted with his doctrines. But there were striking similarities both of method and of doctrine, and the two movements seemed predestined to marriage. Swedenborgianism needed a social programme, and Fourierism needed a metaphysical and religious foundation. It was this reciprocal, complementary fitness that was most important to the reformers of the 1840's, and seems to have suggested itself almost simultaneously to many leaders of the two movements on both sides of the Atlantic.

The doctrines of Fourier attracted James not only because they seemed to provide a social science and a guarantee of fulfillment, but because they confirmed two of his most cherished convictions. The first of these was social solidarity, "the unity or personality of the great race itself." The only important sense in which "good" men differ from "bad" is in their relation to "that great

---

[11] *L.R.H.J.*, 66-7. 69.
[12] Wilkinson to H.J.[1], May 20, 1879.
[13] The *Dial*, I (184-I), 523, 534. Even mediumship and spiritism profited by the general enthusiasm, but Andrew Jackson Davis's lead in this direction was not followed by the group with which James was more immediately associated, and James himself took little interest in it.

unitary life of God in our nature, which we call society, fraternity, fellowship, equality," [14] The second cherished idea for which James found confirmation in Fourier was the idea of human innocence. Fourier ascribed misconduct and the necessity of institutional control to maladjustment, and his programme consisted in devising communities so skilfully organized that within them the individual could enjoy entire spontaneity and be "freely good." Or, as William James expressed it, "In a Society organized divinely our *natures* will not be altered, but our spontaneities, because they then will work harmoniously, will all work innocently, and the Kingdom of Heaven will have come." [15]

In other words, the elder James proclaimed with his characteristic recklessness and hearty whole-souled affirmation the doctrine that human progress and true religion, which are the same thing, look in the direction of vindicating the natural man and delivering him from institutional authority.

The transcendentalists, Brook Farmers, and romantic humanitarians were William James's spiritual uncles. They belonged definitely to the past, and were already beginning to wear the aspect of historic monuments. Although, being reared with a wise tolerance and liberality, he suffered no reaction against the associations of his youth, these men of his father's circle influenced him congenitally, rather than as contemporary and living forces. His friends were their sons, and his teachers were men of another tribe altogether.

[14] Henry James, *Substance and Shadow*, 1863, 145, 369.
[15] Prefatory note to his father's "Emerson," *Atlantic*, XCIV (1904).

II

THE ELDER JAMES AND EMERSON

The birth of William James coincides almost precisely with the beginning of the acquaintance between his father and Emerson. On March 18, 1842, Emerson wrote in his diary: "In New York I became acquainted with Henry James."[1] The following letter to Emerson apparently deals with this event. James had gone to hear Emerson lecture, was attracted to him, and invited him to his house, where he arrived just in time to be taken upstairs to admire "the lately-born babe who was to become the second American William James."[2]

New York City, Thursday Evening [March 3, 1842?]

My dear Sir,—

I listened to your address this evening,[3] and as my bosom glowed with many a true word that fell from your lips I felt erelong fully assured that before me I beheld a man who in very truth was seeking the realities of things. I said to myself, I will try when I go home how far this man follows reality—how far he loves truth and goodness. For I will write to him that I, too, in my small degree am coveting to understand the truth which surrounds me and embraces me, am seeking worthily to apprehend, or to be more worthily apprehended of, the love which underlies and vivifies all the seeming barrenness of our most unloving world; but that yet for every step I have taken I find myself severed from friends and kindred, so that at last, and just when I am become more consciously worthy of love than I ever was, in so far as being more consciously and universally loving may argue me so, I find my free manifestations com-

---

[1] Bliss Perry, *The Heart of Emerson's Journals*, Houghton Mifflin Co., 1926, 173. The names of Horace Greeley and Albert Brisbane also appear in this list of new acquaintances. An unpublished letter, dated March 10, 1842, from Emerson to Margaret Fuller, reports the same fact; and speaks at the same time of Henry James's brother John, and of the fact that Henry James's sister (Jeanette) had married William H. Barker, the brother of Anna (Mrs. Samuel G.) Ward. Mrs. Ward was a friend both of James and of Emerson, and her son, Thomas W. Ward, was one of William's most intimate friends and correspondents. *Cf.* below, 74 ff. In 1904 William James edited for publication in the *Atlantic* (XCIV) a paper of his father's on "Emerson," which opens with the words: "It is now full thirty years ago that I made Mr. Emerson's acquaintance. He had come at the time to New York to read a course of lectures. These I diligently attended, and I saw much of him also in private. He at once captivated my imagination, and I have been ever since his loving bondman." The editor (W.J.) states that this paper was written in "1868, or thereabouts." Either this last statement, or the statement "full thirty years," above, must be in error. The lectures which Emerson was delivering in New York in 1842 were those that afterwards formed the first volume of his *Essays*.

[2] *S.B.O.*, 8.

[3] On Thursday, March 3, Emerson lectured in the Society Library on "The Times."

pressed into the sphere of my own fireside. I will further tell him that to talk familiarly with one who earnestly follows truth through whatever frowning ways she beckons him on, and loves her with so true a love as never to have been baffled from her pursuit by all the wearisome forms of error he may have encountered in the way, has never been my lot for one half-hour even; and that he, therefore, if he be now the generous lover of truth and of her friends which he seems to be, may give me this untasted pleasure, and let me once feel the cordial grasp of a fellow pilgrim, and remember for long days the cheering Godspeed and the ringing laugh with which he bounded on from my sight at parting. I will not insult his reverence for truth equally with my own by saying that I desire his guidance in any way, but I will tell him that when once my voice is known, I may now and then call him back to interpret some of the hieroglyphics which here and there line our way, and which my own skill in tongues may be unequal to,—which slight services he cannot well deny. I will tell him that I do not value his substantive discoveries, whatever they may be, perhaps half so highly as he values them, but that I chiefly value that erect attitude of mind about him which in God's universe undauntedly seeks the worthiest tidings of God, and calmly defies every mumbling phantom which would herein challenge its freedom. And finally, not to try his patience also, I will tell him that should his zeal for realities and his contempt of vulgar shows abide the ordeal I had thus contrived for them, I should gladly await his visit to me whenever he should be pleased to appoint it.

This in substance is what I said to myself. Now that I have told it to you also, you have become a sort of confidant between me and myself, and so in a manner bound to promote harmony there. If you shrink from the confidence thus thrust upon you, *I* shall certainly be blamed by *myself,* for making so indiscreet a communication to you; but if you abide it, *I* shall with equal certainty be highly felicitated by *myself* for achieving a result so undeniably auspicious to both. In every event, I remain, your true well-wisher,

H. JAMES

P.S. My residence is at No. 5, Washington Place. This Place runs from Broadway to Washington Square, and forms, or is formed by, the row of buildings between the University building and Broadway. My occupations are all indoor, so that I am generally at home—always in the evenings.

The letters to Emerson reveal that mixture of admiration, love, and irritation which on James's part is the sign of their quickly ripening friendship. There was every reason why they should differ, or, rather, why James should differ from Emerson. One of the differences was that whereas James *would* differ, Emerson would not. James kept the old Calvinistic habit of theological disputation. His impulse was to argue and persuade, and he hated to let people go whom he thought worth saving. He had his intuitions and convictions, but he wanted reasons for them, and was constantly striving to shape these into a metaphysics. Emerson's eloquence, on the other hand, was affirmative rather than demonstrative. He refused to be drawn into argument, or even to answer questions, and the more he eluded the more he exasperated.[4] To this must be added the profound temperamental difference—the vehemence of the one and the imperturbability of the other.

The following passages refer reminiscently to the period of their first meeting:

> Good heavens! how soothed and comforted I was by the innocent lovely look of my new acquaintance, by his tender courtesy, his generous laudatory appreciation of my crude literary ventures! and how I used to lock myself up with him in my bed-room, swearing that before the door was opened I would arrive at the secret of his immense superiority to the common herd of literary men! I might just as well have locked myself up with a handful of diamonds, so far as any capacity of self-cognizance existed in him. . . . On the whole I may say that at first I was greatly disappointed in him, because his intellect never kept the promise which his lovely face and manners held out to me. He was to my senses a literal divine presence in the house with me; and we cannot recognize literal divine presences in our houses without feeling sure that they will be able to say something of critical importance to one's intellect. It turned out that any average old dame in a horse-car would have satisfied my intellectual rapacity just as well as Emerson. . . . No man could look at him speaking (or when he was silent either, for that matter) without having a vision of the divinest beauty. But when you went to him to hold discourse about the wondrous phenomenon, you found him absolutely destitute of reflective power.[5]

Lectures brought Emerson intermittently to New York and he became a frequent visitor at the James house. One or more of these visits left the following traces on the mind of Henry James, the second son, then under twelve years of age:

> Do I roll several occasions into one, or amplify one beyond reason?—this last being ever, I allow, the waiting pitfall of a chronicler too memory-ridden. I "visualize" at any rate the winter firelight of our back-parlour at dusk and the great Emerson—I knew he was great, greater than any of our friends—sitting in it between my parents, before the lamps had been lighted, as a visitor consentingly housed only could have done, and affecting me the more as an apparition sinuously and, I held, elegantly slim, benevolently aquiline, and commanding a tone alien, beautifully alien, to any we heard round-about.[6]

It was through Emerson that James became acquainted with Thoreau. "I should like," wrote Emerson to James,[7]

[4] "Emerson would listen, I fancy, as if charmed, to James's talk of the 'divine natural Humanity,' but he would never *subscribe;* and this, from one whose native gifts were so suggestive of that same Humanity, was disappointing." (William James, in the prefatory note to his father's "Emerson," *Atlantic,* XCIV, 1904, 740.)

[5] *L.R.H.J.,* 296-7, 300.

[6] *N.S.B.,* 204. The second Henry James was born in 1843, and the above impression must have occurred before 1855, when the family ceased to reside in New York.

[7] May 6, 1843.

both for Mr. Thoreau's and for your own sake that you would meet and see what you have for each other. Thoreau is a profound mind and a person of true magnanimity, and if it should happen that there is some village pedantry and tediousness of facts, it will easily be forgotten when you come at what is better. One can never be sure that these delicatest of all experiments, experiments of men and intercourse, will prosper: but if you remain in the city this summer, which seemed uncertain, I wish you would send your card to him through my brother.

The first meeting between Thoreau and James seems to have been an immediate success, though Thoreau came to have his doubts concerning the usefulness of James's philosophy. He wrote to his parents that he had met "Henry James, a lame man," of whom he "had heard before"; and described his impressions at length in a letter to Emerson of June 8, 1843:—

> I have been to see Henry James, and like him very much. It was a great pleasure to meet him. It makes humanity seem more erect and respectable. I never was more kindly and faithfully catechized. It made me respect myself more to be thought worthy of such wise questions. He is a man, and takes his own way, or stands still in his own place. I know of no one so patient and determined to have the good of you. It is almost friendship, such plain and human dealing. I think that he will not write or speak inspiringly; but he is a refreshing, forward-looking and forward-moving man, and he has naturalized and humanized New York for me. He actually reproaches you by his respect for your poor words. I had three hours' solid talk with him, and he asks me to make free use of his house. He wants an expression of your faith, or to be sure that it is faith, and confesses that his own treads fast upon the neck of his understanding. He exclaimed, at some careless answer of mine, "Well, you Transcendentalists are wonderfully consistent. I must get hold of this somehow." [8]

The James family sailed for Europe on October 19, 1843, on that memorable journey which was to be remembered for the revelation of Swedenborg, and for the beginning of a personal acquaintance with Wilkinson and Carlyle. What James thought of Carlyle he set down afterwards with his usual enthusiastic candor; what Carlyle thought of James, except that he "liked him," is less clearly recorded.[9] In 1845 James and his family returned to America, first to Albany and then, in 1847, to New York. The correspondence with Emerson was resumed together with the old habit of meeting in New York on the occasions of Emerson's lecturing. They met also in Boston, James being a member of the series of clubs which were successively organized there *autour d'Emerson*.

1852 was the year of Kossuth's famous tour. He went to Concord and was

[8] F. B. Sanborn, *Familiar Letters of H. D. Thoreau*, Houghton Mifflin Co., 1894, 95.
[9] *Cf. N.S.B.*, 186-8.

publicly greeted by Emerson as "the foremost soldier of freedom in this age." [10]
It was also the year of the appearance of the *Memoirs* of Margaret Fuller, by
Emerson, William Henry Channing, and others. Both the tour and the book
were events in James's world, and are alluded to in the following letter to his
friend Edmund Tweedy:—

New York, Feb. 24 [1852]

My beloved old Tweedius,—

Hang such weather! weather that overwhelms you with an hourly enchant-
ment, and seduces you from the sacredest duties. How many letters have I written to you lately under its inspiration, to be sure not with mere vulgar pens and
ink, but with the pen of my brain dipped into the inkstand of my heart! Ah!
could you only get some of these letters! they would disqualify you for reading
any of the present sort, as they do me for writing them. For my memory
preserves only what is best and humanest of both of you, and I make you both
sharers in imagination of all that is noblest and divinest in the life of my
thought. . . .

Channing has done himself great credit, I am told, by his account of Margaret Fuller's last years. I have only read Emerson's narrative of her, which is
first-rate and worthy of his youth. . . . The impression the book makes upon
me so far, is that while Margaret was a person of fine intellect and aspiration,
she was also a most uncomfortable neighbour, from the circumstance of her in-
ordinate self-esteem. She thought herself somebody, and a somebody so large as
to attract the gaze of the world, and perhaps bias human destiny. Omnibus
drivers, and my splendid friend Derby the tailor, are sweet in comparison with
that sort of pretension. . . .

Emerson is here lecturing—or rather he has suspended his lectures for a fortnight, in order to resume them when the public attention is less absorbed by
other entertainments. I see a good deal of him. He expresses himself much
interested in my ideas, only he thinks I am too far ahead. He read the proof of
one of my lectures the other day, now printing, and said many pleasant and
apparently sincere things of it, only he would have it that I was (comparatively)
"a modern gentleman in the Saurian era." This is because he has no faith in
man, at least in progress. He does not imagine the possibility of "hurrying up
the cakes" on a large scale. Indeed he denies that any cakes are baking upon
any larger scale than that of the family griddle. He is much interested in the
question of immortality, and pumps one dry thereon. . . . Kossuth . . . on the
whole will gain nothing by his motion in this country but private sympathy.
Nothing will move us but the invasion of England by the powers of (Continental) darkness. Then I think we should fill all our ships. But I beg pardon
for introducing political topics to a mere *virtuoso* and worldling like you. . . .
Believe me, . . . my dear good old Tweedius, ever faithfully, your

H. J.

A picture of this same year and of the New York house at 54 West 14th
Street, from the memory of one who was then a child of six, is contained in a
letter of Robertson James:

[10] G. W. Cooke, *Ralph Waldo Emerson: His Life, Writings, and Philosophy*, 1881, 121.

What a troop of figures come out of the shadows. . . . Uncle William from Albany, who throws his nightgown, nightcap, brushes, etc., from the omnibus window *en passant* from the Albany train to the lower Broadway from which he is to return late in the day,—signaling to the awe-struck servant on the steps that these things are his and that he will return for the night. "Tell Henry and Mary" is lost in the rumble of the wheels on the high cobbles of the roadway. Charles Dana at Saturday dinners. George Ripley. Mr. Bayard Taylor, who tells of his frozen nose in the north. Mr. Bryant's son-in-law—name forgotten—but not forgotten the homeliest countenance in America which was his. Uncle Edward. John and Uncle Gus.[11] The McBrides, the Van Zandts, Grandma James, —her silk dress, peppermints, lace mittens and gentle smile. The Senters, the Costers, the Ironsides. Then also my mother, who walked down Sixth Avenue to Washington Market *with a basket on her arm* (*of this I am sure*)—every morning—for I tagged after her, aged six years, and held to her shawl. The Vanderpoels and the Vanderbergs come next. And then the dancing school. William will remember the name—Gen. Ferano—the master distinguished himself later on in our war as a soldier. . . . I might go on indefinitely writing you of these memories. Some of them are very plain like the sight of Gen. Kossuth seen in a procession of welcome on Broadway.[12]

Another European trip, planned for a variety of personal and domestic reasons, including the children's education, took place in 1855. Although they had been friends for many years, James had never visited Emerson in Concord, or made the acquaintance of his family, and this happy event was to be postponed until the return some years later from his sojourn abroad. The fuller account of this fateful educational Odyssey belongs to a later part of our record, but the following letter gives a fragmentary glimpse of it, together with more of Carlyle. James had met Carlyle in 1843, and now renewed his acquaintance. During both of these periods of residence in England he appears to have been a frequent and welcome visitor in the Carlyle household. When James sailed from America Emerson had written him a letter of farewell.

London [1856]

My dear Emerson,—

I suppose if you hadn't bestowed upon me so generous and noble a valedictory, I should have brought myself to your remembrance half a dozen of times at least. But your letter proved such a quickener of emotion, and so penetrated us all with a sense of the sweetness we had left behind, the sweetness that distils from the divine depths of the human bosom, that we were in some danger of precipitately retracing our steps, and I for my own part felt an actual depressing homesickness every time I thought of you. For really I find every want supplied here but that to which you minister, a want which grows, I hope, out of my American manhood, and which demands in one's cronies an openness of

---

[11] William Cullen Bryant's son-in-law was Parke Godwin. William, Edward, John, and Augustus were brothers of H.J.[1]

[12] To A.H.J., February 24, 1898; for another extract from this letter, *cf.* below, 51.

soul answering to one's own. This is certainly you, a soul full of doors and windows, a well-ventilated soul, open to every breeze that blows, and without any dark closets receptive of ancestral, political and ecclesiastical trumpery. I could sometimes wish indeed to find those gracious doors and windows a little more retentive of what comes in, or a little more humanly jealous of what goes too speedily out; I could wish, indeed, that those stately chambers should afford the hospitality of a frequent and spacious *bed,* in which the weary guest might lie down and sleep till the next breakfast time; but perhaps this is only my sensuality, and sure I am meanwhile that you are a matchless summer house, green with clambering vines, and girt with cool piazzas fit to entertain the democratic host as it marches from the old worn-out past to the beckoning and blossoming future.

But this is the lack of the men here, of all I know, at least. They are all of them depressed or embittered by the public embarrassments that beset them; deflected, distorted, or somehow despoiled of their rich individual manliness, by the necessity of providing for these imbecile old inheritances of church and state. Carlyle is the same old sausage, fizzing and sputtering in his own grease, only infinitely more unreconciled to the blessed Providence which guides human affairs. He names God frequently, and alludes to the highest things as if they were realities; but it almost looks as if he did it only for a picturesque effect, so completely does he seem to regard them as habitually circumvented and set at naught by the politicians. I took our friend McKay[13] to see him, and he came away greatly distressed and *désillusionné,* Carlyle having taken the utmost pains to deny and decry and deride the idea of his having done the least good to anybody, and to profess, indeed, the utmost contempt for everybody who thought he had; and McKay, being intent upon giving him a plenary assurance of this fact in his own case. It strikes me that the Scotch nature does not easily lend itself to the highest conventional culture, and Carlyle would have fared better in personal respects to have remained a Cameronian preacher, if only government persecution had still left a bounty on that career, than to have descended into the circle of London amenities. . . .

But farewell, my dear Emerson, and believe me, ever devotedly, yours,

H. JAMES

After Carlyle's death in 1881 James published his "Personal Recollections," [14] incorporating detailed notes of Carlyle's talk which he had taken down in these early days. Although in this later article he testified to his "affectionate esteem" for Carlyle's memory,[15] the letters that follow prove that his first ardor for Carlyle in the book was somewhat cooled by Carlyle in the flesh, and that his ad-

---

[13] There is an account of this interview in James's published recollections of Carlyle, *L.R.H.J.,* 446 ff. The friend is Col. James Morrison McKay (later changed to MacKaye), 1805-88, artist, abolitionist, and man of affairs, who moved from Buffalo to Newport about 1850. When James came to reside in Newport the two men became close friends, and James later rented McKay's house for two years (1860-61). William and Henry were schoolmates and playfellows of McKay's son, James Steele McKay, the famous dramatist, actor, and theatrical manager, father of Percy MacKaye, the poet, and James MacKaye, the economist. (*Cf.* Percy MacKaye, *Epoch, The Life of Steele Mac-Kaye,* 1927, I.)

[14] *Atlantic,* XLVII (1881), 593; reprinted in *L.R.H.J.*

[15] *L.R.H.J.,* 422.

miration was qualified not only by dissent, but by an element of personal repugnance. Both men enjoyed denunciation, and used a full-blooded style of talk and writing; but James was fundamentally optimistic and eupeptic, Carlyle pessimistic and dyspeptic. Carlyle despised his fellow men, or when he loved them did so with a pitying eye for their weaknesses. "His own intellectual life," writes James,

> consisted so much in bemoaning the vices of his race, or drew such inspiration from despair, that he could not help regarding a man with contempt the instant he found him reconciled to the course of history. Pity is the highest style of intercourse he allowed himself with his kind. He compassionated all his friends in the measure of his affection for them. "Poor John Sterling," he used always to say; "poor John Mill, poor Frederick Maurice, poor Neuberg, poor Arthur Helps, poor little Browning, poor little Lewes," and so on; as if the temple of his friendship were a hospital, and all its inmates scrofulous or paralytic.[16]

James, on the other hand, never forgot the Man in men, and his love was always flavored with respect, if not with reverence. He was a good American, especially when he was in England; while Carlyle did not hesitate to express his poor opinion of Americans both collectively and singly. Carlyle, furthermore, heaped scorn upon reformers in general, and upon Fourier in particular. Here was the head and front of his offending—the lack of that faith and zeal which moved reformers, and to which Americans were by nature predisposed:

> Nothing maddened him so much as to be mistaken for a reformer, really intent upon the interests of God's righteousness upon the earth, which are the interests of universal justice. This is what made him hate Americans, and call us a nation of bores,—that we took him at his word, and reckoned upon him as a sincere well-wisher to his species. He hated us, because a secret instinct told him that our exuberant faith in him would never be justified by closer knowledge; for no one loves the man who forces him upon a premature recognition of himself.[17]

The Saturday Club of which Emerson had proposed James as a charter member, began its regular meetings in the winter of 1855-1856. It was a group of congenial spirits who dined together and dined well, at Parker's Hotel in Boston, at three o'clock in the afternoon of the last Saturday of each month. The original members were Louis Agassiz; Richard H. Dana; John S. Dwight; Emerson; Judge Ebenezer R. Hoar of Concord; Lowell; Motley; Benjamin Peirce, the distinguished Harvard mathematician; Samuel G. Ward, banker and patron of art and letters; Edwin P. Whipple, lecturer and essayist; and Horatio Woodman, the club's most active promoter and organizer. Among others who joined the club in its early years were Longfellow; Dr. Holmes;

[16] *L.R.H.J.*, 424.
[17] *Ibid.*, 451.

W. H. Prescott; Whittier; Hawthorne; John M. Forbes, merchant and builder of railroads; Charles Eliot Norton; Reverend Frederick H. Hedge, Unitarian minister in Bangor, Providence, and Brookline, renowned for his knowledge of German literature and philosophy, professor of ecclesiastical history and afterwards of German at Harvard; Charles Sumner; John A. Andrew, Massachusetts's famous war-time governor; James T. Fields, publisher and friend of famous authors; Jeffries Wyman, professor of anatomy at Harvard; E. W. Gurney, professor of history and dean at Harvard; William Morris Hunt, the painter, who was a Newport neighbor of James; Charles Francis Adams. James, although he had returned definitely from Europe in the autumn of 1860, was not elected to the club until 1863, when he was about to transfer his residence from Newport to Boston.[18] Meanwhile, however, he had been present as an invited guest. On one such occasion, January 26, 1861, he was a fellow guest with William Ellery Channing, the Concord poet. The following letter is an account of his impressions on this occasion, written in his raciest and most extravagant style. Its personalities are strictly Jamesian. He never hesitated to abuse his best friends, or to follow the impulse of his highly pictorial imagination at the cost of all sense of proportion. The fact is, of course, that he never quite meant it, and expected *that* to be understood. There was an unspoken tenderness that shone in his face, or was somehow intimated in the very absurdity of his invective, and which offset the literal meaning of his words.

Boston, Sunday night [1861]

My dear Emerson,—

I am going to Concord in the morning but shall have barely time to see you, if I do as much as that: yet I can't forbear to say a word I want to say about Hawthorne and Ellery Channing. Hawthorne isn't a handsome man nor an engaging one anyway, personally: he had the look all the time, to one who didn't know him, of a rogue who suddenly finds himself in a company of detectives. But in spite of his rusticity I felt a sympathy for him amounting to anguish and couldn't take my eyes off him all the dinner, nor my rapt attention; as that indecisive little Dr. Hedge found, I am afraid to his cost, for I hardly heard a word of what he kept on saying to me, and felt at one time very much like sending down to Mr. Parker to have him removed from the room as maliciously putting his artificial little person between me and a profitable object of study.

Yet I feel now no ill-will to Hedge and could recommend any one (but myself) to go and hear him preach. Hawthorne, however, seemed to me to possess human substance and not to have dissipated it all away as that debauched Charles Norton, and the good, inoffensive, comforting Longfellow. He seemed much nearer the human being than any one at that end of the table, much nearer. John Forbes and yourself kept up the balance at the other end: but that

---

[18] James moved to Boston in the spring of 1864, and from that time on he was a frequent attendant. He liked Dr. Holmes above all his fellow members save Emerson.

end was a desert with him for its only oasis. It was so pathetic to see him, contented, sprawling Concord owl that he was and always has been, brought blindfold into that brilliant daylight, and expected to wink and be lively like any little dapper Tommy Titmouse, or Jenny Wren. How he buried his eyes in his plate, and ate with such a voracity that no person should dare to ask him a question!

My heart broke for him as that attenuated Charles Norton kept putting forth his long antennæ towards him, stroking his face, and trying whether his eyes were shut. The idea I got was, and it was very powerfully impressed upon me, that we are all of us monstrously corrupt, hopelessly bereft of human consciousness, and that it is the intention of the Divine Providence to overrun us and obliterate us in a new Gothic and Vandalic invasion of which this Concord specimen is a first fruits. It was heavenly to see him persist in ignoring Charles Norton, and shutting his eyes against his spectral smiles: eating his dinner and doing absolutely nothing but that, and then going home to his Concord den to fall upon his knees, and ask his heavenly Father why it was that an owl couldn't remain an owl, and not be forced into the dimensions of a canary. I have no doubt that all the tenderest angels saw to his care that night, and poured oil into his wounds more soothing than gentlemen ever know.

William Ellery Channing, too, seemed so human and good, sweet as summer, and fragrant as pine woods. He is more sophisticated than the other of course, but still he was kin; and I felt the world richer by two *men,* who had not yet lost themselves in mere members of society. This is what I suspect; that we are fast getting so fearful one to another, we "members of society," that we shall ere long begin to kill one another in self-defense, and give place in that way at last to a more veracious state of things. The old world is breaking up on all hands: the glimpse of the everlasting granite I caught in Hawthorne and William Ellery, shows me that there is stock enough left for fifty better. Let the old impostor go, bag and baggage, for a very real and substantial one is aching to come in, in which the churl shall not be exalted to a place of dignity, in which innocence shall never be tarnished nor trafficked in, in which every man's freedom shall be respected down to its feeblest filament as the radiant altar of God. To the angels, says Swedenborg, death means resurrection to life; by that necessary rule of inversion which keeps them separate from us and us from them, and so prevents our being mutual nuisances.

Let us then accept political and all other destruction that chooses to come: because what is disorder and wrath and contention on the surface is sure to be the deepest peace at the centre, working its way thus to a surface that shall *never* be disorderly. Yours,

H. J.

P.S. . . . What a world! What a world! But once we get rid of slavery and the new heavens and new earth will swim into reality.[19]

---

[19] This letter has been printed with omissions in Sanborn and Harris, *A. Bronson Alcott,* 1893, 465-8; E. W. Emerson, *The Early Years of the Saturday Club,* Houghton Mifflin Co., 1918, 331-2; and E. D. Hanscom, *The Friendly Craft,* 1908, 152-4. A passage in H.J.[2]'s *Hawthorne* (1880, 78) is reminiscent of part of this letter of his father's: "He [Hawthorne] must have been struck with the glare of her understanding [Margaret Fuller's], and, mentally speaking, have scowled and blinked a good deal in conversation with her."

Some months later Emerson commented on this letter as follows:

> I never thanked you by a written syllable for that happiest letter you wrote of the Club, so nobly true in its broad lights, that one was forced to forgive the perverse shadows you chose to throw on some of our quaintest statues;—but I insisted on reading the entire letter to Ellery Channing, who vainly endeavored to disown his joy. Continue to shine on me, in spite of my ingratitude. If you should now and then send me a letter, I do not think contumacy or old age could long resist you,—the old heart would melt and flow at your command.[20]

The relations between James and Emerson were further cemented, and extended to their families, when, after the return from Europe in 1860, the two youngest James boys, Wilkinson and Robertson, were placed in Mr. Frank Sanborn's school in Concord. A letter from James to Mrs. William A. Tappan describes this episode and at the same time contains a charming picture of Emerson at home:

> Mary[21] and I trotted forth last Wednesday, bearing Wilky and Bob in our arms to surrender them to the famous Mr. Sanborn. . . . Then we drove to Emerson's and waded up to our knees through a harvest of apples and pears, which, tired of their mere outward or carnal growth, had descended to the loving bosom of the lawn . . . until at last we found the cordial Pan himself in the midst of his household, breezy with hospitality and blowing exhilarating trumpets of welcome. Age has just the least in the world dimmed the lustre we once knew, but an unmistakable breath of the morning still encircles him, and the odour of primæval woods. . . . Still I insist that he is a voluntary Pan, that it is a condition of mere wilfulness and insurrection on his part, contingent upon a mercilessly sound digestion and an uncommon imaginative influx, and I have no doubt that even he, as the years ripen, will at last admit Nature to be tributary and not supreme. . . . Then and upon the waves of that friendly music we were duly wafted to our educational Zion and carefully made over our good and promising and affectionate boys to the school-master's keeping. . . . The short of the story is that we left them and rode home robbed of our plumage, feeling sore and ugly and only hoping that they wouldn't die, any of these cold winter days, before the parental breast could get there to warm them back to life or cheer them on to a better.[22]

The Emersons followed the early development and European adventures of William and Henry James, Jr., with an almost familial interest. The proud father sometimes took his sons' letters to Concord and read them aloud. The following letter to William from his father reveals Emerson's interest in Wil-

---

[20] March 29, 1861.
[21] Mary Walsh James, beloved wife of H.J.[1]
[22] These extracts are taken from the letter as published in *N.S.B.*, 221 ff.

liam's impressions of Herman Grimm. It also contains another characterization of Emerson, whom James cannot mention without sketching his portrait:—

Cambridge, March 18 [1868]

My dear Willy,—

Everything goes on from week to week without shock or agreeable surprise to tell you of, so that one's letters become mere love messages. You get plenty of love from us all here, and your friends everywhere abound in your praises. Emerson wants me to take all your letters down to him that touch upon the Grimms to be read there in conclave, and I go next Saturday for that purpose. I happened to read one of your first letters there from Dresden about German women and the language, etc., and Ellen Emerson was near going into fits over the reading. I hope she will escape a catastrophe on Saturday.

Emerson's unreality to me grows evermore. You have got to deal with him as with a child, making all manner of allowances for his ignorance of everything above the senses, and putting such a restraint upon your intellect as tires you to death. I can't find anything but a pedantic intention in him. He has no sympathy with nature, but is a sort of a police-spy upon it, chasing it into its hiding-places, and noting its subtlest features, for the purpose of reporting them to the public; that's all. He is an uncommonly sharp detective, but a detective he is and nothing more. He never for a moment drops his office, loses sight of himself, and becomes drowned in the beautiful illusion, but is sure always to appear as a fisherman with his fish upon the hook. The proof of all this is that he breeds no love of nature in his intellectual offspring, but only the love of imitating him and saying similar 'cute things about nature and man. I love the man very much, he is such a born natural; but his books are to me wholly destitute of spiritual flavour, being at most carbonic acid gas and *water*. . . . Ever your loving DADDY

There is no record of further correspondence after 1872. Emerson was failing; and each man had, no doubt, given to the other all that the other was prepared to receive. Each was to the other one of those "partial minds" which Emerson found his friends to possess, in place of that symmetry he had first looked for.[23] Both men died in the same year—in 1882; but before the end their attachment had already grown increasingly remote and reminiscent.

[23] In his journal for October, 1862, he says this of Thoreau, Charles Newcomb, Alcott, and Henry James. *Cf.* Bliss Perry, *Heart of Emerson's Journals*, 1926, 289.

III

PERSONAL CHARACTERISTICS OF THE ELDER JAMES

In the autumn of 1866 the James family moved from Boston to Cambridge, where they took up their residence at 20 Quincy Street, across the street from Harvard College.[1] Here they lived for fifteen years. James remained in close contact with his New England circle of friends and continued to attend the Saturday Club. Thus Charles Eliot Norton, writing to Carlyle in 1876, immediately after returning from one of its meetings, reports the presence of "your old acquaintance Henry James, with his Swedenborgian enthusiasms and eccentricities."[2] There is a certain pathos in this characterization. When these words were written he was working, at the age of sixty-five, with unabated energy and with unshaken conviction. *Society the Redeemed Form of Man,* a major book in his most vigorous style, was completed three years later, in spite of the paralytic stroke which had already marked the advent of declining health. When the end came in 1882 he was in the midst of a last restatement of his message,[3] no less triumphant than those which had preceded. But to the world at large, and to many who knew him well, he was only "enthusiastic and eccentric."

E. L. Godkin spent the years from 1875 to 1881 in Cambridge, where he had long been a frequent visitor, owing to his close association with Norton and Lowell in the founding and editing of the *Nation.* Towards the end of his life he wrote his recollections of "Old Cambridge," in which is again revealed the impression that James was indubitably a "character," with, however, an exceedingly dubious philosophy:—

> Henry James, the elder, was a person of delightful eccentricity, and a humorist of the first water. When in his grotesque moods, he maintained that, to a right-minded man, a crowded Cambridge horse-car "was the nearest approach to heaven upon earth!" What was the precise nature of his philosophy, I never fully understood, but he professed to be a Swedenborgian, and carried on a correspondence full of droll incidents with anxious inquirers, in various parts

---

[1] This house afterwards became the Colonial Club, and has recently been torn down to make room for the new Faculty Club.

[2] *Letters of C. E. Norton,* ed. by Sara Norton and M. A. De Wolfe Howe, Houghton Mifflin Co., 1913, II, 60.

[3] *Spiritual Creation,* published posthumously in *L.R.H.J.*

of the country. Asking him one day about one of these, he replied instantly, "Oh, a devil of a woman!" to my great astonishment, as I was not then thoroughly familiar with his ways. One of his most amusing experiences was that the other Swedenborgians repudiated all religious connection with him, so that the sect to which he belonged, and of which he was the head, may be said to have consisted of himself alone. He was a writer of extraordinary vigor and picturesqueness, and I suppose there was not in his day a more formidable master of English style.

His son, the author, then a youth of nineteen or twenty, was just beginning to try his literary wings. There could not be a more entertaining treat than a dinner at the James house, when all the young people were at home. They were full of stories of the oddest kind, and discussed questions of morals or taste or literature with a vociferous vigor so great as sometimes to lead the young men to leave their seats and gesticulate on the floor. I remember, in some of these heated discussions, it was not unusual for the sons to invoke humorous curses on their parent, one of which was, that "his mashed potatoes might always have lumps in them!" [4]

James, like Socrates, was picturesque and convivial. But like Socrates he had a mission to mankind—and even, unlike Socrates, a gospel. He can have enjoyed little conviction of the efficacy of his mission or of the acceptance of his gospel. He was not dismayed, nor ever doubted his faith, but it is not surprising that there should have been moments when he doubted himself. His wife wrote on March 17, 1874, to the younger Henry in Europe:

Father came back comfortably from his Providence spree, but rather discouraged, I think, as he always is, after giving a lecture. All that he has to say seems so good and glorious, and easily understood to him, but it falls so dead upon the dull or skeptical ears who come to hear him, that I do not wonder he feels so.

When the James family moved to Boston William James had just entered the Harvard Medical School. When they moved to Cambridge he was still engaged in his medical studies, and after 1873 he was a teacher in Harvard College.

The following letter, written by their father to Henry James, Jr., gives a day of his social life at this time. Professor Ephraim W. and Mrs. Ellen Hooper Gurney were among the closer intimates. Gurney was at this time professor of history, dean of the faculty, and right-hand man of President Eliot; and Henry Adams was an assistant professor of history—both, of course, at Harvard.

[Cambridge], Oct. 17, 1873

My darling Harry,—

Willy is spinning on his way to you in this the seventh day of his voyage,[5] and will probably reach you before this letter. I hope from the style of weather

---

[4] *Life and Letters of Edwin Lawrence Godkin*, 1907, edited by Rollo Ogden, The Macmillan Co., 1907, II, 117-8.

[5] For further details of this voyage, *cf.* below, 138 ff.

we have had since he left, that his voyage has been smooth, at least comparatively. Never was there such an autumn known for blandness in point of air, and gorgeous golden pomp in point of light. The heavens seem bent upon decorating the earth with new beauties every day, and such a sunset of blazing and dazzling crimson as we had last night was enough to make the very cattle cry out, Alleluia. . . .

I lunched in the morning with President Charles Eliot to meet a Mr. Broderick,[6] a writer for the *Times*. Godkin and Agassiz and Henry Adams made up the remainder of the members. Mr. Broderick is most peculiar in appearance and conversation, so much so in fact as to call out your tenderness, and make you wish that his mother and sisters would keep him at home. I think he asked as many as eighty distinct questions in the two hours we were together. Agassiz was in great force, stomach and brain both; Henry Adams, saturnine and silent; Godkin as usual, but sad, very; and Charles Eliot himself very courteous and hospitable. In the evening I dined at the Gurneys' with Mr. and Mrs. Agassiz, Henry Adams and Clover [Hooper],[7] and Godkin. Henry Adams, Clover and Ellen [Gurney] all asked with interest after you, and all expressed pleasure in your literary activity. The hosts, both, and the Agassizs were particularly expressive in regard to Willy, and Mrs. Agassiz desired me particularly to give him her love and say to him that if she had known he was going so immediately, she would have come in to say good-bye to him. . . . In the morning at lunch Mr. Broderick asked President Eliot what sect President Grant favored. He replied, "The Methodist. At least I infer as much," he said, "from a remark he made to me about his boy when he came to put him in college, where he now is. I asked him what profession he destined his son for. He said, 'I think he will be a minister, for he is a *pious* child.'" This raised a laugh among the company, but I liked it. I thought it showed Grant more *simplex munditiis* than the professors and critics about me. . . .

Good-bye, my lovely boys. I have been hearing so many things about you both of late, apropos of Willy's going away, that I am quite set up. Your loving
DADDY

The period of the Quincy Street residence witnessed the growing absorption of the parents in the careers of the children, and especially of William and Henry. "It is a delight above all delights," wrote the father, "to see one's children turn out—as ours have done—all that the heart covets in children; and my delight is so full that I sometimes fancy my heart will have to burst for its own relief."[8] William lived with his parents (the intervals being spent in Europe) during the winter of 1866-1867, from the autumn of 1868 to the autumn of 1873, and from early in 1874 until his marriage in the summer of 1878—after which he continued to reside in Cambridge in his own house, uninterruptedly until 1882. The younger Henry lived at the Quincy Street house from 1866 to 1869,

[6] "Mr. Broderick" was George Charles Brodrick, Fellow and Warden of Merton College, Oxford, and leader writer on the *Times* (London) from 1860 to 1873. He was known in England for his sympathy with the cause of the Union.
[7] "Clover" Hooper was Marian Hooper, whom Henry Adams married in 1872.
[8] To H.J.[2], August 9, 1872.

from the spring of 1870 until the spring of 1872, and from the autumn of 1874
to the autumn of 1875; after which he definitely took up his residence in
Europe and remained continuously until 1881, when he returned for a visit
shortly before his mother's death. These were exciting and somewhat trying
years of pathfinding, and except for the relatively brief periods when *neither*
William nor Henry was in Europe, there were always letters from Cambridge
reflecting the home life there and the watchful, sympathetic, apprehensive interest in the adventures of the distant voyager. Some of these letters we shall
read later, since they form part of the story of William James's vocation. Although the father's advice was freely given and greatly respected, the ultimate
choice of their occupation was left to their own decision. He entered with the
warmest interest into *their* interests and communicated with William's philosophical friends and Henry's literary friends in Europe. Their Cambridge companions, Chauncey Wright, Oliver Wendell Holmes, Jr., Charles Peirce, W. D.
Howells, became intimates of his household.

The wife and mother of this family, Mary Walsh James, died on January 29,
1882, while Henry, her favorite son, was in America after an absence of six
years. What his mother was to her children, and to him in particular—sympathy and selfless love, "soundless and yet absolutely all-saving service and
trust"—can be read in his *Notes of a Son and Brother*.[9] To Godkin he wrote
on February 3: "My dearest mother died last Sunday—suddenly and tranquilly,
from an affection of the heart. . . . You know my mother and you know what
she was to us—the sweetest, gentlest, most natural embodiment of maternity—
and our protecting spirit, our household genius."[10] What Mrs. James meant to
her husband is revealed in the following letter to Henry, Jr., who had just
sailed for England:—

Boston, May 9 [1882]

My darling Harry,—

    I went out early after breakfast to see William yesterday, and he came down
from his bedroom *dancing* to greet me. He was apparently ever so much better.
. . . It was delightful to witness the elasticity of his spirits, and we had a capital talk. . . .

    And now, my darling boy, I must bid you farewell. How loving a farewell
it is, I can't say, but only that it is most loving. All my children have been very
good and sweet from their infancy, and I have been very proud of you and
Willy. But I can't help feeling that you are the one that has cost us the least
trouble, and given us always the most delight. Especially do I mind mother's
perfect joy in you the last few months of her life, and your perfect sweetness
to her. I think in fact it is this which endears you so much to me now. No
doubt the other boys in the same circumstances would have betrayed the same
tender and playful love to her, only they were not called upon to do so. I am

[9] 176-81.
[10] Godkin Collection, Widener Library.

no way unjust to them, therefore, but I feel that I have fallen heir to all dear mother's fondness for you, as well as my proper own, and bid you accordingly a distinctly widowed farewell. That blessed mother, what a link her memory is to us all henceforth! I think none of us who remember her natural unaffected ways of goodness, and especially her sleepless sense of justice, will ever again feel tempted to do a dishonest or unhandsome thing. She was not to me "a liberal education," intellectually speaking, as some one has said of his wife, but she really did arouse my heart, early in our married life, from its selfish torpor, and so enabled me to become a man. And this she did altogether unconsciously, without the most cursory thought of doing so, but solely by the presentation of her womanly sweetness and purity, which she herself had no recognition of. The sum of it all is, that I would sooner rejoin her in her modesty, and find my eternal lot in association with her, than have the gift of a noisy delirious world!

Good-bye then again, my precious Harry! . . . We shall each rejoice in you in our several way as you plough the ocean and attain to your old rooms, where it will be charming to think of you as once more settled and at work. I wish England itself offered a less troubled residence to you than it does. A lingering good-bye, then, dearest Harry, from all of us! and above all from your loving father,

H. J.

James did not long survive his bereavement. As the end approached he refused to take food. "Unfalteringly he claimed his right to the spiritual life, and most characteristically and consistently refused to nourish what he called death, saying *life* is fed by God Almighty." [11] When he died, on December 18, 1882, both of his elder sons were absent, William in London, Henry at sea vainly hoping to arrive before the end. The following letter from Henry in Boston to William in London describes their father's last hours.

Boston, Dec. 26, 1882

My dear William,—
You will already have heard the circumstances under which I arrived at New York on Thursday 21st, at noon, after a very rapid and prosperous, but painful passage. . . . They told me everything—or at least they told me a great deal—before we parted that night, and what they told me was deeply touching, and yet not at all literally painful. Father had been so tranquil and painless, had died so easily and, as it were, deliberately, and there had been none—not the least—of that anguish and confusion which we imagined in London. . . . It appears to have been most strange, most characteristic above all, and as full of beauty as it was void of suffering. There was none of what we feared—no paralysis, no dementia, no violence. He simply, after the improvement of which we were written before I sailed, had a sudden relapse—a series of swoons—after which he took to his bed not to rise again. He had no visible malady—

---

[11] Mrs. Catharine Walsh to W.J., December 23, 1882. Mrs. Walsh, a sister of Mrs. H.J.¹, was a beloved member of H.J.¹'s household until his death. To the children she was "Aunt Kate."

strange as it may seem. The "softening of the brain" was simply a gradual refusal of food, because he *wished* to die. There was no dementia except a sort of
exaltation of belief that he had entered into "the spiritual life." Nothing could
persuade him to eat, and yet he never suffered, or gave the least sign of suffering, from inanition. All this will seem strange and incredible to you—but told
with all the details, as Aunt Kate has told it to me, it becomes real—taking
Father as he was, almost natural. He prayed and longed to die. He ebbed and
faded away—though in spite of his strength becoming continually less, he was
able to see people and to talk. He wished to see as many people as he could,
and he talked with them without effort. . . . Alice[12] says he said the most
picturesque and humorous things! He knew I was coming and was glad, but
not impatient. He was delighted when he was told that you would stay in my
rooms in my absence, and seemed much interested in the idea. He had no belief, apparently, that he should live to see me, but was perfectly cheerful about
it. He slept a great deal and, as Aunt Kate says, there was "so little of the sick-
room" about him. He lay facing the windows which he would never have darkened—never pained by the light. . . . He spoke of everything—the disposition
of his things, made all his arrangements of every kind. Aunt Kate repeats
again and again, that he yearned unspeakably to die. . . . Ever your

H. James

Both of his elder sons felt the disproportion between James's inward greatness and the little that he left behind. There was a sense of sudden shrinkage.
Thus when William first heard the news of his father's death, he saw in swift
retrospect the events of that full and eager life and noted the comparative
slightness of their surviving effects: "What remains is a few printed pages, us
and our children and some incalculable modifications of other people's lives,
influenced this day or that by what he said or did." [13]

The volume of *The Literary Remains of the Late Henry James,* which William edited and published in 1884, and for which he wrote a long Introduction,
worthy alike of its subject and of its author, had a small and rapidly diminishing sale. This the author doubtless anticipated, for in the Introduction he had
already written of his father's maladjustment to his age. Whether he came too
late or too early is difficult to say—perhaps it amounts to the same thing. In
any case he brought a theological message to an untheological age. Those who
believe theologically are not receptive to new ideas,

whilst those of us who have intellectual vitality are either apt to be full of bias
against theism in any form, or if we are theistic at all, it is in such a tentative
and supplicating sort of way that the sight of a robust and dogmatizing theo-
logian sends a shiver through our bones. A man like my father, lighting on such
a time, is wholly out of his element and atmosphere, and is soon left stranded
high and dry. His effectiveness as a missionary is null; and it is wonderful if

[12] Alice James (1848-1892), youngest child and only daughter of the H.J.Srs.
[13] To A.H.J., December, 1882; *L.W.J.,* I, 221.

his voice, crying in the wilderness and getting no echo, do not soon die away for sheer discouragement.[14]

The content was as unseasonable as the method. For James insisted upon the tragic essence of the Christian hope, upon death as the way of life, in an age which was disposed to see only good in both nature and man.

A letter from the younger Henry James, written to his brother after the appearance of the *Literary Remains,* expresses the same sense of the futility of their father's mission.

London, Jan. 2, 1885

Dear William,—

. . . Three days ago . . . came the two copies of Father's (and your) book, which have given me great filial and fraternal joy. All I have had time to read as yet is the Introduction—your part of which seems to me admirable, perfect. It must have been very difficult to do, and you could n't have done it better. And how beautiful and extraordinarily individual (some of them magnificent) all the extracts from Father's writings which you have selected so happily. It comes over me as I read them (more than ever before) how intensely original and personal his whole system was, and how indispensable it is that those who go in for religion should take some heed of it. I can't enter into it (much) myself—I can't be so theological nor grant his extraordinary premises, nor throw myself into conceptions of heavens and hells, nor be sure that the keynote of nature is humanity, etc. But I can enjoy greatly the spirit, the feeling and the manner of the whole thing (full as this last is of things that displease me too), and feel really that poor Father, struggling so alone all his life, and so destitute of every worldly or literary ambition, was yet a great writer. At any rate your task is beautifully and honourably done—may it be as great or half as great a service as it deserves to be, to his memory!

The book came at a bad time for Alice[15] . . . but though she has been able to have it in her hand but for a moment, it evidently gives her great pleasure. She burst into tears when I gave it to her, exclaiming, "How beautiful it is that William should have done it! Is n't it, is n't it beautiful? And how good William is, how good, how good!" And we talked of poor Father's fading away into silence and darkness, the waves of the world closing over this system which he tried to offer it, and of how we were touched by this act of yours which will (I am sure) do so much to rescue him from oblivion. . . . Love to all. Ever your

HENRY

Never, in the case of a man of the world making the necessary concessions to social usage, were living and thinking more completely fused than in Henry James. In speaking once of the theological truths which he proclaimed, he said that they were "truths of the very life of man"; and, as his son said of him after his death, *his* truths were *his life.*[16] Truth being revealed to him in the very

[14] *L.R.H.J.,* 11.
[15] The sister Alice, at this time ill and living in London.
[16] *Nature of Evil,* 1855, 13; *L.R.H.J.,* 10.

living of it, he could not fail either to be what he affirmed, or to affirm what he was. Similarly, he valued others, including his children, for what they *were,* rather than for what they said or did. This profound integrity was the most characteristic thing about him. Such being the case, if the exigencies of consecutive exposition make it necessary to describe the man before we describe his ideas, we must be aware that either without the other is a misleading abstraction.

He was a man with a mission and at the same time dogged by a sense of futility. Like many single-minded men he exalted his cause and debased himself. He proclaimed his own beliefs and denounced other people's errors with the most unqualified dogmatism, but it was as though he were a vehicle and not an author of truths. Together with a positive and colorful individuality he had a "selfless detachment" which claimed no credit or superiority.[17]

Until ill-health began to tell upon him, there was nothing of the ascetic in James, either in his conduct or in his appearance; "a little fat, rosy Swedenborgian amateur," said Ellery Channing, "with the look of a broker, and the brains and heart of a Pascal."[18] He was full-blooded and robust, his invalidism, if such it can be called, being accidental and not constitutional. Speaking of his early boyhood, he said: "The common ore of existence perpetually converted itself into the gold of life in the glowing fire of my animal spirits."[19] Being crippled, he knew suffering and was permanently handicapped; but his animal spirits did not cease to glow. Behind his gifts of intellect and character there was always this organic exuberance. In society it made him, as Emerson said, "expansive,"[20] and not merely witty. He poured forth a profusion of animated talk. It made him playful, and contributed to that art of elaborate nonsense which was so characteristic of his family circle. It made him in all his human relations at one time romantically tender, at another almost boisterously bellicose, and often both at the same time. In fact a sort of bellicose tenderness, or beaming abusiveness, was one of his peculiar achievements.

The curious quality of James's friendships, as of his human relations generally, was not a temperamental accident, but sprang from that truth which was his life. He believed that mankind was one and divine, and that the weakness of mortals constituted a phase in their spiritual progress. Though he might see the individual's weakness with a discerning eye and describe it with telling epithets, he also saw beyond it to the mankind which he loved. All of his quarrels were family quarrels. Hence he could combine reprobation with indulgence—with jollity and warm affection, and even with respect. Such was his

[17] *N.S.B.,* 162.
[18] F. B. Sanborn, *Familiar Letters of H. D. Thoreau,* 1894, 145.
[19] *L.R.H.J.,* 183.
[20] Emerson to Samuel G. Ward, July 12, 1849; *cf.* E. W. Emerson, *Early Years of the Saturday Club,* 1918, 4, 8.

magnanimity that he could reconcile passionate loyalty to his ideas with a most delicate avoidance of pressing them either intrusively or despotically upon others. He had uncompromising convictions and an unusual power both of advocacy and of denunciation, but so strong was his humanity that nothing aroused real hostility in him—except inhumanity. Otherwise difference of opinion might excite his condemnation but not his resentment.

IV

FATHER AND SON

For the elder Henry James the most natural form of art, if art it can be called, was talk. Of all the arts, unless it be dancing, talk is the directest and most contemporaneous form of expression, the least detached and externalized. It is infused with bodily heat: like a blush or a gesture it reflects the feeling and the insight of the moment as it passes. The style of the natural talker is emphatic and mobile—meant to be listened to, with a brief and constantly shifting focus of attention, and not designed for contemplation. When this style is transferred from the spoken to the written word, it takes on an aspect of exaggeration, so that while James's talk was full-blooded, his writing at times seems plethoric. Nevertheless, as representing style of this intensely vital sort, he ranks high among English writers, despite the forbidding character of his subject matter. It is doubtful if Carlyle or Melville could have done better with James's theme. He was a humane Carlyle, an optimistic Melville, writing on theology and metaphysics.

His two elder sons, to each of whom style was a vocation, have set down their impressions of their father's peculiar quality. His books, resembling his talk and his character, could not fail, says Henry, "to flush with the strong colour, colour so remarkably given and not taken, projected and not reflected, colour of thought and faith and moral and expressional atmosphere."[1] We find him, says William,

> in the effortless possession of that style . . . which, to its great dignity of ca-
> dence and full and homely vocabulary, united a sort of inward palpitating hu-
> man quality, gracious and tender, precise, fierce, scornful, humorous by turns,
> recalling the rich vascular temperament of the old English masters, rather than
> that of an American of today.[2]

Garth Wilkinson not only knew James but could respond in kind:

> If eulogy were necessary, I could tell you how I have been dragged along at
> the chariot-wheels of your snorting-sentences, with my hair all streaming out be-

---

[1] *N.S.B.*, 163.
[2] *L.R.H.J.*, 9.

hind, while you were lashing on the speed in front; an attempt too ineffectual, to go my own way, while fastened by the feet to your impetuosity.[3]

The visceral quality of James's style must not be taken to mean a lack of artistry. He had what can only be described as a *command* of the English language. He creates the impression of using language, or even of abusing it, rather than of accommodating himself to it. In the heat of his conviction language was melted out of its stereotyped forms and remoulded or even amalgamated to his thought. Artful he certainly was not. But he had the artist's gift and the artist's flair. Once started on a period he elaborated and embroidered with evident creative joy. He let himself go.

Despite his acknowledged mastery of style, it was a common complaint that James was obscure. "Oh, that I might thunder it out," James once exclaimed, "in a single interjection that would tell the *whole* of it, and never speak a word again!" [4] He found himself compelled to return again and again to the same task, and neither he nor his audience ever felt that he had said what it was in him to say. Obscurity was the price he paid for being a philosopher. Both his talk and his writing were the vehicle of his ideas, and these ideas were inherently difficult to grasp. He was not satisfied to communicate anything less than their full depth and subtlety. No one could understand him who was not prepared to think as searchingly and as boldly as he did. There were many, therefore, who found his manner and his wit entertaining but were baffled by his doctrines, feeling that there was a recondite and hidden meaning that escaped them—as indeed there was.

That William James resembled his father in personal flavor and genius is inescapable. It was said of the father that he was "aninted with the isle of Patmos" [5]—that he was, in other words, both Hibernian and apocalyptic. The son was not apocalyptic, but he was Hibernian. Like his father he was warm-blooded, effervescent, and tenderly affectionate. Both men were unstable and impatient, though in neither case did this quality prevent long periods of intense and fruitful application. Alice James testified to this common quality of her father and her brother. She was writing in 1889 of William's European wanderings:

> William, instead of going to Switzerland, came suddenly back from Paris and went home, having, as usual, exhausted Europe in a few weeks, finding it stale, flat and unprofitable. The only necessity being to get home, the first letter after his arrival was, of course, full of plans for his return *plus* wife and infants; *he is just like a blob of mercury*—you can't put a mental finger upon him. Harry and I were laughing over him, and recalling Father, and William's

[3] Wilkinson to H.J.[1], April 5, 1850; the reference is to James's *Moralism and Christianity*.
[4] *L.R.H.J.*, 16.
[5] M. A. deW. Howe, *Memories of a Hostess*, Atlantic Monthly Press, 1922, 75.

resemblance (in his ways) to him. Though the results are the same, they seem to come from such a different nature in the two; in William, an entire inability or indifference to "stick to a thing for the sake of sticking," as someone said of him once; whilst Father, the delicious infant! could n't submit even to the thralldom of his own whim; and then the dear being was such a prey to the demon homesickness.[6]

According to the daughter's judgment the cause in the father's case was a sort of rebelliousness against control, and in the son's case a chronic infirmity of will—the lack of a capacity for laborious routine. Both were fond of laughter. Both were men of extreme spontaneity, with a tendency to embellishment and immoderate affirmation; both were mobile or even erratic in a degree that made it impossible for them to drive readily in harness or to engage easily in organized activity.

Based on this sameness are two marked differences. The father was fundamentally robust, the son relatively frail, with long periods of bodily disability and neurasthenia. There was more of sheer aboriginal force in the father, while the son depended more on the temper and edge of his instruments. The other difference is no less unmistakable, but more difficult to describe. The father was, as we have seen, an eccentric. His originality was more self-contained— he conceded less. William James was more mundane, more highly socialized, and had more of what men call "taste." He had queer ideas, but *he* was not queer. With all his philosophical detachment he knew instinctively how to meet the world on its own terms, how to make himself understood, and how to be free and spirited without ever transgressing the accepted norms of convention or polite intercourse. While the father had his moments of spiritual inebriety, the son was more securely restrained. There was a warm and explosive emotionality in both men, but in the son the outward expression was further removed from the central fire—more highly elaborated and more subtly controlled.

Their similarity of temperament predisposed father and son to the same style of utterance. William was also a talking writer, with a genius for picturesque epithets, and a tendency to vivid coloring and extreme freedom of manner. William, too, was one who wrote primarily in order to express convictions, giving the result a peculiar quality of sincerity. Like his father he presented philosophy in the form of literature, and invited the attention of lovers of literature, who thereupon found themselves unequal to the philosophy. Hence W. D. Howells, accustomed to literature rather than to philosophy, found that William's *Pragmatism* was brilliant but not clear, "like his father, who wrote the Secret of Swedenborg and kept it." [7] But there was a difference.

---

[6] *L.W.J.*, I, 289-90.
[7] Quoted by C. E. Norton in *Letters*, 1913, II, 379.

The son might be puzzling, but he was not, like the father, recondite or cryptic. He had a better control of his instrument and an infinitely better understanding of his audience. The father was quite capable of delivering jeremiads to an unhearing or even unlistening age; the son would have found any unreciprocal and noncommunicating relation intolerable.

The outstanding fact is the son's loving admiration of his father as a man. It was not only a filial love—it was an idealizing love. He loved the kind of man his father was. And such being the fact he could not fail to grow like him, in his habits, his feelings, his appraisals, his attitudes. There is a letter written by William four days before his father's death and never read by him to whom it was addressed:—

> In that mysterious gulf of the past into which the present soon will fall and go back and back, yours is still for me the central figure. All my intellectual life I derive from you; and though we have often seemed at odds in the expression thereof, I'm sure that there's a harmony somewhere, and that our strivings will combine. What my debt to you is goes beyond all my power of estimating,—so early, so penetrating and so constant has been the influence. . . . As for us; we shall live on each in his way,—feeling somewhat unprotected, old as we are, for the absence of the parental bosoms as a refuge, but holding fast together in that common sacred memory. We will stand by each other and . . . try to transmit the torch in our offspring as you did in us, and when the time comes for being gathered in, I pray we may, if not all, some at least, be as ripe as you. As for myself, I know what trouble I've given you at various times through my peculiarities; and as my own boys grow up, I shall learn more and more of the kind of trial you had to overcome in superintending the development of a creature different from yourself, for whom you felt responsible. I say this merely to show how my *sympathy* with you is likely to grow much livelier, rather than to fade—and not for the sake of regrets. . . . It comes strangely over me in bidding you good-bye how a life is but a day and expresses mainly but a single note. It is so much like the act of bidding an ordinary good-night. Good-night, my sacred old Father! If I don't see you again—Farewell! a blessed farewell! [8]

Turning from the man to his ideas, it is natural to speak first of the elder James as a critic. He criticized by the application of his doctrines, and this procedure was peculiarly characteristic of him. But in his criticism, much of it impromptu, his doctrines appear in the closest fusion with his personal traits.

First of all, he *was* a critic, an inveterate critic, both of men and of ideas. Criticism pervaded his talk; and the interest of his talk lay largely in the fact that he had emphatic, startling, not to say sensational, opinions on any topic that arose. In stating these opinions he was no respecter of persons. Never was a man more opinionative than he who believed that "the curse of mankind, that

---

[8] December 14, 1882; printed in full in *L.W.J.*, I, 218-20.

which keeps our manhood so little and so depraved, is its sense of selfhood, and the absurd, abominable opinionativeness it engenders!" [9] "Truth," he said, is "essentially combative"—and he evidently rejoiced in the fact.[10]

As can easily be imagined, James's methods of criticism have not always been approved. Referring to the relatively flattering picture of Hawthorne contained in the Saturday Club letter of 1861,[11] Hawthorne's biographer speaks of "the late Henry James" as "a humourous rhetorician, over-frank in his besprinkling of adjectives, which sometimes escaped the syringe at random, and hit no mark." [12] In speaking of his friend's harsh comments on Carlyle, Emerson accused him of a "passion for perversity." [13] But James's attacks were neither random nor perverse. They were reckless, but they invariably had a meaning and pointed a moral. They were for the most part directed against arrogance or complacency. As William James said,

> Nothing so endlessly besotted in Mr. James's eyes, as the pretension to possess personally any substantive merit or advantage whatever, any worth other than your unconscious uses to your kind! Nothing pleased him like exploding the bubbles of conventional dignity, unless it was fraternizing on the simplest and commonest plane with all lowly persons whom he met. To exalt humble and abase proud things was ever the darling sport of his conversation,—a conversation the somewhat reckless invective humor of which, when he was in the *abasing* mood, often startled the good people of Boston, who did not know him well enough to see the endlessly genial and humane intuition from which the whole mood flowed.[14]

If there was an implied philosophy in James's abasing, there was an explicit philosophy in his more deliberate criticism. There was, in the first place, a clearly recognizable attitute to art. Inasmuch as, of his two oldest sons, William had a predilection for the art of painting and Henry for the art of letters, this was a matter of some importance in the domestic circle. Fundamentally, James's disparagement of art expressed his sense of the overwhelming importance of religion. This, I take it, underlay his opinion that art was too "narrowing" [15]—literature, or any other art, is so much less than life! The failure of art consists in being spiritually sterile—a mere reiteration of nature and echo of worldliness. But in attacking art as it exists, James was at the same time thinking of art as it ought to be. A fundamental fault of what the world calls art, and esteems as such, is its divorce from honest conviction. The true artist

[9] *L.R.H.J.,* 62.
[10] *The Church of Christ Not an Ecclesiasticism,* 1854, 3.
[11] *Cf.* above, 18-19.
[12] F. B. Sanborn, "The Friendships of Hawthorne," in *The Hawthorne Centenary,* Houghton Mifflin Co., 1905, 192.
[13] Emerson to H.J.[1], September 7, 1869.
[14] *L.R.H.J.,* 75-6.
[15] *Cf.* below, 43, 59.

will "give natural body to spiritual conception"; he will work "only to satisfy an inspiration, thus from attraction, and therefore divinely"—his business being "to glorify MAN in nature and in men." [16]

Such being James's theory of art and literature, his considered judgments of literary men will naturally turn on the extent to which these are vehicles of spiritual truth—as James saw it. Thus Thackeray was ignorant of true religion, but in creating Becky Sharp be builded better than he knew:

> Why do we justify Becky in our inmost hearts, even while condemning her vicious methods? Because it is entirely transparent throughout the book that her evils have not their source in herself, but only in her externally defective fellowship with others. . . . Her whole life was a struggle to get a position, to become herself, to burst the sepulchral environment in which she was born, and come forth into God's genial and radiant air. You might as well expect a drowning man to respect the tails of your coat, if they come within his reach, as expect so vital a soul as this to rest content in that stifling atmosphere, or forego any chance, however conventionally denounced, of freeing herself from it. . . . No, it is sheer error to pronounce the actions ascribed to Becky in this book, *hers*. They were not hers. She was the hand that executed them, but the soul that animated or inspired them was the inharmonic society in which she was born and matured.[17]

As between Dickens and Thackeray, James preferred the latter. Dickens's moralism, being trite and shallow, must needs be seasoned with exaggeration:

> Dickens has no suspicion of astral depths in man. Life is to him a pure surface, bounded on the north by the head, on the south by the belly, on the east by the heart, on the west by the liver, and whatsoever falls without these palpable limits is double-Dutch and moonshine. . . . When one's whole conception of the mystery and majesty of life is limited to the obvious antagonism of virtue and vice, of the church and the play-house, it is evident that the conception will not carry him a great way, and that the jaded palates of novel-readers will speedily crave a more piquant refection. Hence you find all Dickens's virtue to be necessarily tainted. His virtuous men are like game on the turn, appetising to a sophisticated taste, but revolting to a healthy one.[18]

James admired Turgenev[19] because he was radically pessimistic. Since the way to the heights leads through the depths, the sooner one descends to total disillusionment the sooner can one mount again to hope. Writing to Turgenev on June 19, 1874, James said:

---

[16] *Lectures and Miscellanies*, 1852, 117, 118, 125.

[17] From a review of *Vanity Fair*, in the *Spirit of the Age*, edited by William H. Channing, I (1849), 50, 51.

[18] *N. Y. Tribune*, November 13, 1852.

[19] There is no "correct" spelling of this name. The owner of the name himself, in his letters to H.J.[1] and H.J.[2], uses "Turgeniew," "Turgèniew," and "Tourguéneff."

Men and women of great and surprising genius have made romance an instrument second only to the drama, as an educative power over the emotions.
But it must be said of the greatest of these, that the most they do is, either like
Scott to give us stirring pictures of human will *aux prises* with outward circumstance, and finally victorious over it; or else, like George Sand, Thackeray and
George Eliot, to give us an idea of the enervating and palsying effect of social
convention upon the conscience, in rendering men sceptical, self-indulgent and
immoral. But you as a general thing strike a far deeper chord in the consciousness of your reader. You sink your shaft sheer through the world of outward
circumstance, and of social convention, and shew us ourselves in the fixed grasp
of fate, so to speak, or struggling vainly to break the bonds of temperament.
Superficial critics revolt at this tragic spectacle, and pronounce you cynical. They
mistake the profound spirituality of your method, and do not see that what
touches the earnest heart of man, and fills it with divinest love and pity for its
fellow-man, is infinitely more educative than anything addressed to his frivolous
and self-righteous head.

Of much more serious importance was James's criticism of Emerson and
Carlyle. It is natural to couple these two men together as familiar divinities in
the James household. Father and sons must deal with them, and each must settle his account. James regarded Emerson as a spiritual manifestation, and not
as a source of ideas. Even as an imitation of perfection, he could not satisfy
James because of what the latter thought to be a personal incompleteness, an
absence, namely, of "conscience." [20] Emerson embodied innocence of the pre-
natal sort, rather than the seasoned blessedness that accrues from conflict and
struggle. Having no conviction of sin, he was incapable of repentance, and
therefore could not know that supreme joy of being united with God, which
is the highest moment of life and the purpose of creation.

Carlyle, like Emerson, was too little of a philosopher to satisfy James. "He
is an artist, a wilful artist, and no reasoner. He has only genius." [21] But he differed from Emerson in his extravagant manifestation of that very conscience
which Emerson lacked. It was to Carlyle's credit that he recognized evil and
pitted the moral will against it, but he never rose to that higher understanding
in which their opposition is seen as the necessary condition of a fuller spiritual
growth.

It is clear that James did not conceal his opinions of men and of ideas, and
although these opinions were not commonly addressed to his sons, they were
overheard and taken to heart. A sympathetic responsiveness to his father's
judgment accounts for two of William James's most characteristic habits of
thought. In the first place, he shared the same distaste for orthodoxy. As soon
as ideas became established, or were proclaimed with unction and airs of authority, they became repugnant. You could spoil any good thing for him by

[20] *L.R.H.J.*, 294.
[21] M. A. deW. Howe, *Memories of a Hostess*, 73.

converting it into an institution. That was the way the elder James felt about Swedenborgianism and Christianity, and the younger about science. Closely associated with this first attitude is his disposition to champion the weak and assail the strong. Look over the list of those whom William James attacked most severely, of those for whom he refused to make allowances, and they will prove to be men with some pride of office—some touch of insolence, smugness, self-importance, or complacency. In short, William, like his father, was sometimes in an "abasing mood."

How far William James shared, or was affected by, his father's judgment upon art will appear more clearly in the sequel. It belongs to the story of his vocation. Suffice it to say that his abandonment of painting for science and philosophy was in his father's favor, since it meant a search for truth and the use of style as a vehicle of ideas. We shall also learn more later of William James's opinions of literature, since these opinions came to clearest expression in his intercourse with his brother. But his attitude to Carlyle and Emerson concerns his relations with his father. These men were his father's friends and contemporaries, and the first became known to him through his father's personal impressions.

What gifts, then, did these fairy godfathers bestow on William James in his youth? Neither gave him his philosophy, both gave him precepts and apt quotations. They both influenced his style in his most impressionable period. He responded to Emerson in his acquiescent or optimistic moods, to Carlyle in his warlike moods. In 1903 he reread Emerson extensively, "volume after volume," in preparation for his Centenary address at Concord. In that address he confirmed his father's opinion that Emerson was a seer rather than a thinker. What, then, did this seer see? For William James, Emersonian truth consisted essentially in the vision of a deeper unity behind multiple appearances. Even the individualism or nonconformism of Emerson, which was "the hottest side of him," was not pluralistic. If he separated one individual from other individuals morally, it was only to unite them all on their cosmic side, as being potentially "mouthpieces of the Universe's meaning." [22] This teaching is allied to James's teaching of the unique preciousness and valid claim of each individual, however obscure or despised; but it is a different teaching, divided by all that separates monism from pluralism.

The heat which he missed in Emerson, William James found in Carlyle. The essays published in 1898 under the title of *The Will to Believe* were composed in part as early as 1879, and they prove how deeply in his youth their author had drunk of Carlyle. When the moment of solution came it was often Carlyle that provided the solvent. Especially is this true of the problem of evil, where

<hr/>

[22] *L.W.J.*, II, 190, 196-7; *Memories and Studies*, 1911, 25, 32.

the solution was found in the "gospel of work, of fact, of veracity." "The only escape," writes James,

> is by the practical way. And since I have mentioned the nowadays much-reviled name of Carlyle, let me mention it once more, and say it is the way of his teaching. No matter for Carlyle's life, no matter for a great deal of his writing. What was the most important thing he said to us? He said: "Hang your sensibilities! Stop your sniveling complaints, and your equally sniveling raptures! Leave off your general emotional tomfoolery, and get to WORK like men!"

In adopting this gospel William James specifically and with deep conviction rejected that very solution which was his father's: the transcendence, namely, of moral distinctions in a higher or æsthetic flight of the spirit. The father had reproached Carlyle for grimly accepting the finality of the moral struggle; the son says, *with* Carlyle, that "it feels like a real fight." [23]

In proportion as we pass from temperament and personal traits to ideas, the influence of Henry James upon his son William becomes attenuated. By his own contemporaries the elder James was commonly referred to as "the philosopher." Now there are a good many ways of being a philosopher or a metaphysician, and Henry James's was the way of conviction and intuition. This was not an inadvertence on his part. He *believed* in believing: "For he is far likelier to prove a wise man in the long run, whose negations are fed by his beliefs, than he whose beliefs are starved upon his negations." As to intuition, man has "an inward law or light telling him what good and evil, truth and falsity, respectively are, and so insuring all the possibilities of his spiritual destiny." "Truth indeed! How should any man of woman born pretend to such ability? Truth must *reveal itself* if it would be known; and even then how imperfectly known at best!" [24]

William James could not sympathize with this kind of philosophy or with that of his father's contemporaries who argued freely from analogy, took figures of speech literally, and produced a blend of poetry and science which was neither the one nor the other. He had contracted at an early age the scientist's standard of parsimony, which forbids one's spending more in the way of belief than one's income in the form of fact. Although he took liberties with science, he had scientific scruples. To his father "science" was anathema, as were all those thinkers, Sir William Hamilton, Mansel, Herbert Spencer, Comte, Taine, and Mill, who tried to be scientific in philosophy. William's scientific training, on the other hand, predisposed him from his early years in

---

[23] *W.B.*, 61, 87, 173-4.
[24] *Substance and Shadow*, 445; "Faith and Science," *North Amer. Rev.*, CII (1865), 369; *L.R.H.J.*, 63.

favor of precisely these philosophers. Hence, however harshly he might criticize science elsewhere, before his father he was its champion.

When William affirms that his father has no "intellectual sympathies," or that he is no "reasoner," or wishes something could be taken up from him into "a system more articulately scientific," [25] he did not mean to deny that his father philosophized. He meant that his father did not *earn* his beliefs, but freely helped himself to them. "A sceptical state," said the elder James, "I have never known for a moment." [26] But philosophy in the modern and critical sense familiar to William *begins* with scepticism, and must perpetually be tested by it.

There remains one fundamental sense in which William James derived his father's philosophy unqualifiedly from his father. Immediately after his father's death he wrote: "For me, the humor, the good spirits, the humanity, the faith in the divine, and the sense of his right to have a say about the deepest reasons of the universe, are what will stay by me." [27] The insistence on having his "say about the universe" is the profoundest motive of William James's thinking, as well as of his filial gratitude.

As we turn from the method of philosophy to its doctrines, we find father and son sharply divided. In the concluding pages of the Introduction to his father's *Literary Remains*, William James made his most considered statement of this issue. The "most serious enemy" to his father's religious monism, he says, is "the *philosophic* pluralist," [28] the ally of moralism. The former accepts evil as a moral phase of the higher spiritual good, the latter repudiates and destroys it. Writing in 1903 to a European inquirer, he said, "I wish I could see that my philosophy came from my father." [29] His impulse, always strong, to credit other persons with his ideas would have been doubly strong in the case of his father. But the difference was too profound to be annulled even by filial devotion. The issue between monism and a pluralistic moralism was always to the younger James the gravest of philosophical issues, and here, so far as theory and profession went, he and his father were on opposite sides.

But this does not mean that William James unqualifiedly renounced his father's religious philosophy. He set out in another direction. He achieved his own philosophical majority and his own personal salvation through the gospel of moralism. So much is unquestionable. But he did not forget that earlier way of thinking which he had learned at home. In 1897 he remarked, quite

[25] W.J. to H.J.², November 1, 1869; W.J. to Shadworth H. Hodgson, February 20, 1885.

[26] *N.S.B.*, 235.

[27] *L.W.J.*, I, 221.

[28] *L.R.H.J.*, 116.

[29] His correspondent, M. Pierre Bovet, was at this time offering a course on James's philosophy at the Academy of Neuchâtel, perhaps the first such course to be given. The letter is dated October 16, 1903.

casually and parenthetically, "Religion is the great interest of my life." [30] Since it would be unjust to hold a man strictly to a statement made in an unguarded moment, let us say that religion was *one* of the great interests of his life. That being the case, it was not surprising that his father's influence should have been both deep and permanent. "Father's cry," he said, "was the single one that religion is real. The thing is so to 'voice' it that other ears shall hear,—no easy task, but a worthy one, which in some shape I shall attempt." [31]

In short, the father testified most eloquently and memorably to the *reality of religion*, and the son was supremely interested in religion. How was he interested? Not merely as a collector and describer, as might be inferred from the fact that he was a psychologist and wrote a book called *The Varieties of Religious Experience*. No—he was interested in the *justification* of religion. His interest was never an external one, but was the interest of one who felt religion and was concerned for it. He wanted to save a place for his own generalized religious feelings, but above all did he want to save a place for the more concrete beliefs of those more intensely pious fellow creatures with whom he sympathized. He wrote in 1891, "Father would find in me today a much more receptive listener—all *that* philosophy has got to be brought in." [32] What he evidently meant was that his father's religious philosophy, or some portion of it that was sound and true, should be accommodated within a system that should at the same time provide both for the facts of science and for the integrity of the moral will.

[30] *L.W.J.*, II, 58.
[31] Written on January 9, 1883; other parts of this letter appear below, 158-9.
[32] *L.W.J.*, I, 310.

V

BOYHOOD AT HOME AND ABROAD

The youthful development of William James, and his education in the larger, continuing sense, are woven of three strands—schooling, travel, and vocation. His brother Henry, only a year younger, was having a similar threefold experience at the same time, so that the story of the education of the one embraces his intercourse with the other. The whole is a process of immense complexity resulting in two highly individualized human products.

The schooling of William and the younger Henry James seems in retrospect to have been a series of accidents, but that this should have been the case was not itself altogether an accident. It bears a significant relation to their father's domestic philosophy. It was not to be expected that he would be satisfied with the ordinary institutionalized routine, in education or in anything else. He had apparently acquired an antipathy to college from his own experience. He believed, furthermore, in the liberty of his children, within the bounds of what he thought to be their spiritual good.

> I desire my child to become an upright man, a man in whom goodness shall be induced not by mercenary motives as brute goodness is induced, but by love for it or a sympathetic delight in it. And inasmuch as I know that this character or disposition cannot be forcibly imposed upon him, but must be freely assumed, I surround him as far as possible with an atmosphere of freedom.[1]

Parental affection is a dangerous passion, he thought, tending to become possessive. Parents would ideally have no claims upon their children, but would share them with others and recognize their belonging to society as a whole.

The atmosphere of liberty which pervaded the James household was not, however, a mere effect of parental renunciation. The children were free not only from parental tyranny but, through their parents, from the tyranny of the world. There was a general absence of institutional authority. Thus Alice wrote:

> How grateful we ought to be that our excellent parents had threshed out all the ignoble superstitions, and did not feel it to be their duty to fill our minds with the dry husks,—leaving them *tabulae rasae* to receive whatever stamp our

[1] *The Nature of Evil*, 1855, 99.

individual experience was to give them, so that we had not the bore of wasting our energy in raking over and sweeping out the rubbish.[2]

Henry James tells us that his father checked the vocational ardor of his sons, and prevented an abrupt decision in favor of this or that alternative, by asking whether it were not too "narrowing."[3] He subordinated doing to being, having the philosopher's idea of vocation, that men's first calling is to be men. Despite their careers the sons unconsciously obeyed his injunction. Both William and Henry became men before they became anything else, and there is always a peculiar inadequacy in referring to the one as a "psychologist" and to the other as a "novelist," as though to name them by what they did rather than by what they were. The application of such a standard alters the aspect of this extraordinary educational process. That which, when conventionally regarded, is called incoherence becomes variety and depth of living. The very mistakes, even when they teach no evident lesson, become a part of that pathos of life, of that incompetence of the individual to achieve his own destiny, which is the mark of his humanity and the beginning of his salvation.

It would be a mistake, however, to regard the domestic influence as merely negative. The father, as we have seen, was unconsciously commanding and infectious, and the atmosphere of the family life was charged with palpable and active forces, as was vividly recalled by Edward Emerson who had made a visit to Newport in 1860 or 1861:—

> "The adipose and affectionate Wilkie," as his father called him, would say something and be instantly corrected or disputed by the little cock-sparrow Bob, the youngest, but good-naturedly defend his statement, and then, Henry (Junior) would emerge from his silence in defence of Wilkie. Then Bob would be more impertinently insistent, and Mr. James would advance as moderator, and William, the eldest, join in. The voice of the moderator presently would be drowned by the combatants and he soon came down vigorously into the arena, and when, in the excited argument, the dinner knives might not be absent from eagerly gesticulating hands, dear Mrs. James, more conventional, but bright as well as motherly, would look at me, laughingly reassuring, saying, "Don't be disturbed, Edward; they won't stab each other. This is usual when the boys come home."[4]

William James's choice of occupation is worthy of attention because it was the choice of a gifted man, and because it was prolonged and difficult; above all, however, because his choice was a *choosing*. He was the creature or victim of circumstance in none but the most superficial sense. He *fed and nourished*

---

[2] *Alice James. Her Brothers. Her Journal*, ed. by Anna Robeson Burr, Dodd, Mead and Company, 1934, entry of December 31, 1890.

[3] *N.S.B.*, 50-2.

[4] E. W. Emerson, *Early Years of the Saturday Club*, 328.

himself upon circumstance. It is true that he complained of his education, or lack of it, but he referred to formal schooling, and his complaint is in any case evidence of his chronic discontent rather than of any real lack of nutriment. William James began to be William James at a very early age, and began to find and appropriate the food which his characteristic appetites required. But this, it may be added, was not less true of his brother. Getting "settled in life" was a long and painful process for both. With William it was chiefly the question "what," with Henry the question "where"—but neither question was taken lightly or abandoned to fate. The result of this prolongation of choice was that a good many early crops—of deed, or judgment, or other mode of self-expression—were ploughed in, to the greater enrichment of the soil.

Although there was only a year's difference of age between them, William was definitely the "big brother." It was, in fact, not a question of age. Henry, in speaking of his "very first perceptions," says:

> One of these, and probably the promptest in order, was that of my brother's occupying a place in the world to which I couldn't at all aspire . . . wherever it might be that there was a question of my arriving, when arriving at all, belatedly and ruefully; as if he had gained such an advance of me in his sixteen months' experience of the world before mine began, that I never for all the time of childhood and youth in the least caught up with him or overtook him.[5]

It was not, then, a question of temporal age, but of temporal quality, or of tempo. William was more "vividly bright," more daring, and prompter to respond.[6] He was funnier—and so tended to hold the centre of the stage, the younger brother taking his place among those who laughed. "In fact," says the latter, "almost no one but W. J. himself, who flowered in every waste, seems to have struck me as funny in those years." [7] Laughter was a very important element in the family life, and William, next after his father, was its most copious source. When the children and their friends played comedies in the attic, it was William who first composed them and then played the leading role. This he did not through self-assertion, but rather through quickness of wit. When William once put off his brother with the words, "*I* play with boys who curse and swear!" [8] he was using, quite unconsciously, words that symbolized his greater capacity to meet the world on its own terms, his habit of always being equal to the occasion.

Henry James has left a most illuminating and characteristically chivalrous account of their difference of attitude toward humankind. William, who

[5] *S.B.O.*, 8, 9.
[6] *Ibid.*, 16, 22.
[7] *Ibid.*, 204, 253.
[8] *Ibid.*, 259.

showed a discriminating taste otherwise, could stomach almost anything in his social relations. It was not that he overcame his repugnance to this person or that, but rather that he had none. "No man can well have cared less for the question, or made less of the consciousness, of dislike." Now whatever this might imply as to William's judgment, it undoubtedly qualified him for intercourse with his fellows. Henry may have had a more delicate social palate, but William had a stronger social appetite. Hence where Henry shrank away William would enter in with relish and hearty good-will.[9] In later life Henry was often shocked by William's disregard of conventions. The latter did not care what kind of hat he wore at week-end parties, and he climbed a ladder in order to peer at Chesterton over the garden wall.[10] Being less concerned with appearances, he excelled the more circumspect Henry in the freedom and boldness of his action.

In other words, the stage seems to 'have been set for an "inferiority" complex. Incredible as it may seem, nothing of the sort happened. The younger brother accepted the situation quite serenely, without either resentment towards William or loss of confidence in himself. That this should have been the case points to his possessing qualities less glittering perhaps, but not less pure, than his brother's. His unselfishness and goodness were proverbial in the family and earned him the epithet of "angel," employed in all sincerity by his parents, and with teasing but amiable irony by William. He lacked initiative, and the capacity for bold and decisive action; but since his inclination here ran with his capacity, he suffered no self-disparagement. He was not envious of what he did not possess, having unassuming but sturdy confidence in what he did possess.

The difference between these two minds is profound, and evident at so early an age that it passes from the view of the retracing eye and disappears behind the closed door of temperament and heredity. The younger son, in accounting for the fact that his own and his brother's lack of orderly and consecutive education did, nevertheless, somehow educate, says that the indispensable and sufficient condition of anything's being educative is that it shall arouse "some subjective passion." [11] Each of them had such a subjective passion almost from the time when he became an individual. Each had his own spiritual metabolism, his characteristic way of appropriating and incorporating the experiences that he encountered.

As regards the comparative degrees in which the two boys possessed such a subjective passion, appearances are misleading. Henry engaged in literary and

[9] *N.S.B.*, 323-7. Speaking of his brother Henry, just after the latter had arrived for a visit in 1904, James said: "His manners, speech, and voice have become thoroughly Anglicized. He is a shy fellow. I suppose it is a phenomenon of protective coloration." (Reported by Professor Alexander Forbes.)

[10] H. G. Wells, *Experiment in Autobiography*, 1934, 453-4.   [11] *S.B.O.*, 26.

dramatic composition from childhood, just as William engaged in juvenile forms of science and art.[12] But William's characteristic genius showed itself boldly, Henry's furtively. William's educational career was a series of raids, from which he returned sometimes laden with spoils, sometimes empty-handed; but, in any case, he took the initiative. Henry's subjective passion, on the other hand, showed itself in resistance rather than in attack. They tried to make a scientist of him, and they tried to make a lawyer of him. He allowed himself to be moved about as these experiments required. But in the end he tired his educators out and had to be allowed to achieve his own destiny. Meanwhile he accomplished his education not by trying this or that himself, but by keeping his eyes open and taking notes on life and literature while others tried unsuccessful educational experiments upon him.

Henry demanded "just to *be* somewhere—almost anywhere would do—and somehow receive an impression or an accession, feel a relation or a vibration." [13] Experience afforded patterns or *scenes,* having for him some mysterious affinity of order or rhythm, by which they were apprehended feelingly as units, and by which they became possessions to be stored against the day of their literary use. William shared this passion, but though an insistent, it was always a subordinate motive. His own proper and deeper passion was to look *behind* the scenes for causes, or to look beyond in behalf of governing purposes. The one mind was contemplative, the other inquisitive and operative. It would not be untrue, were it not so inadequate, to say that the one was an æsthetic, the other a scientific mind. There is a contemporary philosophical verbiage which suits the matter somewhat better. Henry's interest was in "essences." The standard of his art was veracious reporting—the representation and communication of integral experiences—with the most scrupulous delicacy both in the apprehending and in the conveying of their specific quality. William had the same strain in his being. He had a painter's eye. He had a capacity, perhaps never equaled, of seizing and exposing the evanescent moments and fugitive sequences of conscious life. He could see most cunningly out of the corner of his eye. But he never indulged this interest without a revulsion against it, a revulsion that took one or the other of two forms—either *action* or *explanation.* He was forever harping on the need of an explanatory psychology; and though he collected varieties of religious experience with rare connoisseurship, he rushed impatiently on to what was to him the *real* question, "What shall we say or do about them?"

So while Henry was content with essences, William was avid of existence, of the "that" rather than the "what." In the presence of a problem Henry was interested in its problematic *aspect,* William in its solution. He asked questions

[12] *N.S.B.,* 122, 260.
[13] *S.B.O.,* 25.

about everything. What is the meaning of things, the substance of things, and the destiny of things? What is the good of things, and how may it be brought about? It was this same quality which made William James quite indifferent to ideas as specimens or archetypes of thinking. He had no archæological interest. Although he came to define truth as satisfaction, it is certain that a final truth already arrived at would never have satisfied *him*. Every new insight or theory superseded those that went before, as the best available belief; there being only one important question—namely, what, according to the completest available evidence, is true? But the intellectual life would have made no appeal to him had it not been for the fortunate fact that all solutions promptly required revision.

It is impossible that William James should have written his brother's autobiographical works. He remembered, but what he *merely* remembered did not interest him. "He professed amazement and even occasionally impatience," writes Henry, "at my reach of reminiscence—liking as he did to brush away old moral scraps in favour of new rather than to hoard and so complacently exhibit them." [14]

Their difference is nowhere more evident than in their accounts of their father. [15] To Henry he was a character and a mind, represented by half-forgotten impressions to be revived in their unique concreteness and experienced quality, altered only by a perspective of laborious recollection. To William, too, his father was a dear and singular being. But beyond this he was a symbol and a source of ideas whose truth had to be judged and if possible perpetuated. It would be unjust to say that Henry and William are related to their father as Xenophon and Plato to Socrates. But to say it and withdraw it leaves just the slight savor of truth which the comparison possesses. To the one his father was an image to be enshrined, to the other he was an oracle to be interpreted and judged.

Travel was a fundamental fact in the history of the James family. It was habitually resorted to as a means of education for the young and as a remedy for the old, whatever their affliction, whether of body or of mind. The incidents of travel ceased to be incidental. The frequent exposure to natural scenery, with its various themes of primeval ruggedness or of human culture, became a staple in William James's diet. The comparison of the several types of European civilization, and above all the comparison of Europe with America, became almost an obsession. A facility in the reading and speaking of European languages was acquired early enough to fructify the whole cycle of development. Books were read, books of every description, because books can be read wherever one may be, or even while one is on the way. The very rhythm of

---

[14] *S.B.O.*, 68.
[15] Compare, *e.g.*, *N.S.B.*, 163-81, with the Introduction to *L.R.H.J.*

travel seems to have entered into the soul of William James, where conditions were already favorable to its reception. He was scarcely out of his infancy before he began to be a nostalgic cosmopolitan, flying from perch to perch, now yearning for home, now equally eager to escape—liking it where he was and longing for the better far away.

We shall first witness the travels of William and Henry, Jr., in the year 1844, during that memorable European sojourn when their father experienced conversion. William had reached the age of two years and five months, Henry the age of one year. It will be noted that William was already less "good" than Henry—and more voluble. The letter was addressed by the father to the grandmother, Mrs. William James of Albany.

Windsor, May 1, 1844

My dear Mother,—

. . . . Going to France the weather was rough, and we were all shockingly treated—from me down to poor little Harry. I never was so sea-sick before. Willy didn't know what to make of it all, and screamed incessantly to have "the hair taken out of his mouth." We were delighted enough to get back again to tidy old England. The weather is perfectly delicious, foliage and flowers all out, the grass as green as summer, and the air equal to any barber's shop for fragrance. We went to Clifton after landing, but finding no precisely suitable lodgings there except in the town, we pushed on to Windsor, and here we have found a comfortable resting-place at last. It is a little cottage standing between the Great and Little Parks, next to the residence of the Duchess of Kent, and fronting the entrance to the Little Park. . . . Willy and Harry from the nursery windows may hold delightful converse with the sheep and cattle browsing beneath, the livelong day. I have never seen a more enchanting spot. . . .

The children are well in the main. Harry's teeth are troublesome at times, but he is as good as the day is long, and the night on top of it. Willy is very good, too, when we are quietly settled. Our wretched Paris excursion broke him up a little, but he is now on the mend. He is full of fun—calls me "Hen*wy*" (he can't pronounce the *ry*) and his mother "Ma*wy*"—and talks frequently of his transatlantic experience and acquaintance. . . .

So, dear Ma, believe me at least affectionately mindful of you all, and especially most tenderly and truly yours,

H.

The period between the return from Europe in 1845 and the departure for Europe in 1855, is the period of Henry James's *A Small Boy and Others*—especially of that other but less small boy who is the central subject of the present book. As shadowed forth in the distant retrospect of the younger, the instruction of these two small boys was up to 1851 entrusted to a series of "educative ladies." After 1851 came a series of educational agencies at once more masculine and more organized. There was the Institution Vergnès, on lower Broadway, with its shrill atmosphere of foreign language and temperament; there was the academy of Mr. Richard Pulling Jenks, with Mr. Coe, the drawing master, uncovering the talent of William; and finally there was the establishment of Forest and Quackenboss, where Henry encountered "the dreadful blight of arithmetic." The most evident characteristic of this educational period, as of that which follows, is change. "We couldn't have changed oftener . . . if our presence had been inveterately objected to, and yet I enjoy an inward certainty that, my brother being vividly bright and I quite blankly innocuous, this reproach was never brought home to our house." It would appear, then, that the fault lay not in the small boys but in the schools—as judged by the small boys' father.

The elder James experienced a growing dissatisfaction with the New York schools. Furthermore, there was the question of languages. We may "go to foreign parts . . . and educate the babies in strange lingoes," he wrote to his friends Edmund and Mary Tweedy, who were already in Europe and helping to turn his thoughts in that direction.[16] Finally, after much thought, the momentous decision was made and the whole family sailed for Liverpool, June 27, 1855. They paused long enough in London to nurse the young Henry through an attack of malarial chills and fever; then on to Paris, from Paris to Lyons by rail, and from Lyons, by "travelling carriage," to Geneva, where they settled early in August, and "got the boys all nicely established at school and at Mr. Roediger's." [17] Roediger's "polyglot pensionnat" failed, however, to fulfill its early promise. "We had fared across the sea," writes Henry, "under the glamour of the Swiss school in the abstract, but the Swiss school in the concrete soon turned stale on our hands." October found the family returning on their former route through Lyons and Paris to London, accompanied by the first of a long succession of French governesses. Here they established themselves first on Berkeley Square, and then, sometime before Christmas, at St. John's Wood, where they were neighbors of Wilkinson, and where they "enjoyed a considerable garden and wistful view." [18] Here a certain Robert Thompson, Scotchman and one-time teacher or R. L. Stevenson, became the latest instrument of formal education.

The two brothers put very different estimates on this period of their lives. "I remember," writes Henry,

> how, looking back at it from after days, W. J. denounced it to me, and with it the following year and more spent in Paris, as a poor and arid and lamentable time, in which, missing such larger chances and connections as we might have reached out to, we had done nothing, he and I, but walk about together, in a state of the direst propriety, little "high" black hats and inveterate gloves, the childish costume of the place and period, to stare at grey street-scenery . . .

[16] *S.B.O.*, 16, 222 and *passim*.
[17] August 13 [1855], to Mrs. W.J. of Albany.
[18] *S.B.O.*, 286 ff., 294, 303.

dawdle at shop-windows and buy water-colours and brushes with which to bedaub eternal drawing-blocks.

He adds that while William felt "deeper stirrings and braver needs," he himself had only a "rueful sense" of the absence of such feelings.[19]

When, in June 1856, the scene of London was replaced by that of Paris, Robert Thompson was succeeded by M. Lerambert. "Spare and tightly black-coated, spectacled, pale and prominently intellectual," he administered instruction in a pavilion that hung over the Avenue des Champs-Elysées between the Rond-Point and the Rue du Colisée. At the end of the winter, following a "rupture" with M. Lerambert, the children were enrolled as *externes* in the Institution Fezandié, Rue Balzac. M. Fezandié was a follower of Fourier, and the Institution, embracing persons of diverse nations, ages, and sexes, was "all but phalansteric"—"if not absolutely phalansteric at least inspired, or at any rate enriched, by a bold idealism." [20]

This winter of 1856-1857 in Paris was a year of exposure on the part of sensitive and maturing minds not only to the Parisian scene itself, but to the treasures of the Louvre and Luxembourg. William's growing interest in painting, so soon to assert itself, was richly fed. "I remember," writes Henry,

> his repeatedly laying his hand on Delacroix, whom he found always and everywhere interesting—to the point of trying effects, with charcoal and crayon, in his manner; and not less in the manner of Decamps, whom we regarded as more or less of a genius of the same rare family. They were touched with the ineffable, the inscrutable, and Delacroix in especial with the incalculable; categories these toward which we had even then, by a happy transition, begun to yearn and languish.[21]

With Henry such experiences touched more than his artistic side—they were "educative, formative, fertilising." "Such were at any rate," he goes on to say,

> some of the vague processes . . . of picking up an education; and I was, in spite of the vagueness, so far from agreeing with my brother afterwards that we didn't pick one up and that that never *is* done, in any sense not negligible. . . . I was so far dissentient, I say, that I think I quite came to glorify such passages and see them as part of an order really fortunate.[22]

In the summer of 1857, impelled by motives of economy, the family sublet their Paris residence on the Rue Montaigne and moved to Boulogne, where

[19] *S.B.O.*, 301.
[20] *Ibid.*, 326-7, 364.
[21] *Ibid.*, 345.
[22] *Ibid.*, 349, 352.

the boys attended the local *collège*. Here William, who had reached his six-teenth year, felt for the first time the benefits of good teaching and continual application. Henry, a year younger, found Boulogne a comparatively barren scene. The following passage from the elder James to his mother gives a report of his parental stock-taking:—

> Willy is very devoted to scientific pursuits, and I hope will turn out a most respectable scholar. He has been attending the Collège Impérial here all summer, and one of his professors told me the other day "that he was an admirable stu-dent, and that all the advantages of a first-rate scientific education which Paris affords ought to be accorded him." He is, however, much dearer to my heart for his moral worth than for his intellectual. I never knew a child of so much principle, and at the same time of a perfectly generous and conciliatory de-meanour towards his younger brothers, always disposed to help them and never to oppress. Harry is not so fond of study, properly so-called, as of reading. He is a devourer of libraries, and an immense writer of novels and dramas. He has considerable talent as a writer, but I am at a loss to know whether he will ever accomplish much.[23]

This European sojourn is also preserved in the memory of another of its young adventurers, Robertson James, who was then in his tenth and eleventh years:

> A riot in Regent's Park where the mounted men charge the populace in the Bread Riots. The night in London when it was aflame with fireworks over the Crimean peace. The Queen, who sits in the gilded coach on her way to Parlia-ment. The Christmas pantomime—the "Ratcatcher's Daughter"—Berkeley Square— . . . —Dr. Wilkinson—the Horse Guards. Mr. Thackeray, who car-ried me on his shoulder, and then Boulogne-sur-Mer and the Collège Munici-pale and its stone vaunted ceiling where Wilkie and I went and failed to take prizes. . . . The only thing to say of it is that it was a beautiful and splendid childhood for any child to have had, and I remember it all now as full of in-dulgence and light and color and hardly a craving unsatisfied.[24]

The mind of William, his observations and his soul-searchings during this European Odyssey, was recorded profusely and candidly in letters to his boy-hood friend Edgar B. Van Winkle of New York City.[25] It is evident that he was much preoccupied with the choice of a profession and that he was can-vassing the question in the light of all cosmic possibilities. It is also evident that he had imbibed from his father and from M. Fezandié the optimism of

[23] Dated Boulogne, October 15, 1857.
[24] R.J. to A.H.J., February 24, 1898. Another extract from this letter appears above, 15.
[25] Edgar Beach van Winkle was born in the same year as W.J. (1842), was graduated from Union College in 1860, served in the Civil War, and was for many years Chief Engineer of the Department of Public Parks of New York.

Fourier, who attributed all the evils of the world to the disordered but curable state of human society. Here (in part!) is one of William's "effusions":

29 Grande Rue, Boulogne-sur-Mer, March 1, 1858

Dear Ed,—

I received your kind and prompt reply last week. . . . I want now to tell you plainly what I think. . . . The choice of a profession torments everyone who begins life, but there is really no reason why it should; that is, there is no reason why it should if society was decently ordered. Everyone, I think, should do in society what he would do if left to himself, and I think I can prove it to you conclusively.

In the first place, what ought to be everyone's object in life? To be as much use as possible. Open a biographical dictionary. Every name it contains has exercised some influence on humanity, good or evil, and 99 names out of 100 are good,—that is, useful. But what is use? Analyse any useful invention, or the life of any useful man, and you will see that its or his use consists in some *pleasure*, mental or bodily, conferred upon humanity. In the present day the bodily is most esteemed, and justly. In the damnable way in which society is now ordained,—when a man cannot be sure of that food, shelter and raiment which is afforded to the beasts of the field, and which is his birthright as much as the air which he breathes; when he is stifled and crushed by his brothers, deprived by them of all but his life, and sometimes that, all inventions which tend to put the necessaries of life within his reach take the first place and are the most honored. And at the present time such inventions are alone called "useful."

But suppose that men did [not] behave like devils. Suppose that food and clothing and shelter were *assured* to everyone. What men would then be held in honour? Not only the constructors of bridges and tunnels, the inventors of steam engines and spinning jennies, but all those who afforded some pleasure to others, whether material or spiritual, and in such a state of society (which will soon come, I hope) every man would follow out his own tastes, and excel as much as possible in the particular line for which he was created. It is then the duty of everyone to do as much good as possible. You may say that it's the duty of everyone to live as much like a saint as possible,—to fast and pray and all that. True for you, as the Irish say, but that is not all. A man must do that and something more. The best way to serve God is to serve your fellow men. "He prayeth well, who loveth well both man and bird and beast." For my part, I have the greatest faith in the innate good of mankind. I love every human being and every living and inanimate thing. When I go out on the beach,— when I see the sky and the sea and the glorious old cliff, I feel a sort of wild joy which makes my heart leap to my throat and the tears come to my eyes. And when I come home along the port thronged [with] the dear old dirty fisher[men], I feel as [if] I could hug them all. Yes, mankind is all good, and as soon as governments and priests are abolished such a thing as sin will not be known. There is no such thing as a bad heart. I know that you and everyone else must feel in the same way. All the evil in the world comes from the law and the priests and the sooner these two things are abolished the better.

But now let us see what our duty is. I have already said, I know not how many times, that it's *use*. Which of us would wish to go through life without leaving a trace behind to mark his passage. Who would prefer to live unknown to all but his immediate friends and to be forgotten by all thirty years after his death. For what was life given us? Suppose we do nothing and die; we have swindled society. Nature, in giving us birth, had saddled us with a debt which we must pay off some time or other. I saw today at school a sentence of Rousseau which I agree with perfectly. "What are 10, 20, 30 years for an immortal being? Pleasure and pain both pass like shadows. Life is gone in an instant. In itself it is nothing. Its value depends upon the use to which you put it. The good which you have done is lasting and that alone,—and life is valuable only by that good!" It is hard to translate it into English, but that is the sense. By *good* I do not mean mere *force,* muscle and sinew. A common laborer who digs a canal is of *use* certainly. But of what kind of use? A machine could be invented to supply his place, and the canal would go on just as well as if *he,* the *man* with all his *mind* and *soul* were at work on it. True *use,* or good, does not then consist in mere brute force. For what was our mind given us if not that we should employ it? We should, then, each in his own particular way find out something new, something which without us could not be. . . .

Poets may be laughed at for being useless, impractical people. But suppose the author of the "Psalm of Life" had attempted to invent steam engines (for which I suppose he has no genius) in the hope of being useful, how much time would he have wasted and how much would we have lost! But no, he did better, he followed his taste, and redeemed his life, by writing the "psalm" which is as useful a production as any I know. Astronomy and natural history are of little *practical* use, and as such are not all important at the present day, but they afford inexpressible pleasure to those who are interested in them and therefore are useful. And I think that a man who was urged toward them by his tastes and who, wishing to be more useful, should make discoveries of little importance in practical branches would do very wrong.

I think now you will agree with me that everyone has his own particular use, and that he would be a traitor were he to abandon it for something else for which he had little taste. Thank God! man shall not live by bread alone. I want to be a man and to do some good, no matter what. . . .

If I followed my taste and did what was most agreeable to me, I'll tell you what I would do. I would get a microscope and go out into the country, into the dear old woods and fields and ponds. There I would try to make as many discoveries as possible,—and I'll be kicked if I would not be more useful than if I'd laid out railroads by rules which others had made and which I have learned from them. If in the former case I do not vindicate my existence better than in the latter, then I'm no man. I'll tell you what I think I'll do. I'll be a farmer and do as much good in the natural history line as I can. How much that is, God only knows. I pray that I may do something. . . .

In my first letters there was a great display of miserable prejudice against the French. I am heartily ashamed of it. I like the French more and more every day. Dear Ed, never give way to prejudice. Human nature is the same all over the world. Everywhere it has faults and everywhere it is good at heart. . . .

Please answer me soon, dear Ed, and tell me what you think. God bless you. Good-bye. Write soon. Your friend

W. James

In the spring of 1858 the whole family was removed bag and baggage from Boulogne-sur-Mer, by way of Albany, to Newport, Rhode Island, where they were attracted, no doubt, by the proximity of their close friends, Edmund and Mary Tweedy. Here they remained for fifteen months. The older boys attended the William Leverett School, with Thomas Sergeant Perry and Steele Mac-Kaye among their schoolmates. The former has described his impressions of his companions: their long walks together every afternoon; Henry who "sat on the window-seat . . . with a certain air of remoteness"—"an uninterested scholar," but preoccupied with literature; and William, who was "full of merriment," though he discoursed on Schopenhauer and Renan.[26] But it seems to have been a more significant fact that William took drawing lessons from William Morris Hunt, who with his pupil John La Farge was living in Newport and strengthened in the breast of William that appeal of art which a year later proved too strong to be resisted.

William had been eager to join his friend Van Winkle at Union College, and he had directed his studies abroad largely to this goal. But his father's authority was at this point stronger than his indulgence. On August 12, 1858, William thus communicated his disappointment to Van Winkle:

> When I left you the other day . . . it was with the almost certainty of becoming within a few months a fellow "man" with you at Union College. But I was greatly mistaken; for on coming to speak with my father on the subject I found, to my surprise, that he would not hear of my going to any college whatsoever. He says that colleges are hot-beds of corruption where it is *impossible* to learn anything. I think this opinion very unjust, but of course, much as I should like, myself, to go to Union I must abide by his decision. I think it probable that I shall go to the Scientific School at Harvard. At any rate I must make the best of it, though I am very sorry not to go to Union which I think would be by far the best place for me.

Plans for a return to Europe were made and abandoned. Only one thing was clear, namely, that the movements of the family were dictated by the parental view of the educational requirements of the children. As William expressed it to Van Winkle:

> Father has come to the conclusion that America is not the place to bring up such "ingenuous youth" as myself and brothers,—and consequently this step. Of course this is so in great measure, and so we must make the best of our exile. I was very much disappointed because, having given up all thoughts of Union, I had my heart set on going to Cambridge. However I hope it won't be too late for that when we come home again and, in the meantime, I shall have become a good German scholar, etc. etc. etc. As it is we have been merely making a visit home, and a very pleasant visit it has been. I love dear old America,

[26] *The Letters of Henry James,* edited by Percy Lubbock, Charles Scribner's Sons, 1920, I, 6-8.

and I hope I always shall through thick and thin. I am sure of one thing and that is that a residence abroad will never unfit me for living at home.[27]

The father's state of mind at this time, and the educational philosophy which underlay his somewhat wavering course, appear in the following paragraph from a letter to Mrs. Francis G. Shaw, written from Newport on July 22, 1859. He had referred to his subsequent "return from Geneva":

> For, you must know, we are anxiously thinking of embarking for that educational paradise. We can't get a house in Cambridge, and are disposed to think it would not be the place for us in all respects if we could. Besides, I am not looking forward to giving my boys a college course, our desire after Cambridge having been prompted by the wish to get my oldest boy in the Scientific School. But we *may* not go, as our minds are still undetermined. The truth is, my dear Mrs. Shaw, I have but one *fixed mind* about anything; which is, that whether we stay here or go abroad, and whatever befalls my dear boys in this world, they and you and I are all alike, and after all, absolute creatures of God, vivified every moment by Him, cared for every moment by Him, guided every moment by an infallible wisdom and an irreproachable tenderness, and that we have none of us therefore the slightest right to indulge any anxiety or listen in any conceivable circumstances to the lightest whisper of perturbation.

So they all set out on October 8, 1859 and, the pendulum being at the other end of its trajectory, settled again in Geneva, at the Hôtel de l'Écu, this time with a very determined educational intent. William was sent to the academy (afterwards the university), and here Henry joined him after an abortive attempt had been made to teach him science and mathematics at the Institution Rochette. This treatment was designed to cure Henry of the habit of excessive novel-reading, and he meekly, although quite fruitlessly, submitted to it. The outcome—"an obscure, a deeply hushed failure"—was calculated to intensify his sense of the comparative greatness of his brother:

> Whatever he [William] might happen to be doing made him so interesting about it, and indeed, with the quickest concomitance, about everything else, that what I probably most did, all the while, was but to pick up, and to the effect not a bit of starving but quite of filling myself, the crumbs of his feast and the echoes of his life.[28]

William, apparently, was equal to anything. He was taken into the important students' organization, the Société de Zoffingue, and carried it off (including the scarf and cap) with *élan*. He conducted himself in the family circle with

[27] September 18, 1858.
[28] *N.S.B.*, 4, 13. *Cf.* also William's letter to his father, *ibid.*, 18. The original letter contained "some very beautiful poetry" composed in honor of Alice, which, he said, "loses a great deal by not being sung." "Alice took it very coolly," he added.

his usual high spirits. The following letters were written by two of the younger children, Wilky and Alice, aged fourteen and twelve respectively, to their parents, who had departed for Paris and London.

Geneva [Dec. 1859]

My dear Father,—

We arrived a little while ago from school and have already read your welcome letters that have made one feel very sympathetic for you, but still I cannot help smiling at the easy, graceful and homesick style in which they flow. . . . How do you find Paris and London? I would give a great deal to be there with you, to be arm in arm with you in Regent's Street or St. John's Wood. But I suppose those sweet days have passed and that we are now not to depend so much upon the pleasures that unity or friendship can afford, because we are growing older and must prepare to harden ourselves to deny ourselves the mere affections, so that in the world to come we may have peace and as much of these pleasures as we like. Enough of this, however. . . . How are the Wilkinsons? Give them all my love, and tell Mrs. Wilkinson how glad I was to receive her letter, or something agreeable that would touch her sentimentality (you know what I mean).

Father, you cannot imagine how much we miss you, and what a blank space your absence makes in this house. Even away off at school I feel it. I have a sort of unprotected feeling (not physically so, but mentally)—I feel as if there was something missing—but I have no doubt it does an immense deal of good to both sides to have occasionally these little separations. We received five letters after you left, one of them from La Farge, who gives us four pages of nothing else but Newport gossip and Newport this and thats. . . .

Willie interrupts me here and wants me to go into the parlor with him to hear him deliver a little sonnate on Alice which he has just composed and which he means to perform with much gusto. I will tell you its success when it is finished. . . . Song went off very well, and excited a good deal of laughter among the audience assembled.

As I have exhausted all my news, and as bedtime is approaching and as my eyes are gradually closing, even so must this letter which is meant to tell you how much we love you, how much we miss you, and how much we would give for you to be back under the roof of this hotel. Good-bye, dear Papa. Ever your affectionate son,

G. W. JAMES

March 11 [1860]

My dear Father,—

We have had two dear letters from you and find you are the same dear old good-for-nothing home-sick papa as ever.

Willie is in a very extraordinary state of mind, composing odes to all the family. A warlike one he addressed to Aunt Kate, in which the hero is her husband and dies for her; and he says: "The idea of any one dying for her!!" . . . We have all come to the conclusion that he is fit to go to the lunatic asylum, so make haste home before such an unhappy event takes place. . . . Your affectionate daughter

ALICE JAMES

It is not surprising that Henry, who was cold, hungry, and uncomfortable, and found the Bernese and Bâlois "strange representations of the joy of life," abandoned the idea of rivalry, and lived, so far as he could, "by the imagination, in William's so adaptive skin." [29]

[29] *N.S.B.*, 14, 15.

VI

SHALL HE BECOME A PAINTER?

In the summer of 1860 the scene again shifted, this time to Bonn, where the boys (with the exception of Bob, who remained behind in Geneva) were divided between two tutorial households, William with Herr Stromberg, Henry and Wilky with Herr Doctor Humpert. This was the first glimpse of Germany and the beginning of facility in the German language. With this addition the sum of William's learning now embraced a good knowledge of French, some German and Latin, mathematics through trigonometry, and scattered bits of science.

But the brief residence at Bonn in the summer of 1860 was chiefly notable as the occasion of William's decision to study painting. It was not a surprising decision. Indeed, the last European trip had been taken largely in order to save William from that siren call, which was so clearly audible in Newport. William had sketched and painted from early boyhood, but though his interest and aptitude had long since been proved, even now it was not an unqualified decision. It had been hoped that through travel he might forget art's fatal attractions—and thus avoid a *mésalliance*. He now found that he could not forget her, and that separation only induced restlessness and longing. If the separation were made permanent he might be haunted by regrets all his life. So he would go back to her: it might end in marriage, or it might cure him.

The following letter from the elder James to Edmund Tweedy reveals the former's parental doubts, and his habit of finding reasons to reconcile the interest of the family as a whole with whatever at the moment seemed best for William.

Bonn, July 18 [1860]

My dear old Tweedius,—

. . . We hardly reached here before Willy took an opportunity to say to me—what it seems he had been long wanting to say, but found it difficult to come to the scratch—that he felt the vocation of a painter so strongly that he did not think it worth my while to expend any more time or money on his scientific education! I confess I was greatly startled by the annunciation, and not a little grieved, for I had always counted upon a scientific career for Willy, and I hope the day may even yet come when my calculations may be realized in this regard. But as it was I had nothing to do but to submit; and as our motive to stay in Europe was chiefly derived from the imagined needs of his education, so now we are glad enough to turn homewards, and let him begin at once with Mr. Hunt. The welfare of the other youngsters will, however, be as much consulted by this manœuvre, I am persuaded, as Willy's. They are none of them cut out for intellectual labours, and they are getting to an age, Harry and Wilky especially, when the heart craves a little wider expansion than is furnished it by the domestic affections. They want friends among their own sex, and sweethearts in the other; and my hope for their own salvation, temporal and spiritual, is that they may "go it strong" in both lines when they get home. . . . Love to all and believe me, ever faithfully yours,

H.J.

The following letters from William James to his parents[1] throw light on the life of the divided family during the Bonn period, as well as on the crucial decision which was then their common problem. During August, when the die had already been cast, William wrote from Bonn to his parents in Paris and in London, where they were to be rejoined by their sons before sailing. The father's opposition to art in general, as well as his indulgence of its particular embodiments, was well known to William, and he felt a strong desire to meet that opposition by argument, at the same time that he intended to profit by the indulgence. Although the father's letters are unfortunately missing, his views can be supplied. Art was, he felt, frivolous, irresponsible, narrow, vain, and parasitic, as compared with either the glory of religion or the seriousness of science.

Bonn [Aug. 19, 1860]

My dearest Father,—

I got your letter on Thursday. I wish you would, as you promise, set down as clearly as you can on paper what your idea of the nature of art is, because I do not probably understand it fully, and should like to have it presented in a form that I might think over at my leisure. . . . I wish you would do it as fully as you conveniently can, so that I may ruminate it. I will not say anything about it before I have got your next letter.

As for what your last letter did contain, what can I do but thank you for every word of it and assure you that every word went to the right spot! Having such a father with us, how can we be other than in some measure worthy of him, though not perhaps as eminently so as the distance leads his fond heart to imagine. . . .

I have just got home from dining at the boys' house. . . . They certainly live on the fat of the land, though they do not seem as sensible of their advantages as they should be. As I had been led to expect nothing of the kind, I was surprised at the sumptuousness of the dinner, rich beef, sausages, pigeons, capital vegetables and soup, all cooked just right, and a most delicious cherry pie, with two bottles of costly Rhine wine in honor of the day. The Doctor [Humpert] was as cordial as usual, and the two old ladies perfect characters for Dickens. They have been so shut out from the world and have been melting together so

[1] These letters, together with a third written from Bonn during the same month, have been published in an abbreviated form in N.S.B., 43-7.

long by the kitchen fire that the minds of both have become confounded into one, and they seem to constitute a sort of two-bodied individual. I never saw anything more curious than the way in which they sit mumbling together at the end of the table, each using simultaneously the same exclamation if anything said at our end strikes their ear. The boys say they always speak together, using the same words or else one beginning a phrase, the other ending it. It is a singular life.

Harry studies pretty stoutly, but I do not think you need to be apprehensive about him. There has been no renewal of the stomach aches that I am aware of, and he looks fatter and fresher than when you left. He and Wilky appear to get on very harmoniously together. They enliven themselves occasionally by very good-natured brotherly trials of strength in their bedroom, when study has made them dull and sleepy. In these sometimes one, sometimes the other is victor. . . . We are going to put Harry through a slashing big walk daily. His old white Lordet clothes began to look so shockingly grimy that we have at last induced him to take them to be cleaned. He clung to them with such affection that it was no easy matter. I have got on very well this last week in German, am beginning to understand and to make myself tolerably understood in straightforward matters. . . .

Thousand thanks to the cherry-lipped, apricot-nosed, double-chinned little Bal [2] for her strongly dashed-off letter, which inflamed the hearts of her lonely brothers with an intense longing to kiss and slap her celestial cheeks. . . . Mother, in her precious letter, speaks of having her photograph taken when we get there. I conjure her by all the affection she bears us and by the ties which bind her to the eldest son, not to have it done *before*. When we get there we will have a consultation about it. . . . Now bosom upon bosom full of love to all, from your affectionate

WILLY

Bonn, Aug. [24, 1860]

My dearest Father,—

Your letter came last evening too late for me to have answered it immediately. I hasten to take time to do so this morning in order to quiet your apprehensions about the time of our leaving Bonn. We have never for a moment forgotten that we were to do so on Friday, Aug. 31st. . . .

I was very glad to get your preceding letter, although its contents were not exactly what I had expected. What I wanted to ask you for . . . were the reasons why I should not be an "artist." I could not *fully* make out from your talk . . . what were *exactly* the causes of your disappointment at my late resolve, what your view of the nature of art was, that the idea of my devoting myself to it should be so repugnant to you. Your present letter simply points out the spiritual danger in which a man is if he allows the bent of his æsthetic nature (supposed strong) to direct his activity. It does not, therefore, cover just the ground which I had expected, unless your repugnance was in great measure merely a repugnance to my exposure to such spiritual danger, which can hardly be the case.—But now I perceive that what I was just going to say is not true,

[2] One of W.J.'s nicknames for his sister Alice.

and we had better leave the matter till I get to Paris and we can talk it over.

It of course gives me a sort of gratification to see that in your letter you seem to accept the *fact* of my being an "artist," and limit yourself to showing me what you think an artist is and how he may deceive himself. In as far as you have done so I think I understand you perfectly. I had already gathered the idea from your conversation and have often thought over it and felt all its truth. I think there is small danger of my ever forgetting it. The influence which my dealings with art and works of art hitherto have had upon me is such as would by no means tempt me to forget it. I do not see why a man's spiritual culture should not go on independently of his æsthetic activity, why the power which an artist feels in himself should tempt him to forget what he is, any more than the power felt by a Cuvier or Fourier would tempt them to do the same. Why should not a given susceptibility of religious development be found bound up in a mind whose predominant tendencies are artistic, as well as in one largely intellectual, granting, even, that the former be much the most elementary, the least dignified and useful? My experience amounts to very little, but it is all I have to go upon; and I am sure that far from feeling myself degraded by my intercourse with art, I continually receive from it spiritual impressions the intensest and purest I know. So it seems to me is my mind formed, and *I can see* no reason for avoiding the giving myself up to art *on this score*. Of course if you even agree to let this pass, there remain other considerations which might induce me to hesitate,—those of utility, of duty to society, etc. All these, however, I think ought to be weighed down by strong *inclination* towards art, and by the fact that my life would be embittered if I were kept from it. That is the way I feel *at present*. Of course I may change. I may have misapprehended your position, too, and talked quite uselessly. We will see in a week. I have no more time. Great love to all. Good-bye.

W. J.

The parents were rejoined by their children on September 1, and ten days later the James family sailed for America on the *Adriatic*. As the younger Henry expressed it, "we went home to learn to paint." Not only were his problems subordinated to those of William, but he followed in his brother's wake. For when they all settled again in Newport in order that William might study painting with Hunt, the latter exercised a "fertilising action on our common life"; and "since W. J. for the first six months or so after our return, daily and devotedly haunted his studio, I myself did no less, for a shorter stretch, under the irresistible contagion." [3] In short, while William (together with John La Farge) drew and painted in the foreground, the younger Henry drew and painted in the background.

The vocational experiment was a complete success in the sense that it was altogether decisive. William learned by living with art that he could live without it. That he had talent and interest is unquestionable; but he found the interest to be less compelling than he had thought, and he judged the talent to be less distinguished than his standards required. Having once rejected painting, he rarely looked back, and never with profound regrets.[4]

Though James definitely abandoned painting as a vocation, he did not for that reason lose those qualities, or even those interests, which had led him to make the experiment. He had acquired and retained something of the painter's professional prejudices, leading him, for example, to suspect the connoisseurship of the layman, and to feel the hopeless inadequacy, if not irrelevance, of æsthetics. He retained the painter's sensibility, and something of the artist's detachment. He cultivated style in his scientific and philosophical writing, and was offended by its absence in others. He allowed himself the artist's license. I mean that when a theme took him, it possessed him. His descriptions of people were, like his father's, *portraits,* in which he expressed some tonality of life which the subject conveyed to him. Hence when he was most personal he was often most impersonal. He indulged his moods because they were intuitive, and his playfulness because it was creative.

In analyzing the genius of William James, all this may properly be emphasized, provided in the end it is subordinated. For just as at this critical moment of his life he preferred science to painting, so does his life as a whole signify a preference of explanation and achievement to contemplation and imagination. He saw the landscape with a painter's eye and the artist's senses of plastic form, as in his descriptions of the "full-bodied air" of Edinburgh, its "plane rising behind plane of flat dark relieved against flat light in ever-receding gradation."[5] He had the artist's imagination and acute perception of sensory qualities, as when he paused in his writing to remark that "the light is shrieking away, outside."[6] But the gifts which qualified him to be an artist were from this crucial period of his life unreservedly dedicated to ulterior moral and speculative ends.

[4] The reader who wishes to form his own judgment of James's skill as a draughtsman and painter will find reproductions in *L.W.J.*, *N.S.B.*, and *As William James Said:*, Vanguard Press, 1942.

[5] *L.W.J.*, II, 146.

[6] A.J., *Journal*, October 12, 1890.

VII

SCIENTIFIC STUDIES IN HARVARD

From 1861 William James's range of vocational alternatives was narrowed to science. He was, in short, to pursue knowledge. Whether it should be science in the stricter sense of natural science, or in the broader sense of philosophy; whether, if natural science, it should be science of experiment or of observation; and whether his intellectual vocation should assume the form of research, or of teaching, or of the practice of medicine—all of these questions lay ahead, to be answered only after twelve years of trial and doubt, during which the state of his health played as decisive a role as the self-revelation of interest and aptitude.

The autumn of 1861 found him a student of chemistry in the Lawrence Scientific School at Harvard, where Henry joined him the following year as a "singularly alien member" of the Law School. When he entered upon his academic career, William was nineteen years of age. To us who revive this autumn of 1861 in historical retrospect it was preëminently a time of civil war. Nationalism, the defense of the Union, the abolition of slavery, were the ideas that possessed the public mind. The elder James had been most passionately aroused, and had brought his dearest convictions to the support of these ideas in his July oration at Newport.[1] The enlistment of the two younger boys, as well as of countless cousins and friends, afterwards brought the war directly home to the James family.[2] There is no evidence, however, that William was in the autumn of 1861 preoccupied by the public questions of the day, as he was in later life—for example, at the time of the Spanish War. He expressed himself eloquently on the issues of the Civil War in his oration of 1897 at the dedication of the monument to Colonel Robert Gould Shaw, but this was retrospective and detached rather than contemporary. In 1861 physical frailty precluded the possibility of enlistment. That he did not utter himself more intensely on the subject is due in part, perhaps, to the fact that his social and political interests were not yet ripe; in part also, I suspect, to a feeling that if he could not act he preferred not to talk.

[1] *N.S.B.,* 120; "The Social Significance of Our Institutions," July 4, 1861.
[2] Wilkinson James enlisted in 1862 at the age of seventeen. "To me in my boyish fancy," he afterwards wrote, "to go to war seemed glorious indeed; to my parents it seemed a stern duty, a sacrifice worth any cost." ("The Assault on Fort Wagner," in *War Papers,* Commandery of Wisconsin, Loyal Legion, Milwaukee, 1891.) Robertson James enlisted May 21, 1863.

The year 1861 belongs not only to the age of the Civil War, but also to the age of Barnum. Advertising and Babbittry were not yet refined, but manifested themselves with forceful crudity. There is a certain strident note, an artfulness of first intent, which later sophistication finds naïve; a charlatanry so blatant, a quackery so transparent, as to seem honest; and which somehow enters, whether in visible bulk or as a mere aroma, into all the life of the times. It was the age of the exclamation point, when it was necessary to astonish in order to command attention; when shrillness of accent, the use of superlatives, and simple-minded boasting were still the principal instruments of publicity and propaganda. This was the vulgarism of the age, which James seems wholly to have escaped, whether by his aloofness from the life of the market place and forum, or by an instinctive repugnance.

In short, so far as wider national characteristics are concerned, I can see in William James no evidence whatever of his having entered on manhood in the decade of the 1860's. What shall be said of the local influences of New England? The transcendental movement was manifesting itself vigorously and had assumed institutional form in the Sanborn school, attended by the younger James boys. But to this whole wide current of influences, as well as to its Hegelian aftermath in the "Concord School of Philosophy," William seems to have been insusceptible—except for the case of Emerson, and it was what *divided* Emerson from these influences that commended him to James. The futility of transcendentalism, to Henry as well as to William, lay in its unselfcritical solemnity. It was a series of "experiments in the void," unaware of the actual complications of life.[3] William's mind seems always to have been disillusioned. It seems always to have been the kind of mind which requires an anvil to its hammer, a resistance to overcome—whether unmitigated evil for which to devise a remedy, or stubborn facts on which to think.

Turning, in search of influences, from New England generally to Harvard in particular, we find two groups of remarkable personages, which we may term the humanistic and the scientific groups. Harvard, under President Felton, was an undistinguished institution embracing distinguished men. That which a student remembered in after life was not that he took this or that course, or mastered this or that subject, but that he knew this or that man. The humanistic group intersected that of the literary celebrities of Boston and Cambridge. The *Atlantic Monthly,* edited by James T. Fields, was at this time publishing contributions by Hawthorne, Longfellow, Lowell, Holmes, Emerson, Whittier, Bayard Taylor, Norton, Mrs. Stowe, Harriet Martineau, and others of only slightly less repute. The *North American Review* was edited by A. P. Peabody, and later by Lowell, Norton, Gurney, and Henry Adams. In 1865, E. L. Godkin, who was intermittently a resident of Cambridge, began his fa-

* *N.S.B.,* 217.

mous editorship of the *Nation,* aided and abetted by Norton. Longfellow, Lowell, Holmes, Emerson, and Norton were all at one time or another officially connected with Harvard. This group belonged to the European as well as to the American world of letters. They frequently visited Europe themselves, and were in turn visited by distinguished travelers from abroad. The European contacts of the New England historians and diplomats were even more notable. Prescott, who had been a member of the Saturday Club, had just passed from the scene, but Motley was Minister to Austria and at home in all parts of Europe; while George Bancroft had been Minister in London and was shortly (in 1867) to be appointed to Berlin. Europe was nearer than were the Ohio and Mississippi valleys.[4]

This literary cosmopolitanism of Boston and Cambridge was congenial to James, and no doubt helped to confirm the influence already exerted by his own travel and European contacts. When he began to experiment with his pen, he wrote reviews and short articles for the *Atlantic,* the *North American Review,* and the *Nation;* and his career as a writer, like that of his brother, was greatly facilitated by the fact that he lived among the editors, and numbered such men as Lowell, Fields, Norton, Godkin, and Howells among his friends. But here the parallel ends. To Henry the New England men of letters were masters and colleagues, to William they were friends and sources of entertainment to whom he turned in his hours of relaxation.

There remains the scientific group, including Asa Gray, Benjamin Peirce, Louis Agassiz, Jeffries Wyman, and (after 1863) Wolcott Gibbs—also men of fame and greatness, through whom Boston and Cambridge participated in the thought if not in the life of the world, and were stirred from provincial sluggishness by winds from abroad. Agassiz, in particular, with his irresistible personal force, his disarming enthusiasm, and his unashamed Europeanism, wrought mightily to loosen the grip of local tradition. It was in science, and especially in the field of biological science, that Harvard was most contemporary and prophetic; and it was this emancipating influence, among all the forces of his time and place, that most deeply affected William James during the years of his university studies.[5]

James's interest in the natural sciences, like his interest in painting, dated from boyhood, when he showed an aptitude both for observation and for the use of instruments. He had shown curiosity enough to supplement his meagre scientific studies in Geneva by reading and visits to the museum. His brother testifies to this early bent:—

[4] Edward Everett Hale writes that when Robert Todd Lincoln, bringing a letter of introduction from Stephen A. Douglas, entered Harvard in 1860, Lowell was apparently the only member of the faculty who had heard of his father. (E. E. Hale, *J. R. Lowell and His Friends,* 1899, 200-1.)

[5] Similarly, Henry Adams, who graduated from Harvard in 1858, reports that only Agassiz really stirred him. (*Education of Henry Adams,* 1918, 60.)

As certain as that he had been all the while "artistic" did it thus appear that he had been at the same time quite otherwise inquiring too—addicted to "experiments" and the consumption of chemicals, the transfusion of mysterious liquids from glass to glass under exposure to lambent flame, the cultivation of stained fingers, the establishment and the transport, in our wanderings, of galvanic batteries, the administration to all he could persuade of electric shocks, the maintenance of marine animals in splashy aquaria, the practice of photography in the room I for a while shared with him at Boulogne, with every stern reality of big cumbrous camera, prolonged exposure, exposure mostly of myself, darkened development, also interminable, and ubiquitous brown blot. Then there had been also the constant, as I fearfully felt it, the finely speculative and boldly disinterested absorption of curious drugs. No livelier remembrance have I of our early years together than this inveteracy, often appalling to a nature so incurious as mine in *that* direction, of his interest in the "queer" or the incalculable effects of things. There was apparently for him no possible effect whatever that mightn't be more or less rejoiced in as such—all exclusive of its relation to other things than merely knowing.[6]

James's early scientific studies brought to light a fundamental quality of his mind. He was eagerly but *impatiently* interested. There was that in him which made prolonged application to the same task extremely repugnant. This quality was, as we have seen, temperamental. Its effect was enhanced by his periodic ill-health, which often made sustained effort impossible; but fundamentally it was a trait and not a symptom. He himself was disposed to regard it as a weakness, and whenever, as in the case of the writing of the *Principles of Psychology,* he committed himself to a task of large proportions, he fought and overcame it. But if it was a weakness it was the price he had to pay for his peculiar kind of strength. The power of his mind lay largely in its extreme mobility, its darting, exploratory impulsiveness. It was not a mind which remained stationary, drawing all things to itself as a centre; but a mind which traveled widely—now here and now there—seeing all things for itself, and making up in the variety of its adventures for what it lacked in poise.

James's teacher of chemistry in the Lawrence Scientific School was Charles William Eliot, who was an acute observer of men and one who weighed his words. This is what he afterwards said of his famous pupil:—

James was a very interesting and agreeable pupil, but was not wholly devoted to the study of chemistry. . . . His excursions into other sciences and realms of thought were not infrequent; his mind was excursive, and he liked experimenting, particularly novel experimenting. . . . In 1863-4 [he] changed from the Department of Chemistry to that of Comparative Anatomy and Physiology in the Lawrence Scientific School, and became for one year a pupil of Professor Jeffries Wyman. His tendency to the subject of physiology had appeared clearly during his two years in the Department of Chemistry; so that I

[6] *N.S.B.,* 122-3.

enlisted him, in the second year of his study of chemistry, in an inquiry into the effects on the kidneys of eating bread made with the Liebig-Horsford baking powder, whose chief constituent was an acid phosphate. But James did not like the bread, and found accurate determination of its effects three times a day tiresome and unpromising; so that after three weeks he requested me to transfer that inquiry to some other person. . . . The two interesting points about his education are: first, its irregularity—it did not conform to the Boston and Cambridge traditional method; and secondly, it was in large proportion observational, and particularly in the biological sciences. The systematic part of his education did not foretell his subsequent devotion to philosophical studies; but his unsystematic excursions did.[7]

The central point here is James's tendency to "unsystematic excursions," the movement of his mind curiously duplicating the movements of his body, and giving him a cosmopolitanism of thought and experience—in a genuinely cosmic, and not merely in the usual and more limited, sense. In this tendency Eliot was shrewd enough to recognize a hopeful promise of philosophy and not a mere negation of science.

But Wyman and Agassiz, not Eliot, were the teachers who counted during these years. Jeffries Wyman was Hersey Professor of Anatomy in the Harvard Medical School. As a scientist he represented extreme scrupulousness without narrowness or pedantry. His range of interests was wide. He was a field naturalist as well as an experimentalist, and he addressed himself eagerly to the great controversial topics of his day—evolution and "spontaneous generation." But he was distinguished from his colleague Agassiz by his greater openness of mind and more patient suspension of judgment until such time as the evidence should prove decisive. When Dr. Holmes said of him that "his word would be accepted on a miracle," he testified to his reputation for extreme caution as well as for character.[8] To William James, who was instantly attracted to him and came directly and almost continuously under his influence for five years, he was a scientific paragon. His "unmagisterial manner," his "complete and simple devotion to objective truth," his "disinterestedness," his "accuracy and thoroughness," not only embodied what the scientist ought to be, but contributed greatly to the forming of that scientific conscience which exercised a constant censorship upon James's speculative profligacy.[9]

Louis Agassiz was so conspicuous a figure in the Boston and Cambridge of the '60s that James inevitably felt his power, though it does not appear that until he joined him on his Brazilian expedition in 1865 he had any closer association than that of auditor and casual acquaintance. Agassiz, at this time

[7] These statements are quoted from a memorandum which President Eliot prepared for Mr. Henry James, and from which the latter quotes in *L.W.J.*, I, 31-2.

[8] E. W. Emerson, *Early Years of the Saturday Club*, 427.

[9] "Professor Jeffries Wyman," *Harvard Advocate*, XVIII (October 1, 1874), 8-9; *L.W.J.*, I, 50.

fifty-three years of age, and professor of geology in the Lawrence Scientific School, was at the height of his power and fame. Comparing Wyman with Agassiz, James wrote that the latter was more "widely effective"; and when he suggested that Wyman's fame would have been greater if he had had a little more egotism and ambition, it was Agassiz, no doubt, that was in his mind. Wyman was a saint, Agassiz was a titan—enthusiastic, powerful, irresistibly magnetic. Being masterful, he exercised a natural ascendancy over others. "From his boyhood," wrote William James, "he looked on the world as if it and he were made for each other, and on the vast diversity of living things as if he were there with authority to take mental possession of them all." He had, like Wyman, an interest as broad as all biology; and made, besides, an impression of personal greatness which distinguished him in any company of men, and made it natural that even the Saturday Club, composed almost solidly of celebrities, should be known to some as "Agassiz's Club." He was "recognized by all," continues William James, "as one of those folio copies of mankind . . . who aim at nothing less than an acquaintance with the whole of animated Nature." [10] His genius lay not in abstract reasoning, which he despised, but in a comprehensive massing and organization of facts.

When James began to teach, he drew most heavily upon what he had learned from Wyman. The first philosophical problem to which he devoted himself systematically was the problem of evolution, and here also it was the same teacher who had first shown him the way. This, together with the ideal of scientific purity, was his debt to Wyman. To Agassiz he owed the strong stimulation of his scientific interest. He felt, as did all who came under Agassiz's hypnotic spell, that "natural history must indeed be a godlike pursuit, if such a man as this can so adore it." Above all he learned from Agassiz to believe that abstract knowledge is a second best, transcended in immediate acquaintance. Thus he testified in 1896:

> We cannot all escape from being abstractionists. I myself, for instance, have never been able to escape; but the hours I spent with Agassiz so taught me the difference between all possible abstractionists and all livers in the light of the world's concrete fulness, that I have never been able to forget it.[11]

The letters of this first academic year were written from Cambridge to his family, all now living in Newport except Wilky and Bob, who had been surrendered to "the famous Mr. Sanborn" [12] at Concord and who from there made occasional visits to Cambridge.

[10] M.S., 4, 6.
[11] Ibid., 10, 14.
[12] Cf. above, 20.

[Sept. 7-8, 1861]

Professor Eliot is a fine fellow, I suspect, a man who, if he resolves to do a thing, will do it. I find analysis very interesting *so far.*

Sept. 16 [1861]

This chemical analysis is so bewildering at first that I am entirely "muddled and beat" [13] and have to employ most all my time reading up. Agassiz gives now a course of lectures in Boston, to which I have been. He is evidently a great favorite with his audience and feels so himself. But he is an admirable, earnest lecturer, clear as day, and his accent is most fascinating. I should like to study under him. Prof. Wyman's lectures on the comparative anatomy of vertebrates promise to be very good; prosy perhaps a little and monotonous, but plain and packed full and well arranged (*nourris*). Eliot I have not seen much of; I don't believe he is a *very* accomplished chemist, but can't tell yet. . . . In last year's [class] there is a son of Prof. Peirce, whom I suspect to be a very "smart" fellow with a great deal of character, pretty independent and violent though.[14] . . . We are only about twelve in the laboratory, so that we have a very cosy time. I expect to have a winter of "crowded" life.[15]

[Nov. 1861]

As Wilky has submitted to you a résumé of his future history for the next few years, so will I, hoping it will meet your approval. Thus: one year study chemistry, then spend one term at home, then one year with Wyman, then a medical education, then five or six years with Agassiz, then probably death, death, death with inflation and plethora of knowledge.[16]

Dec. 25 [1861]

The *place,* to me, improves as I go on living here, and if I study with Agassiz four or five years I should like to have you all here, with me, comfortable. I had a long talk with one of his students the other night and saw for the first time how a naturalist could feel about his trade in the same way that an artist does about his. For instance, Agassiz would rather take wholly uninstructed people, "for he has to unteach them all that they have learnt." He does not let them *look* into a book for a long while, what they learn they must learn for themselves, and be *masters* of it all. The consequence is he makes *naturalists* of them, he does not merely cram them, and this student (he had been there two years) said he felt ready to go anywhere in the world now with nothing but his notebook and study out anything quite alone. He must be a great teacher. Chemistry comes on tolerably, but not as fast as I expected. I am pretty slow with my substances, having done but twelve since Thanksgiving and having thirty-eight more to do before the end of the term.[17]

---

[13] From Sir James Stephen's account of the Lincolnshire boor whose dying words were: "What with faith, and what with the earth a-turning round the sun, and what with the railroads a-fuzzing and a-whuzzing, I'm clean stonied, muddled, and beat." *Essays by a Barrister,* 1862, 233. Stephen was a favorite author, frequently quoted by W.J.

[14] This is the first mention of his life-long friend, Charles S. Peirce. *Cf.* below, 129 ff., Ch. XXXI.

[15] *L.W.J.,* I, 34-5.

[16] *Ibid.,* I, 42.

[17] Selections from this letter appear also in *N.S.B.,* 131-4.

[March 1, 1862]

President Felton's death[18] has been the great event of the week, two funerals and I do not know how many prayers and sermons. Today I thought I would go to chapel for the sake of variety, and hear Dr. Peabody's[19] final word on him —and a very long and lugubrious one it was. The prayer was a prolonged moan in which the death (not in its consequences but in itself) was treated of as a great calamity, and the eulogy of the sermon was almost ridiculously overcharged. What was most disagreeable throughout the whole was the wailing tone,—not a bit that of simple pagan grief at the *loss* (which would have been honest), but a whine consciously *put on* as if from a sense of duty, and a whine at *nothing* definite either, but a purposeless clothing of all his words in tears. The whole style of the performance was so false and unpleasant that I have concluded to have nothing more to do with funerals till they improve. . . . I am now studying organic chemistry. It will probably shock Mother to hear that I yesterday destroyed a handkerchief—but it was an old one, and I converted it into some sugar which, though rather brown, is very good. I believe I forgot to tell you that I am shorn of my brightest ornament. That solitary hirsute jewel which lent such a manly and martial aspect to my visage is gone, and the place thereof is naked. Please don't let Father get excited. I don't think anyone will know the difference, and moreover it is not dead, it only sleeps and some day will rise phœnix like from its ashes with tenfold its former beauty.

In his second year at Harvard William continued his studies in chemistry with Eliot, but did not finish the year. The following is to his sister Alice written in his characteristic vein of affectionate banter. His father had come on to arrange for the publication of his *Substance and Shadow,* which appeared in 1863.

Cambridge, Oct. 19, 1862

Dearest Child,—

Although unwell, such is the love I cherish for you and for all the dear folks at home that I cannot resist writing a few words this evening, in order to keep up our affectionate relations and to thank you for your nice letters, which, though rudely and coarsely executed, are rather *more* than *less* delightful for it. Father has been making such a long stay here that you at home must be beginning to think of coming on after him. I think now he will stay till Wilky leaves, *si toujours* he *does* leave, on Tuesday. I think the knocking about and excitement here is doing him good. I have been with him to the printer's, and think that between us three one of the prettiest books of modern times will be produced—plain, unadorned, but severely handsome. . . .

I have had since last Sunday a boil in my elbow. Eliot with voice of absolute certainty told me to keep painting it with iodine, and as he rarely proffers a remark, those which he does let fall have double weight. So how could I help hopefully painting away. The result has been to keep the boil about *in statu quo* until about three days ago, when my arm began to swell voluminously. The io-

---

[18] President C. C. Felton died February 25, 1862. He had been President of Harvard College only two years.

[19] The Reverend Andrew Preston Peabody.

dine seems to prevent the formation of a crater, but what else it does, heaven and Eliot alone know. It is very painful to apply, and seems only to prolong the boil, and having dropped its use I now curse it aloud. I am quite sick and feverish tonight, and sit under my lamp wrapped in my overcoat writing *à la seule que j'aime* and wishing for nothing so much as an hour or two of her voluble and senseless, though soothing and pleasing, talk. Her transparent eyes, soft step, and gentle hands, her genial voice and mood, never seemed to me more desirable or more lovable than now. And what a hallowed warmth and light environs our too fond mother's form, too, as my mind's eye now sees us; she who is always as ready to soothe us in sickness as to guide us in health, and who is as unassuming and gentle in the one function as in the other. Dear old Aunt Kate too, whose self-sacrificing zeal and devotion never seemed so angelic, and whose cool and comfortable fussing around your sickly frame never so exquisitely grateful—and the sprightly, genial Bob, with the healthy breeze of active, moving life he always bears in with him—all—all—rush over me like an aged and mellow sea at the bottom of which my soul lies faintly floating. One sofa is vacant in the parlour of my home, one place unfilled,—'tis mine. Harry just comes in, sweet child, and sends his love to each and all. You shall have Bourdon's arithmetic and anything else you please. Good night—a thousand kisses to all—*le seul qui t'aime,*

WM. JAMES

To conceive James during these years as engaged in the study of chemistry, comparative anatomy, or medicine, is to form a very inadequate idea of his intellectual development. He was perpetually grazing and ruminating, wandering wherever the pasturage was good. Fortunately two notebooks of the year 1862-1863 have been preserved, in which appear—along with items extracted from the lectures of Agassiz on "Geology and the Structure and Classification of the Animal Kingdom," and Joseph Lovering on "Electrostatics, Electrodynamics and Acoustics"—pencil drawings, historical and literary chronologies, sayings of Charles Peirce, an outline of the French Revolution, and abstracts of Büchner's *Kraft und Stoff,* Max Müller's *History of Ancient Sanskrit Literature,* Farrar's *Origins of Language,* and Jonathan Edward's *Original Sin.* The entries in these books, and in an Index Rerum begun in 1864, range over the whole field of literature, history, science, and philosophy. They indicate a mind as energetic and acquisitive as it was voracious and incorrigibly vagrant. The following entry is characteristic:

> Feb'y 12, Read Buckle's essay on Mill. Buckle's noble enthusiasm for truth is inspiring. Read also, or rather skipped through, Balzac's "Lys dans la vallée." Wonderful! There never was such devotion of author to subject before. I will read all Balzac.

Although in September James again registered in the Lawrence Scientific School, the focus of his interest had shifted from chemistry to biology. He began to have "a filial feeling" towards Wyman, and to set his heart on a scientific career, with "natural history" as his subject. Business (perhaps printing) and medicine (perhaps psychiatry) were the more lucrative alternatives.[20] The following paragraph from a letter to his mother best summarizes the state of his mind on the ever-present question of a profession:—

Monday night [Nov. 2, 1863]

I feel very much the importance of making soon a final choice of my business in life. I stand now at the place where the road forks. One branch leads to material comfort, the flesh-pots, but it seems a kind of selling of one's soul. The other to mental dignity and independence; combined, however, with physical penury. If I myself were the only one concerned I should not hesitate an instant in my choice. But it seems hard on Mrs. W. J., "that not impossible she," to ask her to share an empty purse and a cold hearth. On one side is *science;* upon the other *business* (the honorable, honored and productive business of printing seems most attractive), with *medicine,* which partakes of the advantages of both, between them, but which has drawbacks of its own. I confess I hesitate. I fancy there is a fond maternal cowardice which would make you and every other mother contemplate with complacency the worldly fatness of a son, even if obtained by some sacrifice of his "higher nature." But I fear there might be some anguish in looking back from the pinnacle of prosperity (*necessarily* reached, if not by eating dirt, at least by renouncing some divine ambrosia) over the life you might have led in the pure pursuit of truth. It seems as if one *could* not afford to give that up for any bribe, however great. Still, I am undecided. The medical term opens tomorrow and between this and the end of the term here, I shall have an opportunity of seeing a little into medical business. I shall confer with Wyman about the prospects of a naturalist and finally decide. I want you to become familiar with the notion that I *may* stick to science, however, and drain away at your property for a few years more. If I can get into Agassiz's museum I think it not improbable I may receive a salary of $400 or $500 in a couple of years. I know some stupider than I who have done so. You see in that case how desirable it would be to have a home in Cambridge. Anyhow, I am convinced that *somewhere* in this neighborhood is the place for us to rest. These matters have been a good deal on my mind lately, and I am very glad to get this chance of pouring them into yours.[21]

Although James had now entered the Medical School, his studies were chiefly under the direction of Jeffries Wyman. It is clear that the *practice* of medicine did not attract him. "I embraced the medical profession a couple of months ago," he wrote on February 21, 1864, to his cousin, Jeannette Gourlay:

---

[20] *L.W.J.,* I, 50. James's cousin, Katharine Barber James, had married Dr. William Henry Prince, first superintendent of the Northampton State Hospital, and this circumstance no doubt contributed to his interest (both psychological and medical) in the insane. *Cf. L.W.J.,* I, 43-5.

[21] Reprinted from *L.W.J.,* I, 45-6. It is now possible to fix the date of the letter.

My first impressions are that there is much humbug therein, and that, with the exception of surgery, in which something positive is sometimes accomplished, a doctor does more by the moral effect of his presence on the patient and family, than by anything else. He also extracts money from them.

In the spring of 1864, after many doubts and difficulties had been overcome, the James family at last settled upon a house in Boston and moved to 13 Ashburton Place. Although this step happily united James to his family, it put an end for nearly a year to his correspondence.

VIII

MEDICAL STUDIES AND PHILOSOPHICAL BEGINNINGS

James continued his medical studies until the end of March, 1865, when he joined the Thayer Expedition to Brazil. This promised a period of close association with Professor Agassiz and a trial of the career of biology, which was still a live alternative. His letters home reveal his interest in his father's writings (*The Nature of Evil*) and his brother Henry's career, as well as his own brooding preoccupation with philosophy.

> At Sea, April 21-25, 1865
>
> You cannot conceive how pleasant it is to feel that tomorrow we shall lie in smooth water at Rio and the horrors of this voyage will be over. O the vile Sea! the damned Deep! No one has a right to write about the "nature of evil" or to have any opinion about evil, who has not been at sea. The awful slough of despond into which you are there plunged furnishes too profound an experience not to be a fruitful one. I cannot yet say what the fruit is in my case, but I am sure some day of an accession of wisdom from it.

> Rio, May 3-10, 1865
>
> Prof. has given me the marine critters of the bay (except fishes) while I am here, which is delightful, but it will cut me off of most of the excursions which the other men will make while we are here. You can imagine nothing which will equal the profusion of the lower forms of life here at low water. I shall keep on now working as steadily as I can in every way, and trying to be of as much use as I can to the Professor. . . . [He] is a very interesting man. I don't yet understand him very well. His *charlatanerie* is almost as great as his solid worth; and it seems of an unconscious childish kind that you can't condemn him for, as you would most people. He wishes to be too omniscient. But his personal fascination is very remarkable. I don't know whether, after all, our expedition will accomplish as much as it promised to. Prof. himself is a first rate captain, to be sure, and can organize splendidly. But of his eleven assistants, three are absolute idiots; Tom Ward, Dexter[1] and myself know nothing; of the five who know something, one is superannuated and one in such a feeble condition that the least exertion renders him unwell. Remain three whole men. . . . Prof. told me yesterday he was going to send four of us overland to Pará, one, a geologist; the others must settle among themselves who shall go. I think it probable now that Tom Ward and I will make two. . . .
>
> You've no idea how I pine for war news. When I get home I'm going to study philosophy all my days. I hope this letter has not a sombre tone. If it has it is

---

[1] Thomas W. Ward and Simon Newton Dexter, personal friends and fellow students at Harvard.

owing to my digestive derangement. I have only written today from sheer necessity. I never looked forward to anything with more pleasure than to the making of this overland journey.

He did not leave on "this overland journey," but had smallpox (or varioloid) instead. As soon as he recovered he wrote at length to his family, saying that his "coming was a mistake," and that he was evidently "cut out for a speculative rather than an active life":

> Agassiz has treated me very well, and agrees cordially to my going home, though of course I am a pair of hands lost to him. He is an extraordinary being, having with all his foibles, a greater personal fascination than anyone I know. . . . I have seen . . . a most extraordinary and lovely country, and it has been worth a long journey.[2]

The same letter contained an ominous allusion to the "sensitiveness" of his eyes. Although he was promptly reassured as to any permanent impairment of his vision, he suffered for many years, and intermittently throughout the remainder of his life, from an inability to use his eyes without excessive fatigue. His health and spirits improved rapidly, however, and his stay in Brazil was prolonged until March 1866.

> [Rio], July 23, 1865
>
> We start for Pará day after tomorrow without fail, which will bring us 1500 miles or more nearer home. . . . I have seen . . . more scenery and been on two large plantations in the interior. Very interesting. I pine for some conversation of an intellectual character, and I can't read. Would I might hear your articles on Goethe and Arnold. Would I might hear Father's on "Faith and Science" or his letter[3] to the *Evening Post* on Johnson's drunkenness! Would I might hear Chauncey Wright philosophize for one evening, or see La Farge, or Perry, or Holmes." [4]

> In the Xingú River, Aug. 23-25 [1865]
>
> I am very sorry if I have disappointed you by making you hope to see me too soon—but now that the real enjoyment of the expedition is beginning and

---

[2] June 3, 1865. The remainder of this letter is published in *L.W.J.*, I, 60-4.

[3] The "letter" here referred to, and which appeared in the *New York Evening Post* on May 18, 1865, is not the least remarkable of James's polemical utterances. Replying to the charge that President Johnson was intoxicated at the time of the delivery of his Inaugural Address, he pays his respects to the pharisaism and snobbism of the London *Times* and *Saturday Review*, and then contends that Johnson's momentary use of stimulants was not only excusable because of his illness, but justified by the candor and humanity (as referring to his humble origin) of the utterance which resulted. "It is very doubtful to me," he said, "whether President Johnson would have given the frank utterance he did to the divine emotion which glowed in his soul, if he had been left to his ordinary carnal prudence."

"Faith and Science" appeared in the *North Amer. Rev.* for Oct. 1865. The same number contained critical notices of Arnold's *Essays in Criticism* and Carlyle's translation of Goethe's *Wilhelm Meister*, by H.J., Jr.

[4] Thomas Sergeant Perry. For O. W. Holmes, Jr., *cf.* below, Ch. X; for Wright, *cf.* 78, 127 *ff.*

I am tasting the sweets of these lovely forests here, I find it impossible to tear myself away, and this morning I told the Professor that I would see this Amazon trip through at any rate. My eyes are getting better, ard as I begin to be able to look at objects without dreading a jumping toothache in one of them for half the night, I arouse myself from the dismal potato existence I have been leading for the last three months, and begin to feel as if there were a little of the human being left in me. Still in these ashes glow their wonted fires. I see, moreover, a chance of learning a good deal of zoölogy and botany now, as we shall have a good deal of spare time; and I am getting a pretty valuable training from the Professor, who pitches into me right and left and wakes me up to a great many of my imperfections. This morning he said I was "totally uneducated." He has done me much good already, and will evidently do me more before I have got through with him.

Mrs. Agassiz is one of the best women I have ever met. Her good temper never changes and she is so curious and wide awake and interested in all that we see, and so ever busy and spotless, that she is like an angel in the boat. . . . Agassiz is too happy for anything,—I fear the gods are bent upon his ruin. Since we arrived at Pará fourteen days ago, he has found forty-six *new species* of fish, and a total number of fishes greater than the collection which Spix and Martius[5] made in the whole four years of their sojourn! The reason is that he gets everyone to help him. . . . If Harry would keep his promise and send Father's letter to the *Evening Post* about Johnson's ebriety, I would take it very kindly.

Teffé (Amazon), Oct. 21-22, 1865

I wish I could send this letter home by telegraph so as to neutralize instantaneously the effect of some of my past letters, which I recollect for some time after my sickness were calculated to make you think I was discontented. The fact was that my blindness made me feel very blue and desponding for some time. I only rejoice that I was saved from acting on my feeling; for every day for the last two months I have thanked heaven that I kept on here, and put the thing through instead of going prematurely home. . . .

I wrote in my last letter something about the possibility of my wishing to go down south again with the Professor. I don't think there is any more probability of it than of my wishing to explore Central Africa. If there is anything I hate it is collecting. I don't think it suited to my genius at all, but for that very reason this little exercise in it I am having here is the better for me. I am getting to be very practical, orderly, and business-like. That fine disorder which used to prevail in my precincts and which used to make Mother heave a beautiful sigh when she entered my room, is treated by the people with whom I am here as a heinous crime, and I feel very sensitive and ashamed about it. . . .

I pine for Harry's literary *efforts* and to see a number or so of the *Nation*. You can't send too many magazines or papers.[6]

Obidos, Dec. 9, 1865

I seize a moment before the steamer arrives to write you just one line which may possibly reach you a fortnight before I do myself. I am just returned from

---

[5] The reference is to *Reise in Brazilien, 1817-1820*, by J. B. Spix and K. F. Martius, 1823.

[6] For other parts of this letter, *cf. L.W.J.*, I, 67-70.

a short canoe trip for the everlasting old story, *fish,* having had small luck owing to the premature rise in the river. I have now but two weeks more work before me, and then the Sabbath. I am expecting Hunnewell [7] down in this steamer to be companion. I have with infinite trouble succeeded in getting three men, and a good canoe, and tomorrow we shall start up the River Trombetas together. . . . I speak Portuguese like a book now, and am ready to converse for hours on any subject. To be sure the natives seem to have a slight difficulty in understanding me, but that is their lookout, not mine,—*my* business is to *speak,* and understand *them.* . . .

I long to be back to books, studies, etc., after this elementary existence. You have no idea . . . how strange that home life seems to me from the depths of this world, buried as it is in mere vegetation and physical needs and enjoyments . . . The idea of the people swarming about as they do at home, killing themselves with thinking about things that have no connection with their merely external circumstances, studying themselves into fevers, going mad about religion, philosophy, love and sich, breathing perpetual heated gas and excitement, turning night into day, seems almost incredible and imaginary—and yet I only left it eight months ago. Still more remarkable seems the extraordinary variety of character that results from it all—here all is so monotonous, in life and in nature, that you are rocked into a kind of sleep,—but, strange to say, it is the old existence that has already begun to seem to me like a dream. I dare say when I get home I shall have for a time many a pang of nostalgia for this placid Arcadia; even now it often suffices for me to see an orange-tree or one of these mellow sunsets, to make me shrink from the thought of giving them up altogether. . . . But it's all over—and I thrill with joy when I think that one short month and we are homeward bound. Welcome ye dark blue waves! Welcome my native slosh and ice and cast-iron stoves, magazines, theatre, friends and everything! even churches! Tell Harry that I long to see him and hear him, and read him, as one seasick longs for land; and Father, I never knew what he was to me before, and feel as if I could talk to him night and day for a week running. . . .

P.S. It is now night—not a mosquito, but a perfumed air, filled with the music of insects, frogs and whippoorwills. The stars are beating time together, I am writing by a yellow wax candle, in shirt-sleeves, and linen trousers, on a tiled floor, with every door and window open. How different from your circumstances at this moment! what they *may* be, I frequently amuse myself by imagining, but never can know what they are. Good-bye!

After a year's absence James returned to Boston, in March 1866, and resumed his studies at the Harvard Medical School. The family, after much hesitation and debate, finally chose the Quincy Street house in Cambridge, and there they were reunited, excepting the two younger sons, Wilkinson and Robertson, who had recently been discharged from military service with records of bravery. Wilkinson had been wounded at Fort Wagner and both suffered from the aftereffects of physical and nervous strain. Having been officers of Negro regi-

[7] Walter Hunnewell was a senior in Harvard College.

ments, they felt a strong interest in the future of that race, and together acquired a plantation in Florida on which they employed Negro labor. In 1870
they were forced by the industrial depression and by local prejudice to abandon this idealistic enterprise. William and Henry felt towards their younger
brothers an interest which was both solicitous and admiring.[8]

Speaking in later years of this period of his life, James said: "I originally studied medicine in order to be a physiologist, but I drifted into psychology and
philosophy from a sort of fatality. I never had any philosophic instruction, the
first lecture on psychology I ever heard being the first I ever gave."[9]

The flame of James's philosophical interest burned brightly and continuously,
but the fuel was supplied irregularly. His studies, in the sense of systematic
application under expert direction, were in the biological sciences. The philosophical content was supplied by the theoretical part of his scientific studies; by
the sporadic reading of philosophers, beginning with those standing closest to
science, such as Mill and Spencer; and by contact with his personal friends and
contemporaries. These last supplied a counter-influence, in the field of philosophy, to the religious emphasis of his father. Four of them stand out from the
rest: Charles S. Peirce, Chauncey Wright, Wendell Holmes, and Thomas W.
Ward. The first two were philosophers by vocation, the last two friends who
were passing through a philosophical phase of adolescence. All were disposed
to naturalism or scepticism. So it happened that James found himself, in his
relations with his more intimate companions, the fighting champion of metaphysical liberalism. They were rough philosophical playmates—sparring partners, who helped him to strengthen his speculative sinews.

The next phase of James's medical education is described in a letter to his
sister:

Cambridge, Dec. 12 [1866]

The present time is a very exciting one for ambitious young men at the Medical School who are anxious to get into the hospital. Their toadying the
physicians, asking them intelligent questions after lectures, offering to run
errands for them, etc., this week reaches its climax; they call at their residences
and humbly solicit them to favor their appointment, and do the same at the
residences of the ten trustees. So I have sixteen visits to make. I have little fears,
with my talent for flattery and fawning, of a failure. The appointments are
published in January.

Whether James secured his hospital appointment or not, it was impossible
that he should avail himself of it. The following spring brought a new interruption of his medical studies and another period devoted to searching life and

[8] For a fuller account of Wilkinson and Robertson James, cf. A.J. *Journal*, 1-82.
[9] Letter of August 16, 1902, published by A. Ménard, *Analyse et critique des principes de la psychologie*, 1911, 5, note.

considering the alternatives it offered. He sailed for Europe in April 1867, not to return until November 1868.

Several causes combined to bring him to this decision. The first was a condition of ill-health from which he had been suffering since the previous autumn.[10] He was now entering upon a period of partial incapacity, physical suffering, and depression, which lasted for nearly five years. It is impossible in the case of James to regard the state of his health as a mere incident. It provided a decisive reason against experimental research. It limited the amount of his reading, and no doubt was partially responsible for his extraordinary capacity to seize quickly the nourishment which his mind required. In any case it turned him from passive and cumulative erudition toward active rumination. Recurrent ill-health, while it produced periods of depression, did not touch his essential sanity—his nature was too elastic. It did, however, give him a peculiar sympathy for abnormal people. Finally, his ill-health blended in a peculiar way with that fundamental trait to which attention has already been called. James was, as we have seen, almost always restless and discontented. His discontent acted as an irritant and prevented his mind from becoming stagnant. He tasted the good things of life through yearning for them in their absence as well as through enjoying their presence. He was soon sated with what he had, but this condition was always associated with an eager longing for something else; so that on the whole he was insatiable rather than replete. The condition of his health undoubtedly contributed to this instability. Some other activity, some other scene, always furnished a relief from his present discomforts. He found work a cure for too much play, and play a cure for work; nature a cure for social fatigue, and civilization a cure for the emptiness of primitive nature; philosophy a cure for science and science for philosophy; he sought in America a cure for Europe, and went to Europe when he suffered from America.

In 1867 James had a more specific reason for going to Europe. At the Medical School he had acquired an interest in experimental physiology, and he believed that by going to Germany at this time he could both satisfy his scientific needs and perfect his knowledge of the language. In directing his steps to Germany he was following a well-worn pilgrimage route, leading not only from America but from western Europe as well. Germany glowed distantly and enticingly as the home of the great and good things of the spirit, and of the new and interesting things in literature, science, and philosophy. Germans were admired for the lack of precisely those qualities for the possession of which they were later disliked. The Germany that men loved was the Germany reminiscent of the past rather than the Germany prophetic of the future. Thus Henry

---

[10] "Insomnia, digestive disorders, eye-troubles, weakness of the back, and sometimes deep depression of spirits followed each other or afflicted him simultaneously." *L.W.J.*, I, 84.

Adams, who went to Germany in 1860, said that "what he liked was the simple character; the good-natured sentiment; the musical and metaphysical abstraction; the blundering incapacity of the German for practical affairs." [11] To an American in the 1860's political influences could not fail to confirm this cultural predisposition. Germany benefited by the unpopularity of her nearest rivals, and was loved in proportion as they were hated: England for her sympathy with the South; France for the same reason, as well as for the pretensions of the Second Empire and the supposed shallowness and frivolity of the Parisians. It will appear in the sequel that though James was influenced by this Germanophile tendency he was never dominated by it. It is characteristic of him to have loved Germany, France, England, and Italy each in turn, without definitely adopting any of them.

[11] *Education of Henry Adams*, Riverside Press, 1918, 83.

IX

DRESDEN AND BERLIN

James spent the spring and early summer of 1867 in Dresden. This period was marked by a great efflorescence of his æsthetic interests, stimulated both by galleries and by his general reading. His intellectual and emotional adventures—with art and literature, with the language and people, and with fellow travelers—are described with fullness of detail and characteristic self-revelation in the letters which he wrote at this time to his family. All the time he was thinking of those left behind in America, and wanting them, in particular his brother Harry, to share his new-found treasures.

Dresden, July 24, 1867

My dearest Family,—

. . . My uneventful life rolls quietly on, I have plenty of leisure for reading, and see very few people, so that at times, in fact, I rather pine after a heart to beat in unison with; but on the whole I am very contented, and preserve that golden mean between an inane optimism and a stupid pessimism which has always distinguished me. . . .

I have a kind of airy friendship for the people I see in the street, and the study of their physical type is very interesting, although perplexing. The sight of the women here has strengthened me more than ever in my belief that they ought to be made to do the hard labor of the community—they are far happier and better for it. . . . They all have flat, tanned faces, seldom with any color in their cheeks, very small back heads with their scanty and well-greased brown hair in a braid rolled circularly round and clapped like a muffin just above the nape of their very short necks, broad shoulders and short solid sides that remind you of nothing but chops and the possibility of cannibalism, massive hips, feet and ankles, and of a more saturated dirtiness than any race of people I ever remember to have seen. But they are as active and strong as little lionesses, and work from morning till night. . . . The Jews (with all that may be urged against them) are the best looking people here on the whole. There is a decisive character about their face that makes a picture of them immediately, and is extremely refreshing after the somewhat vulgar platitude of the Christian-Germanic type. . . .

Since my last, I have discovered another lovely *vis-à-vis* (whose existence I was not aware of at the time I sent you the portrait of the old lady opposite)[1] in a house a little way down the street, fifth story. Black hair, ruddy complexion,

---

[1] This seems to be the third of these fenestral apparitions. *Cf. L.W.J.*, I, 93 ff., where the "portrait of the old lady" will be found opposite p. 96.

large gold earrings and stout figure—the very picture of robust beauty, and forms now (together with my letter of credit, of course) the consolation of my life. Every evening she sits in her window looking down upon me while I sit looking up at her, and from the modest blush that mantles on her cheek and the ill-repressed smile that gladdens her countenance, it is evident to me that she views me not with perfect indifference. I went down into the market this morning to purchase a bouquet to send to her, but the commissionaires, or *Dienstleute* as they call them here, were all such dirty ragamuffins to serve as Cupid's messengers, and I felt so bashful about buying the bouquet and asking one of them to take it to her, and moreover it was so doubtful whether, in the present state of our acquaintance, she would receive it, that I beat a humiliating retreat back to my room—where I now am. So you see, with all my solitude and reading, Aunt Kate could hardly say I dwell more in the Intellect than in the Affections.

The country about here in every direction is beautiful, so peaceful and cultivated—and there are spots and nooks close to the city of ravishing charms—I have wished so often, and would oftener "if wishing were not vain," that Harry might be here for an hour at a time just to refresh himself with a sight of something new, though not so very *different* from home. . . .

The greatest delight I have had since I've been here was the loan of five *Weekly Transcripts*. . . . I never should have believed that in three months the tone of a Boston paper would seem so outlandish to me. As it was, I was in one squeal of amusement, surprise, and satisfaction until deep in the night when I went to bed tired out with patriotism. The boisterous animal good-humor, familiarity, reckless energy and self-confidence, unprincipled optimism, æsthetic saplessness and intellectual imbecility, made a mixture hard to characterize, but totally different from the tone of things here and, as the Germans would say, whose *"Existenz so völlig dasteht"* that there was nothing to do but to let yourself feel it. It amuses me very much to see Americans here too. They have such a hungry, restless look, and seem so unhooked somehow from the general framework. The other afternoon as I was sitting on the Terrace, a gentleman and two young ladies came in and sat down beside me. I knew them to be Americans at a glance and the man amused me very much by his exceedingly American expression: a red moustache, and tuft on chin, powerful nose, small, light eye, half whimsical, half insolent, and *all* sagacious looking, and a sort of rowdy air of superiority that made me quite proud to claim him as a brother. In a few minutes I recognized him to be Gen. M'Clellan, looking rather different from his photographs, but still no possibility of mistaking him; and I learned afterwards he was here. Whatever his faults may be, that of not being a Yankee is not among them. . . .

Tell Harry to keep up his spirits. If I were he I would not put off all my German reading till I come here—you can do it just exactly as easily at home. Read Goethe's *Faust*—it is a good piece and not without a vein of poetry running through it, and *lässt sich lesen* with enjoyment provided one does not insist on getting a *consistent* "philosophy" out of it. Such at least is my experience so far. I have read nothing since my last, but medicine, Lewes's *Aristotle* (in German translation) and some essays, full of talent, by Herman Grimm; and have no "ideas." Let Harry read (if he wants to) an essay by Grimm on the Venus of Milo . . . and compare it with the St. Victor one.[2] Both are imaginative rhapsodies, but how much solider the German! (if I remember right). It is worth reading, Harry. . . . Adieu! Your affectionate

W.J.

In August, on the advice of a Dresden physician, James tried the baths at Teplitz in the hope of curing his ailing back, and in September went to Berlin. During this and the following month he wrote a series of letters to his father dealing with the philosophical articles which the latter had recently published in the *North American Review*. These letters, together with those addressed to O. W. Holmes, Jr.,[3] furnish abundant evidence of the writer's serious attention to philosophical matters. His other letters reveal ill-health, brooding melancholy, vocational doubts, and dispersion of interests.

The following paragraphs from letters to his brother Henry reveal James's literary occupations and the circumstances of his first literary venture, the review of Grimm's *Unüberwindliche Mächte*.[4]

Berlin, Sept. 26, 1867 [5]

The other day, as I was sitting alone with my deeply breached letter of credit, beweeping my outcast state, and wondering what I could possibly do for a living, it flashed across me that I might write a "notice" of H. Grimm's novel which I had just been reading. To conceive with me is to execute, as you well know. And after sweating fearfully for three days, erasing, tearing my hair, copying, recopying, etc., etc., I have just succeeded in finishing the enclosed. I want you to read it, and if, after correcting the style and thoughts, with the aid of Mother, Alice and Father, and rewriting it if possible, you judge it to be capable of interesting in any degree anyone in the world but H. Grimm, himself, to send it to the *Nation* or the *Round Table*. I feel that a living is hardly worth being gained at this price. Style is not my forte, and to strike the mean between pomposity and vulgar familiarity is indeed difficult. Still, an the rich guerdon accrue, an but ten beauteous dollars lie down on their green and glossy backs within the family treasury in consequence of my exertions, I shall feel glad that I have made them. . . .

I wish you would articulately display to me in your future letters the names of all the books you have been reading. "A great many books, none but good ones," is provokingly vague. On looking back at what *I* have read since I left home, it shows exceeding small, owing in great part, I suppose, to its being in German. I have just got settled down again—after a nearly-two-months' debauch on French fiction, during which time Mrs. Sand, the fresh, the bright, the free, the somewhat shrill but doughty Balzac, who has risen considerably in my esteem or rather in my affection; Théophile Gautier, the good, the golden-mouthed, in turn captivated my attention; not to speak of the peerless

[2] Paul de Saint-Victor's "La Venus de Mile" formed the first chapter of his *Hommes et Dieux*, 1868.

[3] *Cf.* below, Ch. X.

[4] Published in the *Nation*, V (1867).

[5] *L.W.J.*, I, 103-4, 106.

Erckmann-Chatrian, who renew one's beliefs in the succulent harmonies of creation—and a host of others. I lately read Diderot, *Oeuvres choisies,* 2 vol., which are entertaining to the utmost from their animal spirits and the comic modes of thinking, speaking and behaving of the time.

James's review of Grimm's novel had grown, no doubt, out of his personal interest in the author. He had carried with him to Germany a letter of introduction from Emerson. Herman Grimm, son of Wilhelm Grimm, the younger of the famous brothers of the fairy tales, was an essayist and historian of art and literature, who became professor of the history of art in Berlin in 1872.

November, December, and half of January James spent in Berlin, where he attended lectures on physiology by Emil Du Bois-Reymond, and began to entertain the project of approaching psychology from that angle. This new enthusiasm reminded him sharply of his limitations: "Too late! Too late!" he wrote to Tom Ward on November 7, 1867,

> If I had been *drilled* further in mathematics, physics, chemistry, logic, and the history of metaphysics, and had established, even if only in my memory, a firm and thoroughly familiar *basis* of knowledge in all these sciences (like the basis of human anatomy one gets in studying medicine), to which I should involuntarily refer all subsequently acquired facts and thoughts . . . I might be steadily advancing.

Among James's contemporaries at the Lawrence Scientific School and at the Medical School, it was Henry P. Bowditch who influenced him most in the direction of physiology. Bowditch received his M.D. degree in 1868, a year before James, and then went abroad for three years' study in France and Germany, where he was able to *do* what James had eagerly hoped to do in the previous year. In 1871 Bowditch became a professor of physiology at Harvard and instituted in Boston his own physiological laboratory, to which James made frequent visits.[6] Though Bowditch soon outstripped James in physiology, the latter was the first to explore the European field. The numerous letters in which he described his studies were designed to help Bowditch to form plans of his own. And it was to Bowditch that he poured out his heart when it was filled with baffled yearnings after experimental research.

Berlin, Dec. 12, 1867

> I live near the University, and attend all the lectures on physiology that are given there, but am unable to do anything in the laboratory, or to attend the cliniques or Virchow's lectures and demonstrations, etc. Du Bois-Reymond, an irascible man of about forty-five, gives a very good and clear, yea, brilliant, series of five lectures a week, and two ambitious young Jews give six more between them which are almost as instructive. . . . The physiological laboratory, with

its endless array of machinery, frogs, dogs, etc., etc., almost "bursts my gizzard," when I go by it, with vexation. . . . It is very discouraging to get over so little ground. But a steady boring away is bound to fetch it, I suppose; and it seems to me it is worth the trouble. . . .

I suppose you have been rolling on like a great growing snowball through the vast fields of medical knowledge and are fairly out of the long tunnel of low spirits that leads there by this time. . . . Of course I can never hope to practise. . . . But I don't want to break off connection with biological science. I can't be a teacher of physiology, pathology, or anatomy; for I can't do laboratory work, much less microscopical or anatomical.[7]

But if James was penetrating less rapidly and deeply than Bowditch, he was advancing on a broader front. He was not only reading *belles-lettres*, but was studying philosophy. He sent home for "Cousin's lectures on Kant and that other French translation of a German introduction to Kant." "It behooves me," he said, "to learn something of the 'philosopher of Königsberg,' and I want these to ease the way."[8]

In the next letter the subject of psychology, approached from the side of physiology, comes very clearly into view. As he says in another letter of the period, he is "wading" his way towards the psychological field.[9] The following was written to his father,—

> Berlin, Dec. 26, 1867
>
> I don't think I've told you as yet anything about my future plans. Lectures end here near the end of March. I propose then to go to Teplitz again. If it does me then as much good as before, I think I shall probably be about whole. . . . Then, I think now of going to Heidelberg. There are two professors there, Helmholtz and Wundt, who are strong on the physiology of the senses, and I hope I shall be well enough to do some work in their laboratory. . . . My ultimate prospects are pretty hazy. If I only had been well and could have got out here a year or two earlier to one of these physiological laboratories, the way of life would have been singularly simplified for me. At present my health is so uncertain that I cannot look forward to teaching physiology. As a central point of study I imagine that the border ground of physiology and psychology, overlapping both, would be as fruitful as any, and I am now working on to it.

The *Nation* for January 23, 1868, contains an unsigned article entitled "The Manners of the Day," which consists of a temperately hostile commentary on Parisian life as reflected in *La Comtesse de Châlis; ou les mœurs du jour*, by Ernest Feydeau. This article had passed through a brother's expert hands, whose editorial "smoothing" of the style involved a liberal use of scissors as

---

[7] *L.W.J.*, I, 120, 123.

[8] *L.W.J.*, I, 117. The two books are: Victor Cousin, *Leçons sur la philosophie de Kant*, 1844; and, presumably, Johann Schultz, *Erläuterungen über des Hrn. Prof. Kant's "Kritik der reinen Vernunft,"* of which a French translation by Tissot appeared in 1865.

[9] *L.W.J.*, I, 126-7.

well as of the pen. The following is from William's covering letter, written from Berlin, on December 26, 1867:—

> Another fat pseudo-letter. T. S. P.[10] bought the book of Feydeau the other night and, after sitting up to read it, it occurred to me that my irrepressible and venal pen might *compliquer* an article out of it which should be more readable than the other two. So with a mighty sweat and labor I forged the accompanying, which I beg you will take care of and smooth, if possible, the style. I strove to imitate the *Saturday Review,* I fear unsuccessfully, but the writing is good practice. I am now more than ever convinced that I was not born for it. Don't read the book, it is as vile and weak as they make 'em. For the last year, I know not why, I have found myself growing to despise the French in many ways. Paris seems now to be in a state of moral and intellectual debasement, of which it really seems hard to imagine any peaceful issue. Every cord is tightly screwed up, to a hair of the snapping point; everything *screams* falsetto, the point seems coming when pleasure must be bloody to be felt at all. T. S. P. takes the *Figaro* daily. It is the most hideous little sheet I ever saw. One part *bons-mots,* personal *cancans,* and bawdy anecdotes, spun out with that infernal, grinning flippancy and galvanized gaiety ye wot of; the rest devoted to executions, murders and crimes generally in different countries, and theatrical gossip. I seriously think our *Police Gazette* is a higher paper. It is the organ of naturally coarse and low minds, but the *Figaro* is that of minds lost and putrefying. Bah!

The balance of this letter is devoted to minute descriptions for blistering the back. In fact the unpublished parts of the correspondence between William and Henry James are very largely composed of hygienic, symptomatic, and therapeutic details. Their interest in one another's condition of health was equaled only by their faith in their own remedies.

To his sister James wrote this vivid account of his social experiences:—

> Berlin, Jan. 9, 1868
>
> Sweetlington!
>   . . . The last fortnight has been distinguished by a greater social activity than ever on my part. The last of it was on the night of the 6th when H. Grimm was forty years old, and in the manner of his nation had a fandango, at which an allegorical little drama in verse with prologue was performed by some of the friends of the family. The Thieses,[11] or rather Mrs. Thies on a visit to Mrs. Bancroft a few days before, had suggested to Mrs. Bancroft that she should "surprise" Mrs. Grimm by coming in upon them that night. . . . To make the surprise more sudden and unexpected, Mrs. Thies told Mrs. Grimm all about it beforehand, and extra cray-fish were ordered and a few extra people invited. I sat behind Bancroft at the allegorical drama and he looked more like a villain than ever. There is no other word for his expression, especially that of the back of his

[10] Thomas Sergeant Perry.
[11] Old Cambridge friends. Louis Thies was Curator of the Gray Collection of Engravings at Harvard.

neck and ears. His eyes look like those of a lobster, as if they were on stalks, and T. S. P. says you feel as if he ought to have a pin run through him to be stuck up on the wall like an insect. He speaks German fluently (and audibly) and the Germans speak with ever new admiration of his being minister here, as if they were not yet quite able to realize the idea. Mrs. Bancroft is doubtless an excellent lady in private, but the impression of an old limp party kid glove which her appearance suggests is but too well corroborated by the want of body to fill out the form of her conversation. Miss Thies played the part in the drama of a sort of nondescript being answering, as well as I could make out, to the "Genius of Hospitality." She wore a cloud of white muslin and a tin crown on her disheveled hair, and recited very prettily her German verses, with red cheeks, and sparkling eyes. . . .

Mrs. Grimm is a woman of genius, really. . . . There is a freedom and breadth about her ways, combined with a feminine grace that must bring everyone down. . . . Grimm himself is a noble fellow, and you can't think how friendly they have both been to me. At that last party, for the first time since I have been away, I felt for a time at home and really fused with my surroundings, talked away my idiotisms and despoiled phrases to nearly everyone in the room. . . . You've no idea what an intense pleasure it was. If I wanted, I could see all the best society in Berlin with the openings I now have, but with my University work, my back is unequal to the task of a larger visiting circle than I have. T. S. Perry went to the party and naturally found it gloomier than a funeral. One has got here by sheer force of self-sustenance to live down this foreignness. The stranger himself has much more than at home or in France or England to do his own work—and when by chance you meet a Berliner whose manners go out to meet you, as it were, it strikes you so strangely that your impulse is to beg him not to take that extra trouble on your account. When you've crossed the sill, I daresay you're as well off as anywhere else. I made, or rather had made, a "Moore's" Patent Blotter for a birthday present for Grimm which seemed to tickle him.

O my beloved child, how much I would like to be with you and have you "sass" me as of yore. Frequently in the night watches does my spirit fly and bump like a moth against the window panes of Quincy Street, and I think on the whole what a good crowd dwells there, especially in the midst of the ignoble mush of which the majority of the male sex is composed, how refreshing it is to have two persons of moral cleanness and freshness like H. James, Sr., and H. James, Jr., in the family. I would not have you read them this as directly coming from me, but you can somehow leave the letter trailing around where they may be likely to see it, and inadvertently peruse it. . . . 1000 kisses to all, from your loving

WM. JAMES

The consoling and hortatory letters which James wrote at this time to Tom Ward were designed as much for his own cure as for Ward's. There was a dawning realization that since education is a cumulative effect, even a series of abortive undertakings like his own might bear fruit in the end: "Results should not be too voluntarily aimed at or too busily thought of. They are *sure* to float up of their own accord, from a long enough daily work at a given matter." [12]

From Teplitz, to which his health obliged him to return, he communicated similar reflections to his youngest brother:

Teplitz, Jan. 27, 1868

My dear old Bob,—

. . . I feel rather ashamed at my age to stand in the presence of you and Wilky without having earned a cent. But I have not been quite idle notwithstanding, and will, if health only returns, make my living yet. I am very glad I came to Germany on many accounts, in the first place, because I have got command of the literature in a way I hardly think I should have had patience to do at home, so difficult is the language; and in the second place . . . my way of looking on the practical problem of life is a much steadier and simpler one. I feel as if I should be contented to settle down to some one occupation for the rest of my days, and atone for the narrowness of my scope by the thoroughness of my treatment of it—trusting to have life rounded off in the next world if necessary, like the man in Browning's "Grammarian's Funeral." . . .

We Americans are too greedy for *results* . . . and we think only of means of cutting short the work to reach them sooner. I suppose it grows mostly out of the facility with which *material* results of all sorts have been obtainable with us—I am sure it is a destructive temper of mind in purely intellectual pursuits. I think the business of life appears to the vision of an ordinary German about to embark on it rather as a succession of days of a given *occupation,* than as a mere road to some more or less considerable achievement. . . . Most Americans I have seen here have had a peculiar haggard, hungry expression about the eye quite different from anything German. . . .

I confess sometimes the prospect of our scattered and in various ways dilapidated family of old is a little disheartening, but hang it! the world is as young now as it was when the gospel was first preached. And our lives, if we will make them so, are as real as the lives of anyone who ever lived. . . . Pray write me soon . . . again, and tell me of your prospects, and your views of life, and believe me my dearest Bob, ever your loving brother,

WM. JAMES

[12] Written in January 1868; *L.W.J.,* I, 133.

X

WENDELL HOLMES

This was the period of James's greatest intimacy with Oliver Wendell Holmes, Jr. The friendship with Holmes began while the latter was in the Harvard Law School (1864-1866). When James was in Brazil in 1865 he longed for Holmes, and after he returned to his medical studies in 1866 he "wrangled" with Holmes by the hour.[1] In the winter of 1866-1867 the two were deep in a continuing metaphysical discussion, echoes of which are preserved in a memorandum on "materialism," addressed by James to Holmes. It contained a defense of optimism against the negations of agnosticism—a defense which he "was groping for the other evening," but "could not say" until Holmes was gone and he was in bed.[2] It was on April 16, 1867, that James sailed from New York on the *Great Eastern*—bound for that long voyage of exile and discovery which has already been recorded. Suffering from mortification that he should be so unreliable in health and so vacillating in will, he had kept his plan a secret even from his family and friends. But on the eve of his departure he must hold a farewell session at the Holmes house on Charles Street: "Dear Wendy boy,—I will go in tomorrow night, and we will evolve cosmos out of chaos for positively the last time."[3]

During all the time of his homesickness and heart-searching in Germany James felt that Holmes and Tom Ward were his "best friends so far."[4] In September 1867, he wrote from Berlin complaining of Holmes's silence, inquiring after the results of his "study of the *vis viva* question, and referring familiarly to their "dilapidated old friend the Cosmos."[5] He received the following reply:—

Boston, Dec. 15, 1867

Dear Bill,—

I shall begin with no apologies for my delay in writing except to tell you that since seeing you I have written three long letters to you at different intervals on *vis viva*, each of which I was compelled to destroy because on reflection it appeared either unsound or incomplete. But I was talking yesterday with Fanny

---

[1] W.J. to A.J., November 16, 1866; *L.W.J.*, I, 80.
[2] W.J. to O.W.H., Jr., winter of 1866-7; *L.W.J.*, I, 82.
[3] *Ibid.*, "Monday" [April 8, 1867].
[4] W.J. to Tom Ward, May 24, 1868.
[5] September 17, 1867; *L.W.J.*, I, 103, 101.

Dixwell[6] and she told me to fire away anyhow—that she thought it would please you to hear from me even without *vis viva*. So here goes. Writing is so unnatural to me that I have never before dared to try it to you unless in connection with a subject. Ah! dear Bill, do me justice. My expressions of esteem are not hollow nor hyperbolical—nor put in to cover my neglect. In spite of my many friends I am almost alone in my thoughts and inner feelings. And whether I ever see you much or not, I think I can never fail to derive a secret comfort and companionship from the thought of you. I believe I shall always respect and love you whether we see much or little of each other. . . .

For two or three months I debauched o' nights in philosophy. But now it is law—law—law. My *magnum opus* was reading the *Critique of Pure Reason*. . . . It's puerile stuff enough, I admit, to waste energy on. But it seems necessary to read a good deal of useless stuff, in order to know that it is so and not to depend only on a surmise. At present, I say it's nothing but law; though, by the by, I am reading Tyndall's book on *Heat*—what a yellow-whiskered, healthy, florid-complected, pleasant English book it is, to be sure. Aren't the foreigners simpler than we? See what one of the great lights of English law says in the preface to a book I'm reading (he is speaking of Savigny): "I have used great exertions, but without effect, to make myself sufficiently master of the German language to read this work in the original." If a man here had three cents' worth of secondhand knowledge would he confess that he didn't know anything under the sun? . . .

Oh! Bill, my beloved, how have I yearned after thee all this long time. How I have admired those brave, generous and magnanimous traits of which I will not shame thee by speaking. I am the better that I have seen thee and known thee,—let that suffice. Since I wrote the last word I have been to see your father. By a rather remarkable coincidence, your last letter referred to Kant. . . . It is rather strange, isn't it? It is now evening and the whole day has been yours with the exceptions noted and meals. . . . May this get to you in time to wish you a Happy New Year. By Heaven I do,—*vis viva* must wait. There are stickers I can't answer. But I rather think you found difficulty—at least I did—in the insufficiency of facts. As one is shaping his views he wants to say, Is this experiment so or so? . . . What a passion your father has in writing and talking his religion! Almost he persuadeth me to be a Swedenborgian, but I can't go it so far—will see whether the other scheme busts up first, I think. Good-bye, dear Bill—don't forget me quite. Affectionately yours,

O. W. Holmes

Berlin, Jan. 3, 1868[7]

My dear Wendle,—

Ich weiss nicht was soll es bedeuten, dass ich so traurig bin, tonight. The ghosts of the past all start from their unquiet graves and keep dancing a senseless whirligig around me so that, after trying in vain to read three books, to sleep, or to think, I clutch the pen and ink and resolve to work off the fit by a few lines to one of the most obtrusive ghosts of all—namely the tall and lank one of Charles Street. Good golly! how I would prefer to have about twenty-

[6] Afterwards Mrs. Oliver Wendell Holmes, Jr.
[7] Reprinted with omissions from *L.W.J.*, I, 124-7.

four hours' talk with you up in that whitely lit-up room—without the sun rising or the firmament revolving so as to put the gas out, without sleep, food,
clothing or shelter except your whiskey bottle, of which, or the like of which,
I have not partaken since I have been in these longitudes! I should like to have
you opposite me in any mood, whether the facetiously excursive, the metaphysically discursive, the personally confidential, or the jadedly *cursive* and argu-
mentative—so that the oyster-shells which enclose my being might slowly turn
open on their rigid hinges under the radiation, and the critter within loll out his
dried-up gills into the circumfused ichor of life, till they grew so fat as not to
know themselves again. I feel as if a talk with you of any kind could not fail
to set me on my legs again for three weeks at least. I have been chewing on two
or three dried-up old cuds of ideas I brought from America with me, till they
have disappeared, and the nudity of the Kosmos has got beyond anything I
have as yet experienced. . . .

I don't know how it is I am able to take so little interest in reading this
winter. I marked out a number of books when I first came here, to finish. What
with their heaviness and the damnable slowness with which the Dutch still
goes, they weigh on me like a haystack. I loathe the thought of them; and yet
they have poisoned my slave of a conscience so that I can't enjoy anything else.
I have reached an age when practical work of some kind clamors to be done—
and I must still wait!

There! Having worked off that pent-up gall of six weeks' accumulation I feel
more genial. I wish I could have some news of you—now that the postage is
lowered to such a ridiculous figure (and no letter is double) there remains no
shadow of an excuse for not writing—but, still, I don't expect anything from
you. I suppose you are sinking ever deeper into the sloughs of the law—yet
I ween the Eternal Mystery still from time to time gives her goad another turn
in the raw she once established between your ribs. Don't let it heal over yet.
When I get home let's establish a philosophical society to have regular meetings
and discuss none but the very tallest and broadest questions—to be composed
of none but the very topmost cream of Boston manhood. It will give each one a
chance to air his own opinion in a grammatical form, and to sneer and chuckle
when he goes home at what damned fools all the other members are—and may
grow into something very important after a sufficient number of years. . . .

I'll now pull up. I don't know whether you take it as a compliment that I
should only write to you when in the dismalest of dumps—perhaps you ought
to—you, the one emergent peak, to which I cling when all the rest of the world
has sunk beneath the wave. Believe me, my Wendly boy, what poor possibility
of friendship in the crazy frame of W.J. meanders about thy neighborhood.
Good-bye! Keep the same bold front as ever to the Common Enemy—and don't
forget your ally,

W. J.

P.S. . . . Jan. 4. [Written on the outside of the envelope] By a strange coincidence, after writing this last night, I received yours this morning. Not to sacrifice the postage stamps which are already on the envelope (Economical W!)
I don't reopen it. But I will write you again soon. Meanwhile, bless your heart!
thank you! *Vide* Shakespeare: Sonnet XXIX.

Boston, April 19, 1868

Dear Bill,—

The icy teeth have melted out of the air and winter has snapped at us for the last time. Now are the waters beneath my window of a deeper and more significant blue than heretofore. Now do the fields burn with green fire—the evanescent hint of I know not what hidden longing of the earth. Now all the bushes burgeon with wooly buds and the elm trees have put on bridal veils of hazy brown. Now to the chorus of the frogs answers the chorus of the birds in antiphony of morning and evening. Now couples, walking round Boston Common Sundays after sunset, draw near to each other in the dark spaces between the gas lights and think themselves unseen. Now are the roads around Cambridge filled with collegians with new hats and sticks and shining schoolboy faces. Now the young man seeks the maiden nothing loath to be pursued. Spring is here, Bill, and I turn to thee,—not with more affection than during the long grind of the winter, but desiring if it may be to say a word to thee once more.

Since I wrote in December I have worked at nothing but the law. Philosophy has hibernated in torpid slumber, and I have lain "sluttishly soaking and gurgling in the devil's pickle," as Carlyle says. It has been necessary,—if a man chooses a profession he cannot forever content himself in picking out the plums with fastidious dilettantism and give the rest of the loaf to the poor, but must eat his way manfully through crust and crumb—soft, unpleasant, inner parts which, within one, swell, causing discomfort in the bowels. Such has been my cowardice that I have been almost glad that you weren't here, lest you should be disgusted to find me inaccessible to ideas and impressions of more spiritual significance but alien to my studies. Think not, however, that I distrust the long enduring of your patience. I know that you would be the last of all to turn away from one in whom you discerned the possibility of friendship because his vigils were at a different shrine, knowing it was the same Divinity he worshipped. And the winter has been a success, I think, both for the simple discipline of the work and because I now go on with an ever increasing conviction that law as well as any other series of facts in this world may be approached in the interests of science and may be studied, yes and practised, with the preservation of one's ideals. I should even say that they grew robust under the regimen, —more than that I do not ask. To finish the search of mankind, to discover the *ne plus ultra* which is the demand of ingenuous youth, one finds is not allotted to an individual. To reconcile oneself to life—to dimly apprehend that this dream disturbing the sleep of the cosm is not the result of a dyspepsy, but is well—to suspect some of the divine harmonies, though you cannot note them like a score of music—these things, methinks, furnish vanishing points which give a kind of perspective to the chaos of events. Perhaps I am fortunate in what I have often made a reproach to myself.

Harry never lets up on his high aims,—somehow it connects itself with the absence of humor in him which himself avows. *I do.* There are not infrequent times when a bottle of wine, a good dinner, a girl of some trivial sort can fill the hour for me. So for longer spaces, work,—of which only at the beginning and the end do I perceive the philosophic *nexus,* and while performing forget the

Great Task Master's Eye. This makes life easier though perhaps it does not deserve approval. . . .

Dear old Bill, I haven't said anything about your illness to you—there is nothing, perhaps, which particularly belongs to me to say. But for God's sake don't lose that courage with which you have faced "the common enemy" (as you well have it). Would that I could give back the spirits which you have given to me so often. At all events doubt not of my love.

Let me not be sad,—at least for this letter. There is a new fire in the earth and sky. I, who through the long winter have felt the wrinkles deepening in my face and a stoop settling in my back—I, who have said to myself that my life henceforth must and should be given only to severe thought, and have said to youth, *"procul esto,"*—I feel the mighty quickening of the spring.

The larches have sprouted.

I saw a butterfly today just loosed from the bondage of winter, and a bee toiling in sticky buds half opened.

O! passionate breezes! O! rejoicing hills! How swells the soft full chorus—for this earth which slept has awakened, and the air is tremulous with multiplied joyous sound.

Sing, sparrow—kissing with thy feet the topmost tassels of the pines.

Cease not thy too much sound, O! robin. Squirrels grind thy scissors in the woods. Creak, blackbirds. Croak, frogs. Caw, high-flying crows, who have seen the breaking of the ice in northern rivers and the seaward moving booms.

A keen, slender, stridulous vibration—almost too fine for the hearing, weaving in and out, and in the pauses of the music dividing the silence like a knife —pierces my heart with an ecstasy I cannot utter. Ah! what is it? Did I ever hear it? Is it a voice within, answering to the others, but different from them— and like a singing flame not ceasing with that which made it vocal?

Dear Bill, to whom should I vent this madness but to you? Good-bye. You know my sentiments—I will not repeat them. Affectionately yours,

O. W. HOLMES

Apr. 25. It is snowing again. S'help me.

Dresden, May 15, 1868

My dear Wendell,—

Your unexpected letter has just burst into my existence like a meteor into the sphere of a planet, and here I go for an answer while the heat developed by the impact is at its highest. I have got so accustomed to thinking of you as not a writing animal that such an event rather dislocates my mind from its habitual "sag" in contemplating the world. I have of late been repeatedly on the point of writing to you but have paused ere slipping o'er the brink. It is easy to write people whom you have been steadily writing to, for one letter seems to continue the previous ones. But to fire off a letter point blank at a man once in six months has an arbitrary savor. There are so many things of about equal importance for you to tell him that there is no reason for you to begin with any particular one and leave off the rest. Consequently you don't begin at all. However, heaven reward you for this inspired effusion and help you to another some time. It runs through the whole circle of human energy, Shelley, Kant, Goethe, Walt

Whitman, all being fused in the unity of your fiery personality. Were I only in the vein, O! friend, I would answer in the same high strain, but today I grovel in prose. That you firmly embrace like a *Bothriocephalus latus* the very bowels of the law and grapple them to your soul with hooks of steel, is good. That the miasmas thence arising do not forever hide the blue Jove above, is better. I am firmly convinced that by going straight in almost any direction you can get out of the woods in which the young mind grows up, for I have an idea that the process usually consists of a more or less forcible reduction of the other elements of the chaos to a harmony with the terms of the one on which one has taken his particular stand. I. think I might have fought it out on the line of practical medicine quite well. Your image of the ideals being vanishing points which give a kind of perspective to the chaos of events, tickleth that organ within me whose function it is to dally with the ineffable. I shall not fail to remember it, and if I stay long enough in Germany to make the acquaintance of ary a philosopher, I shall get it off at my own, you bet!

Your letter last winter I got and acknowledged on the cover of one I had just written you. Your criticism of Kant seems perfectly sound to me. I hoped to have got at him before now but have been interfered with. I have read only his *Prolegomena* and his little *Anthropology* (a marvellous, biting little work), and Cousin's exposé of him (and of himself at the same time, darn him and the likes of him!—he is a mere politician). I hope soon to begin with the *Kritik,* for which I feel myself now quite prepared. And I reserve any half-ripe remarks I may have made on Kant till after that is done. I think a good five hours' talk with you would probably do me more good than almost any other experience I can conceive of. I have not had any contact out of books with any soul possessed of *reason* since I left home, except, perhaps, Grimm—and I did not, owing to the linguistic wall between us, succeed in putting myself into communication with him. And in personal contact, Wendell, lies a deep dark power. I say "reason," but I have no idea what the thing is. I have slipped so gradually out of sight of it in people that I did not know any particular thing was gone, till the day before yesterday I made the acquaintance of a young female from New York who is here in the house, and suddenly noticed that an old long-forgotten element was present (I mean in her way of accepting the world). It has been a beneficent discovery, and the suddenness and quasi-definiteness of it almost shatters one's empirical philosophy. But probably it, too, may be resolved into other more vulgar elements.

The fact is, my dear boy, that I feel more as if you were my ally against what you call "the common enemy" than anyone I know. As I am writing a grave statement of facts and not an effusion of friendliness, I may say that Tom Ward seems to me to have as great an intuition of the length and breadth of the enemy (which is the place in which most people fail), and perhaps a greater animal passion in his feeling about it, but poor Tom is so deficient in power of orderly thought that intercourse with him hardly ever bears fruit. With Harry and my Dad I have a perfect sympathy "personally," but Harry's orbit and mine coincide but part way, and Father's and mine hardly at all, except in a general feeling of philanthropy in which we both indulge. I have no idea that the particular point of view from which we spy the fiendish enemy *per se* any merit over that of lots of other men. Such an opinion we recognize in other people as "conceit." But merely because it is common to both of us, I have an esteem for you which is *tout particulier,* and value intercourse with you. You have a far more logical and orderly mode of thinking than I (I stand between you and T. Ward), and whenever we have been together I have somehow been conscious of a reaction against the ascendancy of this over my ruder processes—a reaction caused by some subtle deviltry of egotism and jealousy, whose causes are untraceable by myself, but through whose agency I put myself involuntarily into a position of self-defense, as if you threatened to overrun my territory and injure my own proprietorship. I don't know whether you ever noticed any such thing,—it is hard to define the subtleness of it. *Some* of it may have been caused by the feeling of a too "cosmo-centric" consciousness in you. But most of it was pure meanness. I *guess* that were we to meet now I should be less troubled with it. I have grown into the belief that friendship (including the highest half of that which between the two sexes is united under the single name of love) is about the highest joy of earth, and that a man's rank in the general scale is well indicated by his capacity for it. So much established, I will try in a few brief strokes to define my present condition to you. If asked the question which all men who pretend to know themselves ought to be able to answer, but which few probably could offhand,—"What reason can you give for continuing to live? What ground allege why the thread of your days should not be snapped *now?*"

May 18th. Wendell of my entrails! At the momentous point where the last sheet ends I was interrupted by the buxom maid calling to tea and through various causes have not got back till now. As I sit by the open window waiting for my breakfast and look out on the line of *Droschkes* drawn up on the side of the Dohna Platz, and see the coachmen, red-faced, red-collared, and blue-coated, with varnished hats, sitting in a variety of indolent attitudes upon their boxes, one of them looking in upon me and probably wondering what the devil I am,—when I see the big sky with a monstrous white cloud battening and bulging up from behind the houses into the blue, with a uniform copper film drawn over cloud and blue, which makes one anticipate a soaking day—when I see the houses opposite with their balconies and windows filled with flowers and greenery—Ha! on the topmost balcony of one stands a maiden, black-jacketed, red-petticoated, fair and slim under the striped awning, leaning her elbow on the rail and her peach-like chin upon her rosy finger tips! Of whom thinkest thou, maiden, up there aloft? Here, *here!* beats that human heart for which in the drunkenness of the morning hour thy being vaguely longs, and tremulously, but recklessly and wickedly, posits elsewhere, over those distant housetops which thou regardest. Out of another window hangs the form, seen from behind and centre of gravity downwards, of an intrepid servant girl, washing the window. Blue frocked is she, and like a spider fast holding to his thread, or one that gathers samphires on dizzy promontory, she braves the danger of a fall. Against the lamp-post leans the *Dienstman* or *commissionaire,* cross-legged and with tin-badged cap, smoking his cheap morning cigar. Far over the *Platz* toils the big country wagon with high-collared horses, and the still pavement rings with the shuffling feet of broad-backed wenches carrying baskets, and of short-necked, wide-faced men. The day has in fact begun, and when I see all this and think that at the same moment thou art probably in a dead sleep whirled round through the black night with rocks and trees and monuments like an inanimate thing, when I think all this, I feel—*how?*—I give it up myself! After this interruption, which on the ground of local color and my half-awake condition you will excuse, I return to the former subject. But here's the breakfast! Excuse me! Man eats in Germany a very light breakfast, chocolate and dry bread, so it won't take me long.

'Tis done, and a more genial glow than ever fills my system. Having read over what I wrote the day before yesterday I feel tempted not to send it, for I cannot help thinking it does not represent with perfect sincerity the state of the case. Still, if I do not write to you now, it may postpone itself a good while, and I let it go for the general spirit which animates it rather than for the particular propositions it contains. The point which seems to me unwarranted was my assumption of any special battle I was fighting against the powers of darkness, and of your being allied with me therein as the ground of my esteem for you. The truth is painfully evident to me that I am but little interested in any particular battle or movement of progress, and the ground of my friendship for you is more a sort of physical relish for your wit and wisdom, and passive enjoyment of the entertainment they afford, than anything else. Much would I give for a constructive passion of some kind. As it is, I am in great measure in the hands of Chance. Your metaphysical industry and the artistic satisfaction you take in the exercise of it, gives you an immeasurable advantage. In the past year if I have learned little else, I have at least learned a good deal that I previously did not suspect about the limits of my own mind. They are not exhilarating. I will not annoy you by going into the details, but they all conspire to give my thoughts a vague emptiness wherever feeling is, and to drive feeling out wherever the thought becomes good for anything. Bah! My answer to the question I asked at the end of sheet two would be vague indeed; it would vary between the allegation of a dogged desire to assert myself at certain times, and the undermined hope of making *some* nick, however minute, in the pile which humanity is fashioning, at others. Of course I would beg for a *temporary* respite from the inevitable shears, for different reasons at different times. If a *particular* and passionate reason for wishing to live for four hours longer were *always* forthcoming, I should think myself a very remarkable man, and be quite satisfied. But in the intervals of absence of such a reason, I could wish that my general grounds are more defined than they are.[8] . . .

I am tending strongly to an empiristic view of life. I don't know how far it will carry me, or what rocks insoluble by it will block my future path. Already I see an ontological cloud of absolute idealism waiting for me far off on the horizon, but I have no passion for the fray. I shall continue to apply empirical principles to my experiences as I go on and see how much they fit. One thing makes me uneasy. *If* the end of all is to be that we must take our sensations as simply given or as preserved by natural selection for us, and interpret this rich and delicate overgrowth of ideas, moral, artistic, religious and social, as a mere mask, a tissue spun in happy hours by creative individuals and adopted by other men in the interests of their sensations,—how long is it going to be well for us not to "let on" all we know to the public? How long are we to indulge the "people" in their theological and other vagaries so long as such vagaries seem to

---

[8] The paragraph omitted here will be found below, 107.

us more beneficial on the whole than otherwise? How long are we to wear that uncomfortable "air of suppression" which has been complained of in Mr. Mill? Can any men be trusted to dole out from moment to moment just that measure of a doctrine which is consistent with utility? I know that the brightest jewel in the crown of Utilitarianism is that every notion hatched by the human mind receives justice and tolerance at its hands. But I know that no mind can trace the far ramifications of an idea in the mind of the public; and that any idea is at a disadvantage which cannot enlist in its favor the thirst for conquest, the love of absoluteness, that have helped to found religions; and which cannot open a *definite* channel for human sympathies and affections to flow in. It seems exceedingly improbable that any new *religious* genius should arise in these days to open a fresh highway for the masses who have outgrown the old beliefs. Now ought not we (supposing we becomed indurated sensationalists) to begin to smite the old, hip and thigh, and get, if possible, a little enthusiasm associated with our doctrines? If God is dead or at least irrelevant, ditto everything pertaining to the "Beyond." If happiness is our Good, ought we not to try to foment a passionate and bold will to attain that happiness among the multitudes? Can we not conduct off upon our purposes from the old moralities and theologies a beam which will invest us with some of the proud absoluteness which made them so venerable, by preaching the doctrine that Man is his own Providence, and every individual a real God to his race, greater or less in proportion to his gifts and the way he uses them? The sentiment of philanthropy is now so firmly established and apparently its permanence so guaranteed by its beneficent nature, that it would be bold to say it could not take its place as an ultimate motive for human action. I feel no *confidence* (even apart from my doubts as to the theoretical finality of "sensationalism") that society is as yet ripe for it as a popular philosophy and religion combined, but as I said above, no one can measure the effects of an idea, or distribute exactly the shares which different ideas have in our present social order. And certainly there is something disheartening in the position of an esoteric philosopher. The conscientious prudence which would wish to educate mankind gradually instead of throwing out the line, and letting it educate itself, may be both presumptuous and timid. Do you take? I only throw out these as doubts, and would like to know whether you have been troubled by any similar ones on the matter of policy. The breath of my nostrils is doubt, and that is what makes me so the slave of chance. . . .

I have been reading lately in Teplitz in Schiller and Goethe. The possession of those two men's lives and works by a people gives them a great advantage over neighboring nations. Goethe at last has shot into distinct individual shape for me, which is a great relief, and an enormous figure he is. . . . I am sensible to your expression of sympathy with my stove-in condition of back. I shall *endeavor* (by jerks) to keep the upper lip rigid even if the vertebral column yields. An account of a man in a western settlement which I heard from a traveler on the ship coming over has afforded me much satisfaction ever since, and served as a good example. The traveler stopped at a grocery store to get some whiskey, and alarmed at the woebegone appearance of the storekeeper, asked him what was the matter. "Do you see that man sitting in the back shop?" said the other. "He's the sheriff, and has attached all my goods." He then went on to tell his other misfortunes, ending with the story of his wife having run away the day before with another man, but presently wiped his eyes, and with a smile of sweet recollection said: "I don't know, though, as I have any right to complain—I've done pretty well on the whole since I came to this settlement." Comment is needless.

There, my dear boy, I hope you have not begun to thank your stars I don't write oftener, since I write at such length. I wanted to give you a report of my mental condition, I have done so more or less, and trust you will respect the affection and confidence which dictated it. I'd rather my father should not see it. Use your own judgment about showing it to Harry. I leave here in a month or so for Heidelberg. Get my address from Harry whenever you write. And for God's sake do so again before too long. I got a letter in Teplitz from Miss Fanny Dixwell which was a great godsend. Please remember me to all your family, and believe me thy friend

Wm. James

As is intimated in this letter, James's affection for Holmes was not untroubled. He felt a certain constraint in his presence, which was perhaps due at bottom to a difference of emotional "wave-length." James would let himself go, and then recoil when he felt that the circuit was not completed. He was more impulsive, headlong, self-forgetful—Holmes more firmly resolute and self-contained, as well as more ironical. James was sometimes led by this experience to attribute a certain hardness and self-seeking to Holmes. The latter is said to have remarked of another of his friends, "I'm afraid Brandeis has the crusading spirit. He talks like one of those upward-and-onward fellows." [9] So did James, and he never wholly relished the air of flippancy or dry cynicism with which Holmes masked his own service of mankind. After James's return from Europe Holmes continued to be a familiar intimate of the James household. "W. Holmes rings the bell as usual at eight and one-half o'clock on Saturday evenings, and we are all falling into our old ways," wrote the elder Mrs. James to her son Henry. [10] But James was constantly baffled by him—found him "composed of at least two and a half different people rolled into one." [11] That there was something about Holmes's very adherence to his chosen task which was appalling to the other members of the James family, as well as to William, will be seen in this paragraph from a letter written to Henry James by his mother in 1873:

> Wendell Holmes dined with us a few days ago. His whole life, soul and body, is utterly absorbed in his *last* work upon his Kent. He carries about his manuscript in his green bag and never loses sight of it for a moment. He started to go to Will's room to wash his hands, but came back for his bag, and when we went to dinner, Will said, "Don't you want to take your bag with you?" He

[9] S. Bent, *Justice Oliver Wendell Holmes,* Garden City Publishing Co., 1932, 281.
[10] September 21, 1869.
[11] *Cf.* below, 113.

said, "Yes, I always do so at home." His pallid face, and this fearful grip upon his work, makes him a melancholy sight.[12]

A similar comment appears in a letter written by William to his brother Henry on July 5, 1876:

> I spent three very pleasant days with the Holmes's at Mattapoisett. I fell quite in love with she; and he exemplified in the most ridiculous way Michelet's *"mariage de l'homme at de la terre."* I told him that he looked like Millet's peasant figures as he stooped over his little plants in his flannel shirt and trousers. He is a powerful battery, formed like a planing machine to gouge a deep self-beneficial groove through life; and his virtues and faults were thrown into singular relief by the lonesomeness of the shore, which as it makes every object, rock or shrub, stand out so vividly, seemed also to put him and his wife under a sort of lens for you.

As time went on there was a weakening of the philosophical bond that united the two men. Already, as early as 1868, James had felt that their divergent specialization had seriously diminished their community of interest. He had remarked to Ward that "the mystery of the *Total* is a rather empty platform to be the only one to meet a man on." [13] And even within the field of this common interest there was a profound difference which was bound to widen with the years. James and Holmes had been drawn together chiefly through their common negations and defiances, and through their participation in the common problems of youthful emancipation. When James recovered from his weakness he recovered from his doubts; sensationalism and utilitarianism, as is clearly to be seen in all of his momentary avowals of them, were never more than a counsel of desperation. As he grew more constructive and speculative, as his beliefs multiplied, he traveled farther and farther from that crossroads where he and Holmes had met. The latter never lost his philosophical interest, and when James became a writer of books Holmes read them and sent his comment. But he could rarely agree in any point of doctrine. The two men were divided, morally and metaphysically.[14] Their deepest and most durable bond was that "physical relish" for one another's "wit and wisdom" to which James had alluded in his youthful confession.

[12] February 28, 1873. Holmes's edition of Kent's *Commentaries on American Law* was published a few months later.
[13] In a letter dated December 16, 1868.
[14] *Cf.* below, 216, 300.

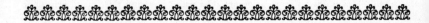

XI

READING AND CRITICISM

During all of this period, but especially during his retreat at Teplitz, James enlarged his acquaintance with literature and exercised himself in the art of literary criticism. There were moral, metaphysical, and recreative motives which limited James's taste, and predisposed him against anything which stressed technique at the expense of subject matter, surface at the expense of depth, or evil at the expense of good. Literature must be true, important, and pleasing. At the same time that James was coming to a clearer consciousness of his literary bias he had a sudden access of fluency, and poured himself out in letters of incredible length. This was not merely the effect of isolation—it is evident that he enjoyed the excitement of having ideas and expressing them. His brother was their favorite recipient and often their object:—

Teplitz, Feb. 12, 1868

My dear Harry,—

. . . I was much pleased the other day by receiving . . . some old *Atlantic Monthlies,* in which I found parts II and III of your "Poor Richard." I found it good much beyond my expectations—story, characters and way of telling excellent, in fact. And hardly a trace of that too diffuse explanation of the successive psychological steps which I remember attacking you for when you read it to me.

The *Atlantics* came in a box which was sent me apparently from a party at the Grimms' house, for it contained three sheets of allegorical contributions in German manuscript signed by seven or eight of the Grimm crowd. The head-senders, however, were Mrs. Grimm, Miss Thies, and Fräulein Bornemann. The contents varied from a big and bully liver sausage to a bottle of champagne —passing through some pots of the most india-rubber-like calves-foot jelly, chocolate, meringues, cologne water, pin cushion, oranges, plaster statuary, etc., forming, with the allegory of the manuscript, a most German mixture. Luckily the allegory was in prose, or it would have been even more insipid. The sapidity of the sausage made amends—and there is in every phenomenon that takes place in the German female nature the most curious coexistence of sausage and what seems to us cold and moonshiny sentimentality. It must be felt, for it cannot be analytically exhibited to a foreigner. . . .

I have not read anything lately worth recording. The bathing weakens one's brain so as to almost prevent all study. I took up Balzac's *Modeste Mignon* the other day. I don't know whether you know it. It must be one of the very early ones, for the extraordinary research and effort in the style is perfectly *cocasse*. It is consoling to see a man overcome such difficulties. But the story was so monstrously diseased morally that I could not finish it, reading novels as I do for the sake of refreshment. Ever your

WMS.

Teplitz, March 4, 1868[1]

My dear Harry,—

. . . Teplitz is as *safe* a place as there is on the globe. Nothing moves at this season save the heavenly bodies, and as one hardly feels tempted to arise and pursue them around their orbits, one can keep very still. In other respects, it is a singularly blameless place, too. This house is excellently kept and I feel exactly like one of the family, and am on the most affectionate terms with the domestics, male and female, who, in sooth, are an excellent crowd. The male, *der alte* Franz, resembles General Washington, both in form and feature and in moral character. He walks at the rate of about half a mile an hour, but never sits down and so in the course of the day gets through a fabulous amount of the most heterogeneous work. When spoken to, he always seems to count twenty-five before answering, and when angry (if that ever occurs) I have no doubt he counts a full hundred. . . .

I have received the second *Galaxy* and *Atlantic* for February, with your story of old clothes.[2] Both stories show a certain neatness and airy grace of touch which is characteristic of your productions (I suppose you want to hear in an unvarnished manner what is exactly the impression they make on me). And both show a greater suppleness and freedom of movement in the composition; although the first was unsympathetic to me from being one of those male *vs.* female subjects you have so often treated, and besides there was something cold about it, a want of heartiness or unction. It seems to me that a story must have rare picturesque elements of some sort, or much action, to compensate for the absence of heartiness, and the elements of yours were those of everyday life. It can also escape by the exceeding "keen"ness of its analysis and thoroughness of its treatment, as in some of Balzac's (but even there the result is disagreeable, if valuable); but in yours the moral action was very lightly touched, and rather indicated than exhibited. I fancy this rather dainty and disdainful treatment of yours comes from a wholesome dread of being sloppy and gushing and overabounding in power of expression, like the most of your rivals in the *Atlantic* . . . and that is excellent, in fact it is the instinct of truth against humbug and twaddle, and when it governs the treatment of a rich material it produces first class works. But the material in your stories (except "Poor Richard") has been *thin.* . . . I don't suppose *your literarisches Selbstgefühl* suffers from what I have said; for I really think my taste is rather incompetent in these matters, and as beforesaid, only offer these remarks as the impressions of an individual for you to philosophize upon yourself. . . . I have no time for more—my veal-time is long foreby. Ever yours affectionately,

WM. JAMES

---

[1] A fragment of this letter is printed in *L.W.J.*, I, 136-7.
[2] "The Story of a Masterpiece," and "The Romance of Certain Old Clothes."

In March James returned to Dresden, where he took up his abode under the motherly care of Frau Spangenberg, and remained until the end of June, except for occasional visits to Teplitz, forty miles away. During these months of comparative rest, in which he hoped for beneficial effects from the Teplitz baths, he experienced a great awakening of interest in art, this time from the point of view of the critic and historian.

[Dresden], March 9 [1868]

Dear Harry,—

Here is the "Darwin" for Charles Norton,[3] which I spoke of in my letter of three days ago. I slung it yesterday and breathe at last free. Nothing new to tell you save that I have finished the *Odyssey,* and been once to see the collection of casts in the Museum here. It is useless to deny that the Greeks had a certain cleverness. Houp la la!—I have gone and bought Renan's *Questions contemporaines.* . . . Renan is—Renan, but abounds in felicitous sayings and suggestive *aperçus.* . . . The more I think of Darwin's ideas the more weighty do they appear to me, though of course my opinion is worth very little—still, I *believe* that that scoundrel Agassiz is unworthy either intellectually or morally for him to wipe his shoes on, and I find a certain pleasure in yielding to the feeling. . . . Adieu! Adieu! Yours,

WM. JAMES

Dresden, April 5, 1868

My dear Harry,—

. . . I have been a number of times in the gallery, you may imagine with what pleasure—like a bath from Heaven; for last summer when I was here I was only able to thrust my nose into it twice, and look for a few minutes at some half dozen pictures. I'd give a good deal to import you and hear how some of the things strike you. . . .

One thing is certain, that the German blood is almost without a sense or a want of the beautiful. . . . I think the real charm in nature which they *sought* to render will be found to be the *agreeable, i.e.,* that by which each separate sense is affected pleasantly, such as brightness, velvetiness; and not at all that higher and more intellectual harmony (consistent with far duller and inferior separate sensations) which leaps at once to one's eyes out of the beginnings of the Italian Schools. . . . With all this there is yet in the old Germans a repose which is analogous in some measure to that of the Greeks . . . inasmuch as both seem to have conceived their subjects as simply *being,* and degenerate schools need to have the being determined in some picturesque and expressive manner. But the general mode of looking at the universe was as wide as East from West between the Greeks and Germans; and I fancy their agreeing in this point may possibly arise from the fact that German *art* . . . may have expressed only a small holy corner of what the Germans call their *Weltanschauung,* while to the Greek it expressed everything.

[3] The review (unsigned) of Darwin's *Variation of Animals and Plants under Domestication* appeared in the *North Amer. Rev.,* 1868 (XVII).

The real brothers of the Greeks are the glorious Venetians: in both does the means of expression the artist is able to dispose of seem to cover all he wants to say,—the artist is adequate to his universe. Finiteness and serenity and perfection—though out of the finiteness in both cases there steals a grace, which pierces the moral hide of the observer, and lays hold of the "infinite" in some mysterious way. It is a touching thing in Titian and Paul Veronese, who paint scenes which are a perfect *charivari* of splendor and luxury, and manifold sensations as far removed from what we call simplicity as anything well can be, that they preserve a tone of sober innocence, of instinctive single-heartedness, as natural as the breathing of a child. . . .

Besides the gallery, I have been enjoying that imperturbable old heathen Homer, lately, and have read twenty books of the *Odyssey*. . . . The *Odyssey* strikes me as very different in spirit from the *Iliad,* though whether such difference necessarily implies a difference of time and production I am too ignorant to have any idea. My South American Indians keep rising before me now as I read the *Odyssey*. . . . But the health! the brightness and the freshness!—and yet "combined with a total absence" of almost all that we consider peculiarly valuable in ourselves.

The very persons who would most writhe and wail at their surroundings if transported back into early Greece, would, I think, be the neo-pagans and Hellas worshipers of today. The cool acceptance by the bloody old heathens of everything that happened around them, their indifference to evil in the abstract, their want of what we call sympathy, the essentially definite character of their joys, or at any rate of their sorrows (for their joy was perhaps coextensive with life itself), would all make their society perfectly hateful to these over-cultivated and vaguely sick complainers. But I don't blame them for being dazzled by the luminous harmony of the Greek productions. The Homeric Greeks "accepted the universe," their only notion of evil was its perishability. . . . To them existence was its own justification, and the imperturbable tone of delight and admiration with which Homer speaks of every fact, is not in the least abated when the fact becomes to *our* eyes perfectly atrocious in character. As long as Ulysses is in the hands of the Cyclop, he abhors him, but when he is once out of danger, the chronic feeling of admiration, or at least indifferent tolerance, gains the upper hand. To the Greeks a thing was evil only transiently and accidentally, and with respect to those particular unfortunates whose bad luck happened to bring them under it. Bystanders could remain careless and untouched—no afterbrooding, no disinterested hatred of it *in se,* and questioning of its right to darken the world, such as now prevail. . . .

I wrote you from Teplitz a long letter relative to your writings. Exactly what escaped me in the ardor of composition I cannot now remember, but I have the impression I assumed a rather law-giving tone. I hope it did not hurt you in any way, or mislead you as to the opinion I may have of you as a whole, for I feel as if you were one of the two or three sole intellectual and moral companions I have. If you could have known how I have ached at times to have you by and hear your opinion on different matters, or see how things would strike you, you would not think I thought lightly of the evolutions of your mind. . . . Yours,

W. J.

Dresden, April 13, 1868

My dear Harry,—

I am just in from the theatre and feel like dropping you a line to tell you I have got your last *Atlantic* story ("Extraordinary Case"), and read it with much satisfaction. It makes me think I may have partly misunderstood your aim heretofore, and that one of the objects you have had in view has been to give an impression like that we often get of people in life: Their orbits come out of space and lay themselves for a short time along of ours, and then off they whirl again into the unknown, leaving us with little more than an impression of their reality and a feeling of baffled curiosity as to the mystery of the beginning and end of their being, and of the intimate character of that segment of it which we have seen. Am I right in guessing that you had a conscious intention of this sort here? . . . You seem to acknowledge that you can't exhaust any character's feelings or thoughts by an articulate displaying of them. You shrink from the attempt to drag them all reeking and dripping and raw upon the stage, which most writers make and fail in. You expressly restrict yourself, accordingly, to showing a few external acts and speeches, and by the magic of your art making the reader *feel* back of these the existence of a body of being of which these are casual features. You wish to suggest a mysterious fulness which you do not lead the reader through. It seems to me this is a very legitimate method, and has a great effect when it succeeds. . . . Only it must succeed. The gushing system is better to fail in, since that admits of a warmth of feeling and generosity of intention that may reconcile the reader. . . . Your style grows easier, firmer and more concise as you go on writing. The tendency to return on an idea and over-refine it, becomes obsolete,—you hit it the first lick now. The face of the whole story is bright and sparkling, no dead places, and on the whole the scepticism and, as some people would say, impudence implied in your giving a story which is no story at all, is not only a rather *gentlemanly* thing, but has a deep justification in nature, for we know the beginning and end of nothing. Still, while granting your success here, I must say that I think the thorough and passionate conception of a story is the highest, as of course you think yourself.

I have been hearing Devrient play in *Hamlet*. . . . The endless fulness of the play never struck me so before,—it bursts and cracks at every seam. I may feel it the more for having been thinking of classical things lately,—I was in the cast collection again yesterday.

The question what is the difference between the classical conception of life and art, and that of which *Hamlet* is an example, besets me more and more, and I think by a long enough soaking in presence of examples of each, some light might dawn. And then the still bigger question is: What is the warrant for each? Is our present only a half-way stage to another classical era with a more complete conception of the universe than the Greek, or is the difference between classic and romantic not one of intellect but of race and *temperament*? I was only thinking yesterday of the difference between the modern flower-in-a-dunghill (*e.g.,* Victor Hugo *passim*) poetry, where often the dirtier the dung the more touching the poetry of the flower, and the Greek idea, which could not possibly have conceived such a thing, but would have either made the flower leaven the heap, or turned back on it altogether, harmony being the *sine qua non;* and here comes to add to my "realizing sense" of the chasm between them, this awful *Hamlet,* which groans and aches so with the mystery of things, with the ineffable, that the *attempt* to express it is abandoned, one form of words seeming as irrelevant as another; and crazy conceits and countersenses slip and "whirl" around the vastness of the subject, as if the tongue were mocking itself. . . . Yours,

W.J.

On April 1, 1868, James began at Dresden a diary in which for two months he recorded his reading and reflections, and in which for several years he formulated his crucial decisions and resolves. In the spring of 1868, he was, as is also revealed in his letters, reading widely and voluminously—Homer, Renan, Shakespeare, Darwin, Taine, Kant, Agassiz, Janet, Goethe, Lessing, "sensible as the northwest wind," and "the beloved" Schiller, whose "magnificent essay," "Über Anmut und Würde," interested him greatly as presenting that antithesis of the moral and the æsthetic which he had inherited from his father.

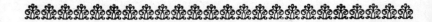

XII

TOWARDS PSYCHOLOGY AND PHILOSOPHY

James's thoughts now turned towards Heidelberg, where he hoped to resume his scientific studies. The correspondent to whom he most fully confided his scientific yearnings was, as ever, Henry Bowditch:—

Teplitz, May 5, 1868

My dear Henry,—

. . . In ten days I start for Dresden, where I shall stay at least one month, and perhaps longer, trying to husband the good effects of this bathing by rest and not work them right off as I have hitherto done. Then it is most probable that I shall go to Heidelberg. I have by this time dropped all hope of doing anything at physiology, for I'm not fit for laboratory work, and even if that were not the only reputable way of cultivating the science at all (which it is), it would be for *me* with my bad memory and slack interest in the details, the only practicable way of getting any honest knowledge of the subject. I go to Heidelberg because Helmholtz is there and a man named Wundt, from whom I think I may learn something of the physiology of the senses without too great bodily exertion, and may perhaps apply the knowledge to some use afterwards. The immortal Helmholtz is such an ingrained mathematician that I suppose I shall not profit much by him. How long I stay in Heidelberg will depend on what I find I can gain there, and on the state of my back. It's a delicious place to live in, people say, although the Swabian German is laughed at by those of the North. So if you are intending to come to Germany this summer and to devote yourself first to the language, which is the common plan, you would hardly choose it for a residence. For my part, I think this universal fastidiousness on the part of Americans about hearing good German the first three months is the most ludicrous phenomenon of the 19th Century. The common people you won't understand, no matter where you are, and your own dialect is so certain to be worse than the very worst you can possibly hear from educated people, that to be particular is as absurd as for a chimney sweep to refuse to sit down because there's dust on the bench. . . . Good-bye and good luck to you till we meet. Yours,

WM. JAMES

A paragraph from a letter written to Holmes from Dresden on May 15 reveals the characteristic educational impediments and vocational doubts, together with the growing interest in psychology:—

I had hoped until the end of my visit to Teplitz last winter that I might be able to get working at physiology, not that I have any special interest in its details, but that there is work there for somebody to do, and I have a (perhaps erroneous) suspicion that psychology is not à l'ordre du jour until some as yet unforeseen steps are made in the physiology of the nervous system; and if I were able by assiduous pottering to define a few physiological facts, however humble, I should feel I had not lived entirely in vain. But I now see that I can probably never do laboratory work, and so am obliged to fall back on something else. The prospective burden of a wife and family being taken off my shoulders simultaneously with the placing of this "mild yoke" upon the small of my back, relieves me from imminent *material* anxiety. I nevertheless feel the want of some particular outward responsibility to prevent my wasting time. I shall continue to study, or rather *begin* to, in a general psychological direction, hoping that soon I may get into a particular channel. Perhaps a practical application may present itself sometime—the only thing I can now think of is a professorship of "moral philosophy" in some western academy, but I have no idea how such things are attainable, nor if they are attainable at all to men of a non-spiritualistic mould.[1]

It was during these Teplitz and Dresden days of 1868 that James *discovered* Goethe, and found in him that "sturdy realism" by which he hoped to steer a middle course between pessimism and supernaturalism. On this theme he wrote as follows to his brother Henry:—

Dresden, June 4, 1868

My dear Harry,—

. . . I have been reading up Goethe a little lately—having finished today Vol. II of Eckermann's conversations with him. . . . I had read previously his and Schiller's correspondence, the perusal of which I strongly urge upon you. . . . The spectacle of two such earnestly living and working men is refreshing to the soul of anyone, but in their æsthetic discussions you will find a particular profit, I fancy. Goethe's ideas of the importance of the *subject-matter* in a work of poetry may perhaps cause you to reflect. I own that there was much in their talk about these matters to which from the want of any technical experience I could do no justice, and which will all be alive to you. . . . I have also read *Wilhelm Meister's Lehrjahre* lately, and wondered more than ever at the life and beauty of the first part. To the latter part I am perhaps not yet *gewachsen,* as they say here. It seems to me too allegorical and coldly invented. . . .

Altogether the old apparent contradiction which bothered me so in Goethe, the seeming want of humor—of that decisive glance in æsthetic and moral matters which separates the wheat from the chaff, the essential from the accidental, *intuitively*—has vanished, I can't say exactly how. He used to bother me by that incessant cataloguing of individual details, which you must have noticed in whatever you have read of his; by his pitiless manner of taking seriously *everything* that came along, as if the world for the time contained nothing else; by his noticing the binding of a copy of *Othello,* for instance, with the same gravity as the poem itself . . . and the somewhat Tennysonian character of the humor in *Hermann and Dorothy,* and in those parts of *Wahrheit und Dichtung* where he relates a joke, strengthened the impression. In spite of the humor

---

[1] The remainder of this letter will be found above, 93.

shown in *Egmont* and the abysses of "all is vanity" etc., opened in *Faust,* he *would* seem to me like a very serious man who, fearing to lose *any*thing of value, and not having an immediate intuition, saved up everything he got, and put the important and the accessory in one sheaf.

Now, as I say, this foolish impression of mine is dissipated, I know not exactly how. In the first place, his objectivity or literalness is to me now a merit in itself (although it may be at times tedious to me to read), and does not offend me as it did in my raw youth. At that time I remember I could not forgive him that he should describe the scenes of his childhood in Frankfurt in a dry light as they *were*. I thought he ought to have lain back and given the public those subjective feelings, sentimental, musical, visceral, whatever you please to call them, with which he recalled them from the old past in his late years. I smile now to think of my unhealthiness and weakness. And, in the second place, I have learned to distinguish between his general philosophic tendency, and his constitutional habit of *collecting*. . . . He could not bear to *waste* or dishonor any item, however small, of that which struck his senses; and as he was alive at every pore of his skin, and received *every* impression in a sort of undistracted leisure which makes the movements of his mental machinery one of the most extraordinary exhibitions which this planet ever can have witnessed, his less healthily endowed reader is often made impatient by his minute seriousness. But he *had* the intuitive glance beside, and the minutiæ he gives you are only *thrown in* extra. A little story of his called the "Novelle" contains him, it seems to me, in all his peculiarity and perfection. You'd better read it in the original, for it is short. Of his poems read all those in elegiac meter. I tell you of them because they happen to be the ones I have just read. They are worth your trouble, epigrams and all. As a wielder of language he was a magician—there is no other word for it. His verses grow fuller with every successive reading. Schiller's, on the contrary, seem most pregnant at first.

About Goethe's "philosophy" I will say nothing now,—it must be felt to be appreciated, and it can only be felt when it is seen applied in detail. . . . I feel pretty certain he did not exhaust human life, but he worked about as wide a stretch of it into an unity as most people have done, and I feel now like passively accepting all I can of positive in him before I begin to define his shortcomings.

Excuse this headlong scrawl. . . . Lots of love to all and plenty for yourself from yours,   W. J.

On the same day James was writing to his sister on the ever-alluring theme of Germanic traits.

Dresden, June 4, 1868

Beloved Sisterkin,—

I take my pen in hand to waft you my love across the jumping waves of the Atlantic, and to express a hope that you are better. . . . Ever since I have been here I have been the object of motherly attentions from all classes of the population, which I might have sought during a long life in the U. S. and never found away from my own hearth. They are a queer race in the abundance and homeliness of their kindness. . . . We at home value people for what they have of productive and positive about them,—and try at most to enjoy them by *abstract-*

ing our attention from their personal defects and unpleasantnesses. The Germans, "enthused" by the perception of some scrap of a good quality, proceed to stir the whole personality of its possessor up with it, making a kind of indistinguishable broth in which they take a sort of unnatural delight, half-ridiculous, half-offensive, to one of our more fastidious race. The gum-boil or the deficient teeth of a hero are thought of with the same romantic affection as his more strictly heroic "points.". This want of what we call "fastidiousness" which leads to refinement of various kinds, spreads all through the German character. . . .

(I was interrupted at this point by dinner, and am just back.) . . . To return to the previous subject, here is an example of the German confounding of everything in a broth of sentiment, though it may seem to you at first sight to belong to a different order of facts. When we got our strawberries I proceeded to eat them in the usual manner—when I was startled by a sudden cry from [Fräulein von] Bose: "Ach! schmecken die Erdbeeren so *wun*derschön!" I looked at her,—her eyes were closed, and she seemed to be in a sort of mystic rapture. She had been smashing her strawberries with her spoon so that they made a sort of pulp on her plate with the cream. I replied: "Ja, wunderschön"; but was rebuked by Mme. Spangenberg for leaving the berries whole on my plate, for when crushed, "Sie schmecken *so* viel schöner!" The *attendrissement* of the expression with which the words were pronounced was the *peculiarly* German part of the occurrence, and that I can't convey to you in writing. It implied a sort of religious melting of the whole emotional nature in this one small experience of the sense of taste. The washing out of all boundary lines is implied in the application of the word *wunderschön* to such an experience. It is employed continually to describe articles of diet and always with an intonation that denotes that the speaker is swimming in sentiment: "Der Kalbsbraten ist aber *wun*derschön! ! ! Ach! ! !" And up go the eyes to heaven. And in the same way when the Germans do what they call *Partie-machen* (that is go out on holidays in the country, and sit for hours over beer and coffee at little tables, in leafy places if possible) they remain speechless and apparently vacant-minded most of the time, but at intervals say with enthusiasm: "Ach! ist es doch hier *wun*derschön zu sitzen! ! !" . . . The sluices of a German's wonder and affection are ever trembling to be unlocked. The slightest touch sets the flood in motion and when it is once going, the creature abandons himself to the sentiment and cares very little about its original exciting cause.

They lack the sense of form throughout. Take, for instance, the word *Kunst* or Art. It has a magical effect on Germans which we are quite incapable of conceiving. They write poems about it, couple it with religion and virtue as one of the sacred things in human life,—lose, in short, their critical power when thinking of it, just as we do when thinking of morality, for instance. But (except, perhaps, in music) they produce no works of art good for anything, nor do I believe that as a rule those who are most struck by the divinity of *Kunst* in the abstract, have the power of discriminative appreciation thereof in the concrete. The tender emotion carries their sagacity and judgment off its legs. They believe that the mission of art is to represent or create in anticipation a regenerate world, and over every so-called work of art, however contemptible, they are apt to cast the halo which belongs to the generic idea, and to accept it without criticizing. . . . How much more pleasing to *this* heart is a good insolent American girl (like yourself), who by her unconcealed repugnance of everything unhealthy about you, and ill-feigned contempt of your person generally, goads you and spurs you to desperate exertions of manliness to keep your head above water at all and in the air of her mere courtesy. . . . Ever your affectionate brother

                                                                W. J.

On June 23 James wrote to his sister: "In three days I start for Heidelberg. . . . I am sanguine after this long lapse to rise in the scale of being . . . as soon as I come in contact with the stern realities of life." But his hopes were again disappointed, and after several weeks of travel he tried another cure, this time at Divonne, in the French Savoy. On May 14 he had written to his sister, "I somehow feel as if I were cheating Harry of his birthright." To this self-reproachful theme he now returns:—

                                                Divonne, Aug. 26, 1868

My dear Harry,—
     You must have been envying me within the last few weeks, hearing that I was revisiting the sacred scenes of our youth, the shores of Léman, the Hôtel de l'Écu de Genève, the Rue de la Corraterie, etc. The only pang I have felt has been caused by your absence, or rather by my presence instead of yours, for I think that your abstemious and poetic soul would have got infinitely more good out of the things I have seen than my hardening and definite growing nature. . . .
     The impression received on gradually coming from a German into a French atmosphere of things was unexpected and in many respects unpleasant. I have been in Germany half amused and half impatient with the slowness of execution, and the uncouthness of taste and expression that prevails there so largely in all things—but on exchanging it for the brightness and shipshapeness of these quasi-French arrangements of life, and for the somewhat tart, firecracker-like speech of the French nation, I found myself inclined to go backwards and for a few days had quite a homesickness for the easy, ugly, substantial ways I had left. . . . I am struck more than I ever was with the hopelessness of us English, and with stronger reason the Germans, ever trying to compete with the French in matters of form or finite taste of any sort. They are sensitive to things which do not exist for us. I notice it here in manners and speech—how can a people who speak with no tonic accents in their words help being cleaner and neater in expressing themselves? On the other hand the limitations of *reach* in the French mind strike me more and more,—their delight in rallying round an official standard in all matters, in counting and dating everything from certain great names, their love of repeating catchwords and current phrases and sacrificing their independence of mind for the mere sake of meeting their hearer or reader on common ground, their metaphysical incapacity not only to deal with questions but to know what the questions are, stand out plainer and plainer the more I read in German. One wonders where the *Versöhnung* or conciliation of all these rival national qualities is going to take place. I imagine

we English stand between the French and the Germans both in taste and . . . spiritual intuition. . . .

The things which have given me the most pleasure have been some traveling sketches by Théophile Gautier. What an absolute thing genius is! That this creature with no more soul than a healthy poodle-dog, no morality, no knowledge (for I doubt exceedingly if his knowledge of architectural terms, etc., is accurate) should give one a more perfect enjoyment than his betters in all these respects, by mere force of good nature, clear eyesight and fit use of language! His style seems to me *perfect* and I should think it would pay you to study it over and over again. . . . Ever yours

W.J.

A few weeks later, in a letter to his father, James records his reading of Kant, and the beginning of his acquaintance with the philosophy of Charles Renouvier, an event whose full significance he could not then appreciate.[2] In a letter to Tom Ward there is the usual confession and moralizing:—

Divonne, Oct. 9 [1868]

My dear old Thomas,—

. . . All I have done in the last six months is to keep up the dribbling I recommend to you, and, little as each day seems, the sum total is not disrespectable. I have not got started properly on any line of work yet, but am hovering and dipping about the portals of psychology. I can't say that I have learned anything yet, or that a single guiding point of view has dawned upon me, but I have a sort of consciousness that this winter the clouds will precipitate and I shall find myself *barboter*-ing about in some little puddle which may grow bigger. I sometimes feel pretty discouraged at the inanity of my activity. The fact is that I am about as little fitted by nature to be a worker in science of any sort as anyone can be, and yet in virtue of that great law of the universe . . . *miscent quadrata rotundis,* etc., my only ideal of life is a scientific life. I should feel as if all value had departed from my life if convinced of *absolute* scientific impotence, whereas in reality a man who should do nothing but keep his grandmother alive would be doing a grand thing, as I read in a book *Rudin* of Turgenev the other day. . . . Ah! Tom, Tom, you well-constructed whelps who travel on their free-will and moral responsibility are more to be envied than anyone in the world. What a solidity the web of their life has—no step they make is trivial. On purely materialistic principles they are the greatest success of any of us, the most susceptible of happiness. To get at something absolute without going out of your own skin! To measure yourself by what you strive for and not by what you reach! They are a superb form of animal, and beat the cows of whom you speak . . . beat 'em hollow, on their own track of finite absoluteness.

I am poisoned with Utilitarian venom, and sometimes when I despair of ever doing anything, say: "Why not step out into the green darkness?" But then I think that, loathsome and grotesque as most of the results of my living may be, and innocent and desirable as the fermentation and crumbling and evaporation

[2] October 5, 1868; *L.W.J.,* I, 138; for Renouvier, *cf.* below, 121, 123, 135, 144, 148, 152-3, 352.

and diffusion which will succeed them seem in comparison, yet interwoven with the former are some tatters and shreds of beauty that may as well last, as long as they have been formed. . . . There will remain and live . . . some shreds of manhood (thoughts, smiles), and, shreds though they be, they are worth more to the world than the fermentations and chemical reactions that might replace them. They are not worth more for the consciousness of your individual self, perhaps,—more of pain than of pleasure will follow in their train—but taken as existence theirs is a nobler category than the other. . . . All in all, even the sweepings of morality are better than chemical reactions.— Thus do I lash my tail and start myself up again. . . . *Adieu chéri, ton*

WM. JAMES

Returning to Cambridge in November, 1868, James was able to pursue his medical studies with sufficient continuity to present himself for the degree in the following spring. At the same time that he resumed his studies he resumed his conversations with his friends; especially with Wendell Holmes, and with Charles Peirce, whose unintelligibilities fascinated him, and whose professional career now became a responsibility which he was destined to carry on his conscience for forty years.

Bowditch being at a distance, James continued to correspond with him, and to follow his physiological studies with keen and envious interest. The following letter is characteristic of the period, irrepressible intellectual interests contending against discouragement and yearning for repose. A thesis being required for the diploma in medicine, he had selected the topic of "cold."

Cambridge, Jan. 24-25, 1869 [3]

My dear Henry,—

. . . I have just been quit by Charles S. Peirce, with whom I have been talking about a couple of articles in the St. Louis *Journal of Speculative Philosophy* by him which I have just read. They are exceedingly bold, subtle and incomprehensible and I can't say that his vocal elucidations helped me a great deal to' their understanding, but they nevertheless interest me strangely.[4] The poor cuss sees no chance of getting a professorship anywhere, and is likely to go into the Observatory for good. It seems a great pity that as original a man as he is, who is willing and able to devote the powers of his life to logic and metaphysics, should be starved out of a career, when there are lots of professorships of the sort to be given in the country, to "safe," orthodox men. He has had good reason, I know, to feel a little discouraged about the prospect, but I think he ought to hang on, as a German would do, till he grows gray. . . .

I continue to "bide my time" here. I have a shrewd suspicion (which I will not put in the form of a categoric declaration, lest the blasted thing should hear

---

[3] Parts of this letter are reprinted from *L.W.J.*, I, 149-50.

[4] Peirce published three articles in this *Journal* in 1868, as follows: "Grounds of Validity of the Laws of Logic," "Questions Concerning Certain Faculties Claimed for Man," "Some Consequences of Four Incapacities." He was at this time employed as assistant at the Harvard Observatory.

it and go back on me as it has done before) that I have begun to get better.
. . . Wendell Holmes comes out and we jaw once a week. . . . My brother
Harry goes abroad in the spring, and will, I hope, strike Paris before you leave.
. . . I hope this letter is *décousue* enough for you. What is a man to write when
a reef is being taken in his existence, and absense from thought and life is all
he aspires to. Better times will come, though, and with them better letters. Good-
bye, ever yours,

WM. JAMES

To Henry Bowditch James continued to write of his medical studies and
prospects:—

Cambridge, May 22, 1869

My dear Henry,—

I am mortified at the long silence I have kept towards you. I have thought of
you often enough with *Sehnsucht,* but I have lacked that cheerful and definite
news to give you without which writing does not seem a natural act. . . . It is
totally impossible for me to study now in any way, and I have at last succeeded
in *genuinely* giving up the attempt to. With all this, I never was so cheerful,—
I've done what I can, and it's a mean thing for a man to fret about what is accidentally and externally imposed upon him. I took in my thesis and tickets to
Hodges[5] yesterday. The examination takes place on June 21st, and I suppose my
star will guide me through it, though I'm ashamed of the fewness of the medical
facts I know. I wrote a thesis on cold, nary experiment and nary chance of
consulting any books on the subject but those I had, and a few I could send for
by name to the library,—so it's of no value. . . .

Charles S. Peirce has been writing some very acute and original psychologico-
metaphysical articles in the St. Louis philosophic *Journal,* though they are so
crabbedly expressed that one can hardly get their exact sense. He is an original
fellow, but with a capacity for arbitrariness that makes one mistrust him. C. W.
Eliot was confirmed President yesterday. His great personal defects, tactlessness,
meddlesomeness, and disposition to cherish petty grudges seem pretty universally
acknowledged; but his ideas seem good and his economic powers first-rate,—
so in the absence of any other possible candidate, he went in. It seems queer that
such a place should go begging for candidates. . . .

My brother Harry is now in England, enjoying the sights thereof mightily.
I hope you may soon meet. . . . Wendell Holmes pays me a weekly visit. John
Ropes[6] told me the other night he had never known of anyone in the law who
studied anything like as hard as Wendell. (This must lead to Chief Justice,
U. S. Supreme Court.) Wendell amuses me by being composed of at least two
and a half different people rolled into one, and the way he keeps them together
in one tight skin, without quarreling any more than they do, is remarkable. I
like him and esteem him exceedingly. . . .

My dear old boy, write soon to a cove and give him your budget of the winter's progress. You don't know how much I want to hear from you. Ever your
friend,

WM. JAMES

[5] Richard Manning Hodges was at this time adjunct professor of surgery at the Medical School.
[6] John Codman Ropes (Harvard LL.B., 1861) was a fellow student of Holmes at the Law School.

The younger Henry James being now in Europe, the position of the brothers was reversed, Henry writing the chronicles of adventure, and William voicing the eager interest and solicitude of the family circle in Cambridge.

Cambridge, June 12, 1869

My dear Harry,—

> O call my brother back to me,
> I cannot play alone.
> The summer comes with flower and bee—
> Where is my brother gone?

Your second letter from Geneva . . . having just arrived has intensified the above familiar sentiment to the point of making me incontinently sit down and write ye a line. . . . Next Friday my clinical examination at the dispensary (which I tried to get exempted from, but failed) takes place and the following Monday the big examination. The thought becomes more grisly every day, and I wish the thing were over. My thesis was decent, and I suppose Dr. Holmes will veto my being plucked no matter how bad my examination may be, but the truth is I feel unprepared. I've no doubt I'll *éprouver* a distinct bodily improvement when it's all over. My feeling of unpreparedness has, so far from exciting me to study, given me a disgust for the subject. . . . I made a discovery in sending my credentials to the Dean which gratified me. It was that adding in conscientiously every week in which I have had anything to do with medicine, I can't sum up more than three years and two or three months. Three years is the minimum with which one can go up for examination; but as I began away back in '63 I have been considering myself as having studied about five years, and have felt much humiliated by the greater readiness of so many younger men to answer questions and understand cases. My physical status is *quo;* but, as I say, I suppose the summer will make some difference. Meanwhile I am perfectly contented that the power which gave me these faculties should recall them partially or totally when and in what order it sees fit. I don't think I should "give a single damn" now if I were struck blind. . . .

You say you mean to write me about what I wrote to you of Germany. I wrote another letter on the same subject a few days ago. . . . I hope the legislative tone of my advice doesn't offend you—it is for the sake of concision. . . . Ever yours affectionately,

WM. JAMES

The passing of his medical examination "with no difficulty" on June 21, 1869, brought James relief in two senses: it was the removal of a burden, and at the same time a prop to his self-confidence. He had long since abandoned any intention of practising medicine. After his success he went with his family to Pomfret for his summer's rest, and while there he summed up this "epoch" as follows:

> So there is one epoch of my life closed, and a pretty important one, I feel it, both in its scientific "yield" and in its general educational value as enabling me

to see a little the inside workings of an important profession and to learn from it, as an average example, how all the work of human society is performed. I feel a good deal of intellectual hunger nowadays, and if my health would allow, I think there is little doubt that I should make a creditable use of my freedom, in pretty hard study. I hope, even as it is, not to have to remain absolutely idle —and shall try to make whatever reading I can do bear on psychological subjects.[7]

During the summer of 1869 James had received frequent letters from his brother Henry, who was making a tour of Switzerland, and was experiencing a surge of bodily vigor. In September he exchanged the physical mountain tops of Switzerland for the emotional and spiritual altitudes of Italy, and worked off his *"éblouissement"* in a series of long and glowing letters, full both of spontaneous joy and of critical appraisal.

Cambridge, Oct. 2, 1869

Dearest Harry,—

Within ten days we have received two letters from you—one from Como, t'other from Brescia, and most luscious epistles were they indeed. It does one's heart good to think of you at last able to drink in full gulps the beautiful and the antique. As Mother said the other day, it seems as if your whole life had but been a preparation for this. Since I wrote you from Pomfret a couple of months since, so many things have happened and I have had so much to say to you of matters personal, moral, spiritual and practical that I hardly know how to begin this letter. Some things will get crowded out anyhow.

First, of my health. It kept wonderful for about six weeks at Pomfret and I began to think that all was saved, but it suddenly caved in a week before I left. . . . The result is that I find myself unable to predict my state as of yore; and I feel on the whole encouraged by it—for it shows that the condition, whatever it be, is mobile and not essential. . . . I am very much run down in nervous force and have resolved to read as little as I possibly can this winter, and absolutely not study, *i.e.,* read nothing which I can get interested and *thinking* about. There is plenty of biographical, historical and literary matter which I have always hoped to read some day, so this is just the time for it. I cal'late likewise to pay a visit every evening when it is possible, and not to stick in the house as hitherto. I cannot tell you, my dear brother, how my admiration of the silent pluck you have exhibited during those long years has risen of late. I never realized till within three or four months the full amount of endurance it must have needed to go through all that literary work, and especially all that unshirking social activity, which you accomplished. I give up like a baby in comparison, though occasionally I find my heart fired and my determination *retrempé'*d by a sudden wave of recollection of your behavior. . . .

Thomas Sergeant Perry is back very well after his vacation. . . . His true modesty, and unreserved kind feeling to everyone, together with his humor and enthusiasm, ought not to let him be lightly estimated. The more I live in the world the more the cold-blooded, conscious egotism and conceit of people afflict me and T. S. P. is sweetly free of them. All the noble qualities of Wendell

[7] W.J. to Henry Bowditch, August 12, 1869; *L.W.J.,* I, 154.

Holmes, for instance, are poisoned by them, and friendly as I want to be towards him, as yet the good he has done me is more in presenting me something to kick away from or react against than to follow and embrace. I have seen him but sparingly since the spring, but expect he will be here tonight. . . .

I am forgetting your "Gabrielle de Bergerac." Very exquisitely touched, but the *dénouement* bad in that it did not end with Coquelin's death in that stormy meeting and her being sent to a nunnery. At least Coquelin ought to have had a *lettre de cachet* and she, resisting still the Viscount, have ended in a nunnery. The end is both humdrum and improbable. I expect to write you more stiddy now. Get your belly full of enjoyment this winter. . . . Ever your loving
                                                                                          W. J.

Early in October, during a visit to Florence, Henry was prostrated by an illness of several weeks, and wrote of his symptoms at great length; evoking medical advice from the new M.D., as well as the following philosophical outburst of fraternal solicitude:—

It makes me sick to think of your life being blighted by this hideous affliction. I will say nothing to the family about it, as they can do you no good, and it will only give them pain, but don't you hesitate hereafter to let me know minutely all about yourself. I hope to God you will soon find a way to make it go better. For what purpose we are thus tormented I know not,—I don't see that Father's philosophy explains it any more than anyone else's. But as Pascal says, *"malgré les misères qui nous tiennent par la gorge,"* there's a divine instinct in us, and at the end of life the good remains and the evil sinks into darkness. If there is to be evil in the world at all, I don't see why you or I should not be its victims as well as anyone else,—the trouble is that there should be any.[8]

Recovering from his illness, Henry moved on to Rome, where he "went reeling and moaning thro' the streets, in a fever of enjoyment," and whence he sent remarkable records of his experiences (objective and subjective) to the family in Cambridge.[9]

                                                                    Cambridge, Dec. 5, 1869

Dear Harry,—
     . . . Your letters from Italy are beyond praise. It is a great pity they should be born to blush unseen by the general public and that just the matter that they contain, in a little less rambling style, should not appear in the columns of the *Nation.* They are read partially to appreciative visitors, and seem to cause "unfeigned delight." Father took some to Emerson at Concord the other day. He pleaded hard to keep them for study, but Father refused. Meeting Edward [Emerson] in the Athenæum the next day, the latter said his father was doing nothing but talk of your letters. That sample ought to be enough for you.
     As for my more humble self, your admirable discriminating remarks on art matters go to the right spot. I can well sympathize with what must be the tur-

moil of your feeling before all this wealth,—that strange impulse to exorcise it by extracting the soul of it and throwing it off *in words;* which translation is in the nature of things impossible, but each attempt to storm its inaccessible heights produces, with the pang of failure, a keener sense of the reality of the ineffable subject, and a more welcome submission to its yoke. I had a touch of the fever at little Dresden, and I can't help hoping that with your larger opportunities there will be a distinct intellectual precipitate from your experience which may be communicable to others. . . . It does not do to trust to the matter remaining in the mind. Nothing can take the place of notes struck off with the animal heat of the fever upon them, and I hope you are making some for your own use all this time.

What you say of the antique and of architecture touches a kindred chord in me. It seems as if the difference of classical and romantic had some metaphysic parallel, and was but a symbol. Soak yourself in the symbol and perhaps the meaning will suddenly dawn upon you. You can't tell how *satisfied* I feel at your being able at last to see these things, or how I pray that you may finally attain the power to lead a working life and let your faculties bear their legitimate fruit. . . .

I have been reading Max Müller's *Chips (from a German Workshop)* lately with much pleasure, likewise a little of Leopardi, the Italian of which is by no means insurmountable, and the matter and manner of which strangely attract me. The extracts from a Persian poet which C. E. Norton sent to the last *North American Review* are mighty things.[10] Borrow the book from him if you have a chance. . . . Time passes with me like a whirlwind . . . and I am beginning to go regularly into the evening visit business. . . . Write good news of yourself to your

W.

On December 21 and 23 Henry had written to his mother an account of the Bay of Naples, of Pompeii and Paestum, and of his arrival in Rome. "Now that I am leaving Italy," he said, "I feel with redoubled force its enchanting eloquence, and fumble over the rich contents of these last four months as fondly as a coin-collector a bag of medals." William's reply on January 19 contained the following passage:

I enjoyed last week the great pleasure of reading *The House of the Seven Gables.* I little expected so *great* a work. It's like a great symphony, with no touch alterable without injury to the harmony. It made a deep impression on me and I thank Heaven that Hawthorne was an American. It also tickled my national feeling not a little to note the resemblance of Hawthorne's style to yours and Howells's, even as I had earlier noted the converse. That you and Howells with all the models in English literature to follow, should needs involuntarily have imitated (as it were) this American, seems to point to the existence of some real American mental quality. But I must spare my eyes and stop. Ever your devoted

WMS.

[10] Norton's citations from Fitzgerald's translation of Omar Khayyám, October, 1869.

To this literary comment Henry replied at the end of a letter written on February 13, ten days after his happy return to England:

> I'm glad you've been liking Hawthorne. But I mean to write as good a novel one of these days (perhaps) as *The House of the Seven Gables*.
>
> Monday, 14th. With the above thrilling prophecy I last night laid down my pen. I see nothing left but to close my letter. When I began I had a vague intention of treating you to a grand summing up on the subject of Italy. But it won't be summed up, happily for you. . . . Farewell. Love to all. Yours most fraternally,
>
> H. JAMES JR.

XIII

DEPRESSION AND RECOVERY

During the autumn and winter of 1869 James's spirits had steadily declined. He wrote to Bowditch of his personal problems and difficulties, as well as of local medical gossip, of that regretted physiology which the latter was so successfully pursuing in his stead, and of the Franco-Prussian War, which touched him deeply. The following letter to Bowditch is characteristic.

Cambridge, Dec. 29, 1869

Dear Harry,—

I am a low-lived wretch, I know, for keeping you all this time unwritten-to. I have been a prey to such disgust for life during the past three months as to make letter writing almost an impossibility. . . . I heard part of a letter from you to Jeffries Wyman read the other night by him, and was glad to know that you were well, and in the midst of such physiological luxury as you represent Ludwig's laboratory to be. To tell you about matters at home: My own condition, I am sorry to say, goes on pretty steadily deteriorating in all respects, in spite of a fitful flash up for six weeks this summer. I have, however, begun to poke about in town and to pay visits in spite of it, which is a great refreshment. But I literally have given up all pretense to study or even to serious reading of any kind, and I look on physiology and medicine generally as dim voices from a bygone time. . . .

Wendell Holmes is hard at work,—I fear too hard, having undertaken a two years' job to edit Kent's *Commentaries;* and being ambitious of excellence he says the time is too short for the amount of work he is resolved to put into it, and it weighs heavy on his soul. . . . I shall trust to you to tell me of any bibliographic news of consequence either in the physio- or the psycho-logic lines. . . . Of Professor Eliot's new courses of lectures,[1] the philosophic course seems to have made a successful beginning, and I hope it may be kept up and improve. The literary one seems to be a sort of mongrel and useless affair. I heard Charles Peirce lecture yesterday, one of his nine on "British Logicians." It was delivered without notes, and was admirable in matter, manner and clearness of statement. He has recently been made assistant astronomer with $2500 a year. But I wish he could get a professorship of philosophy somewhere. That is his forte, and therein he is certainly *très fort.* I never saw a man go into things so intensely and thoroughly.

Now, I confidently expect that you will sit down and write me a long letter

[1] The so-called "University Lectures" designed for "graduates, teachers, and other competent persons."

immediately on receiving this. I will promise to treat you better in future. If you don't, 'twere better you had ne'er been born, for I'll cause you to die by tortures so lingering and horrible that the mind of man has not yet conceived of the like of them,—when you return. What would not I give to spend another ten days with you in Leipzig like unto that blissful spell of time we had together in Paris! I shall never forget the pleasure of those days, nor all you did for me. . . . Ever your affectionate friend,

WM. JAMES

His brother Henry having suddenly returned to Cambridge at the end of April 1870, most of James's former correspondents were for the next few years his neighbors or members of his household. The letters, therefore, provide a very inadequate record of this momentous period. Momentous it was because it marked the low point of James's depression and the beginnings of a permanent improvement. Three forward steps are clearly defined, despite many lesser oscillations: the spiritual crisis of 1870; the commencement of his teaching in 1872; his marriage in 1878.

By James's spiritual crisis I do not refer specifically to the acute attack of melancholia described in the autobiographical passage of *The Varieties of Religious Experience*.[2] The date of this experience cannot be precisely fixed, and it might have occurred at any time between his return from Europe and the definitive improvement of his health in 1872. It was symptomatic of his desperate neurasthenic condition during these years, and contributed to his understanding of religious mysticism and morbid mentality. But it was a pathological seizure rather than a spiritual crisis.

The more fundamental spiritual crisis was the ebbing of the will to live, for lack of a philosophy to live by—a paralysis of action occasioned by a sense of moral impotence. On February 1, 1870, James recorded in his diary a resolve to acknowledge the supremacy of morality:

> Today I about touched bottom, and perceive plainly that I must face the choice with open eyes: shall I *frankly* throw the moral business overboard, as one unsuited to my innate aptitudes, or shall I follow it, and it alone, making everything else merely stuff for it? I will give the latter alternative a fair trial. Who knows but the moral interest may become developed. . . . Hitherto I have tried to fire myself with the moral interest, as an aid in the accomplishing of certain utilitarian ends.

But the personal problem was not yet solved, for the devotee of morals may be driven to despair by the existence of evil:

> Can one with full knowledge and sincerely ever bring one's self so to sympathize with the total process of the universe as heartily to assent to the evil that

[2] *Cf.* below, 363.

seems inherent in its details? Is the mind so purely fluid and plastic? If so, optimism is possible. Are, on the other hand, the private interests and sympathies of the individual so essential to his existence that they can never be swallowed up in his feeling for the total process,—and does he nevertheless imperiously crave a reconciliation or unity of some sort. Pessimism must be his portion. But if, as in Homer, a divided universe be a conception possible for his intellect to rest in, and at the same time he have vigor of will enough to look the universal death in the face without blinking, he can lead the life of moralism. A militant existence, in which the ego is posited as a monad, with the *good* as its end, and the final consolation only that of irreconcilable hatred—though evil slay me, she can't subdue me, or make me worship her. The brute force is all at her command, but the final protest of my soul as she squeezes me out of existence gives me still in a certain sense the superiority.[3]

In other words, if one adopts the alternative of "moralism," whether this assumes the form of a hope to conquer evil or a resolve to die bravely—in either case one needs that "vigor of will" which springs from the belief in its freedom. It was this which James derived from Charles Renouvier, as recorded in his diary on April 30, 1870:

> I think that yesterday was a crisis in my life. I finished the first part of Renouvier's second *Essais* and see no reason why his definition of free will—"the sustaining of a thought *because I choose to* when I might have other thoughts" —need be the definition of an illusion. At any rate, I will assume for the present —until next year—that it is no illusion. My first act of free will shall be to believe in free will.[4]

Thus James felt his old doubts to be dispelled by a new and revolutionary insight. It is important to note two things: first, the fact that he experienced a personal crisis that could be relieved only by a *philosophical* insight; and, second, the specific quality of the philosophy which his soul-sickness required.

That he should have experienced such a crisis at all furnishes the best possible proof of James's philosophical cast of mind. He had for many years brooded upon the nature of the universe and the destiny of man. Although the problem stimulated his curiosity and fascinated his intellect, it was at the same time a vital problem. He was looking for a solution that should be not merely tenable as judged by scientific standards, but at the same time propitious enough to live by. Philosophy was never, for James, a detached and dispassionate inquiry into truth; still less was it a form of amusement. It was a quest, the outcome of which was hopefully and fearfully apprehended by a soul on trial and awaiting its sentence. It is true that the gravity of his philosophical task varied with his moods, and with the condition of his health. In his more

[3] From loose sheets cut from a notebook, apparently of the same date as the Diary.
[4] *L.W.J.*, I, 147.

exuberant moments he relished the play of his speculative and critical faculties, and during long periods of vigorous productivity he became, like any other investigator, interested in special problems for themselves; but behind all this, reasserting itself with every new deepening of reflection, and determining the whole tone and direction of his philosophical career, was his identification of philosophy with personal conviction. His philosophy was never a mere theory, but always a set of beliefs which reconciled him to life and which he proclaimed as one preaching a way of salvation.

It is worthy of remark, then, that James required a philosophy to save him. Not less significant is the particular quality of the philosophy which was needed by his particular soul. To his temperament the counsel of resignation could never be more than a temporary anæsthetic, and he was too profoundly human to find consolaton in heaven. He was too sensitive to ignore evil, too moral to tolerate it, and too ardent to accept it as inevitable. Optimism was as impossible for him as pessimism. No philosophy could possibly suit him that did not candidly recognize the dubious fortunes of mankind, and encourage him as a moral individual to buckle on his armor and go forth to battle. In other words, to cure him from his weakness he needed the strong man's medicine. He *was* a strong man, overtaken by weakness—a man of action cut off from action by bodily incapacity, a man to whom no teaching of acquiescence or evasion could be either palatable or nutritive.

What is the strong man's medicine, diluted to suit his disabled condition? *The gospel of belief.* For belief is action, and yet a sort that may be demanded even of a sick man; and belief may have action as its object. To believe *by* an act of will *in* the efficacy of will—that is a gospel which fits the temper of action, and which may be used to bring the invalid warrior back to fighting trim.

The crisis of April 1870 was a turning point but not a cure. For several years to come the road was hard, with only a very gradual upward incline. In spite of all professions to the contrary James's mind was incessantly active. On December 17, 1870, he wrote to Tom Ward:

> I was sorry not to see you again before your return. Talking with you has clinched my resolve to look into mathematics—not now, but if I ever get able to study. Meanwhile I like to scheme,—so write me a programme of mathematical study, what books I had better go through and in what order, beginning with analytic geometry and logarithms.

This is characteristic both of James's indefatigable industry and of his sincere conviction that he was doing nothing. During these years of felt frustration he read widely and voluminously, as he had always done. And he read to good purpose, having a quite extraordinary capacity for detecting quickly what in a book or article he could appropriate. Nor did he carry out his resolution to avoid study. He maintained his lively interest in physiology, and continued to look longingly, sometimes hopefully, in that direction. As he read he thought, and as he thought he wrote—many pages of analysis and argument, returning again and again to the problems that baffled him.

During the year 1871 James gradually resumed his scientific studies and he eagerly welcomed Bowditch's inauguration of experimental physiology at the Medical School in the autumn of that year. The winter of 1872-1873 was notable for two events—the opening of James's correspondence with Renouvier, and the beginning of his career as a teacher. To his relations with Renouvier we shall return later. His commitment to the teaching career began in April 1872, when he received and accepted an informal offer from Harvard. In August he was appointed instructor in physiology, to give in the following year, in collaboration with the anatomist, Dr. Timothy Dwight, an elective course open to undergraduates of Harvard College on "Comparative Anatomy and Physiology." Thus, at last, after long delays and many uncertainties, when he had reached the age of thirty, James entered upon the professional career to which he thereafter devoted himself for thirty-five years. That he was to be a teacher and scholar was now settled, but what he should teach and investigate was still subject to change. Physiology, psychology, and philosophy all attracted him, and he ended by teaching them all; physiology coming first, not because his interest was greatest, but because the first opportunity came to him in that field. Philosophy and psychology were to have their day, and it was not far distant. Furthermore, the three subjects all interpenetrated. Comparative anatomy and physiology led through the conception of evolution to philosophy of nature, and human physiology led to psychology; while psychology, as James knew it, looked for its causal explanation to physiology and for its deeper implications to theory of knowledge and metaphysics.

James was a good teacher because of the manner of man that he was, and not because of any method which he consciously adopted. In the classroom he was precisely what he was everywhere else—just as unorganized, just as stimulating and irresistibly charming. It has sometimes been supposed that James as a professor was a caged bird, eager to rise into the empyrean, but imprisoned by the pedantry and routine of academic duties. But he regarded it as of the first importance that a man should have a fixed schedule of work and responsibility: he recommended this medicine to others, and believed in its efficacy for himself. He was, furthermore, a man who craved a hearing for the truth that he believed was in him. Teaching provided the (to him) indispensable social aspect of his scholarly vocation. He enjoyed, loved, stimulated, and sometimes berated his students. All of this helped to consume his energy, and June usually found him fagged and eager to escape. Towards the end of his career, when he was contending against the illness that ultimately proved fatal, he rejoiced in his permanent release from the yoke. But on the whole it was with his teaching as it was with everything else—he soon grew weary of whatever he was doing, and with equal promptness missed it when he gave it up.

Even the *prospect* of teaching had an immediately beneficial effect on James's health. In May 1872, his brother Henry had again gone abroad and the brotherly interchange of letters was resumed:—

Scarboro, Aug. 24, 1872

Beloved Henry,—

I got your letter from Grindelwald and Meyringen some ten days ago, just as I was starting for the second time for Mt. Desert. . . . I drove down here yesterday evening from Portland where I . . . could not resist the temptation of stopping and getting three sea baths. I shall return on Monday. The beach shines as of yore—it is really superb—and the wood is delightful even after Mt. Desert. . . . I write in the little parlor opposite the office. . . . The steady, heavy roaring of the surf comes through the open window, borne by the delicious salt breeze over the great bank of stooping willows, field and fence. The little horse-chestnut trees are no bigger, the cow with the board face still crops the grass. The broad sky and sea are whanging with the mellow light. All is as it was and will be. . . .

I do envy you very much what you are going to see in Italy, and a good deal what you are and have been seeing in Switzerland. Though nature as to its *essence* is the same anywhere, and many nervous puckers which were in my mind when I left Cambridge in July have been smoothed out gently and fairly by the sweet influences of many a lie on a hill-top at Mt. Desert with sky and sea and islands before me, by many a row, and a couple of sails, and by my bath and siesta on the blazing sand this morn. But I envy ye the world of art. Away from it, as we live, we sink into a flatter, blanker kind of consciousness, and indulge in an ostrich-like forgetfulness of all our richest potentialities; and they startle us now and then when by accident some rich human product, pictorial, literary, or architectural slaps us with its tail. I feel more and more as if I ought to try to learn to sketch in water-colors, but am too lazy to begin. . . .

Your letters to the *Nation*,[5] of which I have as yet seen three, have been very exquisite, and both I and others . . . have got great refreshment from them. But as one gets more appreciative one's self for fineness of perception and fineness of literary touch either in poetry or prose, one also finds how few there are to sympathize with one. I suppose, moreover, that descriptive writing is on the whole not a popular kind. Your own tendency is more and more to over-refinement, and elaboration. Recollect that for newspaporial purposes, a broader treatment hits a broader mark; and keep bearing that way as much as you can with comfort. I suppose traits of human nature and character would also agreeably speckle the columns. . . .

You will like an account of my own condition. My eyes serve from three to four hours daily. I don't wish in this vacation to use them more—seldom as

[5] The reference is to a series of communications on the places of interest which he visited, reprinted afterwards in *Transatlantic Sketches*.

much—but feel sure they will respond whenever I make the demand. My other symptoms are gradually modifying themselves. . . . The appointment to teach physiology is a perfect godsend to me just now. An external motive to work, which yet does not strain me, a dealing with men instead of my own mind, and a diversion from those introspective studies which had bred a sort of philosophical hypochondria in me of late and which it will certainly do me good to drop for a year. . . . From your ever affectionate

W. J.

Cambridge, Oct. [10] 1872

My dear Harry,—

. . . I begin by saying how good and full of information . . . your letters home have been, leaving, in fact, nothing to be desired. Your letters to the *Nation* have been rather too few, and very much enjoyed by me, and by a number of other people so large that I confess it has rather surprised me; as I thought the style ran a little more to *curliness* than suited the average mind, or in general the newspaper reader. In my opinion what you should *cultivate* is directness of style. Delicacy, subtlety and ingenuity will take care of themselves. . . . I have been of late so sickened and sceptical of philosophic activity as to regret much that I did not stick to painting, and to envy those like you to whom the æsthetic relations of things were the real world. Surely they reveal a deeper part of the universal life than all the mechanical and logical abstractions do, and if I were you I would never repine that my life had got cast among them rather than elsewhere. . . .

Where this gets to you and how, I know not, but suppose you'll feel like making a short stay in England before returning to the South. Happy wretch! I hope you appreciate your lot, to spend the winter in an environment whose impression thickly assails your every sense and interest, instead of this naked vacuous America; and in a climate which in spite of its quantum of chill, on the whole lets you alone in a way that ours never thinks of, and has no northwest winds. Ever your affectionate

WM. JAMES

Cambridge, Nov. 24, 1872

Dear Harry,—

. . . Of the people who experienced a personal dislike, so to speak, of your stories, the most I think will be repelled by the element which gets expression in [certain] phrases, something cold, thin-blooded and priggish suddenly popping in and freezing the genial current. And I think that is the principal defect you have now to guard against. In flexibility, ease, and light power of style you clearly continue to gain. . . . I criticize you so much as perhaps to seem a mere caviler, but I think it ought to be of use to you to have any detailed criticism from even a wrong judge, and you don't get much from anyone else. I meanwhile say nothing of the great delight which all your pieces give me by their insight into the shades of being, and their exquisite diction and sense of beauty. . . .

Wendell Holmes spent an evening here this week. He grows more and more concentrated upon his law. His mind resembles a stiff spring, which has to be abducted violently from it, and which every instant it is left to itself flies tight back. . . . Charles Peirce and wife are going to Washington again for the winter and perhaps for good. He says he is appreciated there, and only tolerated here, and would be a fool not to go there. He read us an admirable introductory chapter to his book on logic the other day. I go in to the Medical School nearly every morning to hear Bowditch lecture, or paddle round in his laboratory. It is a noble thing for one's spirits to have some responsible work to do. I enjoy my revived physiological reading greatly, and have in a corporeal sense been better for the past four or five weeks than I have been at all since you left. . . . Ever yours affectionately,

W.J.

XIV

CHAUNCEY WRIGHT AND CHARLES PEIRCE

In writing the preface of his *Principles of Psychology* in 1890, James recorded his indebtedness to Chauncey Wright and Charles Peirce for "their intellectual companionship in old times." Both of these youthful friends were, like Holmes and Ward, of a relatively rigorous or sceptical turn of mind, and by exposure to their criticism James's germinating metaphysics became a hardier plant.

Of Chauncey Wright, James said, "His best work has been done in conversation." He was a recognized master in the circle of his Cambridge friends, owing not to constructive achievement, but rather to a sheer "power of analytic intellect pure and simple."[1] When, in 1865, James was suffering from intellectual as well as domestic nostalgia in Brazil, he wrote, "Would I might hear Chauncey Wright philosophize for one evening."[2] During the decade that followed, until his death in 1875, Wright was an intimate friend of the James family and held many a Socratic session with both father and son. To William he was a redoubtable champion whom to overthrow in argument was peculiarly sweet: as when in 1872 he wrote triumphantly to his aunt and sister in Europe of "the great Chauncey Wright who now (as to his system of the universe) lies in my arms as harmless as a babe."[3]

As regards the relations of Wright to William James, there was, in the first place, a pervasive and lingering influence, both of thought and of expression. James's remarks were often introduced by the words, "as Chauncey Wright used to say." Wright, like Peirce, had that boldness of ideas which always attracted James, and it was often combined with a happy turn of phrase. James felt him to be a master in the field of scientific thought and tended to accept him as an authoritative exponent of scientific aims and methods. To some extent, like Jeffries Wyman, he represented the ideal scientific temper—restrained, impersonal, and scrupulous. He represented personally and forcefully the contemporary tendency of scientific thinking to assume an experimental and de-

---

[1] *W.J.*, "Chauncey Wright," in *C.E.R.*, 20, 21. Wright's literary remains were edited and published by C. E. Norton in 1877 under the title of *Philosophical Discussions*. A volume of his letters (including correspondence with Darwin) was edited and published by James Bradley Thayer in 1878, under the title of *Letters of Chauncey Wright*. Wright was favorably known in England, especially in the Darwinian circle.

[2] *Cf.* above, 75.

[3] To A.J. and Mrs. Walsh, May 30, 1872.

scriptive rather than a metaphysical form. James accepted this version of science: "The physical order of nature, taken simply as science knows it, cannot be held to reveal any one harmonious spiritual intent"; it is not a divine order, a "divinely aimed at and established thing," but is "mere *weather,* as Chauncey Wright called it, doing and undoing without end." [4]

The agreement went beyond this. Wright adhered firmly to the "experiential philosophy," and unquestionably confirmed the like tendency in James. Wright's notion that the orderly relations and groupings of things do not require any explanation, since they involve nothing surprising or unnatural, is closely allied to James's notion that the connections of things are given with the things themselves. [5] Both Wright and James were prepared to accept a strain of irreducible fatality in existence, a something which it is hopeless and meaningless further to question; both, in short, were empiricists. Wright's essay on the "Evolution of Self-Consciousness," published in 1873, contributed to James's view of the biological role of thought, as set forth in his essay on "Brute and Human Intellect" in 1878, and afterwards incorporated in the chapter on "Reasoning" in the *Principles of Psychology.* Finally we have James's testimony that he did not come to utilitarianism "unaided," but was influenced by Chauncey Wright; whose antireligious teaching, however, he "reacted against." [6] Through Wright James apparently owed to Mill that better understanding of "utility" which frees it from ill-repute, and conceives it as including "the highest motives in which an individual's happiness can consist." [7]

But when all this has been said it remains none the less true that Wright was to James a philosophical adversary. The reason, of course, lay in his "antireligious teaching," and his rejection of the rights of metaphysics. To William James as well as to his father, Wright was the arch-exponent of positivism, with all of its negative implications. There is evidence that in the years 1868-1870 James gave a provisional adherence to this school. He continued to think of Wright as a paragon of that intellectual parsimony which confines itself to the description of phenomena. "Never in a human head was contemplation more separated from desire." Many years later he recalled him as his "tough-minded old friend Chauncey Wright, the great Harvard empiricist of my youth," who used to say that "behind the bare phenomenal facts . . . there is *nothing."* [8] But before 1875 James had already assigned positivists to the class of those who, unconscious of the subjective interests (in economy of thought) by which they were themselves actuated, refused to acknowledge

---

[4] *W.B.,* 52. Wright's notion of "cosmical weather" can be found in *Philosophical Discussions,* 10, 23.

[5] *Cf. C.E.R.,* 23-4.

[6] *Monist,* XIX (1909), 156.

[7] Wright, *op. cit.,* 418.

[8] *C.E.R.,* 23; *Pragm.,* 263.

the differing but analogous preferences of others. He attributed Wright's intellectual parsimoniousness to "a defect in the active or impulsive part of his mental nature," [9] and designed his own study of the "motives which lead men to philosophize" as a proof that positivism was both narrow and arbitrary.

The influence of Holmes was moral and personal—a glow and afterglow of adolescent comradeship; Wright's influence was mainly that of a challenge and an irritant, felt in the initial phase of James's thinking. Charles S. Peirce exerted both of these influences, with immeasurably more beside. He was only three years older than James, but had already graduated from Harvard College in 1859, while James was engaged in his preliminary educational experiments abroad. When James first encountered the "smart," but "pretty independent and violent" son of Professor Peirce, they were fellow students of chemistry in the Lawrence Scientific School.[10] But Peirce was receiving a degree *summa cum laude,* while James was still at the beginning of his intellectual attainment. In addition to being a trained scientist, Peirce manifested signs of genius. For although he was still unknown to the wider philosophical public in America when James introduced him in 1898 as the originator of pragmatism, his originality and promise of greatness had always been recognized by his close associates.

In the early '70s James and Peirce, together with Wright, were fellow members of a small group formed for the purpose of philosophical discussion. Peirce himself has described it as follows:—

> It was in the earliest seventies that a knot of us young men in Old Cambridge, calling ourselves, half-ironically, half-defiantly, "The Metaphysical Club," —for agnosticism was then riding its high horse, and was frowning superbly upon all metaphysics,—used to meet, sometimes in my study, sometimes in that of William James. It may be that some of our old-time confederates would today not care to have such wild-oats-sowings made public, though there was nothing but boiled oats, milk, and sugar in the mess. Mr. Justice Holmes, however, will not, I believe, take it ill that we are proud to remember his membership; nor will Joseph Warner, Esq. Nicholas St. John Green was one of the most interested fellows, a skillful lawyer and a learned one, a disciple of Jeremy Bentham. . . . Chauncey Wright, something of a philosophical celebrity in those days, was never absent from our meetings. I was about to call him our cory pheus; but he will better be described as our boxing-master whom we,—I particularly,—used to face to be severely pummelled. He had abandoned a former attachment to Hamiltonianism to take up with the doctrines of Mill, to which and to its cognate agnosticism he was trying to weld the really incongruous ideas of Darwin. John Fiske and, more rarely, Francis Ellingwood Abbot, were sometimes present, lending their countenances to the spirit of our endeavours,

[9] *C.E.R.*, 24.
[10] *Cf.* above, 69.

while holding aloof from any assent to their success. Wright, James, and I were men of science, rather scrutinizing the doctrines of the metaphysicians on their scientific side than regarding them as very momentous spiritually. The type of our thought was decidedly British. I, alone of our number, had come upon the threshing-floor of philosophy through the doorway of Kant, and even my ideas were acquiring the English accent.[11]

When Peirce went to Paris in 1875 he fell in with Henry James.[12] There were echoes of this strange fellowship in the letters which both parties addressed to Cambridge. On January 11, 1876, Henry wrote to his family:

> The only man I see here familiarly is C. Peirce, with whom I generally dine a couple of times a week. He is a very good fellow—when he is not in ill-humour; then he is intolerable. But, as William says, he is a man of genius, and in such, in the long run, one always finds one's account. He is leading here a life of insupportable loneliness and sterility—but of much material luxury, as he seems to have plenty of money. He sees, literally, not a soul but myself and his secretary.

Of his own impression Peirce had written to William on December 16, 1875:

> I see your brother very frequently. He is a splendid fellow. I admire him greatly and have only discovered two faults in him. One is that his digestion isn't quite that of an ostrich and the other is that he isn't as fond of turning over questions as I am, but likes to settle them and have done with them. A manly trait too, but not a philosophic one.

The following letter closes this early period of familiar intimacy. It reveals the interior of that apparition which Henry James in Paris had contemplated from without:—

Brevoort House, New York, May 1, 1877

My dear Willie,—

. . . I am in process of moving and was forced to come here for the night. Imagine my disgust at seeing in the *Herald* this morning that Prof. C. S. Peirce of Harvard College is sojourning at the Brevoort. Particularly as I am rather ashamed of my partiality for the Brevoort. But I have always come here for many years; I am known to every waiter etc., and find myself at home. It is

---

[11] From a paper (*circa* 1906) published for the first time in Vol. V, §12, of the *Collected Papers of C. S. Peirce*, ed. by C. Hartshorne and P. Weiss, Harvard University Press, 1934. Joseph B. Warner, Harvard '69, a Boston lawyer and lifelong friend of the James family, died in 1923. Green graduated from the Harvard Law School in 1853. He was present at Chauncey Wright's deathbed and survived him only one year. F. E. Abbot (1836-1903), a classmate of Peirce, was for one year (1887-8) an instructor of philosophy at Harvard, but spent most of his life as a private scholar and writer in that subject.

[12] *Cf.* also below, 143, and Chapter XXXI.

frequented by a class of people very *comme il faut* but not in my line. I insensibly put on a sort of swagger here which I hope I have nowhere else, and which is designed to say: "You are a very good fellow in your way; who you are I don't know and I don't care, but I, you know, am Mr. Peirce, distinguished for my varied scientific acquirements, but above all for my extreme modesty in which respect I challenge the world." I notice that if one goes into the niceties, scarcely any one is totally without swagger, and in those few the dryness is disagreeable. Required: an essay on good taste in swaggering.

You don't say how your father and the rest of them are—I had lately a letter from H. James, Jr. Your loving

C. S. P.

Peirce not only occupied an important place, perhaps the first place, in the history of pragmatism, but greatly influenced James's ultimate metaphysics. The personal and temperamental differences between the two men are flagrant. James was instinctively, as well as by breeding and experience, adapted to social intercourse, and, despite his neurasthenic tendencies and intellectual preoccupations, was a man of the world. Peirce was ill at ease, of uncertain temper, and found it increasingly difficult, as life went on, to associate with his fellow men. James was slow to take offense and always gave other people the benefit of the doubt, while Peirce was touchy and prone to suspicion; the one being almost excessively modest and appreciative of others, while the other tended to arrogance.

There were intellectual as well as moral differences. Peirce, both by aptitude and by training, was an exponent of exact science, where a man might be sure of his ground, and where inaccuracy was the deadliest of sins; whereas James was at home in literature, psychology, and metaphysics, where accuracy is likely to be pretentious or pedantic, and where sympathy, insight, fertility, and delicacy of feeling may richly compensate for its absence. It is commonly said that James did not understand Peirce. James himself said so, and Peirce agreed. It seems to be generally assumed that Peirce understood James. But it is to be noted that James rarely claimed to understand anybody, whereas it was characteristic of Peirce to feel that he understood everybody—only too well. The difference is so striking that it is well to discount the word of both on this matter, and at the same time to bear in mind that the feeling of understanding or misunderstanding a doctrine reflects the degree of a man's expectation. James usually expected a good deal, and it was a long time before he could feel confident that his failure to see the light was due to the fact that there was none. With Peirce this was a natural and easy assumption. To this it must be added that James most eagerly desired to be understood, while Peirce was sometimes playfully or maliciously obscure.

At the same time it must be recognized that James was comparatively defective in that formal or symbolic mode of statement[13] which Peirce, as a trained mathematician and logician, regarded as the acme of clearness. Towards the close of his life Peirce wrote down his opinions of his old friend at some length—a spontaneous soliloquizing over old times, with a characteristic blending of emotion and analysis. Having referred to James's "almost unexampled incapacity for mathematical thought, combined with intense hatred for logic," he went on to say:

> After studying William James on the intellectual side for half a century,—for I was not acquainted with him as a boy,—I must testify that I believe him to be, and always to have been during my acquaintance with him about as perfect a lover of truth as it is possible for a man to be; and I do not believe there is any definite limit to man's capacity for loving the truth. . . .
> In speaking . . . of William James as I do I am saying the most that I could of any man's intellectual morality; and with him this was but one of a whole diadem of virtues. Though it is entirely out of place in this connexion, and I must beg the reader's pardon for so wandering from the point under consideration, I really lack the self-command to repress my reflexions when I have once set down his name. Though his lectures were delightful, they not at all exhibited the man at his best. It was his unstudied common behaviour that did so by the perfection of his manners, in their perfect freedom from expressing flattery or anything else false or inappropriate to the occasion. He did not express himself very easily, because rhetoric was his antipathy and logic an inconvenience to him. One always felt that the pencil, not the pen, was the lever with which he ought to have moved the world; and yet no! it was not the externals of things but their souls he could have pictured.
> His comprehension of men to the very core was most wonderful. Who, for example, could be of a nature so different from his as I. He so concrete, so living; I a mere table of contents, so abstract, a very snarl of twine. Yet in all my life I found scarce any soul that seemed to comprehend,—naturally, [not] my concepts, but the mainspring of my life, better than he did. He was even greater in practice than in theory of psychology.[14]

That in their early contact James was more influenced by Peirce than Peirce by James is, I think, undeniable. He was the "maturer companion," who first delivered the young student of science from the spell of Herbert Spencer. James, who never took a day's journey in the realms of thought without *meeting* somebody, and who recorded such encounters, jotted down many of Peirce's sayings from days as early as 1862. Their mutual influence, like their mutual understanding, was largely an inevitable effect of their differences of

---

[13] In the famous essay "How to Make Our Ideas Clear," *Pop. Sc. Mo.*, XII (1877-8), Peirce distinguished three grades of clearness: familiarity, analytical definition, and an apprehension of the object's "practical bearings." He said later that "the third grade is the most important of all and a good example of it is William James who is phenomenally weak in the second grade, yet ever so high above most men in the third."

[14] From "A Sketch of Logical Criticism." *Collected Papers of C. S. Peirce*, Vol. VI.

temperament. Peirce was a more self-sufficient thinker, James a man who nourished his mind by intercourse and by the momentary half-acceptance of a multitude of ideas in which his quick sympathy found something of value. James's mind was both more hospitable and more prodigal, and while his destination was no less fixed than was Peirce's, he arrived at it by more devious routes and halted more frequently on the way.

There were three respects in which James was receptive to the influence of Peirce in the '60s and '70s. In the first place, he relished Peirce's boldness of thought and intellectual irreverence—his shameless way of disregarding the philosophical dogmas and commonplaces. To James originality was always irresistibly fascinating. Then Peirce fed and confirmed James's dissatisfaction with the merely sensationalistic outcome of empiricism. Whatever the stress which the empiricist places upon presentations to sense, he must not ignore the connections of things, the *a priori* element in judgment, and the transcendence of the object of knowledge. Peirce, who despised sensation, never let James overlook these considerations; and the latter's empiricism is distinguished by its provision for them. Finally, Peirce, like James, was interested in the nature of doubt and belief. Peirce's articles of 1868 dealt with doubt, and his articles of 1878 with belief. Nothing could be more opposed to Peirce's doctrine of a belief predestined by fact and social agreement than James's allowance for emotional preference, but it is significant that as early as 1868 both Peirce and James, the one for theoretical and the other primarily for personal and religious reasons, were both interested in the same problem; and were equally ready, for the sake of solving it, to disregard the boundary between philosophy and psychology. It was largely on account of this emphasis that James found Peirce not only "strangely interesting," [15] but also relevant.

[15] *Cf.* above, 112.

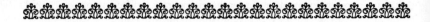

XV

SETTLING INTO THE CAREER

Despite the characteristic misgivings voiced in his letters to his brother, James began his teaching of "Comparative Anatomy and Physiology" in January, 1873. There was little doubt of its success, as judged both from his own point of view and from that of his students. Parental impressions are recorded in letters to Harry:

Cambridge, Jan. 14, 1873

Willy is going on with his teaching. The eleven o'clock bell has just tolled, and he is on his platform expounding the mysteries of physiology. He uses himself up now and then visiting and all the rest of it, such as debating about *Middlemarch* and other transient topics, but on the whole he gets on very well. He often talks of you. We all do that of course, but *he* very often initiates the talk. I needn't say that he always talks of you in the most tenderly affectionate and appreciative way. Yes, we are all your tender lovers, darling Harry, and none more so than your devoted Daddy.

H. J.

Cambridge, Jan. 21, 1873

Will comes in from his lesson, and throws himself in the big green chair in the warm, broad sunshine. I say, "What shall I say to Harry?" He says, "Say I hoped to have written him long ago, but now I cannot say when I will be able to." I think he finds his lessons all that he can do. The intellectual part is easy enough, but the whole thing taxes his weak nerves considerably. With habit and experience this, I hope, will abate. He complains of the loutish character of the young men generally, so few show intelligence or interest,—still there are a few. This is the usual experience of college professors. I remember Mr. Gurney once saying, "Tell William he must be sure to expect nothing from the young men." . . . Your loving MOTHER.

On February 10, 1873, James wrote the following entry in his diary:

I decide today to stick to biology for a profession in case I am not called to a chair of philosophy, rather than to try to make the same amount of money by literary work, while carrying on more *general* or philosophic study. Philosophy I will nevertheless regard as my vocation and never let slip a chance to do a stroke at it."

His teaching had turned him from morbid self-examination, and Renouvier had delivered him from the felt impotence of philosophical determinism. He had a work in the world, and he could undertake it with good heart, since he could now believe in its efficacy. Renouvier, too, had helped to draw the fangs of science so that it could be domesticated without peril to the soul. The following letter from his father to Henry presents an epitome of William's progress:—

March 18 [1873] [1]

My darling Harry,—

. . . Willy goes on swimmingly with his teaching. The students (fifty-seven) are elated with their luck in having such a professor, and next year he will have no doubt a larger class still, attracted by his fame. He came in here the other afternoon when I was sitting alone, and after walking the floor in an animated way for a moment, exclaimed "Dear me! What a difference there is between me now and me last spring this time: then so hypochondriacal" (he used that word, though perhaps in substantive form) "and now feeling my mind so cleared up and restored to sanity. It is the difference between death and life." He had a great effusion. I was afraid of interfering with it, or possibly checking it, but I ventured to ask what specially in his opinion had promoted the change. He said several things: the reading of Renouvier (specially his vindication of the freedom of the will) and Wordsworth, whom he has been feeding upon now for a good while; but especially his having given up the notion that all mental disorder required to have a physical basis. This had become perfectly untrue to him. He saw that the mind did act irrespectively of material coercion, and could be dealt with therefore at first-hand, and this was health to his bones. It was a splendid confession, and though I knew the change had taken place, from unerring signs, I never was more delighted than to hear it from his own lips so unreservedly. He has been shaking off his respect for men of mere science as such, and is even more universal and impartial in his mental judgments than I have ever known him before. . . .

Good-bye, my lovely Harry. Words can't tell how dear you are to my heart; how proud I am of your goodness and truth; of what Mr. Arnold calls your "sweet reasonableness." Truly I am a happy and grateful father at every remembrance of you. Yours ever lovingly,

[H.J.]

When, a few weeks later, Eliot offered James a renewal of his appointment in biology, with a prospect of permanence, his first impulse was to decline it:—

Cambridge, April 6, 1873

My dear Harry,—

I take up my pen once more after this long interval to converse with my in many respects twin brother. We have not heard from you in a fortnight and eagerly expect a letter today, describing new sensual delights and luxuries in

[1] Published in part in *N.S.B.*, 264, and *L.W.J.*, I, 169-70.

which your body and soul shall have alike been wallowing. Alice and I keep up a rather constant fire of *badinage*, etc., of which you furnish the material; she never speaking of you except as "that angel"—and I sarcastically calling you the "angel-hero-martyr." Usually towards bedtime I wander into the parlor where the three are sitting and say "I suppose that angel is now in such and such an attitude," drawing on my imagination for something very "oriental," to which Alice generally finds no better reply than a tirade upon the petty jealousies of *men*. Long may you have the power of enjoying what luxuries you can get! . . .

I have just got through three months of tuition, and have four weeks' holiday before taking them up again for a final month. It has turned out a solider job than I anticipated, both in respect of the effort it has taken to put it through, and in respect of the information I have imparted. . . . Eliot offered me the other day the whole department (*i.e.,* this physiology plus Dwight's anatomy) for next year. But I told him I had resolved to fight it out in the line of mental science, and with such arrears of lost time behind me and such curtailed power of work now, could not afford to make such an expedition into anatomy. It cost me some perplexity to make the decision, for had I accepted, it might easily grow into a permanent biological appointment, to succeed Wyman, perhaps,— and that study, though less native to my taste, has many things in its favor. . . . Ever your affectionate

W.J.

But he soon changed his mind, recording this important decision in his diary for April 10, and communicating it to his brother a month later. It was not that his passion for philosophy had abated, but that he distrusted his power to sustain it, and feared its effect upon his health:—

Yesterday I told Eliot I would accept the anatomical instruction for next year, if well enough to perform it, and would probably stick to that department. I came to this decision mainly from the feeling that philosophical activity as a *business* is not normal for most men, and not for me. To be responsible for a complete conception of things is beyond my strength. To make the *form* of all possible thought the prevailing *matter* of one's thought breeds hypochondria. Of course my deepest interest will as ever lie with the most general problems. But as my strongest moral and intellectual craving is for some stable reality to lean upon, and as a professed philosopher pledges himself publicly never to have done with doubt on these subjects, but every day to be ready to criticize afresh and call in question the grounds of his faith of the day before, I fear the constant sense of instability generated by this attitude would be more than the voluntary faith I can keep going is sufficient to neutralize. . . . That gets reality for us in which we place our responsibility, and the concrete facts in which a biologist's responsibilities lie form a fixed basis from which to aspire as much as he pleases to the mastery of the universal questions when the gallant mood is on him; and a basis, too, upon which he can passively float, and tide over times of weakness and depression, trusting all the while blindly in the beneficence of nature's forces and the return of higher opportunities. A "philosopher" has publicly renounced the privilege of trusting *blindly,* which every simple man owns as a right—and my sight is not always clear enough for such constant duty. Of course one may say, you could make of psychology proper just such a basis; but not so, you can't divorce psychology from introspection, and immense as is the work demanded by its purely objective physiologic part, yet it is the other part rather for which a professor thereof is expected to make himself publicly responsible.

It is not necessary to attack the universal problems directly, and as such, in their abstract form. We work at their solution in every way,—by living and by solving minor concrete questions, as they are involved in everything. The method of nature is patience, and that easy sitting faith, not tense strung, but smiling and with a dash of scepticism in it, which is not in despair at postponing a solution, which Goethe showed in his feeling about philosophy and nature, is no ignoble attitude, and perhaps belongs to a mode of taking life ampler and of longer reach of promise, than the hot imperious tragic way of attack. The ends of nature are all attained through means—perhaps the soundest way of recovering them is by tracking them through all the means.

Despite James's improvement in mind he had not yet acquired sufficient bodily endurance to bear the strain of continuous teaching. The end of May finds him again plunged into doubt, and thinking of another trip to Europe. But this time there is a note of hopefulness even in his discouragement. He feels convinced that health is more nearly within his grasp, and that a period of recuperation may free him permanently from his chronic invalidism. The vocational alternatives, too, have now been narrowed to several concrete possibilities, for any of which he feels himself competent, health permitting. His brother Henry, having been asked for advice, recommended Rome for its "sedative climate," its social distractions, and as "peculiarly adapted to help one get through time." [2] He offered eagerly to join him there if he would come. But first William James enjoyed an American vacation, and experienced in the presence of nature the characteristic exaltation described in the following letter to his mother:—

Magnolia [July 8, 1873]

My dearest Mar,—

. . . I never experienced in five days such a change of feelings as in the last five. The benefits of this place culminated yesterday in a sort of afternoon of rapture. It was a magnificent thought to leave my work behind me for three weeks, as I then no doubt will take it up with appetite, and its presence here now would, I know, have spoiled all the splendor of this careless and free attitude of mind. I have spent all my mornings and afternoons except yesterday morning alone in the woods, fields, and rocks, with the breath of the woods in my lungs, the smell of the laurels in my nose, the surf pounding rhythmically upon my ear, and the beautiful wash of light before my eyes. It takes all the

[2] H.J.[2] to W.J., June 18, 1873.

wrinkles and puckers out of you and washes you whole again, filling you with courage, and independence of what may happen in the future—whereas your ordinary working-day consciousness is all sicklied o'er with fretful solicitudes and apprehensions. I don't see how men can live without a month in the year of this normal life—for taking mankind as a whole the open-air existence, from day to day, has been the normal life, and the liking and need of it has deep roots in our nature. . . . Adieu. Yours ever,

W. J.

On September 2 James wrote his brother:

The die is cast! The six hundred dollars' salary falls into the pocket of another! And for a year I am adrift again and free. I feel the solemnity of the moment, and that I *must* get well now or give up. It seems as if I should, too . . . so you may expect me to rejoin you about November 1.

He secured passage in October on the *S.S. Spain,* landed at Queenstown, and proceeded at once to Florence with only hurried glimpses of London and Paris. On November 28, accompanied by his brother, he went from Florence to Rome, where he experienced a mixture of awe and repugnance—expressing it all most vehemently in his letters home. While impressed by the splendor of Rome and its rich antiquity, he felt a strong moral revulsion to its decay, its paganism, and its traditionalism—a moral revulsion which he thought his father alone could adequately voice. That his health was rapidly improving is indicated by a letter which his brother wrote home a few weeks later:—

Rome, Dec. 22, 1873

Dear Father,—
   . . . Willy will have written you about himself and given you, I hope, as good accounts of his progress as he daily gives me, and as his whole appearance and daily exploits testify to so eloquently. He seems greatly contented with his condition and is sensible of its growing constantly better. He has just been into my room, flushed with health and strength, to see whether I had found any letters at the bankers this morning and to ask where he should go today. Seeing me writing, he says,—"Give them my love and tell them I am doing splendidly." He does in fact, a great deal, and walks, climbs Roman staircases, and sees sights in a way most satisfactory to behold. . . . Willy, who at first hung fire over Rome, has now quite ignited, and confesses to its sovereign influence. But he enjoys all the melancholy of antiquity under a constant protest, which pleases me as a symptom of growing optimism and elasticity in his own disposition. His talk, as you may imagine, on all things, is most rich and vivacious. My own more sluggish perceptions can hardly keep pace with it. Ever, dear Father, with love to all, your loving

H. J.

Compelled by an attack of malarial fever to leave Rome at the end of December, William returned to Florence, his brother following later. Then in February the former began his homeward journey, going first to Venice, whence he addressed the following to his sister:—

Feb. 13, 1874

Beloved Beautlet,—

. . . I bade good-bye to Florence three days ago with many a sting of regret, for I had hardly done it justice in the past month, the sickness of the "angel" and my being out of sorts myself had made me unfit for my opportunities. But Venice has put me on my sight-seeing feet again. Three days have I gondoled and picture-gazed, under a cloudless sky, but a neager and an ipping air—especially in the Academy, where the poor custodians have a cold time of it. Such glory of painting and such actual decay, I never saw. This afternoon I mounted the Campanile and got a view which explained to me much of Venetian art— *i.e.,* the light as one of the *dramatis personæ.* While the gondola . . . makes one understand how figures seen from below against the sky . . . came so natural to them. . . .

Altogether my visit is a great success. . . . Tomorrow to Munich stopping six hours in Verona. At Dresden I must decide whether to return in March or not, a hard step. . . . *Addio,* sweet babe. Ever your loving

WM.

In March James sailed for home from Bremen. The following letter to his brother is characteristic of his *usual* state of mind just after returning from Europe.

Cambridge, April 18, 1874

Dear Harry,—

. . . Any gossip about Florence you can still communicate will be greedily sucked in by me, who feel towards it as I do towards the old Albany of our childhood, with afternoon shadows of trees, etc. Not but that I am happy here,— more so than I ever was there, because I'm in a permanent path, and it shows me how for our type of character the thought of the *whole* dominates the particular moments. All my moments here are inferior to those in Italy, but they are parts of a long plan which is good, so they content me more than the Italian ones which only existed for themselves. I have been feeling uncommonly strong for almost three weeks . . . and done a good deal of work in Bowditch's laboratory. . . . My short stay abroad has given me quite a new sense of what you used to call the provinciality of Boston, but that is no harm. What displeases me is the want of stoutness and squareness in the people, their ultra quietness, prudence, slyness, intellectualness of gait. Not that their intellects amount to anything, either. You will be discouraged, I remain happy!

But this brings me to the subject of your return, of which I have thought much. It is evident that you will have to eat your bread in sorrow for a time here; it is equally evident that time . . . will prove a remedy for a great deal of the trouble, and you will attune your at present coarse senses to snatch a fearful joy from wooden fences and commercial faces, a joy the more thrilling for being so subtly extracted. Are you ready to make the heroic effort? . . . This is your dilemma: The congeniality of Europe, on the one hand, plus the difficulty of making an entire living out of original writing, and its abnormality as a matter of mental hygiene . . . on the other hand, the dreariness of American conditions of life plus a mechanical, routine occupation possibly to be obtained, which from day to day is *done* when 'tis done, mixed up with the writing into which you distil your essence. . . . In short, don't come unless with a *resolute* intention. If you come, your worst years will be the first. If you stay, the bad years may be the later ones, when, moreover, you can't change. And I have a suspicion that if you come, too, and *can* get once acclimated, the quality of what you write will be higher than it would be in Europe. . . . It seems to me a very critical moment in your history. But you have several months to decide. Good-bye.

[W. J.]

A vivid impression of William's activities and personal associations during this period is conveyed by the following letter to his brother Robertson, now living in Prairie du Chien, Wisconsin:—

Cambridge, Sept. 20, 1874

We are established for the winter, Harry very well indeed and seeming glad to be back. The only event that has happened of any interest is the marriage of Edward Emerson and Miss Keyes yesterday at the Keyes' house. I went up with half a car load of people from town,—the Forbes crowd, and various other relatives. The day was warm, drizzly and dripping, bringing out the moist green of the country beautifully. The wedding was a delightful thing, being, with the exception of Aunt Kate's and Wendell Holmes's—which latter took place in a church—the first I ever attended. All my friends have been so high-toned of late, T. S. Perry, Ellen Gurney, John La Farge, Clover Adams, etc., as to get married in secret, so that no mortal eye should profane the ceremony, and I had passively accepted that as the only fitting way for a person of "culture" who respected himself. But the affair of yesterday entirely opened my eyes and when I get married I shall have a cheerful sociable crowd round me. The crowd there all had the worthy, reliable, Concord look—all called each other by their first names, and you felt that the men and especially the woman standing next you, though you did not know them, were people worthy of your esteem. Tom Ward was there, and the famous Miss Lizzie Simmons who is very good looking; the Bartlett family looking all like baked apples; and old Mr. Emerson more gaunt and lop-sided than ever; Mr. Sanborn, who supported himself by leaning his hand against the ceiling and who sent his regards to you and Wilky. All the people seem to remember you, for more asked about you than I can now remember,—Miss Elizabeth Hoar, for example, and Mrs. Simmons. Ellen Emerson looked beautiful in a white dress and lilac crape shawl, and Edith Forbes was there sumptuously attired, with three magnificent looking children. The person that pleased me most was Malcolm Forbes's young wife, who is as pretty faced and voiced as she can be, and a very bright little talker. Edward looked and behaved very well, while Miss Keyes, who had just recovered from a sharp illness, looked a little too bony and had two bright crimson spots on her cheek bones.[3] Will Forbes has asked me to Naushon for a few days at the end of the week. Edward and his bride will be there, and they will have a deer hunt. I will write to Wilky about it. . . . Believe me, dear Bob, always your loving

W.J.

[3] The bride was Miss Annie Shepard Keyes, daughter of Judge John S. Keyes. Dr. Josiah Bartlett was the well-known Concord physician. Miss Elizabeth Hoar, sister of Judge Ebenezer R. Hoar, had been engaged to Charles Emerson, who died a few months before the marriage was to take place. Mrs. George Francis Simmons was formerly Miss Mary Ripley of Concord and Miss Lizzie Simmons was her daughter. Mr. Sanborn was the well-known Frank B. Sanborn whose school the younger James boys had attended. Mrs. John Malcolm Forbes was the former Miss Sarah Jones.

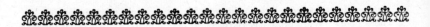

XVI

ESTABLISHED IN LIFE

In 1874-1875 James resumed his teaching, this time in full charge of "Natural History 3," on "The Comparative Anatomy and Physiology of Vertebrates," which he continued to give for five consecutive years. After Jeffries Wyman's death in 1874 James temporarily succeeded to the direction of the laboratory of Comparative Anatomy, which the former had established in Boylston Hall. From that building he was ousted by the chemists in 1875. I am indebted to Professor Charles Loring Jackson for the following account of a visit which James made to the laboratory during the autumn, apparently to remove supplies that he had left behind: "I had just returned from two years in Europe, and, talking of my work, I said that once when I was working with amyl nitrite in Berlin an Englishman who was also in the loggia began singing and laughing as though he were drunk. By the evening I was in the same state. James was immensely interested and asked to try some of it. At first he very properly held the bottle at a distance, and waved the vapor toward himself; but when to his continual questions, 'Is my face flushing?' we answered 'No,' he at last put it against his nose and took a good sniff. Then he felt blindly for the table, put the bottle on it and said, 'O! how queer I feel!' took up two battery-jars full of alcohol (two quarts if I remember) and started across the Yard." It seems that James arrived safely at his destination, which was presumably the Museum of Comparative Zoölogy on Oxford Street.

In this autumn of 1875 James announced a graduate course on "The Relations between Physiology and Psychology," and a similar course for undergraduates was introduced the next year. With his promotion to an assistant professorship in 1876, he was established professionally.

Henry's career was definitely inaugurated almost simultaneously with his brother's. His first long novel, *Roderick Hudson,* was begun in Florence in 1874. He returned to Cambridge in the autumn of that year to settle the momentous question of his permanent residence, while *Roderick Hudson* was appearing in installments in the *Atlantic Monthly*.[1] The great decision having

---

[1] The trials of an author residing abroad, where he had no chance to read his own proofs, are illustrated by the misadventure with his letter to the *Nation* from Pisa, in which "idle vistas and melancholy nooks" appeared as "idle sisters and melancholy monks." *Cf.* letter of H.J.[2] to W.J., June 13 [1874].

been made in favor of Europe, he repaired thither in the fall of 1875, not to return to America for six years. The correspondence between the brothers was thus resumed. From Paris Henry wrote on December 3:

> I have seen few people—chiefly Turgenev. . . . He is a most attractive man and I took a great shine to him. . . . Also Charles Peirce, who wears beautiful clothes, etc. He is busy swinging pendulums at the Observatory, and thinks himself indifferently treated by the Paris scientists. We meet every two or three days to dine together; but though we get on very well, our sympathy is economical rather than intellectual.

William replied on December 12:

> I am amused that you should have fallen into the arms of C. S. Peirce, whom I imagine you find a rather uncomfortable bedfellow, thorny and spinous, but the way to treat him is after the fabled "nettle" receipt: grasp firmly, contradict, push hard, make fun of him, and he is as pleasant as anyone; but be overawed by his sententious manner and his paradoxical and obscure statements—wait upon them, as it were, for light to dawn—and you will never get a feeling of ease with him any more than I did for years, until I changed my course and treated him more or less chaffingly. I confess I like him very much in spite of all his peculiarities, for he is a man of genius, and there's always something in that to compel one's sympathy. . . .
>
> *Roderick Hudson* seems to be a very common theme of conversation. . . . In looking through the volume it seems to me even better than it did, but I must tell you that I am again struck unfavorably by the tendency of the personages to reflect on themselves and give an acute critical scientific introspective classification of their own natures and states of mind, *à la* G. Sand. Take warning once more! . . . The only other thing I have done except mind my anatomy is the squib in the *Nation* which I enclose. In the interval between sending it and seeing it appear in print, I have dipped into Baudelaire and am reluctantly obliged to confess that Scherer is quite as wrong as Saintsbury. It is a pity that every writer in France is bound to do injustice to the opposite "camp." Baudelaire is really, in his *Fleurs du Mal,* original and in a certain sense elevated, and on the whole I can bear no rancor against him, although at times he writes like a person half-awake and groping for words. The most amusing thing about it all is the impression one gets of the innocence of a generation in which the *Fleurs du Mal* should have made a *scandal*. It is a mild and spiritualistic book today. Get it and write about it in the *Nation* or *Atlantic,* if you like, and especially read a letter of Sainte-Beuve's at the end of it, which is the *ne plus ultra* of his diabolic subtlety and malice.[2]
>
> I had an interview with C. W. Eliot the other day, who smiles on me and lets me expect $1200 this year and possibly hope for $2000 the next, which will be

---

[2] James's "squib" was a letter to the *Nation* in which he pretends to be composing a manual of the literature of the nineteenth century and calls attention to the flat contradiction between Saintsbury's favorable (*Fortnightly Review* for Nov. 1875) and Edward Scherer's unfavorable (*Études*) judgment of Charles Baudelaire. *Cf.* the *Nation,* Dec. 2, 1875 (XXI), 255. Sainte-Beuve's letter to Baudelaire appears in the Appendix of the first volume of the latter's *Œuvres complètes,* 1869.

a sweet boon if it occurs. As the term advances I become sensible that I am really better than I was last year in almost every way; which gives me still better prospects for the future. . . . Good-bye! Heaven bless you,—get as much society as you can. Your first letter was a very good beginning, though one sees that you are to a certain extent fishing for the proper tone or level. I should like to accompany you to some of the theatres. Adieu!

W. J.

P.S. Latest American humor, quoted last night by Godkin—child (lost at fair): Where's my mother? I told the darned thing she'd lose me.

That James's philosophical mind was busy during the spring and summer of ·1876 is indicated by his correspondence with Renouvier;[3] and by a letter written to the *Nation* on "The Teaching of Philosophy in Our Colleges," in which he advocated entire freedom of teaching in this field, and contended, in a manner profoundly characteristic of his later thought and practice, that the chief educational value of philosophy lay in a "wider openness of mind and a more flexible way of thinking."[4] As a matter of fact it was many years before this ideal of philosophical teaching triumphed over that of dogmatic edification, and in this change James himself played a leading part.

The autumn of 1876 was notable for the opening of James's first undergraduate course in psychology, which was the "new Spencer elective" referred to in the following letter to Thomas W. Ward:—

Cambridge, Dec. 30, 1876

My dear Tom,—

   . . . My new Spencer elective has proved quite exciting and arduous. . . . How I envy you your fund of energy. I have a little spoonful ready for each day and when that's out, as it usually is by 10 o'clock A.M., I'm good for nothing. Every man ought to have outside of his work a chance to cultivate the ideal. I ought to be able to read biographies, histories, etc., a couple of hours every evening, for I think a professor, in addition to his *Fach,* should be a *ganzer Mensch*—but I can read nothing. A part of Doudan's letters (delightful stuff), and one half of Mlle. Lespinasse's letters[5] are the literal sum total in three months. The latter show the *disease* of love about as completely as anything I ever saw. But I like human nature, and can't breathe without some suggestion of contact with lives of other people—vigorous ones, I mean. All the men here seem so dry and shopboard like. . . . I have some bright boys in my Spencer class,—but I am completely disgusted with the eminent philosopher, who seems to me more and more to be as absolutely worthless in all *funda-. mental* matters of thought, as he is admirable, clever and ingenious in secondary matters. His mind is a perfect puzzle to me, but the total impression is of an intensely two and sixpenny, paper-collar affair. . . . Yours always,

W. J.

---

[3] *Cf.* below, 152-3.

[4] *L.W.J.,* I, 190. For the article in full, *cf. Nation,* Sept. 21, 1876 (XXIII).

[5] The letters of Mlle. Julie Jeanne Elénore de Lespinasse were published in Paris in 1809, second edition in 1876.

Apparently Henry also had heard of William's new elective, for on February 28 (1877) he wrote:

> What is your "Herbert Spencer elective"?—to which you have alluded, but without explaining its sudden genesis. Whatever it is I am glad you like it. I often take a nap beside Herbert Spencer at the Athenæum, and feel as if I were robbing *you* of the privilege. A good speech of Matthew Arnold's, which seems to be classical here: "Oh yes, my wife is a delightful woman; she has all my sweetness, and none of my airs."

In June 1878, James entered into the contract with Henry Holt and Company which led (twelve years later) to the publication of his *Principles of Psychology;* and on the tenth of the next month he married Alice H. Gibbens, whom he had met two years before through his friend Thomas Davidson.[6] Without the second of these contracts there would have been much less likelihood of his fulfilling the first. Mrs. James was a remarkable woman in her own right, distinguished in beauty, wit, and character. Her benign influence upon her husband's happiness and upon the fruitfulness of his career can scarcely be exaggerated. She shared his intellectual and professional interests with sympathetic loyalty: in her absence he spoke of himself as "left alone and deprived of the wonted ear into which to pour all my observations, aphorisms, wishes and complaints." [7] She watched over him with untiring devotion, protecting him against the consequences of his own rash generosity. Above all, she introduced into his household an embodiment and suggestion of the composure which his mobile and high-strung nature greatly needed. There was at the same time a quality of finality in the very fact of marriage itself—the sense of a safe anchorage, and of a steadying purpose in life.

The domestic harbor in which James anchored was not always peaceful. Its waters were ruffled by the usual incidents attending the living together of adults and small children, and James's nervous organization made him peculiarly sensitive to noises, vexations, and anxieties. Thus in 1879 he wrote to his youngest brother, Robertson, "I find the cares of a nursing father to be very different from those of a bachelor. Farewell the tranquil mind!" [8] In 1887, writing from Chocorua, he said:

> It is a good deal of a complication to life to have children! not to speak of the complications to *them!* Mothers-in-law, sisters-in-law, aunts-in-law added to them, "mellow one up" a good deal (as that ancient *massagiste,* Horne, said of my back). I look back at my narrow and brittle-minded bachelor state as the vealiest of epochs, though there was something grateful about the feeling of potentiality attached to it.[9]

[6] *Cf.* below, 166 ff.
[7] W.J. to William M. Salter, May 11, 1893.
[8] August 18, 1879.
[9] To A.J., July 7, 1887.

The following passage, from a letter of 1892, was written with genuine feeling, albeit with James's customary hyperbole:

> It seems to me that the most solemn duty *I* can have in what remains to me of life will be to save my inexperienced fellow-beings from ignorantly taking their little ones abroad when they go for their own refreshment. To combine novel anxieties of the most agonizing kind about your children's education, nocturnal and diurnal contact of the most intimate sort with their shrieks, their quarrels, their questions, their rollings-about and tears, in short with all their emotional, intellectual and bodily functions, in what practically in these close quarters amounts to one room—to combine these things (I say) with a *holiday* for *oneself* is an idea worthy to emanate from a lunatic asylum.[10]

There were times, too, as in the middle nineties, when the financial burden imposed by a growing family led James to multiply popular lectures and articles, and thus to increase the strain from which he already suffered as a consequence of his growing fame and his constantly broadening intellectual interests. But there is no reason to suppose that his domestic life afforded irritating stimuli or temptations to excess that he would not, in its absence, have found elsewhere. That he should have been prudent, and at peace with himself and the world, is unimaginable. His inborn temperament had taken care of that! What his domestic life did was to create the best possible environment for his constitutional tendencies: giving him as much stability as was consistent with his mercurial genius, directing his superabundant nervous energy into productive channels, providing in his own house those tender human relationships which his nature craved, and giving him at the core of his being the all-important sense of living a full and useful life.

The honeymoon, during the summer of 1878, was spent in Keene Valley, New York, in the farmhouse which James (together with Bowditch and the Putnams) had converted into a camp for summer holidays. This and the adjoining region of the Adirondack Mountains played a peculiar role in James's development. "I love it like a peasant," he wrote many years later; "and if Calais was engraved on the heart of Mary Tudor, surely Keene Valley will be engraved on mine when I die." [11] Here, and in the White Mountains, in the vicinity of his summer home at Chocorua, New Hampshire, he found that wild aspect of nature which so deeply satisfied him. "On the whole," he said, "I prefer the works of God to those of man." [12] Although he had a painter's eye for landscape, the appeal of nature was something much deeper. The wide and unobstructed prospect gave him the sense of a breathing space, and favored contemplative detachment. He enjoyed *immersion* in the wilderness, and that

[10] To Grace Ashburner, July 13, 1892; *L.W.J.*, I, 321.
[11] To the author, January 2, 1900.
[12] To H.J.², August 11, 1898; *L.W.J.*, II, 81.

simplification of clothes and personal habits which such life requires. "What I *crave* most," he once wrote from Europe, "is some wild American country. It is a curious organic-feeling need. One's social relations with European landscape are entirely different, everything being so fenced or planted that you can't lie down and sprawl." [13] He enjoyed what he called the American's "wild-animal personal relations" with nature.[14]

A glance at the list of James's published works affords conclusive evidence that the year 1878 was a turning point in his career, as well as in his personal life. During the decade 1867-1877 he had written some forty-five reviews, notices, and short articles. They are of comparatively slight importance, even as evidence of their author's doctrinal tendencies and quality of mind. In the year 1878, on the other hand, he published three major articles, "Remarks on Spencer's *Definition of Mind As Correspondence*," "Brute and Human Intellect," and "Quelques Considérations sur la méthode subjective," all of them highly characteristic, and indicating that certain of his most fundamental ideas in both philosophy and psychology had already crystallized. *After* 1878, the stream of James's production flowed continuously and with increasing volume for thirty years—or until within a few months of his death.

He did not, however, cease to be interested in art and literature, and to express himself about them. Frequent trips to Europe multiplied his contacts and stimulated his interest in national traits. Nor did he ever lose interest in his brother's career, or cease to read and criticize his works. This interest was reciprocated, but not in like proportion. William sent Henry his articles and later his books; they were gratefully acknowledged and sometimes read, but there is little or no comment. It is quite clear that literature was more to William than was science or philosophy to Henry.

Henry had transferred his residence from Paris to London towards the end of the year 1876. William's letters for the next four years are missing, but there are echoes of them in the replies of his brother, who described his impressions of the persons in whom William would be interested—Huxley, Morley, Gladstone, Tennyson, and "the thundering Spencer." Meanwhile William kept up a running fire of criticism against his brother's literary style. *The Europeans* was "thin and empty"; there was no "fatness" or "bigness"—a tendency, in short, to sacrifice subject to form.[15] Henry usually admitted the fact without in the least conceding the principle.

William spent the summer of 1880 recuperating in Europe. It was during this summer that he first made the acquaintance of the two men he regarded as the "foremost philosophers" of his day, Shadworth Hodgson and Charles

[13] To Frances R. Morse, July 10, 1901; *L.W.J.*, II, 158.
[14] *Ibid.*
[15] *L.H.J.*², I, 65-6.

Renouvier.[16] He met the former in London where he spent a few weeks visiting his brother. From London he moved on to Germany where he renewed, in the company of G. Stanley Hall, his associations with physiological psychology. Hall had been James's student and associate at Harvard, and together they had frequented Bowditch's laboratory. He had been studying in Germany since 1878. The following is to Bowditch who had changed his plans and left Germany just before James's arrival.

Heidelberg, July 19 [1880]

Schurke, Lump, Unverschämter, Mensch, Halb-Physiolog, und so weiter! See what you lost by breaking your promise and running off in that cowardly way: I reached Cöln Wednesday midnight; found your letter and cards sent on from London assuring me you would wait Thursday for me in Heidelberg. I accordingly sacrificed one day I expected to spend on the Rhine, telegraphed you at nine o'clock, got to Heidelberg Thursday night only to find your *teuflisch höhnisch, selbstsüchtig,* badly-spelt illegible note saying you couldn't wait and boasting of your shameless carousals with Kühne[17] (which by the way I will report to your poor wife). Meanwhile Hall (who arrived also on Thursday night) and I have been carrying on the highest and most instructive conversation, which we would have let you listen to gratis had you been here. We talked twelve hours steadily on Friday, thirteen with a two-hour intermission at Kühne's lecture on Saturday, and thirteen and a half without an instant's intermission yesterday. He is a *herrlicher Mensch* and singularly solidified since being here. Speaking seriously, I wish to heaven you had stayed; three would have been better than two, even though the third were only an H. P. Bowditch. Hall left this A.M. for Paris via Cöln. He goes soon to London and almost certainly thence in August home, where I hope he'll get a place in Baltimore next winter. I start in an hour for Strassburg . . . and then to Basel and der Schweiz. . . .
Yours ever,

W. J.

From Switzerland he made a pilgrimage to Uriage-les-Bains, a watering-place near Grenoble, where in August he visited Renouvier, as recounted in the following letter to Hodgson from Cambridge on September 25:

Cambridge, Sept. 25, 1880

My dear Hodgson,—

Eyes, eyes, eyes! Not a bit better than when I left home, and you see I am writing by my wife's hand. They broke down entirely as soon as I began to walk in Switzerland, so that I have not read a line of your immortal works since I left you. I returned home three weeks earlier than I intended, and spent but three days in London on my way. I had a delightful day with Renouvier who is the queerest looking old boy you ever saw. He bore with apparent stoic fortitude —save a blinking of the eyes—what I told him of your articles, confessing to a

---

[16] *C.E.R.*, 133. For Shadworth H. Hodgson *cf.* below, 157.
[17] Wilke Kühne was professor of physiology at the University of Heidelberg.

great interest in your writings but saying that he found them *terriblement diffi-ciles à comprendre,* and fancying a part of the difficulty lay in his unfamiliarity with English.

I send you an anti-Spencerian squib of mine which has just appeared.[18] It was written and delivered as a lecture; the editor wiped out traces of this origin, and I did not see the proofs; however, *valeat quantum.* I can write no more now, but shall never forget the hours I spent with you in your room. "Conduit Street" shall be henceforth *dulcissimum mundi nomen* to my exiled Yankee ears. Always faithfully yours,

WM. JAMES

[18] "Great Men, Great Thoughts and the Environment," which appeared in the October number of the *Atlantic.*

XVII

EUROPEAN CONTACTS IN 1882-1883

In the summer of 1882, having secured a year's leave of absence, James went to Europe for a tour which lasted seven months. In its effect on his philosophical development this was the most important of all James's European adventures. He had taught continuously for eight consecutive years and had written numerous articles. But this time rest and health were subordinate motives. Nor did he go to Europe because he had run out of ideas—quite the contrary; he was eager to write, and was seeking an escape from the interruptions by which his time was being fruitlessly dissipated. He did not find this escape, and the amount of writing which he succeeded in doing was small. But in Europe his interruptions were of a more profitable sort, consisting mainly of personal contacts which both stimulated his thinking and fortified his self-confidence.

James was now not only thoroughly committed to the vocation of philosophy and psychology, but beginning to be known in Europe through his published articles. By this time, too, he had earned that reputation which has been so happily described by a recent biographer: "He could pass in America for the most cosmopolitan of philosophers and in Europe for the most American."[1] James was now able to play that important role for which his early training, as well as his personal traits, so admirably fitted him—ambassador of American thought and international "messenger of good will" to the countries of Western Europe. American thought was almost unknown in Europe. James represented both his own and that of others. His command of French and German, his witty and entertaining talk, his quick appreciation of merit, and his glowing kindliness won him the attachment and affection of a wide circle. Those who commended themselves to him he recommended to one another. His European friends, or their friends, visited him in Cambridge, and his American friends took letters of introduction to his European friends. He even introduced Europeans to Europeans. It happened not infrequently that his friends loved him more than they loved one another.

James went first to Germany where he made the acquaintance of the physicist and philosopher, Ernst Mach, with whom he felt a strong intellectual

---

[1] "Il a pu passer en Amérique pour le plus cosmopolite et en Europe pour le plus américain des philosophes"; M. Le Breton, *La Personnalité de William James*, 1929, 35.

affinity, perhaps because Mach, like himself, had arrived at his empirical philosophy by way of science. Here he also laid the foundations of an enduring friendship with the psychologist Carl Stumpf. James's published letters of this period breathe a note of heightened self-confidence. He has no apologies to make—for himself, for Harvard, or for America. His travels in Germany served only to confirm this feeling:

> My native *Geschwätzigkeit* triumphed over even the difficulties of the German tongue; I careered over the field, taking the pitfalls and breastworks at full run, and was fairly astounded myself at coming in alive. . . . We are a sound country and my opinion of our essential worth has risen and not fallen. We only lack abdominal depth of temperament and the power to sit for an hour over a single pot of beer without being able to tell at the end of it what we've been thinking about. . . . I saw in Germany all the men I cared to see and talked with most of them. With three or four I had a really nutritious time. . . . Nowhere did I see a university which seems to do for *all* its students anything like what Harvard does. Our methods throughout are better. . . . I certainly got a most distinct impression of my own *information* in regard to *modern* philosophic matters being broader than that of anyone I met, and our Harvard post of observation being more cosmopolitan.[2]

In October James passed several weeks in Venice, where his old conflicts were revived—the incompatibility between theorizing about art and simply enjoying it, and the alternation between the mood of despising Italy and that of succumbing to its fascination. The following letter reached his father shortly before his death on December 18:[3]

Venice, Oct. 23, 1882

My dear old Father,—

The sight of your robust handwriting in a letter that Harry transmitted to me three or four days ago, made me wish to write to you immediately, but I haven't been able to till now. . . . I have been here in Venice twenty-three days, and leave today reluctantly in the Trieste steamer at midnight. . . . I hate to leave the indescribable Italian charm, and to go back to the harsh North again. The *laissez aller* of everything in Italy is the most comfortable of all possible mediums to be plunged in,—just the antipodes of England. The poor natives are so broken in and inured to all the ups and downs and all the sights of life, that nothing astonishes them any more or shocks them; and they leave everyone alone and expect everyone to dress and talk and eat and drink and act and think, just as he pleases, though no one else should ever have done the like before him. . . .

I hate to leave the glorious pictures, which one has to see in such an infernally unsatisfactory way. They ought to be erected into a circulating library to which one might subscribe and have a masterpiece a month in his own house

---

[2] To A.H.J., November 2 and November 20, 1882; to H.J.[2], November 22, 1882; *L.W.J.*, I, 212, 216-7. For Carl Stumpf *cf.* below, 193 ff.

[3] *Cf.* also above, 34.

throughout the year. If anything can make one a fatalist it's the sight of the inevitable decay of each fine art after it reaches its maturity. I did think I might
scribble something about it for the *Nation,* but have thought better of it, as
the spirit of the cheap young Italian swell has gradually stolen over my soul,
who thinks that the truest philosophy is to straddle about St. Mark's Place and
watch the decay go on, with a pleasant smile on his face, a round topped hat
stuck on the side of his head with a curl escaping beneath it on his forehead, a
ready-made sack coat flung on his shoulders, and a six centime cigar between
his teeth. Whatever he may be, he is not a man of "formulas." I suddenly realized the other evening that I had got into exactly his position, barring the curl,
and felt at the same time how good it was to let the "formulas" rest a while.
But the *canaille* character of the population of St. Mark's Square is something
literally horrible when one thinks of what it once must have been. Cads of every
race, and to the outward eye hardly anything but cads. I imagine some old
patrician starting into indignant life again, merely to drive us away with his
maledictions. I'm sure we should all flee conscience-stricken at the sight of
him; for the energy of old Venice, as I've been reading it, must have been
something prodigious and incessant. . . .

I have felt many a time, dear old Father, in the last few weeks, how lone-
some you must be, and how dreadful a separation is where one can *get no letters.*
But I hope you'll have your recompense. I wish you'd send me the proofs of
what you're writing, as you get them. I would rather read them piecemeal. . . .
I am always your loving

W. J.

From Venice James proceeded through Germany and Belgium to Paris where
he had hoped to spend some weeks, and to see Renouvier later in the winter.
Receiving news of his father's illness, however, he hurried on to London, where
he joined his brother Henry and occupied the latter's apartment after Henry
had left for America. Here he remained until March, and despite family anxieties, nostalgia, and inability to accomplish any considerable amount of writing, this was a highly fruitful period in his philosophical development. It was
during these months that he found himself in the closest philosophical sympathy with Renouvier and Hodgson and entertained the hope that they might
find with one another the same bond which he felt with each.

Although James was at this time prevented from seeing Renouvier in the
flesh, as he had hoped, their proximity stimulated their correspondence, which
had been carried on intermittently since 1872, when James had written from
Cambridge:

> Thanks to you I possess for the first time an intelligible and reasonable con-
> ception of freedom. I accept it almost entirely. On other points of your phi-
> losophy I am beginning to experience a rebirth of the moral life; and I assure
> you, Monsieur, that this is no small thing! [4]

[4] November 2, 1872.

When James wrote this letter he was a young man of thirty, at the beginning of his career, while Renouvier was fifty-seven and long since a distinguished figure in the intellectual life of France. Despite this difference of age they held one another in equal esteem. As editor of the *Critique philosophique* Renouvier published translations of James's papers at frequent intervals. That Renouvier was the greatest individual influence on the development of James's thought cannot be doubted. The dedication of *Some Problems of Philosophy,* published posthumously in 1911, but prepared by James himself before his death, contains the following retrospective judgment:

> He [Charles Renouvier] was one of the greatest of philosophic characters, and but for the decisive impression made on me in the seventies by his masterly advocacy of pluralism, I might never have got free from the monistic superstition under which I had grown up. The present volume, in short, might never have been written. This is why, feeling endlessly thankful as I do, I dedicate this textbook to the great Renouvier's memory.

While it was Renouvier's doctrine of freedom, with its deliverance from the reigning monisms, in which James found his personal and moral salvation, he was no less attracted by Renouvier's theory of knowledge. In the same letter which has just been quoted he said: "Your philosophy seems, on its phenomenist side [*par son côté phénoméniste*] to be peculiarly qualified to appeal to minds trained in the English empirical school." James was here referring to his own training. But while he felt himself to be in the succession of Locke, Berkeley, Hume, and Mill in his acceptance of a philosophy based on experience, and nourished himself on their writings, he could not accept for himself the evil ways of scepticism, materialism, and determinism into which this school had fallen. He wished not only to join the school but save it, and he looked to Renouvier for help—to Renouvier and to Shadworth Hodgson.

During the months which James spent in London in the winter of 1882-1883 the tradition of empiricism was in the ascendancy. Of those who had developed it in that direction of naturalism and positivism which James deplored, W. K. Clifford had died in 1879, and T. H. Huxley was in full vigor. These two men were James's favorite examples of the unconscious passion of science. In the name of the "science" to which they were so intensely loyal they exhorted men to renounce their emotions. But, "How shall I say," asked James, "that knowing fact with Messrs. Huxley and Clifford is a better use to put my mind to than feeling good with Messrs. Moody and Sankey?" [5]

[5] *C.E.R.,* 66. For the most important reference to Huxley and to Clifford, the "delicious *enfant terrible,*" *cf. W.B.,* 8. Clifford's scientific creed is set forth in "The Ethics of Belief" in *Lectures and Essays,* 1879, II. James reviewed this work at length for the *Nation* in 1879 (*cf. C.E.R.,* 137), and, while he conceded its brilliancy, complained of its thinness and inconclusiveness. Clifford was also to James a favorite example of the "mind-stuff theory," and both Clifford and Huxley of the "automaton" theory.

Spencer lived until 1902, and was in these early '80s heroically working towards the completion of his "Synthetic Philosophy." But his great books had long since appeared and his vogue had passed its crest. For James he had served the purpose of a teething ring, and was outlived as an incident of his philosophical infancy. In any case James did not make any attempt to see Spencer.

Alexander Bain, although he lived until 1903, was James's senior by twenty-four years. With Hume, Mill, and Chauncey Wright, he belonged, in James's eyes, to the school of the sceptics and nihilists, who refused to be disturbed by the sheer arbitrariness and manyness of facts. But at the same time James had drawn upon him heavily in 1876-1879 in his thinking and writing on the motives of philosophizing, and later in his examination of the psychology of thought.

The Society for Psychical Research had been founded in England in February 1882, and during James's visit to England the president was Henry Sidgwick. This was the beginning of James's interest in the subject and of his acquaintance with this remarkable man. Their philosophical aloofness was no doubt due to their division of interest, Sidgwick being largely preoccupied with ethics, James with psychology and metaphysics; and to their profound difference of temperament, Sidgwick being as deliberate, rigorous, and critical as James was enthusiastic and speculative. James would have appreciated the full flavor of the feeling which led Leslie Stephen to say, in describing a meeting of the Metaphysical Society: "Sidgwick displayed that reflective candour which in him becomes at times a little irritating. A man has no right to be so fair to his opponents." [6]

The Metaphysical Society of London was one of the many groups which existed in England at this time for the purpose of uniting good fellowship and philosophy. The Aristotelian Society had been founded in 1880, and the Metaphysical Club was designed to have a more informal and intimate character. Writing on January 18, 1883, to his friend Thomas Davidson, James said: "I'm getting into the thick of philosophic society here." At the Aristotelian Society he met the Right Honorable Richard B. Haldane, the afterwards distinguished Chancellor of the Exchequer and War Secretary: "I went to the Aristotelian Society last night and had an instructive time. A . . . pupil of Caird was there, Haldane by name, and for all the world you would have thought it was dear old Palmer talking—same unrivaled fluency, same blamelessness of diction, same purity of thought." [7] But the nucleus of James's "philosophic

[6] F. W. Maitland, *Life and Letters of Leslie Stephen*, 1906, 333-4.
[7] W.J. to A.H.J., Feb. 6, 1883. R. B. Haldane, like Robert Bridges and W. R. Sorley, was a member of "The Tramps," but not of the Scratch Eight. George Herbert Palmer was W.J.'s distinguished elder colleague.

society" was the Scratch Eight, of which he became the ninth member. The first meeting which he attended is described in the following extract from a letter to his wife:—

> Dec. 16, 1882
>
> Last night I dined at Gurney's with the "Scratch Eight," spoken of in the invitation I enclosed to you. Gurney himself, whose *Power of Sound,* which I have now half finished, proves him to be one of the first-rate minds of the time, is a magnificent Adonis, six feet four in height, with an extremely handsome face, voice, and general air of distinction about him, altogether the exact opposite of classical idea of a philosopher. The other seven were Robertson, Hodgson, Sully, Carveth Read, Frederick Pollock, Leslie Stephen, and a certain Maitland, he being, so far as I know, the only one not known to fame. I felt quite at home among them, was asked to the next meeting, invited by Stephen and Pollock, etc. The discussion, carried on by Sully, Hodgson, and Robertson principally, seemed to show me that there was a great opening for my psychology. Story of Carlyle saying just before his death, apropos of Dean Stanley's desire to extend the hospitalities of Westminster Abbey, "that body-snatcher shan't have my corpse." But how tell of all these things when Father's ear, whom they would most interest, will perhaps not be able to hear!—Robertson has come and gone and I must haste to Hodgson's to dine and go afterwards to the Aristotelian Society.

At later meetings of the Scratch Eight James presented his own ideas—the central ideas of his new psychology—and felt a growing confidence both in the ideas and in his power to make them effective.

Of the members of the Scratch Eight, James's earliest and most intimate friend was George Croom Robertson, from 1867 professor of mental philosophy and logic at University College, London, and first editor of *Mind*. He was a man of James's own age and after his own heart. In fact he was one of those men who are fated to be enshrined in the hearts of their friends rather than in monuments of their own making. He was a thorough scholar and a magnetic teacher, but his very conscientiousness and generosity prevented any considerable volume of production.[8] He was essentially a *collaborator*. It was to Robertson that James had owed the revision and publication of several of his earliest philosophical and psychological articles in 1879, when his professorship was at stake.

Robertson's wife died in May 1892, and Robertson himself survived her only four months. Ten days before his wife's death he had written to James that he had given up hope of her recovery. The letter reached James in Europe and the following is his reply:—

---

[8] His scattered writings, other than his volume on *Hobbes,* were published in 1894 under the title of *Philosophical Remains*.

Freiburg, June 15, 1892

My dear old Friend,—

Your heart-rending letter of the 21st of May has just been put into my hands, forwarded from Cambridge. How sorry I am, how sorry I am! And what a burden you both of you have had to carry all these years. . . . But my dear fellow, in all the darkness, "as of night eternal," that girdles us about, there must be *some* ulterior significance in the fact that the hearts of onlookers are so warmed when they see calamities such as yours have been endured with such a staunch and uncomplaining spirit. The experience of which *that* is an integral part cannot interiorly be as bad as it outwardly seems. You of course know your own weaknesses, and your own failures and disgusts; but I assure you that to others your life has been a source of deepest inspiration—and more I cannot say. . . . Good-bye, my dear old Robertson! Warmest love . . . from your friend

WM. JAMES

After 1880 and for the twelve remaining years of his life Robertson was afflicted with a fatal and painful disease which, after the Stoic teaching, he seized as *his* opportunity to live nobly. When James wrote of his death and of the "perfume" which his manliness left behind, he reverted in memory to this season of 1882-1883: "Whom did he not help whom he could help,—even when most needing help himself? I, for one, can never forget what I owe to his encouragement and indefatigable kindliness many years ago, in an otherwise dark London winter." [9]

Let us return to the Scratch Eight as James knew them in 1882-1883. For Leslie Stephen, who was ten years his senior, James felt both admiration and affection. But there could be no profound sympathy between the two men. Stephen inclined to the pessimistic, deterministic, or left wing of empiricism; James to the right. James Sully, whom James met for the first time at a dinner of the Scratch Eight, was a lifelong friend whose judgment he respected in matters of psychology rather than of philosophy. "We took to one another," he wrote, "in a quiet steadfast fashion"; and when, in 1910, James died, Sully spoke of him as "one of the strong supporters of my life." [10] The following was written by James after returning from a European trip in 1908:

My last ten days in England were very tumultuous and hurried. . . . I am very sorry not to have seen you after all. . . . The fact is that my duties as *pater familias* interfered very much with my own inclinations, which were sedentary and sociable towards my old friends. . . . I didn't see dear old Shadworth Hodgson, which I also much regretted. How times have changed! Of all the members of that philosophical dining club, to which you so kindly

[9] *Philos. Rev.*, II (1893), 255.
[10] James Sully, *My Life and Friends*, T. F. Unwin, Ltd., 1918, 221, 249.

admitted me in 1882, you, he and I are the only survivors, if I remember aright. Gurney, Robertson, Stephen and Maitland are gathered in.[11]

The first of the circle to be "gathered in" (in 1888, at the age of forty-one) was Edmund Gurney, he whom James loved the most. Loyalty to Gurney and admiration for "his devotion to this unfashionable work" constituted one of the strong motives that impelled James to stick by the ship of psychical research.[12] But this was by no means the only, or indeed the chief virtue that commended Gurney to James. He saw in him the promise of an "intellectual synthesis" that should be "solider and completer than that of anyone . . . except perhaps Royce." [13] Adding to Gurney's "rare metaphysical power," his "tenderest heart," it is not strange that in Gurney's death "the destroying angel had outdone even himself in heartlessness." [14] To Robertson he wrote on August 22, 1888:

> Poor Gurney! How I shall miss that man's presence in the world. I think, to compare small things with great, that there was a very unusual sort of affinity between my mind and his. Our problems were the same, and for the most part our solutions. I eagerly devoured every word he wrote, and was always conscious of him as critic and judge. He had both quantity and quality, and I hoped for some big philosophic achievement from him ere he should get through. And now—*omnia ademit una dies infesta*—! The world is grown hollower.

The closing words of the posthumous tribute, written by their common friend F. W. H. Myers, might have been uttered by James himself: "Not in vain did his heart grieve for human woe. He beat against the bars of our earthly prison-house, and he has forced a narrow opening through which we seem to breathe immortal air." [15]

On January 13, 1883, James wrote to his wife:

> I had a delightful evening last night at the Scratch Eight. Charming fellows all. Gurney strikes me as a big man with any amount of loose power about him. But Hodgson is simply an incarnate angel, the most exquisite human creature I ever knew, a *gentleman* to his finger tips and a professional philosopher as well. I love the rare combination.

While Gurney became the dearest of the English circle, it was the "divine" Shadworth Hodgson upon whom James drew most heavily for philosophical

[11] November 9, 1908. James had evidently forgotten Frederick Pollock, who still survived.
[12] To Carl Stumpf, February 6, 1887; *L.W.J.*, I, 267.
[13] W.J. to H.J.[2], July 11, 1888; *L.W.J.*, I, 280. For Royce *cf.* below, Ch. XVIII.
[14] *Nation*, XLVII (1888), 53.
[15] *Proc. of Soc. for Psych. Research*, V (1889-9). For Myers *cf.* below, 204 *ff.*

sustenance—Hodgson, "the wealthiest mine of thought" he "ever met with." [16]
Hodgson was a private scholar, ten years older than James, but destined to outlive him; a man respected by his contemporaries with whom he engaged in
talk, and neglected by the posterity which can approach him only through his
books. He was, like James, and before James, a reformed empiricist, who
hoped to restore the prestige of the British tradition. James looked upon him
as an ally in this cause. Like James, and like Renouvier, Hodgson waged war
against all substances and substrata, in behalf of phenomena—things as they are
given in experience. It was James's ardent but vain hope that his two great
philosophers should be as great to one another as they were to him. He strode
cheerfully in the middle, arm in arm with each, and turning now to the one
and now to the other with beaming friendliness; while his half-reluctant partners to right and left responded in kind to James, but greeted one another with
what was at best an amiable grimace. Not only did Renouvier and Hodgson
fail to discover one another as soul-mates, but James himself, despite his un-
dying gratitude, came soon to feel that neither of them fulfilled the destiny to
which he had appointed them. Despite their professions of empiricism they
both, he thought, succumbed in the end to the germs of rationalism—even of
monism—with which they had been infected in their early training.

These months which brought James so much intellectual and personal stimulation, were nevertheless months of discontent. His normal homesickness was
aggravated by bereavement. His mother had died in the preceding January,
and now his father, too, had died, on December 18, before Henry had been able
to reach him. This mood of depression was reflected in his comments on his
surroundings, written to his brother in Boston:

[London] Jan. 9, 1883 [17]

My dear Harry,—
. . . The complete absence of any aggregate and outward expression of pure
and direct intelligence is what is so striking here. After Paris, London seems
like a mediæval village, with nothing but its blanket of golden dirt to take the
place of style, beauty, and rationality. At times one feels as if the former were
a poor substitute. And then one does grow impatient at times with the universal
expression of aggregate stupidity—stupidity heavy and massive, with a sort of
voluntary self-corroboration, the like whereof exists nowhere else under the
sun. Germany is the abode of the purest grace and lucency compared with this
life, clogged with every kind of senseless unnecessariness, and moving down the
centuries under its thick swathings, all unconscious of its load. It appeals to me
as a physical image, with which doubtless the meteorological conditions of my
stay here have something to do: England under a filthy, smeary, smoky fog,
lusty and happy, hale and hearty, with the eternal sunlit ether outside, and she

[16] W.J. to Josiah Royce, February 16, 1879; *L.W.J.*, I, 203.
[17] A paragraph from this letter is cited above, 41.

not suspecting, or not caring to think that with a puff of her breath she might rend the veil and be there.

You ought to have seen the Rossetti exhibition,—the work of a boarding-school girl, no color, no drawing, no cleverness of any sort, nothing but feebleness incarnate, and a sort of refined intention of an extremely narrow sort, with no technical power to carry it out. Yet such expressions of admiration as I heard from the bystanders! Then the theatres, and the hippopotamus-like satisfaction of their audiences! Bad as our theatres are, they are not so massively hopeless as that. It makes Paris seem like a sort of Athens. Then the determination on the part of all who write . . . to do it as amateurs, and never to use the airs and language of a professional; to be first of all a layman and a gentleman, and to pretend that your ideas came to you accidentally as it were, and are things you care nothing about. As I said, it makes one impatient at times; and one finds himself wondering whether England can afford forever, when her rivals are living by the light of pure rationality to so great an extent, to go blundering thus unsystematically along, and trusting to mere luck to help her to find what is good, a fragment at a time. It's a queer mystery. She never *has* failed to find it hitherto in perhaps richer measure than they, by her method of blundering into it. But will it always last? and can she *always* fight without stripping? Won't the general clearness and keenness of a rational age force her to throw some of her nonsense away, or to fall behind the rest? . . . Ever your affectionate brother,

WM. JAMES

To Henry, who took a very different view of England, it was incredible that William should insist on hurrying home. In a letter of January 11 which crossed William's he wrote:

You speak of being "determined to sail at latest in the *Servia* of Feb. 11th." . . . The *pity* of it almost brings tears to my eyes, and when I look upon the barren scene (bating your wife and babes) that awaits you here, I feel as if I were justified in doing almost anything to keep you on the other side. . . . It is a chance, an opportunity, which may not come to you again for years. All this came over me much as this morning I went out to poor *nudified* and staring Cambridge, and thought that *that* and your life there is what you are in such a hurry to get back to! At furthest you will take up that life soon enough; *interpose,* therefore, as much as you can before that day—continue to interpose the Europe that you are already in possession of. . . . Therefore I say, stick to Europe till the summer, in spite of everything, in the faith that you are getting a great deal out of it and that it is a good and valuable thing.

To which William replied on January 23:

The horror you seem to feel at Cambridge is something with which I have no sympathy, preferring it as I do to any place in the known world. Quite as little do I feel the infinite blessing of simply being in London, or in Europe *überhaupt.* The truth is, we each of us speak from the point of view of his own work; the place where a man's work is best done seems and ought to seem the place of places to him. I feel tempted to go back now just to show you how happy a man can be in the wretched circumstances that so distress your imagination.

Some improvement in his health and capacity for work, the ripening of his friendships, and perhaps his brother's exhortations, led James to prolong his London sojourn—but only until March.

XVIII

JOSIAH ROYCE AND IDEALISM

When James resumed his teaching in the autumn of 1883, the Department of Philosophy had been enlarged by the addition of Josiah Royce; called from California to replace James during his absence, but now permanently retained and destined to become one of Harvard's most illustrious scholars and James's intimate colleague and neighbor. The story of James's relations with Royce constitute the central thread of his relations with "idealism"—that philosophy which sprang from Kant, was developed in Germany by Fichte, Hegel, Schelling, and Schopenhauer, and having been transplanted to England, was now rapidly achieving ascendancy in the United States. James's elder colleague George Herbert Palmer was one of its milder advocates, but it was Royce who became its most powerful and to James its most formidable protagonist.

To James in 1883, neither idealism nor Royce was a novelty and he had long since been gathering ammunition with which to combat them. In 1868 he had written to Holmes: "Already I see an ontological cloud of absolute idealism waiting for me far off on the horizon, but I have no passion for the fray." [1] That passion soon developed. At first he attacked idealism with the lighter weapons which he knew so well how to wield. He referred to the group of American idealists as "the white-winged band" whose "sacerdotal airs" contrasted strangely with the "sterility" of their thought.[2] He spoke of resisting the inroads of this philosophy ("too fundamentally rotten and charlatanish to last long") as his principal "amusement" during the winter of 1879-1880.[3] In his famous essay "On Some Hegelisms" published in 1882 he scandalized his idealistic friends by comparing Hegelian dialectic with the experience of nitrous-oxide-gas intoxication. In an article published in 1884 he wrote:

> Certainly, to my personal knowledge, all Hegelians are not prigs, but I somehow feel as if all prigs ought to end . . . by becoming Hegelians. . . . The "through and through" philosophy, as it actually exists . . . seems too but-

[1] May 15, 1868; *cf.* above, 96.
[2] To Royce, February 3, 1880; *L.W.J.*, I, 205.
[3] To Renouvier, December 27, 1880; *L.W.J.*, I, 208.

toned-up and white-chokered and clean-shaven a thing to speak for the vast slow-breathing Kosmos with its dread abysses and its unknown tides. [4]

But as time went on he acquired a growing respect for this philosophy, until at the end of his life he counted Hegelians as one of the "great types of cosmic vision." [5] While he steadily maintained that "the line of philosophic progress" lay "not so much *through* Kant as *round* him," and that "the truth can be built much better by simply extending Locke's and Hume's lines," [6] he came to realize that idealism could not be dismissed lightly. He spent years in earning the right to reject it, and this toughening of his philosophical sinews he owed largely to his relations with Josiah Royce.

In 1888, on July 26, James wrote to Renouvier of Royce: "I am in a measure his sponsor, having discovered him in California and brought him to Harvard College where my feebly burning philosophic star is far eclipsed by his luminary." Royce, who was thirteen years younger than James, was born in Grass Valley, on the slopes of the Sierras, and was educated in the public schools of San Francisco, and at the University of California. He continued his studies at Johns Hopkins University and spent a year in Germany, where he was profoundly influenced by the philosophy and literature of the romantic movement. While he was in the East he called upon James, and this meeting was described by him at a dinner held in the James's house in 1910:

> My real acquaintance with our host began one summer day in 1877, when I first visited him in the house on Quincy Street, and was permitted to pour out my soul to somebody who really seemed to believe that a young man might rightfully devote his life to philosophy if he chose. . . . James found me at once—made out what my essential interests were at our first interview, accepted me, with all my imperfections, as one of those many souls who ought to be able to find themselves in their own way, gave a patient and willing ear to just my variety of philosophical experience, and used his influence from that time on, not to win me as a follower, but to give me my chance. . . . Whatever I am is in that sense due to him. . . .
>
> Sometimes critical people have expressed this by saying that James has always been too fond of cranks, and that the cranks have loved him. Well, I am one of James's cranks. He was good to me, and I love him. The result of my own early contact with James was to make me for years very much his disciple. I am still in large part under his spell. If I contend with him sometimes, I suppose that it is he also who through his own free spirit has in great measure taught me this liberty. [7]

When James went abroad in 1882-1883 he recommended that Royce be appointed for the year, hoping and predicting that once Royce was on the

[4] "Absolutism and Empiricism," *Mind*, IX (1884), 285, reprinted in *E.R.E.*, 276-8.
[5] *P.U.*, 108.
[6] *C.E.R.*, 436-7; Notes made in 1896-7 for an article on Kant which he never published.
[7] *Harvard Graduates' Magazine*, XVIII (1910), 631-2.

ground he would make a permanent place for himself in the Department—as, in fact, he did. In their early correspondence James and Royce found themselves for a time in agreement. Both were interested in "the motives which lead men to philosophize," [8] James having led the way with his essay (written in 1877 and published in 1879) on "The Sentiment of Rationality"; and both found its deeper motives in the will rather than in pure intellect. They had other bonds, philosophical, moral, and neighborly. But as time went on it became more and more evident that agreement between descendants of the British and Kantian schools could be no more than temporary and superficial. Empiricism and pluralism were in James's blood—rationalism and monism in Royce's. When Royce's first book, *The Religious Aspect of Philosophy,* appeared in 1885, James recommended it to Hodgson, Renouvier, and his other philosophical friends not so much for what he agreed with as because it contained an original argument for "The Absolute"—that all-embracing and over-ruling spiritual being which Kant's successors (and notably the Hegelians) found both congenial and demonstrable. James would have none of it, but it took him some years to find answers to the arguments, and especially to Royce's argument, which proceeded from much the same starting-point as his own. Human ideas refer to objects which lie beyond themselves; they are either true or false; and their truth or falsity must therefore lie within a super-consciousness which envelopes both the idea and its object. It was not until the early nineties that, after a "final bout with Royce's theory," [9] James was finally convinced that both the idea and its object, and the reference of the one to the other, could be brought within human experience, thus rendering the Absolute as unnecessary intellectually as it was objectionable morally.

A glimpse of Royce's personality is afforded by passages from a letter to James written when the former was on one of the sea-voyages in which he was accustomed to find refreshment from his academic labors:

> Southern Ocean, circ. 600 miles out of Melbourne
> Lat. circ. 40° S; Long. circ. 135° E.
> May 21, 1888

Dear James,—

It ought to be a long letter, if it were to undertake to tell the whole story of my life since I last saw Boston Light; but it must be a short one, since I have so many others to write. . . . With the winds and the birds of the southern sea came a new life. My wits had been working all along. In the deepest of my nothingness I read mechanics, and mathematics, and Martineau, and even Casanova, with an impartial insight into the essential nothingness of definite integrals, easily conquered maidens, and divine laws—one and all. But while I mused dispassionately upon the world of passion, my head was clear so far as the

[8] *Mind* (IV), 346, footnote.
[9] W.J. to Dickinson S. Miller, November 19, 1893; *L.W.J.*, II, 18.

mere mechanics of thinking went. And now that passion has come again, and the good Lord seems to have some life in his world of *Sonnen und Milchstrassen,* my wits grow more constructive, and I more and more look upon the voyage as a very highly educating experience. In fine, I have largely straightened out the big metaphysical tangle about continuity, freedom, and the world-formula which, as you remember, I had aboard with me when I started. . . .

My companionships aboard the ship have been highly agreeable. The Captain, as Yankee and Cape Cod man, who has read a good deal in the long sea hours of his life, is contemplative. Once in a while I have to explain to him metaphysics, as thus: We sit on deck in the tropics, gazing into the heavens, and talking over Newcomb's *Astronomy,* which Captain has been reading. He grows now more and more meditative over the vast stellar distances, and the rest, and at last observes: "Well, sometimes it seems to me like nothing so much as a dream. Don't it ever occur to you that perhaps the whole thing above there and our life, too, is a dream of ours, and perhaps there ain't anything anyhow, that's real?" I admit having had such thoughts. "Well now, what do you teach your classes at Harvard about all this?" Thus called upon to explain amid the trade-winds, and under the softly flapping canvas, the mysteries of absolute idealism, I put the thing thus: "There was once a countryman," I say, "from Cape Cod, who went to Boston to hear Mark Twain lecture, and to delight his soul with the most mirth-compelling of our humorists. But, as I have heard, when he was in Boston, he was misdirected, so that he heard not Mark Twain, but one of Joseph Cook's Monday Lectures. But he steadfastly believed that he was hearing Mark. So when he went home to Cape Cod, they asked him of Mark Twain's lecture. 'Was it *very* funny?' 'Oh, it was *funny,* yes,—it was *funny,*' replies the countryman cautiously, 'but then, you see, it wasn't so *damned* funny.' Even so, Captain," say I, "I teach at Harvard that the world and the heavens, and the stars are all *real,* but not so *damned* real, you see." The Captain has been a devout student of the *Religious Aspect* from time to time ever since, though in lucid intervals he affirms that the whole is consarned nonsense. . . . The rest of the ship's life is very amusing, on the whole. I escaped altogether sea-sickness, at the outset of the voyage, probably because of my abnormal nerves. God be with thine house. . . . Yours very truly,

JOSIAH ROYCE

As time went on, James passed from the defense to the attack, and from attack to tolerance. In 1899 he wrote:

Since teaching *The Conception of God* I have come to perceive what I didn't trust myself to believe before, that looseness of thought is R's *essential* element. He *wants* it. There isn't a tight joint in his system; not one. And yet I thought that a mind that could talk me blind and black and numb on mathematics and logic, and whose favorite recreation is works on those subjects, must necessarily conceal closeness and exactitudes of ratiocination that I hadn't the wit to find out. But no! he is the Rubens of philosophy. Richness, abundance, boldness, color, but a sharp contour never, and never any *perfection.* But isn't fertility better than perfection? [10]

[10] To Dickinson S. Miller, January 31, 1899; *L.W.J.,* II, 86.

In 1899 Royce delivered his course of Gifford Lectures, and in 1900 James went abroad for the same purpose. Selections from their correspondence reveal a friendship undiminished by profound philosophical disagreement. Royce wrote from Cambridge on September 12, 1900:

> The year to come will be very lonesome without you, and my own interest in Harvard is more bound up with my associations with you than it is with any one other interest. Philosophy I love for itself, and life for its general meaning. But Harvard originally meant to me *you,* and the old association remains still the deepest. I shall go on, and lecture; but the Department can have its real meaning to me personally only when you are here. And I ought the more plainly to say that, because I am so poor a letter writer, and so silent, that you must think me less bound up in you than I always am. My defect as a letter writer is simply a result of my writing so much otherwise. The writing centres rebel at anything but lectures and books. But the heart has its own life too, and I miss you deeply.

To which James replied as follows:

Nauheim, Sept. 26, 1900 [11]

Beloved Royce,—

Great was my . . . pleasure in receiving your long and delightful letter last night. . . . I need not say, my dear old boy, how touched I am at your expressions of affection, or how it pleases me to hear that you have missed me. I too miss you profoundly. I do not find in the hotel waiters, chambermaids and bathattendants with whom my lot is chiefly cast, that unique mixture of erudition, originality, profundity and vastness, and human wit and leisureliness, by accustoming me to which during all these years you have spoilt me for inferior kinds of intercourse. You are still the centre of my gaze, the pole of my mental magnet. When I write, 'tis with one eye on the page, and one on you. When I compose my Gifford lectures mentally, 'tis with the design exclusively of overthrowing your system, and ruining your peace. I lead a parasitic life upon you, for my highest flight of ambitious ideality is to become your conqueror, and go down into history as such, you and I rolled in one another's arms and silent (or rather loquacious still) in one last death-grapple of an embrace. How then, O my dear Royce, can I forget you, or be contented out of your close neighborhood? Different as our minds are, yours has nourished mine, as no other social influence ever has, and in converse with you I have always felt that my life was being lived importantly. Our minds, too, are not different in the *Object* which they envisage. It is the whole paradoxical physico-moral-spiritual Fatness, of which most people single out some skinny fragment, which we both cover with our eye. We "aim at him generally"—and most others don't. I don't believe that we shall dwell apart forever, though our formulas may. . . . Love to you all,

W. J.

It is impossible to understand James's relations with the Kantian-idealistic movement of his time unless we take into account the peculiar prestige which that movement enjoyed. It claimed a sort of apostolic succession, after Leibnitz, in the line of the great philosophers that sprang from Plato. This claim was so widely acknowledged that in the last decades of the nineteenth century philosophers of other schools, especially in England and America, felt themselves on the defensive. This state of mind accounts not only for the time which it took James to throw off the yoke, but for the violence with which he did so. Towards the end of his life emotions of respect and disrespect tended to give place to a more even tone. Once it was deflated and its arrogant pretensions discredited, absolute idealism took its place among the major hypotheses from which the philosopher must make his choice.

It was during this same formative period of the early eighties when he was coming to terms with idealism, that James was most intimately associated with Thomas Davidson and George H. Howison. He hoped to wean them from their idealistic predispositions by appealing to their individualism, since they, like James, repudiated the monistic Absolute; but in spite of his best efforts they declined to accept that wholehearted empiricism which he believed to be the only road to pluralism.

James had a great gift for the memorial essay. This was one of his ways of substituting the pen for that paintbrush he had laid down so many years before. Perhaps the finest of these memorial essays was dedicated to the uprooted Scotchman, Thomas Davidson—"a knight-errant," he calls him, "of the intellectual life"; a man of his own age, a boon companion, with an endearing mixture of traits, homely and ennobling. James speaks of his "broad brow, his big chest, his bright blue eyes, his volubility in talk and laughter" that "told a tale of vitality far beyond the common." He was a man to be out of doors with, in that Adirondack wilderness which both men loved so well. But he was as tender as he was irascible, and as sensitive as he was robust: dictatorial, aggressive, but profoundly human—altogether a man of "massive" proportions.[12]

Although Davidson held no academic post and despised "academicism," he was a man of vast erudition and of strong intellectual enthusiasms, who attached himself to the Continental rather than the British tradition in philosophy, revering Kant and having a low opinion of Spencer and Mill. He had come to Boston in 1875, and it was not long after his arrival that he associated himself with William James's fortunes by introducing him to the Alice Gibbens who afterwards became Mrs. William James.

In St. Louis, where he had taught Greek in the high school, Davidson had participated in the so-called "St. Louis Movement." This remarkable cultural manifestation was the result of the association in that city of two unusual men, Henry C. Brokmeyer and William T. Harris. The former, an extraordinary blend of the scholar, the reformer, the soldier, the artisan, the adventurer, and

---

[12] *M.S.*, 76-7.

the politician, migrated from Germany in 1844. He settled in St. Louis, launched upon a political career during the Civil War, and eventually became lieutenant governor and acting governor of the state (1875-1877). Meanwhile, however, he had been spreading the gospel of Hegel. William T. Harris (afterwards United States Commissioner of Education) had come to St. Louis in 1857, as a teacher in the public schools. He at once met Brokmeyer and placed himself under his instruction. In 1866 the two men organized the so-called St. Louis Philosophical Society, of which Thomas Davidson and George H. Howison became members. Harris, Davidson, and Howison all came afterwards to Boston and thus transplanted Hegelianism from west to east.

In James's philosophical encounters with Davidson in the early eighties he found himself, the empiricist, defending God against Davidson, the rationalist. James was at this time espousing[13] the idea of a temporal, finite God on whose support the moral will of man might rely in its struggle against evil. Davidson, on the other hand, would have none of this God; but deified man himself, and conceived the world as a community of "spirits," eternal in nature and unified by a spirit of harmony and love. Davidson wrote to James on December 14, 1881:

> Of a *real* God we know absolutely nothing, and we are only yielding to an inveterate prejudice and repeating a popular watchword when we say we do. I find, moreover, plenty and more than plenty of aim in the universe, to call out my best efforts, and keep aflame my deepest enthusiasms, without the aid of any such popular idol. Blessedness for myself and others, blessedness for myself through others, and for others through me—that is more than any heaven that an omnipotent God could give. I am eternal, without beginning or end: that is as clear to me today as the fact that I am at this instant. For my highest blessedness I am dependent upon the concurrence of all other *I*'s, in whatever stage of development, whether reciprocally cancelled as matter, or instinct with pure energy, as all-sympathetic spirits. In one sense the positivists are right. Humanity is God; humanity alone, so far as we know, "makes for righteousness" —at least, consciously. But the whole universe is moving toward blessedness; for the most part blindly; in good men, seeingly. God is love, in the strictest sense of the term. Evil is the result of blindness and narrowness, mere false combination, mere disharmony. When we have done away with God and shifted the responsibility for the well-being of the world upon our own shoulders, where it belongs, we shall begin to feel the duties of consciousness to the universe. Not till then!

To which James replied on January 8, 1882:

> It is a curious thing, this matter of God! I can sympathize perfectly with the most rabid hater of him and the idea of him, when I think of the use that has

---

[13] In his essay "Reflex Action and Theism," afterwards incorporated into his *The Will to Believe and other Essays*, 1897.

been made of him in history and philosophy as a *starting-point,* or premise for grounding deductions. But as an ideal to attain and make probable, I find myself less and less able to do without him. He need not be an *all*-including "subjective unity of the universe." . . . All I mean is that there must be *some* subjective unity in the universe which has purposes commensurable with my own, and which is at the same time large enough to be, among all the powers that may be there, the strongest. . . . In saying "God exists" all I imply is that my purposes are cared for by a mind so powerful as on the whole to control the drift of the universe. . . . The only difficulties of theism are the moral difficulties and meannesses; and they have always seemed to me to flow from the gratuitous dogma of God being the all-exclusive reality. Once think possible a primordial pluralism of which he may be one member and which may have no single subjective synthesis, and piety forthwith ceases to be incompatible with manliness, and religious "faith" with intellectual rectitude. . . . What news can I tell you? Nothing in the College, where the old routine prevails. Harris has founded a weekly Saturday afternoon Hegel Club where he expounds the third volume of the *Logik* to ten of us, Palmer, Cabot, Hall, Everett, Emery[14] and some others. I am much won by his innocence and apostolic disposition, but not a word has he said that has any magic for me.

During his unhappy weeks of homesickness and indecision in London in 1883 James was strongly tempted to join Davidson in Italy, and to Davidson he wrote frequently after his return. He had promised to find him, if possible, a teaching position in America, and in December he proposed to President Eliot that Davidson should be appointed at Harvard. This effort failed, as, indeed, James had expected. His misgivings he communicated to Davidson, together with friendly admonition:

Cambridge, Dec. 20 [1883]

Tomasino mio!

   . . . I write now in great haste to tell you this: Sophocles[15] died three days ago, and the day after, I went to the President and told him that if that made a new opening, I wished he would consider your claims, saying that "Ancient Philosophy" was a thing you would like to take care of as much as anything. . . . He seemed struck by what I said of you. . . . But I can not disguise the fact, you rambustious old eternal individual, that the President and Fellows will hear many headshakings as to your *safety* as a *character*. Indiscretion, immoderation, lack of tact, quarrelsomeness, dogmatism, conceit, general red-hotness, will be among the sins of which you will be accused, and will make them doubt, whatever your learning and intellect may be, whether you ought to be set down in such a happy family as the College Faculty. I hear such accusations already often when I mention your name, and they all sum themselves up into this one, that whether you be right or wrong in any particular case, you do, as a matter of fact, succeed in strewing your path with enemies, and that

<hr/>

[14] J. E. Cabot, Emerson's biographer; for G. Stanley Hall *cf.* below, 182 ff.; C. C. Everett, Dean of the Harvard faculty of Theology, S. H. Emery, Jr., was director of the Concord School of Philosophy.

[15] Evangelinus Apostolides Sophocles, tutor and professor of Greek at Harvard, 1842-83.

is, of course, considered a point against you. In vain I say that those enemies know you superficially, and that if they knew you as I did, they would all end by rather preferring you to their own selves. Their mere existence acts as a warning, and is a label "beware" put upon you. I judge it best to talk to you thus frankly, as it makes you acquainted with the direction of the danger you most have to fear, and *may* help you to meet it. I hope to Heaven something may come of this, but am not too sanguine. Don't you be so either. I and others will "work" all we can for you, and do you be very dignified and grandisonian. The disease the College is dying of is the lack of a few men like you in it, but what is one to do in a country in which "safety" is the one principle used to settle intellectual matters? . . . Ever your friend,

WM. JAMES

The years that follow tell the usual story of a friendship that outlives intellectual sympathy. James said that the more he knew Davidson the fonder he grew of him; he would not have said "the more I agreed with him." Each had taken his own way of thinking. Even James's moral individualism was to Davidson only "a happy-go-lucky Stevensonian adventuresomeness." [16] Meanwhile the old love remained, slightly reminiscent in flavor, but showing itself unabated when major events such as books or sickness overtook either of them. Then from Europe on February 16, 1900, to his "Darling old T. D.":

One can meet mortal (or would-be mortal) disease either by gentlemanly levity, by high-minded stoicism, or by religious enthusiasm. I advise you, old T.D., to follow my example and try a playful *durcheinander* of all three, taking each in turn *pro re nata*.[17] . . . We are here for six weeks, along with F. W. H. Myers and family, in Charles Richet's[18] empty château, between Toulon and Hyères, most hospitably lent us by C. R. The climate is glorious, and the conditions excellent for nerve rest. . . . I was *very* low in England until January. Acute nervous prostration on top of the heart trouble. Of course the latter is the serious thing.

To this Davidson replied on May 4:

I need not tell you, my dear fellow, that I am deeply grieved at your condition. It seems more serious than mine, which is not threatening to life. But I am sure you are taking yours too seriously. You will yet be strong, and able to continue your work, if you will give yourself rest and refrain from brooding. That is what I am doing. I don't for a moment think of leaving this blessed life, and even if I knew I had to do so, it would not worry me. . . . Death means to me little more than going into the next room. I have all my life been quite at home with death.

[16] Davidson to W.J., March 29, 1897.
[17] As occasion may require.
[18] The bond uniting Myers, Richet, and James was their common interest in psychical research.

Davidson was well enough to go to Glenmore again shortly after this last and hopeful letter was written. But the following September James learned of his sudden death—

> One September day in 1900, at the "Kurhaus" at Nauheim, I took up a copy of the Paris *New York Herald,* and read in capitals: "Death of Professor Thomas Davidson." I had well known how ill he was, yet such was his vitality that the shock was wholly unexpected. I did not realize till that moment how much that free companionship with him every spring and autumn, surrounded by that beautiful nature, had signified to me, or how big a piece would be subtracted from my life by its cessation.[19]

Although George Holmes Howison was James's senior in age by eight years, they were philosophical contemporaries. In 1872, only a year before James began his teaching at Harvard, Howison became professor of logic and the philosophy of science at the Massachusetts Institute of Technology in Boston. In 1884 he was appointed to the University of California where generations of students were impressed by the strength of his conviction and stirred by his moral earnestness. Despite their wide separation James and Howison maintained a close friendship until the year of the former's death.

During his residence in Boston Howison belonged to the circle of those who, like James, Davidson, and Palmer, were studying Hegel, stimulated if not converted by Harris's sectarian zeal. They were all *discovering* Hegel and, each in his own way, coming to terms with him. As between Hegel and his belittlers, Howison's sympathies at this time were with Hegel. Later he became convinced "that Hegel, with all his robust personal intentions to rout pantheism, never attained to any systematic view compatible with his religious and political aims. Everywhere, he, after all, plants the corporate to the logical obliteration of the individual being." In view of Howison's emphasis on the moral individual in his later advocacy of what he called *"personal* idealism," it was surprising, and a cause of some disappointment to Howison himself, that his philosophy should have played no part in James's pluralism. The explanation lies in their different roots—James being by temperament and association a descendant of British empiricism, while the blood which flowed in Howison's veins was, however much he might quarrel with them, the blood of Kant and Hegel. Many years afterwards, in commenting on Howison's *Limits of Evolution,* James set forth in words that he might equally have addressed to Royce or Davidson, why he could not agree in fundamentals even with the best of the Kantian-Hegelian tribe:

> First of all, the style is a delight and a refresher, in this vulgar world, by its elevation and distinction, along with its rare perspicuity. The book is a gentle-

man (—or a lady?)! What seems to me its strength is the radical and direct and uncompromising way in which it lays down a conception of the world on lines of *rational fitness*. Few today dare to be so aggressively and positively teleological. . . . The weakness of this book seems to me to lie in the *purity* with which the considerations of teleological fitness disport themselves. You seem almost unconscious of the *prima facie* rebelliousness of the world of facts. You simply *override* them, strong in your conviction of the ultimate ideality, whereas with most of us their brutality and madness are the principal stimulus to thought; and *untying* the knot, not *cutting* it, is what we want help in doing. . . . I must say that for my mind your deduction of evil from the logical necessity of some *defect,* in the definition of every finite, doesn't meet the want; and I find myself more and more disposed to believe in irrationality as the *prius,* out of which ideality slowly and empirically emerges by a *de facto* process of evolution—or, if you wish, of improvement by alteration. . . . But no matter! I won't cavil, for the book is a noble book; and you on the right flank and I on the left flank will execute one of Kitchener's sweeping movements, and clear the country of all boors, monists, fatalists, and annex it in the name of the pluralistic philosophy.[20]

[20] Howison to W.J., May 19, 1894; W.J. to Howison, June 17, 1901.

TEACHING, WRITING, AND TRAVEL

After James's return from Europe in March, 1883, he settled down to work on his psychology, "floundered round in the morasses of the theory of cognition," lectured in July at the Concord School ("a Jonah among the prophets"),[1] and transformed the lectures into an important article on "Some Omissions of Introspective Psychology," which was published in *Mind* in the following year.

The next decade was devoted to the writing of the *Principles of Psychology,* together with the edition of his father's *Literary Remains* and the miscellaneous philosophical addresses afterwards printed under the title of *The Will to Believe.* His teaching ranged over a wide field embracing history of philosophy, cosmology, and ethics, as well as psychology, elementary and advanced. In spite of family sorrows, increasing domestic responsibilities, the building of the home at 95 Irving Street, Cambridge, and the purchase of the farm at Chocorua, he found himself on the whole fully equal to his load of teaching and writing. He felt that he was accomplishing little—thus in 1886 he wrote to his brother Henry, "I am killed with small businesses, that stop all progress in the larger interests of life," [2] but college catalogues, bibliographical records, and correspondence tell another story.

Several new literary enthusiasms appear in James's letters of this period. In 1885 he was reading Dostoievski's *Crime and Punishment,* "a wonderful psychological study—and so deep and moral withal that all the French sexual stuff seems mere snicker in comparison," [3] and in February 1886 it was *Anna Karénina* which was being read aloud. "Isn't Tolstoi, after all," he wrote to his brother, "the most complete of novelists? There is a sort of infallability and effortlessness about him which is like impartial mother nature, as if one thing was as easy as another." [4] The third of his new literary idols was Robert Louis Stevenson.

A glimpse of James's activities and mood is afforded by the following, again to his brother:

[1] To Renouvier, August 5, 1883; *L.W.J.,* I, 230; to Davidson, May 2, 1883.
[2] December 2, 1886.
[3] To H.J.[2], April 18, 1885.
[4] February 21, 1886.

Cambridge, Sept. 1, 1887

My dear Harry,—

It is atrociously long since I have writ you. . . . This summer I have lived in such a chaos, trying to do some writing and oversee house construction at one and the same time, that letters were impossible. . . .

Chocorua, N. H., Sept 19. This date is a commentary on the lines which precede. I carried this letter to the Adirondacks with me, and back again, without having really had a minute in which I could complete it, although it was on my mind every day of the time. At last the hour has come. Alice has taken charge of the carpenters and graders and hired man, and I have a clear morning at my desk. I am awfully impeded by not being able to write at night; and the all but complete stoppage of my intellectual work this summer has much depressed my spirits. But the exigency is temporary; and in other respects, walking power and sleeping power, my condition is more satisfactory than it has been for a long time. . . .

After spending nine days in the imperishable beauty of the Keene Valley woods, and getting as great an amount of refreshment as I ever got in the same space of time, I came back *via* Albany and New York. . . . I go back to Cambridge in a week, ready to address the multitude (I have about 100 men in one of my courses) on the twenty-ninth of September. I *hope* to finish the manuscript of my book [the *Psychology*] by Christmas time, if things run smoothly. Anyhow I shall finish it this winter; and then a great load will be taken off me. It must seem amusing to you, who can throw off a *chef d'œuvre* every three months, to hear of my slowness. But my time is altogether taken up by other things, and almost every page of this book of mine is against a resistance which you know nothing of in your resistless air of romance, the resistance of *facts,* to begin with, each one of which must be bribed to be on one's side, and the resistance of other philosophers to end with, each one of which must be slain. It is no joke slaying the Helmholtzes as well as the Spencers. When this book is out I shall say adieu to psychology for a while and study some other things, physics a little, and history of philosophy, in which I'm awfully in arrears. I got Ticknor's account last week—poor Father's *Literary Remains* has sold only one copy in the past six months! It is pitiful, but there's nothing to be done about it.

If I were fond of description, I suppose I should now give you a long account of our little place; but you must wait till you see it yourself. . . . The house is very pretty shaped, shingle-covered with green trimmings, and has eleven outside doors, so that the rooms are all independent of each other. . . . There is nothing *banal* in any sense about the place.

I see that R. L. Stevenson is in this country, and I see by the papers that he has paid you a couple of handsome "tributes" in his new volume of verses. I'm glad of it. I hope I may see him ere he leaves, for if there is an author I love 'tis he; and I'm sure he'll be hereafter reckoned as one of our masters of good classic English. How they hang back with publishing your things! I quite thirst for something new. . . . Believe me yours ever,

W.J.

A letter to his brother and sister resume the account of James's diverse activities:

Chocorua, Oct. 14, 1888 [5]

Dear Harry and Alice,—

. . . I am just up for the Sabbath to see the family, and go down again tomorrow. . . . We are moving the barn from the front of the house, so as to open the view a little more, down to the flat meadow below, with its margin of trees behind which the brook flows. Most people buy a site and then put a house on it. I have bought a house and am now creating a site round about it, lowering the level of the landscape, in order to make the house appear on a little higher ground. . . . Men and oxen, and the brown earth, and the new chopped wood, are goodly things to dwell among; and if one had plenty of money, I can imagine no more fascinating way of throwing it away than in owning a lot of land and playing the "gentleman farmer." . . .

The Cambridge year begins with much vehemence—I with a big class in ethics, and seven graduates from other colleges in advanced psychology, giving me a good deal of work. But I feel uncommonly hearty, and shall no doubt come out of it all in good shape. . . . The College has not perceptibly grown this year, whilst other colleges, Yale, Cornell, etc., have. I'm afraid we have about reached our limits for the present. . . .

I hunger and thirst for more of those short stories which I have purposely avoided reading in their periodical shape. The *Reverberator* is immortal. . . . I don't see how you can produce at such a rate, or how you find time for a line of reading or anything else. I should think you'd feel all hollowed out inwardly, and absolutely need to fill up. I am to have lots of reading and no writing to speak of this year, and expect to enjoy it hugely. It does do one good to read classic books. For a month past I've done nothing else, in behalf of my ethics class—Plato, Aristotle, Adam Smith, Butler, Paley, Spinoza, etc.—no book is celebrated without deserving it for some quality, and recenter books, certain never to be celebrated, have an awfully squashy texture. . . .

Wendell Holmes is going to vote for Harrison, God knows why, except to show the shady side of himself—he couldn't give an articulate reason for it the other night. He made a flying trip to California with his wife, seeing no end of country and being elated thereby, and then he spent two months at the Clifton House in Niagara Falls, very happily as he always does. He's just been reading the Bible through, and as John Gray says, it's a great thing to have a virgin mind turned on to so trite a book—as odd as Gustave Doré's illustrations. I don't see how his judgeship gives him so much leisure. . . . Good-bye to both of you. Receive a brother's blessing from your affectionate

WM. JAMES

It was not until 1889 that James again sailed for Europe—on the *Cephalonia* for Queenstown, with Wendell Holmes on the same ship "making himself delightful to all hands." [6] In England he saw his sister Alice who had been living

---

[5] A paragraph of this letter appeared in *L.W.J.*, I, 283. John Chipman Gray was professor at the Harvard Law School and lifelong friend of James.

[6] W.J. to H.J.[2], July 1, 1889.

there since 1884, under the watchful eye of her brother Henry. Her impression of this visit was recorded on July 18:

> William had got to London only the day before, having been for three weeks in Ireland and Scotland. He doesn't look much older for the three years, and all that there is to be said of him, of course, is that he is simply himself; a creature who speaks in another language, as Henry says, from the rest of mankind, and who would lend life and charm to a tread-mill. What a strange experience it was, to have what had seemed so dead and gone all these years suddenly bloom before one, a flowering oasis in this alien desert, redolent with the exquisite *family* perfume of the days gone by, made of the allusions and the point of view in common, so that my floating-particle sense was lost for an hour or so in the illusion that what is forever shattered had sprung anew, and existed outside of our memories, where it is forever green.

Another sisterly comment recorded on the occasion of this same visit is the following:

> William expressed himself and his environment to perfection when he replied to my question about his house in Chocorua. "Oh, it's the most delightful house you ever saw; it has fourteen doors, all opening outwards." His brain isn't limited to fourteen, perhaps unfortunately.[7]

After ten days in England James went to Paris as American representative at the International Congress of Physiological Psychology, held August 5 to 10.[8] He found the experience both stimulating and reassuring, though he approached it with misgivings. The following was written to his sister on the eve of his departure from London, where a common interest in psychical research had brought him into contact with F. W. H. Myers and Professor and Mrs. Henry Sidgwick.

London, July 29, 1889

My dear Alice,—

I am off tomorrow, *bona fide*, for Boulogne, having been here two days longer than I purposed. I've been to Brighton, to Surrey, etc. The best thing was being *perdu dans la foule* yesterday afternoon on a bus ride to Hampton Court via Kew, Richmond, etc. I find I'm more in the mood for anonymity and democracy than for sitting up straight and talking with folks. Myers and the Sidgwicks fill me with terrible psychic responsibility,—they have such a grip on that subject, and feel so earnestly. How I'm to confront them for ten days in Paris I know not, yet such seems my doom. I have enjoyed being with Harry very much, but of London itself I'm thoroughly sated, and never care to see its yellow-brownness and stale spaciousness again. How sad that nothing is the same to us twice over! I'm glad to say that my *wife* stands the test of meeting

---

[7] A.J., *Journal*, July 18 and December 14, 1889.
[8] James wrote an account of this Congress for *Mind* (XIV), 1889.

again after absence, or at least has stood it so far. A letter from her this morning reports all very well. Harry has been delightful,—easier and freer than when I was here before, and beneath all the accretions of years and the world, is still the same dear, innocent old Harry of our youth. His anglicisms are but "protective resemblances,"—he's really, I won't say a Yankee, but a native of the James family, and has no other country. . . .

I've spent half my children's future on clothes for my own idolatrous carcass, and feel like a sort of bloated Moloch. What a horrid thing this coming abroad is! With much love. Ever yours,

W. J.

After returning to Cambridge James was preoccupied with the completing of his *Principles of Psychology,* which was published in the autumn of 1890. His brother's *Tragic Muse* had begun to appear in January 1889.

Chocorua, June 26 [1890]

My dear Harry,—

At last you've done it and no mistake. *The Tragic Muse* caps the climax. It is a most original, wonderful, delightful and admirable production. It must make you feel jolly to have so masterfully and effortlessly answered the accusation that you could do nothing but the international and cosmopolitan business; for cosmopolitan as the whole atmosphere of the book is, yet the people and setting are most easily and naturally English, and the perfect air of good society which reigns through the book is one of its most salient characteristics. It leaves a good taste in one's mouth, everyone in it is human and good, and although the final winding up is, as usual with you, rather a losing of the story in the sand, yet that is the way in which things lose themselves in real life. . . .

I have nothing to say in detail. The whole thing hangs together most intimately and well; and it is truly a spectacle for rejoicing to see that by the sort of practice a man gives himself he attains the plenitude and richness which you have at last got. Your sentences are straighter and simpler than before, and your felicities of observation are on every page. I wish you had managed to bring in a little more business with Julia ere the end; her love-making scene was exquisite; but it must be a difficult task to tread the crack between her charms and femininity and her hardness and politicality. The whole thing is an exquisite mirage which remains afloat in the air of one's mind. . . . As for the question of the size of your public, I tremble. The work is too refined, too elaborate and minute, and requires to be read with too much leisure to appeal to any but the select few. But you mustn't mind that. It will *always* have its audience. No reason, however, for not doing less elaborate things for wider audiences; which I hope ere long to have direct testimony that you have done.

. . . My proofs have only just begun coming in; but they promise to come thick and fast. I take little pride or pleasure in the accursed book, which has clung to me so long, but I shall be glad to have it out, just to show that I *can* write one book. . . . Yours ever,

W. J.

Chocorua, Aug. 22, 1890

My dear Harry,—

It gave me great pleasure to get your letter from Vallombrosa about a fort-night ago. . . . You see now why I have been urging you all these years to take more of your vacation in the face of nature. Your last two letters have breathed a spirit of youth, a sort of *Lebenslust,* which has long been absent from them, and which nothing but mother earth can give. Alternation between her and the gas-lit life of corrupt capitals is the optimum for man here below. Neither ele-ment alone will do, but both must be there. I'm glad you've had such a vacation from writing. I don't see how either you or Howells can keep it up at such a rate. I am just now in the middle of his *Hazard of New Fortunes,* which is an extraordinarily vigorous production, quite up to Dickens I should say, in hu-mor, detail of observation and geniality, with flexible human beings on the stage instead of puppets. With that work, your *Tragic Muse,* and last *but by no means least,* my *Psychology,* all appearing in it, the year 1890 will be known as the great epochal year in American literature.

I finished and posted my index yesterday, so my mind is free to turn to the universe receptively again. A wondrous boon. I have been six weeks in Cam-bridge all alone in the house, until the last week . . . and corrected fourteen hundred pages of proofs, much of them in small type. I almost never got away from my writing-table till 9 P.M., and then used, in a starving condition, to go booming along through the sultry night on the front seat of an electric car, the finest locomotion in the world, to get my dinner between 9 and 10 at Young's or Parker's, after mailing the proofs in the Boston post-office to catch the late New York mail. It was hard on the digestive organs, but it has left no bad effects, and I look back to the month and a half of it as a most delightful period of time; only one thing to think about, and great strides of progress in that every day,— so different from the college year, with fifty things to think about, and no sen sible progress made at all. . . .

I have just raised $4000— . . . for a psychological laboratory and fixings, so with that and other things I expect to have a hard-working year of it next year. We ought to get abroad for 1891-2 if it be possible to afford it, but nothing will be known about it until next spring. . . . Yours,

W.J.

The interest in psychical research which James had acquired from Frederic Myers, Edmund Gurney, and the Henry Sidgwicks during his English sojourn of 1882-1883 had stirred James to intermittent investigations, especially of the famous medium, Mrs. Piper, on whom he had reported to the American So-ciety for Psychical Research in 1886. In 1890 he sent a written report[9] on the same subject to the parent society in England, and it was read in his absence by his brother Henry; which William thought was "the most comical thing" he had ever heard of. When his wife suggested that he had not "melted enough" over the matter he wrote to Henry: "I *do* melt to perfect liquefaction.

[9] This report was published in the *Proc. of the S.P.R.,* VI (1890).

'Tis the most beautiful and devoted brotherly act I ever knew, and I hope it may be the beginning of a new career, on your part, of psychic apostolicism. Heaven bless you for it! Write short and often!" [10]

In a remarkable letter of July 6, 1891, James wrote to his sister concerning death as a release from suffering and frustration,[11] and hinted at some of the ideas of immortality contained in his Ingersoll Lecture of 1897. The next letter followed soon after, from the neighborhood of Asheville, North Carolina.

Roan Mountain, Aug. 23, 1891

Dearest Sister,—

. . . I walked up here yesterday, and this peaceful sunny morning, with the billowy mountain-world spread out all round and beneath, the air is as round-edged and balmy (in spite of its vitality) as if we were on the plain instead of at a height of 6300-odd feet. Very different from the Mount Washington air!

I got your admirable, inspired and inspiring letter before I left home. It is good to hear you speak of this year as one of the best of your life. It is good to hear you speak of life and death from a standpoint so unshaken and serene, with what one of the Adirondack guides spoke of as such "heaven-up-histed-ness" in the point of view. A letter from Harry, received only a few days later, confirmed me in this impression. He says he is less "anxious" about you than at any former time, and I think we ought all to be so together now. Poor Lowell's disease was cancer.[12] He never knew what it was, and in the shape of positive pain, suffered comparatively little, although he had no end of various discomforts. Now that he is gone, he seems a much more unique and rare individual than before. What a pity it is always so. I do hope that you will leave some notes on life and English life which Harry can work in hereafter, so as to make the best book he ever wrote. Charles Norton, I see, receives the bequest of Lowell's manuscripts, etc. The way that man gets his name stuck to every greatness is fabulous—Dante, Goethe, Carlyle, Ruskin, Fitzgerald, Chauncey Wright, and now Lowell! His name will dominate all the literary history of this epoch. 100 years hence, the *Revue des deux mondes* will publish an article entitled "La Vie de l'esprit aux États-Unis vers la fin du XIXme siècle; étude sur Charles Norton." He is our *foyer de lumières;* and the worst of it is that he does all the chores therewith connected, and practically fills the position rather better, than if he were the genuine article. . . .

I appear to be tougher physically and capable of more continuous head work than in many a long year. The *Psychology* turns out to be a much "bigger" book than I thought it was; and reviews in the technical periodicals (I am given to understand) are erelong to inform the world of its true greatness. . . . Our children grow lovelier every year and more confidence-inspiring. . . . God bless you, dearest sister. Your loving

W. J.

---

[10] October 20, 1890.
[11] This letter will be found in *L.W.J.*, I, 309-11.
[12] James Russell Lowell died on August 12, 1891.

On September 12, 1891, James sailed for Europe on the *S.S. Eider*—swept by a gust of affectionate solicitude, he had gone to see his sister. On October 1 he was on his way home, having had ten days in London!

This gifted and heroic woman died at the age of forty-four, in the following March. She had been an invalid during the greater part of her life, and had suffered greatly, both from physical pain and from the conflict between her bodily infirmity and her high spirits. She resembled her father and her brother William in her gayety, turn of wit, and vividness of style. Her courage assumed the form of neither grim endurance nor evasion of reality, but of a tender irony, in which she both renounced life and at the same time kept her warmth of sympathy. Although she resembled her brother William, it fell to the lot of her brother Henry to be her watchful providence during the last years. The degree and the quality of his devotion can be read in her own words, written in 1890:—

> Henry came on the 10th to spend the day; Henry the Patient, I should call him. Five years ago, in November, I crossed the water, and suspended myself, like an old woman of the sea, round his neck, where to all appearances I shall remain for all time. I have given him endless care and anxiety; but notwithstanding this and the fantastic nature of my troubles, I have never seen an impatient look upon his face or heard an unsympathetic or misunderstanding sound cross his lips. He comes at my slightest sign, and "hangs on" to whatever organ may be in eruption, and gives me calm and solace by assuring me that my nerves are his nerves, and my stomach his stomach,—this last a pitch of brotherly devotion never before approached by the race. He has never remotely hinted that he expected me to be well at any given moment,—that burden which fond friend and relative so inevitably imposes upon the cherished invalid. But he has always been the same since I can remember, and has almost as strongly as Father that personal susceptibility—what can one call it?—it seems as if it were a matter of the scarf-skin, as if they perceived through that your mood, and were saved thereby from rubbing you raw with their theory of it or blindness to it.[13]

During her last years her brother William was her chief link with home, both with the old circle of family and friends and with the country from which she was in her heart never expatriated. New arrivals from America or American friends who saw her on the eve of the homeward journey reminded her poignantly of her exile. It was on one such occasion that she recorded the following impression:—

> What a tide of homesickness swept me under for the moment! What a longing to see a shaft of sunshine shimmering through the pines, breathe in the resinous air, and throw my withered body down upon my mother earth, bury

[13] *Journal*, March 25, 1890.

my face in the coarse grass, worshipping all that the ugly, raw emptiness of the
blessed land stands for,—the embodiment of a huge chance for hemmed-in
humanity; its flexible conditions stretching and lending themselves to all sizes
of man; pallid and naked of necessity; undraped by the illusions and mystery
of a moss-grown, cobwebby past, but overflowing with a divine good-humour
and benignancy, a helping hand for the faltering, and indulgent thought for the
discredited, a heart of hope for every outcast of tradition.[14]

These casual fragments will convey some slight idea of Alice James's quality.
She had both the impulse and the capacity to write. She was keenly interested
in the life about her, full of shrewd insight, and moved by a strong creative
impulse. That she left so little behind her was the fault of her frail body and not
of the spirit that burned so unquenchably within.

[14] *Journal,* May 20, 1890.

XX

JAMES AND THE SCIENCE OF PSYCHOLOGY

The first of James's major works was the *Principles of Psychology,* which appeared in 1890 when the author was forty-eight years old. It was a work of highest importance, not only for James but for the history of psychology—the fruit of over twenty years of study and writing, carried on during a crucial period in the development of the subject to which it was devoted. For whether or no James be regarded as one of the founders of modern psychology, in any case he was present while it was being founded, and experienced in himself the motives which led to its founding. Writing from Berlin to Thomas W. Ward in the autumn of 1867, he said:—

> It seems to me that perhaps the time has come for psychology to begin to be a science—some measurements have already been made in the region lying between the physical changes in the nerves and the appearance of consciousness-at (in the shape of sense perceptions), and more may come of it. I am going on to study what is already known, and perhaps may be able to do some work at it. Helmholtz and a man named Wundt at Heidelberg are working at it, and I hope I live through this winter to go to them in the summer.

James here alluded to the most important signs of the new "experimental psychology." In 1860 Fechner[1] had published his *Elemente der Psychophysik* and had formulated the famous Weber-Fechner Law which related to intensities of the physical stimulus. Helmholtz had approached psychology by way of the physiology of the senses. Wilhelm Wundt was the man in whom experimental psychology was weaned from this physical and physiological parentage. He was James's senior by ten years—in age and in academic status; and he had already, in 1862, published a volume of experimental studies on sense perception[2] and begun to lecture on "psychology as a natural science."

At the same time James's medical training, together with his own personal experiences, implanted in him a deep interest in psychopathology which drew him in the direction of the French school of Charcot.[3] His psychological cosmo-

[1] *Cf.* also below, 331.
[2] *Beiträge zur Theorie der Sinneswahrnehmung.*
[3] James was attending Charcot's lectures in Paris in 1882 when he received news of his father's last illness.

politanism was completed by his direct inheritance of the British tradition, represented by James and John Stuart Mill, Maudsley, Spencer, and Bain.

The fact that James was an American accounts for the peculiar catholicism of his psychology. He benefited by the new movements in German, French, and English psychology without surrendering himself wholly to any of them. His wide acquaintance and mobility, both of person and of mind, enabled him to sit at all of these feasts and combine their several nutritive values. Having imbibed the newer tendencies in Europe, and having followed them up with physiological and empirical studies of his own, James became one of the first American teachers to recognize the existence of psychology as an independent science. Although it was not characteristic of him to make claims for himself, he was drawn into a public controversy over the question of priority by the extravagant counterclaims of one who had been his pupil. In October 1895, G. Stanley Hall, then President of Clark University, published in his *American Journal of Psychology* an editorial in which he gave a long list of men who had at one time or another been associated with him at Johns Hopkins or Clark, and then went on to say: "Under the influence of these men departments of experimental psychology and laboratories were founded at Harvard, Yale, Philadelphia, Columbia, Toronto, Wisconsin and many other higher institutions of learning." When James read Hall's extraordinary editorial he at once (October 12, 1895) wrote the latter a long letter, in which he said:

> As an arm-chair professor, I frankly admit my great inferiority as a laboratory-teacher and investigator. But some little regard should be paid to the good will with which I have tried to force my nature, and to the actual things I have done. One of them, for example, was inducting you into experimental investigation, with very naïve methods, it is true, but you may remember that there was no other place but Harvard where during those years you could get even that. I remember also giving a short course of psychological lectures at the Johns Hopkins years before you went there.[4] They were exclusively experimental, and, I have been told, made an "epoch" there in determining opinion.
>
> I well recognize how contemptible these beginnings were, and that you and your pupils have in these latter years left them far behind. But you are now professing to state history; beginnings are a part thereof, and should not be written down in inverted order. . . . In this world we all owe to each other. My debt to you and to Clark is great, and if only my own person was concerned, I should let you say what you like and not object, for the bystanders generally see truly. In this case, however, the misstatement concerns the credit of my university.

The early history of James's teaching of psychology is briefly as follows. Beginning in 1872 and for the next few years, he gave courses in anatomy and physiology in Harvard College. In these courses he devoted considerable atten-

---

[4] In 1878.

tion to the physiology of the nervous system and some to psychophysics. In 1875 he announced a course for graduates on "The Relations between Physiology and Psychology," and thereafter this course or some equivalent course of advanced grade was given regularly. He began his undergraduate instruction in psychology in 1876-1877. The scope of this earliest undergraduate course was very broad, including physiological psychology, the traditional topics of the associationists, and such philosophical problems as knowledge of the external world and freedom of the will. Indeed its scope corresponds fairly closely to the contents of the *Principles of Psychology,* and most of the author's characteristic views were worked out in his lectures and in his criticisms of the texts which were assigned.

James was clearly advocating the recognition of the new psychology—"new" in the sense of allying itself with science as well as with philosophy, and in combining the methods of observation and experiment with those of speculation and reflection. This was a distinct innovation. Psychology as then taught in the United States was indistinguishable from the philosophy of the soul, embracing a brief account of the senses and of association, but devoted mainly to the higher moral and logical processes. Thus it is not surprising that James's early teaching of physiological psychology at Harvard attracted considerable attention.

In his published reply to Stanley Hall's famous claim of priority, James said that the psychological laboratory at Harvard grew up in connection with these new courses:

> I, myself, "founded" the instruction in experimental psychology at Harvard in 1874-5, or 1876, I forget which. For a long series of years the laboratory was in two rooms of the Scientific School building, which at last became choked with apparatus, so that a change was necessary. I then, in 1890, resolved on an altogether new departure, raised several thousand dollars, fitted up Dane Hall, and introduced laboratory exercises as a regular part of the undergraduate psychology-course.[5]

Just when a psychological laboratory can be said to begin is a question which is incapable of definite settlement, because it is impossible to determine just when a physical or physiological laboratory becomes a *psychological* laboratory; and just when a set of instruments collected and used for demonstration or research in psychology becomes a *laboratory.* James's undergraduate teaching was in the main from texts, but he made use of apparatus for classroom demonstrations, gave his advanced students experimental problems, and carried on a certain amount of experimental research of his own.

As for Stanley Hall, he had begun his advanced studies in 1869 in Germany,

[5] *Science, N.S.,* II (1895), 626.

but had then been chiefly concerned with philosophy and theology. After teaching miscellaneous subjects for four years at Antioch College, he came in 1876 to Harvard, where he was registered for two years, and was closely associated with James in the study of physiological psychology.

When James was in Europe in 1880 he was joined by Hall at Heidelberg, where they carried on much verbal psychologizing together. Hall returned to America this same summer, and was invited, in January 1882, to Johns Hopkins, where he began giving regular instruction (including experimental laboratory psychology) in the following autumn—first as lecturer and then, in 1884, as professor. He was called to Clark University in 1888.

In view of these facts, what shall we say of the relative priority of James's laboratory and Hall's? Professor Boring has made a statement which seems to me to constitute the sum of wisdom on the matter. "Nothing," he says, "that is called 'first' is ever literally first; there always turn out to have been 'anticipations.'" Such anticipations, he adds, are not "founded," they simply occur and exist. James's laboratory was such an anticipation. It was earlier, but it "came into being, whereas Hall founded his. The difference between *having* and *founding* is a difference between the temperaments of the two men." [6] About five years after this "founding" (or ten years after the "anticipation"), owing to the influence of Harvard and Hopkins, and to the independent studies of American psychologists in Germany, laboratories began to multiply rapidly. By 1900 there were twenty-five or more in American universities. In 1905 the Harvard Laboratory was removed from Dane to Emerson Hall, being one of the first, if not the first, psychological laboratory originally designed and built for the purpose.

In judging of James's relations to experimental psychology in general, it is to be remembered that there is more than one sense of the term "experimental." In the broad sense of testing hypotheses by experience, James's mind was instinctively and profoundly experimental. But it is only the more striking that James did not himself make important contributions to experimental psychology in the strict sense. Not more than a fifth of his *Principles of Psychology* can be said to relate even to the experimental work of others. That he could not endure long hours in a laboratory was due to physical reasons. That he did not incline to the use of quantitative methods was due to his nonmathematical cast of mind. That he did not organize experiments and carry them on through years of sustained diligence was due to his impatience. To this threefold incapacity was joined an opinion that the new laboratory method had not yielded significant results.

Whether psychology lost or gained by this incapacity and disinclination, who shall say? That the peculiar quality of James's influence is in some measure due

[6] E. G. Boring, *History of Experimental Psychology*, The Century Company, 1929, 318, 507.

to it seems clear. He could not stand in the laboratory, but he *could* move about outside. Just as he was bound to no national movement, so he was restricted to no technique. He was an exceptionally acute observer of the natural man in all the varied aspects of his life. He had a lively and veracious imagination. He used whatever facts he could thus find for himself or gather from other observers, interpreted them freely, and constructed an image of human nature which after forty years is not yet obsolete.

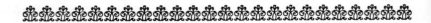

XXI

THE WRITING OF THE *PSYCHOLOGY*

In June 1878, at the close of the year in which he had transferred his under-graduate course to the department of philosophy, and a month before his marriage, James contracted to write a *Psychology* for Henry Holt's "American Science Series." He declined to promise the manuscript in one year, but thought he might have it ready in two. Holt began as early as the autumn of 1878 to have misgivings, and to allude to the possibility of turning to Hall or some other rival author. As a matter of fact, however, the composition of the book took twelve years—and Holt waited!

James's relations with Henry Holt were not merely professional and commercial. They *were* professional and commercial—and, as both men spoke plainly, how a publisher annoys an author and an author a publisher, appears very plainly in their long correspondence extending over a period of twenty-five years. But Holt was a man who had intellectual interests of his own, enabling him to meet his author on his own ground, and he was capable of a humor and pungency of statement which James greatly relished.

Between 1878 and 1890 James was teaching psychology continuously, and the book, as he tells us in the Preface, grew up "in connection with the author's class-room instruction." [1] James's animated and polemical method of teaching is largely accountable for the style of the book—its persuasiveness, its profusion of illustration, and its liberal citation of authors.

The composition of the *Psychology* was, like all of James's writing, laborious. He was easily fatigued; and—having diverse interests, an eager mind, a driving creative impulse, and a generous heart—there was much to fatigue him. If genius implies continuous, frictionless, outpouring spontaneity, then James was not a genius. Periods of outpouring alternated with periods of painful effort. He struggled, and he suffered; and though he achieved much, he always seemed to himself to be achieving little, and extravagantly admired what he took to be the greater fecundity of more gifted contemporaries. Despite his other burdens, his ill-health, his discouragement, his repining and occasional backsliding, he nevertheless steadily added chapter to chapter.

Up to the year 1882-1883, seven months of which James spent abroad, he had

---

[1] *Psychology*, v.

published six articles that may be said to have contributed to the making of the *Psychology,* but only one of them was incorporated as it stood. One of the principal objects of this European sojourn was to obtain an opportunity for the uninterrupted writing of his book. But in December 1882 he was compelled to confess that, though he had "hoped to begin writing about November 1," he had "written as yet *six pages!*" Early after the new year the tide turned. On January 22 and 23, 1883, he had "written some psychology." [2] The following paragraph is from a letter to his wife, written from London on February 10, 1883:—

> Yesterday I was parturient of psychological truth, being in one of my fevered states you wot of, when ideas are shooting together and I can think of no finite things. I wrote a lot at headlong speed, and in the evening, having been appointed, gave an account of it—the difference between feeling and thought—at the Scratch Eight.

This "psychological truth" was apparently the substance of his Concord lectures of 1883, and of his article "On Some Omissions of Introspective Psychology" published in *Mind* in 1884 and later distributed among several chapters of the *Psychology.*

The progress of the work was very uneven, owing to two causes. The first was personal—his limited time and capacity for work, as recorded in such passages as these from letters to his brother:—

> Oct. 18, 1884
>
> College work has begun never for me with so little strain. . . . I hope this will permit me to do something towards my psychology. My working day is sadly short, however—do what I will with my eyes I can't get them to do anything by lamplight without having to pay the piper for it afterwards, and the hunger that arises in me for reading in the evening is sometimes most poignantly severe.

> April 1, 1885
>
> I am running along quite smoothly, and my eyes,—you never knew such an improvement! . . . I have made a start with my psychology which I shall work at, temperately, through the vacation and hope to get finished a year from next fall, *sans faute.* Then shall the star of your romances be eclipst! [3]

The second impediment to steady progress was the difficulty of the task. He had undertaken, not a summary of existing psychological knowledge, but its extension and revision. Every problem, he found, "bristles with obstructions" requiring years for their "mitigation." Every sentence had to be forged "in the teeth of irreducible and stubborn facts." He had to overcome not only "the re-

---

[2] W.J. to Renouvier, December 6, 1882; W.J. to H.J.², January 23, 1883.
[3] Reprinted from *L.W.J.,* I, 242-3.

sistance of facts," but "the resistance of other philosophers." It was "no joke slaying the Helmholtzes as well as the Spencers." [4] The "science" of psychology was "in such a confused and imperfect state" that every paragraph presented "some unforeseen snag." [5] In other words, between 1878 and 1890 James was not only *composing* a systematic work on psychology, but making observations, searching out acceptable hypotheses, and waging a vigorous polemical warfare.

The year 1884 saw the publication of the famous "James-Lange theory" of emotion.[6] In 1885 he wrote the important discussion of "Necessary Truths and the Effects of Experience," which became the concluding chapter of the *Psychology*. The winter of 1886-1887 found him doing his work "easily," writing with more "continuity," the book "two-thirds done," and hopeful of finishing it in a year.[7] Of the chapters which now flew thick and fast many were sent to Croom Robertson for publication in *Mind*.

As the book neared completion James's correspondence with his publisher, Henry Holt, became frequent, voluminous, and intense. Holt was quite alive to the unbusinesslike habits of his authors. He gave and took rebuke indulgently. Thus he once wrote to James that "dear old Royce" had been in the office "professing that the one effort of his life was 'to keep free from the business virtues.' I kind of love the wambling cuss, nevertheless." [8] Holt's authors not only had their own code, which differed from that of the publisher, but felt quite sure that theirs was a loftier code. This feeling was only partially concealed by a mask of pleasantry:—

Cambridge, March 21, 1890

My dear Holt,—

Publishers are demons, there's no doubt about it. How silly it is to fly in the face of the accumulated wisdom of mankind, and think just because one of them appears genial socially that the great natural law is broken and that he is also a human being in his professional capacity. Fie upon such weakness! I shall ne'er be guilty of it again. . . .

As for the manuscript, I confess I don't know why you need the whole of it *en bloc* in your own hands, before printing begins. After this week of recess I shall write a chapter which may take three weeks at the outside and complete the book. Some 1700 pages of manuscript will then be ready for the printer without another touch from me. There will remain five or six chapters, some of which need slight retouches and additions, which can be added by me perfectly well in the intervals of correcting proofs, thereby enabling the latter to begin about the first of May. The *whole* work, as I said, will then be *written*, only those few chapters not *revised*. Time is so precious now that I don't see what

[4] *Cf.* above, 173.
[5] W.J. to H.J.², April 12, 1887; *L.W.J.*, I, 269.
[6] "What Is an Emotion?" *Mind*, IX.
[7] W.J. to H.J.², April 12, 1887; *L.W.J.*, I, 269.
[8] July 24, 1893.

possible thing is risked by proceeding to press with the revised manuscript. The rest *could* be printed without revision, but it will be better to go over it again. Write and tell me what is your decree. I want to get forward now with the least possible delay. . . . I find that I have lost the contract you sent me last spring. I did not even examine it then. Pray send another that I may see what to do. Yours always,

WM. JAMES

New York, April 2, 1890

My dear James,—

If "publishers are not demons," it is a striking instance of long-suffering. I have illustrations here made years ago for manuscript that has never appeared. Your letter makes plain what I took for granted,—that your manuscript will not be ready as early as May 1. *Of course* you "don't know why I need the whole of the manuscript before printing begins." It's not in your line to know. If you were gradually being converted into a demon, however, by the disappointments occasioned by authors, you would know all about it. I *never* began printing an instalment of a manuscript, so far as I can remember, without having to stop work before the book was finished, thus forcing the printer to put away the apparatus in place for it, and giving him excuses (which they always avail themselves of to the full) for dilly-dallying with the rest of the work when it came, and eventually getting out the work later and after vastly more friction than would have been the case if it had not been begun till the manuscript was all ready. . . . One of the things that makes me a demon, is to have to go over this weary explanation again and again. I'm glad that you "want to get forward now with the least possible delay." To accomplish that, believe that I do too; put some faith in my experience; and complete your manuscript before doing anything else.

My demoniacal character has not been developed so much by authors failing to look at contracts and losing them, as by the other thing; so I'm angelic enough to send you duplicates, of which please sign both and return us one. I have just seen a contract signed by you to give us that manuscript June 12, 1880, and yet, you, you, you, Brute (two syllables) revile me for being a demon! I'm awfully sorry, all the same, that you're not coming here and to dine with us, but that all must be in due time. Yours ever,

H. HOLT, Professional Demon,
which being correctly interpreted
meaneth Δαίμων

Cambridge, April 5, 1890

My dear Holt,—

Your letter awaits me on my return from Newport. Poor publisher, poor fellow, poor human being, ex-demon! How those vermin of authors must have caused you to suffer in your time to wring from you such a tirade! Well, it has been very instructive to me to grasp the publisher's point of view. Your fatal error, however, has been in not perceiving that I was an entirely *different kind* of author from any of those whom you had been in the habit of meeting, and that *celerity,* celerity incarnate, is the motive and result of all my plans and deeds. It is not fair to throw that former contract into my face, when you know, or ought to know, that when the ten years or a little more from the time of its signature had elapsed I wrote to you that you must get another man to write this book for you, and that, as things were then going, I didn't see how I could ever finish it.

I would return these contracts signed, herewith, but for two points. First, the provision that the author "shall prepare" matter for new editions "whenever called on" by publishers. I should naturally hope to do that, but certainly can't pledge myself. . . . Secondly, I find in the former contract a manuscript addition to the effect that on publication you deliver me twenty copies free of charge. That seems fair enough. I was calculating the other day that I should have in all to give away at least seventy-five copies of the book, most of them to professors here and abroad. . . . Let me know about these points and I will sign. Yours always,

WM. JAMES

New York, April 7, 1890

My dear James,—

"Celerity" is good. I don't want to "throw anything into your face," but upon my soul I don't see how after agreeing to do a thing, a suggestion that somebody else should do it is to be accounted a valid substitute for doing it; but your sins which are many are forgiven, as you know. Now, don't you be afraid of that provision about new editions. Experience has shown me that it is necessary to have that point settled in advance, and you are not going to be abused on the strength of it. . . . Yours ever,

H. HOLT

Cambridge, April 8, 1890

My dear Holt,—

Here goes a copy of the contract signed by me. Your copy found again. I add as you suggest, the clause about twenty copies; and I leave the clause about new matter for new editions; but I warn you clearly that I shall only consent to furnish such new matter in case it involves no great sacrifice. I can easily imagine myself engrossed in some other work hereafter, and having grown into such a state of disgust for my old psychology book as to find the rehandling of it an intellectually impossible task. In that case I should calmly fold my arms and say, "the book has had its day—let it be republished if at all as an historical monument, not as a show exhibition of my present opinions." There comes a time in all books when a man can't tinker them; he must write a new work altogether. . . . Ever truly yours,

WM. JAMES

Cambridge, May 9, 1890 [9]

My dear Holt,—

I was in hopes that you would propose to break away from the famous "Series" and publish the book independently, in two volumes. An abridgment

[9] Reprinted from *L.W.J.,* I, 293-4.

could then be prepared for the Series. If there be anything which I loathe it is a mean overgrown page in small type, and I think the author's feelings ought to go for a good deal in the case of the enormous *rat* which his ten years' gestation has brought forth. . . . No one could be more disgusted than I at the sight of the book. *No* subject is worth being treated of in 1000 pages! Had I ten years more, I could rewrite it in 500; but as it stands it is this or nothing—a loathsome, distended, tumefied, bloated, dropsical mass, testifying to nothing but two facts: *1st,* that there is no such thing as a *science* of psychology, and *2nd,* that W. J. is an incapable. Yours provided you hurry up things,

WM. JAMES

The writing of the *Psychology* was completed in May and the book appeared in the autumn. The interval between these dates James spent in Cambridge, correcting proof. A letter to his sister affords a glimpse of him:—

Cambridge, July 23, 1890

Dearest Alice,—

. . . I, as you doubtless know, found it necessary to come here a couple of weeks since and correct my proofs. The printers are bent on overwhelming me and making me cry mercy now (I having complained of slowness at first), so that every mail, four times a day, is apt to bring a big bundle. I have stood it so far, but it's bad for head and stomach. I carry the last ones in at night to mail in the Boston Post Office and often don't get at my dinner till 9 o'clock. My breakfasts I usually take in our old home on Quincy St., whose brand-new bright surface together with certain structural alterations have entirely wiped away all old associations. The outlook from the windows, however, is the same, only the trees about the back and sides have grown and closed in the view. I have it pretty much to myself there just now—Jim Myers[10] being the only person whom I am likely ever to meet—and I confess it is pleasant to have that spot again recognizing my tread. Its walls are saturated with my groans and tears, as well as with yours! But the new wallpapers lie close, and let none of them transpire. . . .

But here comes the postman with the proofs, which I've just opened—forty pages in galley and fifty-six of page-proof! I ought to get it all mailed tonight—it's now half past three—but of course I can't. Anyhow, no more dalliance with the likes of *you!* . . . *Adieu. Mille baisers!*

W. J.

While James's first feeling had been one of weariness and disgust, this soon gave way, as the summer wore on, to a happy sense of completed achievement. He was conscious that an epoch was closed. Of course most of the book was "unreadable from any human point of view," but seeing it "as a unit" he felt,

[10] The house at 20 Quincy St. had become the Colonial Club, where one of the most familiar figures was Hon. James J. Myers, Harvard '69, Speaker of the Massachusetts House of Representatives.

nevertheless, "as if it might be rather a vigorous and richly colored chunk." He who had always considered himself "a thing of glimpses, a discontinuity, of *aperçus*," had written a *big book* on psychology—"a good one, as psychologies go." [11]

[11] *L.W.J.*, I, 295-8.

XXII

SOURCES, DOCTRINES, AND INFLUENCE OF THE *PSYCHOLOGY*

No one who considers the sources of James's *Psychology* can fail to be impressed by their number and variety. This plenitude of tributary streams was not an accident, nor does it imply any lack of originality on the part of the author. It goes with his conception of the scope of psychology—the conception which he described as "functional" or "clinical":

> We habitually hear much nowadays of the difference between structural and functional psychology. I am not sure that I understand the difference, but it probably has something to do with what I have privately been accustomed to distinguish as the analytical and the clinical points of view in psychological observation. . . . The clinical conceptions, though they may be vaguer than the analytic ones, are certainly more adequate, give the concreter picture of the way the whole mind works, and are of far more urgent practical importance.[1]

For James, in other words, psychology meant seeing man in the round—as he presents himself to the physician, the biologist, the traveler, the artist, or the novelist. Hence he was willing to learn about man from any source, including psychologists both proper and improper.

The psychologists of whose writings James made the largest use, as judged by citations and references in the *Psychology,* were Spencer, Helmholtz, Wundt, and Bain. Spencer and Wundt he both used and rejected—using them as reservoirs of facts and as texts for discussion, rejecting their characteristic and dominating ideas. Among his own contemporaries he was most influenced by James Ward, of Cambridge University, and Carl Stumpf. Both became his close personal friends. Here, however, the parallel ceases. James was expansive, brilliant, and colorful, while Ward was concise, analytical, and systematic. Ward wholly lacked the radical temper of mind essential to James, and in his *Psychological Principles,* published eight years after James's death, he found little to say in the latter's favor and much to say against his "absurdities." [2] A similar difference of temper divided the two men philosophically, despite the fact that Ward, like Davidson and Howison, professed pluralism. But the two

---

[1] "The Energies of Men," *Philos. Rev.,* XVI (1907), 1, 2.

[2] He declares James's treatment of the emotions and the self to be absurd, and these are the only doctrines of James which he treats at length. (*Cf. Psychological Principles,* 1918, 379, 270.)

men remained close friends, and met frequently towards the close of James's life when his Gifford Lectures and his illness took him to Europe.

James's favorite experimental psychologist was Carl Stumpf, of Würzburg, Prague, Halle, Munich, and finally Berlin. Stumpf had the kind of versatility that James liked. Though he was six years James's junior, he was more precocious, and received his Doctor's degree in 1868 at the age of twenty; so that the '70s and '80s found the two men at the same stage of their scientific and academic development. Stumpf received a thorough philosophical training and remained a philosopher throughout his entire career. His first psychological work was on the perception of space. In writing his acknowledgments to those who had preceded him in this field, James said, "Stumpf seems to me the most philosophical and profound of all the writers; and I owe him much." [3] It was owing to his authorship of this work on space that James looked up "the good and sharp-nosed Stumpf" in Prague at the end of October, 1882, and, after talking with him for twelve hours in three days, came away resolved to engage him in correspondence. [4] This correspondence began at once and continued, with some chills and fevers, until James's death. Intellectual coöperation between the two scholars inevitably declined, but the warmth of their personal friendship was undiminished, and as James moved on to ethics, religion, and metaphysics he tried with characteristic ardor to carry Stumpf with him. Speaking of his *Principles of Psychology* as avoiding spiritualistic, associationist, or other metaphysical theories of explanation, James wrote: "In this strictly positivistic point of view consists the only feature of it for which I . . . claim originality." [5] Notwithstanding this claim, a comparison of the *Psychology* with any subsequent or even contemporary treatise professing to deal with the *science* of psychology reveals James's liberal use of philosophical literature.

The composition of the *Psychology* found James with a half-finished theory of knowledge. If he was not to carry on his philosophizing in the *Psychology,* he must arrange a truce. In other words, his positivism was not a completely thought-out set of presuppositions for psychology, but a half-thought-out compromise designed to give him a temporary respite from philosophizing. This explains his saying in 1900: "I confess that during the years which have elapsed since the publication of the book, I have become more and more convinced of the difficulty of treating psychology without introducing some true and suitable philosophical doctrine." [6]

James's psychological positivism had a constructive and not a merely neg-

[3] *Psychology*, II, 282. Stumpf's work was *Ueber den psychologischen Ursprung der Raumvorstellung,* 1873.

[4] W.J. to A.H.J., September 24, 1882; *L.W.J.*, I, 211, 212.

[5] *Psychology,* vi.

[6] Preface to Italian translation of *Psychology*, xi.

ative sense; it was a professed avoidance of metaphysics, but at the same time betrayed a leaning toward a naturalistic metaphysics. Both motives inclined him, for example, to the acceptance of the so-called theory of the "reflex arc." An essay published in 1888 contains this significant passage:

> The only conception at the same time renovating and fundamental with which biology has enriched psychology, the only *essential* point in which "the new psychology" is an advance upon the old, is, it seems to me, the very general, and by this time very familiar notion, that all our activity belongs at bottom to the type of reflex action, and that all our consciousness accompanies a chain of events of which the first was an incoming current in some sensory nerve, and of which the last will be a discharge into some muscle, blood-vessel, or gland. . . . Viewed in this light the thinking and feeling portions of our life seem little more than half-way houses towards behavior; and recent Psychology accordingly tends to treat consciousness more and more as if it existed only for the sake of the conduct which it seems to introduce, and tries to explain its peculiarities (so far as they can be explained at all) by their practical utility.[7]

The theory of the reflex arc thus commended itself to James because, while it introduces mind into the context of nature, it at the same time recognizes that character of *interestedness* which distinguishes mind.

Turning to James's more specifically *psychological* doctrines, the first place must be given to the "stream of thought."[8] The most signal "omission of introspective psychology," as James saw it, was the relational or transitive state, which, when adequately recognized, gives to consciousness an aspect of streamlike continuity. Except possibly for the dependence of knowledge on will, this was James's most important insight. It implied the rejection of "associationism" and signified a sharp break with tradition. This doctrine pervades the whole work, and he felt it to be original as well as important.

Next in order among James's fundamental doctrines, was his *nativism*— using this term broadly to mean a tendency to emphasize what is original rather than what is acquired. This took two forms. In the first place, influenced by Darwin, he credited the human mind with a liberal share of inborn traits and aptitudes. In the second place, he believed in the diversity and fecundity of first experience. He was sceptical of the possibility of generating one experience out of another, because he was so keenly alive to the unique *qualia* of each experience; and he did not feel the need of such a genetic account, because he was confident of finding the derived experience among the originals.

The seed of James's famous theory that emotions are fusions of organic sen-

[7] "What the Will Effects," *Scribner's,* III (1888), 240.
[8] His "radical empiricism" is a *philosophical* application of this doctrine.

sations aroused by bodily expression—that "we feel sorry because we cry, angry because we strike, afraid because we tremble" [9]—was evidently planted in his mind at a very early date. There were two general influences, which led him in this direction. One was the influence of Darwin, which inclined him to link the emotions with the instincts, and to stress the biological aspect of emotional expression. The other was the influence of British empiricism, inclining him to stress the sensory aspect of mental content.

Many chapters and passages of the *Psychology* attracted attention. Often they were noteworthy and influential, not because of any psychological originality, but because of the brilliancy of style and richness of concrete illustration with which an old theme was given new life. Such was the case, for example, with the discussions of belief and instinct. But the most signal case of this was the famous chapter on habit. In a letter to Robertson he referred slightingly to the article which first treated this subject: "A mere pot-boiler, which I had long had, written, in my drawer. No new thing in it, so I hardly advise you to read it." [10] But James, the artist and teacher, combining vividness with moral conviction, created a popular classic. It is not without bearing on its success that it should have sprung from an early and lifelong faith of his own in the benign effect of routine and the cumulative significance of little acts. At the head of the chapter on habit in his *Briefer Course* he wrote with his own hand: "Sow an action, and you reap a habit; sow a habit and you reap a character; sow a character and you reap a destiny."

The *Principles of Psychology* was successful in a sense that is unusual for a book of science—it was widely read, not only by other psychologists, or by students of psychology, but by people who were under no obligation to read it. It was read because it was readable, and it was read by people of all sorts, often because of the very qualities which condemned it in the eyes of some professional psychologists. It was a tolerant, curious book; and because its author saw so wide a range of possibilities, and was so promiscuously hospitable to them, almost any later development in psychology can trace a line of ancestry there. It has been said that there are three schools of psychology, "the conscious, the unconscious and the anti-conscious," [11] referring to the introspective, the psychoanalytical, and the behavioristic schools. It is easy to find all three in James. The same may be said of the *"Gestalt"* school, or the *"Akt"* school, or the "Functional" school. James promoted the method of introspection traditional in the British school, and imported the results and technique of the ex-

[9] *Psychology*, II, 450. This theory is now commonly called the "James-Lange Theory," because the Danish physiologist C. Lange published a similar view in 1887. James first published his view in *Mind* in 1884 ("What is an Emotion?").

[10] The article, entitled "The Laws of Habit," was published in *Pop. Science Mo.*, XXX (1887); W.J. to Robertson, March 19, 1887.

[11] Grace Adams, "The Babel of the Psyche," *American Mercury*, XX (1930), 463.

perimental school from Germany. He was interested in applied psychology and comparative psychology. His chapter on instinct gave a great impetus to social psychology, and his medical approach and emphasis on "exceptional mental states" gave him a place in the development of abnormal psychology and psychopathology. Hence the *Psychology* was acclaimed by laymen and beginners, by students of other subjects who looked for some special application of psychology to their own problems, and by philosophical or nonsectarian students of psychology who had not yet become addicted to any special method of investigation; while at the same time it was viewed with some shade of disapproval by laboratory experimentalists and by systematizers. One of its reviewers, George Santayana, having commented on its lack of rigor and system, concluded as follows:

> But it would be pedantry to regret the loss of logical unity in a book so rich and living, in which a generous nature breaks out at every point, and the perennial problems of the human mind are discussed so modestly, so solidly, with such a deep and pathetic sincerity.[12]

The completion of the *Psychology* in 1890 moved James to expressions of opinion not only about his own book in particular, but about psychology in general. One of the most interesting of these judgments was written in the summer of 1890 to James Sully, whose paler efforts in psychology had the misfortune to be contemporaneous with those of James's colorful genius:

> It seems to me that psychology is like physics before Galileo's time,—not a single *elementary* law yet caught a glimpse of. A great chance for some future psychologue to make a greater name than Newton's, but who then will read the books of this generation? Not many, I trow. Meanwhile they must be written.[13]

James's judgment that his own psychology would be, and deserved to be, superseded by a more "scientific" psychology had already been made in a letter to his brother and was evidently much in his mind at this time:

> As "Psychologies" go, it is a good one, but psychology is in such an antescientific condition that the whole present generation of them is predestined to become unreadable old mediæval lumber, as soon as the first genuine tracks of insight are made. The sooner the better, for me![14]

It is clear that James did not accept the experimental psychology of his day as marking the advent of the new era. This was clearly not what he was looking for! It is true that he had from the beginning, and never lost, a respect for

[12] *Atlantic*, LXVII (1891), 556.
[13] July 8, 1890.
[14] June 4, 1890; *L.W.J.*, I, 296.

facts. But for experimental psychology he felt a growing distaste owing to physical and temperamental reasons. He lacked the strength to spend long hours in a laboratory; a recurrent lumbago prevented his standing, and trouble with his eyes interfered with his use of the microscope. With his precarious health there went a fitfulness of mood that incapacitated him for continuous routine. And then James had a romantic mind, eager for new adventure, and repelled by detail and repetition. From distaste to disesteem the transition was easy and natural. In such a passage as the following it is impossible to say which of these attitudes dominates:

> The results that come from all this laboratory work seem to me to grow more and more disappointing and trivial. What is most needed is new ideas. For every man who has one of them one may find a hundred who are willing to drudge patiently at some unimportant experiment.[15]

In short, James not only disliked the psychological laboratory, but came to disbelieve in any fruitfulness commensurable with the effort expended.

Did James offer anything in place of the experimental laboratory psychology which he esteemed so lightly? Did he have any intimations of the direction in which a Galileo of psychology would advance? It is clear that James was looking for a psychology that *explained,* and that he believed that the best prospect of a causal explanation was afforded by the connections of mind and body. He complained of a merely introspective psychology that it was *tedious*—"tedious not as really hard things, like physics and chemistry, are tedious, but tedious as the throwing of feathers hour after hour is tedious." [16] He was dissatisfied with such psychology, in other words, because it was too easy; and its easiness lay in the fact that it evaded the problem of causal explanation. Causal laws, then, for the sake of prediction and control—in mental science, as in physical science!

> As constituting the inner life of individual persons who are born and die, our conscious states are temporal *events* arising in the ordinary course of nature,—events, moreover, the conditions of whose happening or non-happening from one moment to another, lie certainly in large part in the physical world. Not only this; they are events of such tremendous practical moment to us that the control of these conditions on a large scale would be an achievement compared with which the control of the rest of physical nature would appear comparatively insignificant.[17]

In 1906 James addressed the Psychology Club at Harvard. "When a student of psychology," his notes for this address read, "I always regarded it as but a

---

[15] W.J. to Theodore Flournoy, December 7, 1896; *L.W.J.,* II, 54.
[16] *C.E.R.,* 343.
[17] *Ibid.,* 318-9.

part of the larger science of living beings. . . . Official psychology is a very *small* part!" He then went on to outline a "concrete" or "functional psychology," which, having discovered the forces that govern the moral and religious life, should develop a technique for their control. In the same year James advocated the study of "dynamo-genesis"—in his presidential address on "The Energies of Men" delivered before the American Philosophical Association:

> We ought somehow to get a topographic survey made of the limits of human power in every conceivable direction, something like an opthalmologist's chart of the limits of the human field of vision. . . . This would be an absolutely concrete study, to be carried on by using historical and biographical material mainly. The limits of power must be limits that have been realized in actual persons, and the various ways of unlocking the reserves of power must have been exemplified in individual lives. . . . Here is a program of concrete individual psychology, at which anyone in some measure may work. It is replete with interesting facts, and points to practical issues superior in importance to anything we know.[18]

Finally, a year before his death, James welcomed psychoanalysis, applauding its aims even when he distrusted its individual exponents:

> I strongly suspect Freud, with his dream-theory, of being a regular *halluciné*. But I hope that he and his disciples will push it to its limits, as undoubtedly it covers some facts, and will add to our understanding of "functional" psychology, which is the real psychology.[19]

That which he recommended to others is what James undertook to do himself, in the limited time which, after 1890, he devoted to psychology. He continued to interest himself in psychical research and in abnormal psychology. The "transmission" theory applied to the question of immortality was the hypothesis of a cerebralist. In his "Energies of Men" he set forth the power of the mind to resist bodily fatigue and overcome physical obstacles. He was interested in types of mentality, in all their fullness, such as those exemplified in religion and war. And he was interested in applied psychology, especially in ethical and educational applications. In all of these essays he kept in view the integral man, and sought for causal explanations through taking account of the body and the environment. He never felt confident that he had found such an explanation, but he practised his own psychological creed.

[18] *Philos. Rev.*, XVI (1907), 19.
[19] To Professor Mary W. Calkins, September 19, 1909.

XXIII

THE AFTERMATH OF THE *PSYCHOLOGY*

Upon the publication of the *Psychology* James undoubtedly experienced a profound sense of relief and a desire to disport himself in other pastures. It is also true that he never afterwards produced any considerable article or book on the standard problems of psychology. To this extent he bore out his own judgment, written in 1894: "There isn't a page more of psychological literature in this child's mental organism. . . . Our reputation first begins as our talent commences to decay." [1] But it would be a mistake to suppose that he abandoned psychology, now or later. He continued his reading, both of treatises and of periodical literature. He wrote a large number of psychological reviews, in fact some fifty-five between 1891 and 1898; with the result that when, in the latter year, he was asked to review Henry Rutgers Marshall's *Instinct and Reason,* he wrote to the author:

> I have been forced by instinct and reason, working together to protect and save my own body and soul, to forswear and renounce book-reviewing forever. I've served my time and bought my freedom, and must employ my ebbing sands of life for things parasitic, insolent, and inconclusive.[2]

In 1892 James published his so-called *Briefer Course,* a short textbook, of which two fifths was new or rewritten—the rest "scissors and paste." [3] In particular, much to his distaste, he added chapters on the psychology of the several senses. His motives were quite frankly commercial, and his expectations were fully justified when the book became and remained for some years the most widely used English text in the subject.

In the decades of the '90s James capitalized his rising fame by giving a large number of popular addresses. Many of these were on ethical and philosophical subjects, but there were two sets of lectures on psychology. The first, published under the title of *Talks to Teachers on Psychology,* was originally delivered in Cambridge in 1892, and afterwards repeated in various parts of the country. The second set was entitled "Exceptional (or, 'Abnormal') Mental States."

[1] W.J. to Henry Rutgers Marshall [1894]
[2] *Ibid.,* November 22, 1898.
[3] *P.B.C.,* iii.

They were first delivered before the Lowell Institute in 1896, and were never published.

The Preface and the contents of the *Talks to Teachers* as it finally appeared make clear how James thought a psychologist could best serve teachers—not by expounding the science of psychology in its technicalities, but by enabling them to "conceive, and, if possible, reproduce sympathetically in their imagination, the mental life of their pupil as the sort of active unity which he himself feels it to be." [4] In this there is not only an echo of the *Psychology,* but perhaps a memory of those far-off days when he was the pupil and had learned something about the mental life of his teachers.

James took a genuine and sympathetic interest in the work of the teacher and contributed substantially to the development of educational psychology. His rejection of the possibility of the transfer of training in memory—his belief, namely, that general retentiveness was unalterable and that one could only improve one's memory in specific fields by one's method of dealing with their materials—exercised a notable influence. More important, because of its wider bearing, was James's emphasis upon interest and action. The pupil, like other human beings, is essentially a reacting organism, which can be affected only by stimuli appropriate to its existing propensities, and which must as a result of its reactions inevitably form habits that will condition its future reactions.

In the autumn of 1892, Hugo Münsterberg, formerly a pupil of Wundt, came from the University of Freiburg to relieve James of the directorship of the Harvard Psychological Laboratory. He remained for three years, and then after a two years' interruption returned to remain at Harvard until his death in 1916. James admired the quality of Münsterberg's work and thought him to be "the ablest experimental psychologist in Germany, allowance made for his being only twenty-eight years old." He also admired the boldness and flexibility of his mind and the vigor of his style. Thus it came about that when in 1892 James looked for a man who might become both his temporary substitute as a teacher and his permanent substitute as director of the psychological laboratory, he turned to "that vigorous young psychologist," "the irrepressible young Münsterberg." [5]

Although Münsterberg actively fomented experimentalism among his students in the laboratory, he, like James, had heard the siren voice of philosophy and was rapidly becoming more interested in the "principles" of psychology than in the discovery of new facts. He became famous in America for his personal brilliancy, his participation in public affairs, his voluminous popular writings, and his innovating applications of psychology to industry, jurisprudence, and medicine. Though James retained both affection and esteem for Münster-

[4] *T.T.,* iv.
[5] W.J. to H.J.², April 11, 1892; *L.W.J.,* I, 318; *Psychology,* II, 189, 500.

berg, he was unquestionably disappointed by this diversion of his interests. At the same time, as the years passed, there emerged the total and irreconcilable difference between their philosophies.

The immediate occasion of Münsterberg's first invitation to Harvard was James's plan for another European sojourn. On June 1, 1891 he wrote to his brother:

> Next year . . . is a bright year, for we shall take our "leave of absence" when it is over, and as at present minded, will go abroad, every soul of us. A sweet and peaceful thought. Incessant "productive activity" needs intervals of reception. "The heart must pause to breathe, and love itself must rest."

The event proved less "sweet and peaceful" than he thought. He had promised himself a "solid holiday" by bringing the whole family to the continent; but discovered that "the wear and tear of continuous exposure to infancy in the narrow quarters with which one has to put up in hotels is something not to be imagined without actual trial." [6] It was a period of broken and scattered activities, of domestic cares, of social distractions, of indulgence in art and literature, and of philosophical reading and thinking, during which, after a long immersion in psychology, he lifted his head above water and looked around. He had his intervals of repose and refreshment during which his spirits recovered their buoyancy. The family settled for the winter in Florence, and from there James made trips to Padua and Venice. At Padua he represented Harvard at the Galileo Tercentenary, "and it was great fun." [7] Of Padua itself he wrote to his wife on November 2:

> I have rarely in my life passed a day of greater contentment. . . . The contentment doesn't come from your absence (far from it, for I've done little else but wish that you were by my side), but from the extraordinary satisfaction which this place yields to the age. It soothes it as stillness soothes the ear or lukewarm water the skin. I surrender to Italy, and I should think that a painter would almost go out of his skin to wander about from town to town. One wants to paint everything that one sees in a place like this—as a *town* Florence can't hold a candle to it. She has her galleries, her palaces and her bridges, but the rest is incumbrance, here it is the entire town that speaks to one in the most charming unpretending way. . . . I understand Giotto's eminence now. It started the tears in my eyes to see the way the little old fellow had gone to work with such joyousness and spirit . . . and it is an honor to human nature that so many people feel under his quaintness that he is a *moral* painter.

[6] To S. Hodgson, July 13, 1892.
[7] To C. Stumpf, December 20, 1892.

From Venice, four days later, James wrote to his brother:

> I spent four hours in the Academy yesterday, and went into some churches, and am presently about to start for the Ducal palace. I find the Academy less splendid than I had remembered it, and altogether get a sort of impression that the Venetian pictures wear less well than those of the Florentine sort. Giovanni Bellini and the earlier ones are the most immortal—the trail of the world, flesh, devil, chic, and conscious ability lying too thick over the others. Moreover too luscious! No matter, they *possess* one's eyes. The odd thing about it is that although my appetite to see them is ravenous, I have practically *no* recollection of how they look an hour after my back is turned. No visual images—a nice equipment for a would-be connoisseur! However, the great thing is to be able to use one's eyes at all. . . . I really enjoy this furiously.

James was less boastful of his linguistic accomplishments in the following paragraph written soon after his return to Florence:

> Our Italian is of the bottommost-infernal quality; and the pathetic resignation of the natives to the like of it, which they get from all us foreigners, is a touching sight. Centuries of servitude have bred in them a spirit very different from that noble mirth and scorn with which the free Anglo-Saxon meets the attacks of outsiders on his mother tongue! [8]

Passing on to Switzerland in the spring, James summed up his Italian visit and his change of mood in a letter written to Stumpf from Meggen on April 24, 1893:

> If you could have seen the confusion in which my last six weeks have been spent, however, you would excuse any derelictions on my part. *Incessant* sociability in Florence, pushed to such an extreme that one pair of young American friends came and *had a baby!!!* in our apartment, there being no other convenient place for the event to take place in. Fortunately my wife came away three days ago, and left them in possession—"mother and child well.". . . We are going to spend most of the summer in England, and have taken the road through Switzerland. . . . We are in this heavenly spot, with the trees all in bloom about is, and shall stay a fortnight at least, before going farther. . . . I am glad to have said good-bye to the sweet rottenness of Italy, of which I shall always preserve the tenderest memories, but in which I shall always feel a foreigner. The ugly Swiss faces, costume and speech seem to me delicious, primeval, pure, and full of human soundness and moral good. And the air! the air! there can be nothing like it in the world.

James returned to Cambridge in September, 1893, feeling that fifteen months was "too long a vacation" for a man like him to take: "teaching is such an

[8] To Francis Boott, November 18, 1892.

artificial discipline that one loses the habit of it almost immediately, and seems to forget all that one ever knew." When he was urged to attend the International Congress of Psychology held in Munich in 1896 he was still in this mood. Writing to Stumpf, he said:[9]

> I ruined myself financially by my last excursion *en famille* to Europe, and nothing but the need of foreign travel for my health could justify so speedy a repetition of the process. Moreover, it unsettles my Americanism (that tender plant) to go too often abroad, and that must be weighed against the intellectual and social advantages of the Congress. It is no light matter to feel foreign in one's native land. I am just beginning to feel American again, when this temptation comes! . . . I am heavily worked this year, but doing nothing original. As I grow older I get impatient (and incompetent) of details and turn to broad abstractions. I wish to get relieved of psychology as soon as possible, but am trying at present to keep Münsterberg's nest warm for him ere his return, which we all pray for; for he proved an efficient, and in fact an invaluable man here. There are many valuable attributes, even in a professor, besides infallibility, and taking one man with another, Münsterberg is about as infallible as anyone who takes as broad a field.

Two of James's activities during the nineties served to connect his psychological interests with his growing absorption in morals, religion, and metaphysics. The first of these was his continuing participation in "psychical research." His interest in "psychical research" was not one of his vagaries, but was central and typical. He grew up in a circle in which heresies were more gladly tolerated than orthodoxies. Men like his father and his father's friends, who were attracted to Fourierism, communism, homœopathy, women's rights, abolition, and spiritism, were not likely to have any prejudices against mediumship, clairvoyance, mesmerism, automatic writing, and crystal gazing. From his youth James contemplated such "phenomena" without repulsion and with an open mind.

Psychical research was only one of many examples of James's fondness for excursions to the scientific underworld. His freedom from prejudice against theories or sects of dubious repute was converted into something more positive by his chivalry. He not only tolerated, but *preferred,* the despised and rejected —in movements as well as in men. Orthodox science was a symbol of arrogance and vulgar success, disposed to exaggerate its claims and to abuse its power. In any dispute between science and a weaker brother in which it appeared that science was the aggressor, James would invariably be found intervening. Hence he proposed as a suitable motto to Myers's posthumous work the scriptural passage, "And base things of the world and things which are despised hath God

[9] To Stumpf, January 24, 1894 and December 18, 1895.

chosen, yes, and things which are not, to bring to naught things that are." [10]

James hoped that psychical research, like other studies of abnormal phenomena, might throw light on the central constitution and deeper causes of human nature. He also saw in it the possibility of a more kindly treatment of suffering humanity. It was connected in his mind with the possibility of mental healing, and this, in turn, with his own personal maladies and recoveries.

The Society for Psychical Research was founded in 1882, the year of James's residence in London and of his close contact with those who, like Gurney, Myers, and the Sidgwicks, were primarily responsible for its success. James became a member in 1884, and remained a member until his death. He was a vice president for eighteen years, and president in 1894-1895 and 1895-1896. The American Society was founded in 1884, and James was one of its supporters and workers.

Frederic Myers was to James not only the leading proponent of psychical research, but the creator of a bold hypothesis, that of a wider sub-liminal and extra-liminal consciousness, of which "the whole system of consciousness studied by the classical psychology is only an extract." But while James felt the liveliest sympathy with this hypothesis he was nevertheless quite aware that the foundations were insecure. As he remarked, apropos of the posthumous work on *Human Personality and Its Survival,* "the piles driven into the quicksand are too few for such a structure." [11]

James never abandoned psychical research. In 1909 he published the most ambitious of all his investigations in this field, a voluminous report on "Mrs. Piper's Hodgson-Control"; and later in the same year, and less than a year before his death, he published a popular article entitled "The Confidences of a 'Psychical Researcher.'" [12] Such, in brief, is the history of James's participation in psychical research. What was his conclusion?

In the first place, it is important to remember that for James this more or less extra-scientific domain of investigation was continuous with psychopathology and abnormal psychology. He had seen phenomena such as hypnotism, hysteria, and multiple personality removed from the realm of charlatanry and superstition and brought within the pale of science; and he saw no reason why the phenomena that were still outlawed should not receive a like recognition. In the late autumn of 1896 he began a course of eight lectures on "Abnormal Mental States" before the Lowell Institute in Boston. The subjects of the lectures were: "Dreams and Hypnotism," "Hysteria," "Automatisms," "Multiple Personality," "Demoniacal Possession," "Witchcraft," "Degenera-

[10] *L.W.J.,* II, 157. The motto was not adopted.

[11] *M.S.,* 163-4; W.J. to F. C. S. Schiller, April 8, 1903; for Schiller *cf.* below, 301 ff.

[12] *Proc. of the Soc. for Psychical Research,* XXIII (1909); and *American Magazine,* October 1909. Richard Hodgson had died in 1905.

tion," and "Genius." These lectures were never written out, but the notes that remain indicate the wealth of their material and the profusion of concrete illustration with which they were made palatable to the audience. He made the following allusion to the field that lay beyond:—

> [I am] at the portal of psychical research, into which I said I would not enter. . . . I myself have no question that the formula of dissociated personality will account for the phenomena I have brought before you. . . . But to say that is one thing and to *deny any other range of phenomena* is another. Whether supernormal powers of cognition in certain persons may occur, is a matter to be decided by evidence.

There remains the question of James's final verdict on these residual, "supernormal," phenomena. He was offended by the vulgarity and scandal which frequently attended mediumistic and spiritist "manifestations." He was perfectly aware of the imposture that was commonly practised, and regarded the greater part of the alleged revelations as "rubbish." And yet, in spite of all, he "found himself believing" [13] that there was "something in it"—a residuum of supernormal knowledge, a pattern of mentality not admitted by orthodox science.

Furthermore, James had a hypothesis for which he claimed a "dramatic probabilit;"—the hypothesis, namely, that "there is a continuum of cosmic consciousness, against which our individuality builds but accidental fences, and into which our several minds plunge as into a mother-sea or reservoir." [14]

This hypothesis was unverified in any sense that would be acceptable to science. It was unsupported by experiment, and afforded no basis for control or prediction. James accepted it as a generalization which most nearly satisfied all the manifold requirements of a philosophy, providing both for the facts of experience and for the subjective demands of the moral subject.

The same hypothesis was applied by James to the topic of immortality, and served here to link psychology with religion. In 1898 James gave the "Ingersoll Lecture on the Immortality of Man," afterwards published under the title of *Human Immortality: Two Supposed Objections.* The first of the "supposed objections" was the argument of science that the mind was dependent on the body and could not, therefore, outlive it. James replied that the facts of physiological psychology require only a "functional" dependence of mind on body. Such a dependence does not necessarily imply that the brain *produces* the mind; it may merely release it, or *let it through.*[15] In that case the larger res-

---

[13] *M.S.,* 196 ff.

[14] *Ibid.,* 204.

[15] This idea that the brain, instead of creating mind, merely strains and canalizes it, was an idea that James had long entertained, and an idea which seemed to him entirely congruent not only with the alleged phenomena of psychical research but with the mystical religious experience.

ervoir of consciousness would remain intact after the dissolution of the brain, and might retain traces of the life history of its individual emanation.

The same hypothesis was playfully presented in a letter to Thomas Davidson. Among the metaphors which James commonly used (and occasionally mixed!) were those of light—"the white radiance of eternity" stained by "a dome of many-colored glass"—and the mother-sea divided by channels or overflowing its barriers.[16]

Cambridge, Oct. 20, 1898 [17]

Dear Thomas,—

If you had the slightest spark of scientific imagination you would see that the mother-sea is of a glutinous consistency, and when she strains off portions of her being through the dome of many-colored glass, they stick so tenaciously that she must shake herself hard to get rid of them. Then, as there is no action without reaction, the shake is felt by both members, and remains registered in the mother-sea, like a "stub" in a check book, preserving memory of the transaction. These stubs form the basis of the immortal account, which we begin when the prismatic dome is shattered. These matters, you see, are ultra simple, and would be revealed to you if you had a more humble and teachable heart. Your whole lot of idle and captious questions proceed so obviously from intellectual pride, and are so empty of all true desire for instructions that I will not pretend to reply to them all. . . . In great haste. Yours affectionately,

W.J.

[16] *H.l.*, 1899, 16.
[17] This letter has also been printed in J. S. Bixler's *Religion in the Philosophy of William James*, 1926, 152.

XXIV

THE WILL TO BELIEVE

In 1899, on September 10, James wrote to Stumpf: "I fear I am ceasing to be a psychologist and becoming exclusively a moralist and a metaphysician." These deeper problems first presented themselves as problems of life rather than of theory, and James was often moved to reaffirm and amplify the faith of his youth. Release from the pressure and discipline imposed by the writing of the *Psychology* rendered him again vulnerable to brooding melancholy; and he again felt the need of a saving gospel. At the same time there was a great expansion of his human sympathies and of his political and social activities. This was the decade of the Spanish War and of the Dreyfus case, both of which deeply stirred his moral emotions. His activities in psychical research revived his old sympathy with religious mysticism, and gave him a new hope of justifying it. All of these reasons conspired to make the decade from 1890 to 1900, or more precisely from 1892 to 1902, James's period of reform and evangelism.

The volume entitled *The Will to Believe, and other Essays in Popular Philosophy,* published in 1897, was made up of articles and addresses which had been written at intervals from 1879 to 1896. The famous address which gave the book its title had been delivered in 1895.[1] The doctrines which the volume sets forth fall naturally into three groups, those, namely, which deal with fideism, with pluralism, and with individualism. Fideism touches theory of knowledge, pluralism metaphysics, and individualism ethics, but in all three cases the personal and practical accent predominates.

Early in his life, perhaps as early as 1868, James recorded the following observation in a notebook: "Philosophies owe their being to two impulses in the mind: (1) that after absolute intellectual unity or consistency; (2) that after an object we guarantee for our interests." In July 1879, James published in *Mind* an article entitled "The Sentiment of Rationality," to which he added the statement that this article was "the first chapter of a psychological work on the motives which lead men to philosophize." These motives James again divided into two groups, the "theoretic or logical" and the "practical and emotional." Fideism has to do with the second of these groups of motives—the extra-theo-

---

[1] ". . . luckless title, which should have been 'Right to Believe' " (W.J. to F. H. Bradley, June 16, 1904).

retical motives which express man's "active powers" and carry belief beyond the data of experience.

It was a plea for conviction and confidence as opposed to scepticism and doubt. That this plea expressed the ardor of James's personal temperament, he himself would have been the last to deny. There is an indubitable connection, also, with James's upbringing. Having committed no excesses of credulity in his youth, there was nothing to repent in his maturity or old age. But while he craved belief, he indulged that craving with restraint and moderation. He urged the case for belief with a certain vehemence, because he was addressing himself to "academic audiences" [2] who lived in the unnatural atmosphere of scientific pursuits. He was also addressing himself. He was not credulous, but *suffered from incredulity*. He was deeply concerned with the need of belief and with the right to believe, but made no considerable use of that right.

The same spirit of unpretentious empiricism prompted James to chill the ardor of friends who took his fideism too seriously:

> As for faith, don't treat it as a technical word. It simply means the kind of belief a person may have in a doubtful case—and may carry a sense of "heat in your throat," readytobackoutness, or a sort of passionate refusal to give up, or anything between; and is the same state, when applied to some practical affairs of your own, or to a theological creed. [3]

Assuming that belief may be dictated by the preferences of our practical nature, what do these preferences dictate? The answer is to be found in "pluralism." This doctrine, in turn, has to be interpreted in the light of its moving appeal. It is not a mere doctrine of plurality, but plurality in its bearing on human feelings and resolves. Thus pluralism means a finite God, who evokes a passionate allegiance because he is in some measure hampered by circumstances, and dependent on the aid of others; or because, the evil of the world being external to him, he may be loved without reserve. In the brilliant essay on "The Dilemma of Determinism" which forms a part of the *Will to Believe,* he is concerned not so much to reject determinism in general as to reject a *monistic* determinism, in which the world, being all of one piece, must be approved or condemned as a unit. The moral will is essentially partisan—recognizing and promoting what ought to be, in a context of things that were better not, and which it seeks with all its might to make as though they had never been.

But the moral will needs a pluralistic environment for another reason: not only because good must be free from any compromise with evil, but also because one moral will must not be compromised by another. The very goodness

---

[2] *W.B.*, x.
[3] To Mrs. Glendower Evans, July 29, 1897.

of life is inseparable from its aspect of privacy. The world is "a sort of republican banquet . . . where all the qualities of being respect one another's personal sacredness, yet sit at the common table of space and time." [4] Pluralism is thus united with individualism.

The pluralism and individualism of James's *Will to Believe* was not only a bond with his old friends, Davidson and Howison, but brought him new friends.

Wincenty Lutoslawski, Platonic scholar, linguist, reformer, exponent of Yoga, Polish patriot, and latterly professor at Wilno, came to America in 1893 to attend the Congress of Religions at the Chicago World's Fair and took the occasion to visit James in Cambridge. This year marked the beginning of a correspondence, personal and philosophical, which continued until 1909. James took a warm interest in his friend's career and personal affairs. He entertained him at his home, endeavored with varying success to obtain lectureships and other appointments for him in America, read and promoted his writings. He applauded both his individualistic-pluralistic philosophy and his heroic moralism. "A perfect passion of friendship, love, brotherhood and loyalty sings through his pages." [5] But Lutoslawski's zeal was a little too much—even for James. "These Slavs," he said, "seem to be the great radical livers-out of their theories"; besides which, the theories themselves lost plausibility through their extravagance. In 1899, Lutoslawski visited James at Nauheim and "read to him in improvised English translation many masterpieces of Polish literature." James's description of this visit gives a summary both of the philosophy and of the philosopher:—

> We have been having a visit from an extraordinary Pole named Lutoslawski, 36 years old, author of philosophical writings in seven different languages . . . and knower of several more, handsome, and to the last degree genial. He has a singular philosophy—the philosophy of friendship. He takes in dead seriousness what most people admit, but only half-believe, *viz.*, that we are *Souls* (Zoolss, he pronounces it), that souls are immortal, and agents of the world's destinies, and that the chief concern of a soul is to get ahead by the help of other souls with whom it can establish confidential relations. . . . He is a *wunderlicher Mensch:* abstractly his scheme is divine, but there is something on which I can't yet just lay my defining finger that makes one feel that there is some need of the corrective and critical arresting judgment in his manner of carrying it out.[6]

Among the most vigorous and sympathetic critics of *The Will to Believe* was Benjamin Paul Blood of Amsterdam, New York—who had heard James's father preach fifty or sixty years before, and had then acquired a "fancy for the

[4] *W.B.*, 270.
[5] James's Preface to Lutoslawski's *World of Souls,* G. Allen and Unwin Ltd., 1924, 8.
[6] The last three quotations are taken from W.J.'s letter to Frances R. Morse of September 17, 1899; *L.W.J.*, II, 103.

family name." [7] He was born in 1832 and lived for eighty-six years. During that time he wrote much, but unsystematically. His favorite form of publication was letters to newspapers, mainly local newspapers with a small circulation. Blood was a man after James's own heart, in temperament and style as well as in the substance of his thought. He was an unacademic philosopher who wrote from the depths or shallows of his own experience, and fitted his vehicle to this content. He was a mystic, which in itself would have commended him to James. But he was also a man of exceptional physical vigor, and sufficiently affected by the diversity and particularity of this world to lean to pluralism rather than to monism.

In the Preface to *The Will to Believe* James had quoted from Blood's pamphlet *The Flaw in Supremacy,* and referred to its author as a "gifted writer" and pluralistic ally.[8]

Amsterdam, April 18, 1897

My dear Doctor,—

Mrs. Blood has gone to church, and I have sat hesitating about longer delay in trying to do some justice to your *Essays,* which I have read and re-read occasionally every day since I received them. . . . Mrs. Blood says this is the only fame I ever had that was any good. . . . She is a thinker and a wag. I was telling her of your notion of the "Sentiment of Rationality" as easily flowing thought, etc.: she said there was more of it than that—something *has* to be, to put any go into the world; and she illustrated from what she was doing by saying, "If you have picked-up codfish for dinner on Friday, you have got to have codfish balls for breakfast on Saturday!" There is an apodictic judgment for you.

But it would take as much matter as your book contains to tell what I think of it, for it is all ahead of the procession, and all along the lines which interest me most. The style is not perfection. The meanings are all classic, but there is a colloquial insouciance which is not as a man would write for his life, unless indeed he didn't give a continental whether he lived or died. . . .

But about the leading animus of the book: "pluralism." I am a pluralist easily enough, believing only in lower-case gods, and in no grand climacteric results of being; there is no finale, no one lesson to be learned. Everything happens in the middle of eternity. All days are judgment-days and creation-morns, and all the hustle and bustle and hurry and worry of the man who had lost a day!— him who had a charge to keep, a God to glorify, a never-dying soul to save, and other ethical chores pressing—stamped him out of "the caste of Vere de Vere":[9] "for the slow planets sun themselves in green immortal leisure." The gods recline on asphodel; no sympathy with these our rushing purposes, ruffles the languor of their patrician repose. Yet will it ever do to put pluralism in the place of philosophy? It is still true, though there be no god with the capital *G,* that "the one remains, the many change and pass."[10]. . .

[7] Blood to W.J., August 9, 1882: ". . . The first man of genius I ever saw alive was Henry James. He preached at the Presbyterian church here." *Cf.* also below, 352, 363.

[8] *W.B.,* viii-ix.

[9] Tennyson's "Lady Clara Vere de Vere."

[10] Shelley's *Adonais.*

"The Dilemma of Determinism" strikes me as the most dramatic "piece of work" in your volume, though possibly "The Sentiment of Rationality" is more original; but all are good and have a future—negative, iconoclastic, perhaps, but powerful. You do not build—how can you build on foundations that run everywhere? and I am not sure that you generalize at all. . . . The world has long believed in limited space (subjective), unity of intelligence, community, a home, a heaven, a duty, an order, a chance for fame that is known of all, not *a* world but *the* world, under control—all facts and possibilities known and realized— imperial peace. Even in pluralism *per se* this must be *sometime;* if we are to have everything we must try the One awhile, however stale it may become, till "there was war in heaven." Pluralism is hard to focus,—it is like sand, or meal. It is a necessary conception, but so is the One. I leave to you and to time the reconciliation, very grateful that something compels you to write about it,— and let me read it. . . . Believe that you have afforded a great pleasure to your humble friend,

BENJ. PAUL BLOOD

Cambridge, April 28, 1897

Dear Blood,—

Your letter is delectable. From your not having yet acknowledged the book, I began to wonder whether you had got it, but this acknowledgment is almost too good. Your thought is obscure,—lightning flashes, darting gleams—but that's the way truth is. And although I "put pluralism in the place of philosophy," I do it only so far as philosophy means the articulable and the scientific. Life and mysticism exceed the articulable, and if there is a *One* (and surely men will never be weaned from the idea of it) it must remain only mystically expressed.

I have been roaring over and quoting some of the passages of your letter, in which my wife takes as much delight as I do. As for your strictures on my English, I accept them humbly. I have a tendency towards too great colloquiality, I know, and I trust your sense of English better than any man's in the country. I have a fearful job on hand just now: an address on the unveiling of a military statue.[11] Three thousand people, Governor and troops, etc. Why they fell upon me, God knows, but being challenged, I could not funk. The task is a mechanical one, and the result somewhat of a school-boy composition. If I thought it wouldn't bore you I should send you a copy for you to go carefully over and correct or rewrite as to the English. I should probably adopt every one of your corrections. What do you say to this? Yours ever,

WM. JAMES

Some years later James wrote to Blood: "You have the greatest gift of superior gab since Shakespeare"; but to his request that Blood revise the Shaw Address the latter's reply was prompt and decisive: "Thanks no! I have not the gall to undertake to improve your English, which for ordinary purposes, whether praying or swearing, will probably be understood; and I infer that it

[11] The monument to Robert Gould Shaw, unveiled in Boston, May 31, 1897. The address is published in *M.S.*

has a charm of its own." Although in later years James's correspondence with Blood languished, it never expired. He continued to admire Blood's style, despite the latter's lack of coherence. "For single far-flung and far-flashing words and sentences," wrote James in 1907, "you're the biggest genius I know; but when it comes to constructing a whole argument or article it seems to be another kettle of fish." [12] Evidence of the tenacity of James's personal attachment appears in the fact that the last of his writings published in his own lifetime was an essay entitled "A Pluralistic Mystic," devoted to the philosophy and genius of his old friend. He had evidently found in this obscure and amateur thinker a *mystical verification of pluralism:*

> I confess that the existence of this novel brand of mysticism has made my cowering mood depart. I feel now as if my own pluralism were not without the kind of support which mystical corroboration may confer. Monism can no longer claim to be the only beneficiary of whatever right mysticism may possess to lend *prestige.*

Blood's philosophy, said James, was "not dissimilar to my own"; and he was willing that Blood's "last word" as a mystic should be *his* last word as a philosopher:

> Let *my* last word, then, speaking in the name of intellectual philosophy, be *his* word:—"There is no conclusion. What has concluded, that we might conclude in regard to it? There are no fortunes to be told, and there is no advice to be given.—Farewell!" [13]

Among the critics of *The Will to Believe* there was one, at least, who complained not of James's boldness but of his excessive caution. A faith so generalized, so consciously and punctiliously justified, was not faith at all! John Jay Chapman was at this time practising law in New York City, and had been for many years a friend and kindred spirit.

New York, March 30, 1897

My dear Mr. James,—

. . . The course of reasoning—or, say, the state of mind of a man who justifies faith by the considerations you mention—is well enough. He makes himself content. His shanty will last his day. He's got some kind of tar or hopes that'll keep faith in him and prevent it from evaporating. But he'll never convey it—arouse it, evoke it—in another. . . . This is a somewhat roundabout way of saying that such a man hasn't got faith at all. The faith you begin to talk about has been so justified and bolstered, and drugged up and down, and ironed and wired—damme if I call that faith! Damned if I call that faith! If I cared about such matters and thought them important, your essay would make me a Roman

[12] W.J. to Blood, November 28, 1909; Blood to W.J., April 29, 1897; W.J. to Blood, March 13, 1907.
[13] *M.S.,* 374-5, 411.

Catholic. I honestly think the Roman system contains a better statement of spiritual truth than this shy at it.

The question is one of expressiveness. You remember that at the "Swarry" in *Pickwick Papers* the Bath butler, to make conversation, asks Sam Weller whether he has noticed the chalybeate in the Bath waters. "I noticed," says Sam, "a taste of warm flat-irons—but I noticed no chalybeate, and I think chalybeate is a very inexpressive word."

Another thing. . . . I kept wondering,—"But why all this pother—what *difference* does it make whether a man believes or not? Why is this question important enough to be discussed?" . . . I had supposed that the idea of that note —the supposed connection between belief and conduct—was one of the busted ideas of the world, like astrology, or the divining rod. . . . Sincerely yours,

JOHN JAY CHAPMAN

Cambridge, April 5, 1897

Dear Chapman,—

Pray continue your epistolary explosions. The latter one did my heart real good. You belong to the Salvation Army party; and the poor little razor-like "thin end of the wedge" which your academic personages twiddle between their fingers must indeed seem loathsome to the robuster temperaments at the other end. You remind me of the farmer who said to his bishop, after a sermon proving the existence of God,—"It is a very fine sermon, but I believe there be a God after all."

Faith indeed! Damme if I call that faith, either. It is only calculated for the sickly hotbed atmosphere of the philosophic-positivistically enlightened scientific classroom. To the victims of spinal paralysis which these studies superinduce, the homeopathic treatment, although you might not believe it, really does good. We are getting too refined for anything; altogether out of touch with genuine life. Therefore I tie to you as a piece of water-closet paper might try to tie to a stone, if it were afraid that the wind would blow it away.

All this rubbish is only for public purposes. In my individual heart I fully believe my faith is as robust as yours. The trouble about your robust and full-bodied faiths, however, is, that they begin to cut each other's throats too soon, and for getting on in the world and establishing a *modus vivendi* these pestilential refinements and reasonablenesses and moderations have to creep in. I am sorry for your paragraph about your supposed connection between belief and conduct. It is by no means busted; on the contrary, it is one of the most tremendous forces in the world.

Now send me another letter soon, and read my Preface if you have not yet read it, and believe me, ever devotedly and affectionately yours,

WM. JAMES

In 1904 L. T. Hobhouse published an article in which he attacked James as holding two doctrines: "The first is, that by believing a thing we make it true; the second is, that we can believe in a thing without asking ourselves seriously whether it is true or false." James replied:

I cry to Heaven to tell me of what insane root my "leading contemporaries" have eaten, that they are so smitten with blindness as to the meaning of printed texts. Or are we others absolutely incapable of making our meaning clear? I imagine that there is neither insane root nor unclear writing, but that in these matters each man writes from out of a field of consciousness of which the bogey in the background is the chief object. Your bogey is superstition; my bogey is desiccation; and each, for his contrast-effect, clutches at any text that can be used to represent the enemy, regardless of exegetical proprieties. In my essay the evil shape was a vision of "Science" in the form of abstraction, priggishness and sawdust, lording it over all. Take the sterilist scientific prig and cad you know, compare him with the richest religious intellect you know, and you would not, any more than I would, give the former the exclusive right of way.[14]

The ground of James's complaint is quite clear. He was accused of encouraging *willfulness* or *wantonness* of belief, or of advocating belief for belief's sake, whereas his whole purpose had been to *justify* belief. He had affirmed that belief was voluntary, but had naturally assumed that, in this as in other cases, volition would be governed by motives and illuminated by reasons. His critics had accused him of advocating *license* in belief, whereas, on the contrary, his aim had been to formulate rules for belief. And whatever one might think of its extensive religious applications, the thesis had been simple. He had argued that in certain cases where both belief and doubt are possible there is a greater likelihood of getting the truth by believing than by doubting—or at least an equal likelihood, with other advantages besides. Over and above the risk of incurring error, to which science is so acutely alive, there is another risk to be considered, the risk, namely, of losing truth. What truth was, he had not undertaken to show; this theme was resumed in *Pragmatism*.

[14] Hobhouse, "Faith and the Will to Believe," *Proc. of the Aristotelian Soc.,* IV (1904), 91; W.J. to Hobhouse, August 12, 1904.

XXV

MORAL INDIVIDUALISM

The Will to Believe, together with his other writings and activities of the same period, gave expression to James's fundamental moralism. It was this moralism that stood in the way of a more perfect sympathy with the most stimulating and congenial of his early friends. On March 7, 1900, Holmes, then Chief Justice of the Supreme Court of Massachusetts, was given a dinner by the Bar Association of Boston. His response was a brief formulation of his philosophy of life:

> We cannot live our dreams. We are lucky enough if we can give a sample of our best, and if in our hearts we can feel that it has been nobly done. . . . The joy of life is to put out one's power in some natural and useful or harmless way. . . . The rule of joy and the law of duty seem to me all one. I confess that altruistic and cynically selfish talk seem to me about equally unreal. . . . From the point of view of the world the end of life is life. Life is action, the use of one's powers. As to use them to their height is our joy and duty, so it is the one end that justifies itself. . . . Life is an end in itself, and the only question as to whether it is worth living is whether you have enough of it." [1]

Having read this speech, James wrote to his friend Miss Frances R. Morse:

> I thank you for the paper with the Chief Justice's speech to the bar dinner. I must say I'm disappointed in O.W.H. for being unable to make any other than that one set speech which comes out on every occasion. It's all right for once, in the exuberance of youth, to celebrate mere vital excitement, *la joie de vivre,* as a protest against humdrum solemnity. But to make it systematic, and oppose it, as an ideal and a duty, to the ordinarily recognized duties, is to pervert it altogether—especially when one is a Chief Justice. It is curiously childish to me, and Wendell always forgets that on his own terms the dutiful people also fulfil his law. Even they live hard, and enjoy the struggle with their opposing devils! So let them alone! W. reminds me of the verse of Browning, which Santayana in his new book says Attila or Alaric might have written: "Bound dizzily to the wheel of Change, to slake the thirst of God." Mere excitement is an immature ideal, unworthy of the Supreme Court's official endorsement. [2]

---

[1] *Speeches by Oliver Wendell Holmes,* Little, Brown and Company, 1913, 83-6.
[2] April 12, 1900; other parts of this letter appear in *L.W.J.,* II, 124-9; and below, 257.

James's strong attachment to Holmes on other grounds makes this dissent the more striking. It derives further significance from the fact that James himself seemed so often to be preaching the same gospel—of action for the action's sake. But there can be no doubt whatever of his sensitiveness to any sceptical slur upon moral earnestness, or to any fainthearted abandonment of the cause of righteousness. If there is to be anything inherently valuable in living, it must be living *of a certain sort,* in which one both serves a moral ideal and *believes in it.* Whether in this James was voicing the genius of his ancestry—their Scotch-Irish levity curbed by the Presbyterian sobriety—I shall not venture to say, but there is an unmistakable connection with James's personal need of a stabilizer for his mercurial temperament.

This same moralism affected James's attitude to his brother's novels, and his enjoyment of the purely lyrical quality in poetry. Replying on August 14, 1907, to Charles Eliot Norton's criticism of the *Oxford Book of English Verse,* he said:

> Your letter . . . gave *me* more than enjoyment—it explained me to myself. I had always supposed myself to "hate" English poetry, because I had never been able to finish reading a poem. You have shown me that the fault lies with the poets, and not with me—they can't finish their own poems. That lets me out, and I agree with you perfectly! I don't know Quiller-Couch's collection, but I think the *Golden Treasury* a dreadful thing in the main— . . . it is so inhuman. Have you seen a little book, *Les cent meilleurs poèmes français?* It seems to me, objectively speaking, superior to any English collection. . . . But I have to admit at the outset that I am *poetry-deaf.*

Closely allied to James's moral earnestness was his strong distaste for anything which he suspected of being decadent. It was not merely that he disapproved of moral irregularities, but that he felt an almost physiological repugnance to anything which was overrefined, overseasoned, or overmature. He applauded Blood's remark that the universe was "game-flavored as a hawk's wing,"[3] but he did not want his game too high. He liked simplicity, purity, and wholesomeness, in life as well as in nature. That at the same time he was tolerant of difference, addicted to morbid psychology, and catholic in his love of art and literature is not to be denied, but rather recognized as proving how deeply rooted was the plant which could resist these opposing influences. There are many evidences of this "wholesome" side of James's moralism. It appears in his admiring antipathy to Santayana's philosophy, with its "perfection of rottenness" and "moribund Latinity."[4] Best of all, there is his feeling toward the seduction of Italy—his alternations of yielding and rejecting. When he

[3] *W.B.,* ix.
[4] *L.W.J.,* II, 122-3.

judged the debility and "sweet decay" [5] of Italy it was usually in contrast with the hygienic "insipidity" of Switzerland. "Switzerland is *good!* Good *people!*" [6] This feeling appears in a letter written to Charles Ritter from Florence on October 5, 1892:

> Florence seems to me even more attractive than it was when I was here eighteen years ago. . . . But how sovereignly *good* is Switzerland! It meets all the major needs of body and soul as no other country does, in summer time. After the æsthetics, the morbidness, the corruptions of Italy, how I shall want again in *ihrem Thau gesund mich zu baden!* You have doubtless been shocked by Renan's death. A true magician, but a man who caused legitimate disappointment by the form which his intellect finally found most congruous. He used the vocabulary of the moral and religious life too sweetly and freely for one whose thought refused to be *bound* by those ideals. Moral ideals go with refusals and sacrifices, and there is something shocking about the merely *musical* function they play in Renan's pages. So I call him *profoundly* superficial! But *what* an artist!

The strength of the æsthetic motive in James is well known and abundantly attested. In his youth he was deeply impressed by Goethe's amoralism, and this impression was repeated and confirmed as late as 1902. He respected canons of taste, both in his conduct and in his judgment. His own artistic impulse, transferred from painting, found expression in philosophizing, which involved the same "sacrificial element" and (for James, at least) the same inseparable fusion of style and matter. From time to time, notably in Paris and Dresden in his youth, and again in Florence twenty-five years later, he indulged a ravenous appetite for the visual arts. He often remarked that he had no visual *memory,* but the effect of this was to make him more rather than less dependent upon immediate visual experience.

If James felt the futility of theoretical æsthetics, it was not, then, for lack of artistic sensibility or owing to any disparagement of the value of art. Nor did he neglect the problem. He returned to it again and again, but always with the same sense of failure. As time went on this feeling of futility was converted into a definite judgment that the æsthetic experience was insuperably personal and subjective. It was not that James regarded this experience as one of undiscriminating emotionality—quite the contrary. In the *Psychology* he describes an aged couple who sat for more than an hour before Titian's "Assumption" in Venice, supported by "a glow of spurious sentiment that would have fairly made old Titian sick." They had missed the point. "In every art, in every science, there is the keen perception of certain relations being *right* or not, and there is the

[5] *L.W.J.,* I, 342.
[6] *Ibid.,* I, 328; *Journal,* May 10, 1905.

emotional flush and thrill consequent thereupon."[7] But it is this "flush" or "thrill" which is the ultimate criterion, and this is too hopelessly relative to the individual observer to permit of any general formulation.

Apart from its relativity, the æsthetic experience resists formulation because it consists in *feeling*. Writing later to Henry Rutgers Marshall, he said:

> The difference between the first- and second-best things in art absolutely seems to escape verbal definition—it is a matter of a hair, a shade, an inward quiver of some kind—yet what miles away in point of preciousness! Absolutely the same verbal formula applies to the supreme success and to the thing that just misses it, and yet verbal formulas are all that your æsthetics will give.[8]

This objection is an application of the most general principle in James's philosophy, the priority, namely, of original experience over representations or descriptions—"the contrast between the richness of life and the poverty of all possible formulas."[9] He insisted on this priority wherever his own original experience was peculiarly vivid. There is food for reflection in the fact that while he wrote at length about religious experiences he shrank away from any account of æsthetic experiences. I suspect that the explanation is to be found in the fact that he *had* the æsthetic experience, and borrowed the religious—which was thus, even in his "sources," already verbalized.

So much for James's æsthetics, or his rejection of the "universal," "objective" æsthetics of his day. This in itself implies no subordination of the æsthetic experience, or of art, in the hierarchy of values. To account for this subordination we must turn to other considerations, and note, in the first place, that there was in James a *primitivism* which always disputed for possession of his soul. Assuming that art and even landscape imply some regard for form, their enjoyment was opposed in James to his relish for the *unformed*—the raw and crude.

> I enjoy an occasional thing when it comes in my way, like York or Durham, but a methodical pursuit of the picturesque—heaven remove me sooner! The only thing that does me real good is the *country* in the American sense, as something that you can go *into*, and lie on the ground with a book all day. *This* [English] country is splendid if one have proper legs and wind, which I haven't. It is full of crags and climbs and possible loneliness, but the entire foreground is cocknified in the extreme, solidly built up and walled round.[10]

In a limited, orderly world, whether made by the hand of man or by his thought and imagination, James felt a sort of claustrophobia. The *historic*

[7] *Psychology,* II, 471-2.
[8] [February 7, 1899?]; *L.W.J.,* II, 87.
[9] *Nation,* LIX (1894), 49.
[10] To Charles A. Strong, June 28, 1909.

aroused a similar feeling. The cult of art lovers was associated in his mind with traditionalism, especially in Italy; whereas James preferred the boundless future or the opportune present. He was an exponent of contemporaneousness. There is something to be done *now* to make the world better. It was in this vein that he wrote to his sister from Rome on December 24, 1873:

> Italy is a very *delightful* place to dip into but no more. I can't imagine how, unless one is earnestly studying history in some way, it can in the long run help injuring all one's active powers. The weight of the past world here is fatal,— one ends by becoming its mere parasite instead of its equivalent. This worship, this dependence on other men is abnormal. The ancients did things by doing the business of their own day, not by gaping at their grandfathers' tombs,—and the normal man today will do likewise. Better fifty years of Cambridge, than a cycle of Cathay! Adieu. Your brutal and philistine Brother.

We are thus brought back again to the priority of the moral will—over feeling, as well as over thought. James was far from proposing to abolish feeling. He recognized it as composing a large part of that inwardness of life from which the individual derives his uniqueness and dignity. He even advocated intensity of feeling:

> It is a consequence of the "law of stimulation" that, apart from motor effect and *per se,* feeling is reckoned as a good. Which lives most, this orderly man whose life runs on oiled rails of propriety, who never does ill or makes a mistake or has a regret, or a pang, because on every occasion the right *action* presents itself to his mind and he simply does it; or the passionate tumultuous blunderer, whose whole life is an alternation of rapturous excitement, and horrible repentance and longing for the ruined good? He *feels;* the other *does.* If his type should be extinguished, surely would not one of the divinest of human gifts, the gift of intense feeling, be lost from life? [11]

But James, as he said, was a "motor." [12] It was an essential feature of his psychology, furthermore, that emotion was an unnatural terminus of mind. A completed cycle of conscious life will always culminate in action—feelings merely enjoyed lead to the atrophy of will:

> Even the habit of excessive indulgence in music, for those who are neither performers themselves nor musically gifted enough to take it in a purely intellectual way, has probably a relaxing effect upon the character. One becomes filled with emotions which habitually pass without prompting to any deed, and so the inertly sentimental condition is kept up. The remedy would be, never to suffer one's self to have an emotion at a concert, without expressing it afterward in *some* active way.[13]

[11] From a loose undated note entitled "Æsthetics."
[12] To Pauline Goldmark, September 14, 1901; *L.W.J.,* II, 163.
[13] *Psychology,* I, 125-6.

"What does the moral enthusiast care for philosophical ethics?" asked James in 1879.[14] "The Moral Philosopher and the Moral Life," originally an address given in 1891, and afterwards included in *The Will to Believe,* is his answer to this question and his only published discussion of theoretical ethics. He recognized its uniqueness, and was disappointed at its reception. His conclusions grew out of the reading and thinking done for his lectures when he took over Philosophy 4 from Palmer in 1888-1889. The outline of these lectures has been preserved, and the following selections serve to supplement the published address:—

> So far as I feel anything good, I make it so. It *is* so, for me. . . . *Prima facie,* goods form a multifarious jungle. Must we so leave them, or can they be unified? . . . The abstract best would be that *all* goods should be realized. That is physically impossible, for many of them exclude each other. The whole difficulty of the moral life consists in deciding, when this is the case, which good to sacrifice and which to save. . . . The solution is [to] consider *every* good as a real good, and *keep as many as we can.* That act is the best act which *makes for the best whole,* the best whole being that which prevails at least cost, in which the vanquished goods are least completely annulled. . . . Follow the common traditions. Sacrifice all wills which are not organizable, and which avowedly go against the whole. No one pretends in the main to revise the decalogue, or to take up offenses against life, property, veracity, or decency into the permanent whole. If those are a man's goods, the man is not a member of the whole we mean to keep, and we sacrifice both him and his goods without a tear. When the rivalry is between real organizable goods, the rule is that the one victorious should so far as possible keep the vanquished somehow represented. Find some innocent way out.

The principle is clear: value derives ultimately from the interests of the individual; and the social whole is justified by the inclusion and reconciliation of its individual parts. Individualism is fundamental.

Between 1893 and 1899 James gave a large number of public lectures and addresses in different parts of the United States—Hot Springs (Virginia), Chautauqua, Buffalo, Chicago, Lake Geneva (Wisconsin), Colorado Springs, and California. In the course of his travels he made human as well as geographical discoveries. The exterior unattractiveness and apparent meaninglessness of what he saw was a challenge to his sympathy. One of the addresses which he gave was entitled, "A Certain Blindness in Human Beings," in which he insisted that the view of the outsider should be corrected by an imaginative understanding of the inner experience. Then the aggregate life of man, otherwise monstrous, repetitive, and trivial, would take on an aspect of dignity and rich diversity. Writing in 1899 to Mrs. Glendower Evans about the *Talks to*

[14] "Sentiment of Rationality," *Mind,* IV (1879), 338.

Teachers, which contained this address[15] and which he had just sent to her, James said:

> Pray don't wade through the Teacher part, which is incarnate boredom. I sent it to you merely that you might read the essay "On a Certain Blindness," which is really the perception on which my whole individualistic philosophy is based.

"I care very much," he wrote in the same year to another friend, "for the truth which it so inadequately tries . . . to express." [16] In the Preface to the *Talks with Teachers,* we read:—

> I wish I were able to make the second, "On a Certain Blindness in Human Beings," more impressive. It is more than the mere piece of sentimentalism which it may seem to some readers. It connects itself with a definite view of the world and of our moral relations to the same. Those who have done me the honor of reading my volume of philosophic essays will recognize that I mean the pluralistic or individualistic philosophy. According to that philosophy, the truth is too great for any one actual mind, even though that mind be dubbed "the Absolute," to know the whole of it. The facts and worths of life need many cognizers to take them in. There is no point of view absolutely public and universal. . . . The practical consequence of such a philosophy is the well-known democratic respect for the sacredness of individuality.[17]

Peirce and Royce, who were lonely souls and more or less disqualified for social and public relations, emphasized the community, both as a reality and as an ideal; James, the most sociable and urbane of men—actively, eagerly, almost painfully interested in the state of his country and the world—proclaimed the supreme value of those strivings which are unique in each individual, and whose authentic quality is immediately revealed to him alone. This quality is a *redeeming* quality in so far as it possesses some flavor of fidelity or courage, and the common "blindness in human beings" is their failure to discern its inward glow. James wrote to his daughter of a dog who was once his housemate: "His tail keeps wagging *all* the time, and he makes on me the impression of an angel hid in a cloud. He longs to do good." [18] Human beings as well as dogs usually wagged their tails in James's presence, and wanted to do good, which no doubt confirmed his gospel that every man is an angel hid in a cloud.

In proportion as one appreciates the inward significance of other people's lives one attaches importance to differences:

[15] In an appended portion referred to in the sub-title: *and to Students on Some of Life's Ideals.*
[16] Reprinted from *Atlantic,* CXLIV (1929), 377; to Pauline Goldmark, April 18, 1899.
[17] *T.T.,* v.
[18] August 8, 1895; *L.W.J.,* II, 26.

The obstinate insisting that tweedledum is *not* tweedledee is the bone and marrow of life. Look at the Jews and the Scots, with their miserable factions and sectarian disputes, their loyalties and patriotisms and exclusions,—their annals now become a classic heritage, because men of genius took part and sang in them. A thing is important if anyone *think* it important.[19]

The institutional life of men must necessarily be based on their likenesses, but its purpose is to make room for their differences. It is what slips through the meshes of classification and resists organization that justifies either classification or organization: "The memory of Davidson," said James,

> will always strengthen my faith in personal freedom and its spontaneities, and make me less unqualifiedly respectful than ever of "civilization," with its herding and branding, licensing and degree-giving, authorizing and appointing, and in general regulating and administering by system the lives of human beings. Surely the individual, the person in the singular number, is the more fundamental phenomenon, and the social institution, of whatever grade, is but secondary and ministerial. Many as are the interests which social systems satisfy, always unsatisfied interests remain over, and among them are interests to which system, as such, does violence whenever it lays its hand upon us. The best commonwealth will always be the one that most cherishes the men who represent the residual interests, the one that leaves the largest scope to their peculiarities.[20]

The inward, felt value of a human life is independent of the esteem of the world, or of such standards as fame and importance. From this insight sprang James's endorsement of democracy. Whereas, taken wholesale and externally, mankind form an unedifying spectacle; taken as individuals, one by one, each with his own spark of idealism, they may be respected and valued.

Tolerance is an essential part of the same gospel. When one sees the inward value of other lives one acknowledges their right to exist, or even exults in their existence. James felt a tolerance of mankind even in the aggregate. He dealt with this question in the latter part of his lecture on *Human Immortality*. He had no fear of an overcrowded Heaven:

> The Deity that suffers us, we may be sure, can suffer many another queer and wondrous and only half-delightful thing. For my own part . . . I am willing that every leaf that ever grew in this world's forests and rustled in the breeze should become immortal.[21]

[19] *Psychology*, II, 674-5, note.
[20] *M.S.*, 102-3.
[21] *H.I.*, 43-4. This is a very old motive in James's thought. In the "Sentiment of Rationality," where, referring to "a too infinite accumulation of population in the heavens," he goes on to say that the real wonder of existence is not that there should be so many, but that there should be *any*. *Mind*, IV (1879), 344.

Tolerance was a maxim of James's youth—not only the sympathetic tolerance for what is different, but the intellectual tolerance or humility which arises from a sense of the *limits* of sympathy. Thus he wrote in 1873:

> Sight of elephants and tigers at Barnum's menagerie whose existence, so individual and peculiar, yet stands there, so intensely and vividly real, as much so as one's own, so that one feels again poignantly the unfathomableness of ontology, supposing ontology to be at all. They *are, eodem jure* with myself, and yet I with my pretensions or at least aspirations to adequately represent the world, can never hope to *sympathize* in a genuine sense of the word with their being. And the want of sympathy is not as in the case of some deformed or loathsome human life, for their being is admirable; so admirable that one yearns to be in some way its sharer, partner or accomplice. Thus their foreignness confounds one's pretension to comprehend the world,—while their admirableness undermines the stoic or moral frame of mind in which one says the real meaning of life is *my* action. This great world of life in no relation with my action, is so real! [22]

In the same period of James's life in which he thus praises the acknowledgment of ignorance, he set himself a standard of liberality in his moral judgment:

> The "man of the world's" scepticism . . . is at its finest in those generous characters who show it with regard to fortune, what she gives and what she withdraws. . . . Such people can laugh at fate, are flexible, sympathize with the free flow of things, believe ever in the good, but are willing that it should shift its form. They do not close their hand on their possessions. When they profess a willingness that certain persons should be free they mean it not as most of us do —with a mental reservation, as that the freedom should be well employed and other similar humbug—but in all sincerity, and calling for no guarantee against abuse which, when it happens, they accept without complaint or embitterment as part of the chances of the game. They let their bird fly with no string tied to its leg.

The inwardness of the individual's passion is precious—but in what consists its preciousness? The sequel to "A Certain Blindness in Human Beings" was addressed to the question, "What Makes a Life Significant?" The answer is that it is courage, struggle, risk—in a word, heroism, that makes life significant, and is revealed to the eye of sympathy. Chautauqua had led James to feel that "the higher heroisms and the old rare flavors are passing out of life," until it suddenly dawned upon him that there were "great fields of heroism lying round about"—"in the daily lives of the laboring classes." [23] This is a familiar and

---

[22] This note is dated May 16, 1873, and the following is probably of the same year.
[23] *T.T.*, 265, 273-4; *L.W.J.*, II, 40 ff.

persistent theme in James. It is the old gospel of Carlyle, with which James had been impregnated in his childhood. It is the answer which he gave in the *Will to Believe* to the question, "Is Life Worth Living?" Yes, because it can be *made* worth living, by imparting to it the quality of bold and strenuous action.

The martial spirit was implied in James's moral dualism. Good is good and evil is evil, and it is the part of righteousness to love the one and to hate the other with equal whole-heartedness. To a "motor," hating can only mean attacking and destroying. This was James's attitude from early youth:

> To hate evil does not mean to indulge in a brooding feeling against particular evils; that is, to be possessed by it. No, it is to avert the attention, till your chance comes, and then strike home. My trouble is that its existence has power to haunt me. I still cling to the idol of the unspeckled, and when evil takes permanent body and actually sits down *in* me to stay, I'd rather give up all, than go shares with her in existence.[24]

This heroic motive in James was connected with his tendency to neurasthenia. He would be driven in upon himself by illness, and then with a powerful revulsion of feeling would burst into a plea for action. An incident of this sort was recorded in his Dresden diary in 1868, when he was a youth of twenty-six:

> Tonight while listening to Miss Havens' magic playing, and the Doctor and the Italian lady sing, my feelings came to a sort of crisis. The intuition of something here in a measure absolute gave me . . . an unspeakable disgust for the dead drifting of my own life for some time past. . . . Oh God! an end to the idle, idiotic sinking into *Vorstellungen* disproportionate to the object. Every good experience ought to be interpreted in practice. . . . Keep sinewy all the while,—and work at present with a mystical belief in the reality, interpreted somehow, of humanity!

That James's preaching of the martial spirit reflected his *need* rather than his achievement is admitted with characteristic candor in a letter of August 18, 1899, to Lutoslawski:

> Of course I know, as well as anybody that he who verbally celebrates and glorifies a function writes himself down for the time as one who doesn't exercise it, but aspires towards it rather, and seeks to animate himself and keep his courage up. . . . In so far forth every *writer* is what you call a "weakling." But man as man is essentially a weakling. Heroism is always on a precipitous edge, and only keeps alive by running. Every moment is an *escape*. And whoever is sensitive as well as motor well knows this, and ought not to be ashamed of it.

[24] From a loose undated note, *circ.* 1868.

James's later article of 1907 on "The Energies of Men" might be considered as his psychology of heroism. There is a limit of power for the everyday life of everyday men; beyond this lie ranges of activity that are infrequently attained—excitements that carry us over the usually effective dam. There is a common thread running through James's observations on religion, neurasthenia, war, earthquakes, fasting, lynching, patriotism—an interest, namely, in human behavior under high pressure, and the conclusion that exceptional circumstances generate exceptional inner power. These phenomena have a bearing on metaphysics because such exceptional power suggests the sudden removal of a barrier and the tappings of a greater reservoir of consciousness; and they have a bearing on ethics, since this power differs in degree rather than in kind from that moral power—that fighting and adventurous spirit, that heroic quality—which gives to life the color and radiance of value.

It is characteristic of individualism that it should be divisible into two divergent motives which create a tension even when they do not break into open antagonism. There is the motive of self-assertion, and the motive of sympathy: the expression of one's own individuality, and the appreciation of the individuality of others. In the case of James both motives were native and strong. There is, therefore, an oscillation between the ethics of conciliation, peace, and social utility, and the ethics of aggression, militancy, and romanticism. His literary enthusiasm followed these motives—now the one and now the other. He praised poets and writers of fiction for their sensitiveness to the inwardness of nature or their creation of characters that *live*. Tolstoi, Howells, Wordsworth, and Whitman are all cited as witnesses testifying to the worth of life as revealed to an emancipated sympathy. Three new luminaries joined them later—W. H. Hudson, Robert Louis Stevenson, and H. G. Wells. He spoke of Hudson with an almost reverential enthusiasm. Writing in 1901 to a friend through whom he had received Hudson's photograph, he said, "If I could only believe that he had sent it himself! He is no mere dog, but a supernatural being—a reincarnation of the Buddha or something like that. I hope to get nearer him in a future life." [25] To Stevenson's "Lantern-Bearers" James owed the metaphor underlying his whole doctrine of the inward illumination of humble lives. To Wells, "a sunny and healthy-minded Tolstoi"—whose limpid style, moral enthusiasm, "tridimensional human heart," melioristic philosophy, and Anglo-empirical method James keenly relished—he owed in his later years a powerful reënforcement of his wavering optimism. [26] His old loves, Carlyle and Emerson, on the other hand, continued to be the favorite oracles of the opposite gospel, declaring the inalienable right of the individual to affirm *himself* and his duty to execute

---

[25] To Mrs. E. L. Godkin, September 21, 1901.
[26] *T.T.*, 234-40; To H. G. Wells, November 28, 1908 and June 5, 1905; *L.W.J.*, II, 316, 231. James visited Wells at Sandgate in July 1908.

his *own* ideal. The strangest occupant of James's literary pantheon was Rudyard Kipling, the prophet of imperialism. The following letter to his brother throws light on the origins of this attachment:—

Cambridge, Feb. 15, 1891

Dear Harry,—

. . . Last Sunday I dined with Howells . . . and was much delighted to hear him say that you were both a friend and an admirer of Rudyard Kipling. I am ashamed to say that I have been ashamed to write of my adoration of that infant phenomenon, not knowing, with your exquisitely refined taste, how you might be affected by him and fearing to *jar*. The more rejoiced am I at this, but why didn't you say so ere now? He's more of a Shakespeare than anyone yet in this generation of ours, as it strikes me. And seeing the new effects he lately brings in in "The Light That Failed," and that Simla Ball story with Mrs. Hauksbee in the *Illustrated London News,* makes one sure now that he is only at the beginning of a rapidly enlarging career, with indefinite growth before him. Much of his present coarseness and jerkiness is youth only, divine youth. But *what* a youth! Distinctly the biggest literary phenomenon of our time. He has such human entrails, and he takes less time to get under the heart-strings of his personages than anyone I know. On the whole, bless him.

All intellectual work is the same,—the artist feeds the public on his own bleeding insides. Kant's *Kritik* is just like a Strauss waltz, and I felt the other day, finishing "The Light That Failed," and an ethical address to be given at Yale College simultaneously,[27] that there was no *essential* difference between Rudyard Kipling and myself as far as that sacrificial element goes. . . .

I have had this afternoon a two hours' visit from Mrs. H. of Princeton, Mass. . . . Her husband is the victim of one of those hideous mockeries of our civilization, and now serves out a two years' sentence in state prison for sending obscene matter through the mails; the matter consisting in a minute sheet called the *Voice,* which, of all imaginable causes of oppressed things, has taken up that of defending certain Saxon words not usually mentioned in polite society. These few words are martyrs and victims of injustice and prejudice, and one must die to reinstate them! *Grandeur et Néant de l'Homme!* Could anyone imagine such a crusade? Mrs. H. is a gifted creature in her way but practically quite mad. The Almighty must have laughed to see her *aux prises* with Dr. Peabody[28] whilst the trial was going on. She came out here to get some scholars to stand up for her husband. Knowing no names she called at a house, and asked who were "liberal" in the college. "Do you mean in the way of *giving?*" "No, in the way of thought." Peabody and C. C. Everett were named. She goes to Peabody. He says "Your husband is a *bad,* a very *bad* man. He deserves to be imprisoned." . . . She told him she hated to cry, and forgave him. Outside the door the tears rained on the ground. . . . The two opposite lacks of humor, for her "the words" absolutely good, for Peabo "the words" absolutely bad,— what fools we all are! . . .

W. J.

---

[27] "The Moral Philosopher and the Moral Life."
[28] Dr. Andrew Preston Peabody, former Plummer Professor of Christian Morals.

In the summer of 1896, when the recent experience of Chautauqua had repelled James towards the heroic pole of his moral philosophy, he turned to Kipling as his collaborator and exhorted him to "devote himself to the laboring classes." He wrote from Bagg's Hotel, Utica, New York, on August 26—where he stopped overnight en route from the Adirondacks to Chicago—expounding the high romance of lowly people in the vein of the lecture on "What Makes a Life Significant?": "Divinity lies all about us, and culture is too hide-bound to even suspect the fact. Could a Howells or a Kipling be enlisted in this mission?" [29] Kipling was about to sail for Europe on the *S.S. Lahn*:—

> Morristown, N. Y. [Aug. 31, 1896]
>
> Dear James,—
>
> It was just and luminous (but why, in God's name, Bagg's Hotel of all places?) and the thing that made it more impressive to me mineself was because I have just finished off a long tale wherein I have deliberately travelled on the lines you suggest—*i.e.* I have taken the detail of a laborious and dangerous trade (fishing on the Grand Banks) and used it for all the romance in sight.[30] Also, I have thought along those lines—*and* also, I have been four days in Chautauqua, seven years ago, when I thought unspeakable things. Half your trouble is the curse of America—sheer, hopeless, well-ordered boredom; and that is going some day to be the curse of the world. The other races are still scuffling for their three meals a day. America's got 'em and now she doesn't know what she wants but is dimly realizing that extension lectures, hardwood floors, natural gas and trolley-cars don't fill the bill. The Chautauquan "civilization" is to my mind precisely on the same plane as the laborious, ordered ritual of drum, dance and sacred pollen that the Zuñi (with other races) has evolved to fence off his bored soul from the solitude and loneliness of his own environments (I am not a psychologist, but you are and you'll see what I mean). Down below among the men of the trades you get, for proof that there is incident and colour in their lives, the melodramatic form of speech which is always resorted to in moments of stress or passion. We the bourgeoisie, become inarticulate or inept. It is a vast and fascinating subject and you'll see later how I purpose to use it. Your wail and "eructation" was delightful to my soul. . . . Yours ever sincerely,
>
> RUDYARD KIPLING

In the last analysis James preferred the humanity of peace to the cruel heroism of war. The grip of the hand on the sword is relaxed by the reflection that the other's cause is as real and warm to him as is mine to me, and has its own inner and equal justification. If the principle of sympathy be given priority over the principle of self-assertion it is still possible, however, to save the militant and heroic qualities. The principle of sympathy is itself a cause which

[29] *T.T.*, 277.
[30] *Captains Courageous*, which appeared in *McClure's Magazine* in November and December, 1896.

calls for moral and even for physical courage. There are two enemies which may be fought without inhumanity. First, physical nature: "The . . . ideal of the field of ethics being that of the human interests allied against the material environment, and the consequent appeal to reasonableness all round, seems to me unconquerable truth and common-sense." [31]

The second enemy which remains when humanity is enthroned is inhumanity—whatever weakens, resists, or opposes the moral will. The major issue of life is the war of good and evil. This war calls for the fighting virtues, such as courage, endurance, fidelity, energy, and loyalty. Though war in the literal sense provides conditions peculiarly favorable to these virtues, especially in their heroic intensity, they appear in all life when this calls for the enduring of hardship or the overcoming of resistance.

It is clear, however, that James did not believe peace in itself to be "the moral equivalent of war." When he composed the essay bearing that title, it was because he believed the admirable martial qualities to be so dependent on war that they could be preserved only by its deliberate simulation. The essay was published in 1910 by the Association for International Conciliation, and had a great *succès de réclame*. Over 30,000 copies of the leaflet were distributed, and it was twice republished in popular magazines. Letters of approval poured in from all quarters, not only from confirmed pacifists, but from many, including army officers, who were attracted by James's candid recognition of the psychological and moral claims of war. He made no bones of the natural blood-thirstiness of man, and could understand those who apologized for war as the great preserver of the ideals of hardihood and daring:—

"Its 'horrors,'" they argue,

> are a cheap price to pay for rescue from the only alternative supposed, of a world of clerks and teachers, of coeducation and zoöphily, of "consumer's leagues" and "associated charities," of industrialism unlimited, and feminism unabashed. No scorn, no hardness, no valor any more! Fie upon such a cattle-yard of a planet! So far as the central essence of this feeling goes, no healthy-minded person . . . can help to some degree partaking of it.

But the purpose of the essay was to support the cause of peace by suggesting a way of sublimating this martial spirit:

> We must make new energies and hardihoods continue the manliness to which the military mind so faithfully clings. Martial virtues must be the enduring cement; intrepidity, contempt of softness, surrender of private interest, obedience to command, must still remain the rock upon which states are built.

[31] W.J. to the author, July 17, 1909.

By "a conscription of the whole youthful population to form for a certain number of years a part of the army enlisted against *Nature*," James thought that "the military ideals of hardihood and discipline could be wrought into the growing fibre of the people," but without the callousness, cruelty, and degradation that attend war.[32]

[32] *M.S.*, 276, 287-8, 290-2.

XXVI

SOCIAL AND POLITICAL SENTIMENTS

Though there are two well-marked principles in James's moral philosophy, that of militant self-assertion and that of humanity, it is, as we have seen, the second which is the more fundamental both in theory and in practice.

James's sentiment of humanity sprang from several sources. First, he had the sufferer's sensitiveness to the suffering of others. There were moments when this sensitiveness assumed in James, as in his father, an almost morbid aspect. A study of his relations with his sister Alice through her lifelong illness and lingering death furnishes a most revealing record of this trait. But what might easily have become a weakness was, through the compensating and moderating effect of other qualities, ultimately a source of strength. The extreme delicacy of his sympathetic response, instead of leading to an evasion of life, was compounded with other elements into loving friendships, an active loyalty to mankind, and even a pluralistic metaphysics.

The presence in James of an irrational compassionateness to which both ideas and his practice had to accommodate themselves is exemplified by his total inability to drop a case of distress from his mind when once it had been brought to his attention. He would swear off only to yield again to an irresistible impulse. This obsessive compassion led James to the verge of agreeing that "pity is a vice to be exterminated along with its object." "I believe that to be a lie," he said, "but I admit the canalization of pity to be a difficult engineering problem." [1]

The other side of pity is the hatred of cruelty, which was to James most hateful when combined with a profession of high purpose. Even duty forfeits its claims when it hardens the heart. Hence the temper of his judgment on the Inquisition, in which he alludes to the "curious rat-hole feeling" which it inspires—its "combination of authority with feebleness of intellect—powers of life and death with a mental make-up that is almost idiotic for its meanness, timorousness and unmanliness—a mind not bigger than a pin's head, guiding a will that stuck at nothing in the way of cruelty." [2]

The effect of pity was to cause James invariably to side with the "under

---

[1] To Mrs. Glendower Evans, April 13, 1900.
[2] Notes for the Lowell Lectures of 1896-7.

dog"—with the Boers and the Irish against England, with the Filipinos against the United States, with religion or psychical research against science, with privates or laymen against officers, with the disreputable against the respectable, with heresy against orthodoxy, with youth against age, or with the new against the old.

Another and quite independent source of James's humane sentiment was his sociability. He was a highly socialized individual, not in the sense of being impregnated with tradition, or dominated by the group, but in the sense of his peculiar relish and gift for human intercourse. He was *concretely* humane. He tolerated mankind not in principle merely, but in practice; and he did not merely tolerate them, but enjoyed their presence in the flesh. When he was in the mood he was free, open, and expansive in his relations with others, but this mood, like all of James's moods, was liable to periodic fluctuations. He hated formal or crowded occasions, when pleasant human relations were at one and the same time encouraged and rendered impossible. Knowing the utter desolation of a sensitively social individual in an insensitive social milieu, he sometimes sympathized on this score even with his own guests. It will be remembered that he once hustled hatless through his back door one of his students whom he mistakenly supposed to be yearning for escape from the rigors of hospitality. Another instance of the sort is recorded:—

> During one of my courses with him, James invited me to an afternoon reception or tea at his house. I was a shy youth and dreaded going, but thought I ought to go. When I went in there seemed to be a good many people there and I was decidedly uncomfortable. I met James in the entrance hall. There was something about him which invited entire confidence and I found myself telling him just how I felt. "Yes, I know," said he, "when I see these people who know exactly what to do and say at one of these things, I feel like smashing their heads with a paving stone." The sympathetic understanding of my feelings and his characteristically forcible language gave me great satisfaction.[3]

There is an aspect of James's humanity that is more difficult to describe. The term "promiscuity" would be too strong, while to describe it negatively as an absence of fastidiousness would be too weak. From certain pages of *Notes of a Son and Brother* we gather that Henry James felt that William James lacked taste in his choice of associates. The fact was that William had something of the clinician's freedom from prejudice—a suffering mortal is a suffering mortal. He had his chosen comrades, and none was quicker than he to perceive the difference between the congenial and the uncongenial. But he went behind and beyond this impression. He was not unoffended by externals, but the of-

---

[3] From a letter to the author by George D. Burrage, Harvard '83.

fense was negligible if there was something to be found within. It was a part of his genius to find something within when others failed to find it, and a part of his philosophy to believe that there is always something within to find. The generalization of James's tenderheartedness into a humanitarian sentiment and creed was in no small measure due to his lack of squeamishness. His character was somehow capable of uniting a selective taste which chose his intimate friends and preferred companions with the indiscriminate sympathy which gave sincerity to his humanitarian creed.

All of James's humane qualities appear in his friendships. Strangeness and formality quickly melted in his presence, acquaintance ripening into affection and affection into enduring love. His gift for friendship is illustrated by his youthful relations with Ward and Holmes, and by his later relations with Hodgson, Robertson, Renouvier, Davidson, Gurney, and Stumpf. The warmth which fructified the seed of friendship and quickened the growing plant is found in letters to Mrs. Francis J. Child and to Charles Eliot Norton. The first was written in reply to a letter of congratulation on his appointment to a full professorship of philosophy. Mrs. James was at this time ill with scarlet fever.

[Cambridge], March 27 [1885]

Dear Mrs. Child,—

Your letter is the best thing about my promotion—worth more than all its honors, powers and emoluments. It lights up our home with the effulgence of affection and sympathy. I have just read it to Alice through the door with the cracks stuffed with cotton which is the channel of our communion, and all I get from her is a sort of inarticulate cooing and purring, in a voice "choked with tears" of joy. She feels, as I do, that one note of true sympathy is worth all the philosophies and professorships thereof in the world. With love to your blessed family, believe me ever affectionately yours,

WM. JAMES

P.S. As the immortal Schopenhauer says, "Anyone can feel Mit*leid;* aber zur Mit*freude* gehört ein Engel! [4]

Twelve years later James presented the same friend with his *Will to Believe,* inscribed to "Mrs. Child from her loving W.J.," and accompanied by the note: "This is *not to be read,*—simply *owned,* and smiled at occasionally for love of the author."

The old friendship between the James and the Norton families was continued throughout William James's life in his intimacy with Grace Norton and Charles Eliot Norton:—

[4] "Anyone can sympathize with another's sorrow, but to sympathize with another's joy is the attribute of an angel."

Cambridge, Nov. 16, 1907

Dear Charles,—

I cannot let your eightieth birthday pass without the meed of some melodious tear. You will probably be having *Glückwünsche* innumerably showered upon you today, but none will be heartier or more sincere than Alice's or mine,— or our children's either, for they "were nursed upon the self-same hill," and to their minds you have been the tutelary genius of the neighborhood—a sort of benignant half-uncle, always with a word or a present for them, and ever to be remembered among the friendly powers that overarch the universe of childhood. It seemed to me a great achievement to have lived down eighty solid years, each panting to devour one, "trampling their strata with æonian tread" and storing up all that experience. Even with the experience passive, the achievement is great; but when it has been as active as yours, with a part played energetically in every better effort and enterprise that was going, and when one has given help and countenance to so many others who were struggling, retrospect of the whole career ought to yield contentment. You are among those who in the best sense have made of their life a success. . . . That your future years will be many, and increase the tide of general good-will that sets in towards you, is the prayer of your affectionate friends,

WILLIAM AND ALICE JAMES

What James's friendship meant to others is illustrated by a letter from a friend of his youth, Charles Ritter, in acknowledgment of his latest book:

Geneva, June 15, 1902 [5]

Dear and illustrious Friend,—

Your magnificent volume (*The Varieties of Religious Experience*) reached me last Monday, June 9, and filled me with joy, as a sign of life from an old friend, as proof that you have been able to carry out a project in which I was so much interested, and, finally, for its own sake. . . . And now, dear Friend, crown your kindness to an old invalid of the rue St. Léger by sending him the photograph of your dear self, of Madame William James, and of your dear children. If you (or Madame) could add a short account of your present life that would be perfect. . . . Give to an old friendship, after forty-two years, a St. Martin's summer, a glorious late autumn sun. All this week, while running through your beautiful volume, I have paused to recall the stages of that friendship:

First the fine days of 1860, "quand sur ton beau front riait l'adolescence," days all too short, alas! and in particular the springtime fête at Moudon, when you made fun of my youthful enthusiasm for Renan, and when you cited his words: "pour moi je pense qu'il n'est pas dans l'univers d'intelligence supérieure à celle de l'homme"—certainly not a very orthodox formula!

Then your visit to Geneva in 1868, and our interview in a hotel bedroom.

Then the charming reunion at the Berne railway station in June, 1892, ten years ago.

[5] Translated by the author.

Then the delicious day at Meggen on the shores of Lake Lucerne in May, 1893.

Finally the good times of April, 1900, . . . and the brief meeting in the autumn.

And now in fifteen days I shall be reaching my sixty-fourth year, having been born on June 29, 1838. . . . I cannot complain too much,—on the contrary, I ought to regard myself as privileged in this adventure of human life, so difficult and so subject to chance. In any case, one of the happiest chances which have fallen to my lot was that of meeting in my twenty-second year the charming friend who was destined to become an illustrious man, and whose hand I press with all tenderness and the most loyal affection. . . .

CHARLES RITTER

The last of these evidences of friendship is from Charles Peirce, written shortly after James's death to the latter's son Henry:—

Milford, Sept. 21, 1910

My dear Mr. James,—

Your father was the very last of those few men who pulled much upon my heart-strings; and no man ever did so much as he, not even his father. Few days passed without my longing to be with him, and when I was in Prescott Street, and would look out the window and would see him at length pass by, how I used to wish he would come in! . . . His penetration into the hearts of people was most wonderful; and he was not one of those who chiefly see the evil things in hearts. . . .

I know that my letter must sound to you very egotistical; but he was such an exquisitely lovable fellow, that it is in vain that I tell myself how much more those must suffer who saw him every day; I cannot help being overwhelmed with my own grief. . . . It seems as if La Fontaine must have known him when he wrote:

> Qu'un ami véritable est une douce chose.
> Il cherche vos besoins au fond de votre cœur;
> Il vous épargne la pudeur
> De les lui découvrir vous-même.

His last three books may be criticized; but all the sound heads and sound hearts will forever honour and love the MAN.

C. S. P.

The softness of James's heart did not spread to his head. It involved him in acts of kindness which often cost him much trouble, but he was not more fallible than others in his personal judgments. The difference was that while he saw men's weakness as well as their strength, he admired them for their strength instead of despising them for their weakness. He is supposed to have been *blinded* by compassion, especially his compassion for "cranks." The fact is that long experience gave him a shrewd knowledge of the species, and when he was kind to a crank he was perfectly aware that it was a crank to whom he was being kind. But even in cranks of the lower orders he found *something* that touched his heart. The following was to Henry Holt:—

Cambridge, June 19, 1896

Dear Holt,—

A poor crank of a Russian Jew, a regular Spinosa . . . has been melting the heart out of me by his desire to get his *magnum opus* (which is only 300 type-written pages, boiled down from an original 1400) published. He is literally dying of grief because he can't. The stuff might have made some stir in 1650, but of course it is hopeless now. Nevertheless as a fellow crank I am moved by human sympathy to subscribe with the aid of friends $50 towards its pub-lication, and I have written him that I would consult a publisher of my ac-quaintance, meaning you. About how much ought a publisher to require as a guarantee in such a case—say a 300 page book, 500 copies, got out cheaply and of course not stereotyped? Should you be willing to let it bear your name? The old fellow has quite a grand style in his way. Always truly yours,

WILLIAM JAMES

This habit of addressing his regard to the admirable part of a man had a profound influence on James's professional relations. The rays of his affection fertilized the soil they shone on—often a hitherto barren soil hidden away unsus-pected in some obscure and timid soul. Students and colleagues tried to live up to the good that James thought of them. He once wrote to Münsterberg: "I am reading Ostwald's *Vorlesungen über Naturphilosophie,* and find it a most delectable book. I don't think I ever envied a man's mind as much as I have envied Ostwald's—unless it were Mach's." [6] This reservation in favor of Mach gives James away entirely. He envied nearly everybody's mind; for he saw *some* good quality there which he didn't have himself, and acknowledged its value by expressing the wish that he had it.

James believed and practised the maxim that people flourish most in the sun-shine of approval. When a friend congratulated him warmly on one of his books James replied:

Imagine how delighted I am at receiving your post-card this morning, the first real *praise* that I have yet had for this work, and from such a quarter. . . . What my friend Howison said is true: "What your genuine philosopher most craves is *praise,* rank, coarse praise." Harris . . . calls it *recognition,* but it's *praise* which we all need and work for. Since your praise I feel that my book is *certain* to be a success.[7]

[6] July 23, 1902.
[7] To Theodore Flournoy, June 2, 1902; the book was *The Varieties of Religious Experience.*

The result of James's presence was usually to raise the general temperature of cordiality. Men said pleasant things to one another, and being in turn recipients of good-will they instinctively sought to earn it—which illustrated his philosophical maxim that if you *will* believe well of your fellow men you may create the good you believe in.

"The great use of a life," James said in 1900, "is to spend it for something that outlasts it." [8] This outlasting cause was then, as in earlier days, the happiness of mankind. But he was not a utopian. "I devoutly believe," he said, "in the reign of peace and in the gradual advent of some sort of socialistic equilibrium." [9] This was written in 1910. A dozen years before he had said:

> Society has . . . undoubtedly got to pass toward some newer and better equilibrium, and the distribution of wealth has doubtless slowly got to change: such changes have always happened, and will happen to the end of time. But if, after all that I have said, any of you expect that they will make any *genuine vital difference,* on a large scale, to the lives of our descendants, you will have missed the significance of my entire lecture. The solid meaning of life is always the same eternal thing,—the marriage, namely, of some unhabitual ideal, however special, with some fidelity, courage, and endurance; with some man's or woman's pains.—And, whatever or whenever life may be, there will always be the chance for that marriage to take place.[10]

Between these dates there was, I believe, a change of emphasis, induced in part by the Fabian socialism of H. G. Wells.[11] But the change was not radical enough to remove the fundamental ambiguity to which attention has been called above. Was the good life to be found in that state of things that would begin *after* the victorious conquest of evil, or was it to be found in the conquest itself? On the one hand, James loathed evil, and loathed the condoning of evil. On the other hand, he felt that the redeeming quality of life was that heroism which can exist only when there is a live evil to be resisted and overcome; and thus to recognize in evil an indispensable condition of good is to condone it, and to lapse into that "subjectivism" whose insidious philosophical charms he had so well understood and so sternly repulsed in the still earlier eighties.[12] There is a way, a Jamesian way, by which this seeming contradiction can be avoided. What is needed to make life significant is a "real fight," actual risks and genuine obstacles. If one thought that the risks and obstacles were merely put there for their moral effect, one's adventurous spirit would be undermined. The best of all possible worlds from a moral point of view is,

[8] To W. Lutoslawski, November 13, 1900.
[9] *M.S.,* 286.
[10] *T.T.,* 298-9.
[11] Especially this author's *First and Last Things,* which James read with high approval.
[12] *W.B.,* 169 ff.

therefore, a world which is not designed for that purpose—a world in which the conditions of the significant life are accidental and not intended. Since as a matter of fact these conditions do occur, and occur equally in every age, there is no progress as regards the heroic possibilities of life. But the heroic life may be more or less humane; and it is here that one should look for progress—in rendering the heroic quality of one individual's life less costly to others. "We are all ready to be savage in *some* cause. The difference between a good man and a bad one is the choice of the cause." [13]

The root of James's practical politics is to be found not in his ethics and philosophy, but in the fact that he belonged to the educated class, and accepted on that account a peculiar role and a peculiar responsibility. He was a mug-wump, an anti-imperialist, a civil-service reformer, a pacifist, a Dreyfusite, an internationalist and a liberal. What physiognomy do these features compose? Clearly, the advocate of light as opposed to force and emotion. Neither his democracy nor his gospel of action implied a leveling of differences. He did not believe either that one man was as good as another, or that all causes were equally worthy. His politics was governed by the principle of discrimination. The educated man was the man who knew how to criticize, and it was his role in politics to offset to the best of his power both the self-seeking of the ambitious and the blind passion of the crowd.

Undoubtedly the greatest single influence upon James's political thinking was that exerted by E. L. Godkin. During Godkin's residence in Cambridge in the late seventies he had been an intimate of the James household. William and Henry James and the circle of their Cambridge friends read the *Nation* and the *Evening Post,* and wrote for them. Godkin's papers were the most important medium of the day by which the emancipated and disinterested mind found effective political expression. There were periodic lapses and revivals of attachment on James's part, the lapses being due to a dislike of Godkin's negations and polemics, the revivals to a feeling that on important issues Godkin was always fighting valiantly on the right side. The following was written by James to Godkin in 1889:—

> In the earlier years I may say that my whole political education was due to the *Nation;* later came a time when I thought you looked on the doings of Ter-ence Powderly and Co. too much from without and too little from within; now I turn to you again as my only solace in a world where nothing stands straight. You have the most curious way of always being *right,* so I never dare to trust myself now when you're agin me.

And writing six years later, at the time of the Venezuela incident, James pledged his loyalty and warmly congratulated Godkin on his courage, but

[13] To E. L. Godkin, December 24, 1895; *L.W.J.,* II, 28.

urged him in the interest of effectiveness to be as "non-expletive" and patiently explanatory as possible: "Don't curse God and die, dear old fellow. Live and be patient and fight for us a long time yet in this new war." [14]

James was a "mugwump" both in the historical and in the generalized sense. The following letter touches on the Blaine campaign during which this label first came into vogue. F. G. Bromberg had been a classmate at the Lawrence Scientific School and a member of Congress from Alabama:—

Springfield Centre, N. Y., June 30, 1884

My dear Bromberg,—

. . . . What you say of Blaine is . . . moving. I had hoped to find you in the "young" Republican party. It is quite true Blaine has never been confounded with the grosser pecuniary corruptionists. . . . But it's less for what he *is* than for what he *isn't* that we are ready to bring the Democrats in to defeat him. He is blind, and the whole section of Republicans whom he represents are blind, to the real life of the country today. Old dead shibboleths are all they can think of. They live on hatred and prejudice against the Democratic name, as the Democrats live on hatred of the Republican name. If any decent Democrat be nominated, I shall be too happy to vote him in, in order to get the present fossil Republican party permanently killed, and to be able four years later to drive out the Democrats in the same way in the name of a new national party with something of an intellectual character in purpose, which will devote itself to civil service and economical reform, and perhaps ultimately to certain constitutional changes of which we are in pressing need. Look at the Barnum advertisement called the Republican platform! Can you possibly wish to see a party like *that* cumber the earth any longer? I hope not. . . . Always your friend,

WM. JAMES

James was also, quite consciously and avowedly, a mugwump in the more generalized sense. He allied himself with that minority whose function it was to apply critical reflection to public affairs, and whose destiny it was—to remain a minority. In economic matters the mugwump would look beyond the immediate motive of gain to underlying ethical principles or the broad humane purpose of social institutions. Emancipated from a purely national outlook or a chauvinistic patriotism, he would esteem superior human qualities regardless of their place or power. In domestic politics he would be bound by no party allegiance, but would use his vote to tip the scales in favor of rationality and righteousness.

As regards the mugwump's duty James had no doubt, and as regards his effectiveness no illusions. He questioned whether education really made any difference for the good, since educated men seemed to be on both sides of all questions, and to lend or sell the fruits of their education for the support of any passion however base. His qualified appraisal of higher education caused

[14] April 15, 1889 and December 24, 1895; *L.W.J.*, I, 284, II, 30.

some misunderstanding, and in 1905 on July 12 he was compelled to write to Eliot from Chicago and explain that he had not meant to say that the colleges "were training schools of crime!" "I only saw one newspaper report, a single paragraph—but that was diabolical. It was sent me by an unknown correspondent who said he thanked God for raising 'one man courageous enough to tell the truth about the colleges'—adding, 'I never had a college education, the blood of Jesus is enough for me.'"

James realized the power of the professional politician: "the strongest force in politics is human scheming, and the schemers will capture every machinery that you can set up against them." He understood propaganda, that "curious auto-intoxication which society practises upon itself with the journalistic secretion."[15] But he refused to despair, believing that the party of critical intelligence might offset their lack of heat by their greater steadiness. On January 9, 1902, he delivered an address before the Graduate School at Harvard, in which he dwelt upon the critical function that the educated classes might exercise in public affairs:—

> So far, then, as the mission of the educated intellect in society is not to find or invent reasons for the demands of passion, it reduces itself to this small but incessant criticizing, or equalizing function. . . . For this it has to blow cold upon the hot excitement, and hot upon the cold motive; and this judicial and neutral attitude sometimes wears, it must be confessed, a priggish expression and is generally unpopular and distasteful. The intellectual critic as such knows of so many interests, that to the ardent partisan he seems to have none—to be a sort of bloodless bore and mugwump. Those who anticipate the verdict of history, the abolitionists, *les intellectuels,* as the university professors were called who stood out for Dreyfus, the present anti-imperialists etc., excite an almost corporeal antipathy. . . . Often their only audience is posterity. Their names are first honored when the breath has left their bodies, and, like the holders of insurance policies, they must die to win their wager. . . .
>
> Speaking broadly, there are never more than two fundamental parties in a nation: the party of red blood, as it calls itself, and that of pale reflection; the party of animal instinct, jingoism, fun, excitement, bigness; and that of reason, forecast, order gained by growth, and spiritual methods—briefly put, the party of force and that of education. . . . The Tories in any country and the mob will always pull together in the red-blood party, when the catchwords are properly manipulated, as a while ago they were by Disraeli; and liberalism will be between the upper and the nether millstone if it have no magnetic leader. . . . The chronic fault of liberalism is its lack of speed and passion. Over and over again generalizations get into such a deadlock that a hole in the dam must be made somewhere,—then the flowing water will enlarge it. A rifle bullet makes a hole by its mere speed, where the dead pressure of a weightier mass does nothing. But occasionally a leader with liberal ambitions has the *vis viva* of the rifle

[15] W.J. to Lutoslawski, March 20, 1900; and recollection by Professor A. Forbes, letter to the author of March 29, 1932.

bullet. He may be a fanatic, a Cromwell, a Garibaldi, or he may be a Bismarck, or he may be an adventurer like Napoleon. Happy the country that proves able to use such men for what they are worth, and to cast them off before they victimize it. That country indeed is educated!

The mature definition of James's political role is to be found in an address entitled "The Social Value of the College-Bred." [16] It is the function of the college-bred to guard the "tone" of society, to promote the "critical sensibilities" or "admiration of the really admirable," and to "divine the worthier and better leaders":

> We ought to have our own class-consciousness. *"Les Intellectuels!"* What prouder club-name could there be than this one, used ironically by the party of "red blood," the party of every stupid prejudice and passion, during the anti-Dreyfus craze, to satirize the men in France who still retained some critical sense and judgment! [17]

[16] Delivered November 7, 1907. First published in *McClure's Magazine* in February 1908, and reprinted in *M.S.*
[17] *M.S.*, 314, 319-20, 323.

XXVII

JAMES AS A REFORMER

In the light of James's general ethical creed and conception of his role in social and political reform, it is now in order briefly to review his activities.

As early as 1881 James addressed the students of Harvard College on the subject of temperance, and twice thereafter he spoke before the Total Abstinence League. In his early address he dealt mainly with the injurious effect of alcohol as demonstrated by experimental physiology.[1] It is evident that he had a fundamental antipathy to the use of stimulants—the more remarkable because of his curious and open-minded interest in all exceptional experiences (among which intoxication might naturally have been included), and his sympathy with that deliverance from inhibitions which is thought to be one of the merits of alcohol. His fundamental maxim of purity and wholesomeness was no doubt at the root of the matter, but there was at the same time a counterattraction: he found abstinence more intoxicating than indulgence. The following note was made in preparation for an address of 1894 or 1895:—

> The great *excuse* is conviviality. . . . Even here you *pay*. But here if anywhere is what you pay for worth the price. . . . The whole bill against alcohol is its *treachery*. Its happiness is an illusion and seven other devils return. . . . From every point of view we see one conclusion. It is *safer* to drink cold water, or hot water, or any kind of water. In this over-burdened [age], especially here in America, every ounce of handicap that is added should be avoided, and the daily use of even the smallest amount of alcohol is probably a real handicap, increasing the fatigue and wear and tear of life, diminishing reserve force and elasticity, and tending to shorten existence. Say what you will about quality of existence . . . the gas-lit spurious hilarity with sickness afterwards is not the real quality. . . . It seems . . . a mean way of deciding a question like this, by fear. . . . The best way to wean people from intemperance is to fill them with a love of temperance for its own sake. In other words, replace the drink idol and ideal by another ideal. What is the other ideal? It is the ideal of having a constitution in perfect health that is as elastic as cork, and never cracks or runs rusty or finds any situation that it can't meet by its own buoyancy.

During the '90s James was occupied with such educational problems as confronted a member of the Harvard faculty. His individualistic and liber-

---

[1] "William James on Temperance," *Independent*, June 23, 1881.

tarian creed brought him, as a rule, to the support of Eliot's policies. His scientific training and general modernism inclined him to favor the liberalization of the curriculum at the expense of the privileged position of the ancient languages. "We must," he said, "shake the old double reefs out of the canvas into the wind and sunshine, and let in every modern subject, sure that any subject will prove humanistic, if its setting be kept only wide enough." [2]

Between 1890 and 1909 there was a prolonged attempt to reduce the normal period required for the A.B. degree from four to three years. James was a member of the various committees of the faculty which deliberated upon the proposal,[3] and in 1891 he defended the new plan in an article on "The Proposed Shortening of the College Course," contributed to the *Harvard Monthly*. The following passages are characteristic:

> Every teacher soon has forced upon his attention a certain anthropological fact. That fact is that there is a deeply rooted distinction between two sorts of student. . . . The one sort of man is born for the theoretic life, and is capable of pressing forward indefinitely into its subtleties and specialties. . . . The other class of men may be intelligent, but they are not *theoretical,* and their interest in most subjects reaches its saturation-point when the broader results and most general laws have been reached. . . . And their teacher also realizes heavily enough the weight of those eternal laws which render it impossible to make an herbivorous animal out of a carnivorous one by offering the latter a continuous diet of hay. . . . These excellent fellows need contact of some sort with the fighting side of life, with the world in which men and women earn their bread and butter and live and die; there must be the scent of blood, so to speak, upon what you offer them, or else their interest does not wake up; the blood that is shed in our electives, fails to satisfy them very long. The A.B. degree should be accommodated to the needs of students of this second category, and for them the three-year course is long enough.[4]

In 1894 and 1898, James used his influence against bills before the Massachusetts Legislature designed to require the examination and licensing of medical practitioners. Medical knowledge, he said, is highly imperfect and rapidly changing, and experience should be welcomed from any source. He preferred education to legislation, tolerance to prohibition, and experiment to prejudgment.[5] His appearance at a legislative hearing caused much scandal to his colleagues of the Medical School; but he could "face their disapproval much more easily" than that of his own conscience. He wrote to John Jay Chapman

---

[2] *M.S.,* 321.

[3] The result of the agitation was to make the three-year degree *possible* by an increase of the number of courses taken each year. This possibility having proved more and more unrealizable, the number of men who thus obtained the degree soon became negligible.

[4] *Harvard Mo.,* 11-2 (1890-1), 132-5.

[5] *Boston Evening Transcript,* March 24, 1894; March 2, 1898. "I assuredly hold no brief for any of these healers." (*L.W.J.,* II, 69.)

on March 4, 1898: "Says I to myself, Shall civic virtue be confined entirely to
Zola, J. J. C., and Col. Picquart? Never, says I, so in I goes."

President Cleveland's Venezuela message was dispatched December 17, 1895.
The crisis which followed seems to have impressed James for the first time
with the danger which lurked in "the fighting instinct"—"three days of fighting mob-hysteria at Washington can at any time undo peace habits of a hundred years." [6] It was a political crime, James felt, to take any steps which would
arouse these passions. He contributed a letter to the *Harvard Crimson*. Theodore Roosevelt, who was at this time President of the Board of Police Com-
missioners of New York City, had previously written in the same columns to
protest against the pressure exerted on Congress by opponents of the administration's policy. To this James replied:

> We are evidently guilty of *lèse-majesté* in Mr. Roosevelt's eyes; and though
> a mad President may any day commit the country without warning to an ut-
> terly new career and history, no citizen, no matter how he feels, must then
> speak, not even to the representative constitutionally appointed to check the
> President in time of need. May I express a hope that in this University, if no
> where else on the continent, we shall be patriotic enough *not* to remain passive
> whilst the destinies of our country are being settled by surprise. Let us be for
> or against; and if against, then against by every means in our power, when a
> policy is taking shape that is bound to alter all the national ideals that we
> have cultivated hitherto. Let us refuse to be bound over night by proclamation,
> or hypnotized by sacramental phrases through the day. Let us consult our rea-
> son as to what is best, and then exert ourselves as citizens with all our might.[7]

The following was written to Frederic Myers on January 1, 1896, during
these same stirring days:

> Well, our countries will soon be soaked in each other's gore. . . . It will be
> a war of extermination when it comes, for neither side can tell when it is beaten,
> and the last man will bury the penultimate one, and then die himself. The
> French will then occupy England and the Spaniards America. Both will unite
> against the Germans, and no one can foretell the end. But seriously, all true
> patriots here have had a hell of a time. It has been a most instructive thing
> for the dispassionate student of history to see how near the surface in all of us
> the old fighting instinct lies, and how slight an appeal will wake it up. Once
> *really* waked, there is no retreat, so the whole wisdom of governors should be
> to avoid the direct appeals.

On the merits of the Monroe Doctrine as affirmed by Cleveland and Olney,
James wrote on February 13 to his wife's brother-in-law, W. M. Salter:

[6] W.J. to E. L. Godkin, December 24, 1895; *L.W.J.*, II, 28-9.
[7] *Harvard Crimson*, January 7, 9, 1896.

Such affirmations of "our will shall be law" form an integral part of nation's lives, and this "doctrine" may in *some shape* be considered a part of ours. They are primarily expressions of ambition, but naturally they seek [by] precedent and argument to justify themselves. Cleveland had not only a right but a duty (considering all things) to worry England into willingness to arbitrate, and of course he could have done so. . . . *That* policy would have made us real apostles of civilization, and it needn't in the least have gone out of the limits of the particular case, or flourished any hardened theory like Olney's unspeakable rot . . . about the moral interests of America being irreconcilably diverse from those of Europe, about permanent political union between European and American states being unnatural and inexpedient, about South American republics being our natural congeners and allies, about our invariable wisdom and justice and equity, and the rest. Things were in a state where a nascent dogma could harden or not harden, and in my eyes the whole wisdom of disinterested critics at such a time consists in resisting the hardening process.

The political issue which stirred James most deeply and exacted from him the greatest expenditure of time and effort was that of imperialism. He published eight or more articles and letters, including an address before the Anti-Imperialist League of which he was at one time vice president. The Spanish War, like the Venezuela incident, impressed James with the irresistible power of the war fever. The following was written to his Swiss friend Theodore Flournoy on June 17, 1898, when the war was two months old:

It is the worst blow at the *prestige* of popular government that I have *erlebt*. . . . Our Congress was *absolutely* sincere in disclaiming any desire of conquest or annexation. But see how in the twinkling of an eye a nation's ideals will change! With Dewey's sudden victory, an "imperialist" party has arisen here, which, as it will command all the crude and barbaric patriotism of the country, will be a hard thing to resist. After all, it is on that pure instinctive masterfulness and ambition, that sense of a great destiny, that the greatness of every great nation is based; and we have it in a great measure. But one must "live up" to a great destiny, and alas! our education as a nation, so far, little fits us for success in administering islands with inferior populations. Spain deserves to lose them, but do we deserve to gain them? Whatever happens, in any event, will happen not as the result of any particular reason, but as the result of passion, and of certain watchwords that nations have learned habitually to obey.

James saw imperialism as an outlet for blind passion masked by a profession of benevolence:

We gave the fighting instinct and the passion of mastery their outing . . . because we thought that . . . we could resume our permanent ideals and character when the fighting fit was done. We now see how we reckoned without our host. We see . . . what an absolute savage . . . the passion of military conquest always is, and how the only safeguard against the crimes to which it will infallibly drag the nation that gives way to it is to keep it chained forever. . . . We are now openly engaged in crushing out the sacredest thing in this great human world—the attempt of a people long enslaved to attain to the possession of itself, to organize its laws and government, to be free to follow its internal destinies according to its own ideals. . . . Why, then, do we go on? First, the war fever; and then the pride which always refuses to back down when under fire. But these are passions that interfere with the reasonable settlement of any affair; and in this affair we have to deal with a factor altogether peculiar with our belief, namely, in a national destiny which must be "big" at any cost. . . . We are to be missionaries of civilization, and to bear the white man's burden, painful as it often is! . . . The individual lives are nothing. Our duty and our destiny call, and civilization must go on! Could there be a more damning indictment of that whole bloated idol termed "modern civilization" than this amounts to? Civilization is, then, the big, hollow, resounding, corrupting, sophisticating, confusing torrent of mere brutal momentum and irrationality that brings forth fruits like this![8]

On April 11, 1899, Roosevelt made his famous speech on "The Strenuous Life," which evoked a reply from James:—

Shall Governor Roosevelt be allowed to crow all over our national barnyard and hear no equally shrill voice lifted in reply? Even the "prattlers who sit at home in peace with their silly mock-humanitarianism" must feel their "ignoble" and "cowardly" blood stirred by such a challenge; and I for one feel that it would be ignominious to leave him in uncontradicted possession of the field. . . . Of all the naked abstractions that were ever applied to human affairs, the outpourings of Governor Roosevelt's soul in this speech would seem the very nakedest. Although in middle life . . . and in a situation of responsibility concrete enough, he is still mentally in the *Sturm und Drang* period of early adolescence, treats human affairs, when he makes speeches about them, from the sole point of view of the organic excitement and difficulty they may bring, gushes over war as the ideal condition of human society, for the manly strenuousness which it involves, and treats peace as a condition of blubberlike and swollen ignobility, fit only for huckstering weaklings, dwelling in gray twilight and heedless of the higher life. Not a word of the cause,—one foe is as good as another, for aught he tells us; not a word of the conditions of success. . . . He swamps everything together in one flood of abstract bellicose emotion.[9]

James's active participation in the anti-imperialist movement came to a close with his address before the Anti-Imperialist League in Boston in the fall of 1903 in which he said:

Angelic impulses and predatory lusts divide our heart exactly as they divide the hearts of other countries. . . . Political virtue does not follow geographical divisions. It follows the eternal division inside of each country between the

[8] Letter to *Boston Evening Transcript*, March 1, 1899.
[9] Letter to *Springfield Republican*, June 4, 1900.

more animal and the more intellectual kind of men, between the tory and the liberal tendencies, the jingoism and animal instinct that would run things by main force and brute possession, and the critical conscience that believes in educational methods and in rational rules of right. . . . The great international and cosmopolitan liberal party, the party of conscience and intelligence the world over, has, in short, absorbed us; and we are only its American section, carrying on the war against the powers of darkness here, playing our part in the long, long campaign for truth and fair dealing which must go on in all the countries of the world until the end of time. Let us cheerfully settle into our interminable task. Everywhere it is the same struggle under various names,—light against darkness, right against might, love against hate. The Lord of life is with us, and we cannot permanently fail.[10]

Interesting and instructive are James's alterations of attitude to Theodore Roosevelt. In the year 1877-1878 the latter was a member of James's course on the "Comparative Anatomy and Physiology of Vertebrates." He could already boast of some attainment as a field naturalist, having frequently made excursions to the country for birds and to the Boston wharves for specimens of lobsters and fish. I quote from the recollections of another member of the class:

Many were the *rencontres* between him and Dr. James. T. R. *always* had the last word. . . . Those little sparring matches I think threw considerable light on his characteristics. He was a great lime-lighter! My impression of his material, in these instances, was that it was largely irrelevant and far-fetched. At all events, Dr. James would never continue the argument, and I can see him now in his double-breasted blue coat and flowing tie, settling back in his chair, in a broad grin . . . and waiting for T. R. to finish.[11]

As a fighter for ideals Roosevelt was a man after James's own heart; while the roughness of his methods—his lack of taste, sympathy, and discrimination —was profoundly offensive. In 1902 he wrote: "On the whole I have rejoiced in Roosevelt so far, but I've done with the man who can utter such brazen and impudent lies. . . . His moral fibre is too irredeemably coarse. . . . If only one had the pen of a Voltaire!"[12]

Three years later James was advocating the election of Roosevelt to the presidency of Harvard:

Think of the mighty good-will of him, of his enjoyment of his post, of his power as a preacher, of the number of things to which he gives his attention, of the safety of his second thoughts, of the increased courage he is showing, and above all of the fact that he is an open, instead of an underground leader, whom

[10] *Report* of Fifth Annual Meeting of the New England Anti-Imperialist League, November 28, 1903.
[11] From a letter to the author by Dr. Samuel Delano, Harvard '79.
[12] To Charles E. Norton, August 23, 1902.

the voters can control once in four years, when he runs away, whose heart is in the right place, who is an enemy of red tape and quibbling and everything that in general the word "politician" stands for. That significance of him in the popular mind is a great national asset, and it would be a shame to let it run to waste until it has done a lot more work for us.[13]

Two years later the pendulum had swung again. On February 23, 1907, Roosevelt had made a speech at the Harvard Union in which he had humorously derided scholarship to the delight of the students and at the expense of the members of the faculty who sat in the gallery. This was too much for James. Though he preached the gospel of robustness, he cared very deeply what one was robust about. There was always a prior condition of legitimate belligerency—namely, the purity of one's cause.

James's anti-imperialism was an application of his pluralism and individualism. Dickinson S. Miller once wrote of James: "Not detachment, but attachment, was his quality." [14] This is a profound observation. James's wide and almost promiscuous sociability did not detach him from his family, but simply multiplied his attachments. Similarly his cosmopolitanism did not detach him from America, but enriched and diversified his attachments by presenting new human objects to his apparently insatiable appetite. Though he was by no means blind to their faults, he found something to respect and like in every nation that he knew. Once after praising Italy and England, he added: "Yet I believe (or suspect) that ours is eventually the bigger destiny, if we can only succeed in living up to it. . . . Meanwhile, as my brother Henry once wrote, thank God for a world that holds so rich an England, so rare an Italy!" [15] He would have said the same of so vigorous a Germany, so polite a France, or so honest a Switzerland. Thank God for a world that is generous enough to hold them all!

James was fond of saying that he "went in for small nations and small things generally." "Damn great Empires! including that of the Absolute. . . . Give me individuals and their spheres of activity." [16] Here is a completer statement of the matter:

> I am against bigness and greatness in all their forms, and with the invisible molecular moral forces that work from individual to individual, stealing in through the crannies of the world like so many soft rootlets, or like the capillary oozing of water, and yet rending the hardest monuments of man's pride, if you give them time. The bigger the unit you deal with, the hollower, the more brutal, the more mendacious is the life displayed. So I am against all big organizations as such, national ones first and foremost; against all big successes

---

[13] W.J. to Henry L. Higginson, July 18, 1905; *L.W.J.*, II, 232.
[14] "Mr. Santayana and William James," *Harvard Graduates' Magazine*, XXIX (1920-1), 351.
[15] To Pauline Goldmark, July 2, 1908; *L.W.J.*, II, 305.
[16] W.J. to W. Lutoslawski, August 10, 1900, and to Mrs. Glendower Evans, February 15, 1901.

and big results; and in favor of the eternal forces of truth which always work in the individual and immediately unsuccessful way, under-dogs always, till history comes, after they are long dead, and puts them on the top.[17]

James's Americanism was never seriously shaken. He was instinctively loyal to his own, whether family, friend, or country. In 1901, when his illness, together with the Gifford Lectures, had kept him abroad for the better part of two years, he said: "I long to steep myself in America again and let the broken rootlets make new adhesions to the native soil. A man coquetting with too many countries is as bad as a bigamist, and loses his soul altogether." [18] This was his characteristic and invariable reaction to any prolonged absence from home.

His patriotism ran with two of his fundamental moral attitudes. America, was, he thought, less highly institutionalized, less subject to control by impersonal, corporate entities, than Europe. As an individualist James had an antipathy to organization, mechanization, and officialdom. The other attitude which strongly reënforced James's Americanism was his repugnance to the decadent and effete—his preference of the simple, the natural, the vigorous, the forward-looking. He found these qualities in America, and in the end they outweighed the counterattractions of European countries, powerful as these were: "Still, one loves America above all things, for her youth, her greenness, her plasticity, innocence, good intentions, friends, everything." [19]

On July 23, 1903, James contributed a long letter to the *Springfield Republican* on the subject of lynching. This letter was widely reprinted and received so much comment that on July 29 James gave an interview to the *Boston Journal* on the same subject. These published utterances brought him many letters of commendation from the North and of protest from the South.

To James lynching and mob rule were psychological as well as moral phenomena, illustrating the powers of emotional forces, when socially stimulated, to sweep away all ordinary restraints.

> The average church-going civilizee realizes, one may say, absolutely nothing of the deeper currents of human nature, or of the aboriginal capacity for murderous excitement which lies sleeping even in his own bosom. . . . The watertight compartment in which the carnivore within us is confined is artificial and not organic. It never will be organic. The slightest diminution of external pressure, the slightest loophole of licensed exception, will make the whole system leaky, and murder will again grow rampant. It is where the impulse is collective, and the murder is regarded as a punitive or protective duty, that the peril to civilization is greatest. Then, as in the hereditary vendetta, in dueling, in re-

---

[17] W.J. to Mrs. Henry Whitman, June 7, 1899; *L.W.J.*, II, 90.

[18] W.J. to C. E. Norton, June 26, 1901; *L.W.J.*, II, 152.

[19] W.J. to Mrs. Henry Whitman, October 5, 1899; *L.W.J.*, II, 105.

ligious massacre, history shows how difficult it is to exterminate a homicidal custom which is once established.[20]

In the case of the "lynching epidemic," as in the case of militarism and chauvinism, James was profoundly disturbed by the new role of the popular newspaper:—

> Our American people used to be supposed to have a certain hardheaded shrewdness. Nowadays they seem smitten with utter silliness. Their professed principles mean nothing to them, and any phrase or sensational excitement captivates them. The sensational press is the organ and the promulgator of this state of mind, which means . . . a new "dark ages" that may last more centuries than the first one. Then illiteracy was brutal and dumb, and power was rapacious without disguise. Now illiteracy has an enormous literary organization, and power is sophistical; and the result is necessarily a new phenomenon in history— involving every kind of diseased sensationalism and insincerity in the collective mind.[21]

The last of the causes that enlisted James's support was Mental Hygiene. The reasons which actuated James are best set forth in the long letter which he addressed in 1909, on June 2, to Mr. John D. Rockefeller, Sr., in the hope of obtaining financial support for the cause:

> During my life as a "psychologist" I have had much to do with our asylums, and I have had so painfully borne in upon me the massiveness of human evil which the term "insanity" covers, and the inadequacy of our arrangements for coping with it, that I long ago registered a vow that if I myself, by Heaven's grace, should ever be able to leave any money for public use it should be for "insanity" exclusively. . . . Our usual arrangements take no heed either of prophylaxis or of after-care; what should be regarded as a common functional disease is handled as a social stigma. . . . The occasion of bringing my own dissatisfaction . . . to a practical head, has been the recent publication of a very remarkable book, *A Mind That Found Itself*, by Clifford W. Beers of New Haven. . . . It is he who has convinced the rest of us that the hour for doing something—and not merely feeling and wishing—has struck.

James's active support of "causes" reveals the precise nature of his practical idealism. The good is not something to be contemplated, but something to be brought to pass. It is to be felt, yes—but as the agent and not as the spectator feels it. Ideals are objects of will, rather than of taste. It is this view that underlies his vigorous reaction to Santayana. In 1900, having read Santayana's *Poetry and Religion*, James wrote to Palmer as follows:—

---

[20] *Springfield Daily Republican*, July 23, 1903.
[21] July 27, 1903, to Dr. Samuel Delano, who in a letter on lynching, *Evening Post*, July 24, 1903, had emphasized the importance of public opinion.

The great event in my life recently has been the reading of Santayana's book. Although I absolutely reject the Platonism of it, I have literally squealed with delight at the imperturbable perfection with which the position is laid down on page after page. . . . It is refreshing to see a representative of moribund Latinity rise up and administer such reproof to us barbarians in the hour of our triumph. . . . Nevertheless, how fantastic a philosophy!—as if the "world of values" *were* independent of existence. It is only as *being,* that one thing is better than another. The idea of darkness is as good as that of light, as ideas. There is more value in light's *being*. . . . When . . . you come down to the facts, what do your harmonious and integral ideal systems prove to be? in the concrete? Always things burst by the growing content of experience. Dramatic unities; laws of versification; ecclesiastical systems; scholastic doctrines. Bah! Give me Walt Whitman and Browning ten times over, much as the perverse ugliness of the latter at times irritates me, and intensely as I have enjoyed Santayana's attack. The barbarians are in the line of mental growth, and those who do insist that the ideal and the real are dynamically continuous are those by whom the world is to be saved. But I'm nevertheless delighted that the other view, always existing in the world, should at last have found so splendidly impertinent an expression among ourselves.[22]

The letter containing these paragraphs was sent by Palmer to Santayana, who replied on Easter Day as follows:—

I see that you have discovered me in the *Poetry and Religion* more than in my verses or the *Sense of Beauty,* although I fancy there is no less of me in those other books. . . . I think you will find that, apart from temperament, I am nearer to you than you now believe. What you say, for instance, about the value of the good lying in its *existence,* and about the continuity of the world of values with that of fact, is not different from what I should admit. Ideals would be irrelevant if they were not natural entelechies, if they were not called for by something that exists and if, consequently, their realization would not be a present and actual good. . . .

You tax me several times with impertinence and superior airs. I wonder if you realize the years of suppressed irritation which I have passed in the midst of an unintelligible, sanctimonious and often disingenuous Protestantism, which is thoroughly alien and repulsive to me, and the need I have of joining hands with something far away from it and far above it. My Catholic sympathies didn't justify me in speaking out because I felt them to be merely sympathies, and not to have a rational and human backing; but the study of Plato and Aristotle has given me confidence and, backed by such an authority as they and all who have accepted them represent, I have a right to be sincere, to be absolutely objective and unapologetic, because it is not I that speak but human reason that speaks in me. Truly the Babel in which we live has nothing in it so respectable as to put on the defensive the highest traditions of the human mind. No doubt, as you say, Latinity is moribund, as Greece itself was when it transmitted to the rest of the world the seeds of its own rationalism; and for that reason there is

[22] April 2, 1900; *L.W.J.,* II, 122-3.

the more need of transplanting and propagating straight thinking among the peoples who hope to be masters of the world in the immediate future. Otherwise they will be its physical masters only, and the Muses will fly over them to alight among some future race that may understand the gods better.

While James vigorously opposed a Platonic divorce of the good from the realm of existence, and insisted that the "ideal and the real are dynamically continuous," he was not less opposed than Santayana to any *reduction* of the ideal to the real. The ideal is a preferred form of life—something *to be made real* through the energy of the will. Thus James consistently refused to identify meanings with origins, differences of value with physical differences, importance with magnitude, or moral progress with natural history.[23]

[23] *W.B.*, 100; *L.W.J.*, II, 345-6.

XXVIII

VARIETIES OF RELIGIOUS EXPERIENCE

The period of James's preoccupation with practical philosophy culminated in the Gifford Lectures of 1901 and 1902, and their publication in the latter year under the title of *The Varieties of Religious Experience*. This was, in the first place, an act of filial piety. Writing to his wife on January 6, 1883, immediately after his father's death he said:

> You have one new function hereafter, or rather not so much a new function as a new intellectualization of an old one: you must not leave me till I understand a little more of the value and meaning of religion in Father's sense, in the mental life and destiny of man. It is not the *one* thing needful, as he said. But it is needful with the rest. My friends leave it altogether out. I as his son (if for no other reason) must help it to its rights in their eyes. And for that reason I must learn to interpret it aright as I have never done, and you must help me.

The *Varieties* is the fulfillment of this pledge, after the lapse of almost twenty years. It is perhaps surprising that there should be in these lectures so few specific indications of his father's influence.[1] But that influence did not extend to details, nor did it embrace the theological doctrines which filled his father's works. James once said: "I myself believe that the evidence for God lies primarily in inner personal experiences." The father's influence appears in James's general inclination to credit these "personal experiences," of which the chief was the sustaining sense of support from a higher power.[2]

As regards James himself the ideas which are developed in the *Varieties* represent one of two threads which can be traced back continuously to his youth. There were always two kinds of faith, the fighting faith and the comforting faith; or, as they might be called, the faith upstream and the faith downstream. The former is the faith that springs from strength. Preferring the good to the evil, the moral person fights for it with the sort of confidence

---

[1] He refers to his father's conversion at Windsor in 1844 as an instance of "panic fear," but did not introduce it because there was "too much context required." (*V.R.E.*, 161; W.J. to F. Abauzit, June 12, 1904.) There is something reminiscent of his father in the vivid thrust at Calvinism in a footnote: "The very notion that this glorious universe, with planets and winds, and laughing sky and ocean, should have been conceived and had its beams and rafters laid in technicalities of criminality, is incredible to our modern imagination." (*V.R.E.*, 448.)

[2] *Pragm.*, 109; cf. *L.R.H.J.*, 13-4, 72.

that the brave man feels in himself and his allies, exulting in the danger and in the uncertainty of the issue. This is the faith of James's tough-mindedness,[3] the bracing air which he prefers to breathe when his hygienic tone is good; and it is also the faith of last resort, when scepticism has deprived him of every other support. It is the kind of religion that is characteristic of *The Will to Believe*. The second is the faith that springs from human weakness, and asks for refuge and security.[4] In the fighting faith religion is a stimulant to the will; the comforting faith, on the other hand, is at the bottom of one's heart, relaxing. Though one may row with great earnestness, one is aware of being carried to port—safely, inexorably—by the very current in which one floats. The need for this sort of faith James understood both from his own periodic weariness and from his sympathy with that extremity and tragic plight which is the common lot of man. To this second faith, the comforting faith, James devotes special attention in the Gifford Lectures.

There is also a close relation between James's view of religious conversion and his own "crisis" in 1870-1872. His sense of black despair and morbid fear is used in the *Varieties* to illustrate the state of "the sick soul." He tells us that the experience made him "sympathetic with the morbid feelings of others"; and that both his melancholy and his emergence from it had "a religious bearing." His own "salvation" came through self-reliance and the idea of moral freedom, rather than through a sense of supporting grace—but he experienced a marked alteration of mood, and a feeling of renewed life similar to that of "the twice-born." [5]

At the same time that the Gifford Lectures sprang from James's filial piety and from his personal experiences, they also expressed the psychological interest which had governed him during the nineties. Religion afforded the greatest single group—greatest both in volume and in dignity—of those "exceptional mental states" with which he was also concerned in his "psychical research," in his observation of war and mob violence, and in his studies of psychopathology. "I regard the *Varieties of Religious Experience*," he wrote in 1902, "as in a sense a study of morbid psychology, mediating and interpreting to the philistine much that he would otherwise despise and reject utterly." James had already in his Ingersoll Lecture on *Human Immortality* advanced the hypothesis of a "mother-sea" of consciousness from which the finite consciousness of man might receive support and a guarantee of survival.[6]

Nor must it be forgotten, though the exigencies of orderly arrangement permit only a passing reference to it here, that the first public announcement

---

[3] Opposed to "tender-mindedness," *cf. Pragm.*, Lect. I; not to be confused with "healthy-mindedness," as James discusses it in the *Varieties*.

[4] This alternative appears clearly as early as 1861; *cf. L.W.J.*, I, 128 ff.

[5] *Cf.* above, 135, and below, 360; *V.R.E.*, 160-1; *L.W.J.*, I, 145-8.

[6] To Boris Sidis, September 11, 1902; *cf.* above, 206.

of pragmatism took place in 1898, shortly after James had embarked on the preparation of the Gifford Lectures. In the California lecture on "Philosophical Conceptions and Practical Results" he made a special application of pragmatism in a passage which clearly defines the field of religious investigation:

> What keeps religion going is something else than abstract definitions and systems of logically concatenated adjectives, and something different from faculties of theology and their professors. All these things are after-effects, secondary accretions upon a mass of concrete religious experiences, connecting themselves with feeling and conduct that renew themselves in *sæcula sæculorum* in the lives of humble private men. If you ask what these experiences are, they are conversations with the unseen, voices and visions, responses to prayer, changes of heart, deliverances from fear, inflowings of help, assurances of support, whenever certain persons set their own internal attitude in certain appropriate ways.[7]

Although James's appointment to a Gifford Lectureship was not formally made until 1898, it was proposed as early as 1896, and he began in his characteristic way to collect bibliographies, books, clippings, citations, descriptions, letters—material which he did not begin to put into finished written form until 1900. This period coincided with a severe physical collapse. It was in the summer of 1898 that James, after extraordinary physical exertion, spent his *"Walpurgis Nacht"* in the Adirondack Mountains.[8] While it is no doubt true, as he reported, that his projected Edinburgh lectures on religion had "made quite a hitch ahead," [9] the strain of ten hours and a half of hard walking with a pack, coming after a fatiguing year, caused an irreparable valvular lesion of his heart. He had paid a high price for the enrichment of his experience. In the late summer of the same year he again over-exerted himself in the high Sierras. Then, in June 1899 he "got lost in the Adirondacks and converted what was to have been a 'walk' into a thirteen-hours scramble without food and with anxiety."

Thus by a singular irony of fate he twice suffered misfortune in the spot he loved best in the world, and was thenceforth cut off from that form of recreation which he considered his "main hold on primeval sanity and health of soul." [10] From July 1899 he entered upon a period of invalidism of his own peculiar sort—a period during which he *felt* only frustration, but in which he somehow managed by utilizing fragments of time and intermittent pulsations of strength to stride forward both in scholarship and in writing. It will be noted that the major part of James's philosophical achievement, not only

---

[7] *C.E.R.*, 427-8.
[8] *Cf.* below, 364.
[9] To A.H.J., July 9, 1898; *L.W.J.*, II, 76.
[10] To H.J.², August 8 and June 21, 1899.

the *Varieties,* but the whole development of pragmatism and the culminating phase of his metaphysical fruition, with all the lecturing, journeying, controversy, and correspondence that these involved, occurred after he had thought his career ended, and when he was already afflicted with that disability which ultimaely proved fatal. It is not strange that he should have testified to the latent "energies of man."

Much of the actual writing was done in bed, at times when two or three hours a day was the maximum of work which his strength would support. It was necessary to postpone the lectures from 1900 to 1901, and there was always the haunting fear that he might not be able to deliver them even if he could complete their preparation. The first series of lectures began at Edinburgh, on May 16, 1901. Only two weeks before he had written:

> As for my sad self, I feel reasonably sure now of reading my lectures myself (they begin May 16,—on which date please offer up silent prayer). If I can stand the sociability it will be a great thing,—I have grown so pusillanimous in the past two years about everything, that I dread that like a nightmare. I have become a vegetable, a suffering vegetable if there be such a thing; and, as like seeks like, I shan't get seriously better until I can get my back onto some American vegetation with an American tree over my head and an American squirrel chittering at me.[11]

The lectures were a success, both in the number and in the interest of the auditors, and success restored the lecturer's confidence in himself. After a winter at home he returned to Edinburgh again in the spring of 1902. On June 9 he wrote to Theodore Flournoy in Switzerland:

> The last lecture went off today,—about 400 auditors, very silent and attentive, and tremendous enthusiasm at the end. But *how* glad I am it is all over! Hereafter I will make no such contract again. I am *deadly* tired and going home to my own normal conditions, to get well.

The lectures had been prepared for the press before James left America for Edinburgh, and appeared in June under the title, *The Varieties of Religious Experience, a Study in Human Nature.* The book, like the lectures, was signally successful. Writing again to Flournoy, on the ninth of the following January, he said:

> The book has sold extraordinarily well in English, for a book that costs over three dollars. The ten thousand is already being printed; I get enthusiastic letters from strangers; and the reviewers, although, *without a* single *exception,* they all use the word "unsatisfactory," having eased their conscience by that term, they proceed to handle me with sympathy and praise.

[11] To Frances R. Morse, April 30, 1901.

This success was not unexpected; indeed, James had anticipated it with some misgivings when he said, it "will doubtless be a popular book,—too biological for the religious, too religious for the biologists." [12]

The thesis of the *Varieties* is best stated in a letter to Miss Frances R. Morse:

> The problem I have set myself is a hard one: *first,* to defend . . . "experience" against "philosophy" as being the real backbone of the world's religious life . . . and *second*, to make the hearer or reader believe, what I myself invincibly do believe, that, although all the special manifestations of religion may have been absurd (I mean its creeds and theories), yet the life of it as a whole is mankind's most important function. [13]

In other words, religion is not a secondary product, a mode of feeling or action evoked by a secular view of the world, but has its own direct and independent evidence. There are religious *data,* or *facts,* and not merely religious ideas or sentiments. As early as 1884 James had written to Davidson that he rather despaired of any "popular religion of a philosophic character," and found himself wondering

> whether there can be any popular religion raised on the ruins of the old Christianity without the presence of . . . a belief in new *physical* facts and possibilities. Abstract considerations about the soul and the reality of a moral order will not do in a year what the glimpse into a world of new phenomenal possibilities enveloping those of the present life, afforded by an extension of our insight into the order of nature, would do in an instant. [14]

It was with such "phenomenal possibilities" that the *Varieties* was concerned. But while James identified religion with certain specific experiences, and with specific facts, events, forces, and entities which these experiences revealed, he did not identify religion with any particular creed. By religion he meant historic religions, but in respect of their common content and not their particular dogmas.

Religion is something more primordial than reason and of equal authority. "Faith branches off from the high-road before reason begins," said James to a sceptical student. [15] In notes made during the preparation of the Gifford Lectures, he wrote, under the heading of "Faith":

> The struggle seems to be that of a less articulate and more profound part of our nature to hold out, and keep itself standing, against the attempts of a more superficial and explicit or loquacious part, to suppress it. The profounder part be-

[12] To C. Stumpf, July 10, 1901.
[13] April 12, 1900; *L.W.J.*, II, 127; for other parts of this letter *cf*. above, 216.
[14] March 30, 1884; *L.W.J.*, I, 236-7.
[15] Reported to the author by Francis G. Allinson, Harvard '77.

lieves; but it can *say* so little. Ought it to be cowed? to submit? or ought it to stand by its own lights? . . . One *can't* convert a genuine disbeliever in religion any more than one can convert a Protestant to Catholicism. . . . My exhibition of extravagant and irrational instances will probably confirm such disbelievers entirely. Just see, they will say, *how* absurd! Yet I must shape things and argue to the conclusion that a man's religion is the deepest and wisest thing in his life. I must frankly establish the breach between the life of articulate reason, and the push of the subconscious, the irrational instinctive part, which is more vital. . . . In religion the vital needs, the mystical overbeliefs . . . proceed from an ultra-rational region. They are *gifts*. It is a question of *life*, of living in these gifts or not living. . . . There is a chance to do something strong here, but it is extremely difficult."

The original paragraph which James wrote for the opening of the Gifford Lectures stressed the uniqueness of the religious experience and the breach with "articulate reason":

There is something in life, as one feels its presence, that seems to defy all the possible resources of phraseology. . . . Life defies our phrases, not only because it is infinitely continuous and subtle and shaded, whilst our verbal terms are discrete, rude and few; but because of a deeper discrepancy still. Our words come together leaning on each other laterally for support, in chains and propositions, and there is never a proposition that does not require other propositions after it, to amplify it, restrict it, or in some way save it from the falsity by defect or excess which it contains. . . . Life, too, in one sense, stumbles over its own fact in a similar way; for its earlier moments plunge ceaselessly into later ones which reinterpret and correct them. Yet there is something else than this in life, something entirely unparalleled by anything in verbal thought. The living moments—some living moments, at any rate—have somewhat of absolute that needs no lateral support. Their meaning seems to well up from out of their very centre, in a way impossible verbally to describe. If you take a disk painted with a concentric spiral pattern, and make it revolve, it will seem to be growing continuously and indefinitely, and yet to take in nothing from without; and to remain, if you pay attention to its actual size, always of the *same* size. Something as paradoxical as this lies in every present moment of life. Here or nowhere, as Emerson says, is the whole fact. The moment stands and contains and sums up all things; and all change is within it, much as the developing landscape with all its growth falls forever within the rear windowpane of the last car of a train that is speeding on its headlong way. This self-sustaining in the midst of self-removal, which characterizes all reality and fact, is something absolutely foreign to the nature of language, and even to the nature of logic, commonly so-called. Something forever exceeds, escapes from statement, withdraws from definition, must be glimpsed and felt, not told. No one knows this like your genuine professor of philosophy. For what glimmers and twinkles like a bird's wing in the sunshine it is his business to snatch and fix. And every time he fires his volley of new vocables out of his philosophic shot-gun, whatever surface-flush of success he may feel, he secretly kens at the same time the finer hollowness and irrelevancy. . . . Especially is this the case when the topic is named as the philosophy of religion. Religion is the very inner citadel of human life, and the pretension to translate adequately into spread-out conceptual terms a kind of experience in which intellect, feeling and will, all our consciousness and all our subconsciousness together melt in a kind of chemical fusion, would be particularly abhorrent. Let me say then with frankness at the outset, that I believe that no so-called philosophy of religion can possibly begin to be an adequate translation of what goes on in the single private man, as he livingly expresses himself in religious faith and act.

Religion is irrational, and it is also individual. It has to do with "what goes on in the single private man." The social or institutional side of religion did not interest James or seem to him important. Religion concerns "the way an individual's life comes home to *him*, his intimate needs, ideals, desolations, consolations, failures, successes." [16] This, at any rate, was what counted—the rest was merely the instrument.

From James's emphasis upon the uniqueness of the religious experience, and its specific factual implications, arose his paradoxical relation to contemporary Christianity. Religion of the sort in which he was interested was closer to the simple piety of the evangelical sects than to that of modern religious liberalism. To James, as to Methodism, religion was a clearly recognizable and memorable event in the history of the individual. He was fond of more or less playfully mentioning his evangelical orthodoxy to his friends among the liberal clergy, and especially to his friend Borden P. Bowne, professor of philosophy at Boston University who was a Methodist of so modern and philosophical a type that he was tried for heresy. In sending a copy of the *Varieties* to his colleague Professor Francis G. Peabody, James wrote: "You will class me as a Methodist, *minus* a Saviour!" To Flournoy he reported: "An enthusiastic clergyman wrote me yesterday that I am of the company of Isaiah and St. Paul. I have just replied (after Whistler): 'Why drag in St. Paul and Isaiah?' " [17] Masked by this pleasantry there lay the serious meaning of James's whole endeavor. He believed that liberalism had saved the intellect at the cost of repudiating the great historic phenomenon of religion. In notes for his lectures he said:

> Remember that the whole point lies in really *believing* that through a certain point or part in you you coalesce and are identical with the Eternal. This seems to be the *saving* belief both in Christianity and in Vedantism. . . . It *comes home* to one only at particular times. . . . The more original religious life is always lyric—"the monk owns nothing but his lyre"—and its essence is to dip into another kingdom, to feel an invisible order . . . *au prix duquel* the common sense values really vanish. Hence, indeed, the genuine antagonism between common sense religion . . . and that of the more extravagant prophets of what-

[16] "Theological School Lectures" of 1902 or 1906.
[17] To Peabody, June 21, 1902; to Flournoy, July 23, 1902.

ever kind. Each is foolish to the other, for each lives in the light of a different world.

In the summer of 1902 James gave two lectures before the Harvard Summer School of Theology. Writing to Münsterberg from Chocorua on July 11, he said: "I lecture in Cambr. on Monday and Tuesday. If I go on at this rate, they'll make me a bishop. As for my book, don't read it till you're on your deathbed, when it will save your soul. I fancy you're destined to abhor it if you look at it now." [18] In these lectures and the series of five lectures which he gave in the summer of 1906, he continued to stress the antithesis between the modern rationalizing tendency and the essence of historic religion:

> Between the ordinary church-goer and the passionate saint, there is the inveterate feud of those who instinctively tend to keep religion "reasonable" and those who would obey it in ways that are uncompromising and inconvenient. At bottom it is the feud between a naturalism with a softened outline, and a positive supernaturalism with its centre of emphasis outside the margin of this world altogether. My own solution seems to favor this latter view.

Even within the party of supernaturalism James identified himself with the left wing. There is a "natural supernaturalism" (after Carlyle)—an "immanent or universal supernaturalism." It distinguishes value from fact, is indifferent to the scientific description of particular existences, and construes the totality as supernatural. James does not absolutely reject this tendency—in discussing religion he rejects *no* tendency, since it is an essential part of his view to accept and respect as religious any form of piety whatsoever that carries with it a sense of salvation. But he proceeded, for his part, to defend the cause of the old "dualistic," "particular," or "piecemeal supernaturalism," which admits the supernatural into the same realm of fact with the natural. He revived this "as a possibility," adducing abnormal psychology and the religious experiences of mankind as evidences in its support. To most people such concreteness was shocking, but with James himself it was just the reverse. *He* was shocked at "abstract and remote ways of considering individual facts." [19]

It will have been noted that the *Varieties* bore the subtitle, "A Study in Human Nature." It was originally intended that the first series should be "descriptive" and the second "metaphysical," but the descriptive task expanded so greatly that the metaphysical task had to be postponed to another occasion. Such, at least, is the statement of the author. He professed to present the facts and leave the reader to draw his own conclusions. "There is lots of human nature in it," he wrote to a friend, "and I think it must be written rather 'objectively,' for both God's friends and his enemies appear to find in it ample jus-

---

[18] M. Münsterberg, *Hugo Münsterberg: His Life and Work*, D. Appleton and Company, 1922, 89.
[19] The same theme, of "crass" *vs.* "refined" supernaturalism, is briefly presented in *V.R.E.*, 520 ff.

tification for their differing views." [20] The impression left on the reader, however, is that God's friends get much the best of it. James's description was not of the sterilized variety which is commonly called scientific. It is true that he introduced distinctions such as "once-born" and "twice-born," for purposes of classification. But he attached little importance to them, and he made no systematic use of the explanatory hypotheses of general psychology—either those which he had himself introduced in the *Psychology,* or those in vogue at the time when he published the *Varieties*—with the exception of the unorthodox notion of the "subliminal consciousness." He let his religious documents speak for themselves; or, rather, he *helped* them to speak for themselves. Thus while he regarded the *Varieties* as "in a sense a study of morbid psychology," he took great pains in the opening lecture to rid his auditors of any prejudice they might feel against a state of mind merely because it was pathological. "Mere sanity," he said on another occasion, "is the most philistine and (at bottom) unessential of a man's attributes." [21] The reader received the impression that James regarded religious experiences, even though they be judged pathological by strict psychiatric standards, as in some sense and in some degree inspired. Their "exceptional" character commended them to him.

Unquestionably James was justifying, and not merely describing, the religious experience. He stationed himself at the centre of the believer's consciousness and tried to convey its warmth and appeal as they were originally felt. He was concerned with religious values, with the hope or exaltation of concrete individuals, which must be rendered sympathetically if they are to be conveyed at all. And then, especially in the latter part of the book, the author *defended the claims* of religious experience. Philosophy, in the person of William James, confirmed its truth.

There are three tests which are applicable to religious truth: "immediate luminousness," "philosophical reasonableness," and "moral helpfulness." These are new names for criteria of knowledge which appear repeatedly in James's philosophy. There is the direct evidence of fact, as in perception; there is the consistency of alleged fact with beliefs already accepted—in short, the indirect evidence of fact; and there is the congruence of belief with the passional nature, especially with the moral will. The universal claim of religious faith, "that the conscious person is continuous with a wider self through which saving experiences come," satisfies all of these criteria. "Mystical experiences are . . . direct perceptions of fact for those who have them." They are consistent with science, thanks to the psychological hypothesis, advanced by Frederic Myers of a subliminal self. [22] Their consistency with philosophy is obtained through

[20] To Pauline Goldmark, August 1, 1902.
[21] *Letters of Charles Eliot Norton,* 1913, II, 348.
[22] *V.R.E.,* 18, 515, 423-4, 242; *cf. P.U.,* 299, 309.

the hypothesis of pluralism. Mysticism is commonly monistic, and supernaturalism is commonly dogmatic; but James proposes a radical departure: a pluralistic mysticism, and an experimental supernaturalism. This was not a special pleading on James's part, but the proper culmination of one of the lines of his philosophical development. As early as 1874 he had read Benjamin Paul Blood's *Anæsthetic Revelation,* one of the "stepping-stones" of all his thinking thereafter. In 1888 he had been attracted by Edmund Gurney's "hypothetical supernaturalism"—with its idea of an "invisible order continuous with the present order of nature"; and from this there is a natural transition to the "piecemeal" or "crass" supernaturalism of 1902.[23]

Finally, the "moral helpfulness," or passional congruence, of such a pluralistic religious faith lies in its imparting a sense of open opportunity and of serious responsibility to the individual agent. With it goes that "ordinary moralistic state of mind" which makes the salvation of the world dependent upon "the success with which each unit does its part." [24]

The *Varieties* evoked many comments, favorable and unfavorable, published and unpublished, from professional colleagues and from personal friends. In his replies James summarized and appraised his own work. Among these replies the most illuminating is that which he wrote to his Cambridge neighbor and old friend, Grace Norton:

Chocorua, Sept. 12, 1902

My dear Grace,—

. . . Your letter about my book arrived duly and filled me with mixed feelings of interest and sorrow. . . . I don't wonder that the mouldiness and measliness of so many of my saints gave you a revulsion away from other-worldliness to naturalism and humanism. Yours is much the best letter I have received from that point of view, because it is the most gravely expressed and the most profoundly felt. The two points of view, I believe, must work upon each other until they acquire a common content and way of living together, the *material* of the blessed life being thought of in terms of humanity, exclusively, the *inspiration* being felt as a relation to a higher portion of the universe now out of sight. But it will be long ere different persons' formulas will not produce misunderstandings in each other's minds. A real practical difference, so far, is between the healthy-minded (among whom I count you as writer of your letter) and those who seriously despair of straightforward healthy-mindedness as a radical solution. I myself don't see how it can be a *universal* solution, when the world is the seat of so much unhappiness really incurable in ordinary ways, but *cured* (in many individuals) by their religious experience. One can neither ignore the unhappy individuals nor the peculiar form of their relief, as facts of human history; and I, surveying human history objectively, couldn't help seeing *there* its possibly most characteristic manifestation. But I am intensely an individualist,

[23] James's review of Gurney's *Tertium Quid,* in *Nation,* XLVI (1888). The *Varieties* ends with a reference to this writer.

[24] *V.R.E.,* 526.

and believe that as a practical problem for the individual, the religion he stands by must be the one which he finds best for *him,* even though there were better individuals, and their religion better for them. Such Stoicism as you stand up for is one of the noblest all-round attitudes yet found out, and as against the insanities of theistic devotion, certainly has an immense part yet to play.

The summer wanes, and I wane too. Possibly 'tis only "need of change," but it is discouraging, in conditions that seem quite paradisiac, to find that the progress of so many weeks gives way to retrogression. I have no doubt that things will move upward again when the term recommences. Thank you again, dear Grace, a thousand times for your good letter, and all the good advice contained in it, and believe me, with loving regards from Alice, your ever affectionate

WM. JAMES

XXIX

JAMES'S PERSONAL FAITH

It is difficult to distinguish between James's own personal faith and those faiths of others which he not only tolerated and respected, but understood with so much sympathy that he felt their echo in his own breast. Furthermore, it was a part of his creed that there should be many gospels, and it is not easy to tell when he was illustrating this general principle and when he was expounding that particular gospel by which *he* was saved. In a sense his whole genius lay in multiplying differences and alternatives, and in justifying each idiosyncrasy in its own terms. Finally, he was a man of fluctuating moods. The sort of faith which he relished depended on the state of his spiritual palate, and this, in turn, reflected his general bodily and mental tone.

In James's youth he was wont to preach the gospel of Stoicism, especially to his friend Tom Ward, whom he exhorted, in the midst of "December darkness," to remember that the world is "really" as full of life and joy as ever.[1] This motive persisted. Having a tendency to hypochondria himself, James was touched and stirred to admiration by the uncomplaining fortitude of others. Being himself peculiarly subject to moods, he sought to dispel them and to purge his view of their distorting effect:

> Our consolation has to be found in falling back upon the general. It is mean to complain, in one's own case, of that which all flesh—even the most decorative members of the species—have to suffer; and after all, the world is as full of youth and maidenhood as it ever was, if we would but realize the fact when our own beards are grizzling.[2]

There is, then, a last reserve of manliness and objectivity by which a philosopher is reconciled to his world however little it may suit him. This was a persistent part of James's gospel, but the least characteristic part. The following confession, written in 1876, reveals both his dissatisfaction with a gospel of sheer fortitude, and the supplementary motives that actuated him with increasing strength as the years passed—acceptance of religion as a historic fact, the justification of belief by subjective need, the reservation of religious belief for the moments when this need is most extreme:

[1] *L.W.J.*, I, 128.
[2] To S. H. Hodgson, June 25, 1902.

The hardness of my Stoicism oppresses me sometimes. My attitude towards religion is one of deference rather than adoption. I see its place; I feel that there are times when everything else was to fail and that, or nothing, remain; and yet I behave as if I must leave it untouched until such times come, and I am drawn to it by sheer stress of weather. I am sure I am partly right, and that religion is not an every day comfort and convenience. And yet I know I am partly wrong.

The most characteristic element in James's gospel is his insistence that where human subjectivity is sufficiently deep and universal it may properly impose its demands on the environment. What was the subjective demand which James felt most profoundly and deemed most valid? It was, as we have seen, the demand of the moral will for a world in which the cause of righteousness, being freed from complicity with evil, is dependent for its realization on the daring and zeal of its devotees. But there was another motive which James understood, both vicariously through sympathy, and directly through his own suffering. This was the longing for safety and security. This longing never ceased to move James even though it was clearly subordinated to his keener relish for novelty and danger. Thus, although in 1885, in "The Dilemma of Determinism," he declared for a war of extermination against evil, he hesitated to close every door to peace. In the same year in *The Literary Remains of Henry James,* he expounded pluralism and healthy-mindedness in his own behalf, and the monism of the sick soul in behalf of his father. But then he went on to say:

> We are all *potentially* such sick men. The sanest and best of us are of one clay with lunatics and prison-inmates. And whenever we feel this, such a sense of the vanity of our voluntary career comes over us, that all our morality appears but as a plaster hiding a sore it can never cure, and all our well-doing as the hollowest substitute for that well-*being* that our lives ought to be grounded in, but, alas! are not.

"Pluralism is a view to which we all practically incline when in the full and successful exercise of our moral energy"; and this was James's gospel when he was at his best.[3] But a man is not always at his best, and the failure of pluralism *in extremis* is an argument against it. In 1907, comparing his moralistic pluralism with the monistic philosophy of the Absolute, he said:

> Both beliefs confirm our strenuous moods. . . . [Monism] suits sick souls and strenuous ones equally well. One cannot say thus of pluralism. Its world is always vulnerable, for some part may go astray; and . . . its partisans must always feel to some degree insecure. . . . The needs of sick souls are surely the most urgent; and believers in the absolute should rather hold it to be great merit in their philosophy that it can meet them so well. The pragmatism or pluralism

[3] *L.R.H.J.*, 118, 116.

which I defend has to fall back on a certain ultimate hardihood, a certain willingness to live without assurances or guarantees.[4]

Since man is not always hardy, the gospel of pluralism does not always meet
his needs. But James was, on the whole and in the long run, spiritually hardy,
hence *his* gospel was pluralism. Furthermore, since he uses the term "healthy"
for pluralism and "sick" for monism, it is impossible to avoid the inference
that a proper spiritual hygiene would bring man to that better state in which
pluralism is palatable—that the strong man eager for battle and enjoying the
risk is the more ideal type.

James's essential religion, then, is of the moralistic-pluralistic type. The value
of God is as "a more powerful ally of my own ideals." It is this felt *need* of
God and of religion as a reënforcement of the moral will that is the chief cause
of his personal belief. James was not a man to shun the rigors of the intellect.
He kept his intellectual muscles fit. "After taking a bath in religion," he once
said to his students, "come out and take another bout with philosophy."[5] But
as to religious truth itself, he attached comparatively little importance to philosophical arguments, even his own. The *convincing* evidence, he thought, was
practical and immediate.

In 1904, on April 17, James wrote to the psychologist James H. Leuba:

> My personal position is simple. I have no living sense of commerce with a
> God. I envy those who have, for I know that the addition of such a sense would
> help me greatly. The Divine, for my active life, is limited to impersonal and ab-
> stract concepts which, as ideals, interest and determine me, but do so but faintly
> in comparison with what a feeling of God might effect, if I had one. This, to be
> sure, is largely a matter of intensity, but a shade of intensity may make one's
> whole centre of moral energy shift. Now, although I am so devoid of *Gottes-
> bewusstsein* in the directer and stronger sense, yet there is *something in me*
> which *makes response* when I hear utterances from that quarter made by others.
> I recognize the deeper voice. Something tells me:—"*thither lies truth*"—and I
> am sure it is not old theistic prejudices of infancy. Those in my case were Chris-
> tian, but I have grown so out of Christianity that entanglement therewith on
> the part of a mystical utterance has to be abstracted from and overcome, before I
> can listen. Call this, if you like, my mystical *germ*. It is a very common germ. It
> creates the rank and file of believers. As it withstands in my case, so it will
> withstand in most cases, all purely atheistic criticism.

Thus although James did not himself have an experience of the presence of
God, he felt justified in accepting testimony to that effect from those whom
he "envied." He was impressed by "the extraordinary vivacity of man's psychological converse with something ideal that *feels as if* it were also actual."[6]

---

[4] *M.T.*, 226-9.
[5] *L.W.J.*, 11, 214; author's notes in Philos. 3, 1896-7.
[6] To James H. Leuba, April 17, 1904; *L.W.J.*, II, 211; to Charles A. Strong, April 9, 1907;
L.W.J., II, 269.

He was persuaded to accept this feeling of actuality because, though he did not experience it himself, he did have *analogous* experiences: not merely the normal experiences which formed the central feature of his philosophical and psychological empiricism, but also "exceptional" experiences of the mystical type. There was, for example, that night in the Adirondack forest, when he received the "boulder of impression" of which he left so vivid a description. He did not claim that he felt God, but only that he was thereafter enabled to understand how people might feel if they did feel God. "Doubtless," he said, "things in the Edinburgh lectures will be traceable to it." This is but one of many instances of that "mystical germ" [7] which led James to credit the full-flowered mysticism of others; or of that acquaintance with the genus of mysticism which led him to accept its religious species.

Did James believe in the immortality of the soul? It is evident that here, as in the case of the belief in God, he first defended the *legitimacy* of the belief, not on his own private account, but for mankind generally. In his lecture on *Human Immortality* he argued that immortality was not incompatible with the brain-function theory of our present mundane consciousness.

He was there concerned to defend the theoretical possibility of immortality. But what of his own personal attitude? He tells us that the belief was never "keen." He was not one of those who find the thought of their own death intolerable. It is true that when he felt the rush of the creative impulse he disliked the thought of being interrupted: "But, lord! how I do want to read as well as write; and with so much left undone, I am getting really anxious lest I be cut off in the bud." [8] There was always, however, an underlying resignation. Writing of his illness in 1899, he said:

> What the outcome will be, Heaven only knows. It is rather discouraging, for I should like to get out these two volumes of Gifford Lectures before turning my back on this world's vanities. But "man appoints, God disappoints," to use a little Cambridge Negro's version of the French proverb, and I shan't fret over the event whatever it turns out to be. Of all the vanities, when you come to look penetratingly at them, lectures on the philosophy of religion by mortal men may take the first prize. [9]

It was thus a part of James's code that a man should meet death bravely, or even casually. In his youth, when the Stoical teachings made a strong appeal to him, he wrote the following entry in his diary upon learning of the death of his cousin, Minnie Temple:

[7] *Cf.* below, 364; *L.W.J.*, II, 269.
[8] *L.W.J.*, II, 214; W.J. to F. C. S. Schiller, April 8, 1903.
[9] W.J. to Theodore Flournoy, November 13, 1899.

By that big part of me that's in the tomb with you, may I realize and believe in the immediacy of death! May I feel that every torment suffered here passes and is as a breath of wind,—every pleasure too. Acts and examples stay. Time is long. One human life is an instant. Is our patience so short-winded, our curiosity so dead or our grit so loose, that that one instant snatched out of the endless age should not be cheerfully sat out. Minny, your death makes me feel the nothingness of all our egotistic fury. The inevitable release is sure; wherefore take our turn kindly whatever it contain. Ascend to some sort of partnership with fate, and since tragedy is at the heart of us, go to meet it, work it in to our ends, instead of dodging it all our days, and being run down by it at last. *Use your death* (or your life, it's all one meaning), "tut twam asi." [10]

Although he came to view the matter less solemnly, this motive never ceased to govern him. In 1900 he proposed that the attitude to death should be a blend of "gentlemanly levity," "high-minded Stoicism," and "religious enthusiasm." As regards the moral significance of immortality, he took the negative view from which Stumpf dissented. He did not see why we might not be willing to resign the care of our ideals "to other hands." [11]

But as James grew older he came to *believe* in immortality. In 1904 he had acquired a feeling of its "probability." On July 17th of this year he wrote to Stumpf:

I never felt the *rational* need of immortality . . . ; but as I grow older I confess that I feel the practical need of it much more than I ever did before; and that combines with reasons . . . to give me a growing faith in its reality.

What was the practical motive of this faith? In explaining why he was now, late in life, acquiring the belief for the first time, he said, "Because I am just getting fit to live." Five years later he wrote: "I had often said that the best argument I knew for an immortal life was the existence of a man who deserved one as well as Child did." [12] With his temperamental love of the living, his affectionate sympathies, and his glowing moral admirations, he had come more and more to feel that death was a wanton and unintelligible negation of goodness. This motive or mixture of motives appears in comments on the death of two of his friends. The first two were written in 1904, and the third in 1906:[13]

I came down to Sarah Whitman's funeral, and being here, have stayed till Commencement, but return today. I can't go without an overflow to you, Sarah Whitman's death was so abrupt and bewildering. Pathetic, inscrutable, lover of life, outreacher to the good, spreader of friendliness,—where is she now? And

[10] "Thou art that." Entry for March 22, 1870.
[11] Above, 169; *V.R.E.*, 524.
[12] *L.W.J.*, II, 214; *Proc. of the Amer. Soc. for Psychical Research*, III (1909), Pt. I, 580.
[13] To Frances R. Morse, June 30, 1904; to Pauline Goldmark, June 28, 1904; and to F. C. S. Schiller, January 16, 1906.

what does it all mean? I never had the pathos or the mystery brought so sharply home, and one's thought of her now is all one tenderness. How much more real are people's lives than all our criticisms of them! It is a lesson to cultivate each other, all of us, while we yet have each other.

Everything in this beautiful world is good except old age and death if one supposes no "behind the veil" of any kind. Mrs. Whitman's funeral was wonderful for beauty. The crowd of friends at the grave were all swayed by the one pathetic emotion. And now she seems in retrospect like a little slender, lonely, trustful, blind creature, passionately curving and twisting her naïf little life to that black coffin as its terminus. It's queer!

Poor [Richard] Hodgson's death was the event, before I left. Absolutely sudden, dropt dead while playing violent handball. Had said to a friend, a week before, that he thought he could count reasonably on twenty-five more years of life. All his work unfinished. No one can ever learn those records as he knew them—he would have written certainly two or three solid books. Too bad, too bad! And the manliest, unworldliest, kindliest of human beings. May he still be *energizing* somewhere—it's not a case for *requiescat.*"

Very early in his life James expressed his dissatisfaction with funerals, and his resolution to have "nothing more to do with them" until they improved. He did not find the institutional forms of Christian worship either natural or agreeable. He could not pray because he felt "foolish and artificial." [14] Writing to F. C. S. Schiller from Edinburgh on May 17, 1902, he said: "Just been to Church!—automatisms throughout! Let us beware of the day when pragmatism becomes automatism in *our* mouths." He attended daily prayers in the Harvard Chapel, but he was no doubt attracted by the simplicity of the worship and the paucity of the congregation. And as a neglected and somewhat forlorn cause, Chapel may have appealed to his chivalry! He endeavored to acquaint his children with the scriptural teachings, as has been recorded by his sister. Writing in her Journal on October 10, 1890, she said:—

William has, for several years past, read the Bible to his boys, and expounded (!) as he went. The other day Billy exclaimed: "But, Father, who is Jehovah, anyhow?" This must have been a blow, after three years of complacently supposed lucidity. Some years ago, when Harry was five or thereabouts, William undertook to explain to him the nature of God, and hearing that He was everywhere, asked whether He was the chair, or the table. "Oh, no! God isn't a thing; He is everywhere about us; He pervades." "Oh, then, He is a skunk." How could the word "pervade" suggest anything else to an American child?

When James was asked whether the Bible was authoritative, he said, "No. No. No. It is so human a book that I don't see how belief in its divine author-

[14] *Cf.* above, 70; *L.W.J.*, I, 212.

ship can survive the reading of it." He felt the antithesis between nature and the church:

> The spirit of the two systems is so utterly diverse that to an imagination nurtured on the one it is hardly conceivable that the other should yield sustenance. . . . I must personally confess that my own training in natural science has completely disqualified me for sympathetic treatment of the ecclesiastic universe. . . . It is impossible to believe that the same God who established nature should also feel a special pride at being more immediately represented by clergymen than by laymen, or find a sweet sound in church-phraseology and intonation, or a sweet savor in the distinction between deacons, archdeacons and bishops. He is not of that prim temper.[15]

James's religion took the form neither of dogma nor of institutional allegiance. He was essentially a man of faith, though not a man for any one church or creed against the rest. Unlike his father, he was not interested in the elaboration and specific formulation even of his own personal beliefs. He confined himself to the intellectual acceptance of what he regarded as the substance of all religions, and to highly generalized emotional attitudes. He insisted upon retaining not only the ideality but also the *actuality* of God—as a conscious power beyond, with which one may come into beneficent contact; he believed in the triumph, through this same power, of the cause of righteousness to which his moral will was pledged; and he entertained a hopeful half-belief in personal immortality. These specific doctrinal affirmations, together with his belief in believing, his sympathy with every personal belief which brought to an individual the consolation or the incentive that he needed, and the quality of tenderness and ardent good will which pervaded all of his relations with his fellow men, make up the substance of his personal religion.

The following letter, added to what has gone before, conveys the peculiar flavor of his attitude. It was addressed to Charles Eliot Norton when the latter was afflicted with the illness of which he died four days later:—

Cambridge, Oct. 17, 1908

Dear Charles,—

. . . I was . . . grieved at the account . . . of all your sufferings and frustration. What a wrong-way-foremost thing senescence seems to be, and how strange the inharmonious share our different organs take in it! Your brain appears to have no appreciable share, and one hardly knows whether to congratulate or to condole with you, for its functions being so little blunted. I am as convinced as I can be of anything that this experience of ours is only a part of the experience that is, and with which it has something to do; but *what* or *where* the other parts are, I cannot guess. It only enables one to say "behind

[15] *L.W.J.*, II, 214; and notes for lectures at Harvard Summer School of Theology, 1902, 1906.

the veil, behind the veil!" more hopefully, however interrogatively and vaguely, than would otherwise be the case.

I thank you, dear Charles . . . for the superb chrysanthemums, which show that however bedridden a man may be, he can still play a part in the graciousnesses of the world. "Toujours le soleil poudroie par quelque trou." . . . I'm going to Chocorua in a couple of hours. . . . I hope and trust that when I come back I shall be able to come and "hold your hand." Believe, dear Charles, in your present straits, in the deep and warm reverence and affection in which you are held—by no one more profoundly than by yours ever lovingly,

WM. JAMES

XXX

RADICAL EMPIRICISM

There is a common opinion that philosophers spend their declining years in reclaiming the beliefs which in the full vigor of their faculties they have doubted or rejected. Being arterially sclerotic and preoccupied with the salvation of their souls, they are supposed to lapse from criticism into edification and dogmatic piety. If there be any such rule, James is the exception. Although the stream of his interests was never confined to any narrow channel, the last decades can be clearly distinguished by their emphasis: in the eighties on general psychology, in the nineties on ethics and religion, and between 1900 and 1910 on systematic philosophy. Instead of devoting his last years to faith, practice, and sermonizing, he gave them to the technicalities of theoretical inquiry. He wrote to a friend in 1902: "I want now if possible to write something serious, systematic, and syllogistic; I've had enough of the squashy popular-lecture style." [1]

That his attempt was largely frustrated was due to a series of accidents of a sort to which he was peculiarly susceptible. He was perpetually being invited to lecture, and he usually, with much groaning and dread, accepted. The agencies primarily responsible for James's failure to produce his systematic metaphysics were the trustees of the Gifford and Hibbert Foundations, and of the Lowell Institute, to which should perhaps be added the authorities of Harvard and Stanford Universities. Lectures drained off the flow of ideas which might otherwise have gone into the production of a systematic work. It was his fame that brought him these invitations, and their acceptance brought him greater fame. To have declined them would have required an inhuman and un-Jamesian degree of asceticism. But it is tempting to speculate on the contents of that "Principles of Philosophy" which might have resulted from a decade of rigorous and consecutive philosophizing, similar to that psychologizing of the eighties which resulted in the *Principles of Psychology*.

None of the five books which James wrote in the first decade of the century *was* the systematic metaphysics which he projected and to which he made such frequent allusions. This work was to be technical—designed for his colleagues

---

[1] August 25; to Mrs. Glendower Evans.

or for advanced students, rather than for the layman. But when James wrote lectures he wrote them for hearers, and not for readers; and he was not a man to overestimate the capacity either of public audiences or of immature students. The result was that while he attained a vogue and influence almost unique among philosophical writers, he persisted in his "squashy popular-lecture style," and failed to produce that "something serious, systematic, and syllogistic" which he intended. To this judgment certain exceptions should be made. The articles which were published after his death under the title of *Essays in Radical Empiricism* were written for philosophical periodicals, to be read by scholars. The same is true of some of the replies to his critics, published in *The Meaning of Truth*. It should also be said that portions of *Some Problems of Philosophy*, such as those dealing with the topic of infinity, are probably as "serious" and "syllogistic" as anything that James was likely to write under any conditions. But the fact remains that no systematic treatise, in which his doctrines were assembled and set forth both rigorously and consecutively, was ever completed. Happily his unpublished remains throw some light on what it might have been.

James's philosophical ideas were, of course, maturing steadily during the nineties, and there were already grumblings from his intellectual conscience. To James M. Baldwin he wrote in 1894: "I am at present trying to dig some rational truth out of myself . . . but it comes hard and has to be blasted, and I fear will result in shapeless débris." [2] In December of this year he delivered before the American Psychological Association his presidential address on "The Knowing of Things Together," in which he specifically anticipated some of the central ideas of his radical empiricism. He still professed idealism of the Berkeleyan type, but it was clear that his thought was already disloyal to that creed. In the *Psychology* he had allowed himself the conveniences of dualism. But the whole trend of his philosophical thought both before and after the publication of the *Psychology* had been *against* that provisional makeshift. He now saw with increasing clearness that he could not hold one view as a psychologist and another as a philosopher; and as his rejection of dualism became a more and more dominant motive in his thought, he saw that he would have to correct his psychology.

In the year 1895-1896 James devoted the second half of his Psychological Seminary to the "Discussion of Theoretic Problems, as Consciousness, Knowledge, the Self, the Relation of Mind and Body etc." His notes indicate that he was resolved to adopt the hypothesis of "radical empiricism" and to carry it through. The "phenomenon" was also called the "datum" or "the pure experience." The central idea was to substitute "fields" of pure experience—homo-

[2] August 25, 1894.

geneous and in some sense continuous, but standing in peculiar functional relations—both for the dualistic antithesis of mind and matter, and for the monistic reductions of mind to matter or matter to mind.

In the Preface of *The Will to Believe,* written in December 1896, James says (somewhat apologetically) that his radical empiricism "admits of being argued in as technical a shape as any one can desire," and that possibly he "may be spared to do later a share of that work." [3] It is evident that he was already doing it. In 1897-1898 this work was resumed in his seminary under the heading of "Philosophical Problems of Psychology." In the main he was preoccupied with "the pure experience hypothesis"—in a determined effort to resolve certain *substantive* traditional thought into *relational* or *functional* differences.

On August 26, 1898, James gave his address on "Philosophical Conceptions and Practical Results" at the University of California. This was the lecture in which he launched the philosophical movement to which he gave the name of "practicalism" or "pragmatism." The movement did not gather headway at once. In fact the lecture did not excite much comment until after 1904, when it was reprinted with slight changes, under the title of "The Pragmatic Method." [4] Even then, as this revised title indicates, the address revealed only that part of "pragmatism" which touches the *method* of philosophy. It did not embrace the pragmatic doctrine of truth, which later became the great polemical issue. "Pragmatism" occupied the centre of the philosophical stage in England and America only after the appearance in 1907 of James's book bearing that title. But this must not be allowed to obscure the fact that the pragmatic motive was one of the original roots of James's thought, asserting itself strongly from 1898, and playing an important part in the formation of his "system of metaphysics" after 1902.

In 1898-1899 James gave a course on metaphysics, in which he announced that he would discuss "The Fundamental Problems of Theoretical Philosophy; The Unity or Plurality of the World-Ground, and Its Knowability or Unknowability; Realism and Idealism; Freedom, Teleology and Theism." From the scanty notes which survive it does not appear that this course marked any significant forward movement in James's thought. His central theme was the defense of "a restless, moralistic world," against monism and the timeless Absolute. The years 1899-1902 were years of broken health during which his working hours were, as we know, devoted to the composition, delivery, and publication of the Gifford Lectures on religion. In these lectures he "suggested rather than stated" his philosophical conclusions, and expressed the hope of developing them further "at some later day." "All facts and no philosophy,"

[3] *W.B.,* ix-x.
[4] *Jour. of Philos.,* I (1904).

he wrote to his friend F. C. S. Schiller of Oxford.[5] The present volume was to be "followed by another . . . in which not only Professor Royce's arguments, but others for monistic absolutism shall be considered with all the technical fulness which their great importance calls for."

In the autumn of 1902 circumstances seemed to favor this undertaking. There was loss of time from illness, fatigue, and the usual interruptions (including the rereading of Emerson for the purpose of a "fifteen-minute address!").[6] But it is evident that he believed his metaphysics to be ripe for delivery. Ten years before, he had written in reply to Howison, who had alluded expectantly to a "book on metaphysics": "I have never attained to the dream of the possibility of such a thing, much less to the execution, and I now foresee that I never shall. . . . My intellectual higgledy-piggledyism can never lead to a system of metaphysics." [7] Now he wrote to Henri Bergson: "I am going, if I live, to write a general system of metaphysics." [8] This change of attitude reflects his steady development during the nineties, both in the comprehensiveness of his view and in the firmness of his grasp. Two fertile principles now offered a way of rounding up his diverse doctrines, at the same time that they suited the genius of his mind and strengthened his self-confidence. These were pragmatism, and radical empiricism, or the doctrine of pure experience. James felt, in other words, that he had something to say to philosophers, something to contribute to the stream of philosophic enlightenment.

Meanwhile, during this same college year, 1902-1903, James set his fundamental thought in order for a course on "The Philosophy of Nature" (Philosophy 3). The syllabus which he prepared for this course, although it consists in large part only of headings, is perhaps the most *comprehensive* statement of his philosophy that James ever made. It corresponds closely to the description of his system which James gave a year later to Renouvier's friend, François Pillon:

> My philosophy is what I call radical empiricism, a pluralism, a "tychism," [9] which represents order as being gradually won and always in the making. It is theistic, but not *essentially* so. It rejects all doctrines of the Absolute. It is finitist; but it does not attribute to the question of the infinite the great methodological importance which you and Renouvier attribute to it. I fear that you may find my system too *bottomless* and romantic. I am sure that, be it in the end judged true or false, it is essential to the evolution of clearness in philosophic thought that someone should defend a pluralistic empiricism radically.

[5] *Cf.* V.R.E., 454 (note); to Schiller on April 20, 1902; *L.W.J.*, II, 165.
[6] W.J. to Th. Flournoy, April 30, 1903, *L.W.J.*, II, 187.
[7] October 28, 1893; Howison's letter is missing.
[8] December 14, 1902; *L.W.J.*, II, 178. For Bergson, *cf.* below, Ch. XXXVI.
[9] A term borrowed from Charles Peirce to signify there is an element of pure chance in nature. *Cf.* below, 282. This letter, quoted from *L.W.J.*, II, 203-4, was written on January 20, 1904.

Such a view of the world, he believed, is not only the most economical description of the discoverable facts, but commands itself as the best postulate for action. It eliminates the problem of evil, and "goes with empiricism, personalism, democracy and freedom."[10]

James circulated the "Syllabus of Philosophy 3" among his philosophical colleagues. To Schiller, who received a copy and wrote to congratulate him on the "progress of his system," James replied:

> I have just composed the first sentence of my forthcoming book—the only one yet written: "Philosophy is a queer thing—at once the most sublime and the most contemptible of human occupations." There is nothing like having made your start! I shouldn't be surprised if the rest were like rolling down hill. I am sure that a book of the systematic sort *can* be written—a philosophy of pure experience, which will immediately prove a centre of crystallization and a new rallying-point of opinion in philosophy. The times are fairly crying aloud for it. I have been extraordinarily pleased at the easy way in which my students this year assimilated the attitude, and reproduced the living pulse of it in their examination and other written work. It is the first time I ever tried to set it forth *ex cathedra*. My success makes me feel very sanguine.[11]

Although "the first sentence of the forthcoming book" had been written in April, this seems not to have been counted, to judge by the following report to Howison, written July 4, 1903, on the eve of James's departure for Chocorua:

> I have been getting one obstruction after another out of the way, and on my return to the country tomorrow shall start my new "System der Philosophie." It will be a genooine empiricist pluralism and represent the world in such gothic shape that people will wonder how any philosophy of classic form could ever have been believed in. You, dear H., are a classicist, in spite of your pluralism.

There cannot have been much time for consecutive writing during this summer, since in August James was on his way to Davidson's "school" at Glenmore in the Adirondacks, where, towards the end of the month, he delivered five lectures on "Radical Empiricism As a Philosophy." His mind was "working on the infernal old problem of mind and brain, and how to construct the world out of pure experiences."[12] He began the college year with high hopes of rapid composition, as his teaching schedule was light. But in the spring of 1904 he was complaining to his friends of the frustration of his plans. To Lutoslawski he wrote:

[10] "Syllabus of Philosophy 3."
[11] Schiller to W.J., February 4, 1903; W.J. to Schiller, April 8, 1903.
[12] W.J. to Dickinson S. Miller, August 18, 1903; *L.W.J.*, II, 198. The lectures were not written out and his notes have disappeared.

Two years ago, the *Varieties* being published, I decided that everything was cleared and that my duty was immediately to begin writing my metaphysical system. Up to last October, when the academic year began, I had written some 200 pages of *notes, i.e.* disconnected *brouillons*. I hoped this year to write 400 or 500 pages of straight composition, and could have done so without the interruptions. As a matter of fact, with the best will in the world, I have written exactly 32 pages! [13]

The personal and external difficulties were not the only hindrances to the completion of James's metaphysical task. There were the inherent difficulties of the problems themselves. Instead of advancing to the summary conquest of the domain of metaphysics, the author divided his forces, and laid siege to fortresses and walled towns which had to be reduced before he could pass them by. The record of these local engagements, including the "200 pages of disconnected *brouillons*" above referred to, is to be found in a series of notebooks, containing miscellaneous jottings together with memoranda for the Metaphysical Seminary on "A Pluralistic Description of the World," given in 1903-1904; and in a set of manila envelopes, bearing labels such as "Continuity," "Common Object of Two Minds," "Necessity," "World of Pure Experience." The manila envelopes contained a manuscript on "A World of Pure Experience," and headed "Chapter I." The book of which this was to form the first chapter was to be called "Radical Empiricism"—signifying the "refusal to go beyond concrete experience," and the "insistence that conjunctive and disjunctive relations are, when experienced, equally real."

This winter of 1903-1904, during which James felt himself to be perpetually foiled, was a period of gestation which soon bore fruit—though not of the sort for which he had hoped. His spearhead had not been stopped, but it had been splintered. Between July 1904 and February 1905, he prepared and delivered a new set of lectures and wrote "eight new philosophical articles." [14] These eight articles were published after James's death under the title (already chosen by James) of *Essays in Radical Empiricism*. Upon their completion James wrote to a European friend: "I am interested in a metaphysical system ('Radical Empiricism') which has been forming itself within me, more interested, in fact, than I have ever been in anything else." [15]

It is clear from this statement that radical empiricism was so dear to his heart and so central to his thought that James did not hesitate to give its name to his entire system; also, that it forced him into contact with those technical aspects of philosophy from which he felt a periodic revulsion of feeling.

[13] *L.W.J.,* II, 171-2.
[14] W.J. to Th. Flournoy, February 8, 1905.
[15] To G. C. Ferrari, February 22, 1905.

He could never be as clear, in this context, as *he* liked to be. But the notion of pure experience was his deepest insight, his most constructive idea, and his favorite solvent of the traditional philosophical difficulties. Pragmatism provided his method or technique, and pluralism the architecture of the finished product; but radical empiricism gave him his building material.

The *purity* of "pure experience" means its original or pristine character—its priority to distinctions; and in particular to the distinction between subject and object. It was difficult for James's readers to realize that he had abandoned idealism, and construed experience as a larger area *within* which the boundaries of consciousness and self can be defined. For this misunderstanding he himself was largely to blame. He was a recent convert from idealism, and lapsed readily into its habits of speech. Nor did he ever become perfectly clear in his own mind on the crucial issue between idealism and realism—the status, namely, of those parts of nature that lie beyond the mental reach of man. They consisted of further experiences, no doubt—but *whose?* It would have been more consistent if James had rejected this as a false question. For if pure experience is prior to consciousness and self, then the personal pronoun is not applicable to it. But he hesitated between imputing these further reaches of experience to lower forms of mind (after the manner of panpsychism), and treating them as the "possible" experiences of man. It is not surprising that he was obliged constantly to reiterate his adherence to realism.

The positivists of his day—Richard Avenarius and Henri Poincaré, appealed to James through their identifying the content of the physical and mental realms. Positivism is either sceptical of all metaphysics, or is under suspicion of begging the metaphysical question in favor of naturalism. To James, proponent of a spiritualistic metaphysics, either alternative would be objectionable. "I can't make out," he said, "what becomes of the universe." [16] Thus while James had much in common with contemporary positivism—namely, the appeal to experience and the recognition of a standard of utility or convenience in the framing of hypotheses—he was profoundly unsympathetic to its negations

The first of the *Essays in Radical Empiricism* bore the arresting title, "Does Consciousness Exist?" and set forth the fundamental thesis of "pure" or "neutral" experience. The essays that followed dealt with the applications of this thesis: the relation of cognition to its object; the role of concepts and percepts; the general problem of relations; the sense in which two minds can be said to have the same object; the place of feeling in experience; the relation of mind and body; the question of causal activity and efficacy; the nature of truth. There is a new tone of intellectual self-confidence in these essays. He had achieved a sufficient nucleus of doctrine and a sufficient degree of clearness to warrant his promulgating a system of his own.

[16] W.J. to S. H. Hodgson, June 14, 1900.

Over a period of two and a half years, beginning in the autumn of 1905, James kept a sort of intellectual journal of his thinking. On the flyleaf of a note-book devoted to this purpose, he wrote: "The writhing serpent of philosophy, to use a phrase of Blood's, is one gigantic string of mares' nests." Underlying this prolonged and doubly figurative self-torture there lay a conflict of doctrine so fundamental as to require a reconsideration of almost all of James's philo-sophical ideas. In the *Psychology* he had done everything to accentuate the uniqueness and indivisibility of the individual stream of consciousness. James could then take this view without prejudice to the existence of a common and permanent world because of his distinction between thoughts and their *objects,* the latter possessing the commonness and permanence which the former lacked. But now he had definitely renounced this dualism, and in place of thoughts *and* things there were only "experiences." How to conceive experience so that it could retain both sets of properties, composing both the immediate and the transient life of the subject *and* the stable world of common objects—that was James's problem.

At the same time that James was endeavoring to solve this problem he was engaged in deciding whether or not to accept the "panpsychism" pressed upon him by his friend Charles A. Strong. He had always been attracted to panpsy-chism, and had for brief periods succumbed to its charms. But in the end he re-jected it. Panpsychism was a variety of substantialism—it gave things a core—whereas James had been reared on the empiricist doctrine that a thing is the sum of its appearances. In Strong's panpsychism the real physical object could be directly presented only to itself, or was what it felt itself to be, while in James's radical empiricism the physical object was directly presented to human perceptions, or was what it was perceived to be. This was a far-reaching differ-ence. Nevertheless James owed much to Strong, especially in the development of pragmatism. It was largely owing to Strong's insistent realism that James refused to be drawn by his left-wing associates into the pitfalls of subjectivism, and repeatedly affirmed that human knowledge and practice must accommo-date themselves to an external environment not of their own making.

XXXI

FRIENDLY DISPUTES WITH CHARLES PEIRCE

Charles Peirce, lifelong intellectual friend and irritant, continued to play an important role in James's intellectual life. *The Will to Believe* was dedicated "To my old friend, Charles Sanders Peirce, to whose philosophic comradeship in old times and to whose writings in more recent years I owe more incitement and help than I can express or repay."

In the lecture "Philosophical Conceptions and Practical Results," delivered in 1898, James writes that he heard Peirce enunciate "the principle of practicalism, —or pragmatism, as he called it," in Cambridge in the early seventies. The reference is apparently to "The Metaphysical Club" of which James, Wright, and Peirce were members, and of which Peirce himself said later: "It was there that the name and doctrine of pragmatism saw the light."[1] In the lecture of 1898, James credits Peirce with giving his thought "the most likely direction in which to start up the trail of truth," and defines this "direction" as the idea that

> the effective meaning of any philosophic proposition can always be brought down to some particular consequence, in our future practical experience, whether active or passive; the point lying rather in the fact that the experience must be particular, than in the fact that it must be active.[2]

In this address and in an allusion of 1902 James identifies pragmatism with "the great English way of investigating a conception," namely, to look for its "cash-value in terms of particular experience"; and credits Peirce with singling out and naming the principle by which English and Scotch philosophers "were instinctively guided."[3] In 1904 he credits Peirce with the word "pragmatism," and says that he (James) uses it to indicate "a method of carrying on abstract discussion," according to which "the serious meaning of a concept lies . . . in the concrete difference to someone which its being true will make."[4]

---

[1] Letter to Mrs. Ladd-Franklin, written in 1904-5, and published in the *Jour. of Philos., Psych. and Sc. Methods*, XIII (1916), 718-20. Peirce here dates the club "in the sixties."

[2] *C.E.R.*, 412.

[3] Peirce states, in his contribution to the article on "Pragmatist and Pragmatism" in the *Dictionary of Philos. and Psychol.*, 1902, that he derived this view from Kant. But it would be equally correct to attribute his view to Duns Scotus, or to the influence of scientific technique. Though the origin of pragmatism be obscure, it is clear that the idea that pragmatism originated with Peirce was originated by James.

[4] *C.E.R.*, 448; *M.T.*, 51.

It appears from these passages that Peirce made James acutely conscious of an idea which he had already imbibed, and continued to imbibe, from many sources; and that this idea was to the effect that the meaning of a concept lay in its putting a particular face on a situation and thereby provoking a particular action. James assumes that when perceived facts are altered, something is done about it, and that the meaning of a concept consists in perceptual (and therefore practical) expectations. If these expectations are the same, two concepts mean the same; if there are none, a concept is meaningless.

But while it is clear that this is the idea which Peirce helped to lodge firmly and centrally in James's mind, it is by no means clear that this was Peirce's idea. Writing to Mrs. Ladd-Franklin in 1905, he said: "Although James calls himself a pragmatist, and no doubt he derived his ideas on the subject from me, yet there is a most essential difference between his pragmatism and mine." [5] In the same year, speaking of the current misuses of the term, he said:

> So then, the writer, finding his bantling "pragmatism" so promoted, feels that it is time to kiss his child good-by and relinquish it to its higher destiny; while to serve the precise purpose of expressing the original definition, he begs to announce the birth of the word "pragmaticism," which is ugly enough to be safe from kidnappers. [6]

Now it is a nice question whether it is possible to "derive" from a philosopher ideas which he has never had; or whether one may not reasonably doubt the paternity of a bantling which, as it grows older, becomes increasingly dissimilar to its father. Perhaps it would be correct, and just to all parties, to say that the modern movement known as pragmatism is largely the result of James's misunderstanding of Peirce.

According to his own definition, Peirce's pragmatism (or pragmaticism) differs from that of James in two respects. In the first place, the meaning of a concept is construed in terms of conduct, and not in terms of sensation; and, in the second place, it is construed in terms of generality and not in terms of particularity. With James, thought points to sensory acquaintance. Peirce, on the other hand, interprets thought not in terms of immediacies to which it leads, but in terms of operation and control. A second difference reflects Peirce's emphasis on generalization. "Practical bearings" mean bearings on the *purpose* of action —which turns out to be "concrete reasonableness," or becoming "governed by law," or "instinct with general ideas." [7]

In short, for Peirce a conception has meaning only in so far as it expresses and promotes the idea of a well-ordered life. It is a habit reflecting the stability and

[5] *Jour. of Philos.*, XIII (1916), 718.
[6] *Monist*, XV (1905), 165-6.
[7] *Dict. of Philos. and Psychol.*, loc. cit.; *Monist*, XV (1905), 481.

uniformity of things; and its formation is at once an adaptation to this stability and uniformity, and a participation in its growth. With James, on the other hand, the significance of a conception lies in its leading into the field of particulars and adapting the agent to the exigencies that arise therein. It is not merely that Peirce is more explicit in linking pragmatism to an ethical ideal, but also that there is an important difference *in* that ideal. For Peirce the good lies in coherence, order, coalescence, unity; for James in the individuality, variety, and satisfaction of concrete interests.

Another group of Peirce's ideas influenced James's radical empiricism. These ideas had seen the light in a series of articles published in the *Monist* in the years 1891-1893, and which James predicted would "prove a gold-mine of ideas for thinkers of the coming generation." [8] "Tychism," "synechism," and "agapism" were Peirce's terms for his doctrines of chance, continuity, and love, respectively. Their relation to James's corresponding doctrines is parallel to the case of pragmatism: James found labels, as well as stimulation and confirmation, in Peirce, but the two sets of ideas were profoundly different. James, who liked to dwell on doctrinal similarities and philosophical coöperation, emphasized the likeness; while Peirce, who cared more for the precision of his views than for their general physiognomy, emphasized the unlikeness.

With James, tychism, or the doctrine of chance, first commended itself as providing for moral freedom. It was also agreeable to his fundamental empiricism—to his view that in the last analysis existence is inexplicable. But Peirce was not interested in either of these ideas. To him tychism was acceptable primarily because it reflected the logic of probability, or the statistical and approximative method of science. As time went on James's view of chance as the sheer impact of the inexplicable, a happening out of the blue, gave way to the idea of "novelty." The novel is in a sense inexplicable, but it need not be abrupt; it may *grow out* of what precedes it, and in that way *belong* to the context in which it arises. "Synechism" meant for James that reality, in being thus continuous and flowing, escapes the logic of identity. For Peirce, on the other hand, synechism was a way of reconciling chance with logic. The continuity of things means that there is always room for further analysis. For James there is an unexplained which is inexplicable, and which *needs* no explanation because experience conveys it adequately. For Peirce this same residuum of the unexplained means that the universe is forever explicable.

Peirce gave the name of "agapism" to his doctrine of "evolutionary love." But the disagreement in detail is very striking. For Peirce embraces hate within love as one of its necessary aspects, thus solving the problem of evil in that monistic fashion which James so emphatically repudiated; and Peirce lays stress on the

---

[8] *P.U.*, 398. In this passage James goes on to identify Peirce's ideas with Bergson's; *cf.* below, 291-2.

social or corporate personality in a manner quite incompatible with James's uncompromising individualism.

The correspondence between James and Peirce was one-sided, Peirce's letters being literally *voluminous*. It was not that James had less to say, but that he had other channels of distribution. To James, Peirce was one among dozens of correspondents, hundreds of friends, and thousands of readers; while to Peirce, James served both as confidant and as public. And when James wrote to Peirce he was usually so preoccupied with Peirce's personal problems that his mood was unsuited to philosophizing.

In 1893 Peirce drew up the prospectus of a treatise on "The Principles of Philosophy," in twelve volumes. In reply to a request for a letter expressive of interest in the project, James sent the following, which Peirce printed and circulated:

> I am heartily glad to learn that you are preparing to publish the results of your philosophizing in a complete and connected form. Pray consider me a subscriber to the whole series. There is no more original thinker than yourself in our generation. You have personally suggested more important things to me than perhaps anyone whom I have known; and I have never given you sufficient public credit for all that you have taught me. I am sure that this systematic work will increase my debt.

James was indefatigable in his efforts to improve Peirce's situation. He succeeded in finding him temporary lectureships, but an effort made in 1895 to persuade President Eliot to offer Peirce a regular appointment at Harvard was fruitless.

Cambridge, March 3, 1895

Dear President,—

I hate to hunt you down with disagreeable college problems, but how is a Supreme Being to hide from his creatures? The problem is this. The Philosophic Department has met to arrange the courses for next year, and my taking charge of psychology means . . . that the important course in "Cosmology" or "Philosophy of Nature" . . . must either be dropped for next year or given to some outsider. Now I want to propose to you no less a person than Charles S. Peirce, whose name I don't suppose will make you bound with eagerness at first, but you may think better of it after a short reflection. . . . The better graduates would flock to hear him—his name is one of mysterious greatness for them now —and he would leave a wave of influence, tradition, gossip, etc. that wouldn't die away for many years. *I* should learn a lot from his course. Everyone knows of Peirce's personal uncomfortableness; and if I were President I shouldn't hope for a harmonious wind-up to his connection with the University. But I should take that as part of the disagreeableness of the day's work, and shut my eyes and go ahead, knowing that from the highest intellectual point of view it would be the best thing that could happen for the graduates of the Philosophical Department. It would also advertise us as doing all we could, and making the best of every emergency; and it would be a recognition of C. S. P.'s strength, which I am sure is but justice to the poor fellow. I truly believe that the path of (possibly) least comfort is here the *true* path, so I have no hesitation in urging my opinion. . . . Always truly yours,

WM. JAMES

Eliot was courteous but unmoved: "All that you say of C. S. Peirce's remarkable capacities and acquisitions is true, and I heartily wish that it seemed to me possible for the University to make use of them." [9]

The intellectual relations between James and Peirce were most intimate in the decade of 1897-1907. Peirce was much touched by James's dedication of *The Will to Believe,* and as James began to put together his system of metaphysics he felt that Peirce was on his side, as a partisan not only of practicalism, but of "cosmic variableness." [10] As the years passed, however, the surface of agreement was rubbed away, exposing the hard ribs of difference, both in method and in detail. A subordinate, but persistent and illuminating theme is provided by the problem of Peirce's public lectures at Harvard—when, where, what, how?

Writing to James on May 30, 1897, Peirce said:

> I heard some months ago through Dr. [Paul] Carus that you were endeavoring to get me some opportunity to teach logic in Cambridge. . . . In the main— that is, in holding that belief is fundamentally a practical matter—you and I seem to be in full accord; and if we were together there, we would make an impression upon the philosophical world, and thus upon scientific men, upon teachers, and ultimately upon the current of the world's thought.

In December, Peirce sent James an outline of the proposed eight lectures. The headings were as follows: 1. Logical Graphs. 2. Lessons of the Logic of Relatives. 3. Induction and Hypothesis. 4. The Categories. 5. The Attraction of Ideas. 6. Objective Deduction. 7. Objective Induction and Hypothesis. 8. Creation. The following is James's acknowledgment:—

Cambridge, Dec. 22 [1897]

Dear Charles,—

. . . I am sorry you are sticking so to formal logic. I know our graduate school here, and so does Royce, and we both agree that there are only three men who could possibly follow your graphs and relatives. Are not such highly abstract and mathematically conceived things to be read rather than heard; and ought you not, at the cost of originality, remembering that a *lecture* must succeed *as such,* to give a very minimum of formal logic and get on to metaphysic, psychology and cosmogony almost immediately?

[9] Eliot to W.J., March 26, 1895.
[10] Expression used by W.J. in 1897, Philos. 3.

There is stuff enough in the first two volumes of the prospectus of your system,[11] to give a short course without infringing on any mathematical symbolism, I am sure—to say nothing of the other volumes. Now be a good boy and think a more popular plan out. I don't want the audience to dwindle to three or four, and I don't see how one can help that on the program you propose. . . . *You* can hardly conceive how little interest exists in the purely formal aspects of logic. Things on that subject ought to be *printed* for the scattered few. You are teeming with ideas, and the lectures need not by any means form a continuous whole. Separate topics of a vitally important character would do perfectly well. . . . What *I* should like is anti-nominalism, categories, attraction of ideas, hypothesis, tychism and synechism. . . . Write, now, that you accept all these conditions, and pray keep the lectures as unmathematical as in you lies. With the best of hopes, I am yours ever,

WM. JAMES

New York, Dec. 26, 1897

My dear William,—

I accept all your conditions. I have no doubt you gauge the capacity of your students rightly. It agrees with all I hear and the little I have seen of Cambridge, though the method of graphs has proved quite easy to New Yorkers, whose minds are stimulated by New York life,—people as remote from the mathematical world as anybody in New York. My philosophy, however, is not an "idea" with which I "brim over"; it is a serious research to which there is no royal road; and the part of it which is most closely connected with formal logic is by far the easiest and least intricate. People who cannot reason exactly (which alone *is* reasoning), simply cannot understand my philosophy,—neither the process, methods, nor results. The neglect of logic in Cambridge is plainly absolute. . . . Your Harvard students of philosophy find it too arduous a matter to reason exactly. Soon your engineers will find it better to leave great works unbuilt rather than go through the necessary calculations. And Harvard is only a little in advance of the rest of the country on this road, and this country a little in advance of Europe. The Japanese will come and kick us out, and in the fulness of time *he* will come to the questions which my philosophy answers, and with patience will find the Key, as I have done. . . .

I am perfectly indifferent about times and hours. I shall be clay in the hands of the potter. I wish I had to sing comic songs and dance, though I should do *it* badly. But I am not puritan enough to understand the pleasure of these chins on "topics of vitally important character." The audience had better go home and say their prayers, I am thinking.

C. S. P.

The eight lectures were eventually delivered (beginning February 12, 1898) at the residence of Mrs. Ole Bull on Brattle Street, Cambridge. The title announced for the whole course was, "Reasoning and the Logic of Things." It was of these lectures that Royce wrote to James on June 21, 1901:

---

[11] According to the prospectus, the title of Vol. I was "Review of the Leading Ideas of the Nineteenth Century," and of Vol. II, "Theory of Demonstrative Reasoning."

As for thoughts, of late I seem to myself to be on the track of a great number of interesting topics in logic. Those lectures of poor C. S. Peirce that you devised will always remain quite epoch-making for me. They started me on such new tracks.

The following was written by Peirce in acknowledgment of James's *Varieties of Religious Experience:*

Milford, June 12, 1902

My dear William,—

I owe you the expression of my gratitude for what you have done to induce the Carnegie Institution to aid me to produce my Logic. Try to think of something further to do; for things look blue. . . .

There is a point of psychology which has been interesting me. . . . The question is what passes in consciousness . . . in the course of forming a new belief. . . . I had got to that point when the expressman came in bringing me the copy of your new book. I have spent five minutes turning over the leaves. I can see what the general feature of your position is, sufficiently to say that I am heartily in accord with you. I say to people—imaginary interlocutors, for I have nobody to talk to—you think that the proposition that truth and justice are the greatest powers in this world is metaphorical. Well, I, for my part, hold it to be *true*. No doubt truth has to have defenders to uphold it. But truth creates its defenders and gives them strength. The mode in which the idea of truth influences the world is essentially the same as that in which my desire to have the fire poked causes me to get up and poke it. There is efficient causation, and there is final, or ideal, causation. If either of them is to be set down as a metaphor, it is rather the former. Pragmatism is correct doctrine only in so far as it is recognized that material action is the mere husk of ideas. The brute element exists, and must not be explained away. . . . But the end of thought is action only in so far as the end of action is another thought. . . . With your notions of spiritual influence, why don't you join the Church? Surely you won't allow metaphysical formulæ, dead as the dust of the catacombs, to deprive you of your RIGHT to the influences of the Church. I have been studying Royce's [*World and the Individual*]. The ideas are very beautiful. The logic is most execrable. I don't think it very good taste to stuff it so full of the name of God. The Absolute is, strictly speaking, only God in a Pickwickian sense, that is, in a sense that has no effect. Forgive the garrulity that comes of my eremitical life and God bless you!

C. S. PEIRCE

In the spring of 1903 (March 26-May 14) Peirce again lectured in Cambridge, this time under the auspices of the University, and on the subject of "Pragmatism"; and in the autumn of the same year (November 23-December 17) he gave a course of Lowell Lectures in Boston on "Logic and Other Philosophical Subjects." There were the usual preliminaries between him and James. Thus "William" to "Charles" on March 13:

At last, "under Providence," I have been able to give a slight boost to your affairs. The Corporation of Harvard University have voted to authorize six university lectures by you. . . . You can *name* them as you like. The fifty students whom I have had in Philosophy 3 (of which I sent the syllabus) are well primed with "pragmatism" and "tychism," and would be glad to hear of them from you direct. For "synechism" you have virgin soil.

To which Peirce replied on March 16:

I just received your letter this afternoon. Nothing could be so gratifying to me. . . . I . . . think that the six lectures had better be confined to the single subject of pragmatism, which, as I understand it, is one of the propositions of logic. Its foundation, definition and limitation, and applications to philosophy, to the sciences, and to the conduct of life will make quite enough for six lectures. . . . My dear William, I do not yet thank you. . . . You are of all my friends the one who illustrates *pragmatism* in its most needful forms. You are a jewel of pragmatism.

None of these lectures were published during Peirce's lifetime, but they were written out and preserved. The manuscript of two of them was left in James's possession.[12]

Chocorua, June 5, 1903

Dear Charles,—

I return your two lectures under a separate envelope to Milford, but send this to Cambridge, thinking you may possibly still be there. They are wonderful things—I have read the second one twice—but so original, and your categories are so unusual to other minds, that, although I recognize the region of thought and the profundity and reality of the level on which you move, I do not yet assimilate the various theses in the sense of being able to make a use of them for my own purposes. . . . You spoke of publishing these lectures, but not, I hope, *tel quels*. . . . As things stand, it is only highly skilled technicians and professionals who will sniff the rare perfume of your thought, and *after you are dead,* trace things back to your genius. You ought to gain a bigger audience *when living;* and, if next year you can only score a popular success, it will do much to help your later prospects. I fear that if you make a new course of lectures altogether, they will prove too technical and wonder-arousing and not flagrantly illuminating enough. Whereas, by revising these, you will not only give yourself less trouble, but also do the best possible thing for your audience. You cannot start with too low an idea of their intelligence. Look at me, as one! . . .

WM. JAMES

The spectacle of two philosophers complaining that they do not understand one another is not uncommon, nor is it always edifying. The interest of the present case lies in the association of misunderstanding with so much agreement, sympathy, and good will. After 1903, James's letters (and he appears to

[12] The Cambridge lectures on "Pragmatism" appear in *Collected Papers,* Vol. V, with short extracts in other volumes.

have written only briefly and intermittently) are almost entirely missing. Peirce, on the other hand, kept up a running fire of comment on James's writings, attempting to clarify his own views to James and lamenting the latter's reckless inaccuracies.

The letters immediately following deal mainly with the articles on pure experience or radical empiricism, beginning with "Does Consciousness Exist?" In September 1904, Peirce wrote a letter in which, having complained of the obscurity of James's notion that "consciousness is often regarded as an 'entity,'" he advanced a counterview of his own. James replied that he didn't "understand a word,"[13] and the following is Peirce's rejoinder:—

                                                          Milford, Oct. 3, 1904
Dear William,—
    . . . It is very vexatious to be told at every turn that I am utterly incomprehensible, notwithstanding my careful study of language. When I say it is vexatious, I don't mean that I don't wish to be told so. On the contrary, I am aware that my modes of thought and of expression are peculiar and gauche, and that twenty years of a recluse life have made them more so, and am grateful to people who help me by correcting me. But when, as in the present case, I am able to show that the accusation is a mere auto-suggestion due to your having told yourself that everything that Peirce says is unintelligible, and really having commanded yourself not to understand, it gives me a certain glee to feel authorized to yield to my natural vexation. You will be gratified, with your truly kind nature, to have afforded me so much innocent pleasure. . . . Your mind and mine are as little adapted to understanding one another as two minds could be, and therefore I always feel that I have more to learn from you than from anybody. At the same time, it gives great weight in my mind to our numerous agreements of opinion. . . .
    What you call "pure experience" is not experience at all, and certainly ought to have a name. It is downright bad morals so to misuse words, for it prevents philosophy from becoming a science. One of the things I urge . . . is that it is an indispensable requisite of science that it should have a recognized technical vocabulary, composed of words so unattractive that loose thinkers are not tempted to use them; . . . and that it is vital for science that he who introduces a new conception should be held to have a *duty* imposed upon him to invent a sufficiently disagreeable series of words to express it. I wish you would reflect seriously upon the moral aspect of terminology. . . . Ever faithfully,
                                                          C. S. PEIRCE

On April 30, 1905, James read a communication in French before the International Congress of Psychology held in Rome. It contained a summary of the ideas expressed in James's articles on radical empiricism. The articles, together with the summary, were sent to Peirce.

[13] C.S.P. to W.J., September 28, 1904; W.J. to C.S.P., September 30, 1904.

Milford, July 23, 1905

My dear William,—

. . . To begin with I want to emphasize my particular gratitude for your papers. . . . I read the French paper[14] first. . . . I found it entirely clear as well as beautifully written. When you write English (it is better to say the disagreeable thing) I can seldom at all satisfy myself that I know what you are driving at. Your writing would, I can see, be immensely forcible if one knew what you meant; but one (No. 1) don't. Now, for example, when you talk about doubting whether "consciousness" exists, you drive me at once to consulting a lot of books . . . to see what you could mean; and they left me as much in the dark as ever. But now that you are tied down to the rules of French rhetoric, you are perfectly perspicuous; and I wish, and I am sure lots of others do, that you would consider yourself so tied down habitually. Because one sees that it only aids your force of style. Of course, you can smile at my undertaking to advise you about anything whatever. The fact that you can do so, if you like, emboldens me to say what I say.

I also agree to every word you say in this French article to the full, with one exception, that is that I am quite sure the doctrine is not at all so novel as you say. Of course it is all the better for not being novel. . . . I have myself preached immediate perception, as you know. . . .

I hope the word "pragmatism" may be accepted . . . as the term expressive of those things (perhaps we cannot be sure just what they are) in which the group of us are in agreement, as to the interpretation of thought. As for humanism, it appears to me to be an allied doctrine, in perfect harmony with pragmatism, but not relating exactly to the same question. . . . I prefer the word "anthropomorphism," as expressive of *the scientific opinion*. . . . To . . . anthropomorphism I subscribe in the main. . . . Pluralism, on the other hand, does not satisfy either my head or my heart. . . .

As for the "problem of evil," and the like, I see in them only blasphemous attempts to define the purposes of the Most High . . . There is . . . nothing more wholesome for us than to find problems that quite transcend our powers, and I must say, too, that it imparts a delicious sense of being cradled in the waters of the deep,—a feeling I always have at sea. It is, for example, entirely inscrutable to me why my . . . categories have been made so luminous to me without my being given the power to make them understood by those who alone are in a condition to see their meaning—*i.e.* my fellow-pragmatists . . . and the blackest depression under which I suffer . . . comes from that very thing. Yet when I lay the wail before my God, I see that as long as I can say that I have exhausted all my endeavours, it is a happy thing that my responsibility ends, and that the matter is in the hands of the Author of all thought. When I began this letter I was suffering agonies at the non-realization of the hope of that week in the summer school, as well as with some lesser but great woes. . . . But simply setting down and running over these few points concerning the true theism has brought a joy that already begins to reduce the pain. I perceive that I am not to hope for a class. How inscrutable! . . .

C. S. P.

---

[14] "La Notion de conscience"; *cf.* E.R.E.

The following reply was written from the Adirondacks, where James was lecturing at Davidson's school:

Hurricane, Aug. 1, 1905

Dear Charles,—

I wrote to you in a great hurry as I was leaving Cambridge, and now, having re-read your letter, feel like writing again. Your encouragement to me to become a French classic both gratifies and amuses. *I* will if *you* will,—we shall both be clearer, no doubt. . . . The queer thing about that effort of mine was that I wrote it twice as fast as I ever wrote anything in English. . . . When I write English I have a choice of possible ways of expressing myself, and forever seek to improve. In French the first sentence was my only possible shot, and had to stay; and I was so tickled at having been able to write it at all that it seemed perfect at once, so I rushed on to another of the same kind,—all of them stored-up reminiscences of sentences that I had read, automatically reproduced.

My starting point is, of course, the doctrine of immediate perception; but the farther elaboration I haven't met elsewhere, except recently in two Germans, where the non-dualistic view explaining "mental state" and "physical thing" by different relations to context is made much as I make it. . . . I've given up reading Wundt,—he gets up philosophy as Winston Churchill *et al* get up historical novels.

When you wrote of the "summer school" I thought you meant either Harvard or Chicago. It appears you meant this place. Have no regrets. I have given two lectures to about a dozen auditresses . . . and two men who can understand philosophy. It's lamentable; and the cash would doubtfully cover your journey. Shed no tears for that! I come here because I love the place, and bought long ago a building lot here that I like to come and gloat upon.

I'm awfully sorry, dear Charley, for your hard plight. . . . Believe me, ever faithfully yours,

WM. JAMES

When James's volume on *Pragmatism* appeared Peirce was in Cambridge lecturing before the Philosophy Club at Harvard.

Cambridge, June 13, 1907

My dearest William,—

. . . I have just this minute received your book, *Pragmatism*. I just turned to the index and looked out Peirce, C. Santiago[15] S. I found a statement of my own thoughts, which I can appreciate, having been laboring and crowding my way for months and months—crowding through throngs of technicalities, objections, and stupidities—to try to express. There you have put it on your page with the utmost lucidity and apparent facility. Nothing could be more satisfactory. . . .

C. S. PEIRCE

---

[15] A name adopted by Peirce, presumably in honor of James.

P.S. . . . Believe me, my dearest William, that I would not give you pain for the world, and the day is past when I wanted *anything* for my personal satisfaction. That is more true than you think; but never mind, think what you like. I just have one lingering wish, for your sake and that of the countless minds that, directly or indirectly, you influence. It is that you, if you are not too old, would try to learn to think with more exactitude. If you had a fortnight to spare I believe I could do something for you, and through you to the world; but perhaps I do not sufficiently take account of other psychical conditions than purely rational ones. . . . I have often, both in my lectures and in my printed papers, pointed out how far higher is the faculty of reasoning from rather inexact ideas than of reasoning from formal definitions; and though I am so bound up in my narrow methods as often to lament that you could not furnish me with the exact forms that I am skilled in dealing with, yet I see myself, with admiration and wonder, how you, nevertheless, come to the right conclusions in most cases, and still more wonderfully how you contrive to impart to audiences as near to the exact truth as they are capable of apprehending. That faculty makes one useful, while I am like a miser who picks up things that *might be* useful to the right person at the right time, but which, in fact, are utterly useless to anybody else, and almost so to himself. What is utility, if it is confined to a single accidental person? Truth is public.

The same theme was resumed two years later apropos of an Appendix C to the *Pluralistic Universe*, in which James likened Peirce to Bergson, as believing that real novelty occurs in the continuous train of natural events.

Milford, March 9, 1909

My dear William,—

The instant I got the proof sheets you sent me I sat down and studied them, and as soon as I had mastered Appendix C I sat down to write to you about it. But I write slowly on account of the need of weighing every word when I discuss points of logic, and when I had filled forty sheets and was going on to the forty-first, I concluded that the matter would not interest you. I hold to my "tychism" more than ever; but on that account to liken me to a person who talks about *devenir réel* strikes me much like a doctor who should pronounce that a patient had something like *locomotor ataxia* because he had a soft corn under his heel. . . .

I thought your *Will to Believe* was a very exaggerated utterance, such as injures a serious man very much, but to say what you now do is far more suicidal. I have lain awake several nights in succession in grief that you should be so careless of what you say. . . . The only thing I have ever striven to do in philosophy has been to analyze sundry concepts with exactitude; and to do this it is necessary to use terms with strict scientific precision. . . . But that being my only claim to consideration, and it being a deeper conviction with me that philosophy is either a science or is balderdash, and that a man who seeks to further science can hardly commit a greater sin than to use the terms of his science without anxious care to use them with strict accuracy, it is not very grateful to my feelings to be classed along with a Bergson who seems to be doing his prettiest to muddle all distinctions. . . . Very faithfully, lovingly, and gratefully,

C. S. PEIRCE

Cambridge, March 10, 1909

Dear Charles,—

Before whom have I cast that pearl of an Appendix? I imagined it to be in the purest spirit of your synechistic tychism; and I think still that my only mistake was in sending it to you without the whole text that introduced and justified it. Of course you are right in the logical world, where every term is changeless to eternity, but the real world is incongruent, as I always thought you held (it being indeterminate, except partly), and the logical terms only mark static *positions* in a flux which nowhere is static. But wait till you see the book, of which I enclose a circular! I hope to send it to you in four weeks, and repent now of having stirred you to such a troublesome premature reaction. Forty sheets! Lord help us! . . . Affectionately yours. . . .

WM. JAMES

Milford, March 14, 1909

My dear William,—

I must have been in a hazy condition of mind when I wrote to you, if I did not make it clear, as I intended to do, that you had skilfully stated my position so far as the universe of existence goes. But I wish you would consider—as a vitally important, and quite indispensable condition of making yourself clear—that you must have some invariable or exactly certain yardstick. . . . 'Twas that acute but shallow fellow, Chauncey Wright, whom I only availed myself of as a whetstone of wits, but whom you looked up to far too much, who probably entrapped you in his notion that in some part of the universe one and one perhaps do not make two. . . .

My dear William, there is *something* about your mode of expressing yourself that makes plain folk like me unable to comprehend what you mean; and I think that *this* is what it is. You want to make the universe of the possible (because it indubitably is a real universe) as inexact as I hold the existential universe to be. But that can't be, because the possible is our only *standard* of expression. . . . I could make the whole matter clear to you as the noonday sun, if it were not that you are *wedded* to the theory that you can't understand mathematics! If you would only allow that *perhaps* you are mistaken about that, I guarantee I would make a mathematician of you. But when a person lays it down, as Axiom I, that he can't understand mathematics, that is to say, can't understand the *evident*, that blocks the road, don't you see? . . .

C. S. P.

Cambridge, March 21, 1909

Dear Charles,—

I don't deserve as elaborate and instructive a letter as you have written, nor do I fully deserve all your censure, even though I was conceived and born in philosophic sin, for I expressly *do* believe with you that in the universe of possibles, of merely mental truth, as Locke calls it, relations *are* exact. Time that *equabiliter fluit* is a conceptual entity, against which your time felt as tedious and mine felt as flashing by, can be artificially plotted out and equated, to the great convenience of human practice; and all their exact relations form a splendid artificial scheme of tabulation, on which to catch whatever elements of the existential flux can be made to stick there. My tychism, like yours, relates only to the flux. But wait till you see my forthcoming book! . . .

WM. JAMES

XXXII

PRAGMATISM

In the autumn of 1906 James wrote to his brother:

> This is definitely my last year of lecturing, but I wish it were my first of non-lecturing. Simplification of the field of duties I find more and more to be the *summum bonum* for me; and I live in apprehension lest the Avenger should cut me off before I get my message out. Not that the message is particularly needed by the human race, which can live along perfectly well without any one philosopher; but objectively I hate to leave the volumes I have already published without their logical complement. It is an esthetic tragedy to have a bridge begun and stopped in the middle of an arch.[1]

During James's late years his desire to round out his system and his weakness for public lecturing were perpetually at war. In the spring and summer of 1905 he delivered a series of five lectures, successively at Wellesley, at Chicago, and at Glenmore. They were successful, especially at Chicago, where he attracted an audience of five hundred. "I felt them," he wrote to Eliot, "pulling on my line like one fish." [2] He lectured during this period as one having a message to deliver. He was evidently moved by a characteristic impulse to communicate his latest ideas to others without waiting to give them technical or systematic form; and he was at the same time eager to put his private thoughts to the social test.

These lectures set forth what James called "the individualistic philosophy." He began with praise of philosophy in general, as consisting in the exercise of "the critical function" by the individual, and defended it against the charge of being unprogressive. He repudiated the prevailing opposition between philosophy and science—"both are just man thinking, by every means in his power." The best philosophy will avoid "smugness," and endeavor always to keep in touch with "the character of vulgar reality." The lecturer then reviewed pragmatism—naming Locke, Berkeley, and Hume as "the first pragmatists," and citing Kant's conception of God as an illustration of the pragmatist method in contrast with that of mediæval theology. Pluralism he developed by applying the pragmatic method to the problem of "the one and the many." All views of

---

[1] September 10, 1906; *L.W.J.*, II, 259.
[2] July 12, 1905.

the universe as a whole are based on the analogy of one of its parts. Some have chosen "the lower necessities," others "the higher ideals": thus the world has been conceived as a thought, a sentence, a piece of music, a dream, a work of art, a grab bag. Radical empiricism, said James, proposes

> the social analogy: plurality of individuals, with relations partly external, partly intimate, like and unlike, different in origin, in aim, yet keeping house together, interfering, coalescing, compromising, finding new purposes to arise, getting gradually into more stable habits, winning order, weeding out.

This is the tychistic world, which is in agreement with the new "individualistic" ideas of science (uniformity being only statistical); and which provides for novelty, freedom, real efficacy of the will, and the uncompromising rejection of evil. God is not the whole—but only "the ideal part. He helps us and we can help him." In its moral implications this individualistic philosophy is melioristic, libertarian, tolerant, democratic, militant, humane.

In his course on metaphysics in 1905-1906 James restated and amplified the same philosophy. The "congenial" features of the pluralistic hypotheses be summarized as follows:

> It redeems us from abstraction, from carrying on our book-keeping in two accounts, like Sunday Christianity. It restores to philosophy the temper of science and of practical life, brings the ideal *into things*. It allows order to be increasing,—therefore is a philosophy of *progress*. It makes *us* factors of the order. It frankly interprets the universe after a *social* analogy. It admits different systems of causation relatively independent,—*chance,* therefore, in so far forth.

We are to "take evolution *au grand sérieux,*" providing for real change, real novelty, and real advance. "If evolution, God may be one of the results." Religion is essentially a reliance on "reserve" or "vital resource," "a life in us finding an answering life." Finally, there was a discussion of the nature of the humanistic doctrine of truth. *"Pragmatic method* asserts that what a concept *means* is its consequences. Humanism says that when these are satisfactory, the concept is *true."* [3]

During the first half of the academic year 1905-1906, James also gave a systematic outline of his philosophy in a form adapted to beginners. The course was repeated during the second half-year at Leland Stanford University, and also at Harvard in 1906-1907, as Philosophy D, James's last regular course of instruction. While at Stanford (on January 8, 1906), he wrote in his diary, "Feel lonely and scared"; but on January 10, "Funk is over! It went all right." It continued to go "all right," and led to a varied and exhausting life, full of

---

[3] These lectures were never published, but full notes have been preserved.

social engagements, and of miscellaneous lectures in San Francisco and Berkeley as well as at Stanford. His letters express his enthusiasm over Stanford University and the "freshness and eagerness" of his auditors.

> The human vacuum is curious . . . the historic silence rings in your ears. . . . But this generation is only the first coat of paint, the fallow clover-crop ploughed into the soil. . . . Such simplification! Such freedom from distraction, and such pure, severe and noble surroundings! [4]

The content of this last course was determined first of all by its introductory character. Nevertheless the course played an important part in James's philosophical development. It led to the writing of the unfinished volume, published after James's death but in accordance with his instructions, on *Some Problems of Philosophy*. It also forced James to think of his philosophy as a whole, and was more comprehensive than any one of his published works. It can be looked upon as an essay in systematization.

During the year 1905-1906, when James was so busily occupied with popular lectures, "The Book" still occupied his thoughts, and he prepared two sketches of it. But instead of executing them, he allowed himself to be again drawn into popular lecturing. During the summer of 1906, he gave a brief course before the Harvard Summer School of Theology; and then in the autumn he gave the Lowell Lectures on "Pragmatism," which he repeated at Columbia University, January 29 to February 8, 1907. In the interval he had begun the composition of the book on *Pragmatism,* and had given (January 22) his last college lecture. The Columbia lectures were delivered before an audience of over one thousand, and he spoke of those few days in New York—the lectures and his reception—as "certainly the high tide of my existence, so far as *energizing* and being 'recognized' were concerned." [5] Nevertheless both the lectures and the ensuing volume were dictated by personal and by strategic reasons rather than by the logic of his philosophical development. And the public attention which they received involved the author in so great a volume of acknowledgment, interpretation, and controversy that the technical treatise had again to be postponed. Such was the penalty of success!

To the title of his *Pragmatism* James appended the subtitle: "A New Name for Some Old Ways of Thinking." James meant, no doubt, that he had not himself invented these ways of thinking; not only could their roots be traced far into the past, but they represented a broad contemporary tendency which James shared with others. This tendency embraced: the newer logic, with its

[4] W.J. to Pauline Goldmark, February 13, 1906.
[5] W.J. to H.J.² and W.J., Jr., February 14, 1907; *L.W.J.*, II, 265.

emphasis on the instrumental as distinguished from the representative function of ideas; the doctrines of evolution and historical relativism, stressing change, plasticity, and adaptation in human knowledge; the vogue of probability and hypothesis in scientific method. James also meant that he had himself been familiar with these "ways of thinking" and had espoused them from the beginning of his own philosophical career. There are two of them which transcend the rest in importance, and may fairly be called the cardinal principles of pragmatism. The first, the pragmatic method, proposes to interpret concepts in terms of their consequences for experience or practice. The second is the pragmatic theory of truth: to the effect, namely, that truth is an attribute of ideas rather than of reality; and that it attaches to ideas in proportion as these prove useful for the purpose for which they are invoked. But when these two cardinal principles are stated, it is at once evident that they coincide broadly with the two doctrines which constitute James's "empiricism," and which had constituted it from the beginning of his philosophical maturity: his reliance, namely, on experience and on experiment.

In the early seventies James was already disposed to recognize that if a concept cannot be translated into terms of experience or practice, it is meaningless. His preoccupation with the British empiricists followed soon after, and the public announcement of the pragmatic doctrine in 1898, in the address on "Philosophical Conceptions and Practical Results," identified that doctrine with "the great English way of investigating a conception," exemplified by Locke, Berkeley, Hume, and their lesser followers. Although this address had something of the character of a *pronunciamento,* it is clear that James was not aware of having reached any new stage in his philosophical development. The topic which he selected resulted from his desire to select something "sufficiently popular and practical" from his existing arsenal of ideas.[6] It served as a review of his philosophical beginnings, and as an acknowledgment of indebtedness to Charles Peirce, who in "the early seventies" had enunciated explicitly the method which the English empiricists had followed "instinctively." [7]

With James himself the method soon ceased to be merely "instinctive." Upon his first thorough reading of Locke's *Essay,* perhaps as early as 1876, he wrote the term "practicalism" in the margin opposite the passage in which that author argues that it does not matter of what substance the self is made, provided its functions remain the same—the term "practicalism" which he later employed as a synonym for "pragmatism." Replying in 1878 to the positivistic contention that the question of materialism was insoluble or meaningless, he said:

[6] W.J. to G. H. Howison, July 24, 1898; *L.W.J.,* II, 79.
[7] *C.E.R.,* 410, 434.

Every question has sense and imposes itself unmistakably, when it produces a clear practical alternative, in such wise that according as one answers the question one way or the other, one is obliged to adopt one or the other of two lines of conduct.[8]

Pragmatism in the first or methodological sense, as a canon of meaning, thus dates from the time when James first began to have a philosophical mind of his own. It reappears more or less explicitly in all of his later writings.

The second or experimentalist principle was not less deeply rooted in James's philosophical past. As soon as he had any doctrine of his own concerning the human mind he insisted on its activity, initiative, and congenital bias. Man thinks because he is prompted to do so by the interests and the purposes which govern him. Here again James found the way prepared by the great empiricists. Reading Locke's *Essay,* he applauded that writer's view of "nominal essences" as "teleological" instruments. He was quick to note Locke's recognition of the practical motives in knowledge; and selected the following passage as a suitable "motto for practicalism":

He that will not eat till he has demonstration that it will nourish him, he that will not stir till he infallibly knows the business he goes about will succeed, will have little else to do but sit still and perish.[9]

At approximately the same time (soon after 1875) James set down the following note, indicating his disposition to regard truth as *pro*spective rather than *retro*spective:

The truth of a thing or idea is its meaning, or its destiny, that which grows out of it. This would be a doctrine reversing the opinion of the empiricists that the meaning of an idea is that which it has grown from. . . . Unless we find a way of conciliating the notions of truth and change, we must admit that there is no truth anywhere. But the conciliation is necessarily made by everyone who reads history and admits that an [earlier] set of ideas . . . were in the line of development of the ideas in the light of which we now reject [them]. . . . In so far as they tended to induce these they were true; just as these will induce others and themselves be shelved. Their truth lay in their function of continuing thought in a certain *direction*. Had they tended out of that direction they would have been false.

Taken as *prospective,* truth is to be interpreted in terms of the *purposes* or *ends* which govern thinking. This was the theme of the first systematic work which James planned to write, and of which "The Sentiment of Rationality," first published in 1879, is the most important fragment. How far it is *legitimate*

---

[8] *C.E.R.,* 76; translated by the author.
[9] Locke's *Essay,* 1853, 499; and inside front cover of W.J.'s copy.

that these ends should govern the acceptance of an idea, especially when the ends are practical and emotional rather than theoretic, is the central question of the essay on "The Will to Believe." Meanwhile in the *Psychology* James not only had elaborated his general teleological view of mind, but in the last chapter, on "Necessary Truths and the Effects of Experience," had developed *in extenso* his view that the mind is governed by innate predispositions which, like Darwinian variations, owe their survival to their function of adaptation.

Among the earlier statements of the pragmatic theory of truth, however, James attached unique importance to the essay "On the Function of Cognition," published in 1885. It is "the *fons et origo* of all *my* pragmatism," he wrote in 1907; he gave it the leading place in the volume on *The Meaning of Truth;* and cited Charles Peirce as an exponent of the same doctrine.[10] The historic significance of this essay is due to several facts. It marks the definitive and final identification of "truth" with the success of ideas. It applies this notion not to the grossly practical situation, but to the so-called *theoretical* situation, showing that this, in a more subtle sense, is also practical. It shows just how in such a situation the idea points to a suitable terminus or practical *dénouement;* how it leads to its object through intermediaries, all of which lie within the same field of experience; and how its success may be interpreted in terms of safe arrival at its destination. In short, this essay surpassed previous utterances on the subject in the degree to which it subsumed theoretical and practical processes under a common formula, and in the effectiveness with which the formula was applied to the concrete details of cognition.

Pragmatism appeared in May 1907. It is abundantly evident that James was drawing upon his own past; giving a name, an emphasis, and a new formulation to doctrines which he had held for over thirty years. It does not follow that he experienced no sense of innovation and leadership. Quite the contrary was true. He felt that he might now make these ideas *effective* by his mode of presenting them and in conjunction with the trend of the times. There is a note of exhilaration in his comments and predictions, written on January 2, 1907, in a letter to Theodore Flournoy:

> I want to make you all enthusiastic converts to "pragmatism" . . . on which I gave eight Lowell lectures to a fine audience in Boston this winter. . . . I didn't know, until I came to prepare them, how full of power to found a "school" and to become a "cause," the pragmatistic idea was. But now I am all aflame with it, as displacing all rationalistic systems—all systems, in fact, with rationalistic elements in them; and I mean to turn the lectures into a solid little cube of a book which I hope to send you by next October, and which will, I am confident, make the pragmatic method appear, to you also, as the philosophy of the future. Every sane and sound tendency in life can be brought in under it.

[10] W.J. to C. A. Strong, September 17, 1907; *M.T.,* 1, 136; *Mind,* X (1885), 43, note.

James attributed the success of *Pragmatism* in part to its historic timeliness—it was "like one of those secular changes that come upon public opinion overnight, as it were, borne upon tides 'too deep for sound or foam.' " [11] But at the same time he felt that his own style would ensure the book's receiving public attention. Thus he wrote to his brother:—

> I have just finished the proofs of a little book called "Pragmatism" which even you *may* enjoy reading. It is a very "sincere" and, from the point of view of ordinary philosophy-professorial manners, a very unconventional utterance, not particularly original at any one point, yet, in the midst of the literature of the way of thinking which it represents, with just that amount of squeak or shrillness in the voice that enables one book to *tell,* when others don't, to supersede its brethren, and be treated later as "representative." I shouldn't be surprised if ten years hence it should be rated as "epoch-making," for of the definitive triumph of that general way of thinking I can entertain no doubt whatever—I believe it to be something quite like the protestant reformation.[12]

Evidence of the success of *Pragmatism* is to be found not only in the number of its followers and the volume of their applause, but also in the passionate opposition which it evoked. As a critique of certain authoritative and traditional tendencies in philosophy, it clearly reached its mark. Others, who read the book without resentment, complained of its ambiguity. James and his allies were thus called upon both to defend and to restate their doctrine.

Among the many pragmatists, old and new, who allied themselves with James was his old friend Wendell Holmes. Of what was relativistic and sceptical in James's view, Holmes felt confident; but of James's confidence, metaphysical and religious, Holmes was sceptical. In both spring and fall he "fired off a reflection or two" to his "dear Bill":

> I have been in the habit of saying that all I mean by truth is what I can't help thinking. . . . But I have learned to surmise that my *can't helps* are not necessarily cosmic can't helps—that the universe may not be subject to my limitations; and philosophy generally seems to me to sin through arrogance. It is like the old knight-errants who proposed to knock your head off if you didn't admit that their girl was not only a nice girl but the most beautiful and best of all possible girls. I can't help preferring champagne to ditch water,—I doubt if the universe does. . . . The great act of faith is when a man decides that he is not God. But when I admit that you are not my dream, I seem to myself to have admitted the universe and the *ding an sich*,—unpredictable and only guessed at, as somewhat out of which I come rather than coming out of me. But if I did come out of it, or rather, if I am in it, I see no wonder that I can't swallow it. If it fixed my bounds, as it gives me my powers, I have nothing to say about its possibilities or characteristics except that it is a kind of thing . . . that has me

in its belly and so is bigger than I. It seems to me that the only promising activity is to make *my* universe coherent and livable, not to babble about *the* universe. . . . It is as absurd for me to be spearing my old commonplaces at you as it would be for an outsider to instruct me in the theory of legal responsibility, but you see, *mon vieux,* although it is years since we have had any real talk together, I am rather obstinate in my adherence to ancient sympathies and enjoy letting out a little slack to you. . . . I heartily agree with much, but I am more sceptical than you are. You would say that I am too hard or tough-minded,— I think none of the philosophers sufficiently humble.[13]

Of James's immediate disciples the closest and most enthusiastic was F. C. S. Schiller, of Corpus Christi College, Oxford. Schiller's *Riddles of the Sphinx,* published in 1891, was described by James as "A pluralistic theistic book, of great vigor and constructive originality . . . that of a young man, and crude and disproportioned, but very suggestive, and quite in the lines which I incline to tread." [14] In 1897 Schiller wrote a laudatory review of the *Will to Believe,* and congratulated its author on having "thrown his bomb shells into the stifling *aura* which surrounds many a hoary prejudice of the philosophic world.[15] This review encouraged James to believe that he already had a philosophy, and that (with the collaboration of others such as Schiller) he might found a school.

The following correspondence throws light on the origin of the name "humanism," which Schiller proposed and which James recognized, although he refused to accept it as the best name of the movement *as a whole.* Schiller admitted pragmatism as a species of humanism, while James admitted humanism as a species of pragmatism!

Oxford, April 24, 1903

Dear James,—

. . . I have been inspired this morning, *à propos de rien,* with THE *name* for the only true philosophy! You know I never cared for "pragmatism" . . . it is much too obscure and technical, and not a thing one can ever stampede mankind to. Besides the word has misleading associations and we want something bigger and more extensive (inclusive). It does not express the whole meaning of what we are saying, and I feel that I'm constantly stretching the term. But why should we not call it HUMANISM? "Humanism" as opposed to scholasticism; "humane" as opposed to barbarous (in style and temper); human, living and concrete as opposed to inhuman, fossil, and abstract; in short, not "anthropomorphism" (horrid word!) but "humanism." Consider, *e.g.,* how much better your remark about *"rehumanizing* the universe" sounds! [16] I propose, therefore, to call myself henceforth a humanist, and my volume of essays "Humanism:

---

[13] March 24, 1907 and (last two sentences) October 13, 1907.

[14] W.J. to S. M. Ilsley, September 23, 1897.

[15] *Mind, N.S.,* VI (1897), 554.

[16] James had spoken of "a re-anthropomorphized Universe," as the outcome of personal idealism (*C.E.R.,* 443).

Philosophical Essays by F. C. S. S.," or something of the sort, and shall devote the preface to expounding what I mean. Not that we need drop "pragmatism" on that account as a technical term in epistemology. Only pragmatism will be a species of a greater genus,—humanism in theory of knowledge. . . . As ever thine,

Canning Schiller

Oxford, June 9, 1903

Dear James,—

. . . I have lived in hopes of receiving from you an answer to what is just now the most important question in the philosophic universe, *viz.*—are you a humanist? I am—more than ever, having meanwhile worked out some of the implications of the term in the Preface to *Humanism*. They are beautiful, and I should like, if it doesn't worry you too much, to send you the said Preface in manuscript. Meanwhile I append a new Pythagorean "table of contraries" under the head of

1. *The Good and Finite* vs.	*The Evil and Infinite*
2. Humanism	Scholasticism
3. Pragmatism	Verbalism
4. Personal Idealism	Naturalism
5. Pluralism	Absolutism
6. Radical Empiricism	Apriorism
7. Voluntarism	Intellectualism
8. Anthropomorphism	Amorphism
9. Briticism	Germanism
10. Witticism	Barbarism

That is comprehensive enough, don't you think? . . . It appears to me . . . that the thick of the fight (once we get to close quarters) is going to be about the indetermination of truth and reality prior to experiment. The other side all hold to a rigid preëxistent system which is not made, but only found, and try to fasten upon us a belief in chaotic indetermination. I reply that a *plastic* universe cannot be either, and try to make them see how the nature of the question goes to determine the answer, and how our behaviour therefore helps to shape reality. . . . Ever thine,

Canning Schiller

To which James replied on July 5:

I owe you for three letters, but from my graphophobic personality this post-card must suffice. Don't *you* be discouraged, however, but keep up the correspondence. . . . "Humanism" doesn't make a very electrical connection with my nature, but in appellations the individual proposes and the herd adopts or drops. I rejoice *exceedingly* that your book is so far forward, and am glad you'll call it "Humanism"—we shall see if the name sticks. All *other* names are bad, most certainly—especially "pragmatism."

James's difference with Schiller turned on the latter's relatively subjectivistic and voluntaristic emphasis as opposed to his own realism. According to Schiller *all* knowledge is pragmatic and provisional, including the knowledge of so-called facts. The object is always what it is, *for* a subject, and *on the ground* of the satisfaction afforded by so conceiving it. James, on the other hand, stresses the original and ineradicable aspect of objective givenness, without which the pragmatic operation would have no application or meaning; and which is itself known, independently of that operation, in immediate experience. He spoke of Schiller's "butt-end-foremost statement of the humanist position." He said of Schiller that "he starts from the subjective pole of the chain, the individual with his beliefs, as the more concrete and immediately given phenomena"; whereas he, James, starts with two things, "the objective facts and the claims." [17] James also urged Schiller to "tone down a little the exuberance of his polemical wit." [18] In particular, he felt that Schiller's perpetual baiting of F. H. Bradley was bad strategy. To the former James wrote on May 18, 1907:

> It was so easy to let Bradley with his approximations and grumblings alone. So few people would find these . . . statements of his seductive enough to build them into their own thought. But you, for the pure pleasure of the operation, chase him up and down his windings, flog him into and out of his corners, stop him and cross-reference him and counter on him, as if required to do so by your office. . . . Leave him in his *dunklem Drange*—he is drifting in the right direction evidently, and when a certain amount of positive construction on our side has been added, he will say that that was what he had meant all along—and the world will be the better for containing so much difficult polemic reading the less.

The most distinguished critic of pragmatism was the Englishman F. H. Bradley, whose *Logic* James had greatly admired twenty years before. The correspondence between these champions of opposing schools testifies to their magnanimity. Bradley was a formidable and often supercilious controversialist, an acute dialectician, and an invalid somewhat withdrawn from human intercourse. Philosophically he was one of the foremost champions of absolutism, who greeted every fresh philosophical opinion with the claim that it was to be found in Hegel, and whose rejection of the categories of experience and common sense has led to his being parodied by Schiller as the author of "The Disappearance of Reality." [19] Although these qualities could scarcely have commended him, the strength of James's respect and attachment was unmistakable.

[17] *Pragm.*, 243; *M.T.*, xix, 169, 242.
[18] *C.E.R.*, 443.
[19] *Mind!* a parody of *Mind*, published in 1901, 51.

Indeed there was more than this—a personal sympathy which led him to say of Bradley (in a manner more gentle than ironical): "He is, really, an extra humble-minded man, I think, but even more humble-minded about his reader than about himself, which gives him that false air of arrogance." [20] Bradley, on his part, testified in 1895 that James held "an honored place among those from whom he has learnt and hopes to learn." Of Bradley's *magnum opus* James wrote in 1894:

> I have just read a book *Appearance and Reality* . . . published a year ago, which is destined to bring the whole of English philosophical discussion up to a higher plane, dialectically, than it has ever known before. I mistrust it, both premises and conclusions, but it is one of those vigorous and original things that have to be assimilated slowly. . . . It undoubtedly will be epoch-making in our literature.[21]

On the issue of pragmatism James and Bradley exchanged many letters. Bradley, like Royce, would have consented to be called a "pragmatist" if he were allowed to qualify it by the adjective "absolute." To James this meant two things, both of which he was willing to concede: an insistence on the peculiar claims of theoretical procedure, as distinguished from practice in general; and the recognition of an ideal truth, to which human truth was at best only an approximation. To James these qualifications were not a serious point of difference. Speaking for Schiller and himself he wrote to Bradley: "Nothing debars you from believing in our humanism, bag and baggage—you need only throw your Absolute round it." [22] But while James continued his efforts to convert Bradley, and Bradley continued respectfully attentive, between Bradley's incorrigible intellectualism and James's incorrigible empiricism there was no ultimate reconciliation.

[20] W.J. to Schiller, April 13, 1901; *L.W.J.*, II, 142.
[21] Bradley to W.J., August 23, 1905; W.J. to Th. Flournoy, August 1894.
[22] June 16, 1904; a fragment of this letter is all that remains of James's long and numerous letters to Bradley.

XXXIII

JAMES AND DEWEY

The leadership of the pragmatist movement was shared by James with his younger and surviving colleague, John Dewey. James refused to admit that the differences between them were more than the differences of emphasis or approach. To Dewey himself the differences were more fundamental and more explicit.[1]

James regarded pragmatism as a method to be freely used, and applied it to the standard doctrines of metaphysics, as though any of these might be considered available. It is true that the metaphysics which he adopted—the metaphysics of change, freedom, and manyness—does to some extent reflect the exigencies of a pragmatic theory of knowledge; but pragmatism is much less exigent with James than with Dewey. James's philosophical thinking, both his ethics and his metaphysics, abounds in ideas which are irrelevant, if not alien, to his pragmatism. He felt misgivings on this score, and was disposed to regard Dewey as more radical and more self-consistent.

These differences are no doubt related to the general philosophical temper of the two men, as well as to their early influences. James was more conciliatory and hospitable to ideas, Dewey more systematic. The interest of James was strongly metaphysical and religious, that of Dewey social and logical. To James the ultimate vision was intuitive, while to Dewey it is discursive. Or, while James *was* percipient, artistic, and religious, Dewey elaborates ideas *about* perception, art, and religion. With James the essence of life and experience could be grasped only in the living and in the experiencing, and this conviction sprang from the abundance and vividness of personal living and experience; whereas with Dewey the essence of things emerges only upon reflection, and this conviction springs from his characteristic and perpetual thoughtfulness.

The correspondence between James and Dewey extends over a period of eighteen years, beginning in 1886 with an exchange of friendly comments on one another's psychology and ethics. The group which formed around Dewey

---

[1] James's fullest statements of his philosophical relations to Dewey and Schiller are found in *M.T.*, xvi-xix, 42, 56, 169. For Dewey's views of the matter, *cf.* the articles by him in *Jour. of Philos.* II (1905) and V (1908); *cf.* also "The Development of American Pragmatism," Columbia *Studies in the History of Ideas*, II (1925).

at the University of Michigan and afterwards at the University of Chicago, forming the nucleus of the so-called "Chicago School," and of the general movement known as "instrumentalism," began to attract James's attention and excite his enthusiasm at the beginning of the century. The correspondence which follows reflects James's eager interest and sympathy. On March 11, 1903, James wrote to Dewey: "I have just read, with almost absurd pleasure, A. W. Moore's *Existence, Meaning and Reality*. . . . I see an entirely new 'school of thought' forming, and, as I believe, a true one. Who and what is Moore, and how old?" Dewey replied as follows:—

[Chicago, March 1903]

[My dear James,—]

. . . [I walked] on air for a long time after getting such a letter from you. Moore . . . has taught here since about '95. . . . The flexibility and freedom of his mental operations I needn't speak of,—his articles do that. . . . Lloyd and Mead [2] were both at it in Ann Arbor ten years ago. Did you ever read Lloyd's *Dynamic Idealism*? I can't see much difference between his monism and your pluralism,—barring a little exaggeration of the plural on its own account, if I may venture. Mead has difficulty of articulation in written discourse, as you know; but I suppose he is more effective than any man in our Department in giving capable advanced students independent method. He works himself (and *it*) out mainly in biological terms. "Life-process" is his terminology for the developing reality. We have turned out some doctors who are beginning to do more or less. . . . They are all young, all busy with teaching; and I think on the whole it speaks well for them (and for their standpoint) that they have been fairly conservative in publishing. . . .

As for myself,—I don't know whether you ever read my psychological articles . . . but I have evolved them all from the same standpoint. . . . I am sending you, herewith, some proof from a forthcoming Decennial volume, *Studies in Logical Theory*. . . . You may not have time nor inclination to read, but I wish you would glance the pages over enough to see whether you could stand for a dedication to yourself. Unfortunately my own things come first and are the only ones in page proof yet. (Overlook the disrespectful allusion to your pluralism in a foot-note,—I can but feel that your plurality as it now stands it æsthetic rather than logical.) But so far as I am concerned your *Psychology* is the spiritual *progenitor* of the whole industry; and while we won't attempt to father you with all the weak kidlets which are crying in the volume to be born, it would afford us all (and me in particular, if that doesn't reflect on the pleasure of others) very much satisfaction if you will permit us to dedicate the volume to you. . . . Faithfully yours,

JOHN DEWEY

Cambridge, March 23, 1903

Dear Dewey,—

Thanks for your amazingly obliging and interesting letter. . . . What you write of the *new school of truth* both pleases and humiliates me. It humiliates

[2] A. H. Lloyd and G. H. Mead.

me that I had to wait till I read Moore's article before finding how much on my own lines you were working. Of course I had welcomed you as one coming nearer and nearer, but I had missed the central root of the whole business, and shall now re-read you . . . and try again a hack at Mead and Lloyd of whom I have always recognized the originality, but whom I have found so far unassimilably obscure. I fancy that much depends on the place one starts from. You have all come from Hegel and your terminology *s'en ressent,* I from empiricism, and though we reach much the same goal it superficially looks different from the opposite sides. . . . Yours faithfully,

WM. JAMES

Chicago, March 27, 1903

My dear James,—

. . . I feel rather ashamed to have given you the impression that I was writing about a new school of thought. I do not think you will find it worth while rereading the articles I mentioned; or, if you do, that you will find anything in them that is in any way indicative of new developments. It is simply that upon the psychological side the articles all go back to certain ideas of life activity, of growth, and of adjustment, which involve teleological and dynamic conceptions rather than ontological and static ones. . . . I have been at work with my classes more or less on the metaphysical—or logical side, as I prefer to call it— for some years, but I never felt until this year that I had anything in shape to publish. . . .

It may be the continued working of the Hegelian bacillus of reconciliation of contradictories in me, that makes me feel as if the conception of process gives a basis for uniting the truths of pluralism and monism, and also of necessity and spontaneity. . . . I cannot help feeling that an adequate analysis of activity would exhibit the world of fact and the world of ideas as two correspondent objective statements of the active process itself,—correspondent because each has a work to do, in the doing of which it needs to be helped out by the other. The active process itself transcends any possible objective statement (whether in terms of fact or of ideas) simply for the reason that these objective statements are ultimately incidental to its own ongoing—are for the sake of it. It is this transcendence of any objectified form, whether perceptual or conceptual, that seems to me to give the clue to freedom, spontaneity, etc.; and to make it unnecessary to have recourse to such a hypostatizing of chance as Peirce seems to me to indulge in. I always feel as if he were engaging . . . in just the same sort of conceptual construction he is protesting against. I must say, however, that I can see how far I have moved along when I find how much I get out of Peirce this year, and how easily I understand him, when a few years ago he was mostly a sealed book to me, aside from occasional inspirations. . . . Yours sincerely,

JOHN DEWEY

The spring of 1903 saw the appearance of *Studies in Logical Theory,* by John Dewey, "with the coöperation of Members and Fellows of the Department of Philosophy" of the University of Chicago. The Preface contained the following words: "For both inspiration and the forging of the tools with which the writers have worked there is a preëminent obligation on the part of all of us to William James, of Harvard University, who, we hope, will accept this acknowledgment and this book as unworthy tokens of a regard and an admiration that are coequal."

Cambridge, Oct. 17, 1903

Dear Dewey,—

I was about to write to you in any case this afternoon when your ultra friendly letter came. On returning from the country yesterday, one of the first things that greeted my eyes was your *Logical Studies,* and the to me surprising words that close its Preface. What have I done to merit such a tribute? The Lord, who knoweth all things, knows doubtless about this too, but I accept it rather blindly, and most delightedly, as one of the good things that life sometimes strews in one's way. I feel so the inchoateness of all my publications that it surprises me to hear of anything definite accruing to others from them. I must do better, now that I am "looked up to" so. I thank you from the bottom of my heart! . . .

It rejoices me greatly that your School (I mean your philosophic school) at the University of Chicago is, after this long gestation, bringing its fruits to birth in a way that will demonstrate its great unity and vitality, and be a revelation to many people, of American scholarship. I wish now that you would make a collection of your scattered articles. . . . It is only books that tell. They seem to have a penetrating power which the same content in the shape of scattered articles wholly lacks. But the articles prepare buyers for the books. My own book, rather absurdly cackled about before it is hatched, is hardly begun, and with my slow rate of work will take long to finish. . . . Ever gratefully and faithfully yours,

WM. JAMES

On November 15, 1903, James wrote to Schiller:

I have had all sorts of outside things shoved upon me since my return a month ago to Cambridge. . . . The best of the lot was reading up the output of the "Chicago School of Thought." . . . It is splendid stuff, and Dewey is a hero. A real school and real thought. At Harvard we have plenty of thought, but not school. At Yale and Cornell, the other way about.

James's enthusiastic review of the *Logical Studies* appeared early in 1904 under the title of "The Chicago School"—enthusiastic save for the remark that the book contained no "cosmology" or explanation of the "common world." In his prompt acknowledgment, Dewey wrote:

I need hardly say what I have said before, such approval as you feel drawn to give means more to us than that of anybody else. None the less as far as I am concerned I have simply been rendering back in logical vocabulary what was already your own.[3]

When in 1906 he turned to the composition of the lectures and volume on "Pragmatism," James was acutely and enthusiastically aware of the support which he was receiving from different quarters. He was eager to consolidate the movement, if not by agreement, then by a frank recognition of differences. Dewey contributed to this clarification and mutual understanding.

New York, Nov. 28, 1907

Dear James,—

I have just finished . . . an account of the pragmatic movement, based on your book.[4] . . . I have not attempted a review of the book, but rather of the pragmatic movement with reference to what present controversy seems to me to indicate as the points which require more explicit statement and development. Among other things I have become conscious of some points of possible divergence between Schiller, yourself and myself, taken two by two all the way around; and I am not sure that some misunderstandings among our critics might not be cleared away, if our points of respective agreement and possible disagreement were brought out. For example, the antecedents of humanism, via personal idealism, were distinctly an idealistic metaphysics. My own views are much more naturalistic, and a reaction against not merely intellectualistic and monistic idealism but against all idealisms, except, of course, in the sense of ethical ideals. Now, I seem to myself to be nearer you than I am to Schiller on this point, yet I am not sure. On the other hand, Schiller in his later writings seems to emphasize that the good consequence which is the test of an idea, is *good* not so much in its own nature as in meeting the claims of the idea, whatever the idea is. And here I seem to be nearer to him than to you; and yet again I am not sure. If there are real differences, and our critics are inclined to make combinations of our respective doctrines which no one of us alone would stand for, this may account for some of the unsatisfactory misunderstandings in the present state of controversy. Yours sincerely,

JOHN DEWEY

It will be recalled that in 1907 James had delivered his lectures on pragmatism at Columbia University. In 1908, James was presented with a volume of *Essays Philosophical and Psychological,* written in his honor by "his colleagues at Columbia University," and "intended to mark in some degree its authors' sense of Professor James's memorable services in philosophy and psychology, the vitality he has added to those studies, and the encouragement that has flowed from him to colleagues without number." To this volume Dewey contributed the essay entitled, "Does Reality Possess Practical Character?" and which to James seemed the most "weighty."[5] It served, together with the

---

[3] *Psychol. Bulletin,* I (1904); *cf. C.E.R.,* 445-7; Dewey to W.J., January 20, 1904.
[4] "What Does Pragmatism Mean by Practical?" *Jour. of Philos.,* V (1908).
[5] Title-page and prefatory note; W.J. to Dewey, August 4, 1908; *L.W.J.,* II, 310.

previous article "What Does Pragmatism Mean by Practical?" to define the author's interpretation of James and of the doctrine which they held in common.

In 1908 and 1909 James was busily engaged in the double task of refuting critics and smoothing the way to agreement. In the former year he published an article entitled " 'Truth' *versus* 'Truthfulness,' " at the conclusion of which he proposed to appease his critics by surrendering the word "truth" to those who wished to emphasize "the preliminary and objective conditions of the cognitive relation," while reserving the term "truthful" for that functional value of ideas which pragmatism emphasized. Dewey disapproved of the proposal, and it was withdrawn by James when he afterwards reprinted the article.[6] Knowledge of the past provided a case in point,—Dewey insisting that the term "truth" was not properly applicable to the past event itself, but only to subsequent affirmations made about the event. Thus he wrote to James on February 24, 1909:

> "Is it true that Napoleon landed in Provence on the last day of March, 1814?" If this means anything, it means either (*a*) Is the *statement, idea or belief* that Napoleon landed etc., true? or, (*b*) Is the landing (the bare existential fact) of Napoleon a truth? Now the thoroughgoing rationalist . . . holds, as I understand him, that the bare existential fact *qua* fact *is* itself of the *nature* of truth. . . . It seems to me that we need only hold the critics . . . up to the distinction between brute existences or occurrences (which certainly are not "truths") and the intellectual . . . statements *about* those existences (to which alone the character of truth-falsity does appertain), to make them see that the confusion lies with them, and that truth . . . may well be a relation between the *effects* of the existence in question and the *effects* of the intellectual position or assertion in question. And the case of the truth of a historic statement . . . seems to be a particularly strong case on your side. "Cæsar's existence" is, then, in no sense a *"truth* 2000 years old"; the question is whether a belief or statement that Cæsar did certain things 2000 years ago is true.

In the Preface to *The Meaning of Truth,* a compilation of his restatements and replies to objectors, James undertook to represent the views of Dewey, Schiller, and himself as complementary rather than conflicting. Schiller's universe was "psychological," his own "epistemological," and as for Dewey's—it was "the widest of the three," but he "refrained from giving his own account of its complexity." James had originally written Dewey down as "ontological" to complete the trilogy, but having submitted the passage to Dewey he had "refrained," at the latter's earnest request. "Even the humblest and most obscure writer," wrote Dewey, "has perhaps a natural reluctance, while he is still vocal, to be authoritatively explained by others, even though he recognize that he is fair game for criticism." James's request for further explanation evoked the following:

> Of course I had no intention of passing upon your references to Schiller. No, I don't think your statement about me is false; but, pragmatically, falsity and inadequacy run into each other. The "ontological" reference is, I think, misleading, considering the historic and conventional associations of that term. My most serious objection is that I do not think such summary resolutions of complicated matters really clarify the discussion. They create as many new questions as they resolve and often produce a new crop of misunderstandings.[7]

In the same Preface, James insisted that Schiller, Dewey, and he absolutely agreed "in admitting the transcendency of the object (provided it be an experienceable object) to the subject, in the truth-relation." He was concerned to defend Dewey and Schiller as well as himself against the common charge of subjectivism. Dewey did not feel that he was in need of any defense: since he not only assumed that thought operated in an external environment of experience to which it was answerable, but regarded experience itself as nonsubjective. And in this he claimed the support of James:

> Of course I am not trying to supply *you* with language; but I have never been able to see why a critic . . . if he really believed (except for controversial purposes) that I do not believe in anything beyond mental states, should not point out the self-contradiction that that involves me in. Of course I have repeated *ad nauseam* that there are existences prior to and subsequent to cognitive states and purposes, and that *the whole meaning of the latter* is the way they intervene in the control and revaluation of the independent existences. . . . In fact, I find (in conversation) that many critics regard your doctrine as much more subjectivistic than mine, because I, following the lead of your *Psychology* . . . emphasize (more than do your later writings) the biological *origin* of ideas and intellectual operations. In short, you will find (unless I am mistaken badly) that the critics who make this charge . . . *always* shift the ground from the analysis of *truth* to the meaning of *experience*, and having themselves a thoroughly subjective (and hence dualistic) notion of experience, they read it into us.[8]

It is clear that these discussions led to no breach between James and Dewey, but tended rather to confirm their agreement. James continued to follow the development of Dewey's thought with interest and admiration. The temper of their correspondence was worthy of their common vocation. They were wholly unlike in the genius of their minds; and if it be true that the style re-

---

[7] Dewey to W.J., March 15, 19, 1909.
[8] Dewey to W.J., March 21, 1909.

veals the man, then they were certainly different men. James had great difficulty in understanding Dewey's ideas with their "unchained formlessness of expression" [9]—Dewey must have found James precipitate and overexuberant. But to both these were trivial considerations, and they sought by sympathy and understanding to emphasize what they held in common, rather than by disputation to aggravate their differences.

[9] W.J. to Th. Flournoy, February 9, 1906; *L.W.J.*, II, 244.

XXXIV

PRAGMATISM IN ITALY AND GERMANY

In the spring of 1905, being in Rome for the purpose of attending the Fifth International Congress of Psychology, James wrote as follows:

> I have been having this afternoon a very good and rather intimate talk with the little band of "pragmatists," Papini, Vailati, Calderoni, Amendola, etc., most of whom inhabit Florence, publish the monthly journal *Leonardo,* at their own expense, and carry on a very serious philosophic movement, apparently *really* inspired by Schiller and myself (I never could believe it before, although Ferrari had assured me), and show an enthusiasm, and also a literary swing and activity that I know nothing of in our own land. . . . It has given me a certain new idea of the way in which truth ought to find its way into the world. The most interesting, and in fact genuinely edifying, part of my trip has been meeting this little *cénacle,* who have taken my own writings, *entre autres, au grand sérieux.*[1]

These men, together with Prezzolini and others, formed a group which met informally for philosophical discussion, and which was sometimes referred to as "The Pragmatic Club." Thus did James stumble, quite unawares, upon a band of devotees already engaged in the practice and propagation of the new gospel. The period of their collective enthusiasm coincides with the life of *Leonardo,* from 1903 to 1907. In its pages they published numerous articles on pragmatism—its history and its leaders—reviewed James's works as they appeared, and acclaimed the sale of 2000 copies of the translation of his *Psychology.* Giovanni Vailati died in 1909, Mario Calderoni in 1914. Their articles, representing a relatively sober and moderate version of pragmatism, were published after their death with a Preface by Papini.[2] Of the others, Giovanni Amendola became a liberal statesman, opposed Fascism, and died in 1926 of the effects of "lessons" supposed to have been administered by unofficial agents of the government. Giuseppe Prezzolini veered away from pragmatism in the direction of the idealism of Croce, and Giovanni Papini himself passed through a succession of phases culminating in Christian piety. The latter's book *Sul Pragmatismo,* "the doctrine which had from Peirce its name,

---

[1] W.J. to A.H.J., April 30; to Santayana, May 2; *L.W.J.,* II, 227, 228.
[2] Lanciano, 1920. Largely reprinted from *Leonardo* and *Rivista di psicologia.*

from James its fame," [3] was designed to appear in 1906, simultaneously in Italian, French, and English—there was talk of a preface by James for the English edition. But it did not see the light until 1913, and was then a record of the past rather than a declaration of faith.

So long as the movement lived it was very much alive. It was this liveliness, especially as embodied in Papini, that stirred James to one of his characteristic enthusiasms. He liked the spirit of the group, their "frolicsomeness," and even their "literary swagger and conscious impertinence." He liked their "tone of feeling, well fitted to rally devotees and to make of pragmatism a new militant form of religious or quasi-religious philosophy." [4] He liked their style, and that of Papini in particular: "What a writer! and what fecundity! and what courage! . . . and what humor and what truth!" This feeling seems to have been reciprocated. Papini speaks of James's "simplicity," "charm," and "profundity." It was he who "conquered" at the Psychological Congress of 1905, of which his paper on "La Notion de conscience" was the "high light." [5]

The following exchange of letters reveals the spirit of this relationship, so characteristic of James in its unhesitating ardor and in its disregard of the disparity of ages:—

Del Monte, April 27, 1906

My dear friend and master, Papini,—

I have just been reading your *Crepuscolo dei filosofi* and the February number of *Leonardo,* and great is the resultant fortification of my soul. What a thing is genius! and you are a real genius! Here have I, with my intellectual timidity and conscientiousness, been painfully trying to clear a few steps of the pathway that leads to the systematized new *Weltanschauung* and you with a pair of bold strides get out in a moment beyond the pathway altogether into the freedom of the whole system,—into the open country. It is your *temper of carelessness,* quite as much as your particular formulas, that has had such an emancipating effect on my intelligence. You will be accused of extravagance, and *correctly* accused; you will be called the Cyrano de Bergerac of Pragmatism, etc., but the . . . program . . . *must* be sketched extravagantly. "Correctness" is one of the standards of the older way of philosophizing, that looks in the particular fact for the ghost of some "principle" that legitimates its being, and takes *creation* out of reality. If creation takes place in particulars, as I have always "seen reasons for believing" but now "believe," "correctness" is not a category for judging anything real. . . . I shall soon write a notice of the *Crepuscolo* and *Leonardo* for Woodbridge's *Journal* [6] and call you the master

[3] "Quella dottrina ch'ebbe dal Peirce il nome e dal James la fama" (*Sul Pragmatismo,* 1913, viii).

[4] "G. Papini and the Pragmatist Movement in Italy," originally published by James in 1906; *C.E.R.,* 460, 465. The writings of Papini which chiefly interested James were *Il Crepuscolo dei filosofi* (1906) and the *Leonardo* articles afterwards republished in *Sul Pragmatismo.*

[5] W.J. to F. C. S. Schiller, April 7, 1906; *L.W.J.,* II, 246; "Gli Psicologi a Roma," *Leonardo,* III (1905), 123-4.

[6] *The Journal of Philosophy, Psychology and Scientific Method,* edited at this time by Professor F. J. E. Woodbridge of Columbia University.

of the movement now. You're such a brilliant, humorous and witty writer! It is splendid to see old Italy renovating us all in this way. I have just written to John Dewey of Columbia University in New York, calling his attention to these writings of yours. You must immediately read his article "Beliefs and Realities" in the *Philosophical Review* for March. It is a little obscure in style, but very powerful, and the weightiest pragmatist pronouncement yet made in America! Continue to think and write! Yours faithfully,

WM. JAMES

Florence, May 3, 1906 [7]

Dear Master,—

I have received your letter from Del Monte, and assure you that it has almost overwhelmed me. To hear the master whom I have studied and whom I admire say to me things that seem too flattering even for my pride (which, I might say, is not inconsiderable) has been for me one of the most intense joys of my intellectual life. I know well that your sympathy for what I am trying to do predisposes you to enthusiasm, but I would not hope to be able to give my dearest master in return a fraction, however small, of the intellectual excitement which he had given me. I am still quite young, dear master—only twenty-five years old—and I am eager to go on working in *your* path. I hope that you will continue to support me—your confidence in me will be one of my sustaining forces.

Only a few days ago I published a little book of philosophical fables: I am sending it to you. I am working on the new Italian edition of your *Psychology*. In June this will be finished. I am working also on my book on pragmatism—I shall send you the proofs. Write me again. Will your metaphysics soon appear? Cordially yours,

G. PAPINI

When Papini had received and read James's promised article in "Woodbridge's *Journal*," he wrote on July 3, 1906:

> You can well imagine the emotion I have felt in reading it, not only for what you say of my ideas but above [all] for the heartfelt sympathy that animates your words. Theories may die and you and I may very well, in two days or two years, have opposite opinions, but the inclination you show for my way of thinking and writing gives me a pleasure of a special kind that men of mere knowledge perhaps never feel.

In a chapter of his *L'altra metà*, Papini says that pragmatism, affirming the utility of knowledge, may be taken in two quite opposite ways according as one does or does not cleave to utilitarianism. To a utilitarian, the utility of knowledge will commend it, and confirm its authority; but to a non-utilitarian the utility of knowledge will disparage it and bring deliverance from its yoke. Papini is of the latter persuasion. "The true greatness of man," he says, "lies

---

[7] This letter was written in French and is translated by the author. Papini's "little book" was *Il tragico quotidiano*.

in his doing the useless precisely because it is useless." [8] In proportion as science is useful it becomes a positive duty to despise it, and to turn one's activity into more disinterested channels! There is a similar distinction between the "puritanic" and "conciliatory" pragmatisms, the former manifesting itself in restraint and economy of thought, and thus continuing the tradition of positivism; the latter being exuberantly speculative, as a result of having discovered and escaped the limits of science. Another of Papini's distinctions is that which he draws between "pragmatisti sociali" and "pragmatisti magica." The former are sober men and find in pragmatism an instrument of organization and policy; while the latter are intoxicated with the creative spirit.[9]

Papini himself represented in each of these antitheses the freer and bolder alternative. His appeal to James lay both in his recognition of the many doors which open out from the pragmatist corridor,[10] and also in his choosing for himself the door of heroic imprudence, free speculation, and aggressive faith. He was the "dithyrambic" voice that aroused men's "divinely-creative functions." [11] He was the "youthful and *empanaché* Papini, who has . . . put himself at the centre of equilibrium whence all the motor tendencies start." [12] This was the pragmatism which adopted "action" as the standard by which to judge all human instruments, truths among the rest;[13] and the James to whom this gospel appealed was the James who found "life worth living" because of its heroic moments.

Papini's distinctions suggest two connections of pragmatism with modern social and political developments. Communism, so far as its motives are technological, will readily accept a philosophy in which all knowedge is judged by its applications, in which these applications are construed in terms of a control of environment, and in which both knowledge and its applications are socialized. This is *one* of the strains in pragmatism, albeit more characteristic of Peirce and of Dewey than of James. But the more powerful impulse communicated by pragmatism to social and political thought seems to spring from another source, namely, from its exaltation of direct action, and hence both of revolution and of dictatorship. While a Papinian pragmatist would have had only contempt for a purely economic state, he would have found himself much in sympathy with a cult of violence and danger.

---

[8] "La vera grandezza dell-uomo deve consistere nel fare l'inutile, appunto perchè inutile," *L'altra metà*, 1922, 203. The first edition appeared in 1910.

[9] *Leonardo*, IV (Feb. 1906), 58-61.

[10] *C.E.R.*, 462.

[11] *Pragm.*, 257.

[12] W.J. to Th. Flournoy, March 26, 1907; *L.W.J.*, II, 267.

[13] "Energies of Men," *Philos. Rev.*, XVI (1907); published in *Leonardo*, V (Feb. 1907). Here pragmatism offers no *Weltanschauung* of its own, but permits man to choose any that suits his moral and æsthetic demands, and arouses an *"eccitamento mentale"* by making man conscious of his creative power and superiority to science. (*Op. cit.*, 34.)

In April 1926, Mussolini gave an interview to the press in which he named James, along with Nietzsche and Sorel, among his philosophical masters. Being asked which influence was the greatest, he replied:

> That of Sorel. Nietzsche enchanted me when I was twenty, and reinforced the anti-democratic elements in my nature. The pragmatism of William James was of great use to me in my political career. James taught me that an action should be judged rather by its results than by its doctrinary basis. I learnt of James that faith in action, that ardent will to live and fight, to which Fascism owes a great part of its success. . . . For me the essential was to act. But, I repeat, it is to Georges Sorel that I owe the greatest debt. It was that master of Syndicalism who by his rugged theories on revolutionary tactics contributed most decisively to the forming of the discipline, the energy and the power of the Fascist cohorts.[14]

It would be unwise to take this statement too literally. The list of Mussolini's acknowledged masters is already long and is growing longer.[15] That which he found in James he could easily have found elsewhere, as it was widely disseminated and had many parallels. And James was a prophet on the other side as well. The fate of Amendola has already been alluded to. In his account of life among the political prisons on the island of Lipari, Emilio Lussu describes the time spent in discussing James, and the suspicions excited in the breast of the police agent who "intervened one day and inquired, in the name of the law, who Signor James was." [16] But there is no good reason for doubting that the young Mussolini knew at least fragments of Jamesian doctrine and found them to his liking. He remembers also to have made James's personal acquaintance.

The time and the means of Mussolini's contact with pragmatism are obscure. There is a current story that towards the end of the first decade of the present century (1908 or 1909) Mussolini spent some six months in Paris and went frequently to Péguy's shop on the Rue de la Sorbonne to hear Sorel expound Bergson. According to the story, Lenin was meeting Sorel at the same time, so that both of these great revolutionists were imbibing anti-intellectualistic doctrine from the same source.[17] Lenin read and wrote philosophy voluminously. He was attracted by Sorel's syndicalism, in which class war was defended as a heroic myth—*una interpretazione will-to-believ-istica* of Marxism, as Papini ex-

[14] *Sunday Times,* London, April 11, 1926. The interview was obtained by the Spanish journalist, Dr. André Révesz.

[15] Machiavelli, Schopenhauer, Strindberg, etc., *cf.* H. W. Schneider, *Making the Fascist State,* 1928, 230-1.

[16] The agent referred the matter to his superiors, who apparently thought James to be, if not a teacher of the true gospel, at any rate innocuous. "The Flight from Lipari," *Atlantic,* CXLVI (1930), 31.

[17] I owe this story to Professor M. Mauss of the Collège de France, who does not vouch for its accuracy. I have been unable to verify it.

pressed it.[18] But any reference to Lenin's pragmatistic affiliations has to be qualified by the fact that in the name of materialism he roundly denounced and elaborately refuted the "empirio-criticism" of Ernst Mach espoused by his rival, A. A. Bogdanov. He was suspicious of this philosophy because it seemed to open a fideistic way to "the God-makers," and because of its general spirit of "conciliatory quackery." The followers of Mach were a "wretchedly pulpy . . . contemptible party of middle-roaders," who concealed the irreconcilable conflict between idealism and realism. Lenin was instinctively, and perhaps strategically, opposed to modernist interpretations of Marx; preferring the premise of materialistic determinism to more flexible philosophical doctrines having no fixed economic and political implications.[20]

Mussolini, whether he did or did not meet Sorel in 1908, was in any case familiar with his writings, and through them he undoubtedly heard of Bergson. But that he should have heard of James from the same source is altogether improbable. Sorel's most famous work, *Réflexions sur la violence,* contains many allusions to Bergson, but none to James, despite the striking similarity of the doctrine of the soul-sustaining myth to that of *The Will to Believe.* To the second edition of *Les Illusions du progrès* Sorel added an appendix on "Grandeur et décadence" in which he drew upon James's *Varieties of Religious Experience,* but this was not until 1911. His attention does not appear to have been attracted to James's *Pragmatism* until after the French translation of that book appeared—also in 1911. Then, in 1921, having read the French translations of *The Meaning of Truth* and *A Pluralistic Universe,* Sorel published a book entitled *De l'Utilité du pragmatisme.* The *Avant-propos* was written in 1917, and announces the author's acceptance of the doctrine with reservations. He thinks that James has been ill-served by disciples like Papini, "mystifiers whose special function it is to make a smoke-house of any paradoxical novelty," and who find their proper haven in futurism. He thinks that James's pragmatism is provincial, impregnated with the atmosphere of an American, Protestant, and academic environment, and that it needs to be rethought by a European brain. This being done, however (and Sorel proceeds to do it), he concludes that pragmatism may take its place among the classics of philosophy and render an important service to modern thought.[20]

Everything points to 1908 as the year of Mussolini's affair with philosophy. It was in 1908 that he published in *Il Pensiero romagnolo* an article on Nietzsche, entitled "La Filosofia della forza," and wrote a "Storia della filosofia" which

---

[18] *Leonardo,* IV (1906), 60.

[19] Nikolai Lenin, *Materialism and Empirio-Criticism* (Vol. XIII of *Collected Works*), 1927, 294 and *passim.*

[20] Sorel, *De l'Utilité du pragmatisme,* 1921, III, 21-2.

was never published.[21] This was the year of his doubtful visit to Paris, and of the undoubted publication of Sorel's *Réflexions sur la violence* (followed a year later by its translation into Italian). And it was in this year that Mussolini came into contact with the *Leonardo* group of Florence, from whom he can scarcely have failed to hear the name, if not the doctrines, of William James. *Leonardo* itself came to an end in 1907; but it was succeeded the following year by *La voce,* and while this was primarily political and literary rather than philosophical in its interest, it blossomed from the same stem. Prezzolini was its editor; Papini was a frequent, and Mussolini an occasional, contributor. Here Fascismo seems to have associated for a time with Pragmatismo, under the somewhat questionable auspices of Vocismo and Futurismo.

Whatever be the channels of transmission through which individual leaders have been influenced, there can be no doubt of the broad fact that pragmatism and Fascism (as well as Bolshevism) held some ground in common; and that Mussolini had a right to cite James, even if it be an afterthought. The contemporary political revolution, construed broadly, was a rejection of liberalism. It was the gospel of force consciously opposed to the gospel of humanitarianism and political democracy. It explicitly rejected the widely accepted dogma that the several individuals who compose society, since it is *their* interests which are at stake, shall be the final judges both as to what is good and as to what means shall be adopted for its realization. William James *was* a liberal in precisely this sense. That he would have had the least sympathy with either Bolshevism or Fascism is unthinkable. We have to do, then, not with a coherent revolutionary philosophy of which James was a forerunner, but with a group of ideas and sentiments, shifting and often unrelated, which here and there overlap the ideas and sentiments of pragmatism.

Fascism sprang from an emergency and expressed the need of prompt and decisive action, ideologies being disparaged because they promote discussion, delay, and irresolution: pragmatism was, therefore, a welcome ally, for having boldly challenged the prestige and authority of the intellect. Fascism was opportunistic, arising as a measure of safety, and continuing to be preoccupied with urgent questions of public and partisan necessity: pragmatism had taught that ideas which do not have an application to the practical situation in which they arise are meaningless and unprofitable. Fascism employed force, both against opposing force and against constitutional rights, was merciless and lawless, excited martial ardor among its own members and threatened its neighbors: pragmatism had taught that ideas and policies may rightly be adopted for

---

[21] The manuscript was destroyed, so the story goes, by a jealous young woman who mistook the jargon of philosophy for the names of her rivals. (*Life of B. Mussolini,* by M. G. Sarfatti, Eng. trans., 1925, 149.)

their tonic effect upon the will, and that the justification of action may lie, not in its happy consequences, but in the fervor or exaltation of the action itself. For all these ideas with which pragmatistic philosophy supports the exigencies of Fascist policy, it would be possible to cite innumerable texts from James.

There remains the central idea of Fascism, namely, its subordination of the individual to the organic solidarity of the state. This idea was anathema to James, and belongs in the opposite tradition of Fichte and Hegel. It was to a Gentile, rather than to a James, that Fascism looked for the philosophical elaboration of this idea, and as it assumed increasing importance the rationalization of Fascism shifted more and more to Fichtean or Hegelian grounds.[22] There is a reason why a political movement which found pragmatism congenial in its early and revolutionary stages should look to Post-Kantian idealism in its maturity. Pragmatism of the type represented by the youthful Papini encourages the individual or casual group to become heroes and martyrs in behalf of *any* cause. Its tendency is disruptive and anarchical. But when a revolutionary movement has seized upon the agencies of the state it becomes automatically the champion of the state. For the subjective principle of freedom it is now necessary to substitute the objective principle of common action. For a plurality of militant loyalties which ennoble life diversely, it is necessary to substitute one loyalty, and to give that an exclusive title to nobility. When revolutionists become rulers they can no longer pride themselves on their private force—for that would encourage a like pride in dissidents—but must claim that *their* force possesses a peculiar sanction, as springing from something greater than themselves. Their wills can no longer be merely theirs, but must be channels of a higher will; the blood of a greater organism must flood their veins, and a mightier voice speak out of their mouths. Fascism was a party, held together by discipline and sectarian enthusiasm; when the party became the state, these mental characteristics, already developed, were carried over to the state. As a revolution, Fascism created a breach with the past; the doctrine of statism restored and satisfied the sentiment of historic self-identity. This is not pragmatism—on the contrary, it derives its philosophical sanction from pragmatism's dearest foe—but it is an authoritarian form of the gospel of action, by which the conquests of violence can be preserved, consolidated, and moralized.[23]

---

[22] G. Gentile, "The Philosophic Basis of Fascism," *Foreign Affairs,* VI (1928), 290. This nation-worship, submission of the individual to the state, idealization of patriotism, etc., was, of course, a vigorous cult in France with Charles Maurras and *L'Action française.* But although this influence was considerable, it was not philosophical. For Maurras's nationalistic creed, *cf.* his *Au Signe de flore,* 1931, 256-7, 291-3. Maurras goes back to Renan for his creed of nationality.

[23] I may add that, so far as I can see, these pragmatistic and idealistic ideas have nothing to do with the cult of Mazzini, who believed that action should follow swiftly upon thought, because it is of the very nature of thought that it should illuminate action and of action that it should

Although Ernst Mach was an important forerunner of pragmatism, while Georg Simmel and Wilhelm Ostwald were greeted by James as allies, pragmatism gained only a slight foothold in Germany, and that mainly in Austria. Even the three philosophers just mentioned accepted it as an interpretation of method in the physical or social sciences rather than as a philosophy. Mach, it is true, has recently been canonized and made the father of a new school of philosophy in Vienna. But this Mach *redivivus* is the positivistic and not the pragmatistic Mach. The substitution of logistics for ethics and metaphysics, as proposed by Mach's latest disciples, is profoundly alien to James in temperament as well as in doctrine.

A German translation of *Pragmatism* appeared in 1908, by Wilhelm Jerusalem,[24] whose motive was to make it known to a hitherto unsuspecting philosophical public. The translator had arrived independently at a similar view, and had carried on a sympathetic correspondence with James since 1900. In the *Vorwort* of his translation he now proclaimed his adherence to the pragmatic school, while expressing his preference for a greater emphasis on the *social* conditions of knowledge. Professor Julius Goldstein,[25] who afterwards published articles expounding and defending pragmatism, wrote James several enthusiastic letters, to which the latter replied:—

> Schiller had already written to me about you as the only pragmatist now living in Germany. I hope that this will not long be true, but that you may succeed in inoculating your fellow-countrymen with a taste for more empirical philosophy, or rather with a *dis*taste for the elements of absolutism which so many Germans still leave to flourish in the midst of an otherwise very empirical way of thinking.
>
> I am getting numerous acknowledgments of my book, but only one so far has been as enthusiastically sympathetic as yours. It is evident that your mind and mine are cut on the same pattern. . . . The Germans, as you say, are given over to monism—monism in the depths, however empiricist they may appear on the surface. *My* empiricism and pluralism are in the depths also.[26]

Any summary of the influence and later development of pragmatism must take account not only of the several things which it may itself mean, but of the several philosophical destinations to which it may indirectly lead. The unique importance of James lay not only in the initial impulse which he gave to the movement, but in the fact that he foresaw and countenanced so many of the directions which the movement might take. In its narrowest and strictest sense

realize thought. This is in no sense opposed to the liberal tradition. It finds the justification of action in the ends which thought forecasts, and not in the action itself or in its subjective authority.

[24] W. Jerusalem (1854-1923) was at this time teaching philosophy at the University of Vienna, where he was later made full professor.

[25] Professor of philosophy at the University of Darmstadt.

[26] W.J. to J. Goldstein, October 11, 1906 and August 6, 1907.

his pragmatism was a description of discursive knowledge, including the role of ideas, how they refer to their objects, and what makes them true. All three of these questions are answered in practical terms: an idea is an instrumentality; it refers to its object by inaugurating a train of activities leading thereto, or theretowards; and it is true in so far as it enables the knower to cope with its object successfully. Assuming some such description of discursive knowledge to be correct, what is the metaphysical sequel? One may regard the practical character of discursive knowledge as equivalent to its disparagement. If discursive knowledge is *merely* practical, then it behooves the metaphysician to look for a deeper or purer theoretic insight elsewhere. This is the way of intuitionism and mysticism, exemplified by Bergson. Or, having discovered that discursive knowledge is *practical,* one may pass on to the underlying will and assert the general priority of practice to theory. This is the way of activism, exemplified by Papini, Schiller, Sorel, and Catholic Modernism. Or, having accepted a practical interpretation of the discursive process, one may take this process itself as the prototype of all activity, not only scientific, but moral and æsthetic as well. This is the positivistic instrumentalism of the school of Dewey. This list of alternatives is not complete, nor are they mutually exclusive. In James himself all three alternatives are retained. Indeed it was the indeterminate richness of its possibilities that commended pragmatism to him. Nevertheless, while he joined hands with Papini and Dewey and greeted them as allies in the same cause, it is quite clear that he felt a deeper allegiance to the army of the mystics and intuitionists. It was a metaphysics of vision and insight, rather than either activism or positivism, that sprang from the ancient roots of his thought.

XXXV

RETIREMENT FROM TEACHING

Pragmatism was published in 1907. This was also the year of James's retirement from teaching. As early as 1900 he had seemed "about withdrawing from the career." [1] Foreseeing that he would be unable to renew his teaching in the following autumn, he wrote to President Eliot regarding a second year's leave of absence. There then began seven years of correspondence during which James was perpetually seeking to withdraw, while Eliot, with the most sympathetic consideration for his health and the most jealous regard for the reputation of the university, was trying to hold him.

This proposed resignation, and the thought that their old relations were about to be broken off, occasioned the following exchange of letters between James and his colleague George Herbert Palmer:—

Boxford, Christmas Day [1900]

Dear James,—

. . . My thoughts go back over the long years of our association—twenty-five years I think they must be—and I recall the first time I ever saw you, as you entered the railroad car somewhere near Beverly, accompanied by a dog or two. I did not then know your name, but was introduced to you shortly after. Then came my fight with Bowen[2] over your proposal to offer a course on Spencer. And soon your marriage and my first sight of lovely Mrs. James, sitting on a low stool in the window of your rooms on Harvard Street, when I made my wedding call. These were the days when you used to visit my course on Locke, the days when you encouraged my Readings in Homer, the many hours of comradeship and difference in Department meetings, chance walks, calls at each other's house. We began at the opposite poles, you in anatomy, I in divinity. Perhaps in that early time each was narrow. I know I distrusted you and thought you ought to dislike me. But how steady the growth of confidence and affection has been! Hardly anybody in Harvard has given me so much as you. . . .

It is a common and delusive dream that the professional man's output is but the completed expression of his private life. . . . Of course it is an unreasonable fancy. Professionalism has its own exactions which often run quite outside the personal element. But where, as in your case, the two are largely united and the big man expands undistorted into the solid professional, there comes a charm

---

[1] W.J. to the author, January 2, 1900.
[2] Francis Bowen, teacher of philosophy at Harvard from 1835-39 and from 1853-89.

and weight of influence which the mere amateur or technicist never acquires. It is a vast contribution you have made to our Harvard life, ennobling and intelligizing it just at this time of transition when, but for influences like yours, it might easily have become chaotic. You have given seriousness without humbug, rationality without dilettantism, daily courage without rudeness. Because of men like you Harvard is now taking a chief place in shaping the ideals of this country. That you withdraw from our teaching will be lamented almost as much by men outside the college as by us, your loving colleagues within it.

And yet I cannot blame you. I see that in writing you can better adjust your work to your powers, and with a given expenditure of force can probably have a wider influence than by spending yourself in the classroom. For a year I have had no thought of your coming back to full work. But I have hoped you might offer a single course, or at least a seminary, and so keep yourself an official member of our staff—the greatest, certainly, that any English-speaking university has ever had in philosophy. But undoubtedly there would be difficulties in this plan. . . . No, I am sorry to think you are probably right in resigning. . . . The years of writing which will now become possible will put us under new and glad debts to you. But good as I know all this may be, I cannot help mourning for the happy old arrangements. . . . We can let you off from instruction only on the condition of your doubling the years to be given to Cambridge friendship. Affectionately,

G. H. Palmer

Rome, Feb. 1, 1901

Dear Palmer,—

Your letter written from Boxford on Christmas day was one of the pleasantest things I ever received, coming as it did from an eye as unused to flow (at least in outward show of lachrimosity) and a tongue as sincere as yours; and speaking of the past in a way that made of it a gold framed picture; and emblazoning my character as 'twere a figure on historic tapestry; and treating my lack of training for my profession as if so chosen, by a deliberate stroke of genius; but above all, dear Palmer, by its straight words of recognition of me as a valued co-worker and of affection from your heart. From a man as critical minded as yourself and as absolutely frank when truths are bitter, such expressions have more significance to a fellow than you yourself can probably comprehend, and your letter will surely form one of the brightest features in the "archives" to be handed as a legacy to my children. But "I ain't dead yet"—far from it—and hope still to write your obituary notice, which I will, after this, make "handsomer" than ever. I think the delightful thing about us all in the philosophical department, where each has so distinct and positive a temperament, and each has a set of "ideas," both practical and theoretical, which are the outcrop of his irresistible idiosyncrasy, is our deep appreciation of one another, and our on the whole harmonious coöperation towards the infusion of what probably is objective truth into the minds of the students. At any rate it's genuine liberalism and non-dogmatism, with more and more joints to hang the whole mass of views together with, and more and more flexibility in them every year; and I for one hate to drop out of so healthy and complex, and I verily believe eventually *fertile* a philosophic organism, while reason still holds a seat within my cranium.

So, clutching at a desperate chance, I wrote yesterday to Münsterberg, accepting his suggestion that I should offer Philosophy 6,[3] but realizing the possibility of my breaking down, and trusting the Committee to squelch the plan if the question of the casual substitute proved too hard a one to crack. The fact is I am now crammed to overflowing with just the matter for that course, and of all tasks it would be the easiest. . . . If anyone ought to have a year away it is [Royce]—though possibly half a year would be even better. What I am afraid of is that he will spoil the quality of himself—the freer, simpler touch with deepest relations—in this unremitting close-quarter dealing with the details necessary for rapid publication. He can't get far enough away to see his own relations to the subject, and his mind will lose its spring, wonderful organ as it is. Münsterberg's is wonderful too: *Il sue le talent*—but I believe his whole construction in this great book of his to be utterly artificial. Perhaps for that very reason he will found a school as Kant did, and I shall then become as immortal as Zedlitz![4] . . . Of course my mind, bad enough at the best, is as good as ever it was in point of quality. It's the *quantity* that leaves so much to be desired. But I have blackened paper with a sufficient quantity of stuff to fill more than ten hours in the reading, so I'm safe at Edinburgh in May, though for the book I ought to write possibly 250 more pages of manuscript. It goes direfully slow. When I *do* anything, either writing or walking, I run down. When I rest I come up. But on the whole I more than hold my own, and my heart proper is now, thanks to these injections which I have been taking, apparently in quite normal condition. The rest is probably a matter of time, and possibly of more injections. . . . Good-bye, dear old Palmer! You don't know what a priceless letter yours was. . . .

W. J.

In spite of this and subsequent resignations, actual or threatened, James resumed his teaching in 1901-1902 and continued in active service, though on a reduced schedule, for six years! During the first half of the college year 1905-1906 he was in doubt about resuming his teaching in the autumn of 1906. His diary records for six weeks the diurnal fluctuations of his mind, thus: Oct. 26, "Resign!" Oct. 28, "Resign!!!!" Nov. 4, "Resign?" Nov. 7, "Resign!" Nov. 8, "Don't resign." Nov. 9, "Resign!" Nov. 16, "*Don't* resign!" Nov. 23, "Resign." Dec. 7, "Don't resign." Dec. 9, "Teach here next year." Finally, in the spring of 1907, he again sent in his resignation and this time it was reluctantly but definitively accepted.

When the question of his retirement was settled, James experienced a profound sense of relief. He was as glad to end his teaching as he had been glad to begin. In a letter to his friend Professor Theodore Flournoy he wrote in March:

[3] Hugo Münsterberg was at this time Chairman of the Department. Philosophy 6 was a course in "The Psychological Elements of the Religious Life."

[4] Münsterberg's "great book" was the *Grundzüge der Psychologie,* dedicated to James; Kant's *Kritik der reinen Vernunft* (1781) was dedicated to "Freiherrn von Zedlitz, Sr. Excellenz, dem Königl. Staatsminister."

I thank you for your congratulations on my retirement. It makes me very happy. A professor has two functions: (1) to be learned and distribute bibliographical information; (2) to communicate truth. The 1st function is the essential one, officially considered. The 2nd is the only one I care for. Hitherto I have always felt like a humbug as a professor, for I am weak in the first requirement. Now I can live for the second with a free conscience.[5]

And on May 18 to Schiller:

For thirty-five years I have been suffering from the exigencies of being [a professor], the pretension and the duty, namely, of meeting the mental needs and difficulties of other persons, needs that I couldn't possibly imagine and difficulties that I couldn't possibly understand; and now that I have shuffled off the professional coil, the sense of freedom that comes to me is as surprising as it is exquisite. I wake up every morning with it: "What! not to have to accommodate myself to this mass of alien and recalcitrant humanity, not to think under resistance, not to have to square myself with others at every step I make —hurrah! it is too good to be true. To be alone with truth and God! *es ist nicht zuglauben!* What a future. What a vision of ease!"

There was something in William James which was profoundly opposed to the whole life of scholarship, whether teaching, research, or the making of books. This was his emphasis on the incommunicable, or at least indefinable and indescribable, aspects of life. Thus he sympathized with the artist's prejudice against those who talked or wrote *about* art. "But you can't keep science out of anything in these bad times," he wrote from Florence in 1892.

Love is dead, or at any rate seems weak and shallow wherever science has taken possession. I am glad that, being incapable of anything like scholarship in any line, I still can take some pleasure from these pictures in the way of love. . . . What an awful trade that of professor is,—paid to talk, talk, talk! I have seen artists growing pale and sick whilst I talked to them without being able to stop. . . . It would be an awful universe if *everything* could be converted into words, words, words.[6]

James's peculiar art of teaching sprang not only from the qualities of his temperament and genius, but from a deliberate purpose—of which he was conscious as early as 1876, when he said that "philosophic study means the habit of always seeing an alternative, of not taking the usual for granted, of making conventionalities fluid again, of imagining foreign states of mind." "What doctrines students take from their teachers," he continued, "are of little consequence provided they catch from them the living, philosophic attitude of mind,

[5] March 26, 1907; *L.W.J.*, II, 268.
[6] To Grace Norton, December 28, 1892; *L.W.J.*, I, 337-8.

the independent, personal look at all the data of life, and the eagerness to harmonize them." [7]

This was clearly James's personal creed as a teacher, and he both obeyed and justified it in practice. He also exhibited its complementary defects. "Let me advise you in your teaching to be as methodical as possible," he wrote in 1900 to one of his former students, "let them see the plan of the forest as well as the individual tree. I find that my incurable disorderliness of method always stood in my way. Too incoherent and rambling." [8] Methodical James was not, and in advising others to be methodical he was in effect advising them not to be James—which advice they perforce accepted. Spontaneity comes in flashes, and between the flashes there are likely to be periods of darkness. There were unprofitable moments, even unprofitable hours, in James's classes. There were times when he was evidently fumbling. But his students remembered his flashes when the more steady and duller illumination of their other teachers had long since faded from their minds.

James was aware of the lecturer's illusion. To one who proposed that, in the Medical School, lectures be replaced by the "case-system," he said:

> I think you're entirely right, but your learned professor would rebel. He much prefers sitting and hearing his own beautiful voice to guiding the stumbling minds of the students. I know it myself. If you know something and have a little practice there is nothing easier than to hear yourself talk, while to direct the stumbling minds of the students soon becomes intolerable. [9]

But if teaching which is subjectively satisfying to the teacher himself can be unprofitable to the student, the reverse is also true. In James's case teaching that felt ineffective was often in reality effective, because of the candor and personal vividness with which he gave utterance to his difficulties or even to his boredom. Since no method stood between James and his students, his teaching was essentially a personal relation infused with his personal qualities. His humor, his playful exaggeration, directness, above all his generosity and comradeship, made him loved by his students as he was by his friends.

Writing of his brother William, Henry James once said that "the varieties of his application had been as little wasted for him as those of my vagueness had really been for me." [10] This was intended to refer to the youth and preparatory period of William James's life, but it might have been said with equal truth of his later years, when education was succeeded by career, or rather when education took the form of career. It is easy to point to the fact that

---

[7] "The Teaching of Philosophy in Our Colleges," *Nation*, XXIII (1876), 178.
[8] To the author, January 5, 1910.
[9] Professor Alexander Forbes, "Talk with Professor James," April 1, 1909.
[10] *N.S.B.*, 444.

James was fatigued by his professorial duties, but dangerous to suggest that he would therefore have been less fatigued without them. A man who is highly fatigable is fatigued by whatever he does, and also by what he does not do. James was fatigued by teaching, but so he was by writing, by reading, by traveling, by social intercourse, and even by recreation. He was instinctively prodigal of his energy, so that the effect of accumulated reserve was to induce a greater recklessness of spending. He also suffered intermittently from those vague maladies which in our ignorance we group together as nervous and mental. There is not, so far as I can see, the slightest reason to believe that his professional life was here unfavorable. Of course it exhausted him, and of course it depressed him, as did everything else in its turn. But it provided him with a variety of activities, and permitted a frequent change of scene, while at the same time involving fixed duties from which he derived a sense of stability and usefulness. His profession brought him agreeable and diverse human relations, and a continuous stream of appreciative audiences. Above all it secured his continuous growth, in competence and in fame. Progressively successful as a writer and teacher, he was saved from a sense of futility and enjoyed a belief in his own genius and mission.

Needless to say, James's retirement from Harvard brought no cessation of his lecturing and writing. The Hibbert Lectures, which were published under the title of *A Pluralistic Universe,* were given at Manchester College, Oxford, May 4-26, 1908. "The audiences were surprisingly large, several hundreds," and "very attentive." The invitation had been received in the autumn of the previous year, and accepted after much hesitation. The writing of the lectures was begun on December 7, and not yet completed when James sailed for Europe on April 21. His hesitation had been due largely to the uncertain condition of his health, and after he had engaged himself he feared that he could not go through with it. He was also reluctant to "relapse into the popular style," just when he thought he had "done with it forever." The strength of this reluctance appears in a letter to Schiller, written in January:[11]

> I accepted because I was ashamed to refuse a professional challenge of that importance, but I would it hadn't come to me. I actually *hate* lecturing; and this job condemns me to publish another book written in picturesque and popular style when I was settling down to something whose manner would be more *strengwissenschaftlich, i.e.,* concise, dry, and impersonal. My free and easy style in *Pragmatism* has made me so many enemies in academic and pedantic circles that I hate to go on increasing their number, and want to become tighter instead of looser. These new lectures will have to be even looser; for lectures *must* be prepared for audiences; and once prepared, I have neither the strength to rewrite them, nor the self-abnegation to suppress them.

[11] January 4, 1908. The phrases quoted in the first paragraph are also from letters to Schiller— of May 15 and 24, 1908.

"The Present Situation in Philosophy," used as the subtitle of the book, was the original title of the lectures. His major purpose was to present an alternative to monistic idealism, and thus to consolidate the opposition. This he delighted to do at Oxford—in the very stronghold of monistic idealism. But though James threatened "the scalp of the Absolute," and uttered dire threats against that august being's "clerical defenders," [12] his belligerency was largely playful—signifying exuberance of spirits rather than homicidal intent.

The exponents of monistic idealism whom he honored as his chief adversaries were all of them old friends with whom he had often done battle before, and from whom he had learned much: Royce, Bradley, and Hermann Lotze, whom in the eighties he had considered the "deepest philosopher" [13] of the day. He brought the same general charge against them all, namely, that they present philosophy with a false dilemma between utter unity and utter irrelevance.

Though James was uncompromisingly opposed to an extreme monism, and especially to the proofs advanced in its support, he was not less opposed to a doctrine of bare manyness and irrelevance. He believed that the world was full of intimacies—indeed, that the most characteristic feature of experience is the interpenetration of one thing with another. This accounts for his friendly overtures to Hegel, the very fountainhead of the doctrine which in Royce, Bradley, and Lotze he repudiated. He had always had a sneaking fondness for Hegel, but insisted on taking liberties with him. He liked him in undress, stripped of his logical regalia. There was, he thought, a homely Hegelian insight: the fact that things contaminate one another, thus becoming something other than themselves. The Hegelian Absolute was to be credited with another merit, namely, the sense which it gives its believers that "at bottom all is well with the cosmos," and which permits them to enjoy "moral holidays." But this merit was, he thought, more than offset by the problem of evil—which confronted Hegelianism in a most aggravated form. [14]

There are two connections between the metaphysics of *A Pluralistic Universe* and the *Pragmatism* which preceded it. First, the former is an application of the latter: the pragmatic method and standard of truth are repeatedly applied to the proof of pluralism and the disproof of monism. Second, the latter is an application of the former: that is, the pragmatic account of knowledge affords a special case of the pluralistic metaphysics. The Preface to the *Meaning of Truth* was written in August 1909, over a year after the delivery of the Hibbert Lectures. In that Preface James justified the assembling of his polemical articles on pragmatism by saying that he regarded the acceptance of the pragmatic

[12] W.J. to H.J.[2] April 29, 1908; *L.W.J.*, II, 303.

[13] Student's notes in Philos. 5, 1884-5, by R. W. Black.

[14] *P.U.*, 114, 116. *Cf.* the Preface to *M.T.* viii-x, where James withdraws this last concession to monism.

account of truth as removing an obstacle to that "radical empiricism" in which he was primarily interested. Pragmatism does not merely provide a method which can be employed in metaphysics—it provides a metaphysics of truth which is consistent with that general metaphysics which James advocates, through bringing the entire process of knowledge within the field of experience.

It will be recalled that in 1904, when James was summarizing his metaphysics, he spoke of it as composed of four doctrines: pluralism, radical empiricism, tychism, and theism. *A Pluralistic Universe* is primarily concerned with the first and second of these doctrines, though the fourth is reaffirmed. The third constitutes the most distinctive feature of the later work, *Some Problems of Philosophy,* on which James was engaged at the time of his death.

Pluralism is, as we know, almost coeval with James's philosophical maturity. Its personal roots lay in his love of variety and change; its moral roots in his unwillingness to compromise good with evil, or the individual with the universal; and its philosophical roots in his empiricism. Motives of the first sort led to his picturesque representations of a world which was unfenced, uncultivated, untidy, and unpredictable—a world which slipped through every ideal container, and resisted the impression of every logical mould. Motives of the second sort led in the direction of an ethical pluralism or monadism—a "republic of semi-detached consciousnesses," with a finite God whose limitations and external relations acquitted him of responsibility for evil. It was the third motive which dominated the *Pluralistic Universe.* In the world as it is given in experience, the connections among things are *de facto,* rather than necessary or constitutional. There is a "free play" of the parts of the world on one another; they "lean on" one another; exist *together,* but without loss of their identity. Things are real *severally,* in their "*each*-form," rather than as taken together, in their "*all*-form." Everything in the world has a real environment, that is, a relation to something which is genuinely other than itself, and which it is compelled to meet and take account of without any sort of antecedent complicity.[15]

Pluralism in this sense is indistinguishable from "radical empiricism," which thus forms the main theme of the book. Radical empiricism consists essentially in converting to the uses of metaphysics that "stream of consciousness" which was designed originally for psychology. Some alterations were necessary, and it was for a long time doubtful whether these were possible. The *Pluralistic Universe* announces that the doubt is dispelled. The result is to silence those qualms of his intellectual conscience which had hitherto prevented a step to

[15] *P.U.,* 34, 321-3, 358-9.

which his speculative passion had impelled him—the adoption, namely, of the Fechnerian[16] hierarchy of souls.

There were for James, as there were in fact, two Fechners. When James was writing the psychology, Fechner's *Psychophysik* was already a recognized classic in modern experimental psychology. From it James derived many suggestions bearing on imagination, attention, discrimination, and perception. But with the fundamental doctrine of the book he was in profound disagreement. Fechner was "a man of great learning and subtlety of mind," but as regards the great "psychophysical law" on which his fame as a psychologist mainly depended, it was a "patient whimsey" of "the dear old man," which had inspired a literature so dreadful that James refused even to admit it to a footnote.[17]

The second Fechner was the metaphysical Fechner, who conceived the universe as a series of overlapping souls from God down through the earth-soul to man, and from man to the psychic states that lie below the threshold of his consciousness. This daring speculation excited James's imagination, and at the same time satisfied two motives in his thought: he had always been tempted by the panpsychistic view of physical nature, and his religious thought had steadily moved towards the hypothesis of a superhuman consciousness. In 1907, he wrote to his friends in praise of Fechner's *Zend-Avesta,* "a wonderful book, by a wonderful genius," [18] and he devoted a whole chapter of *A Pluralistic Universe* to the sympathetic exposition of its doctrine.

But the old difficulty which had led James to reject associationism had its application here also. The field of consciousness is not a mere aggregate of separable parts, but a continuous stream. Each moment of consciousness is a unique whole. Fechner's metaphysics, on the other hand, was based throughout on a pyramiding of consciousness, a series of levels in which the unity of the higher was composed of the plurality of the lower.

In *A Pluralistic Universe* James describes his earlier rejection of "the compounding of consciousness," and the gradual changing of his mind. In his doctrine of "pure experience" James was definitely committed to the view that reality and the field of consciousness were one and the same. This implied that portions of the field could be common to two or more minds; that they could, in other words, be identical parts of different conscious wholes. It was clear that something had to break—either the new metaphysics of experience, or the old psychological scruples. This was the crisis which gave rise to the remarkable document to which reference has already been made, and which in

---

[16] G. T. Fechner, *cf.* above, 181.
[17] *Psychology,* I, 534-49.
[18] To Th. Flournoy, January 2, 1908; *L.W.J.,* II, 300.

the form of an intermittent diary extends from 1905 to 1908—from the moment of his definitive adoption of the position of radical empiricism, down to the writing of the Hibbert Lectures. It is to this difficulty, and apparently to this document, that James refers in *A Pluralistic Universe* when he says, "I struggled with the problem for years, covering hundreds of sheets of paper with notes and memoranda and discussions with myself over the difficulty." [19]

He found his solution, after his own characteristic manner, in a closer scrutiny of experience; and in the same insight which had been reported, as early as 1884, in the famous essay "On Some Omissions of Introspective Psychology." The several units of experience have both their difference and their sameness, and they may be conceived under either aspect. They are different, taken as wholes, but they overlap and interpenetrate. There is an "endosmosis of adjacent parts of living experience." [20] The world is a scene of perpetual transition, in which the parts, instead of merely succeeding, inherit one another and usher one another in. No event expires until after another has already begun, so that there is always a zone of commingled dawn and twilight through which the one leads over into another. But while each object is thus woven into the fabric of reality, its threads extend only for a limited distance, so that it is only indirectly connected with remoter regions.

Despite its title, *A Pluralistic Universe* is designed to emphasize *both* plurality and unity. If James wished to escape the practical implications of monism, he was not less anxious to escape the theoretic difficulties of atomism, monadism, dualism, or any view in which unity was excluded in advance. He sought a view which *permitted* unity—as much as theoretic demands might require, or as the facts might yield, or as the religious consciousness might crave. Hence while there is no "universal co-implication, or integration of all things *durcheinander*," there is unity of "the strung-along type, the type of continuity, contiguity, or concatenation." [21] The universe is not a block or an organism, but an all-navigable sea—a great neighborhood embracing lesser neighborhoods, in which accessibility is universal and intimacy proportional to propinquity.

This is the picture of concrete existence. There is another picture which James also knew well how to paint—the picture, namely, of a *selected* world, "dipped out from the stream of time." [22] This motive of selection is one of the aboriginal motives in James's thought. It dominated his conception of mind, his interpretation of concepts, and his pragmatic theory of discursive knowledge. That it should have been subordinated in this last of James's systematic works provides conclusive evidence that metaphysics was his central philo-

---

[19] *P.U.*, 207-8. See above, 279.
[20] *Mind*, IX (1884).
[21] *P.U.*, 325.
[22] *Ibid.*, 235.

sophical interest, and that empiricism was his central philosophical conviction—
a new empiricism in which philosophy shall depict or suggest reality in terms
as close as possible to the sensible flux of unreconstructed experience.

Another element of James's philosophy which was largely ignored in this
work is his realism. There is no reason to suppose that he had abandoned a
creed so frequently reaffirmed, and so vigorously defended against the critics
of pragmatism at the very time when he was writing *A Pluralistic Universe*.
But in the absence of any reëxamination of the question, James's position remained uncertain on a metaphysical point of first importance. Must reality be
perceived, sensed, or felt in order to be? Rejecting a solipsistic or even humanistic limitation of existence, James represented it as stretching off beyond the
horizon of human consciousness—accessible, but out of range. In what, then,
consists this ulterior existence? In rejecting the Absolute, James had eliminated
one alternative—the alternative, namely, that all existence is housed within the
experience of a universal mind expressly provided for the purpose. There remain three alternatives. Residual existence may consist in the *possibility* of experience, a view which is hard to reconcile with James's frequent admission
that a possibility must always be construed in terms of actuality. Or, residual
existence may consist in experience of infra-human minds, everything which is
not for man or some higher subject being conceived as "for itself." This is panpsychism, which James was repeatedly on the verge of accepting, which he constantly praised, but to which he never gave his explicit and unreserved assent.
There remains only one last alternative, which is to distinguish *experience*
from the *experienced*. Existence would then coincide with the *content* of experience, but would be independent of any *act* of experiencing on the part of
mind. This alternative would be the most consistent with James's theory that
mind is a peculiar type of relationship among terms which in themselves are
neither physical nor mental.[23] *A Pluralistic Universe* does not clearly affirm
this alternative, and even compromises it through identifying the continuum
of experience with consciousnesses great and small.

It is in *A Pluralistic Universe* that James speaks most explicitly of the union
between empiricism and religion as inaugurating a new era both for religion
and for philosophy. The virtue for religion of this union lies in its providing
for an intimacy between man and God that does not prejudice either the freedom of man or the innocence of God. It may be described as a pluralistic pantheism: pluralistic because, as James had already expressed it in an earlier work,
"God . . . is no absolute all-experiencer, but simply the experiencer of widest
actual conscious span," having like other finite beings an external environment

---

[23] This is the view, sometimes referred to as "neutralism," which has been explicitly developed
by those later realists who have taken James's "Does Consciousness Exist?" as their point of departure.

for which he is not responsible;[24] pantheism because God is, so far as his limits extend, "the intimate soul and reason of the universe," in whose life man participates directly through the mystical state. When that state occurs, a certain character of isolation which formerly distinguished man's consciousness disappears, leaving that *co*-consciousness which was formerly only God's, but is now shared by man.[25]

In the concluding pages of *A Pluralistic Universe,* James related his final metaphysics to the earlier versions of his philosophy. Its doctrine is the hypothesis of "radical empiricism," defended against "intellectualistic" objections, and verified by experience. But its verification is not conclusive enough to exclude the rival hypothesis of monism. It is to James himself "the most probable hypothesis," but he does not expect that his opponents will recognize this probability as coercive. What he really hopes to obtain, especially on the part of younger thinkers, is a receptivity to the pluralistic alternative, and, in the inevitable exercise of their "will to believe," a pragmatist attention to concrete experiences and the *"particulars of life."*

James felt confident of the success of his latest book, and his expectations were promptly verified. Soon after its appearance he wrote to Flournoy:

> It is already evident from the letters I am getting about the *Pluralistic Universe* that the book will 1st, be *read;* 2nd, be *rejected* almost unanimously at first, and for very diverse reasons; but, 3rd, will continue to be bought and referred to, and will end by strongly influencing English philosophy.[26]

Among the first to applaud this latest work was his ever faithful brother Henry.

The sympathy and affection which had bound William and Henry from boyhood continued throughout their lives despite growing preoccupation and prolonged physical separation. But William's comments on Henry's writings had at length culminated in an undisguised difference of opinion. Henry had never been seriously deflected from his course by William's criticisms; quietly, modestly, but steadfastly, he had gone his own way. At last he spoke out, in a refusal which was no less firm for being colored by a lifelong and ineradicable habit of subordination.

William wrote, on October 22, 1905:

> I read your *Golden Bowl* a month or more ago, and it put me, as most of your recenter long stories have put me, in a very puzzled state of mind. . . . The method of narration by interminable elaboration of suggestive reference . . .

[24] *M.T.,* 125; *P.U.,* 310-11.
[25] Cf. *P.U.,* 28-31, 299, 309, etc.; *V.R.E.,* 388, and *Mind,* VII (1882), 206; *M.S.,* 201-6; *C.E.R.,* 489-90.
[26] June 18, 1909; *L.W.J.,* II, 324.

goes agin the grain of all my own impulses in writing; and yet in spite of it all, there is a brilliancy and cleanness of effect, and in this book especially a high-toned social atmosphere that are unique and extraordinary. Your methods and my ideals seem the reverse, the one of the other—and yet I have to admit your extreme success in this book. But why won't you, just to please Brother, sit down and write a new book, with no twilight or mustiness in the plot, with great vigor and decisiveness in the action, no fencing in the dialogue, no psychological commentaries, and absolute straightness in the style? Publish it in my name, I will acknowledge it, and give you half the proceeds. Seriously, I wish you *would,* for you *can;* and I should think it would tempt you, to embark on a "fourth manner."

To which Henry replied:[27]

I mean (in response to what you write me of your having read the *Golden Bowl*) to try to produce some uncanny form of thing, in fiction, that will gratify you, as Brother—but let me say, dear William, that I shall greatly be humiliated if you *do* like it, and thereby lump it, in your affection, with things, of the current age, that I have heard you express admiration for and that I would sooner descend to a dishonoured grave than have written. Still I *will* write you your book, on that two-and-two-make-four system on which all the awful truck that surrounds us is produced, and *then* descend to my dishonoured grave—taking up the art of the slate pencil instead of, longer, the art of the brush. . . . But it is, seriously, too late at night, and I am too tired, for me to express myself on this question—beyond saying that I'm always sorry when I hear of your reading anything of mine, and always hope you won't—you seem to me so constitutionally unable to "enjoy" it, and so condemned to look at it from a point of view remotely alien to mine in writing it, and to the conditions out of which, *as* mine, it has inevitably sprung—so that all the intentions that have been its main reason for being (with *me*) appear never to have reached you at all—and you appear even to assume that the life, the elements forming its subject-matter, deviate from felicity in not having an impossible analogy with the life of Cambridge. I see nowhere about me done or dreamed of the things that alone for me constitute the *interest* of the doing of the novel—and yet it is in a sacrifice of them on their very own ground that the thing you suggest to me evidently consists. It shows how far apart and to what different ends we have had to work out (very naturally and properly!) our respective intellectual lives. And yet I can read *you* with rapture—having three weeks ago spent three or four days with Manton Marble[28] at Brighton and found in his hands ever so many of your recent papers and discourses, which having margin of mornings in my room, through both breakfasting and lunching there (by the habit of the house), I found time to read several of—with the effect of asking you, earnestly, to address me some of those that I so often, in Irving St., saw you address to others who were not your brother. I had no time to read them there. Philosophically, in short, I am "with" you, almost completely.

[27] November 23, 1905; *L.H.J.*[2], II, 43-4.
[28] Manton Marble of Brighton, England, writer on politics and history.

There is no evidence that Henry James had enjoyed either the mood or the leisure to imbibe his brother's *Psychology,* or that he had been especially interested in the *Will to Believe,* when that volume appeared in 1897. In July 1902, he was "reading *Varieties of Religious Experience* with rapturous deliberation," [29] but he did not comment on it. It was not until the publication of *Pragmatism* in 1907 that he was sufficiently interested in the content of his brother's thought to expound his own. Then, on October 17, he announced his adhesion, as follows:

> Why the devil I didn't write to you after reading your *Pragmatism*—how I kept from it—I can't now explain save by the very fact of the spell itself (of interest and enthralment) that the book cast upon me; I simply sank down, under it, into such depths of submission and assimilation that *any* reaction, very nearly, even that of acknowledgment, would have had almost the taint of dissent or escape. Then I was lost in the wonder of the extent to which all my life I have (like M. Jourdain) unconsciously pragmatised. You are immensely and universally *right.* . . . I feel the reading of the book, at all events, to have been really the event of my summer.[30]

William's later writings evoked similar expressions of discipleship. When Henry received a copy of *A Pluralistic Universe,* he wrote on July 18, 1909:

> I read it, while in town, with a more thrilled interest than I can say; with enchantment, with pride, and almost with comprehension. It may sustain and inspire you a little to know that I'm *with* you, all along the line—and can conceive of no sense in any philosophy that is not yours! As an artist and a "creator" I can catch on, hold on, to pragmatism and can work in the light of it and apply it; finding, in comparison, everything else (so far as I know the same!) utterly irrelevant and useless—vainly and coldly parallel!

The final response was evoked by the publication of *The Meaning of Truth* in the autumn of 1909:

> I broke this off last night and went to bed—and now add a few remarks after a grey soft windless and miraculously rainless day . . . which has had rather a sad hole made in it by a visitation from a young person from New York . . . [who] stole from me the hour or two before my small evening feed in which I hoped to finish *The Meaning of Truth;* but I have done much toward this since that repast, and with a renewed eagerness of inglutition. You surely make philosophy more interesting and living than anyone has ever made it before, and by a real creative and undemolishable making; whereby all you write plays into *my* poor "creative" consciousness and artistic vision and pretension with the most extraordinary suggestiveness and force of application and inspiration.

Thank the powers—that is, thank *yours!*—for a relevant and assimilable and referable philosophy, which is related to the rest of one's intellectual life otherwise and more conveniently than a fowl is related to a fish. In short, dearest William, the effect of these collected papers of your present volume—which I had read all individually before—seems to me exquisitely and adorably cumulative and, so to speak, consecrating; so that I, for my part, feel Pragmatic invulnerability constituted.[31]

It is evident from these letters that Henry let William do his philosophizing for him. I can only conclude, as might have been supposed, that his mind was quite naïve on that side, and that his profession of agreement was an extension of that admiring pride with which he had from childhood viewed all of William's superior attainments. The relation was not symmetrical. As to Henry's work, William freely offered both advice and criticism; while as to William's, Henry could offer only an undiscriminating praise. Science offered them no common ground. This they could find in literature and art, in their experience of life and of the world about them, and, above all, in a deeply rooted familial devotion that grew stronger with the years.

[31] H.J.[2] to W.J., November 1, 1909; *L.H.J.*[2], II, 141.

XXXVI

JAMES AND BERGSON

Without doubt the most important philosophical and personal attachment of James's later years was that which he formed with Henri Bergson. A French report of the Fifth International Congress of Psychology, held at Rome in 1905, and at which James had read his paper on "La Notion de conscience," contains the following statement:

> No one is unaware—he has himself continually proclaimed it—of what our eminent philosopher, our master-analyst, M. Bergson, owed at the beginning of his career to the works of Americans. . . . If we have borrowed a psychology from America, we have given them back a philosophy,—for it was impossible to see in the paper of William James anything other than the Bergsonian doctrine of the primacy of action.[1]

This statement evoked from Bergson the following prompt and conclusive reply:

> I come to the reference to William James, a philosopher my love and admiration for whom I can never adequately express. His *Principles of Psychology* appeared in 1891. My essay[2] . . . was worked out and written between 1883 and 1887, and published in 1889. At that time I knew nothing of James except his fine studies of effort and emotion. (I was not acquainted with the article which appeared in *Mind* in January, 1884, which already contained a part of the chapter on the "stream of thought.")[3] In other words the theories of the *Essai* could not have been drawn from James's psychology. I hasten to add that the conception of the *durée réelle* developed in my *Essai*, coincides on many points with James's description of the "stream of thought." . . . But if one examines the texts one will easily see that the description of the "stream of thought" and the theory of the *"durée réelle"* have not the same significance and cannot spring from the same source. The first is clearly psychological in source and signification. The second consists essentially in a critique of the idea of *homogeneous time*, as one finds it among philosophers and mathematicians. Now, although I am not qualified to speak for William James, I believe I can

[1] Translated from *Revue philos.*, LX (1905), 84; Bergson's reply is from *op. cit.*, 229-30.
[2] *Essai sur les données immédiates de la conscience*, Bergson's first important work.
[3] "Some Omissions of Introspective Psychology," *Mind*, IX (1884). The "studies of effort and emotion" were "The Feeling of Effort," 1880, and "What Is an Emotion?" 1884. The former had appeared also in French in the *Critique philos.*

say that the "Bergsonian" influence counts for nothing in the development of his philosophy. . . . I believe that I ought to insist on these two points because the article . . . presents as an accidental and local fact . . . a movement of ideas which has for some years been in evidence everywhere and which arises from causes that are general and profound. In every country, and with many thinkers, the need has been felt for a philosophy more genuinely empirical, closer to the immediately given, than the traditional philosophy, worked out, as the latter has been, by thinkers who were primarily mathematicians.

This statement should be accepted as disposing permanently of the question of priority. Neither philosopher ever made any claims of priority; each rejoiced to find the other in possession of the truth, and was almost extravagantly appreciative of the other's merit. The similarity of their doctrine is not complete or extraordinary—and does not disparage the originality of either.

There is every reason why James and Bergson should have been attracted to one another. They were both men of profound humanity. They both possessed a degree of artistic sensibility unusual among philosophers, and were distinguished masters of prose style. Their styles are very different, it is true. James uses broader strokes, is more colloquial, humorous, and emphatic; while Bergson's style is chaste, impersonal, restrained. James has something of the quality of a pamphleteer. After the *Psychology,* all of his works were either lectures or special articles, written with a view to their immediate effect upon an audience or a philosophical opponent. He was eager to be understood immediately, and was always willing to speak the language of his auditor in order to obtain a hearing. Bergson, on the other hand, composed systematic works, perfected according to their own inner requirements, and expecting like monuments to be approached and studied in their own terms. Even so, both writers are rich in metaphors and imagery, and in their power of intuitive suggestion. According to their common creed reality cannot be analyzed or described, but only *conveyed,* and they both possessed a very unusual capacity to convey it.

In their philosophical doctrines, also, there are many differences. Their systems, being developed quite independently, met, exchanged salutations and gifts, and then proceeded on their way. In no sense did they *coincide,* either as systems or in their particular theorems. It is true that James professed his conversion to Bergsonism, but this was James's way of expressing his moods of personal discovery and agreement. He had in the same sense been converted by Renouvier, Hodgson, Fechner, and almost converted by half a dozen others, but it is clear that the term of discipleship would scarcely apply to any of these relations. His profound sociability led him to look for a personal embodiment of his ideas, whom he could love and admire; and he liked to expound his ideas by quoting with enthusiastic approval the words of others.

Furthermore, James's Bergsonism was of the spirit and not the letter, so that to enumerate their differences of detail would be to traverse their entire philosophies. Suffice it to mention certain major topics. Bergson took as his point of departure the logico-mathematical way of thinking, which, in neglecting *real time,* missed, he believed, the very essence of things. James began with British empiricism, which, in neglecting *felt relations,* also missed the essence of things. In other words, while for Bergson the crucial truth was temporal passage, for James time was only one of many cases of that transitiveness or continuity which was *his* crucial truth. Both thinkers found the key to metaphysics in a certain aspect of conscious experience, namely, its continuity. James saw in this continuity a way of coping with the hereditary difficulties of empiricism —such as dualism, and the problem of the one and the many. Bergson, on the other hand, used it first as a means of correcting the abstract timelessness of the intellectualistic view, whether in physics or in metaphysics.

Both philosophers attached importance to biological evolution, but with differences. Bergson was more biological than James, and there would be a certain point in saying that James developed a biological psychology while Bergson developed a psychological biology. Furthermore, James's biology was profoundly Darwinian—stressing accidental origins, variations, adaptation, and survival; while Bergson's biology had more affinities with Lamarck, and emphasized the dynamic and creative character of the vital impulse. Finally, the general pattern of the evolutionary process tends to be for Bergson divergent and for James convergent. James's unity is in the making—lies ahead as a goal of achievement; while for Bergson there is always a sense of the *aboriginal* unity, as well as of the qualitative sameness, of the stream of life.

For both philosophers, on the other hand, reality is immediately given in experience—*is* experience, when that term is properly construed. Both find that thinking, since it distinguishes, specifies, and arrests, is alien to the genius of existence, which is interpenetrative and flowing. Both men have the same sense of the *copiousness* of reality, and of the pathetic thinness of the concepts with which the human mind endeavors to represent it. They measure the inadequacy of thought by the standard of intuition. The reality which is felt or intuited is a temporal, changing continuum from which the mind, governed by its practical interests, selects what is relevant. By a change of attitude from thought to feeling, from action to insight, from periphery to centre—or whenever one *yields* oneself to things instead of making demands upon them— one becomes aware of the plenum of being in which the part is immersed. Whenever either Bergson or James adopts this mode of philosophizing he becomes the perfect exponent of the other. Bergson found himself in James's *Pluralistic Universe;* James, if he had lived to read them, would have rejoiced at the clarity and understanding with which his likeness was portrayed in

Bergson's introductions to the French translations of *Pragmatism* and the *Letters*.

A reference in the *Psychology* indicates that James read Bergson's *Données immédiates de la conscience* immediately after its publication in 1889. It appears, however, to have made little or no impression on him. When Bergson's *Matière et mémoire* appeared in 1896 he sent an inscribed copy to James, and although it was promptly read it struck no sparks. Then, in 1902, James reread both books with kindling admiration. "Nothing that I have read in years," he wrote on January 27, 1903, to Flournoy,

> has so excited and stimulated my thought. Four years ago I couldn't understand him at all, though I felt his power. I am sure that that philosophy has a great future. It breaks through old *cadres* and brings things into a solution from which new crystals can be got.

In the spring of 1907 he received and read Bergson's *L'Évolution créatrice*. The effect was immediately made known to his friends. Thus to Strong on June 13: "Have you read Bergson's *Évolution créatrice*? It seems to me the absolutely *divinest* book on philosophy ever written up to this date. I can assimilate it as yet only in part; but he has killed the beast Intellectualism dead!"

The two men met for the first time in 1905, when James was sixty-three and Bergson forty-six. This difference of age seems to have made little difference, either in their enjoyment of one another or in the mingled affection and respect which both of them felt. The date of this first meeting was only five years before James's death, and during the latter's subsequent visits to Europe he was constantly hampered by declining health. Had he been spared, there is every reason to believe that there would have been a growing intimacy, both personal and philosophical.

The correspondence opens with a letter from James that appears to have been prompted by his rereading of Bergson's first two books:—

Cambridge, Dec. 14, 1902[4]

> My dear Sir,—
>
> I read the copy of your *Matière et mémoire* which you so kindly sent me, immediately on receiving it, four years ago or more. I saw its great originality, but found your ideas so new and vast that I could not be sure that I fully understood them, although the *style*, Heaven knows, was lucid enough. So I laid the book aside for a second reading, which I have just accomplished. . . .
>
> It is a work of exquisite genius. It makes a sort of Copernican revolution as much as Berkeley's *Principles* or Kant's *Critique* did, and will probably, as it gets better and better known, open a new era of philosophical discussion. It

[4] Reprinted from *L.W.J.*, II, 178-80.

fills *my* mind with all sorts of new questions and hypotheses and brings the old into a most agreeable liquefaction. I thank you from the bottom of my heart. The *Hauptpunkt* acquired for me is your conclusive demolition of the dualism of object and subject in perception. I believe that the "transcendency" of the object will not recover from your treatment, and as I myself have been working for many years past on the same line, only with other general conceptions than yours, I find myself most agreeably corroborated. My health is so poor now that work goes on very slowly; but I am going, if I live, to write a general system of metaphysics which, in many of its fundamental ideas, agrees closely with what you have set forth, and the agreement inspires and encourages me more than you can well imagine. . . . How good it is sometimes simply to *break away* from all old categories, deny old worn-out beliefs, and restate things *ab initio,* making the lines of division fall into entirely new places!

I send you a little popular lecture of mine on immortality,—no positive theory but merely an *argumentum ad hominem* for the ordinary cerebralistic objection,—in which it may amuse you to see a formulation like your own that the brain is an organ of *filtration* for spiritual life. I also send you my last book, the *Varieties of Religious Experience,* which may sometime beguile an hour. Believe, dear Professor Bergson, the high admiration and regard with which I remain, always sincerely yours,

Wm. James

Paris, Jan. 6, 1903 [5]

My dear confrère,—

I have just completed the reading of the book which you were kind enough to send me,—*The Varieties of Religious Experience,* and I am anxious to tell you what a profound impression the reading of it has made on me. I began it at least a dozen days ago, and since that moment I have been able to think of nothing else, so captivating and—if you will permit me to say it—so moving, is the book from beginning to end. You have, it seems to me, succeeded in extracting the quintessence of the religious emotion. No doubt we already felt that this emotion is both a joy *sui generis* and the consciousness of a union with a superior power; but it was the nature of this joy and of this union which appeared to be capable neither of analysis nor of expression, and which nevertheless you have been able to analyze and express. . . .

If you have had occasion during the last ten or twelve years to talk with French students visiting Cambridge, they must have told you that I have been one of your admirers from the beginning, and that I have lost no opportunity of expressing to my hearers my great sympathy for your ideas. When I wrote my essay on *Les Données de la conscience* . . . I had been led, by an analysis of the idea of time and by reflection on the rôle of that idea in mechanics, to a certain conception of the psychological life which is entirely consistent with that of your *Psychology.* . . . You will therefore understand that no approval could be to me more precious than that which you are kind enough to give to the conclusions of my book *Matière et mémoire.* Here I have sought—without thereby sacrificing the results of cerebral physiology—to show that the relation of consciousness to cerebral activity is quite different from what the physiologists and

---

[5] The letters from Bergson have been translated by the author.

philosophers suppose: and I see that on this point, also, we follow two very close and probably convergent routes. That, at least, is the impression left upon me by the reading of the very interesting lecture on *Human Immortality* that you were good enough to send me. The more I think about the question, the more I am convinced that life is from one end to the other a phenomenon of attention. The brain is that which directs this attention; it marks, delimits and measures the *psychological contraction* which is necessary for action; in short, it is neither the duplicate nor the instrument of conscious life, but its most advanced point, the part which inserts itself in events,—something like the prow in which the ship is narrowed to cleave the ocean. . . . I wish most eagerly that I might have an opportunity of discussing all this with you. May I ask you, in case you come to France, to be good enough to send me word in advance so that we can arrange a *rendez-vous?* I beg you, my dear confrère, etc.,

H. BERGSON

The following exchange of letters illustrates the cross-fertilization of two philosophies sharing the same fundamental bias:

Cambridge, Feb. 25, 1903[6]

Dear Professor Bergson,—

. . . I am convinced that a philosophy of *pure experience,* such as I conceive yours to be, can be made to work, and will reconcile many of the old inveterate oppositions of the schools. I think that your radical denial . . . of the notion that the brain can be in any way the [maker] of consciousness, has introduced a very sudden clearness, and eliminated a part of the idealistic paradox. But your unconscious or subconscious permanence of memories is in its turn a notion that offers difficulties, seeming in fact to be the equivalent of the "soul" in another shape, and the manner in which these memories "insert" themselves into the brain action, and in fact the whole conception of the difference between the outer and inner worlds in your philosophy, still need to me a great deal of elucidation. But behold me challenging you to answer me *par écrit!* . . . How exquisitely you do *write!* Believe me . . . yours most sincerely,

WM. JAMES

Paris, March 25, 1903

My dear confrère,—

. . . The difficulties which you call to my attention in certain parts of *Matière et mémoire* are only too real, and I am far from having succeeded in completely surmounting them. But I believe, nevertheless, that among these difficulties some are the effects of inveterate habits of our mind. . . . Such, for example, is the difficulty of admitting present unconscious memories. If we reduce memories to the category of things, it is clear that there is no mean for them between presence and absence: either they are unqualifiedly present to our mind, and in this sense conscious; or, if they are unconscious, they are absent from our mind and should no longer be considered as present psychological realities. But in the world of psychological realities I do not believe that there is occasion for presenting the alternative "to be or not to be" so exclusively. The more I try to grasp myself by consciousness the more do I perceive myself as the totalization . . . of my own past, this past being contracted with a view to action. "The unity of the self" of which philosophers speak, appears to me as the unity of an apex of a summit to which I narrow myself by an effort of attention—an effort which is prolonged during the whole of life, and which, as it seems to me, is the very essence of life. But to pass from this apex of consciousness or·from this summit, to the base, that is to say, to a state in which all the memories of all the moments of the past would be scattered and distinct, I realize that one would have to pass from the normal state of concentration to a state of dispersion like that of certain dreams; there would, therefore, be nothing positive to be done, but simply something to be undone—nothing to gain, nothing to add, but rather something to lose: it is in this sense that all my memories are there when I do not perceive them, and that nothing really new is produced when they reappear in consciousness.

The résumé[7] which you kindly sent me of the course which you are now conducting interested me profoundly. It contains so many new and original views that I do not yet sufficiently succeed in grasping the ensemble, but one dominant idea stands out so far: the necessity, namely, of transcending concepts, or mere logic, or the procedure, in short, of that over-systematic philosophy which postulates the unity of everything. The path which I am myself following is analogous to this, and I am quite convinced that if a really *positive* philosophy is possible, it can only be found there. . . . How much I regret that I cannot have the talk with you for which I had hoped. But you will not fail to come to France or England one of these days, and in that case I could always arrange to meet you, at any time and place, provided you give me notice a little in advance. I beg you, etc.,

H. BERGSON

In April 1905, as we know, James sailed for a "holiday" in Europe. After visiting Athens, and attending the Congress of Psychology in Rome, he went north through Switzerland and France and sailed back to America in June:—

Cannes, May 13, 1905

Dear Professor Bergson,—

I am staying at the Hôtel du Parc here . . . and expecting to spend a week in Paris, probably from the 25th of May to the 1st of June. . . . I have to confess that, although I am cerebrally in a rather good-for-nothing condition, *one* of the things that makes me choose my way home via Paris rather than straight from the Mediterranean, is the possibility that, once in Paris, I may see you face to face, and perhaps gain a little better understanding of some of the points in your philosophy that are still to me obscure. This is rather a formidable sounding announcement, as you are a modest man. But pray don't take alarm at it,—my intentions are most innocent, and my curiosities will probably seem to you very superficial. The gist of the matter is that I think it must be always good for two philosophers who are *near* each other to come into personal contact. They

---

[7] The "Syllabus in Philosophy 3"; *cf.* above, 275 *ff.*

will understand each other better, even if they should only gossip away their hour. I hope then that you are to be in Paris at the time when I shall be there, and that you will have time and disposition to give me an hour or two. I shall go to the Hôtel des Saints Pères, in the street of the same name. . . . I have a number of different things to do in Paris, and if my date with you is fixed first, everything else can be regulated with reference to that. Hoping that this will find you at home and in good health and not *unsociable!*—I am, with highest esteem and regard, yours truly,

WM. JAMES

The first conjunction of these two luminaries took place on May 28, 1905. There is no contemporary record of it save the entry in James's diary for that date: "Visit from Beautiful Bergson." Twenty years later Bergson himself recalled the occasion. He was speaking of James's preoccupation with the things of the spirit: "I believe that we did indeed, say '*Bonjour,*' but that was all; there were several instants of silence, and straightway he asked me how I envisaged the problem of religion." [8]

The spring of 1907 brought the publication of Bergson's *L'Évolution créatrice,* and James's characteristic postal-card acknowledgment:—

Cambridge, May 19, 1907

Your new book is just arrived—hurrah! hurrah! hurrah! and thanks. You will receive my little book on *Pragmatism* in a couple of weeks.

WM. JAMES

After reading the book James wrote more fully:—

Chocorua, June 13, 1907 [9]

O my Bergson, you are a magician, and your book is a marvel, a real wonder in the history of philosophy, making, if I mistake not, an entirely new era in respect of matter, but unlike the works of genius of the "transcendentalist" movement (which are so obscurely and abominably and inaccessibly written), a pure classic in point of form. You may be amused at the comparison, but in finishing it I found the same after-taste remaining as after finishing *Madame Bovary,* such a flavor of persistent *euphony,* as of a rich river that never foamed or ran thin, but steadily and firmly proceeded with its banks full to the brim. Then the aptness of your illustrations, that never scratch or stand out at right angles, but invariably simplify the thought and help to pour it along! Oh, indeed you are a magician! And if your next book proves to be as great an advance on this one as this is on its two predecessors, your name will surely go down as one of the great creative names in philosophy.

There! have I praised you enough? What every genuine philosopher (every genuine man, in fact) craves most is *praise*—although the philosophers generally call it "recognition"! If you want still more praise, let me know, and I

---

[8] Translated from Bergson's Preface to the French translation of James's *Letters,* by F. Delattre and M. Le Breton, 1924, 9.

[9] Reprinted from *L.W.J.,* II, 290-4.

will send it, for my features have been on a broad smile from the first page to the last, at the chain of felicities that never stopped. I feel rejuvenated.

As to the content of it, I am not in a mood at present to make any definite reaction. There is so much that is absolutely new that it will take a long time for your contemporaries to assimilate it, and I imagine that much of the development of detail will have to be performed by younger men whom your ideas will stimulate to coruscate in manners unexpected by yourself. To me at present the vital achievement of the book is that it inflicts an irrecoverable death-wound upon Intellectualism. It can never resuscitate! But it will die hard, for all the inertia of the past is in it, and the spirit of professionalism and pedantry as well as the æsthetic-intellectual delight of dealing with categories logically distinct yet logically connected, will rally for a desperate defense. The *élan vital,* all contentless and vague as you are obliged to leave it, will be an easy substitute to make fun of. But the beast *has* its death-wound now, and the manner in which you have inflicted it . . . is masterly in the extreme. . . . You will be receiving my own little "pragmatism" book simultaneously with this letter. How jejune and inconsiderable it seems in comparison with your great system! But it is so congruent with parts of your system, fits so well into interstices thereof, that you will easily understand why I am so enthusiastic. I feel that at bottom we are fighting the same fight, you a commander, I in the ranks. . . . Altogether your reality lurks so in the background, in this book, that I am wondering whether you *couldn't* give it any more development *in concreto* here, or whether you perhaps were holding back developments, already in your possession, for a future volume. They are sure to come to you later anyhow, and to make a new volume; and altogether, the clash of these ideas of yours with the traditional ones will be sure to make sparks fly that will illuminate all sorts of dark places and bring innumerable new considerations into view. But the process may be slow, for the ideas are so revolutionary. . . . I can see that, when the tide turns in your favor, many previous tendencies in philosophy will start up, crying "This is nothing but what *we* have contended for all along." Schopenhauer's blind will, Hartmann's unconscious, Fichte's aboriginal freedom . . . will all be claimants for priority. But no matter—all the better if you are in some ancient lines of tendency. Mysticism also must make claims and doubtless just ones. I say nothing more now—this is just my first reaction; but I am so enthusiastic as to have said only two days ago, "I thank heaven that I have lived to this date—that I have witnessed the Russo-Japanese war, and seen Bergson's new book appear—the two great modern turning-points of history and of thought!" Best congratulations and cordialest regards!

WM. JAMES

Paris, June 27, 1907

Dear Professor James,—

Your letter gave me great happiness, and I must thank you for it at once. You are right in saying that the philosopher likes praise, and that in this he resembles the general run of mortals; but allow me to say that the support for which I was especially eager, was that of the thinker who has so powerfully contributed to the refashioning of the soul of the new generations, and whose work has always excited in me such profound admiration. And the letter in which you declare yourself ready to adopt the essential ideas of my work, in which you defend them in advance against the attacks which they are sure to provoke, touches me above all. I keep it by me, as a sufficient recompense for the ten years of effort which this book has cost me.

I began to read your *Pragmatism* the very moment the post placed it in my hands, and I could not put it away until I had finished reading it. It is the program, admirably traced, of the philosophy of the future. By very diverse lines of consideration, which you have always been able to make converge to the same focal point, by suggestions as well as by explicit reasons, you convey the idea, above all the feeling, of that supple and flexible philosophy which is destined to take the place of intellectualism. . . . When you say that "for rationalism reality is ready-made and complete from all eternity, while for pragmatism it is still in the making," [10] you provide the very formula for the metaphysics to which I am convinced we shall come, to which we should have come long ago if we had not remained under the spell of Platonic idealism. . . . Believe me, I beg you, etc.,

H. BERGSON

When, in May, 1908, James arrived in Oxford to give his Hibbert Lectures he wrote at once to Bergson. One of the lectures was to be on "Bergson and His Critique of Intellectualism," and he asked for biographical data, including "any remarkable adventures, romantic or heroic, as well as philosophic, in which you have taken part (!) etc., etc. Details help interest!"

Bergson replied on the following day:

Paris, May 9, 1908

Dear Professor James,—

I cannot tell you how much pleasure I felt when, last evening, I recognized your handwriting on an envelope bearing an English stamp. Here at last, I hope, is an opportunity of talking with you. . . . You do me great honor in devoting one of your Oxford lectures to me. How happy I should have been could I have heard you, both in this and in the other lectures. At any rate I hope that you will not delay bringing them together in a volume. . . .

Now as to events worthy of note, there have been none in the course of my career,—at least nothing *objectively* remarkable. On the subjective side, however, I cannot but attribute great importance to the change which took place in my way of thinking during the two years which followed my leaving the École Normale, from 1881 to 1883. I had remained up to that time wholly imbued with mechanistic theories, to which I had been led at an early date by the reading of Herbert Spencer, a philosopher to whom I adhered almost unreservedly. It was my intention to devote myself to what was then called the philosophy of the sciences, and to that end I had undertaken, after leaving the École Normale, to examine some of the fundamental scientific notions. It was the analysis of the notion of time, as that enters into mechanics and physics, which overturned all my ideas. I saw, to my great astonishment, that scientific time does not *endure,* that it would involve no change in our scientific knowledge if the totality of the

[10] *Pragm.,* 257.

real were unfolded all at once, instantaneously, and that positive science consists essentially in the elimination of duration. This was the point of departure of a series of reflections which brought me, by gradual steps, to reject almost all of what I had hitherto accepted and to change my point of view completely. . . .

Of all this, and much more besides concerning your last work on Pragmatism, I hope soon to be able to talk with you. Meanwhile, dear Professor James, I send you my affectionate and faithful regards,

                                                              H. BERGSON

In July James sent Bergson the proof of the lecture devoted to the latter's philosophy, which Bergson acknowledged as follows:

                                   Chaumont-sur-Neuchâtel, July 23, 1908

Dear Professor James,—

I must tell you at once the great joy which it has given me to read you. Never have I been in this way fathomed, understood, penetrated. Never have I been so aware of the sympathy and of the sort of "preëstablished harmony" which brings your thought and mine into accord. Let me add that you have not confined yourself to analyzing my ideas; you have transfigured them, without ever in any way disfiguring them. I kept thinking, while reading your exposition of my theses, of those superb reproductions which the masters of engraving have derived from pictures which in themselves were sometimes quite ordinary. . . . I believe that I perceive the essential idea of your book,—an idea important above all others, which will dissipate the difficulties which have been accumulated by philosophers around the question of the relation of the parts of experience to experience as a whole. I hope soon to be able to read the whole of this book, which will form the connecting link between the *Principles of Psychology* and the *Varieties of Religious Experience,* and at the same time give definite shape to the philosophy to which pragmatism seems to point,—a philosophy destined, beyond any doubt, to supersede the old metaphysical dogmatism. . . . Believe me, dear Professor James, etc.,

                                                              H. BERGSON

Meanwhile James and Bergson had been trying to see one another, but owing to the accidents of health and travel the meeting did not take place until October 4, in London, two days before James sailed for home. A record of this interview is contained in a letter of James to Flournoy of the same date. Speaking of the various philosophers whom he had been seeing in Oxford and London, he said:

The best of all these meetings has been one of three hours this very morning with Bergson, who is here visiting his relatives. So modest and unpretending a man, but such a genius intellectually! We talked very easily together, or rather *he* talked easily, for he talked much more than I did; and although I can't say that I follow the folds of his system much more clearly than I did before, he has made some points much plainer. I have the strongest suspicions that the tendency which he has brought to a focus will end by prevailing, and that the present epoch will be a sort of turning-point in the history of philosophy. So many things converge towards an anti-rationalistic crystallization. *Qui vivre verra!* [11]

In the spring of 1909 Bergson received a copy of *A Pluralistic Universe,* and read it with his characteristic enthusiasm and sense of agreement:

Paris, April 30, 1909

Dear William James,—

I awaited your new book with impatience, and I thank you for sending it to me. It is an admirable book, which I shall reproach only for being far too modest and for putting forward the names of Fechner and Bergson, when it is with William James—with the word, the thought and the very soul of William James—that we have to do. The book says many things, but it suggests still more than it says. It defines and justifies pluralism, it enables us to place the finger on the concrete relation of beings one with another, it definitely lays the foundations of "radical empiricism"; this is what it *says*. But it suggests something beyond that,—a certain consoling emotion drawn from the very heart of reality. You speak, in your conclusion, of those "saving experiences" which some souls have been privileged to enjoy; unless I deceive myself, your book, combined with the *Varieties of Religious Experience,* will generalize experiences of this sort, introducing them among those who had no idea of them, or developing them where they exist only in a nascent state. That is where the religion of tomorrow is to be found, and the philosophy of tomorrow likewise. . . .

H. BERGSON

A Pluralistic Universe was followed soon by *The Meaning of Truth,* which Bergson acknowledged as follows:—

Paris, Oct. 28, 1909

My dear James,—

. . . What appears to me to stand out in the book as a whole is chiefly the very clear distinction between reality and truth;—and in consequence the possibility, and almost the necessity, that the pragmatist should be at the same time a realist. It is not to be wondered at that people should have so much trouble understanding this; all our habits of mind, and our habits of speech as well, work in the opposite direction, no doubt because they are both formed in the Platonic mould. When once we have represented to ourselves a world of *things,* we cannot help considering truth as constituted by the set of all the love-matches which cause these things (or these ideas) to be coupled forever;—so as to make reality and truth terms of the same order. Much time will be required to dissipate this mirage completely. . . . Once more, in haste, all my compliments. Believe me, etc.,

H. BERGSON

[11] *L.W.J.,* II, 314-5.

Early in 1910 James published his popular address on "The Moral Equivalent of War," and an article[12] in which he described four peculiar experiences of his own "within the last five years," which he thought might throw light on mysticism. In all of these experiences, three developing from reminiscence and the fourth from dreams, there seemed to be a sudden "uncovering" of hidden tracts of reality, continuous with, but lying beyond, the subject's normal world.

Paris, March 31, 1910

My dear James,—

. . . I have not yet told you how much I enjoyed reading your two articles: "The Moral Equivalent of War" and "A Suggestion about Mysticism." The former is certainly the finest and most persuasive thing that has been said concerning the non-necessity of war, and concerning the conditions under which it would be possible to abolish it without thereby diminishing human energy. As to your article on mysticism, it will, I am sure, be the point of departure for much fresh observation and research. I am not sure that I have ever experienced an "uncovering" myself, but perhaps there was something of the kind in the following phenomenon which I have sometimes (though rarely) experienced in dreaming. I believed that I was present at a superb spectacle,—generally a vision of an intensely colored landscape through which I was travelling at great speed, and which gave me so profound an impression of reality that I could not believe, for the first few moments of waking, that it had been a mere dream. Indeed, during the very short time that the dream seemed to last (two or three seconds at most) I had each time the very clear feeling that I was about to have a *dangerous* experience, that it depended on me to prolong it and to learn the sequel, but that something was stretching and swelling in me more and more and would burst if I did not relieve the situation by waking up. And upon waking I had at the same time both a feeling of regret to have had such a dream interrupted and a perfectly clear sense that it was I who had willed its interruption. I give you this experience for what it is worth! It has, perhaps, some relation with yours in so far as it suggests the idea of a momentary extension of the field of consciousness,—due, however, to an intense effort. How I wish that you would pursue further this study of "the noetic value of abnormal states." Your article, taken together with what you have said in the *Varieties of Religious Experience*, opens up great perspectives in that direction. *À bientôt*, I hope. Affectionately and devotedly yours,

H. BERGSON

In the spring of 1910 James was again in Europe. He arrived in Paris May 5, and lunched with Bergson on two occasions. This was their last meeting.

In June 1911, ten months after James's death, Bergson wrote to Mrs. William James that he had just reread all of her husband's recent works in order to prepare himself for the writing of the Introduction to the French translation of the *Pragmatism*. He added that while he had attempted to write of James

---

[12] "A Suggestion about Mysticism," *Jour. of Philos.*, VII (1910).

quite impersonally, he could not avoid betraying something of the peculiar feeling which he had for his memory. To this Introduction Bergson gave the title of "Truth and Reality," and, as this title suggests, he was primarily concerned to show that pragmatism was—in its implications, if not in its explicit affirmations—a metaphysics. It implies that reality is "redundant and super-abundant," differing from the simplified systems of philosophy and common sense as life in all its fecundity and irrelevance differs from the selected and unified representations of it on the stage. The origin and inspiration of pragmatism is to be found, says Bergson, in this notion of a reality in which man *participates*—a reality whose nature is revealed to him only when he feels it flowing through his veins, or whose deeper currents he detects in the transports of the mystical experience. Pragmatism is the theory of truth suitable to such a metaphysics. Truth is an aid to action, a guiding thread by which man finds his way and keeps his footing in the midst of perceptual novelty. With this doctrine of truth, as well as with its complementary metaphysics, Bergson himself was broadly in agreement—and he testified to its profundity, originality, and moral elevation. The vulgar disparagement of pragmatism as sceptical or utilitarian, he said, can only *astonish* those who have known James himself; for no one ever loved truth more ardently or sought it more persistently and self-forgetfully.[13]

The affection and esteem which united James and Bergson provide a remarkable example of friendship without submergence of individual differences. Each paid homage to the other, but without loss of independence or of separate fame. They discovered their doctrinal agreement and their deep personal affinity with no suggestion whatsoever of rivalry, but with a grateful sense of confirmation and a strengthened hope that the truth might prevail.

[13] W. James, *Le Pragmatisme,* trans, by E. le Brun, 1911, 1-16.

XXXVII

THE UNFINISHED TASK

In the Preface which Bergson wrote in 1924 for the French translation of James's letters he said of James: "Un foyer ardent était là, dont on recevait chaleur et lumière." [1] In the closing year of his life, despite his rapidly declining health, James's spirit continued to burn brightly, and to radiate both warmth and light. He experienced a revival of interest in the mystical experience. The "Suggestion about Mysticism" appeared in February 1910. The last of his writings published during his own lifetime was the essay entitled "A Pluralistic Mystic," devoted to an exposition of the philosophy and genius of his old friend Benjamin Paul Blood. That his interest in current problems was as strong as ever is attested by the writing, and publication in February, of "The Moral Equivalent of War."

The serious philosophical enterprise of James's last days, however, was the composition of the most technical and carefully reasoned of all his books. It grew out of introductory courses at Harvard and Stanford and, under the title of *Some Problems of Philosophy,* was designed to serve as a college textbook having a wide circulation. But it was written for readers, and not for an audience; differing in this respect from all of his philosophical works except *Essays in Radical Empiricism* and *The Meaning of Truth,* and differing from these in being conceived as a unified treatise rather than as a volume of independent articles.

This "Introduction," as James at first called it, was begun on March 28, 1909, and was continued intermittently. Parts of the manuscript were read and criticized by his friends in Europe during the summer of 1910. It was never completed, but James left written instructions to publish it: "Say it is fragmentary and unrevised. . . . Say that I hoped by it to round out my system, which now is too much like an arch built only on one side." [2] It was dedicated to "the great Renouvier's memory." Thus at the end James was faithful to his beginnings.

This volume represents a definite turning away from polemics, popular and literary appeal, mysticism, and flights of imaginative speculation. Writing to a

---

[1] Delattre et Le Breton, *William James: extraits de correspondence,* 1924, 7.
[2] *S.P.P.,* vii, viii.

friend in Germany shortly after the appearance of his article on Blood, he referred to it as "a wonderful *Sturm und Drang* utterance for pluralism," but added, "this . . . will be the last of my *Sturm und Drang* period." [3] Now at the close of his life, he wrote from a mood of restraint and sobriety. He met logic on its own ground, and went far to repudiate that "anti-logicality" which, though he had first claimed it as a merit, he did not suffer gladly when applied as a reproachful epithet by others. This work represented, in other words, an effort to anticipate that "greater distinctness and clearness" which James had believed would follow the romantic phase of the new philosophy; while at the same time it discussed certain specific and traditional topics of metaphysics which the author had heretofore neglected from a desire to promulgate his general point of view.

The first eight chapters dealt with questions which James had already treated fully elsewhere, such as the distinction between "percepts and concepts." There must always, he said, be a discrepancy between concepts and reality, because the former are static and discontinuous while the latter is dynamic and flowing. The failure of conception is made good by perception. Concepts are "real" in their "eternal way," they enter into close union with perception, and they play an important role in experience; but they are "secondary . . . imperfect and ministerial." This affirmation of the priority of perception to conception, both genetically and cognitively, is *"the tendency known in philosophy as empiricism"*; to which, in the remainder of the book, the author will "hold fast." [4] Empiricism implies particularism, pluralism, and *novelty*—it is at this point that important additions are made to the author's thought.

Freedom had always been one of the cardinal tenets of James's philosophy, and his metaphysics had in this respect always been adapted to his ethics. But James came to look upon his earliest "tychism," with its emphasis on sheer chance, as only a negative form of intellectualism. According to intellectualism, the units of which reality is composed either are or are not identical: determinism says that they are, tychism that they are not. The paradox of tychism—its odiousness to the philosophic mind—lies in its leaving different existences in a state of total irrelevance one to another. It is permissible, however, to say that two successive events both are and are not identical: the first develops into the second, the second emerges from the first. There is novelty, but it is a novelty which, when it comes, seems natural and reasonable, like the fulfillment of a tendency. This notion of a "really growing world" is the general

[3] To J. Goldstein, June 29, 1910.
[4] *S.P.P.*, 93 ff., 98-101, 106-7, 218. James reiterates his rejection of nominalism and harks back to the view which he had announced as early as 1879; *cf. C.E.R.*, 109-15.

theme of the latter part of the *Problems of Philosophy,* the theme which bound him closely to Bergson, and the theme with which he was increasingly occupied during the last years and months of his life.

The problem of causation has remained unsolved, James thinks, because philosophers have oscillated between the two impossible views that cause and effect are identical and that they are external and mutually exclusive. This is intellectualism again, with its sharp alternatives and logical antitheses. If we turn to the *"experience* of activity," on the other hand, we find a "transitive" efficacy, which neither unites cause and effect nor divides them—but carries the one over into the other. If we ask whether all causes are of this experiential sort, the answer must depend on how we conceive the relation of mind and body, and on whether we accept or reject the panpsychistic view of the physical world.

Here James stopped. He promised a discussion, in later chapters, of idealism, of psychophysics, and of Bergson. These promises were, unhappily, never fulfilled. Had he fulfilled them some of the gravest difficulties and doubts which his philosophy raises would perhaps have been removed.

During the time when his physical strength was ebbing, James's capacity for friendship, new as well as old, remained undiminished. Émile Boutroux, Director of the Fondation Thiers in Paris, had published as early as 1874 a work *On the Contingency of the Laws of Nature.* This work had brought him almost instant recognition, and he was already ripe in years and in fame when his intimacy with James began. For though there had already been a letter or two exchanged, James did not "make his acquaintance" until the autumn of 1908. He at once found him *"simpatico."* [5] Boutroux, like James, was a champion of freedom against the claims of science; and like James he held that truth expresses the moral and æsthetic, as well as the more narrowly intellectual, part of man. As holding these congenial doctrines, and as being the simple and upright man that he was, he made a strong appeal to James. As though to make up for the wasted opportunity of past years, their friendship ripened quickly into love, and formed one of the most significant episodes of the last two years of James's life. In January 1910, as president of the French Academy of Moral and Political Sciences, Boutroux had the pleasure of announcing the election of James as a foreign associate for America, and in March he gave at Harvard a series of lectures which James heartily applauded.

On April 23, 1910, soon after his return to Paris, Boutroux delivered an address before the Academy of Moral and Political Sciences, and took as his theme "observations on his voyage to America." The address was delivered in the presence of ex-President Theodore Roosevelt as well as other notables.

[5] W.J. to Th. Flournoy, October 4, 1908; *L.W.J.,* II, 314.

It was, he said, with the university world that he had come into contact in America:

> The more so since I had the good fortune to stay with Professor William James, whom we have recently elected an associate member of this group. How charming was the house of the illustrious philosopher! Standing by itself amidst lawns and trees, built of wood in the colonial style like most of the houses of the university part of Cambridge; large, filled with books from top to bottom, a dwelling-place marvelously suited to study and meditation. Reflection, furthermore, is here in no danger of degenerating into egotism. For there reigns a most amiable sociability. The "library," which serves as Professor James's place of work, contains not only a desk, tables and books, but couches, window-seats, morris-chairs, welcoming visitors at all hours of the day, so that it is in the midst of merry conversations, among ladies taking tea, that the profound philosopher meditates and writes.

Although James's own health was already alarming, his last trip to Europe, in May 1910, was due to his concern for his beloved brother and lifelong companion, Henry. When he reached Europe, however, his condition rapidly deteriorated, and he now felt that the end was near. From London he wrote to Boutroux on July 16:

> Ever since leaving Nauheim I had been getting worse and worse. . . . Spasmodic attacks, in the early morning hours . . . leave me ill all day. I say this not by way of complaint, but of excuse, rather! Don't waste "sympathy" on me, for I deserve on the whole more misery than I am having! To have known you is one of the pleasantest episodes of my life, and the memory of it will always be a satisfaction.

On the eve of his departure to America, on August 8, 1910, less than three weeks before his death, James wrote a last letter to Schiller in which he said:

> I leave the "Cause" in your hands . . . Good-bye, and God bless you. You shall hear of our safe arrival. Keep your health, your splendid health! It's better than all the "truths" under the firmament.

His last message was to James Ward, written in London on August 11:

> We have been in England for two months this summer, and the natural order of things would have made me look you up, but I have fallen so acutely ill with cardiac asthma that human intercourse has been impossible. We sail tomorrow for home . . . and I send you all these regretful greetings.

Ward's reply is dated August 16:

> Well, all the same we shall "hope for the best" or what we think the best, and if that is not to be—well still. Yours, my dear friend, has been a successful life

and surely it has been a happy one, for I know of no one more universally beloved. I, at least, never heard an ill word of you from anyone. . . . I seem to see clearly that speculation in our day has turned over a new leaf, wherever you have made your mark.

Ward's letter reached its destination, but it could scarcely have been read. After landing in Quebec, James was taken directly to his beloved Chocorua, where he sank rapidly, and died on August 26, 1910.

The "angel of death" did in fact strike James down before he had said all that he had to say. Not only was much left unsaid, but there were many problems that he had neither thought out nor worked out. When death brought him down he was in full flight. But the nature of James's latest preoccupations and the direction of his latest efforts bear out his own statement: "I think the centre of my whole *Anschauung,* since years ago I read Renouvier, has been the belief that something is doing in the universe, and that *novelty* is real." [6]

His philosophy being so interpreted, there is even a certain propriety in the fact that James's task was unfinished. Writing in 1908, he said, "I've grown fearfully old in the past year, except 'philosophically,' where I still keep young." [7] Philosophically he did not merely *keep* young—he seemed to grow younger. Certainly at no period of his life was he so curious, so receptive, so ardently speculative, as in his last years. While his philosophical powers grew —his fertility and his self-confidence—his universe also grew more complex and more interesting. It was inevitable, therefore, that his last glance should look beyond the horizon and that his last act should be a question rather than an answer.

James's philosophy as a whole can be subsumed under the conception of empiricism. But I shall have failed if I have not at the same time created the impression that there is a kind of incongruity in applying any label to James. To oversimplify him would be to offend against the spirit of a philosopher who never objected to an experience as too rich, a public Heaven as too crowded, or a tolerant mind as too promiscuous. He always felt imprisoned by doctrinal limitations, even when he applied them to himself. He undertook to be a rigorously scientific psychologist, and yet he exceeded all of the psychologists of modern times in the frequency of his metaphysical infidelities. If the quarry that he was pursuing fled out of scientific bounds he went after it, with no feeling whatever that he was trespassing. In fact he crossed the line between psychology and philosophy so many times that it was totally obliterated. He called himself empiricist, pluralist, pragmatist, individualist, but whenever he did so he began at once to hanker after the fleshpots of rationalism, monism,

[6] To James Ward, June 27, 1909.
[7] To Pauline Goldmark, May 31, 1908.

intellectualism, socialism. He liked body in his philosophizing, and he hated to leave out anything that had either flavor or nutritive value. He was much more afraid of thinness than he was of inconsistency. To measure such a philosopher by systematic standards is to omit an essential part of him. He enlivened everything that he touched, fertilized every idea that passed through his mind, carried a blazing torch in all his meanderings, zigzags, and circles. This was felt even by his nonphilosophical friends, such as Albert Venn Dicey:—

> So he is gone. . . . There is one good and able man the less among the living to help us. What may be the merit or the truth of his theories I cannot judge. My suspicion is that he hit some weak points in prevailing moral and philosophical systems, but did not establish any coherent theory in their place. He had, however, I am pretty sure, one quality which in my judgment belongs to all great thinkers, in whatever line and in whatever school. He made incidental remarks which have great merit, whatever be the ultimate worth of his general system.[8]

These "incidental remarks" of "great merit," a merit which Dicey certainly did not exaggerate, account for the peculiar vitality of James's influence. It spread like the branches of a banyan tree and took root in divers places. His mind was abundantly fruitful and he scattered its riches far and wide. He lost no chance of exploration from fear of departing too far from the main highway. The result is that while there are very few pure Jamesians, in the sense of direct descent, the world is full of mixed Jamesians, who acknowledge their common relationship to him without feeling any bond with one another.

James's thought has remained green when that of many of his contemporaries is withered. This is due not only to the sheer quality of his work, but to its pioneering spirit and prophetic insight. There *are* elements of James's thought that are at present under an eclipse—psychical research, for example, and individualistic-humanitarian liberalism. But if we compare the year 1947 with the year 1885, in which James may be said to have come of age, and plot the movement of the human mind and spirit during these three score years, it is remarkable how much of James falls on the line. The attention to "experience"; the free intermingling of psychology and philosophy in the study of perception, thought, and other forms of knowledge; the revolt against the dualisms of subject-object and of body-mind; the passing of scientific dogmatism, in both its mechanistic and its evolutionary forms; the empirical study of religion, and the tendency to ascribe noetic value to the mystical consciousness; the rise of the theory of value; the recognition of the emotional and other personal contaminations of thought and of its intimate relation to action; the de-

---

[8] To Mrs. Dicey, August 30, 1910, reprinted from *Memorials of Albert Venn Dicey,* ed. by Robert S. Rait, Macmillan and Company, London, 1925, 209-10.

throning of the Absolute and the decline of all forms of extreme monism; indeterminism; the stream of consciousness; the clinical approach to psychology, with its emphasis on personality and on the unconscious; the rejection of associationism, together with the emphasis on integral motor response, and on the organic unity of the conscious field; the development of applied and of social psychology; relativity, in all its wide range of meanings—these are some of the ideas whose vogue would make it quite possible for James to breathe the air of the present time, and whose proponents find it natural to quote him.

XXXVIII

MORBID TRAITS

The character of James, like his thought, escapes simple formulation. "What a real person he is!" said Minnie Temple.[1] He had, in fact, the reality of his own pluralistic universe—abounding and unbounded.

I shall attempt no clinical diagnosis, but observe him with a layman's eye, and with no predetermined set of categories. It would be natural to apply his *own* categories, and to ask whether he was a tough-minded accepter of facts (a "Rocky Mountain tough"), or a tender-minded respecter of principles (a "tender-foot Bostonian").[2] The fact is that he was both; or perhaps it might be more accurate to say that he was tough-minded with many tender-minded concessions, as he may be said to have been a pluralist with concessions to monism. He would not have made the distinction had his own experience not embraced both sorts of mindedness—had he not had his tough moods and his tender— and his philosophy, as a way of being true to himself, was under an inner compulsion to satisfy them both.

Another of his famous distinctions is that which he made in *The Varieties of Religious Experience*, between the "healthy-minded" and the "sick soul." The former enjoys a sense of easy or certain triumph over evil; he imposes terms on it, regarding it as alien and conquerable. He enjoys, as James expresses it, "a temperament organically weighted on the side of cheer and fatally forbidden to linger, as those of opposite temperament linger, over the darker aspects of the universe."[3] The sick soul, on the other hand, accepts evil not only as incurable but as *essential,* and has to make his peace with the world on terms which evil dictates; suffering is itself a part of the deeper meaning of life, sublimated into resignation, repentance, purification by pain, or the exaltation of self-sacrifice. Now James had his times of healthy-mindedness and his times of soul-sickness, and he knew both; but when he was healthy he was healthy-minded, and when he experienced soul-sickness he was sick. His *norm,* in other words, and his *salvation* lay in the recovery of healthy-mindedness. His own favorite tonic, a sort of open-air exposure to the perilous adventure of combat-

---

[1] *N.S.B.*, 511. *Cf.* above, 267-8.
[2] *Pragm.*, 12-3.
[3] *V.R.E.*, 83.

ing evil, would not do for sick souls. He did, however, have a physician's interest in the soul-sickness of others, and since his own soul sometimes needed the medicine which he prescribed, he knew its virtue.

As to the distinction between the "once" and the "twice-born," James's life was punctuated by abrupt crises, and his recoveries tended to assume the form of a dramatic regeneration. Especially notable was the "crisis" of April 29, 1870, when as a young man of twenty-eight he found not only philosophical insight but a way of life in the reading of Renouvier's second *Essai*.[4] There is some reason, surely, to be reminded of that older young man of thirty-two, Saint Augustine, who, having heard the words *"tolle lege"* in his garden at Milan, found a way of salvation, philosophical as well as personal, in the reading of Saint Paul's Epistles. But there was in James no such sharp disassociation between the unregenerate and regenerate phases as marks the twice-born type in its authentic cases. Had there been, he would not have been a detached observer of his own experience, or a psychologist of religion.

In short, James transcended his own classifications in the act of creating them. They cannot be used to define his limits, but only to prove his many-sidedness. His recognition of them, his understanding of them in terms of his own experience, inclined him also to admit a provisional plurality of truths. That any man should find a remedy good, whether it be medicine for the body or medicine for the soul, created a presumption in its favor. And James not only made an allowance for diverse truths in the final accounting, but reserved the liberty of tasting them all himself. It will be recalled that when Thomas Davidson was, like himself, afflicted with an incurable malady, James wrote: "One can meet mortal (or would-be mortal) disease either by gentlemanly levity, by high-minded stoicism, or by religious enthusiasm. I advise you, old T. D., to follow my example and try a playful *durcheinander* of all three, taking each in turn *pro re nata*."[5] Discount whatever of light-mindedness was designed to cheer the heart of his friend, and this statement contains a residual philosophical conviction that the whole truth somehow includes all gospels whose remedial value is proved in the profounder moments of human experience.

James was never robust and there were many times, short or protracted, when he was disabled by illness. During the Civil War, when he was a young man of from nineteen to twenty-three years of age, he was clearly incapacitated for military service. There were two long periods, one in his youth and one towards the end of his life, when he was unable to use his eyes. From 1867 to 1873 (that is, from his twenty-fifth to his thirty-first year), he suffered from insomnia, weakness of the back, and digestive disorders, and for the next five years he was convalescent. He strained his heart in 1898, twelve years before

[4] *Cf.* above, 135.
[5] Above, 169.

his death, and from this injury he never recovered. In point of physical health, the best years of his life were the twenty from his marriage in 1878 to the injury of his heart in 1898, but even during these years he suffered frequently from nervous fatigue and from recurrent attacks of grippe, insomnia, and eye strain. There was always a ghost or a premonition of disability. "We are all well," he once wrote to Howison, "I suffering much from the sense of my inadequacy, both intellectual and corporeal, to my tasks; but the years elapse, notwithstanding, with no public exposure." And similarly to Davidson: "There is nothing like being regularly ill or regularly well, the *vermischt* condition is the most unsatisfactory." [6]

Despite these facts, invalidism is about the last word with which to describe William James. He was perpetually expending energy, physical as well as mental; he was alert, quick, and elastic in all of his reactions. He was the sort of man that runs upstairs—two steps at a time. His periods of illness were often the effect of the overwork to which his nature constantly tempted him. There was, furthermore, a notable discrepancy between the incapacity of which he complained and the record of his achievement. Somehow long lists of long books got read when he was unable to use his eyes, and a considerable flow of ideas poured out of him when he was unable to use his mind. The fact is that a working day of twenty-four hours would never have been long enough—however large the area enclosed, he would have been fretting at the barrier.

His neurasthenia conspired with his impatience to exaggerate his illness—not only the illness itself, but his feeling of it and his expression of that feeling to others. He was very highly charged, and his body was in a peculiar measure the instrument of his will. It is little wonder that he was unable to accept the hypothesis of automatism. Spencer's description of life as "adjustment of inner and outer relations" failed utterly to fit James's own case. He was, and must have known himself to be, a centrifugal person, whose outward life took on the color of its inner source. This meant that he was the creature of his own moods, and while these were normally buoyant, they were subject to frequent alterations. Of his tendency to hypochondria, his mother wrote in 1874 (during his period of deepest depression):

> The trouble with him is that he *must express* every fluctuation of feeling, and especially every unfavorable symptom, without reference to the effect upon those about him. . . . Wherever he speaks of himself he says he is no better. This I cannot believe to be the true state of the case, but his temperament is a morbidly hopeless one, and with this he has to contend all the time, as well as with his physical disability.[7]

[6] To Howison, March 3, 1894; to Davidson, October 3, 1896.
[7] To H.J.³, March 17 and July 6, 1874.

I begin, then, with what would be regarded as the more malignant of James's mental traits, though reserving doubts as to whether, through the alchemy of genius, they were not in reality benign.

"At . . . moments of energetic living," says James, "we feel as if there were something diseased and contemptible, yea vile, in theoretic grubbing and brooding. In the eye of healthy sense the philosopher is at best a learned fool." [8] An essential element in James's practical philosophy is this eulogy of action and external experience. He once wrote to his brother Robertson in playful earnestness, "My dying words are, 'outward acts, not feelings.'" [9] He accepted Carlyle's gospel of work in his answer to the great question, "What Makes Life Worth Living?" With Carlyle he admired heroic action, and felt that in its absence life was flat and unprofitable. He conceived morality and even religion in terms of risk and combat. He inferred from the principle of "reflex action" that any completed operation of mind culminated in an overt response, and in his theory of truth he was a pragmatist.

When, however, one looks below the surface—and it requires no deep psychoanalytic probing—one finds that James's exhortation to action was addressed primarily to himself. He entered upon a philosophical career with deep misgivings because he feared that it would develop a tendncy to morbid self-preoccupation. He found teaching to be a "godsend," because it diverted him from "those introspective studies which had bred a sort of philosophical hypochondria." He turned at first to science because he needed "some stable reality to lean upon"; he was "not strong enough . . . to choose the other and nobler lot in life." [10] In other words, he had a very definite tendency to brooding melancholy. He knew it, fought it, and triumphed over it, but he never rooted it out of his nature. It was a permanent, though intermittent and subordinate, phase of his experience and character. His gospel of heroism was a moral which he drew for himself from his own experience. His praise of action and scorn of the unventilated chamber of inner thought and feeling was a call to arms, or a shout of triumph, proceeding from the arena of his own moral struggle where his strength was engaged in combat with his weakness.

In the second place, James was interested throughout his life in what he called "exceptional mental states." His promotion of psychical research and of abnormal psychology generally, his studies of the "hidden energies" of men suddenly revealed in times of stress, his collection and description of religious experiences in all their variety, but with special emphasis on their oddity, his disposition to credit mysticism as a source of knowledge—all testify to this preoccupation. How far did James *himself* experience "exceptional mental states"?

[8] *W.B.*, 74.
[9] September 15, 1877.
[10] *Cf.* above, 125, 136, W.J. to H.J.[2], May 11, 1873 (*L.W.J.*, I, 171).

Sometime in the early eighties he was prompted by the writing of his friend Blood to experiment with nitrous-oxide-gas intoxication, and he caused some scandal among his philosophical friends by likening the effect to the insight of Hegel. He recorded the following as the most coherent and articulate truth revealed to him in this state: "There are no differences but differences of degree between different degrees of difference and no difference." He said that this had "the true Hegelian ring," and described the "ecstasies of cognitive emotion" with which it was bathed.[11] Now this incident suggests the child playing with matches, or irreverently mocking the devout. It was, in fact, both of these things. James was incorrigibly and somewhat recklessly curious, and he derived enjoyment from deflating the solemnity of the pundits. There is no doubt that this experiment, and his psychopathological approach generally, did make him sceptical of the import of the mystical experience of others and slow to credit his own. Nevertheless, the very fact that he used his experience under anæsthetics as a key to the interpretation of Hegel indicates his recognition of its noetic claims. Later, in his *Varieties of Religious Experience*,[12] he took pains to point out that the causes of an experience "have nothing to do with its truth or value, which are determined by its fruits." And there can, I think, be no doubt that other experiences, which were not artificially induced, left in his mind an increasing precipitate of conviction. For he had engaged in extraordinary adventures of this sort—adventures having that character which the unbelieving describe as hallucinatory, and the believing as intuitive. It was probably in 1870, just prior to his conversion to Renouvier, that he suffered the memorable hallucination of fear which he has so vividly described in the *Varieties*:—

I went one evening into a dressing-room in the twilight to procure some article that was there; when suddenly there fell upon me without any warning, just as if it came out of the darkness, a horrible fear of my own existence. Simultaneously there arose in my mind the image of an epileptic patient whom I had seen in the asylum, a black-haired youth with greenish skin, entirely idiotic, who used to sit all day on one of the benches, or rather shelves against the wall, with his knees drawn up against his chin, and the coarse gray undershirt, which was his only garment, drawn over them, inclosing his entire figure. . . . This image and my fear entered into a species of combination with each other. *That shape am I,* I felt, potentially. Nothing that I possess can defend me against that fate, if the hour for it should strike for me as it struck for him. . . . After this the universe was changed for me altogether. I awoke morning after morning with a horrible dread at the pit of my stomach, and with a sense of the insecurity of life that I never knew before, and that I have never felt since. It was like a revelation; and although the immediate feelings passed away, the experience has made me sympathetic with the morbid feelings of others ever since.[13]

A less morbid but not less vivid experience is that which befell him in the Adirondack Mountains in 1898. He had at all times a sense of intimate communion with nature, and especially with nature in its natural states. On this particular occasion he spent a sleepless night on the slopes of Mt. Marcy, in what he described as "a state of spiritual alertness of the most vital description." Writing of this night to his wife, he said:—

> I spent a good deal of it in the woods, where the streaming moonlight lit up things in a magical checkered play, and it seemed as if the Gods of all the nature-mythologies were holding an indescribable meeting in my breast with the moral Gods of the inner life. . . . The intense significance of some sort, of the whole scene, if one could only *tell* the significance; the intense inhuman remoteness of its inner life, and yet the intense *appeal* of it; its everlasting freshness and its immemorial antiquity and decay; its utter Americanism, and every sort of patriotic suggestiveness, and you, and my relation to you part and parcel of it all, and beaten up with it, so that memory and sensation all whirled inexplicably together. . . . It was one of the happiest lonesome nights of my existence, and I understand now what a poet is. He is a person who can feel the immense complexity of influences that I felt, and make some partial tracks in them for verbal statement. In point of fact, I can't find a single word for all that significance, and don't know what it was significant of, so there it remains, a mere boulder of *impression*.[14]

In the last year of his life, as we have seen, James described four "abnormal" experiences of his own, all of which had occurred after 1905, and which he hoped would throw light on the topic of mysticism. He *believed* that "there is a continuum of cosmic consciousness, against which our individuality builds but accidental fences, and into which our several minds plunge as into a mother-sea or reservoir." [15] This belief was to some extent founded on normal observation, on the reports of others, and on the theory of the subliminal consciousness which he adopted from Myers. But the impression is irresistible that it was his own unusual experiences that put the seal of conviction on what would otherwise have been an alluring but open hypothesis. It is true that he refused to credit himself with the mystical experience, or at most admitted that he had a "mystical germ." But in view of all the evidence it seems more correct to say that he did in fact have experiences of the type called mystical; adding that these experiences were infrequent, lacked the character of overwhelming authority with which they are commonly invested, and played only a minor role in his philosophy as a whole.

---

[13] *V.R.E.*, 160-1.
[14] *Cf.* above, 255.
[15] *Cf.* above, 350; *M.S.*, 204.

The third of James's morbid traits is his extreme *variability*—the frequency of the barometric and thermometric changes in his temperamental weather. The only published statement which he made about the personal sources of his philosophy contains the following, addressed in 1909 to a writer who had undertaken to make a diagnosis:

> I think you overdo my personal mysticism. It has always seemed to me rather a matter of fair play to the various kinds of experience to let mystical ecstasy have its voice counted with the rest. As far as I am personally concerned it is the ordinary sense of life that every working moment brings, that makes me contemptuous of rationalistic attempts to substitute thin logical formulas for it. My *flux*-philosophy may well have to do with my extremely impatient temperament. I am a motor, need change, and get very quickly bored.[16]

The Jamesian universe was not a Great State of Things, or architectural monument of cosmic bulk and infinite complexity—it was a stream, a passage, a becoming, a history in the making. Now it is certain that whether the universe was really so or not, it would necessarily have *looked* so to James because he was perpetually in motion himself. There was an outward projection of an inward restlessness and nostalgia. He was peculiarly subject to the mirage of absent and distant joys. He became tired of whatever he did long before it was finished, and felt a most powerful revulsion toward it after it was finished. A minor but not insignificant symptom of this was a detestation of proofreading, such as found expression in the following outburst to the editor of the *Psychological Review*:

> Send me no proofs! I will return them unopened and never speak to you again. As Mrs. R. says, "Remove the cuticle from your own polecats," or get your entrapped victims to help you. I am of the eagle's race and free![17]

After the publication of the *Principles of Psychology* poor Palmer prepared several pages of *errata*, but he could never persuade James to look at them.

His sister Alice, who was an indulgent but acute diagnostician, found James "just like a blob of mercury"—lacking in power or inclination to "stick to a thing for the sake of sticking."[18] Describing to this same sister his experiences with a "mind-cure doctress" in 1887, James said:

> I sit down beside her and presently drop asleep, whilst she disentangles the snarls out of my mind. She says she never saw a mind with so many, so agitated, so restless, etc. She said my *eyes*, mentally speaking, kept revolving like wheels

[16] Letter to E. Tausch, *Monist*, XIX (1909), 156.
[17] To J. M. Baldwin, January 10, 1898.
[18] *L.W.J.*, I, 289-90.

in front of each other and in front of my face, and it was four or five sittings ere she could get them *fixed*. . . . I thought it might please you to hear an opinion of my mind so similar to your own.[19]

That James's mercurial temperament made him at times difficult to live with was no secret, at any rate within the family. There is an inverted allusion to it in the following passage from a letter written on June 1, 1891 by William in Chocorua to Henry and Alice in London:

> I am becoming more patriarchal than ever: Last week we had three nurses at once,—nine women in all,—in the house. . . . I think that even (sister) Alice would feel compunction if she could see me, the idol of the group of relatives and dependents, dignified and serene, never worrying or "wishing," never depreciating present possessions, never protesting against the injustice of others' opinions, or contradicting or pinning them down, never discussing personal anecdotes from the point of view of abstract reasoning and absolute truth, never seeking a second metaphor, or a third, when the first or second were good enough, breathing, in short, an atmosphere of peace and rest wherever I go. A *noble et forte personnalité* indeed! But enough of this: since you can't *see* it, it is well that you should *hear* of it at least; and my Alice is, I fear, too shy to write such things.

James complained constantly of a multitude of distractions. "The constitutional disease from which I suffer," he wrote, "is what the Germans call *Zerrissenheit* or *torn-to-pieces-hood*. The days are broken in pure zigzag and interruption. . . . Give me twelve hours of work on *one* occupation for happiness."[20] Although he usually imputed this state to his environment, and sought to escape it *somewhere,* he knew in his heart that it was his own nature, and not outward circumstance, that tormented him.

Over and above these symptoms of volatility—restlessness, impatience, dispersion of attention and perversity—there were deeper alternations of mood. Thus in June 1865, he was sure that his voyage to Brazil was a "mistake," while in October he was in high spirits and thanking heaven that he had come.[21] In the autumn of 1887, although his courses were large and successful, and he was writing busily on his *Principles of Psychology,* and his "eyes, sleep and working and walking powers" were all restored, his zest for life was strangely dulled.[22] On October 16 he wrote to his sister:

> The Eliots have just returned from a year of absence abroad. I have not seen 'em yet. Whether it be his cold figure at the helm, or what not; whether it be perhaps the fact that I myself never graduated here, I know not; one thing is

[19] *L.W.J.,* 261.
[20] To Mrs. Glendower Evans, *Atlantic,* CXLIV (1929), 380.
[21] *Cf.* above, 75, 76.
[22] W.J. to H.J.², November 24, 1887.

certain, that although I *serve* Harvard College to the best of my ability, I have no *affection* at all for the institution, and would gladly desert it for anything that offered better pay.

The following was written to his brother Henry, on November 24, showing the persistence of the mood:

I am glad you write so sanguinely of your work. That's the way to feel. If only one *can* feel so. A strange coldness has come over me with reference to all my deeds and productions, within the past six months. I don't know whether it be the passage under the meridian of forty-five years, or due to a more reparable cause, but everything I've done and shall do seems so *small*.

By the autumn of 1888 this mood seems to have vanished:

The Cambridge year begins with much vehemence—I with a big class in ethics, and seven graduates from other colleges in advanced psychology, giving me a good deal of work. But I feel uncommonly hearty, and shall no doubt come out of it all in good shape. . . . I am to have lots of reading and no writing to speak of this year and expect to enjoy it hugely.[23]

Oscillation, then, of the quick and darting variety, or with the longer rhythm of exaltation and depression, is profoundly characteristic of James's nature. It is reflected in his world, which is a scene of abrupt as well as of continuous change; and in his mind, which is variable, versatile, and itinerant—perpetually crossing over, turning corners, or embarking on new voyages.

Finally, there was in James a temperamental repugnance to the processes of exact thought. Whether it can be regarded as a symptom of soul-sickness to be relatively incompetent in logic and mathematics, I do not presume to say. There is also doubt as to whether James was so incompetent in this direction as he felt himself to be. In any case, incompetent he did *feel* and *profess* himself to be. He made belated efforts to advance his mathematical education. In 1893 he wrote to Flournoy:

Can you name me any simple book on differential calculus which gives an insight into the philosophy of the subject? . . . I have just been through a short treatise by one of my colleagues, but it is a thicket of particular formulas and calculations without one general idea, and I want ideas and not formulas.[24]

But on the whole he was easily consoled. He was much pleased when one of his students characterized algebra as "a form of low cunning." [25] To Peirce he wrote:

[23] To H.J.², October 14, 1888; *L.W.J.*, I, 283.
[24] May 5 and May 12, 1893.
[25] *L.W.J.*, II, 237.

I am *a*-logical, if not illogical, and glad to be so when I find Bertie Russell trying to excogitate what true knowledge means, in the absence of any concrete universe surrounding the knower and the known. Ass! [26]

Thus a lack of mathematics and logic did not exclude James from intimate relations with the universe—at any rate, with the Jamesian universe. On the contrary!

With Charles Peirce this more or less self-righteous plea of incompetence was no laughing matter. Towards James he felt a little as the friends of Mr. Skimpole felt when the latter so blandly remarked that he was a "child" and "could not understand money." Not only did Peirce belong to a tribe of mathematicians and logicians, and practise both subjects with eminent skill, but he thought that they represented the perfection of clarity, and therefore the supreme height of intelligibility. Hence his complaint that when a person "lays it down," as James does, "that he can't understand mathematics, that is to say, can't understand the *evident,* that blocks the road" to further explanations.[27]

In the Hibbert Lectures of 1908 James solemnly and publicly renounced logic. It is true that there is some question as to the precise scope of this renunciation, since he repeatedly referred to the logic which he renounced as the "intellectualistic logic" or the "logic of identity," as though there might be some better logic to which he remained faithful.[28] It is also true that at the very times when he was resolving to renounce logic he was engaged in mental operations of extreme rigor bearing a remarkable resemblance to what other people called logic. His very refutation of the "intellectualistic logic" was, whether right or wrong, certainly not either dogmatic, impressionistic, or empirical, but a notable demonstration of painstaking analysis. Again, despite the reiteration of his incompetence in mathematics, he examined the new mathematical theory of the infinite with much care, and rejected it not because he disliked it, but because it seemed to him to be invalid. But while James was thus perpetually driven to the processes of exact thought by his desire for clearness and cogency, he was at the same time repelled by a temperamental aversion and distrust; and these feelings, combined with a natural impulse to find metaphysical justification for them, led him to sweeping and extravagant assertions of the irrationality of being.

An inventory of James's pathological traits would embrace, then, tendencies to hypochondria and hallucinatory experience, abnormally frequent and intense oscillations of mood, and an almost morbid alogism, or antipathy to the mode

[26] December 24, 1909.
[27] *Cf.* above, 292.
[28] *P.U.,* 208, 212.

of thinking which employs definitions, symbols, and trains of inference. In terming these traits "pathological," I mean only that taken in themselves they would commonly be regarded as defects. In relation to the character and thought of James, they are *ingredients,* essential to the substance as well as to the flavor of the compound.

XXXIX

BENIGN TRAITS

Turning to James's benign traits, I find four that are peculiarly pervasive: sensibility, vivacity, humanity, and sociability. When I say that they are benign I mean not only that in themselves they would commonly be regarded as merits rather than as defects, but also that they dominated James when he enjoyed a sense of well-being, or when he felt himself to be most himself.

In speaking, first, of James's sensibility, I do not mean his susceptibility to feeling or emotion, but the acuity of his *senses*—the voluminousness and richness of the experience which he received through them, and the prominence of that experience and of its underlying motive in his life as a whole. He tells us that he was not a visualizer so far as his memory and imagination were concerned. On the other hand, it is the unanimous testimony of all who knew him that he lived much through the eyes. He wanted to *see* people whom he knew. He exchanged photographs with his friends and made a large "anthropological collection" in order to study the human physiognomy.[1] He was ceaselessly and interestedly observant of all that lay about him—of nature and art, as well as of life. Being a painter, the eye was no doubt his major sense: to use his own expression, he "took in things through the eyes." But although he described himself as a "musical barbarian,"[2] he was quick also to discriminate nuances of sound, especially in the quality of a human voice. His psychological writings testify to his discrimination of organic sensations.

Having a high sensuous endowment and being avid of sensory experience, it is not surprising that he should have felt such experience to convey the authentic revelation of reality. It is the unsaid but fundamental premise of his whole metaphysics that only he can speak authoritatively of the universe who is most sensitively attuned to it. Metaphysics is an apprehending of reality in its most immediate and lifelike aspect, or a listening to hear "the pulse of Being beat." When he said that he found "no good warrant for even suspecting the existence of any reality of a higher denomination than that distributed and strung-along and flowing sort of reality which we finite beings swim in,"[3] he was placing his ultimate reliance on the human sensorium.

[1] *L.W.J.*, I, 51.
[2] W.J. to G. H. Howison, March 3, 1894; to T. Davidson, October 3, 1896.
[3] *W.B.*, 141; *P.U.*, 213.

The same motive appears in all of James's pet philosophical aversions. He was constantly attacking verbalism. How much better, he said, a bill of fare "with one real egg instead of the word 'egg.'" He hated abstractions, and would be like Agassiz, one of the "livers in the light of the world's concrete fulness."[4] He seemed to be forever scooping reality up in his hands in the hope of catching it alive. Caring more for actuality than for ancestry, he took relatively little interest in origins and histories. He thought that the question "why?" was sooner or later a futile question, the last answer being a "what" or "that" for which there is no "why." The world has an ultimate physiognomy, rhythm, flavor, or quality, which, having been discerned, must be accepted as it is. His metaphysics was a perpetual striving to sense that ultimate quality.

James's metaphysics, then, reflects the sensuous, pictorial character of his mind. But this interpretation must not be taken too simply. Intuition, according to Bergson, is immediate, but is not on that account easily attained. So in the case of James the authentic experience of reality is uncommon and difficult. The painter tells us that he paints the scene as he sees it—which sounds very simple, until we discover that only the eye of the painter can really see. Something like this is the case with James's metaphysical vision. There are occasional moments when experience is most fully tasted—in the exhilaration of a fresh morning, in moments of suffering, or in times of triumphant effort, when the tang is strong, when every nuance or overtone is present. James would arrest us at such moments, and say, "There, *that* is it. Reality is like *that*." But our worldly minds are filled with ready-made ideas, and when we experience reality it usually has these ideas already stamped upon it. Our minds are accustomed to various short cuts, omissions, and abbreviations dictated by practical convenience, and what these omit we do not commonly apprehend. Hence the metaphysical vision, like the seeing of the painter, involves a recovery of innocence, a capture of the elusive, an unnatural access of sensitiveness.

The quality which is revealed to James when this metaphysical vision is achieved is *transitivity*. It is characteristic of the mind in its routine operations to dwell upon termini, goals, conclusions; and philosophy usually reflects this characteristic by treating reality as a finished product. Or, revolting at such perfectionism, philosophy may swing to the other extreme and declare reality to be the mere negation of completeness. Both of these views, James thought, are abstract and dialectical. Concretely—when you seize the sense of it, or get the feel of it—reality is movement from terminus to terminus, a pursuing of goals, and *arriving* at conclusions. It is on its way to something. Reality is not the destination, nor is it mere movement, but just that concrete character which is so likely to be missed by the analytic mind, namely, directional or

[4] *V.R.E.*, 500; *M.S.*, 14.

meaningful change. It is neither form nor matter, nor a mere combination of the two, but a plasticity in which matter is in the act of assuming form. James did not invent this view to suit his theoretical exigencies—it was what he discerned when he experienced experience. So whenever the intellect makes distinctions we find him endeavoring to restore the primitive concreteness, not by piecing the distinctions together, but by recovering the original as it was before these were selected and detached.

The following passage will illustrate James's pictorial manner of philosophizing, his effort to convey as faithfully as possible the immediately presented aspect of a situation, and also that peculiar quality of synthesis which distinguishes his way of seeing things. He has been arguing that reality is neither absolutely one nor absolutely many, but a stream whose parts coalesce where they touch, and exclude one another as their interval increases. At the same time he is endeavoring to describe the relations of the private experiences of individuals to the common world in which they live:—

> *Prima facie,* if you should liken the universe of absolute idealism to an aquarium, a crystal globe in which goldfish are swimming, you would have to compare the empiricist universe to something more like one of those dried human heads with which the Dyaks of Borneo deck their lodges. The skull forms a solid nucleus; but innumerable feathers, leaves, strings, beads, and loose appendices of every description float and dangle from it, and, save that they terminate in it, seem to have nothing to do with one another. Even so my experiences and yours float and dangle, terminating, it is true, in a nucleus of common perception, but for the most part out of sight and irrelevant and unimaginable to one another. . . . The distant parts of the physical world are at all times absent from us, and form conceptual objects merely, into the perceptual reality of which our life inserts itself at points discrete and relatively rare. Round the several objective nuclei, partly shared and common and partly discrete, of the real physical world, innumerable thinkers, pursuing their several lines of physically true cogitation, trace paths that intersect one another only at discontinuous perceptual points, and the rest of the time are quite incongruent; and around all the nuclei of shared "reality," as around the Dyak's head of my late metaphor, floats the vast cloud of experiences that are wholly subjective, that are non-substitutional, that find not even an eventual ending for themselves in the perceptual world—the mere daydreams and joys and sufferings and wishes of the individual minds. These exist *with* one another, indeed, and with the objective nuclei, but out of them it is probable that to all eternity no interrelated system of any kind will ever be made.[5]

Owing to his sensibility, James was extraordinarily receptive to impressions. But he met his impressions more than halfway—acted on them and sought them out. He was naturally *vivacious.* He said of himself, "I'm a 'motor,' and

[5] *E.R.E.,* 46-7, 65-6.

morally ill-adapted to the game of patience." [6] He meant, first, that he was one
of those who "in memory, reasoning, and all their intellectual operations,"
make use of "images derived from movements" rather than from sight, hearing, or touch. But he meant also that this motor type of imagery was associated
with comparative quickness of reaction. It is impossible to read James's description of the "explosive will," as represented by the man who will be "the king
of his company, sing all the songs and make all the speeches, lead the parties,
carry out the practical jokes, kiss all the girls, fight the men, and, if need be,
lead the forlorn hopes and enterprises"—without catching a note of sympathy
and understanding on the part of the writer himself.[7]

This *vivacity,* this eagerness and gusto, marked James from an early age—as
a "son and brother." His sister Alice once said of him that he seemed "to be
born afresh every morning." [8] "He came down from his bedroom *dancing* to
greet me," said his father, who had gone out to Cambridge in 1882 to see him.[9]
He was an overflowing and inexhaustible fountain—a fountain, be it remarked,
and not a channeled stream. For a fountain scatters itself wantonly. That
which was so striking about James was not his capacity for work, though this
was remarkable, but his capacity for play. Whatever he did he did with good
measure, and with no nice calculation of its utility. It was this more than any
other trait that gave the impression of genius. There was a fecundity, a prod-
igality, an upward rush from hidden depths, that suggested a prime source
rather than an artifact or instrument.

There were light as well as serious forms of James's vivacity. He wore bright
neckties. He had a highly developed sense of fun, and was usually himself its
principal fomenter. He had his days of feeling "particularly larky," but some
degree of larkiness might be expected at any time. Thus he wrote to Flournoy
on December 26, 1901 as he was completing his second course of Gifford Lectures, "The old spirit of mischief revives in my breast, and I begin to feel a
little as I used to." In the family circles to which James belonged laughter was
a major activity. Its waves and detonations not only cleared away the vapors of
neurasthenia, but were fatal to any "airs" of pretension or pose. There was wit,
but it was gayety and elaborate nonsense which was the characteristic domestic
product. In the days of James's boyhood, when juvenile theatricals were in
order, it was he, according to the testimony of his brother, that supplied "the
motive force," imagined "the comprehensive comedies," and served as "the
constant comic star." [10]

His way of making fun of people, himself included, his delightful absurdity

[6] W.J. to Pauline Goldmark, September 14, 1901; *L.W.J.,* II, 163.
[7] *Psychology,* II, 61-5, 538.
[8] A.J. to H.J.[2], June 3, 1888.
[9] *Cf.* above, 25.
[10] *L.W.J.,* I, 305; *S.B.O.,* 253.

and peculiar art of loving caricature, appear in one of the letters to his family, written in his nineteenth year. He describes his "vision of those at home just going in to dinner":

> My aged, silvered mother leaning on the arm of her stalwart yet flexible Harry, merry and garrulous as ever, my blushing aunt with her old wild beauty still hanging about her, my modest father with his rippling raven locks, the genial auld Rob and the mysterious Alice, all rise before me, a glorified throng.

On this passage—its "pleasantry of paradox," and "evocation of each familiar image by its vivid opposite"—we fortunately have the authoritative commentary of his brother Henry:—

> Our mother, e.g., was not at that time, nor for a good while yet, so venerably "silvered"; our handsome-headed father had lost, occipitally, long before, all pretense to raven locks, certainly to the effect of their "rippling"; the beauty of our admirable aunt was as happily alien either to wildness or to the "hanging" air as it could very well be; the "mystery" of our young sister consisted all in the candour of her natural bloom, even if at the same time of her lively intelligence; and Harry's mirth and garrulity appear to have represented for the writer the veriest ironic translation of something in that youth, I judge, not a little mildly —though oh so mildly!—morose or anxiously mute.[11]

James's correspondence abounds in evidence of the gayety of his spirits, and the rich diversity of their quality and tone. Especially characteristic is the delicious mockery of the early letters to his sister Alice, such as those written in an interval between his cure at Teplitz and his studies at Heidelberg, when he was twenty-six and she was twenty;[12] or the following, written five years later from Florence, upon receiving news of the birth of the first child of his brother Robertson:

> We got . . . from Father . . . a letter . . . announcing to us that we had given birth to a nephew. So the third generation of the James family is in full swing! We are uncles, grandmothers, aunts, etc., all drawing our subsistence as such from that one worm-like being in Wisconsin. It seems to me the pyramid points the wrong way, and the spreading end ought to be the youngest, instead of the trunk being more numerous than the twiggery.[13]

A more serious form of James's vivacity was his curiosity. His mind darted like a humming bird. From boyhood he was "addicted to experiments," there being, as his brother Henry remarked, "no possible effect whatever that

[11] N.S.B., 132-5.
[12] Cf. above, 86, 108; for other letters of the same period and in the same vein, cf. L.W.J., I.
[13] To A.J., December 11, 1873.

mightn't be more or less rejoiced in as such." [14] It was this same liveliness of mind that enabled him to enjoy novelty. It is obvious that he was himself an interesting man, but more significant that he found other things interesting. On that fatal day in 1898 when he overexerted himself in the Adirondacks he fell in with a group of young people, including several Bryn Mawr girls, "dressed," as he described them, "in boys' breeches, and cutaneously desecrated in the extreme." He afterwards apologized for the "impudence" with which he had commented on their clothes: "I remember so vividly," writes one of the party,

> the occasion he mentions, and the keen charm and vigor of his presence,—his laugh ringing out at the end of that long, wonderful, mountain-forest day (and night) with such gayety and spontaneity that I think now with a pang of how little I dreamed he was over-taxing his strength. The "impudence" to which he refers was, I think, his praise of us . . in that Victorian—or Edwardian—era for wearing knickerbockers. I remember especially that he made us all feel in the van of progress . . . by saying of the convenience of our clothes for climbing,—"I'm glad it's come. I'm glad I've lived to see it." [15]

Innovations require readaptations, and they are resented by sluggish or habituated minds for the effort they cost. Not so with James. He enjoyed such expenditures of energy. If change did not come, he went out and looked for it. He was perpetually embarking on voyages of discovery. His travels, which, inaugurated in his childhood, became an essential part of his life, were always voyages of discovery—in new worlds of people, ideas, art, or "life." If his body remained in one place his mind made voyages. He "tried" things—nitrous-oxide gas, mescal, Yoga, Fletcherism, mental healers. He imagined and speculated. He entertained hypotheses and played with ideas. His mind was of the roving-animal, rather than the rooted-vegetable variety; and he required an element in which such an unplanted mind could navigate, breathe, and find its nourishment. It is no wonder that the culminating phase of his philosophy, with which he was preoccupied when death overtook him, was the vision of "a really growing world," of which continuous novelty was the central figure.

James's vivacity was tempered by his equally fundamental *humanity,* or tenderness of heart. He admired the spirit of adventure and the bold fighting qualities, but only provided no one was hurt. That hardness which is said to be a condition of supermanly eminence was utterly lacking in him. Humanity exercised a final veto upon heroism; or, the only kind of heroism that was ultimately tolerable to him was a heroic battle against inhumanity. Similarly, that liveliness of temper that led him sometimes to assume a tone of mockery

---

[14] *N.S.B.,* 123.
[15] To A.H.J., July 9, 1898, *L.W.J.,* II, 76; Edith Franklin Wyatt to W.J.'s son, Henry James.

was sure to be, if not commingled with, then remorsefully succeeded by, a melting mood. It was his sister again who could best evoke this familiar blend of banter and affection—seasoned, in this case, with a characteristic touch of homesickness:—

Rome, Dec. 24, 1873

Sweet Beautlington,—

I cannot resist, in spite of strong objections to spoiling you with too frequent letters, taking my pen in hand on this pearly-lighted Christmas Eve and inscribing with its point on thy tender and loving heart some words of kindness and sympathy. Thou seemest to me so beautiful from here, so intelligent, so affectionate, so in all respects *the thing* that a brother should most desire, that I don't see how when I get home I can do anything else than sit with my arm round thy waist appealing to thee for confirmation of everything I say, for approbation of everything I do, and admiration for everything I am, and never, never for a moment being disappointed. What I shall do for you in return for this excellence 'tis for you rather than me to say, but I hope not to fall short of any of your exactions. I can imagine the darkling light in the library at this hour, with you lonely three sitting watching the embers and wishing for a fuller house to pass the so-called merrie Christmas Eve. . . . Adieu to dear old Father and Mother, the boys and Aunt Kate, and believe, under the form of impertinent self-conceit, in the true love of your brother

WILLIAM

This same note of playful adoration appears in a letter written by James thirty-five years later to his niece Rosamond Gregor, then eight years of age. Mrs. James was visiting her sister in Montreal.

Cambridge, Jan. 14, 1908

Darling Rosymouth (for you know that *Mund* is the German for mouth) you dear lovely extra—
ordinary
  wonderfle
    beautifle
      intellectual
        heavenly
          practical
            affectionate
              obedient
                industrious
                  obliging
                  gifted
                  witty
                    maddeningly
charming THING!

How nice it was for you to write such a letter to your 66 year old uncle and make him feel about 6 years old again! I agree with you about Agamemnon being a fool, but I'm sorry that you love Achilles, for he is a regular *hound,* nothing but pride and sulks. I would spank him if I were able. I hope you didn't read about those tedious fights. Perhaps you read an abridgment.

I hope that you enjoy your Aunt Alice. Underneath all her apparent severity there is a real soft spot, on which you can snuggle down. I am sorry that you give her such cold weather. But the dear spring weather is sure to come, birds and buds and grass and sunshine.

I am glad to hear from my wife that you are so gloriously splendid. Try to make everyone happy about you. Kiss your dear and placid mother for your waspish uncle. She has a big soul, no pettiness or paltriness about *her!* That is the best thing you can say of anyone, except all them things I said of you on the front page. . . .

So now, my own darling lovely, etc., etc., Rosymouth, good-bye, with tenderest regards to your father as well as yourself,

WM. JAMES

There was a flavor of buoyant humanity in all of James's writings which, combined with the directness of his style, gave a peculiarly personal quality to his influences. Thus a distant and casual reader of the *Psychology* once experienced a sense of conversion similar to that which the elder Henry James felt on reading Swedenborg. As her conviction deepened she shared it with a friend:

> I came to know another mind such as my own had been, a mind sick with doubt, dumb with negations, starved on barren philosophies, and, even as I, so this hungry mind fed greedily upon the tonic truths and came to new courage and hope. . . . Thus two souls are facing the East together and living with Pragmatism and William James for the watchword, and where there had been the depths of darkness, there shines the perfect day.[16]

James's life was as notable for its friendships as for the strength of its family ties. Two weeks before his death he wrote to Howells: "One's ancient affections seem the abidingly real part of it all." And to another correspondent: "Wherever you are it is your own friends who make your world." [17] It is this feeling which accounts for the volume of his correspondence. When he was physically isolated from his friends, he must nevertheless live in their companionship. His friendships, with Tom Ward, and Wendell Holmes, in the early days, and later with Renouvier, Hodgson, Howison, Davidson, Gurney, Robertson, Myers, Stumpf, Royce, Ward, Flournoy, Boutroux, Bergson and others, were distinguished by their quality as well as by their number. They partook both of love and of admiration. There were an intellectual commerce and a moral comradeship, together with a simple, warmhearted attachment of man to man. James's official or professional relationships—with colleagues, col-

---

[16] M.T.M. (Mrs. Wade MacMillan), "The Pragmatic Test," *Harper's Weekly*, April 18, 1914.
[17] To W.D. Howells, August 10, 1910; to Pauline Goldmark, May 25, 1899.

laborators, students, teachers, executives, editors, publishers—almost immediately changed into friendships; the man being to William James so much more vivid and important than the particular role in which he might happen to be acting.

He took the initiative in the making of friendships. He had a warm heart, and it was not insulated. There was a look of affection in his eyes; and no one knew better than he how to woo the affection of others by translating his affection into spoken and written words. He recognized no barrier of creed or race, his strongest prejudice being that which he felt against prejudice itself. In 1899, on May 2 he wrote to Davidson concerning a favorite hotel: "The circular appears this year with the precious addition: 'Applications from Hebrews cannot be considered.' I propose to return the boycott." He found almost everybody interesting and worthy of sympathy if they would admit him into their inner lives. His was a compassionate love, conditioned by his own suffering, and based on fellow feeling, but with a delicate discernment of the unique flavor of each individual, and a respect for the residual inwardness which must transcend even the most intimate understanding. It was an outgoing and a confident love, which often found in its objects more than up to that moment they had found in themselves.

James liked variety in the objects of his affection, and liked each with a separate liking. Thus he delighted in his juniors because of their promise. Writing to Julius Goldstein, the young and unrecognized German disciple with whom he talked during his last illness at Nauheim, he said, "It has been an exquisite pleasure to me to meet a 'rising genius' like you, trying his wings like 'an eagle dallying with the wind.'"[18] He delighted in those whom the world called cranks, either because he relished their idiosyncrasies, or from sheer, unconquerable pity. He was a great lover of animals. The history of the dogs who succeed one another as members of the James household would form a chapter in itself. In 1897 he bought a St. Bernard puppy, of whom he wrote on December 26 to Miss Pauline Goldmark:

> He is a violet, a Saint. I have borne him here so far in my arms, and feel like a nursing mother towards him. Tomorrow I take him to Cambridge in the baggage car. If, in the inscrutable leadings of Providence, a perfect sympathy between him and my wife and babes should fail to develop, or, developing, should undergo retrograde metamorphosis, *he is yours next June,* big, intelligent, *salonfähig,* but still (I am sure) the Saint which he is now. He is absolutely incorruptible and unvulgarizable. But if my children develop such a love for him that to lose him would be like losing their mother or me, you can easily see that with them he must remain,—and, alas! I feel that this is the more likely case of the two.

[18] June 22, 1910.

James's sympathy for animals was an almost physical reaction. His pleasure from driving in the mountains was largely destroyed by his feeling for the horses on the long upward grades, and he was perpetually leaping out to reduce the load. Though he believed that the dog in the physiological laboratory would, if he could know what it all meant, "religiously acquiesce" in the experiments, he was haunted by the thought that this meaning of future good to others was precisely what must remain absolutely beyond the sacrificial victim's ken.[19]

James felt a sympathy for dogs and meditated upon their inner lives. He also felt a sympathy for underdogs and invariably sided with them. It is clearly impossible to be a partisan of the underdog without sharing the underdog's antipathies. This is the chief root of James's antipathies. He hated hardness, coldheartedness, complacency, airs of easy superiority. Above all things he hated cruelty. When in his "Dilemma of Determinism" he was casting about in his mind for an instance of unmitigated evil, he chose a recent crime in which a man had murdered his loving and trusting wife. The brutality of the deed itself, the prisoner's self-satisfaction and the mild sentence which he received, not only aroused James's personal detestation, but marked his universe with an indelible stain. He could never bring himself to worship the *whole* of such a universe. "There is something wrong with the world";[20] and the incontrovertible proof of this indictment was the suffering of mankind together with the cruelty or fatality by which it was inflicted.

> There is no *full* consolation. Evil is evil and pain is pain; and in bearing them valiantly I think the only thing we can do is to believe that the good power of the world does not appoint them of its own free will, but works under some dark and inscrutable limitations, and that we by our patience and good will, can somehow strengthen his hands.[21]

The philosophical outcropping of James's tenderness of heart thus appears in his pluralism—in his recognition of the inward significance of individual lives in all their incomprehensible diversity, in his finding a glow of preciousness within every forbidding exterior, and in his absolutely unrelenting condemnation of inhumanity. James's modesty is allied with his tenderness. He frankly enjoyed the honors which were heaped upon him in his later years, but they did not make him self-important. He was fond of quoting John La Farge as saying that fame comes to those who wait, and increases in proportion to their growing imbecility. He was not so much humble as self-forgetful, the reason being that he was preoccupied with other people. This, at least, was his healthy-minded attitude. Now a person who is interested in what he sees and in whom

[19] *W.B.*, 58.
[20] Author's notes in Philos. 3, December 12, 1896.
[21] To Mrs. Glendower Evans, May 24, 1886; *Atlantic*, CXLIV (1929), 375.

he meets, whose mind *goes out,* may very properly be an empiricist in his philosophy. He does not regard himself or any of his faculties as the source of truth; he is never sure enough of himself to claim finality for his results; he listens respectfully to other judges; and he never loses his sense that there is more to come—both from the wisdom of his fellow men and from the teeming universe.

James's extraordinary *sociability* is no doubt associated with his vivacity and his tenderness, but it would be a mistake to treat it as though it were a secondary trait. It is characteristic of him that he should in later years have referred to his three months' hospital internship in 1866 as valuable not because of any pathology that he had learned, but because the "dramatic human relationship" with certain people had helped him in the way of understanding human nature.[22] For stiff, artificial, or noisy social relations he felt a strong loathing, and he sought to avoid them. But this is as though a musically sensitive person should avoid bad music. He had a great love and a great capacity for social relations where these were spontaneous and sincere.

When the atmosphere was favorable—and he could usually make it so—he was a great talker, with an abundant flow of wit and wisdom directed very personally and with great good will to those about him. He considered conversation as a kind of joyful recreation, capable of refinement and subtlety like any art, but requiring openheartedness and fellow feeling as its first condition. The following was written to Howells in 1894, on March 19, apropos of a letter which the latter had received from an enthusiastic admirer of the elder James:—

> I [am] much pleased to learn of one more reader of poor old H. J. whose readers in these latter days seem so few. . . . Only as for "one real American not being afraid of any other," I fear Father would have snorted at the lack of reality in the dictum. If there is anyone *I* am really afraid of it is the dry-hearted American whom you meet in traveling, and to whom the sort of trivial conversation you engage in with everybody you meet in Europe, is an object of nothing but disdain. I dined yesterday at New Bedford, whither I had rushed for a snatch of Sabbatical rest, at a table with four others. Each of us gulped his food in silence, each fearing the other's contemptuous or painful reception of a sudden remark. I was immensely struck in the south two years ago by the uncomfortable state I threw everyone into to whom I spoke at table. They looked away, became uneasy, and hastened to leave. Speech must have an object, for the "real" American to tolerate it.

The same complaint is made in a letter of 1900 to Francis Boott:

> I confess that one of the things at home that most draws me is the remembrance of your laugh and everlasting sociability and good humor. For you, talk-

[22] Talk with Professor Alexander Forbes, April 1, 1909.

ing is a substantive enjoyment. For my other colleagues and playmates, except perhaps Mrs. Whitman,[23] it is only a useful and often tiresome means to some ulterior end.

The following recollection by a former student indicates James's desire to establish a human in place of an official relationship:

> We found that unless his positions were challenged his lectures might become prosy, whereas the challenge was sure to bring the lightning flashes of his wit and make it extremely interesting. Well do I remember how another student and myself framed a friendly conspiracy alternately to take the dangerous role of lightning conductor by trying to badger him. He also at that time had a curious habit of going around to his classes under the pretext of some trouble with his eyes and getting them to read his examination papers to him when, of course, if there was any lack of lucidity it could be at once explained. I think, however, his real object was to get in close touch and friendly contact with the men.[24]

It is clear from this description that James preferred to converse with people who had minds of their own, and who could give as well as receive. It was in 1896 from Chautauqua that James wrote his wife this impression, and this characteristically indulgent judgment, of certain serious and docile people whom he respected but did not enjoy:

> I'm put in conceit of college training. It certainly gives glibness and flexibility, if it doesn't give earnestness and depth. I've been meeting minds so earnest and helpless that it takes them half an hour to get from one idea to its immediately adjacent next neighbor, and that with infinite creaking and groaning. And when they've got to the next idea, they lie down on it with their whole weight and can get no farther, like a cow on a door-mat, so that you can get neither in nor out with them. Still, glibness is not all. Weight is something, even cow-weight.[25]

These, James's natural benign gifts—his sensibility, his vivacity, his humanity, and his sociability—united to compose his personal charm. They were all engraven on his face and embodied in his appearance and bearing: in the erectness and firmness of his posture, in his "irascible blue eyes," in his "pleasant and manly voice," [26] and above all in the confident friendliness of his expression. "I still remember vividly," writes one of his students,

> how James used to arrive at class with hat and gloves but no overcoat on fairly cold mornings, and how handsome he looked standing on the edge of the plat-

[23] August 9, 1900; Mrs. Henry Whitman of Boston and Beverly.
[24] A. C. Lane, "The Trilemma of Determinism," *Western Journal of Education,* IV (1911), 161-8.
[25] July 24, 1896; *L.W.J.,* II, 41.
[26] *L.W.J.,* I, 25; *Letters of C. E. Norton,* 1913, I, 264.

form and saying in a casual conversational tone: "There is no primal teleological reagibility in a protoplasm." [27]

James's radioactive personality not only warmed and illuminated, but ignited; bringing him both lasting friendships, and also a wide circle of acquaintances and readers whose admiration glowed with affection. His personal qualities reached his readers, as well as his hearers, not only because these qualities infused his writing, but because his writing was addressed to his readers as though they were acquaintances or hearers.

Hence the same qualities which afford the key to James's character and personal magnetism also explain his style. He was much concerned with literary form both in others and in himself. Writing in 1894 of Stevenson's *Wrecker,* he said: "It seemed to me that the matter had decidedly overflowed and slopped round the form. Too much inchoate frontierism of event, character and language. Literature has to assimulate her stuff slowly to get it plastic." [28] James's own most characteristic species of writing was the lecture or public address. A being as sensitively socialized as he could not utter monologues in the presence of his kind—he must reach out to them, touch them, and feel their response. So whatever he wrote began as talk. His letters were more artful than his talk. [29] When it came to his published writings, they had to satisfy this social requirement and at the same time expound their subject matter with orderly completeness. To accomplish both of these results at the same time cost James much labor. He wrote, corrected, and rewrote. "Everything comes out wrong with me at first; but when once objectified in a crude shape, I can torture and poke and scrape and pat it till it offends me no more." [30] When his writing was thus finally acceptable to James, its subject matter was clarified and at the same time so humanized that he could enjoy a sense of common understanding and of friendly intercourse with his audience.

Of course he had his moments of dissatisfaction with this style. In 1908, when it was too late to change his habits even had it been temperamentally possible, he wrote:

> I find that my free and easy and personal way of writing, especially in *Pragmatism,* has made me an object of loathing to many respectable academic minds, and I am rather tired of awakening that feeling, which more popular lecturing on my part will probably destine me to increase.

But as a rule his style represented his own opinion of what philosophical style should be. "I don't care how incorrect language may be," he once said,

---

[27] Daniel G. Mason to the author, November 21, 1929.
[28] To Francis Boott, September 5, 1894.
[29] "My letters, I find, tend to escape into humorisms, abstractions and flights of fancy." (*L.W.J.,* II, 111.)
[30] To Mrs. Henry Whitman, July 4, 1890; *L.W.J.,* I, 297.

"if it only has fitness of epithet, energy and clearness." He hailed Papini with joy, as one in whom he found "instead of heaviness, length and obscurity, lightness, clearness and brevity, with no lack of profundity or learning." James's canons of style, in other words, were dictated by a consideration for his reader and a desire to *reach* him. He hated to be bored himself and he dreaded to give such offense to others. He once wrote to his brother Henry of Bryce's *American Commonwealth:* "A perfect bog of reasonableness, as you once said. One fairly longs for a *screech* of some kind." [31]

James's style was also determined by the fact that he wrote both philosophy and psychology in literary or colloquial English. "Technicality seems to me to spell 'failure' in philosophy." He proposed to Santayana that they unite their forces in an assault on "the desiccating and pedantifying" [32] processes of the American Ph.D. This condemnation of technicality no doubt reflected James's distaste for logic and mathematics, but it also reflected his conviction that all inquiries are directed to the same world, which lies open and accessible; and that there is only one way of knowing, namely, by hypothesis and verification. There is, he said, "just man thinking, whether he be greengrocer or metaphysician." There is no mysterious kind of being or truth behind the known world. There is only that sort of thing with which we are familiar, and which we overlook or despise because it is familiar, and there is *more of the same kind.*[33] Reality being of this intimate sort, revealing its innermost character in the human experience of every day, the appropriate style of philosophical exposition is that which vivifies the familiar, and extends its horizon without altering its essential character.

James felt a peculiar aversion towards the translations of his writings. "It is no doubt a piece of neurasthenic perversion of sensibility," he wrote to Flournoy in 1900,

> but I confess that translations of my own writings always give me a kind of horror, and the best thing for me is in no way to coöperate. I haven't read a single page of the German translation of my *Essays* or of the Italian translation of my *Psychology.*

This feeling was in part his characteristic desire to escape to something new from what had long been on his mind, and in part a feeling of humility that anyone should go to so much trouble on his account. But when he did advise his translators it was to urge them to subordinate literal accuracy to sense. He wanted the French translation of the short *Psychology* to read as if it were

---

[31] To Th. Flournoy, January 2, 1908, *L.W.J.,* II, 300-1; to Francis Boott, January 30, 1893, *L.W.J.,* I, 341; *C.E.R.,* 460-1; to H.J.², February 1, 1889.
[32] To G. H. Howison, July 24, 1898, *L.W.J.,* II, 79; to Santayana, May 2, 1905, *L.W.J.,* II, 229.
[33] Student's notes in Philos. 3, 1896-7.

originally composed in the French language. When Flournoy was intending to translate the *Varieties,* James wrote: "Feel absolutely free to abridge, invent, expand, paraphrase in *any* way, solely from the point of view of making the French reader content." [34] Again it is the social motive which outweighs every consideration of verbal precision.

Among the most technical of James's writings were the articles collected under the title of *Essays in Radical Empiricism.* They were designed as papers to be published in a philosophical journal and read by his professional colleagues. But before he published them he seized the opportunity to present them in his five lectures before Davidson's summer school at Glenmore in 1904, "just to hear how the stuff would sound when packed into that bulk. It sounded *queer,* and I must make it sound less so to the common mind." [35] In short, James did not write for posterity, still less for eternity, but spoke audibly to those who were visibly present.

[34] July 6, 1900; June 9, 1902.
[35] To F. C. S. Schiller, September 4, 1904.

CONCLUSION

We have met two William Jameses: the neurasthenic James, with his unstable nervous equilibrium, his sometimes morbidly vivid and lawless imagination, his oscillation of mood and aversion for rigorous intellectual procedure; and the radiant James, vivid, gay, loving, companionable, and sensitive. We have, in fact, met a third James, in whom the second of these is deepened and enrichened through being united with the first. To this third James must be assigned two remarkable essays in self-revelation. The first was written about 1878, when James was thirty-six years of age:—

> I have often thought that the best way to define a man's character would be to seek out the particular mental or moral attitude in which, when it came upon him, he felt himself most deeply and intensely active and alive. At such moments there is a voice inside which speaks and says: "*This* is the real me!" . . . Now as well as I can describe it, this characteristic attitude in me always involves an element of active tension, of holding my own, as it were, and trusting outward things to perform their part so as to make it a full harmony, but without any *guaranty* that they will. Make it a guaranty—and the attitude immediately becomes to my consciousness stagnant and stingless. Take away the guaranty, and I feel (provided I am *überhaupt* in vigorous condition) a sort of deep enthusiastic bliss, of bitter willingness to do and suffer anything, which translates itself physically by a kind of stinging pain inside my breast-bone (don't smile at this—it is to me an essential element of the whole thing!), and which, although it is a mere mood or emotion to which I can give no form in words, authenticates itself to me as the deepest principle of all active and theoretic determination which I possess.[1]

The following paragraphs were written in a notebook twenty-five years later:—

> How can I . . . justify the strong antithesis I constantly feel, namely, that certain philosophic constructions . . . are subjective caprices, redolent of individual taste, while other constructions, those which work with concrete elements, with change, with indeterminism, are more objective and cling closer to the temperament of nature itself. . . . What, on pragmatist terms, does "nature itself" signify? To my mind it signifies the non-artificial; the artificial having

[1] To A.J.H., *L.W.J.*, I, 199-200.

certain definite æsthetic characteristics which I dislike, and can only apperceive in others as matters of personal taste,—to me bad taste. All neat schematisms with permanent and absolute distinctions, classifications with absolute pretensions, systems with pigeon-holes, etc., have this character. All "classic," clean, cut and dried, "noble," fixed, "eternal," *Weltanschauungen* seem to me to violate the character with which life concretely comes and the expression which it bears of being, or at least of involving, a muddle and a struggle, with an "ever not quite" to all our formulas, and novelty and possibility forever leaking in.

Münsterberg's Congress-program[2] seems to me, *e.g.,* to be sheer humbug in the sense of self-infatuation with an idol of the den, a kind of religious service in honor of the professional-philosophy-shop, with its faculty, its departments and sections, its mutual etiquette, its appointments, its great mill of authorities and exclusions and suppressions which the waters of truth are expected to feed to the great class-glory of all who are concerned. To me "truth," if there be any truth, would seem to exist for the express confusion of all this kind of thing, and to reveal itself in whispers to the "meek lovers of the good" in their solitude —the Darwins, the Lockes, etc.,—and to be expressly incompatible with officialism. "Officials" are products of no deep stratum of experience. Münsterberg's Congress seems to be the perfectly inevitable expression of the system of his *Grundzüge,* an artificial construction for the sake of making the authority of professors inalienable, no matter what asininities they may utter, as if the bureaucratic mind were the full flavor of nature's self-revelation. It is obvious that such a difference as this, between me and Münsterberg, is a splendid expression of pragmatism. I want a world of anarchy, Münsterberg one of bureaucracy, and each appeals to "nature" to back him up. Nature partly helps and partly resists each of us.

"Active tension," uncertainty, unpredictability, extemporized adaptation, risk, change, anarchy, unpretentiousness, naturalness—these are the qualities of life which James finds most palatable, and which give him the deepest sense of well-being. These are at the same time the qualities which he deems most authentic, the accents in which the existent world speaks to him most directly. It seems clear that this metaphysical insight, profoundly temperamental as it is, cannot be imputed to any single element of James's nature, morbid or benign. There is something of his restlessness in it, something of his preference of the unusual to the orderly; it is to some extent his way of escape from a tendency to morbid self-preoccupation. On the other hand, it is a direct expression of his creative and richly imaginal fancy; a projection of his vivacity; and the cosmic sympathy by which he rejoiced in strange and varied otherness.

There is still a fourth James, the James of experience and discipline—a transformation of native qualities into dispositions and habits. One is, perhaps, surprised to discover that a man of James's speculative interests was also a man of

---

[2] Written in 1903. "Münsterberg's Congress" was the "Congress of Arts and Sciences" held at the St. Louis Exposition in the summer of 1904. His *Grundzüge der Psychologie,* dedicated to W.J., appeared in 1900.

the world. He was not, like the proverbial Thales, forever falling into wells while gazing at the stars; nor was he one of those childlike innocents, well-known in the European academic world, who need a guardian to manage their affairs. He knew his way around. As was once remarked of his father, he knew how to go close to the edge of impropriety without stepping off.[3] Despite his bold indiscretions, his easy manners, and a mischievous delight in shocking the pedants, he never strayed beyond the bounds of good taste. Or if he did, he knew it. His breeding gave him that sense of security which permits occasional liberties. He took liberties with the English language, but they were clearly privileged liberties, which derived a certain authority from the fact that he took them. He associated with strange characters, and frequented the intellectual underworld; but he did not lose caste, or compromise his essential dignity. Here, in short, was a man who seemed to let himself go, or to be *willing* to make a fool of himself, and who, owing to some unconscious inner check, never did make a fool of himself. He was original, spontaneous, but never "queer."

We think of James as cosmopolitan, and of course he was. He began his almost ceaseless travels at the age of two, and learned to feel at home in all parts of Western Europe. Yet he was so crudely patriotic as to make his more emancipated friends feel a sense of superior detachment. It was characteristic of him to write to Norton of England's "magnificently fine state of civilization," to say that "everything here seems about twice as good as the corresponding thing with us"; and then to add, "but I suspect we have the bigger eventual destiny after all"—thereby betraying, as Norton said, his "invincible Americanism."[4] In short, though James moved freely and wandered far, he was never uprooted. His "heart" remained at home.

Worldly wisdom, taste, breeding, domesticity, patriotism—these were some of the forces of control, entering into what we may call the conscience of James, as distinguished from his native traits. There remain the two major constituents of that conscience, the moral and the intellectual.

James was a moralist in the good old-fashioned sense of one who believes that right is right and wrong is wrong, and he enrolled himself under the first in order to combat the second. "Tell him to live by yes and no,—yes to everything good, no to everything bad," was the message he once sent to his youngest son.[5] I shall not attempt to trace this moralism to its source. It is natural to attribute it to his Calvinistic ancestry, though such an explanation loses much of its force when it is remembered that his father, the immediate embodiment

[3] MS. report of G. H. Howison's "St. Louis Reminiscences," January 6, 1916, University of California Library.
[4] *Letters of C. E. Norton*, 1913, II, 412.
[5] To his mother-in-law, Mrs. Eliza P. Gibbens, August 2, 1899.

of that ancestry, was in antinomian revolt against Calvinism. More important than the question of creed is the fact that his father was a good man and a moral partisan; and there was an image of maternal saintliness which, could it be brought into a clearer light, would no doubt explain much. It is plain, also, that a sense of deportment, associated with those checks of taste and breeding already noted, disposed him to accept traditional moral standards. The intensity of his moral feeling was reënforced by his sympathies, since morals for James were always in the end translated into humanity.

The strength of James's moralism is proved by the fact that it outweighed the warm attachment of old friendships; prevented his ever becoming a mere psychologist of morals, as might have been expected from his interest in the history and pathology of the mind; set limits to his love of life, and sometimes even to his tolerance; and definitely triumphed over his æsthetic sensibility and artistic impulse.

Moralism is only one name for James's fundamental seriousness. With all his gayety and playfulness, he exceeded most of his contemporaries in his sense of responsibility. He refused to use any of the methods, so well known among philosophers, by which a man justifies his leaving the arena and taking a seat among the spectators:

> I can't bring myself, as so many men seem able to do, to blink the evil out of sight, and gloss it over. It's as real as the good, and if it is denied, good must be denied too. It must be accepted and hated and resisted while there's breath in our bodies.[6]

In short, unlike a later and faltering generation, James united liberalism, tolerance, and humanity with a resolve that these principles should, so help him God, prevail.

James had an intellectual as well as a moral conscience. He had a regard, almost a reverence, for facts. In his early days as a student at Harvard, it was Jeffries Wyman with his scrupulous and modest adherence to the results of observation, rather than Louis Agassiz with his bolder and more dogmatic mind, who was his scientific paragon. His philosophical heroes were always men like Renouvier or Mill whom he believed to be honest and disinterested in the sense of reporting faithfully what they found. He did not object to invention and wishful thinking, but he did object to the pretense that they were anything else. He was an empiricist because he believed empiricism to be the only *open-minded* and *candid* philosophy.

His intellectual conscience appears in his vast erudition, his indefatigable industry, and in the patience with which he controlled his own impatience and devoted years to the untying of a philosophic knot. It took him ten years to answer Royce's argument for the Absolute, and another ten years to solve the problem of the compounding of consciousness. When he died he had just forsworn his *Sturm und Drang* propensities forever in order that he might satisfy his intellectual scruples and the "respectable academic minds" of his colleagues.[7]

James took philosophy as he took life—seriously. He felt that, like tragic poetry, it was distinguished by its noble theme. Philosophy was not a form of play or craftsmanship, though it might add those values to its own. It was the pursuit of truth. And truth is not worth pursuing unless what you apprehend you also believe. It is by belief that one makes truth one's own—absorbs its nutriment. Hence in his philosophizing James was a believer; and was moved by the believer's missionary zeal. Thus he once wrote to a fellow pluralist: "We must all go to work to counteract the *Absolute One,* which has its way so freely in metaphysics, and I hope you'll play your part actively." [8]

There is a simple earnestness in this plea that is of the very essence of James. His power in philosophy and over philosophers was due in no small measure to his teaching that in theory as in practice a man must take his part, believing something, fighting for what he believes, and incurring the risk of being wrong. And with all this eagerness of pursuit and strength of conviction there was no suspicion of complacency. He always left the impression that there was more; that he knew there was more; and that the more to come might, for all one knew, throw a very different light on the matters under discussion. He respected his universe too much to believe that he could carry it under his own hat. These saving doubts arose from the same source as his tolerance and respect for his fellow man. The universe, like one's neighbor, is never wholly disclosed to outward view, and the last word must be a consent that the *other* should be *itself.* In metaphysics, as in human relations, the chief source of illumination is sympathy. The conclusion of the matter was unconsciously formulated by James himself:—

> I merely point out to you that, as a matter of fact, certain persons do exist with an enormous capacity for friendship and for taking delight in other people's lives; and that such persons know more of truth than if their hearts were not so big.[9]

[7] Above, 353, 382.
[8] To James Ward, May 13, 1897.
[9] *T.T.,* 267.

ABBREVIATIONS

I. WORKS OF WILLIAM JAMES

Principles of Psychology, 1890	*Psychology*
Psychology. Briefer Course, 1892	*P. B. C.*
The Will to Believe, and Other Essays in Popular Philosophy, 1897	*W. B.*
Human Immortality: Two Supposed Objections to the Doctrine, 1898	*H. I.*
Talks to Teachers on Psychology: and to Students on Some of Life's Ideals, 1899	*T. T.*
The Varieties of Religious Experience: A Study in Human Nature, 1902	*V. R. E.*
Pragmatism: A New Name for Some Old Ways of Thinking, 1907	*Pragm.*
The Meaning of Truth, A Sequel to "Pragmatism," 1909	*M. T.*
A Pluralistic Universe: Hibbert Lectures on the Present Situation in Philosophy, 1909	*P. U.*
[1]*Some Problems of Philosophy: A Beginning of an Introduction to Philosophy*, 1911	*S. P. P.*
[1]*Memories and Studies*, 1911	*M. S.*
[1]*Essays in Radical Empiricism*, 1912	*E. R. E.*
[1]*Collected Essays and Reviews*, 1920	*C. E. R.*

II. OTHER WORKS, RELATING TO JAMES

Henry James, *A Small Boy and Others*, 1913	*S. B. O.*
Henry James, *Notes of a Son and Brother*, 1914	*N. S. B.*
Henry James, *Letters of*, edited by Percy Lubbock, 1920	*L. H. J.*[2]
William James, *Letters of*, edited by his son Henry James, 1920	*L. W. J.*
Henry James, *The Literary Remains of the Late*, edited by William James, 1885	*L.R.H.J.*

III. FAMILY NAMES

William James (1842-1910)	W. J.
Henry James (1811-1882), father of W. J.	H. J.[1]
Henry James (1843-1916), brother of W. J.	H. J.[2]
Garth Wilkinson James (1845-1883), brother of W. J.	G. W. J.
Robertson James (1846-1910), brother of W. J.	R. J.
Alice James (1848-1892), sister of W. J.	A. J.
Alice Howe Gibbens James (1849-1922), wife of W. J.	A. H. J.

[1] Posthumous.

INDEX

harper ✦ torchbooks

HUMANITIES AND SOCIAL SCIENCES

American Studies

JOHN R. ALDEN: The American Revolution, 1775-1783.† *Illus.*　　　TB/3011

RAY STANNARD BAKER: Following the Color Line: *American Negro Citizenship in the Progressive Era.*‡ *Illus. Edited by Dewey W. Grantham, Jr.*　TB/3053

RAY A. BILLINGTON: The Far Western Frontier, 1830-1860.† *Illus.*　　　TB/3012

JOSEPH L. BLAU, Ed.: Cornerstones of Religious Freedom in America. *Selected Basic Documents, Court Decisions and Public Statements. Enlarged and revised edition with new Intro. by Editor*　TB/118

RANDOLPH S. BOURNE: War and the Intellectuals: *Collected Essays, 1915-1919.*‡ *Edited by Carl Resek*　　　TB/3043

A. RUSSELL BUCHANAN: The United States and World War II. † *Illus.*　Volume I　TB/3044
　　　　　　　　　　　　　Volume II　TB/3045

ABRAHAM CAHAN: The Rise of David Levinsky: *a novel. Introduction by John Higham*　TB/1028

JOSEPH CHARLES: The Origins of the American Party System　　　TB/1049

THOMAS C. COCHRAN: The Inner Revolution: *Essays on the Social Sciences in History*　　　TB/1140

T. C. COCHRAN & WILLIAM MILLER: The Age of Enterprise: *A Social History of Industrial America*　　　TB/1054

EDWARD S. CORWIN: American Constitutional History: *Essays edited by Alpheus T. Mason and Gerald Garvey*　　　TB/1136

FOSTER RHEA DULLES: America's Rise to World Power, 1898-1954.† *Illus.*　TB/3021

W. A. DUNNING: Reconstruction, Political and Economic, 1865-1877　　　TB/1073

A. HUNTER DUPREE: Science in the Federal Government: *A History of Policies and Activities to 1940*　　　TB/573

CLEMENT EATON: The Growth of Southern Civilization, 1790-1860.† *Illus.*　TB/3040

HAROLD U. FAULKNER: Politics, Reform and Expansion, 1890-1900.† *Illus.*　TB/3020

LOUIS FILLER: The Crusade against Slavery, 1830-1860.† *Illus.*　TB/3029

EDITORS OF FORTUNE: America in the Sixties: *the Economy and the Society. Two-color charts*　TB/1015

LAWRENCE HENRY GIPSON: The Coming of the Revolution, 1763-1775.† *Illus.*　TB/3007

FRANCIS J. GRUND: Aristocracy in America: *Jacksonian Democracy*　　　TB/1001

ALEXANDER HAMILTON: The Reports of Alexander Hamilton.‡ *Edited by Jacob E. Cooke*　TB/3060

OSCAR HANDLIN, Editor: This Was America: *As Recorded by European Travelers to the Western Shore in the Eighteenth, Nineteenth, and Twentieth Centuries. Illus.*　TB/1119

MARCUS LEE HANSEN: The Atlantic Migration: 1607-1860. *Edited by Arthur M. Schlesinger; Introduction by Oscar Handlin*　TB/1052

MARCUS LEE HANSEN: The Immigrant in American History. *Edited with a Foreword by Arthur Schlesinger, Sr.*　TB/1120

JOHN D. HICKS: Republican Ascendancy, 1921-1933.† *Illus.*　　　TB/3041

JOHN HIGHAM, Ed.: The Reconstruction of American History　　　TB/1068

DANIEL R. HUNDLEY: Social Relations in our Southern States.‡ *Edited by William R. Taylor*　TB/3058

ROBERT H. JACKSON: The Supreme Court in the American System of Government　TB/1106

THOMAS JEFFERSON: Notes on the State of Virginia.‡ *Edited by Thomas Perkins Abernethy*　TB/3052

WILLIAM L. LANGER & S. EVERETT GLEASON: The Challenge to Isolation: *The World Crisis of 1937-1940 and American Foreign Policy*　Volume I　TB/3054
　　　　　　　　　　　　　　Volume II　TB/3055

WILLIAM E. LEUCHTENBURG: Franklin D. Roosevelt and the New Deal, 1932-1940.† *Illus.*　TB/3025

LEONARD W. LEVY: Freedom of Speech and Press in Early American History: *Legacy of Suppression*　　　TB/1109

ARTHUR S. LINK: Woodrow Wilson and the Progressive Era, 1910-1917.† *Illus.*　TB/3023

ROBERT GREEN McCLOSKEY: American Conservatism in the Age of Enterprise, 1865-1910　TB/1137

BERNARD MAYO: Myths and Men: *Patrick Henry, George Washington, Thomas Jefferson*　TB/1108

JOHN C. MILLER: Alexander Hamilton and the Growth of the New Nation　TB/3057

JOHN C. MILLER: The Federalist Era, 1789-1801.† *Illus.*　　　TB/3027

---

† The New American Nation Series, edited by Henry Steele Commager and Richard B. Morris.

‡ American Perspectives series, edited by Bernard Wishy and William E. Leuchtenburg.

* The Rise of Modern Europe series, edited by William L. Langer.

❚ Researches in the Social, Cultural, and Behavioral Sciences, edited by Benjamin Nelson.

§ The Library of Religion and Culture, edited by Benjamin Nelson.

Σ Harper Modern Science Series, edited by James R. Newman.

ᵒ Not for sale in Canada.

PERRY MILLER: Errand into the Wilderness   TB/1139
PERRY MILLER & T. H. JOHNSON, Editors: The Puritans: *A Sourcebook of Their Writings*
Volume I   TB/1093
Volume II   TB/1094
GEORGE E. MOWRY: The Era of Theodore Roosevelt and the Birth of Modern America, 1900-1912.† *Illus.*
TB/3022
WALLACE NOTESTEIN: The English People on the Eve of Colonization, 1603-1630.† *Illus.*   TB/3006
RUSSEL BLAINE NYE: The Cultural Life of the New Nation, 1776-1801.† *Illus.*   TB/3026
RALPH BARTON PERRY: Puritanism and Democracy
TB/1138
GEORGE E. PROBST, Ed.: The Happy Republic: *A Reader in Tocqueville's America*   TB/1060
WALTER RAUSCHENBUSCH: Christianity and the Social Crisis.‡ *Edited by Robert D. Cross*   TB/3059
FRANK THISTLETHWAITE: America and the Atlantic Community: *Anglo-American Aspects, 1790-1850*
TB/1107
TWELVE SOUTHERNERS: I'll Take My Stand: *The South and the Agrarian Tradition. Introduction by Louis D. Rubin, Jr.; Biographical Essays by Virginia Rock*   TB/1072
A. F. TYLER: Freedom's Ferment: *Phases of American Social History from the Revolution to the Outbreak of the Civil War. Illus.*   TB/1074
GLYNDON G. VAN DEUSEN: The Jacksonian Era, 1828-1848.† *Illus.*   TB/3028
WALTER E. WEYL: The New Democracy: *An Essay on Certain Political and Economic Tendencies in the United States.‡ Edited by Charles Forcey*   TB/3042
LOUIS B. WRIGHT: The Cultural Life of the American Colonies, 1607-1763.† *Illus.*   TB/3005
LOUIS B. WRIGHT: Culture on the Moving Frontier
TB/1053

Anthropology & Sociology

BERNARD BERELSON, Ed.: The Behavioral Sciences Today   TB/1127
JOSEPH B. CASAGRANDE, Ed.: In the Company of Man: *20 Portraits of Anthropological Informants. Illus.*   TB/3047
W. E. LE GROS CLARK: The Antecedents of Man: *An Introduction to the Evolution of the Primates.*° *Illus.*
TB/559
THOMAS C. COCHRAN: The Inner Revolution: *Essays on the Social Sciences in History*
TB/1140
ALLISON DAVIS & JOHN DOLLARD: Children of Bondage: *The Personality Development of Negro Youth in the Urban South*▮   TB/3049
ST. CLAIR DRAKE & HORACE R. CAYTON: Black Metropolis: *A Study of Negro Life in a Northern City. Introduction by Everett C. Hughes. Tables, maps, charts and graphs*   Volume I   TB/1086
Volume II   TB/1087
CORA DU BOIS: The People of Alor. *New Preface by the author. Illus.*   Volume I   TB/1042
Volume II   TB/1043
LEON FESTINGER, HENRY W. RIECKEN & STANLEY SCHACHTER: When Prophecy Fails: *A Social and Psychological Account of a Modern Group that Predicted the Destruction of the World*▮   TB/1132
RAYMOND FIRTH, Ed.: Man and Culture: *An Evaluation of the Work of Bronislaw Malinowski* ▮°
TB/1133

L. S. B. LEAKEY: Adam's Ancestors: *The Evolution of Man and his Culture. Illus.*   TB/1019
KURT LEWIN: Field Theory in Social Science: *Selected Theoretical Papers.*▮ *Edited with a Foreword by Dorwin Cartwright*   TB/1135
ROBERT H. LOWIE: Primitive Society. *Introduction by Fred Eggan*   TB/1056
BENJAMIN NELSON: Religious Traditions and the Spirit of Capitalism: *From the Church Fathers to Jeremy Bentham*   TB/1130
TALCOTT PARSONS & EDWARD A. SHILS, Editors: Toward a General Theory of Action: *Theoretical Foundations for the Social Sciences*   TB/1083
JOHN H. ROHRER & MUNRO S. EDMONSON, Eds.: The Eighth Generation Grows Up: *Cultures and Personalities of New Orleans Negroes*▮   TB/3050
ARNOLD ROSE: The Negro in America: *The Condensed Version of Gunnar Myrdal's An American Dilemma. New Introduction by the Author; Foreword by Gunnar Myrdal*   TB/3048
KURT SAMUELSSON: Religion and Economic Action: *A Critique of Max Weber's The Protestant Ethic and the Spirit of Capitalism.*▮° *Trans. by E. G. French; Ed. with Intro. by D. C. Coleman*   TB/1131
PITIRIM SOROKIN: Contemporary Sociological Theories: *Through the First Quarter of the Twentieth Century*   TB/3046
MAURICE R. STEIN: The Eclipse of Community: *An Interpretation of American Studies. New Introduction by the Author*   TB/1128
SIR EDWARD TYLOR: The Origins of Culture. *Part I of "Primitive Culture."*§ *Introduction by Paul Radin*
TB/33
SIR EDWARD TYLOR: Religion in Primitive Culture. *Part II of "Primitive Culture."*§ *Introduction by Paul Radin*   TB/34
W. LLOYD WARNER & Associates: Democracy in Jonesville: *A Study in Quality and Inequality*⁑
TB/1129
W. LLOYD WARNER: A Black Civilization: *A Study of an Australian Tribe.*▮ *Illus.*   TB/3056
W. LLOYD WARNER: Social Class in America: *The Evaluation of Status*   TB/1013

Art and Art History

EMILE MÂLE: The Gothic Image: *Religious Art in France of the Thirteenth Century.*§ *190 illus.*   TB/44
MILLARD MEISS: Painting in Florence and Siena after the Black Death. *169 illus.*   TB/1148
ERWIN PANOFSKY: Studies in Iconology: *Humanistic Themes in the Art of the Renaissance. 180 illustrations*   TB/1077
ALEXANDRE PIANKOFF: The Shrines of Tut-Ankh-Amon. *Edited by N. Rambova. 117 illus.*   TB/2011
JEAN SEZNEC: The Survival of the Pagan Gods: *The Mythological Tradition and Its Place in Renaissance Humanism and Art. 108 illustrations*   TB/2004
OTTO VON SIMSON: The Gothic Cathedral: *Origins of Gothic Architecture and the Medieval Concept of Order. 58 illus.*   TB/2018
HEINRICH ZIMMER: Myths and Symbols in Indian Art and Civilization. *70 illustrations*   TB/2005

Business, Economics & Economic History

REINHARD BENDIX: Work and Authority in Industry: *Ideologies of Management in the Course of Industrialization*   TB/3035

2

THOMAS C. COCHRAN: The American Business System: *A Historical Perspective, 1900-1955* TB/1080

ROBERT DAHL & CHARLES E. LINDBLOM: Politics, Economics, and Welfare: *Planning and Politico-Economic Systems Resolved into Basic Social Processes* TB/3037

PETER F. DRUCKER: The New Society: *The Anatomy of Industrial Order* TB/1082

ROBERT L. HEILBRONER: The Great Ascent: *The Struggle for Economic Development in Our Time* TB/3030

ABBA P. LERNER: Everybody's Business: *A Re-examination of Current Assumptions in Economics and Public Policy* TB/3051

ROBERT GREEN McCLOSKEY: American Conservatism in the Age of Enterprise, 1865-1910 TB/1137

PAUL MANTOUX: The Industrial Revolution in the Eighteenth Century: *The Beginnings of the Modern Factory System in England*° TB/1079

WILLIAM MILLER, Ed.: Men in Business: *Essays on the Historical Role of the Entrepreneur* TB/1081

PERRIN STRYKER: The Character of the Executive: *Eleven Studies in Managerial Qualities* TB/1041

PIERRE URI: Partnership for Progress: *A Program for Transatlantic Action* TB/3036

Contemporary Culture

JACQUES BARZUN: The House of Intellect TB/1051

JOHN U. NEF: Cultural Foundations of Industrial Civilization TB/1024

PAUL VALÉRY: The Outlook for Intelligence TB/2016

History: General

L. CARRINGTON GOODRICH: A Short History of the Chinese People. *Illus.* TB/3015

BERNARD LEWIS: The Arabs in History TB/1029

SIR PERCY SYKES: A History of Exploration.° *Introduction by John K. Wright* TB/1046

History: Ancient and Medieval

A. ANDREWES: The Greek Tyrants TB/1103

P. BOISSONNADE: Life and Work in Medieval Europe.° *Preface by Lynn White, Jr.* TB/1141

HELEN CAM: England before Elizabeth TB/1026

NORMAN COHN: The Pursuit of the Millennium: *Revolutionary Messianism in medieval and Reformation Europe and its bearing on modern Leftist and Rightist totalitarian movements* TB/1037

G. G. COULTON: Medieval Village, Manor, and Monastery TB/1022

HEINRICH FICHTENAU: The Carolingian Empire: *The Age of Charlemagne* TB/1142

F. L. GANSHOF: Feudalism TB/1058

J. M. HUSSEY: The Byzantine World TB/1057

SAMUEL NOAH KRAMER: Sumerian Mythology TB/1055

FERDINAND LOT: The End of the Ancient World and the Beginnings of the Middle Ages. *Introduction by Glanville Downey* TB/1044

STEVEN RUNCIMAN: A History of the Crusades. Volume I: *The First Crusade and the Foundation of the Kingdom of Jerusalem. Illus.* TB/1143

HENRY OSBORN TAYLOR: The Classical Heritage of the Middle Ages. *Foreword and Biblio. by Kenneth M. Setton* [Formerly listed as TB/48 under the title *The Emergence of Christian Culture in the West*] TB/1117

J. M. WALLACE-HADRILL: The Barbarian West: *The Early Middle Ages, A.D. 400-1000* TB/1061

History: Renaissance & Reformation

R. R. BOLGAR: The Classical Heritage and Its Beneficiaries: *From the Carolingian Age to the End of the Renaissance* TB/1125

JACOB BURCKHARDT: The Civilization of the Renaissance in Italy. *Introduction by Benjamin Nelson and Charles Trinkaus. Illus.* Volume I TB/40 Volume II TB/41

ERNST CASSIRER: The Individual and the Cosmos in Renaissance Philosophy. *Translated with an Introduction by Mario Domandi* TB/1097

EDWARD P. CHEYNEY: The Dawn of a New Era, 1250-1453.* *Illus.* TB/3002

WALLACE K. FERGUSON, et al.: Facets of the Renaissance TB/1098

WALLACE K. FERGUSON, et al.: The Renaissance: *Six Essays. Illus.* TB/1084

MYRON P. GILMORE: The World of Humanism, 1453-1517.* *Illus.* TB/3003

JOHAN HUIZINGA: Erasmus and the Age of Reformation. *Illus.* TB/19

ULRICH VON HUTTEN, et al.: On the Eve of the Reformation: *"Letters of Obscure Men." Introduction by Hajo Holborn* TB/1124

PAUL O. KRISTELLER: Renaissance Thought: *The Classic, Scholastic, and Humanist Strains* TB/1048

NICCOLÒ MACHIAVELLI: History of Florence and of the Affairs of Italy: *from the earliest times to the death of Lorenzo the Magnificent. Introduction by Felix Gilbert* TB/1027

ALFRED VON MARTIN: Sociology of the Renaissance. *Introduction by Wallace K. Ferguson* TB/1099

MILLARD MEISS: Painting in Florence and Siena after the Black Death. *169 illus.* TB/1148

J. E. NEALE: The Age of Catherine de Medici° TB/1085

ERWIN PANOFSKY: Studies in Iconology: *Humanistic Themes in the Art of the Renaissance. 180 illustrations* TB/1077

J. H. PARRY: The Establishment of the European Hegemony: 1415-1715: *Trade and Exploration in the Age of the Renaissance* TB/1045

HENRI PIRENNE: Early Democracies in the Low Countries: *Urban Society and Political Conflict in the Middle Ages and the Renaissance. Introduction by John Mundy* TB/1110

FERDINAND SCHEVILL: The Medici. *Illus.* TB/1010

FERDINAND SCHEVILL: Medieval and Renaissance Florence. *Illus.* Volume I: *Medieval Florence* TB/1090 Volume II: *The Coming of Humanism and the Age of the Medici* TB/1091

G. M. TREVELYAN: England in the Age of Wycliffe, 1368-1520° TB/1112

VESPASIANO: Renaissance Princes, Popes, and Prelates: *The Vespasiano Memoirs: Lives of Illustrious Men of the XVth Century. Introduction by Myron P. Gilmore* TB/1111

3

History: Modern European

FREDERICK B. ARTZ: Reaction and Revolution, 1815-1832.* *Illus.*   TB/3034
MAX BELOFF: The Age of Absolutism, 1660-1815   TB/1062
ROBERT C. BINKLEY: Realism and Nationalism, 1852-1871.* *Illus.*   TB/3038
CRANE BRINTON: A Decade of Revolution, 1789-1799.* *Illus.*   TB/3018
J. BRONOWSKI & BRUCE MAZLISH: The Western Intellectual Tradition: *From Leonardo to Hegel*   TB/3001
GEOFFREY BRUUN: Europe and the French Imperium, 1799-1814.* *Illus.*   TB/3033
ALAN BULLOCK: Hitler, A Study in Tyranny.[o] *Illus.*   TB/1123
E. H. CARR: The Twenty Years' Crisis, 1919-1939: *An Introduction to the Study of International Relations*[o]   TB/1122
WALTER L. DORN: Competition for Empire, 1740-1763.* *Illus.*   TB/3032
CARL J. FRIEDRICH: The Age of the Baroque, 1610-1660.* *Illus.*   TB/3004
LEO GERSHOY: From Despotism to Revolution, 1763-1789.* *Illus.*   TB/3017
ALBERT GOODWIN: The French Revolution TB/1064
CARLTON J. H. HAYES: A Generation of Materialism, 1871-1900.* *Illus.*   TB/3039
J. H. HEXTER: Reappraisals in History: *New Views on History and Society in Early Modern Europe*   TB/1100
A. R. HUMPHREYS: The Augustan World: *Society, Thought, and Letters in Eighteenth Century England*   TB/1105
HANS KOHN, Ed.: The Mind of Modern Russia: *Historical and Political Thought of Russia's Great Age*   TB/1065
SIR LEWIS NAMIER: Vanished Supremacies: *Essays on European History, 1812-1918*[o]   TB/1088
JOHN U. NEF: Western Civilization Since the Renaissance: *Peace, War, Industry, and the Arts*   TB/1113
FREDERICK L. NUSSBAUM: The Triumph of Science and Reason, 1660-1685.* *Illus.*   TB/3009
RAYMOND W. POSTGATE, Ed.: Revolution from 1789 to 1906: *Selected Documents*   TB/1063
PENFIELD ROBERTS: The Quest for Security, 1715-1740.* *Illus.*   TB/3016
PRISCILLA ROBERTSON: Revolutions of 1848: *A Social History*   TB/1025
ALBERT SOREL: Europe Under the Old Regime. *Translated by Francis H. Herrick*   TB/1121
N. N. SUKHANOV: The Russian Revolution, 1917: *Eyewitness Account. Edited by Joel Carmichael*
Volume I   TB/1066
Volume II   TB/1067
JOHN B. WOLF: The Emergence of the Great Powers, 1685-1715.* *Illus.*   TB/3010
JOHN B. WOLF: France: 1814-1919: *The Rise of a Liberal-Democratic Society*   TB/3019

Intellectual History

HERSCHEL BAKER: The Image of Man: *A Study of the Idea of Human Dignity in Classical Antiquity, the Middle Ages, and the Renaissance*   TB/1047
J. BRONOWSKI & BRUCE MAZLISH: The Western Intellectual Tradition: *From Leonardo to Hegel*   TB/3001

ERNST CASSIRER: The Individual and the Cosmos in Renaissance Philosophy. *Translated with an Introduction by Mario Domandi*   TB/1097
NORMAN COHN: The Pursuit of the Millennium: *Revolutionary Messianism in medieval and Reformation Europe and its bearing on modern Leftist and Rightist totalitarian movements*   TB/1037
ARTHUR O. LOVEJOY: The Great Chain of Being: *A Study of the History of an Idea*   TB/1009
ROBERT PAYNE: Hubris: *A Study of Pride. Foreword by Sir Herbert Read*   TB/1031
BRUNO SNELL: The Discovery of the Mind: *The Greek Origins of European Thought*   TB/1018
ERNST LEE TUVESON: Millennium and Utopia: *A Study in the Background of the Idea of Progress.*[||] *New Preface by Author*   TB/1134

Literature, Poetry, The Novel & Criticism

JAMES BAIRD: Ishmael: *The Art of Melville in the Contexts of International Primitivism*   TB/1023
JACQUES BARZUN: The House of Intellect   TB/1051
W. J. BATE: From Classic to Romantic: *Premises of Taste in Eighteenth Century England*   TB/1036
RACHEL BESPALOFF: On the Iliad   TB/2006
R. P. BLACKMUR, et al.: Lectures in Criticism. *Introduction by Huntington Cairns*   TB/2003
ABRAHAM CAHAN: The Rise of David Levinsky: *a novel. Introduction by John Higham*   TB/1028
ERNST R. CURTIUS: European Literature and the Latin Middle Ages   TB/2015
GEORGE ELIOT: Daniel Deronda: *a novel. Introduction by F. R. Leavis*   TB/1039
ETIENNE GILSON: Dante and Philosophy   TB/1089
ALFRED HARBAGE: As They Liked It: *A Study of Shakespeare's Moral Artistry*   TB/1035
STANLEY R. HOPPER, Ed.: Spiritual Problems in Contemporary Literature[§]   TB/21
A. R. HUMPHREYS: The Augustan World: *Society, Thought, and Letters in Eighteenth Century England*[o]   TB/1105
ALDOUS HUXLEY: Antic Hay & The Gioconda Smile.[o] *Introduction by Martin Green*   TB/3503
ALDOUS HUXLEY: Brave New World & Brave New World Revisited.[o] *Introduction by C. P. Snow*   TB/3501
ALDOUS HUXLEY: Point Counter Point.[o] *Introduction by C. P. Snow*   TB/3502
HENRY JAMES: The Princess Casamassima: *a novel. Introduction by Clinton F. Oliver*   TB/1005
HENRY JAMES: Roderick Hudson: *a novel. Introduction by Leon Edel*   TB/1016
HENRY JAMES: The Tragic Muse: *a novel. Introduction by Leon Edel*   TB/1017
ARNOLD KETTLE: An Introduction to the English Novel. Volume I: *Defoe to George Eliot*   TB/1011
Volume II: *Henry James to the Present*   TB/1012
JOHN STUART MILL: On Bentham and Coleridge. *Introduction by F. R. Leavis*   TB/1070
PERRY MILLER & T. H. JOHNSON, Editors: The Puritans: *A Sourcebook of Their Writings*
Volume I   TB/1093
Volume II   TB/1094
KENNETH B. MURDOCK: Literature and Theology in Colonial New England   TB/99
SAMUEL PEPYS: The Diary of Samuel Pepys.[o] *Edited by O. F. Morshead. Illustrations by Ernest Shepard*   TB/1007

4

ST.-JOHN PERSE: Seamarks TB/2002
O. E. RÖLVAAG: Giants in the Earth. *Introduction by Einar Haugen* TB/3504
GEORGE SANTAYANA: Interpretations of Poetry and Religion§ TB/9
C. P. SNOW: Time of Hope: *a novel* TB/1040
DOROTHY VAN GHENT: The English Novel: *Form and Function* TB/1050
E. B. WHITE: One Man's Meat. *Introduction by Walter Blair* TB/3505
MORTON DAUWEN ZABEL, Editor: Literary Opinion in America Volume I TB/3013
Volume II TB/3014

Myth, Symbol & Folklore

JOSEPH CAMPBELL, Editor: Pagan and Christian Mysteries. *Illus.* TB/2013
MIRCEA ELIADE: Cosmos and History: *The Myth of the Eternal Return*§ TB/2050
C. G. JUNG & C. KERÉNYI: Essays on a Science of Mythology: *The Myths of the Divine Child and the Divine Maiden* TB/2014
ERWIN PANOFSKY: Studies in Iconology: *Humanistic Themes in the Art of the Renaissance. 180 illustrations* TB/1077
JEAN SEZNEC: The Survival of the Pagan Gods: *The Mythological Tradition and its Place in Renaissance Humanism and Art. 108 illustrations* TB/2004
HELLMUT WILHELM: Change: *Eight Lectures on the I Ching* TB/2019
HEINRICH ZIMMER: Myths and Symbols in Indian Art and Civilization. *70 illustrations* TB/2005

Philosophy

HENRI BERGSON: Time and Free Will: *An Essay on the Immediate Data of Consciousness*° TB/1021
H. J. BLACKHAM: Six Existentialist Thinkers: *Kierkegaard, Nietzsche, Jaspers, Marcel, Heidegger, Sartre*° TB/1002
ERNST CASSIRER: Rousseau, Kant and Goethe. *Introduction by Peter Gay* TB/1092
FREDERICK COPLESTON: Medieval Philosophy° TB/76
F. M. CORNFORD: From Religion to Philosophy: *A Study in the Origins of Western Speculation*§ TB/20
WILFRID DESAN: The Tragic Finale: *An Essay on the Philosophy of Jean-Paul Sartre* TB/1030
PAUL FRIEDLÄNDER: Plato: *An Introduction* TB/2017
ETIENNE GILSON: Dante and Philosophy TB/1089
WILLIAM CHASE GREENE: Moira: *Fate, Good, and Evil in Greek Thought* TB/1104
W. K. C. GUTHRIE: The Greek Philosophers: *From Thales to Aristotle*° TB/1008
F. H. HEINEMANN: Existentialism and the Modern Predicament TB/28
IMMANUEL KANT: The Doctrine of Virtue, *being Part II of The Metaphysic of Morals. Translated with Notes and Introduction by Mary J. Gregor. Foreword by H. J. Paton* TB/110
IMMANUEL KANT: Lectures on Ethics.§ *Introduction by Lewis W. Beck* TB/105
WILLARD VAN ORMAN QUINE: From a Logical Point of View: *Logico-Philosophical Essays* TB/566

BERTRAND RUSSELL et al.: The Philosophy of Bertrand Russell. *Edited by Paul Arthur Schilpp*
Volume I TB/1095
Volume II TB/1096
L. S. STEBBING: A Modern Introduction to Logic TB/538
ALFRED NORTH WHITEHEAD: Process and Reality: *An Essay in Cosmology* TB/1033
WILHELM WINDELBAND: A History of Philosophy I: *Greek, Roman, Medieval* TB/38
WILHELM WINDELBAND: A History of Philosophy II: *Renaissance, Enlightenment, Modern* TB/39

Philosophy of History

NICOLAS BERDYAEV: The Beginning and the End§ TB/14
NICOLAS BERDYAEV: The Destiny of Man TB/61
WILHELM DILTHEY: Pattern and Meaning in History: *Thoughts on History and Society*.° *Edited with an Introduction by H. P. Rickman* TB/1075
RAYMOND KLIBANSKY & H. J. PATON, Eds.: Philosophy and History: *The Ernst Cassirer Festschrift. Illus.* TB/1115
JOSE ORTEGA Y GASSET: The Modern Theme. *Introduction by Jose Ferrater Mora* TB/1038
KARL R. POPPER: The Poverty of Historicism° TB/1126
W. H. WALSH: Philosophy of History: *An Introduction* TB/1020

Political Science & Government

JEREMY BENTHAM: The Handbook of Political Fallacies: *Introduction by Crane Brinton* TB/1069
KENNETH E. BOULDING: Conflict and Defense: *A General Theory* TB/3024
CRANE BRINTON: English Political Thought in the Nineteenth Century TB/1071
EDWARD S. CORWIN: American Constitutional History: *Essays edited by Alpheus T. Mason and Gerald Garvey* TB/1136
ROBERT DAHL & CHARLES E. LINDBLOM: Politics, Economics, and Welfare: *Planning and Politico-Economic Systems Resolved into Basic Social Processes* TB/3037
JOHN NEVILLE FIGGIS: Political Thought from Gerson to Grotius: 1414-1625: *Seven Studies. Introduction by Garrett Mattingly* TB/1032
F. L. GANSHOF: Feudalism TB/1058
G. P. GOOCH: English Democratic Ideas in the Seventeenth Century TB/1006
ROBERT H. JACKSON: The Supreme Court in the American System of Government TB/1106
DAN N. JACOBS, Ed.: The New Communist Manifesto *and Related Documents* TB/1078
DAN N. JACOBS & HANS BAERWALD, Eds.: Chinese Communism: *Selected Documents* TB/3031
ROBERT GREEN McCLOSKEY: American Conservatism in the Age of Enterprise, 1865-1910 TB/1137
KINGSLEY MARTIN: French Liberal Thought in the Eighteenth Century: *A Study of Political Ideas from Bayle to Condorcet* TB/1114
JOHN STUART MILL: On Bentham and Coleridge. *Introduction by F. R. Leavis* TB/1070
JOHN B. MORRALL: Political Thought in Medieval Times TB/1076

Philosophy of Science

R. B. BRAITHWAITE: Scientific Explanation   TB/515

J. BRONOWSKI: Science and Human Values. *Illus.*
                                         TB/505

ALBERT EINSTEIN: Philosopher-Scientist. *Edited by
Paul A. Schilpp*   Volume I TB/502
                              Volume II TB/503

WERNER HEISENBERG: Physics and Philosophy: *The
Revolution in Modern Science. Introduction by F. S.
C. Northrop*   TB/549

JOHN MAYNARD KEYNES: A Treatise on Proba-
bility.º *Introduction by N. R. Hanson* TB/557

STEPHEN TOULMIN: Foresight and Understanding:
*An Enquiry into the Aims of Science. Foreword by
Jacques Barzun*   TB/564

STEPHEN TOULMIN: The Philosophy of Science: *An
Introduction*   TB/513

G. J. WHITROW: The Natural Philosophy of Timeº
                                         TB/563

Physics and Cosmology

DAVID BOHM: Causality and Chance in Modern
Physics. *Foreword by Louis de Broglie*   TB/536

P. W. BRIDGMAN: The Nature of Thermodynamics
                                         TB/537

A. C. CROMBIE, Ed.: Turning Point in Physics TB/535

C. V. DURELL: Readable Relativity. *Foreword by Freeman J. Dyson*   TB/530

ARTHUR EDDINGTON: Space, Time and Gravitation:
An outline of the General Relativity Theory TB/510

GEORGE GAMOW: Biography of Physics∑   TB/567

MAX JAMMER: Concepts of Force: *A Study in the
Foundation of Dynamics*   TB/550

MAX JAMMER: Concepts of Mass *in Classical and
Modern Physics*   TB/571

MAX JAMMER: Concepts of Space: *The History of
Theories of Space in Physics. Foreword by Albert
Einstein*   TB/533

EDMUND WHITTAKER: History of the Theories of
Aether and Electricity
          Volume I: *The Classical Theories* TB/531
          Volume II: *The Modern Theories*   TB/532

G. J. WHITROW: The Structure and Evolution of the
Universe: *An Introduction to Cosmology. Illus.*
                                         TB/504

Philosophy of Science

R. B. BRAITHWAITE: Scientific Explanation ᴛʙ/515

J. BRONOWSKI: Science and Human Values. *Illus.* ᴛʙ/505

ALBERT EINSTEIN: Philosopher-Scientist. *Edited by Paul A. Schilpp* Volume I ᴛʙ/502 Volume II ᴛʙ/503

WERNER HEISENBERG: Physics and Philosophy: *The Revolution in Modern Science. Introduction by F. S. C. Northrop* ᴛʙ/549

JOHN MAYNARD KEYNES: A Treatise on Probability.º *Introduction by N. R. Hanson* ᴛʙ/557

STEPHEN TOULMIN: Foresight and Understanding: *An Enquiry into the Aims of Science. Foreword by Jacques Barzun* ᴛʙ/564

STEPHEN TOULMIN: The Philosophy of Science: *An Introduction* ᴛʙ/513

G. J. WHITROW: The Natural Philosophy of Timeº ᴛʙ/563

Physics and Cosmology

DAVID BOHM: Causality and Chance in Modern Physics. *Foreword by Louis de Broglie* ᴛʙ/536

P. W. BRIDGMAN: The Nature of Thermodynamics ᴛʙ/537

A. C. CROMBIE, Ed.: Turning Point in Physics ᴛʙ/535

C. V. DURELL: Readable Relativity. *Foreword by Freeman J. Dyson* ᴛʙ/530

ARTHUR EDDINGTON: Space, Time and Gravitation: *An outline of the General Relativity Theory* ᴛʙ/510

GEORGE GAMOW: Biography of Physicsꙅ ᴛʙ/567

MAX JAMMER: Concepts of Force: *A Study in the Foundation of Dynamics* ᴛʙ/550

MAX JAMMER: Concepts of Mass *in Classical and Modern Physics* ᴛʙ/571

MAX JAMMER: Concepts of Space: *The History of Theories of Space in Physics. Foreword by Albert Einstein* ᴛʙ/533

EDMUND WHITTAKER: History of the Theories of Aether and Electricity Volume I: *The Classical Theories* ᴛʙ/531 Volume II: *The Modern Theories* ᴛʙ/532

G. J. WHITROW: The Structure and Evolution of the Universe: *An Introduction to Cosmology. Illus.* ᴛʙ/504